MEDIA/IMPACT

AN INTRODUCTION TO MASS MEDIA

*

TWELFTH EDITION

From the Cengage Series in Communication Arts

General Mass Communication

Belmas/Overbeck, *Major Principles of Media Law*, 2016 Edition

Biagi, *Media / Impact: An Introduction to Mass Media*, Twelfth Edition

Fellow, *American Media History*, Third Edition

Lester, *Visual Communication: Images with Messages*, Sixth Edition

Straubhaar/LaRose/Davenport, *Media Now: Understanding Media, Culture, and Technology*, Ninth Edition

Zelezny, *Cases in Communications Law*, Sixth Edition

Zelezny, *Communications Law: Liberties, Restraints, and the Modern Media*, Sixth Edition

Journalism

Bowles/Borden, *Creative Editing*, Sixth Edition

Davis/Davis, *Cengage Advantage Books: Think Like an Editor: 50 Strategies for the Print and Digital World*, Second Edition

Hilliard, *Writing for Television, Radio, and New Media*, Eleventh Edition

Kessler/McDonald, *When Words Collide: A Media Writer's Guide to Grammar and Style*, Ninth Edition

Rich, *Writing and Reporting News: A Coaching Method*, Eighth Edition

Public Relations and Advertising

Diggs-Brown, *The PR Styleguide: Formats for Public Relations Practice*, Third Edition

Drewniany/Jewler, *Creative Strategy in Advertising*, Eleventh Edition

Hendrix/Hayes, *Public Relations Cases*, Ninth Edition

Newsom/Haynes, *Public Relations Writing: Strategies and Structures*, Eleventh Edition

Newsom/Turk/Kruckeberg, *Cengage Advantage Books: This Is PR: The Realities of Public Relations*, Eleventh Edition

Radio, Television, and Film

Albarran, *Management of Electronic and Digital Media*, Sixth Edition

Alten, *Audio Basics*, First Edition

Alten, *Audio in Media*, Tenth Edition

Eastman/Ferguson, *Media Programming: Strategies and Practices*, Ninth Edition

Gross/Ward, *Digital Moviemaking*, Seventh Edition

Hausman/Messere/Benoit, *Modern Radio and Audio Production: Programming and Performance*, Tenth Edition

Hilliard, *Writing for Television, Radio, and New Media*, Eleventh Edition

Hilmes, *Only Connect: A Cultural History of Broadcasting in the United States*, Fourth Edition

Mamer, *Film Production Technique: Creating the Accomplished Image*, Sixth Edition

Lewis, *Essential Cinema: An Introduction to Film Analysis*, First Edition

Osgood/Hinshaw, *Cengage Advantage Books: Visual Storytelling: Videography and Post Production in the Digital Age*, Second Edition

Zettl, *Sight Sound Motion: Applied Media Aesthetics*, Eighth Edition

Zettl, *Television Production Handbook*, Twelfth Edition

Zettl, *Video Basics*, Seventh Edition

Research and Theory

Baran/Davis, *Mass Communication Theory: Foundations, Ferment, and Future*, Seventh Edition

Sparks, *Media Effects Research: A Basic Overview*, Fifth Edition

Wimmer/Dominick, *Mass Media Research: An Introduction*, Tenth Edition

TWELFTH EDITION

MEDIA/IMPACT
AN INTRODUCTION TO MASS MEDIA

SHIRLEY BIAGI
California State University, Sacramento

CENGAGE
Learning·

Australia • Brazil • Mexico • Singapore • United Kingdom • United States

CENGAGE Learning

Media/Impact: An Introduction to Mass Media, Twelfth Edition

Shirley Biagi

Product Director: Monica Eckman

Product Manager: Kelli Strieby

Associate Content Developer: Rachel Smith

Associate Content Developer: Rachel Schowalter

Product Assistant: Colin Solan

Marketing Manager: Sarah Seymour

Senior Content Project Manager: Jill Quinn

Senior Art Director: Marissa Falco

Manufacturing Planner: Doug Bertke

IP Analyst: Ann Hoffman

IP Project Manager: Farah Fard

Production Service/Compositor: Lachina

Text and Cover Designer: Lisa Kuhn, Curio Press

Cover Images: FRONT COVER: App logos: AP Images/Picture-alliance/dpa/Jens Büttner; Lily James: Kevin Winter/Getty Images; Net neutrality: The Washington Post/Getty Images; Big Bang Theory: CBS Photo Archive/Getty Images; Chicago Bulls Mascot: Jonathan Daniel/Staff/Getty Images Sport/Getty Images. BACK COVER: iHeartRadio: Isaac Brekken/Getty Images; Samsung headphones ad: Trevor Snapp/Bloomberg/Getty Images; Russell Westbrook: Layne Murdoch/NBAE via Getty Images; Stop Killing Journalists sign: AP Images/Anjum Naveed

For product information and technology assistance, contact us at **Cengage Learning Customer & Sales Support, 1-800-354-9706**

For permission to use material from this text or product, submit all requests online at **www.cengage.com/permissions**. Further permissions questions can be emailed to **permissionrequest@cengage.com**.

Library of Congress Control Number: 2015955054

Student Edition:
ISBN: 978-1-305-58098-5

Loose-leaf Edition:
ISBN: 978-1-305-87540-1

Cengage Learning
20 Channel Center Street
Boston, MA 02210
USA

Cengage Learning is a leading provider of customized learning solutions with employees residing in nearly 40 different countries and sales in more than 125 countries around the world. Find your local representative at **www.cengage.com**.

Cengage Learning products are represented in Canada by Nelson Education, Ltd.

To learn more about Cengage Learning Solutions, visit **www.cengage.com**.

Purchase any of our products at your local college store or at our preferred online store **www.cengagebrain.com**.

Printed in the United States of America
Print Number: 01 Print Year: 2015

BRIEF CONTENTS

CONTENTS

PART ONE: THE MASS MEDIA INDUSTRIES

Zoran Milich/Reuters

Layne Murdoch/NBAE
via Getty Images

2 | *Books: Rearranging the Page*

Courtesy of Shirley Biagi

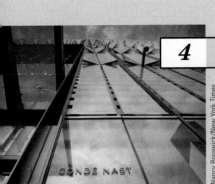

Nancy Borowick/New York Times

4 *Magazines: Chasing the Audience*

Stefano Buonamici/
The New York Times

5 *Recordings: Streaming Sounds*

Bryan Steffy/Getty Images

6 Radio: Riding New Waves

Chad Ress/The New York Times/Redux

7 | *Movies: Digitizing Dreams*

CBS Photo Archive/Getty Images

8 *Television: Switching Channels*

Tina Fineberg/The New York Times

9 | *Internet Media: Widening the Web*

AP Images/Charles Rex Arbogast

10 *Advertising: Catching Consumers*

Courtesy of The San Diego Union Tribune

11 Public Relations: Promoting Ideas

Spencer Platt/Getty Images

AP Images/David Goldman

14 *Law and Regulation: Reforming the Rules*

The Washington Post/Getty Images

IMPACT BOXES

PREFACE

Welcome to the world of *Media/Impact*.

Media/Impact's energetic new design—inside and out—reflects the excitement and intensity inherent in the study of mass media today. Dozens of new charts, illustrations and photographs in this 12th edition enhance the totally revised and updated text, making *Media/Impact*, 12th edition, the most current, accessible, challenging way for students to study the central role that America's mass media play in the global media marketplace.

Accompanying this new edition are many new digital tools offered by Cengage Learning, including MindTap, to organize and enhance student thinking. The result for students and teachers is *Media/Impact*'s best edition ever.

New Features in the 12th Edition

▶ **More than 40 new Impact Boxes**—The Impact Boxes feature current articles and information on the latest topics and trends from the best sources covering the media business, such as *The New York Times*, *The Washington Post*, *The Guardian*, *Wired*, *CNN*, *The Financial Times* and the *Los Angeles Times*.

▶ **Five Impact Box Subject Areas**—Impact Boxes are now divided into five essential subject areas: Convergence, Money, Society, Profile and Global. For example:

- **Impact/Convergence.** "Radio Listening Goes Digital and Mobile."

- **Impact/Money.** "What It Costs: Ad Prices from TV's Biggest Buys to the Smallest Screens."

- **Impact/Society.** "Average Time Americans Spend Using Mass Media Each Day."

- **Impact/Profile.** "BuzzFeed Co-Founder Jonah Peretti Wants to Take Its Content Far Beyond Lists."

- **Impact/Global.** "Primavera Sound Sets the Stage for Music Festivals Worldwide."

▶ **Current Statistics on the Mass Media Industries**—Statistical information is beautifully displayed in more than 30 new and updated illustrations to reflect current research on key issues such as the global box office, 10 most popular social media sites, top 10 U.S. digital "replica" magazines, political figures on social media, 10 most frequently challenged books and top 10 global advertising agencies.

▶ **Timely Photographs, Cartoons and Illustrations to Capture Students' Attention**—More than 230 carefully selected new photos, cartoons and illustrations throughout the book emphasize timely trends and critical topics in today's media business.

▶ **Impact/Action Videos**—Three new Impact/Action videos make contemporary issues in mass communication come alive for students, with customized content that expands on the text and animates the illustrations. Specialized narration accompanies images and videos to tell the story of how mass communication is changing and transforming the world. These three Impact/Action videos, matched to chapters throughout the book, expand student understanding of how mass communication affects today's world:

- Learn how social networks are changing global communication in *Social Media: Communicating Change*.

- Discover the importance of—and dangers facing—journalists reporting from around the world in *Reporters at Risk*.

- Explore the mass media's ongoing digital transformation in *Caught in the Net*.

Continuing Features in the 12th Edition

▶ **Comprehensive Coverage of the Latest Trends in Digital Media.** *Media/Impact* details the latest innovations and controversies surrounding the Internet, mobile media, video games, intellectual property rights, government regulation and social networks.

▶ **Analysis of Changing Delivery Systems for News and Information.** Chapter 9 and Chapter 12 have proven extremely popular with faculty and students. Chapter 9, Internet Media, was first introduced in the 6th edition, when few people understood how consumers' changing habits would affect the delivery of news and entertainment. In the 12th edition, Chapter 9 continues its role as the book's centerpiece, with critical analysis of the most important developments in today's global media transformation. Chapter 12, News and Information, chronicles the declining audience for broadcast news as consumers personalize their information and use the Internet to stay current, as well as social media's central role in creating communities and sharing information.

▶ **Discussion of Current Media Issues.** Beginning with the first graphic illustration in Chapter 1, "Average Time Americans Spend Using Mass Media Each Day," *Media/Impact* helps students understand the ubiquitous presence of mass media in their lives today.

▶ **Margin Definitions.** Designed to help students build a media vocabulary while they read, key terms and definitions are highlighted separately, giving students concise definitions that are incorporated into the text.

▶ **Comprehensive End-of-Chapter Review.** Each chapter's concluding materials include these essential resources:

■ **Chapter Summaries.** Organized by headings that correspond to the chapter's major topics, **Review, Analyze, Investigate** uses bullet points to summarize major concepts.

■ **Key Terms.** A list of important terms with corresponding page numbers appears at the end of each chapter and in the comprehensive **Glossary** at the end of the book.

■ **Critical Questions.** Following the key terms, five questions focus students' analysis of each chapter to help deepen their understanding and engage their critical thinking skills.

■ **Working the Web.** Finishing each chapter, a list of ten Web sites specific to the chapter includes brief annotations that describe each site and encourage students to pursue further research.

▶ **Media Information Resource Guide.** This invaluable student reference beginning on page 366 provides hundreds more resources to help students explore media topics and to assist them with media research, including an alphabetical listing of more than 200 Web site references from the text.

Formal Reviewers Keep Media/Impact's Focus on Students

A special thank you to the many professors who contributed valuable ideas in their formal reviews of *Media/Impact*. I especially appreciate the extra time and dedicated effort the video reviewers gave, which greatly helped shape the new concept of **Impact/Action Videos** as an integral part of *Media/Impact* for students. The 12th edition's reviewers are:

Mary Alice Adams, Louisiana Tech University
Monica Bartoszek, The College of Saint Rose
Richard Cameron, Cerritos College
Kat Cannella, Columbus State University
Michelle Christian, College of Southern Maryland
Henry Dunn, Austin Peay State University
Doug Ferguson, College of Charleston
Amy Lenoce, Naugatuck Valley Community College
Bill Lewis, Alvin Community College
Robert McKeever, University of South Carolina
Judy Noble, City University of New York–Borough of Manhattan Community College
Pamela O'Brien, Bowie State University
Dorren Robinson, Belmont University
Ted Schwalbe, SUNY Fredonia
Richard Tiner, Belmont University
Nicole Turner, Langston University
Sherry Williford, Stephen F. Austin State University

Cengage Teaching and Learning Tools for Teachers and Students

MindTap® Cengage Learning's MindTap for *Media/Impact* brings course concepts to life with interactive learning, study and exam preparation tools that support the printed textbook. Student comprehension is enhanced with the integrated eBook and interactive teaching and learning tools including learning objectives, interactive activities, quizzes and—exclusive to *Media/Impact*—Impact/Action videos. A career guide and social media guide give students insight into the practical applications of their coursework.

Instructor's Edition (IE): Examination and desk copies of the Instructor's Edition of *Media/Impact*, 12th Edition, are available upon request.

Instructor's Web site: This dedicated online resource for instructors provides access to the Instructor's Manual and Microsoft PowerPoint lecture slides covering key concepts from the text. There's also a Test Bank powered by **Cognero**, a flexible, online system that allows you to author, edit and manage test bank content from Cengage Learning; create multiple test versions in an instant; and deliver tests from your Learning Management System, your classroom or wherever you want.

Instructor's Manual: *Media/Impact*'s Instructor's Manual provides a comprehensive teaching guide featuring the following tools for each chapter: chapter outlines; suggestions for integrating print supplements and online resources; suggested discussion questions; handouts for classroom activities and a comprehensive Test Bank with an answer key that includes multiple choice, true/false, essay and fill-in-the-blank test questions. This Manual is available on the password-protected instructor's Web site.

Thank you for your continuing support of *Media/Impact*. Comments? Questions? Suggestions? Please contact your local Cengage sales representative or our Customer Service Team at (800) 354-9706.

FOREWORD

Media/Impact, 12th Edition, is a beautiful, engaging book. It was created under an unbelievably tight production schedule and for that I owe many, many thanks to the people at Cengage, Lachina and Lumina Datamatics who made that work:

At Cengage: Product Manager Kelli Strieby, Associate Content Developer Rachel Smith, Associate Content Developer Rachel Schowalter, Senior Content Project Manager Jill Quinn, Senior Art Director Marissa Falco, IP Analyst Ann Hoffman, IP Project Manager Farah Fard, Marketing Manager Sarah Seymour, Product Assistant Colin Solan.

At Lachina: Chris Black and Whitney Philipp.

At Lumina Datamatics: Manojkiran Chander and Kanchana Vijayarangan.

Also, thank you to Tom Biondi for his important research assistance.

The greatest additions to the 12th edition lineup are three newly produced Impact/Action Videos. For the first time, Vic Biondi and I were given the opportunity to create the videos with the help of the truly exceptional media crew at LAD Post Production: Producer Scott Back, Associate Producer David Biondi, Video Editor Tom Nichols and Electronic Production Coordinator Dennis Sherwood. Thank you.

For her enthusiasm and continuing support for the Impact/Action Videos, I thank Kelli Strieby. Rachel Smith contributed greatly with her dynamic, on-deadline video coordination. And, as always, my all-time favorite photo researcher and video producer, Vic Biondi, provided unmatched vision, creative wisdom and a great sense of humor.

And to all the students and teachers who continue to value *Media/Impact* as a way to explore the exciting field of mass media, I continue to be very grateful for your enduring support.

Shirley Biagi

ABOUT THE AUTHOR

Christopher Briscoe

SHIRLEY BIAGI is Emeritus Professor in the Department of Communication Studies at California State University, Sacramento. Her bestselling text, *Media/Impact*, also is published globally in Canadian, British, Spanish, Chinese and Korean editions.

Biagi has authored several other Cengage Learning communications texts, including *Media/Reader: Perspectives on Mass Media Industries, Effects and Issues* and *Interviews That Work: A Practical Guide for Journalists.* She is co-author, with Marilyn Kern-Foxworth, of *Facing Difference: Race, Gender and Mass Media.*

From 1998 to 2000, she was editor of *American Journalism*, the national media history quarterly published by the American Journalism Historians Association.

She has served as guest faculty for the University of Hawaii, the Center for Digital Government, the Poynter Institute, the American Press Institute, the National Writers Workshop and the Hearst Fellowship Program at the *Houston Chronicle.* She has also been an Internet and publications consultant to the California State Chamber of Commerce.

She also was one of eight project interviewers for the award-winning Washington (D.C.) Press Club Foundation's Women in Journalism Oral History Project, sponsored by the National Press Club. Interviewers completed 57 oral histories of female pioneers in journalism, available free on the Press Club's Web site at http://www.wpcf.org.

Biagi served as a delegate to the Oxford Round Table's conference on Ethical Sentiments in Government at Pembroke College in Oxford, England. Her other international experience includes guest lectureships at Al Ahram Press Institute in Cairo, Egypt, and at Queensland University in Brisbane, Australia.

MASS MEDIA
AND EVERYDAY LIFE

Zoran Milich/Reuters

Today's mobile media, such as smartphones,
have become essential elements of everyday life.
On January 1, 2015, a group in New York's Times
Square uses their new iPhone to take a "selfie" to

What's Ahead?

- Mass Media Are Everywhere You Are
- Mass Communication Becomes Wireless
- How the Communication Process Works
- What Are the Mass Media Industries?
- Three Key Concepts to Remember

- Mass Media Are Profit-Centered Businesses
- Convergence Dominates the Media Business
- Why Media Properties Converge
- Advertisers and Consumers Pay the Bills
- Technology Changes Mass Media Delivery and Consumption

- Media Take Advantage of Digital Delivery
- How Today's Communications Network Operates
- Mass Media Both Reflect and Affect Politics, Society and Culture
- Why You Should Understand Mass Media and Everyday Life

"(The Internet of Things) is going to create disruption and opportunity in every imaginable field, and it's entirely up to you whether you're going to be one of the disrupted or the disruptors."

—DANIEL BURRUS, CEO AND FOUNDER OF BURRUS RESEARCH, TECHNOLOGY FORECASTER AND INNOVATION EXPERT

You are interactive—connected to mass media in a more personal way than ever before. At the center of your personal, interactive connections today is the Internet, where mass media and social media are waiting to bombard you every waking hour. When was the last time you spent 24 hours without the media? From the moment you wake up until the time you go to sleep, mass media and social media overwhelm you with news and information, keep you entertained and—most importantly for the mass media industries—sell you products.

Mass Media Are Everywhere You Are

Online news offers national and local news with constant updates and alerts for breaking stories. Radio news gives you traffic reports on the freeway. Magazines describe new video games, show you the latest fashion trends and help plan your next hiking trip.

Should you power up your Kindle to read the latest romance novel or stream a video on your iPad from Netflix? Maybe you should grab your iPhone to check Facebook or use your CBS app to catch up on the latest episode of your favorite TV sitcom. Perhaps you should check Snapchat for the latest ten-second photo message from your friends or use Spotify to find the newest release from your favorite music artist.

According to industry estimates, adults spend an average of 12 1/2 hours each day using mass media—more than three-fourths of their waking hours. (See **Illustration 1.1**, p. 4.) Some form of mass media touches you every day—economically, socially and politically. Mass media can affect the way you vote and the way you spend your money. Sometimes mass media influence the way you eat, talk, work, study and relax. This is the impact of mass media on you individually and, collectively, on American society.

The media's wide-ranging global presence means today's mass media capture more time and attention than ever. The media affect almost all aspects of the way people live, and the media earn unprecedented amounts of money for delivering information and entertainment.

Today's American society has inherited the wisdom, mistakes, creativity and vision of the people who work in the mass media industries and the society that regulates and consumes what the mass media produce. Consider these situations:

▶ You are an executive with city government working with a limited budget, trying to expand access to the local public library. How can you use technology to help maximize the library's reach? (See **Chapter 2**.)

▶ A friend texts you a link to new song from your favorite recording artist, which you download and use on your Web site. The music works great, but the artist's licensing company sues you because you haven't paid to use the song. Will you be prosecuted? (See **Chapter 5**.)

TimeFrame
3500 B.C.–Today

3500 B.C. The first known pictographs are carved in stone.

2500 B.C. The Egyptians invent papyrus.

1000 B.C. **The First Information Communications Revolution: Phonetic Writing**

200 B.C. The Greeks perfect parchment.

A.D. 100 The Chinese invent paper.

1300 Europeans start to use paper.

1445 The Chinese invent the copper press.

1455 **The Second Information Communications Revolution: Movable Type**

1640 The first American book is published.

1690 The first American newspaper is published.

1741 The first American magazine is published.

1877 Thomas Edison first demonstrates the phonograph.

1899 Guglielmo Marconi first uses his wireless radio.

1927 The *Jazz Singer*, the first feature-length motion picture with sound, premieres in New York City.

1939 NBC debuts TV at the New York World's Fair. On display are 5-inch and 9-inch television sets priced from $199.50 to $600.

1951 **The Third Information Communications Revolution: Digital Computers That Can Process, Store and Retrieve Information**

1980 The Federal Communications Commission begins to deregulate the broadcast media.

1989 Tim Berners-Lee develops the first Internet Web browser.

2007 Amazon introduces the Kindle e-reader. Apple introduces the iPhone.

2008 Internet advertising income reaches $23 billion annually, more than twice what it was in the year 2000.

2010 Apple introduces the iPad tablet.

2013 Wearable technology, including the Smartwatch, debuts.

2014 Facebook has 1.4 billion users. Twitter reaches 300 million. Snapchat boasts 100 million.

2015 Internet advertising income reaches $51 billion annually.

TODAY Wireless digital technology is the standard for all mass media. Mass media are interactive and mobile.

IMPACT

Society

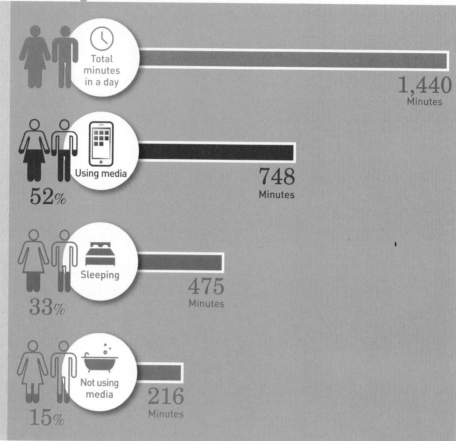

ILLUSTRATION 1.1

Average Time Americans Spend Using Mass Media Each Day

On average, Americans spend more waking time each day with the mass media than without them.

Total minutes in a day — 1,440 Minutes

52% — Using media — 748 Minutes

33% — Sleeping — 475 Minutes

15% — Not using media — 216 Minutes

Advertising Age Marketing Fact Pack 2015, "Time Spent Using Media," December 29, 2014, p. 17.

▶ You work for an advertising agency that wants to use Twitter to create enthusiasm for a new product. What would you recommend as the best way to be most successful on social media? (See **Chapter 10**.)

▶ You are an anchor for a major news organization. During several public appearances you exaggerate the danger you faced reporting from a war zone. How does your company respond when it learns what you've done? (See **Chapter 15**.)

People who work in the media industries, people who own media businesses, people who consume media and people who regulate what the media offer face decisions like these every day. The choices they make continue to shape the future of the American mass media.

Mass Communication Becomes Wireless

In the 1930s, for you to listen to the radio, your house needed electricity. You plugged your radio into an electrical outlet, with the furniture positioned near the radio so the family could listen to the programs. In the 1950s, you had to add an antenna to your roof so you could watch your new TV set, which was connected at the wall to an electrical outlet and the antenna. To be wired was to be connected. In the 1990s, you still needed an electrical outlet at home and at work to be connected to your computer, and the furniture in your family room at home was arranged to accommodate the cable, satellite and/or telephone connection for your television set.

Today's technology makes mass media wireless (**Wi-Fi**, an abbreviation for *Wireless Fidelity*). New technologies give you access to any mass media in almost any location without wires. You can:

▶ Check Twitter for public officials' comments on news events.

Wi-Fi An abbreviation for *Wireless Fidelity*, which makes it possible to transmit Internet data wirelessly to any compatible device.

▶ Stream a first-run movie or a classic TV sitcom or download new and classic books—even your textbook—to a mobile device you carry with you.

▶ Play the newest video game on your smartphone with three people you've never met.

▶ Check your family ancestry to create an online family tree, leading you to connect with overseas relatives you didn't know existed.

▶ Stop on the street corner in a new town, use your smartphone to find the closest Italian restaurant, then order pizza ahead on the restaurant's Web site so it's ready when you arrive there.

You and your mass media are totally mobile. Today's digital environment is an intricate, webbed network of many different types of communications systems that connects virtually every home, school, library and business in the United States and around the world. Most of the systems in this digital environment are invisible. Electronic signals have replaced wires, freeing people to stay connected no matter where or when they want to communicate.

This global communications system uses broadcast, telephone, satellite, cable and electronic technologies,

On February 8, 2015, British singer Sam Smith collected four Grammys. If a friend texts you a link to Smith's latest hit song, and you use it on your Web site without permission, can you be prosecuted for violating music copyright?

Jason LaVeris/FilmMagic/Getty Images

and eventually this communications system will be accessible and affordable everywhere in the world.

How the Communication Process Works

To understand mass media in the digital age, first it is important to understand the process of communication. Communication is the act of sending messages, ideas and opinions from one person to another. Writing and talking to each other are only two ways human beings communicate. We also communicate when we gesture, move our bodies or roll our eyes.

Three ways to describe how people communicate are

▶ *Intrapersonal communication*

▶ *Interpersonal communication*

▶ *Mass communication*

Each form of communication involves different numbers of people in specific ways. If you are in a grocery store and you silently debate with yourself whether to buy an apple or a package of double-chunk chocolate chip cookies, you are using what scholars call *intra*personal communication—communication within one person.

To communicate with each other, people rely on their five senses—sight, hearing, touch, smell and taste. This direct sharing of experience between two people is called *inter*personal communication. **Mass communication** is communication from one person or group of persons through a transmitting device (a medium) to large audiences or markets.

In *Media/Impact* you will study *mass communication*. To describe the process of mass communication, scholars use a communications model. This includes six key terms: *sender, message, receiver, channel, feedback* and *noise.* (See **Illustration 1.2**, p. 6.)

Pretend you're standing directly in front of someone and say, "I like your Detroit Tigers hat." In this simple communication, you are the sender, the message is "I like your Detroit Tigers hat" and the person in front of you is the receiver (or audience). This example of interpersonal communication involves the sender, the message and the receiver.

In mass communication, the *sender* (or *source*) puts the *message* on what is called a *channel*. The sender (source) could be a local business, for example. The channel (or

> **Mass Communication** Communication from one person or group of persons through a transmitting device (a medium) to large audiences or markets.

IMPACT

Society

ILLUSTRATION 1.2

Elements of Mass Communication

The process of mass communication works like this: A *sender* (source) puts a message on a *channel* (medium) that delivers the message to the *receiver*. *Feedback* occurs when the receiver responds, and that response changes subsequent messages from the source. *Noise* (such as static or a dropped connection) can interrupt or change the message during transmission.

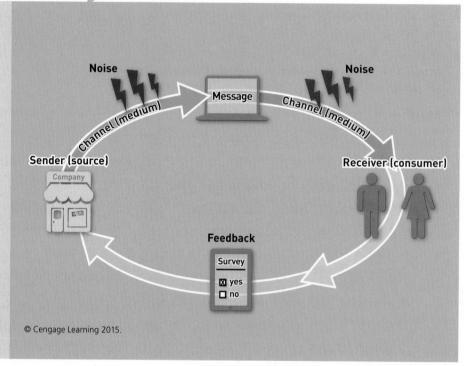

© Cengage Learning 2015.

medium) delivers the message (electronic signal). The channel could be the cable, satellite or Internet provider. A medium is the means by which a message reaches an audience. (The plural of the word *medium* is *media*; the term **media** refers to more than one medium.) Your television set, computer or mobile device is the medium that delivers the message simultaneously to you and many other people.

The *receiver* is the place where the message arrives, such as you, the consumer. **Noise** is any distortion (such as static or a briefly interrupted signal) that interferes with clear communication. **Feedback** occurs when the receiver processes the message and sends a response (such as a survey) back to the sender (source).

As a very simple example, say your satellite company (sender/source) sends an ad for a new movie release (the message) through the signal (channel) into your TV set (medium). If you (the receiver) use the controls on your TV remote to stream the movie, the order you place (feedback) ultimately will bring you a movie to watch. This entire loop between sender and receiver, and the resulting response (feedback) of the receiver to the sender, describes the process of mass communication.

Using a general definition, mass communication today shares three characteristics:

1. A message is sent out on some form of mass communication system (such as the Internet, print or broadcast).

2. The message is delivered rapidly.

3. The message reaches large groups of different kinds of people simultaneously or within a short period of time.

So a telephone conversation between two people does *not* qualify as mass communication, but a message from the president of the United States, broadcast simultaneously by all of the television networks and streamed live via the Internet, would qualify because mass media deliver messages to large numbers of people at once.

Medium   The means by which a message reaches the audience. Also, the singular form of the word *media*.

Media   Plural of the word *medium*.

Noise   Distortion (such as static) that interferes with clear communication.

Feedback   A response sent back to the sender from the person who receives the communication.

Nicolas Asfouri/AFP/Getty Images

Wireless technology means you can carry your media with you and send and receive messages globally. In Queenstown, Singapore, people use their cell phones to try to get a picture of Britain's Prince William and his wife, Catherine, the Duchess of Cambridge, during their visit to the country on September 12, 2012.

What Are the Mass Media Industries?

The term **mass media industries** describes eight types of mass media businesses. The word *industries*, when used to describe the media business, emphasizes the primary goal of mass media in America—to generate money (see **Illustration 1.3**, p. 8).

The eight mass media industries are

▶ Books

▶ Newspapers

▶ Magazines

▶ Recordings

▶ Radio

▶ Movies

▶ Television

▶ The Internet

Books, newspapers and magazines were America's only mass media for 250 years after the first American book was published in 1640. The first half of the 20th century brought 4 new types of media—recordings, radio, movies and TV—in fewer than 50 years. The late-20th-century addition to the media mix, of course, is the Internet. To understand how each medium fits in the mass media industries today, you can start by examining the individual characteristics of each media business.

Books

Publishers issue about 200,000 titles a year in the United States, although many of these are reprints and new editions of old titles. Retail bookstores in the United States account for one-third of all money earned from book sales, but the majority of books are sold online. The rest of book publishing income comes from books that are sold in college stores, through book clubs, to libraries and to school districts for use in elementary and high schools.

U.S. book publishing, the country's oldest media industry, has been revived recently by the introduction of e-books (downloaded copies of traditional books), transforming the book publishing business from print-only sales to print-and-digital online sales.

Newspapers

Newspapers today are struggling to make a profit. Advertising revenues in the last ten years have plummeted, primarily because newspaper readers have migrated to other sources for their news. Between 2008 and 2010, eight major newspaper chains declared bankruptcy, and many laid off reporters and cut salaries.

Advertising makes up more than two-thirds of the printed space in daily newspapers. Most newspapers have launched Internet editions to try to expand their reach, and a few newspapers have converted to online-only publication, but increased Internet ad revenue has not compensated for advertising declines in the printed product.

Magazines

According to the Association of Magazine Media, 75 percent of magazine readers still prefer the printed magazine, although 16 percent read their magazines on a computer and 9 percent read the magazine on a tablet or smartphone. To maintain profits, magazines are raising their subscription and single-copy prices and charging for online access.

Many magazines have launched Internet editions, and a few magazines (such as *Slate*) are published exclusively online. Still, magazine subscriptions and newsstand sales are down. Magazine income is expected to decline over the next decade, primarily because a

Mass Media Industries Eight types of media businesses: books, newspapers, magazines, recordings, radio, movies, television and the Internet.

IMPACT

Money

ILLUSTRATION 1.3

U.S. Mass Media Industries Annual Income 1987–Today

This historical graphic shows how the distribution of media industry income since 1987 has shifted from print media (books, newspapers and magazines) to television and the Internet.

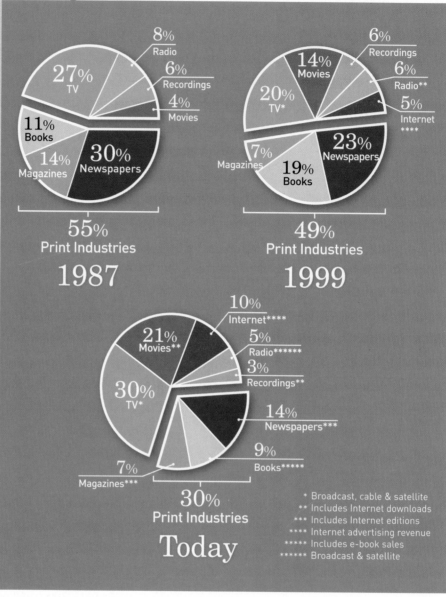

Sources: *U.S. Industrial Outlook 1987; McCann-Erickson Insider's Report 1987; The Veronis, Suhler & Associates Communications Industry Forecast, 1997–2001; Advertising Age Marketing Fact Pack*, December 29, 2014; publishers.org; mpaa.org; naa.org; adage.com; riaa.org; iab.org.

significant portion of magazine advertising revenue has migrated to the Internet.

Recordings

Recording industry revenue overall is declining. CDs account for one-third of industry revenue, while digital downloads, subscriptions and streaming account for the rest. Industry income has been declining sharply because new technologies allow consumers to share music over the Internet rather than pay for their music. Instead of selling albums, as in the past, artists must rely on sales of singles, which of course bring in less revenue.

Radio

About 15,000 radio stations broadcast in the United States, with fewer AM stations than FM. About 4,000 radio stations are public stations, most of them FM. The satellite radio service Sirius XM generates revenue through subscriptions, offering a variety of music and program choices without commercials.

As a result, broadcast radio revenue from advertising is declining because the price of a commercial is based on the size of the audience, which is getting smaller. To expand their audience, many traditional radio stations distribute their programs online. The Internet radio services Pandora, Rhapsody and Spotify have also stolen younger listeners from traditional radio stations.

Movies

There are about 40,000 indoor movie screens in the U.S., and, surprisingly, about 600 outdoor screens still exist. The major and independent studios combined make about 500 pictures a year. The industry is collecting more money because of higher ticket prices, but more people watch and stream movies at home rather than go to theaters, so the number of movie theaters is declining.

Fewer people are buying DVDs and instead are getting movies through Redbox and streaming them through services like Netflix. The increased income to the U.S. movie industry has been primarily from overseas movie sales and streaming. Overall movie industry income began declining in 2005, and that trend continued until 2012. Since then industry income has stabilized.

Television

About 1,700 television stations operate in the U.S. One out of four stations is a public station. Many stations are affiliated with a major network—NBC, CBS, ABC or Fox—although a few stations, called *independents*, are not affiliated with any network. More than 90 percent of the homes in the United States are wired for cable or satellite delivery. To differentiate cable and satellite TV from over-the-air television, cable and satellite television services are now lumped together in one category, called ***subscription television.***

TV network income is increasing while income to cable operators and satellite companies for subscription services has stabilized. Recently, the television networks have all invested heavily in subscription TV programming. The nation's largest cable operator is Comcast Corp. In 2014, Comcast bought Time Warner Cable. AT&T began offering subscription television services through its U-verse system in 2008, and in 2015 AT&T bought satellite provider DirecTV. Total television industry revenue—including cable, satellite and fiber delivery—continues to grow steadily.

The Internet

The newest media industry also is growing the fastest. About 80 percent of all U.S. adults have Internet access, and the amount of money businesses spent for Internet advertising, which totaled $8 billion in 2000, is projected to reach to $51 billion in 2015.

Internet media have become a new mass medium as well as an integrated delivery system for traditional print, audio, video and interactive services (such as streaming). The Internet also offers access to many other consumer

Tom Toro/The New Yorker Collection/Cartoon Bank.com

"Apparently they hand out awards for something called 'television.'"

services, such as shopping and social networking, and a place for businesses to sell their products using advertising and product promotion.

Three Key Concepts to Remember

The mass media are key institutions in our society. They affect our culture, our buying habits and our politics. They are affected in turn by changes in our beliefs, tastes, interests and behavior. Three important concepts can help to organize your thinking about mass media and their impact on American society:

1. The mass media are profit-centered businesses.

2. Technological developments change the way mass media are delivered and consumed.

3. Mass media both reflect and affect politics, society and culture.

Mass Media Are Profit-Centered Businesses

What you see, read and hear in the mass media may tease, entertain, inform, persuade, provoke and even confuse you. But to understand the American mass media, the first concept to grasp is that the central force driving the media business in America is the desire to make money. American media are businesses, vast businesses.

> **Subscription Television** A new term used to describe consumer services delivered by cable and satellite.

American mass media are very popular overseas, representing substantial income potential for U.S. media companies. On February 15, 2015, the *SpongeBob SquarePants* movie premiered at the Cinema Gaumont Capucines in Paris, France.

The products of these businesses are information and entertainment that depend on attracting an audience of media consumers to generate income. Of course, other motives shape the media in America: the desire to fulfill the public's need for information, to influence the country's governance, to disseminate the country's culture, to offer entertainment and to provide an outlet for artistic expression. But American media are, above all, profit-centered.

To understand the mass media industries, it is essential to understand who owns these important channels of communication. In the United States, all media are privately owned except the Public Broadcasting Service (PBS) and National Public Radio (NPR), which survive on government support, private donations and corporate sponsorship. The annual budget for all of public broadcasting (PBS and NPR combined) is less than 2 percent of the amount advertisers pay every year to support America's commercial media.

In some media industries, the same number of companies control ownership today as in the 1950s. There are five major movie studios today, for example, compared to the same number of major studios in the 1940s. The number of broadcast stations and the number of magazines has increased since the 1940s, but the number of newspapers and recording companies has declined.

Overall, American media ownership has been contracting rather than expanding. This is because large companies are buying small companies. The trend is for media companies to cluster together into big groups, which means that a small number of companies now control many aspects of the media business. This trend,

called *concentration of ownership*, takes four different forms: chains, broadcast networks, conglomerates and vertical integration.

CHAINS. Benjamin Franklin established America's first newspaper chain in the 1700s, when he was publishing his own newspaper, the *Pennsylvania Gazette*, as well as sponsoring one-third of the cost of publishing the *South Carolina Gazette*. (He also collected one-third of the *South Carolina Gazette*'s profits.) William Randolph Hearst expanded this tradition in the 1930s. At its peak, the Hearst newspaper chain accounted for nearly 14 percent of total national daily newspaper sales and 25 percent of Sunday sales. Today's U.S. newspaper chain giant is Gannett Co., with 82 daily newspapers, including *USA Today*. The word *chain* is used to describe a company that owns several newspapers.

BROADCAST NETWORKS. A broadcast network is a collection of radio or television stations that offers programs during designated program times. Unlike newspaper ownership (which is not regulated by the government), the Federal Communications Commission (**FCC**) regulates broadcast station ownership and operations. The FCC is a government regulatory body whose members are appointed by the president.

The four major TV networks are ABC (American Broadcasting Co.), NBC (National Broadcasting Co.), CBS (originally the Columbia Broadcasting System) and Fox. NBC, the oldest network, was founded in the 1920s. NBC and the two other original networks (CBS and ABC) first were established to deliver radio programming across the country and continued the network concept when television was invented. Fox is the youngest major network, founded in 1986, and delivers only television programming.

Broadcast networks can have as many *affiliates* as they want. Affiliates are stations that use network programming but are owned by companies other than the networks. No network, however, can have two affiliates in the same geographic broadcast area, due to government regulation of network affiliation.

In 2006, the TV networks announced they would offer shows on demand. Apple and Disney agreed to make series programming available through video downloads. One month later, CBS and NBC announced they planned to offer series programs on demand through Comcast

Concentration of Ownership The current trend of large companies buying smaller companies so that fewer companies own more types of media businesses.

FCC Federal Communications Commission.

Affiliates Stations that use network programming but are owned by companies other than the networks.

Kristy Sparow/Getty Images Entertainment/Getty Images

CBS Photo Archive/Getty Images

CBS is one of the original U.S. broadcast networks and earned an early reputation as the nation's best TV news operation, beginning in the 1960s. In 1968, CBS news anchor Walter Cronkite reported on the Tet Offensive in Vietnam.

and DirecTV. Today broadcast network programming is available by streaming on all mobile media, such as smartphones and tablets. To generate revenue, the broadcast networks today take the programming to their viewers instead of waiting for viewers to come to them.

CONGLOMERATES. When you watch a Sony Pictures Entertainment film or listen to Sony music, you might not realize that Sony also owns Micronics, a medical diagnostics company. Sony is a *conglomerate*—a company that owns media companies (Sony Pictures Entertainment, Sony Music Entertainment and Sony Electronics) as well as other businesses that are unrelated to the media business.

VERTICAL INTEGRATION. Another widespread trend among today's media companies is *vertical integration*—a business model in which one company controls several related aspects of the media business at once, with each part of the company helping the others. Many media companies own more than one type of media property: newspapers, magazines, radio and TV stations, for example.

Gannett, which owns the nation's largest chain of newspapers, also owns television and radio stations, so

Gannett is a newspaper chain that is also a vertically integrated company.

The media company Viacom owns MTV, Comedy Central, Nickelodeon and Black Entertainment Television (BET). The Walt Disney Co. owns Disneyland amusement parks, Walt Disney Motion Pictures Group, the ABC TV network, the ESPN cable network and *ESPN: The Magazine*. Time Warner owns Warner Bros. Pictures, HBO, Turner Broadcasting, CNN, TNT, TBS and the Cartoon Network.

Convergence Dominates the Media Business

To describe the financial status of today's media industries is to talk about intense competition. Media companies are buying and selling each other in unprecedented numbers and forming media groups to position themselves in the marketplace to maintain and increase their income. Since 1986, all three original TV networks (NBC, CBS and ABC) have been sold to new owners—sometimes more than once—making each of the three original networks smaller parts of giant publicly owned media companies.

Fox Broadcasting Co. is part of a larger international media company, Rupert Murdoch's News Corp., which also owns *The Wall Street Journal*, TV stations, magazines and Twentieth Century Fox Film Corp. In 2013, the leading cable operator Comcast acquired full ownership of NBC Universal, with its cable channels, theme parks and the NBC broadcast network. Since shares in most of today's media companies are publicly traded on the nation's stock exchanges, they face heavy pressure to deliver hefty profits to their shareholders.

Media companies today also are driven by media *convergence*. The word *convergence* describes two developments taking place simultaneously. First, it means the melding of the communications, computer and

Conglomerates Companies that own media companies as well as businesses that are unrelated to the media business.

Vertical Integration An attempt by one company to simultaneously control several related aspects of the media business.

Convergence The melding of the communications, computer and electronics industries. Also used to describe the economic alignment of the various media companies with each other to take advantage of technological advancements.

The Walt Disney Company is a vertically integrated media corporation—a company that owns several different types of media businesses, with each part of the company contributing to the others. On April 15, 2013, Mickey, Minnie and Goofy helped celebrate the 30th anniversary of Tokyo Disneyland.

electronics industries because of advances in digital technology. Second, *convergence* also means the economic alignment of different types of media companies with each other so they can offer the variety of services that technical advancements demand.

The people who manage U.S. media companies today want to make money. As in all industries, there are people who want to make money quickly and people who take the long-term view about profits, but certainly none of them wants to lose money. One way to expand a company to take advantage of technological and economic convergence is to acquire an already established business that's successful. Such media acquisitions have skyrocketed for two reasons—public ownership and deregulation.

PUBLIC OWNERSHIP. Most media companies today are publicly traded, which means their stock is sold on one of the nation's stock exchanges. This makes acquisitions relatively easy. A media company that wants to buy another publicly owned company can buy that company's stock when the stock becomes available.

The open availability of stock in these public companies means any company or individual with enough money can invest in the American media industries, which is exactly how Australian Rupert Murdoch, owner of Fox Broadcasting, joined the U.S. media business and was able to accumulate so many media companies in such a short time.

DEREGULATION. Beginning in 1980, the Federal Communications Commission gradually deregulated the broadcast media. *Deregulation* means the FCC withdrew many regulatory restrictions on broadcast media ownership. Before 1980, for example, the FCC allowed a broadcast company to own only five TV stations, five AM radio stations and five FM radio stations. Companies also were required to keep a station for three years before the owners could sell it.

The post-1980 FCC eliminated the three-year rule and raised the number of broadcast holdings allowed for one owner. Today, there are very few FCC restrictions on broadcast media ownership.

Why Media Properties Converge

Ownership turnover is highest in the newspaper and broadcast industries. Six factors have affected the economic alignment of these properties:

1. Media properties can be attractive investments. Many broadcast companies have historically earned profits of 10 percent or more a year, for example, which is about double the average amount that a U.S. manufacturing company earns.

2. Newspapers and broadcast stations are scarce commodities. Because the number of newspapers has been declining and the government regulates the number of broadcast stations that are allowed to operate, a limited number of established media outlets are available. As with all limited commodities, this makes them attractive investments.

3. Newspapers and broadcast stations have moved past their early cycle of family ownership. If the heirs to the founders of a family business are not interested in running the company, the only way for them to collect their inheritance is to sell the business, and the only companies with enough money to buy individual media businesses are large corporations and investment companies.

4. Newspapers and broadcast stations are easier businesses to buy than to create. Because these businesses require huge investments in equipment and people, they are expensive to start up. In broadcasting, the major factor that encouraged ownership changes, beginning in the 1980s, was deregulation. This allowed investors who had never been in the broadcast business before to enter the industry, using bank loans to pay for most of their investment. Some new owners of broadcast media companies see these

Deregulation Government action that reduces government restrictions on the business operations of an industry.

companies the way they would look at any business—hoping to invest the minimum amount necessary. They hold onto the property until the market is favorable, planning to sell at a huge profit.

5. In the 1990s, the introduction of new technologies, especially the Internet, changed the economics of all the media industries. Each industry had to adapt to the Internet quickly, and the fastest way to gain Internet expertise was to buy a company or to invest in a company that already had created an Internet presence or a successful Internet product.

6. The economic downturn that began in 2007 hit the newspaper business especially hard. Heavily dependent on real estate advertising and classifieds and challenged by the dynamics of the Internet, many publicly owned newspaper companies began losing money at an unprecedented rate. This fall in profits drove their stock prices to new lows, which made them vulnerable to takeovers and buyouts as the companies struggled to survive. Several newspaper companies, such as the Tribune Company (which publishes the *Chicago Tribune* and the *Los Angeles Times*), filed for bankruptcy protection, and in 2013 the investors who owned the Tribune Company put it up for sale.

Supporters of concentrated ownership and convergence say a large company can offer advantages that a small company could never afford—training for the employees, higher wages and better working conditions.

The major arguments against the concentration and convergence of group ownership are that concentration of so much power limits the diversity of opinion and the quality of ideas available to the public and reduces what scholars call **message pluralism**. More than 40 years ago, Ben H. Bagdikian, dean emeritus, Graduate School of Journalism at the University of California, Berkeley, described how the loss of message pluralism can affect every aspect of communication:

> It has always been assumed that a newspaper article might be expanded to a magazine article which could become the basis for a hardcover book, which, in turn, could be a paperback, and then, perhaps a TV series and finally, a movie. At each step of change an author and other enterprises could compete for entry into the array of channels for reaching the public mind and pocketbook. But today several media giants own these arrays, not only closing off entry points for competition in different media, but influencing the choice of entry at the start.

Today, ownership concentration is an ongoing trend in the media business.

Advertisers and Consumers Pay the Bills

Most of the income the American mass media industries collect comes from advertising. Advertising directly supports newspapers, radio and television. Subscribers actually pay only a small part of the cost of producing a newspaper. Advertisers pay the biggest portion. Magazines receive more than half their income from advertising and the other portion from subscriptions. Income for movies, recordings and books, of course, comes primarily from direct purchases and ticket sales.

This means that companies that want to sell you products pay for most of the information and entertainment you receive from the Internet, TV, radio, newspapers and magazines. You support the media industries *indirectly* by buying the products that advertisers sell. General Motors Corp. and AT&T each spend more than $3 billion a year on advertising. Multiply the spending for all this advertising for all media, and you can understand how easily American media industries accumulate $200 billion in annual revenue.

You also pay for the media *directly* when you buy a book or a video game or go to a movie. This money buys equipment, underwrites company research and expansion, and pays stock dividends. Advertisers and consumers are the financial foundation for American media industries because different audiences provide a variety of markets for consumer products.

Technology Changes Mass Media Delivery and Consumption

The channels of communication have changed dramatically over the centuries, but the idea that a society will pay to stay informed and entertained is not new. In Imperial Rome, people who wanted to find out what was going on paid professional speakers a coin (a *gazet*) for the privilege of listening to the speaker announce the day's events. Many early newspapers were called *gazettes* to reflect this heritage.

The history of mass communication technology involves three information communications revolutions: phonetic writing, printing and computer technology. (See Time-Frame, p. 3.)

> **Message Pluralism** The availability to an audience of a variety of information and entertainment sources.

Phonetic Writing: The First Information Communications Revolution

Early attempts at written communication began modestly with *pictographs*. A pictograph is a symbol of an object used to convey an idea. If you have ever drawn a heart with an arrow through it, you understand what a pictograph is. The Sumerians of Mesopotamia carved the first known pictographs in stone in about 3500 B.C.

The stone in which these early pictographic messages were carved served as a medium—a device to transmit messages. Eventually, people imprinted messages in clay, and then they stored these clay tablets in a primitive version of today's library. These messages weren't very portable, however. Heavy clay tablets don't slip easily into someone's pocket.

In about 2500 B.C., the Egyptians invented papyrus, a type of paper made from a grasslike plant called sedge, which was easier to write on, but people still communicated using pictographs.

Pictographs as a method of communication developed into *phonetic writing* in about 1000 B.C. when people began to use symbols to represent sounds. Instead of drawing a picture of a dog to convey the idea of a dog, scholars represented the sounds d-o-g with phonetic writing. The invention of phonetic writing has been called *the first information communications revolution*. "After being stored in written form, *information could now reach a new kind of audience, remote from the source and uncontrolled by it*," writes media scholar Anthony Smith. "Writing transformed knowledge into information."

About 500 years later, the Greek philosopher Socrates anticipated the changes that widespread literacy would bring. He argued that knowledge should remain among the privileged classes. Writing threatened the exclusive use of information, he said. "Once a thing is put in writing, the composition, whatever it may be, drifts all over the place, getting into the hands not only of those who understand it, but equally of those who have no business with it."

In about 200 B.C., the Greeks perfected parchment, made from goat and sheep skins. Parchment was an even better medium on which to write. By about A.D. 100, before the use of parchment spread throughout Europe, the Chinese had invented paper, which was much cheaper to produce than parchment. Europeans didn't start to use paper until more than a thousand years later, in about A.D. 1300. The discovery of parchment and then paper meant that storing information became cheaper and easier.

As Socrates predicted, when more people learned to write, wider communication became possible because people in many different societies could share information among themselves and with people in other parts of the world. But scholars still had to painstakingly copy the information they wanted to keep or pay a scribe to copy

Two folios from the Gutenberg Bible, printed in the workshop of Johannes Gutenberg, 1455 (parchment), German School, (15th century) / Universitatsbibliothek, Gottingen, Germany / Bildarchiv Steffens / Bridgeman Images

The Gutenberg Bible, published by Johannes Gutenberg in Germany in 1455, was the first book printed using movable type. Although the printing was done mechanically, hand-colored decorative drawings (called *illuminations*) often were added to artistically enhance the text.

for them. In the 14th century, for example, the library of the Italian poet Petrarch contained more than 100 manuscripts that he himself had copied individually.

In Petrarch's day, literate people were either monks or members of the privileged classes. Wealthy people could afford tutoring, and they also could afford to buy the handwritten manuscripts copied by the monks. Knowledge—and the power it brings—belonged to an elite group of people.

Printing: The Second Information Communications Revolution

As societies grew more literate, the demand for manuscripts flourished, but a scribe could produce only one copy at a time. What has been called *the second information communications revolution* began in Germany in 1455, when Johannes Gutenberg printed a Bible on a press that used movable type.

More than 200 years before Gutenberg, the Chinese had invented a printing press that used wood type, and the Chinese also are credited with perfecting a copper press in 1445. But Gutenberg's innovation was to line up individual metal letters that he could ink and then press onto paper to produce copies. Unlike the wood or copper presses, the metal letters could be reused to produce new pages of text, which made the process much cheaper.

The Gutenberg Bible, a duplicate of the Latin original, is considered the first book printed by movable type (47 copies survive today, 559 years later). As other countries

---

Pictograph A symbol of an object that is used to convey an idea.

Phonetic Writing The use of symbols to represent sounds.

adopted Gutenberg's press, the price for Bibles plummeted. In 1470, the cost of a French, mechanically printed Bible was one-fifth the cost of a hand-printed Bible.

The second information communications revolution—printing—meant that *knowledge, which had belonged to the privileged few, would one day be available to everyone.* The key development of printing was one of the essential conditions for the rise of modern governments, as well as an important element of scientific and technological progress.

Before the Gutenberg press, a scholar who wanted specialized information had to travel to the place where it was kept. But once information could be duplicated easily, it could travel to people beyond the society that created it. The use of paper instead of the scribes' bulky parchment also meant that books could be stacked end to end. *For the first time, knowledge was portable and storable.*

Libraries now could store vast amounts of information in a small space. And because people could easily carry these smaller, lighter books, all different kinds of people in many different cities could read classical works simultaneously. Another benefit of the development of printing was that societies could more easily keep information to share with future generations. *Knowledge now was accessible to many; knowledge no longer belonged to just the chosen few.*

This effort to communicate—first through spoken messages, then through pictographs, then through the written word and finally through printed words—demonstrates people's innate desire to share information with one another. *Storability, portability and accessibility* of information are essential to today's concept of mass communication. By definition, *mass communication is information that is available to a large audience quickly.*

Computer Technology: The Third Information Communications Revolution

Today's age of communication has been called the *third information communications revolution* because computers have become the electronic storehouses and transmitters of vast amounts of information that previously relied on the written word.

Electronic technology, which processes and transmits information much more efficiently than mechanical devices, is driving the majority of changes affecting today's media. This has become possible with the development of digital computers, beginning around 1950. Digital delivery means that changes in today's media industries happen much faster than in the past. Satellite broadcasts, digital recordings and the international electronic network called the Internet are just three examples of the third information communications revolution.

Although each medium has its own history and economic structure, today all of the media industries compete for consumers' attention. Digital technology is

The introduction of digital delivery represents the third information communications revolution and affects every aspect of politics, society and culture. The interconnectivity of all types of digital products is on display at the 2015 Consumer Electronics Show in Las Vegas, where car manufacturers showcase how they have integrated mobile media into their latest designs.

Michael Nagle/Bloomberg/Getty Images

transforming the media business more than we can foresee—enabling faster transmission of more information to more people than ever before.

Media Take Advantage of Digital Delivery

The economics of the communications industries makes digital delivery very important. All the industries involved in building and maintaining this interconnected network—broadcast, cable, telephone, computer, software, satellite and the consumer electronics industries—want a piece of the estimated $1 trillion in global revenue that digital delivery represents.

Leaders of the media industries in the United States are among the central driving forces in this network because many of the companies that are developing digital products—such as Apple, Microsoft, Intel and Facebook—are based in the U.S.

Because the U.S. already contributes so many of the digital environment's necessary elements, it has become logical—and very profitable—for the media industries in this country to drive converging technologies that package and deliver information worldwide.

One-Way Versus Two-Way Communication

The classic model of mass communication (see **Illustration 1.2** on p. 6) describes a process that begins with a *sender* (or source), who puts a *message* on a *channel* (a medium).

Illuminations Hand-colored decorative drawings used to enhance printed text.

The channel then delivers the message to the *receiver*. This is the equivalent of a one-way road—sender to receiver.

Digital delivery begins in the same way. The *channel* carries information and entertainment (*messages*) from many different sources (*senders*) to many different people (*receivers*). The messages that return from the receiver to the sender are called *feedback*. In the digital environment, messages and feedback can occur almost instantly because the sender and the receiver can communicate with each other simultaneously. This makes digital systems **interactive**.

To take advantage of this interactivity, today's delivery system has evolved from a communications system that works like an ordinary television (sending messages and programming one way from the sender to the receiver) into a two-way, interactive system that can send and receive messages simultaneously and that works more like a combination television, telephone and computer.

Dumb Versus *Smart* Communication

A standard television set is a "dumb" appliance; it can only deliver programming. You can change the channel to receive different programs, but you can't talk back to the people who send the programming to your television set to tell them when you'd like to see a particular program.

You can record something to watch later or pick a specific program to watch. But you can't rearrange a television network schedule to show all your programs exactly when you want to see them. You also can't add anything to the programs on your TV, such as your personal commentary about a football game or a bad movie. This type of mass communication—in which the programs are sent to you on an established schedule with you as a passive receiver (a couch potato) for the program—is *one-way*.

As communications devices, however, telephones are smarter. When you talk on the telephone, the person on the other end of the conversation can listen to you and talk back right away (and, in the case of a teleconference, this can involve several people at the same time). This makes telephone communication interactive, giving you the ability to talk back—to transmit as well as to receive messages. Telephone communications are *two-way*.

To communicate rapidly, telephone communication uses a system of digitized information. When you talk, the telephone system uses electronic signals to transform your voice into a series of digits—ones and zeroes—and then reassembles these digits into an exact reproduction of your voice on the other end of the line. This method of storing and transmitting data is called **digital communication**.

Like telephone communications, computers operate using digitized information and are interactive. Written words, audio and video are translated and stored as *bits*. These bits can easily be transmitted, using two-way communication. This is the reason that someone can, for

instance, connect to the Internet on a computer and receive and send information. To communicate via the Internet, a computer uses a *modem* to connect to a telephone line or a cellular signal, making two-way communication possible.

And, unlike television and telephones, computers can store digital information for future use. This ability to store information makes the computer different from broadcast, cable, telephone and satellite communications.

How Today's Communications Network Operates

Today's communications network combines many different elements from existing media industries. The broadcast industry produces content and delivers one-way communication by antenna and satellite; the cable industry delivers one-way communication and two-way communication by underground (or overhead) cable; the telephone companies deliver digital two-way communication using fiber, satellite and cellular technology; and the electronics industry offers digital storage capability.

A digital communications network combines all these elements: content, two-way digital communication and digital storage. **Illustration 1.4** on page 17 shows how this global communications network operates.

The Receiver (You, the Subscriber)

A digital network begins with you, the receiver/subscriber. For example, you use your smartphone and

Interactive A message system that allows senders and receivers to communicate simultaneously.

Digital Communication Data in a form that can be transmitted and received electronically.

Convergence

ILLUSTRATION 1.4

How the Global Communications Network Works

Today's communications network combines different elements of broadcast, cable, telephone, satellite, cellular and computer technology to create a global digital communications service.

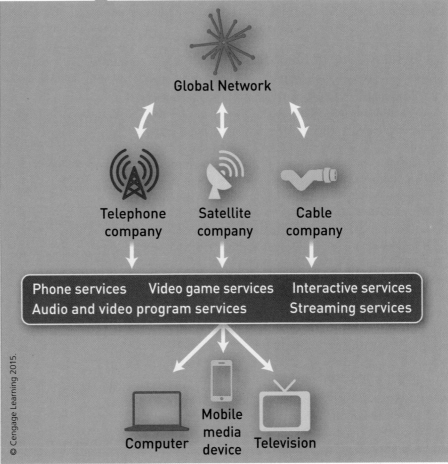

Global Network

Telephone company

Satellite company

Cable company

Phone services   Video game services   Interactive services
Audio and video program services   Streaming services

Computer

Mobile media device

Television

© Cengage Learning 2015.

---

seamlessly shift between texts, video, music and news. You can, for example, choose

▶ First-run movies, TV episodes and music concert streaming

▶ Worldwide video news feeds, including access to overseas channels in a variety of languages

▶ Newspaper and video services, offering live access to today's stories from news and sports outlets around the globe on topics you've preselected

▶ Internet video games and gaming sites

▶ Twitter feeds, social networks, blogs and YouTube videos.

As you glance through the offerings of each service and make your choices, you can use various services at the same time. For example, you can check your bank balance while you play poker online and read your text messages while you watch an overseas soccer match.

All these simultaneous services, which you take for granted today, weren't available 15 years ago. The Internet's digital communications network makes all this possible.

The Channel (Cable, Telephone, Satellite and Cellular Companies)

Cable, telephone, satellite and cellular companies provide Internet communications delivery, acting as a conduit—gathering all the services from national and international networks. Some companies offer only specific services, or they package services together (local, national and international news services, for example), or they offer an unlimited menu of all the available services and let you choose what you want. Cable, telephone, satellite and cellular companies are competing today for consumers' Internet business.

You can choose the type of service you want based on each company's offerings and pricing. Some services are billed as pay-per-use (a $6 charge to view a first-run movie, for example) or per retrieved item (to use a newspaper's archive to retrieve a single research article, for example).

This international communications network and the satellite system to support it already are in place—long-distance carrier networks run by a communications company such as AT&T or a satellite service such as DirecTV or Dish Network. The **Internet**, as an international web of electronic networks, forms the backbone of this communications network, which is available to any consumer who has a screen and a cable, satellite, cellular or telephone connection to the system.

The Sender (Internet Service Providers)

Internet service providers (**ISPs**), such as AT&T, offer a way of organizing the information to help you find what you want. Today's broadcast networks, as well as cable and satellite channels, essentially are video program services, offering a group of programs for a specific subscription fee. Telephone companies also are beginning to compete to deliver programs directly to consumers.

Program services are moving toward a different model, however, which eventually will make it possible for you to choose programs from NBC and ABC and not CBS, for example, or pick ten channels from a list of available channels, rather than having to accept a large number of channels—many that you don't necessarily want to watch—packaged together as they are now. When the complete communications network is in place, the ISP will offer customized **bundles**, and you will be able to select the specific bundle you want.

The Message (Content)

All text, audio and video that are digitized into bits are potential content for an electronic communications system. In a world of networked, rapid, digitized communications, *any* digitized textbook, novel, movie, magazine article, recording, video segment or news story, for example, qualifies as content.

Information and entertainment that already have been produced, stored and digitized form the basic content for this communications network. Companies that hold the copyrights for information and entertainment can quickly and easily sell the content they already own as products, along with the ongoing information-entertainment they are producing, because they own the rights to their content and don't have to buy the rights from someone else.

Today, media companies that traditionally have produced content, such as newspaper publishers, book publishers, TV program producers and movie producers, are busy creating and buying more "inventory" for the online world. "Movie companies have been increasing production," says *The Wall Street Journal*, "because there is a general feeling that as 'content providers' they will be big winners."

Once information and entertainment products are digitized, they are available in many different formats. This is the reason a music video of Disney songs is available online as soon as—even before—Disney releases a new movie; a

profile of a well-known musician, complete with video, can be made available on the musician's Internet site during the musician's worldwide concert tour; and a publisher can assemble excerpts and photos from a new book, along with a video interview with the author, and make them available on the Internet to promote the book before it hits the bookstores. With convergence, the availability of digital content means all the mass media industries have become technologically interdependent and interconnected.

Mass Media Both Reflect and Affect Politics, Society and Culture

The media industries provide information and entertainment, but mass media also can affect political, social and cultural institutions. Although the media actively influence society, they also mirror it, and scholars constantly strive to delineate the differences.

Current news events often focus attention on the role of mass media in society. For example, when President Obama announced in February 2015 that he planned to move ahead with immigration reform despite Congress' objections, the public conversation about the relationship between Congress and the presidency played out through public events scheduled by both sides in the debate. If you were a scholar studying the role of the mass media in public policy, how

Saul Loeb/AFP/Getty Images

Current news events often focus attention on the role mass media play in the development of public policy. On February 4, 2015, President Obama invited media coverage of his meeting with a group of young immigrants at the White House to bring public attention to the need for immigration reform.

Internet   An international web of computer networks.

ISP   Internet service provider.

Bundle   The combination of telecommunications services that the media industries can offer consumers.

would you analyze the role that mass media play in setting the agenda surrounding public topics such as immigration?

This example shows the difficulty scholars face when analyzing mass media's political, social and cultural effects. Early media studies analyzed each message in the belief that once a message was sent, everyone would receive and react to the message in the same way. Then studies proved that different people process messages differently—a phenomenon described as **selective perception**. This occurs because everyone brings many variables—family background, past experiences, interests and education, for example—to each message.

Complicating the study of mass media's political, social and cultural effects is the recent proliferation of media outlets and social networks. The multiplying sources for information and entertainment today mean that very few people share identical mass media environments. This makes it much more difficult for scholars to analyze the specific or cumulative effects of mass media on the general population.

Still, scholars' attempts to describe mass media's political, social and cultural roles in society are important because, once identified, the effects can be observed. The questions should be asked so we do not become complacent about the role of mass media in our lives, so we do not grow immune to the possibility that our society may be cumulatively affected by mass media in ways we cannot yet accurately quantify.

Advertising also is often the focus of media analysis—does advertising cause you to buy products you don't need? Is there a one-to-one relationship between how much money a company devotes to advertising a product and the success of that product? And, if so, how does an advertiser reach a specific customer for a product when mass media delivery today is so diffused? "Marketers used to try their hardest to reach people at home, when they were watching TV or reading newspapers or magazines. But consumers' viewing and reading habits are so scattershot now that many advertisers say the best way to reach time-pressed consumers is to try to catch their eye at literally every turn," reports *The New York Times*.

The market research firm Yankelovich reports that a person living in a city 30 years ago saw up to 2,000 ad messages a day, compared with up to 5,000 today. According to *The New York Times*, about half the people surveyed by Yankelovich said they thought marketing and advertising today were "out of control." How does advertising affect your buying choices?

Why You Should Understand Mass Media and Everyday Life

In the United States, Europe and Asian countries that have encouraged technological advancements, communications changes are moving faster than ever before. For the media industries, this means increasing costs to replace old equipment and expand to meet demand. For consumers, this means a confusing array of products that need to be replaced soon after purchase—video streaming replacing Blu-ray Disc players, which replaced DVD players, which replaced VCRs; curved HDTVs replacing flat-screen HDTVs, which replaced conventional TVs; and smartphones replacing iPods, which replaced CD players, for example.

Forecasters today envision an even bigger technology imprint on people's everyday lives. They describe a future called the **Internet of Things (IoT)**, where all aspects of consumers' lives—from media, to medical information to fitness to home security to the temperature of their air conditioners—will be managed through their connection to the Internet. (see **Impact/Convergence**, p. 20.)

The development of communications technology directly affects the speed with which a society and culture evolve. A town with only one telephone or one radio may be impossible for people in the United States to imagine, but there still are many countries in which ten families share a single telephone, and people consider a television set to be a luxury.

By today's standards, the earliest communications obstacles seem unbelievably simple: how to transmit a single message to several people at the same time and how to share information inexpensively. Yet it has taken 5,500 years to achieve the capability for instant communication that we enjoy today.

After you understand how each type of media business works, you can examine why people who work in the media make the business decisions they do and the effects these decisions have on the United States and the global economy. With a better grasp of technology's role in the evolving mass media landscape, you can see how technological change affects the media business.

Once you understand the history of mass media development, you can consider the mass media's present-day effects on you and on society as a whole. Only then—once you understand the mass media's evolutionary path from 3500 B.C. to today—can you truly begin to analyze the *impact* of mass media on your everyday life.

Internet of Things (IoT) A computing concept that envisions a society where all electronic devices are interconnected through the Internet and, in turn, can process and share information and interact globally.

Selective Perception The concept that each person processes messages differently.

IMPACT

Convergence

The Internet of Things Is Far Bigger Than Anyone Realizes

By Daniel Burrus, Wired

When we truly consider the ramifications of connecting a vast array of data-gathering sensors, devices, and machines together, what's important to realize is that information will be translated into action at a rate that we have never seen before. We are closing in on a world with infinitesimal reaction times, immediate responses to changing conditions, and unparalleled control in managing assets and resources.

The key is not to think small. The Internet of Things (IoT) is not merely about creating savings within current industry models. It's about upending old models entirely, creating new services and new products. There is no one sector where the Internet of Things is making the biggest impact; it will disrupt every industry imaginable, including agriculture, energy, security, disaster management, and healthcare, just to name a few.

How do you make this intelligence useful? Take a look at your own home. What parts can you make smart? Here's a simple one. I once observed a video conferencing system that allowed a dog owner to actually talk to his dog, call it over, and feed it remotely through a smart appliance. Think bigger. A house that knows when you're coming home because it's connected to a sensor in your car or smartphone. A home that links smoke alarms,

Skott Ahn, president and chief technology officer at electronics manufacturer LG, discusses the Internet of Things at the 2015 Consumer Electronics Show in Las Vegas.

Robyn Beck/AFP/Getty Images

security systems, and infotainment consoles to your phone.

This is a huge and transformational shift. It won't stop with intelligent homes and businesses. We're going to end up with intelligent highways and vehicles, intelligent factories and farms, intelligent utility and power grids. This is not some flight of fantasy, or one of many potential outcomes (what I call a soft trend). This is a hard trend: it's a projection based on measurable facts, facts that cannot be changed.

I haven't even come close to listing all the ways this technology is going to impact us. It's going to create disruption and opportunity in every imaginable field, and it's entirely up to you whether you're going to be one of the disrupted or the disruptors. Because this is going to happen. It's time to learn about it now.

Daniel Burrus, CEO and President of Burrus Research, is a leading technology forecaster and innovation expert.

Excerpted from Daniel Burrus, "The Internet of Things Is Far Bigger Than Anyone Realizes," Part 2. Wired.com, November 26, 2014.

REVIEW, ANALYZE, INVESTIGATE

CHAPTER 1

Mass Media Are Everywhere You Are

- Adults spend three-fourths of their waking lives with the media.
- Some form of media touches your life every day—economically, socially and politically.

Mass Communication Becomes Wireless

- Historically, to be connected to media meant that you had to be near an electrical outlet.
- Because of the development of digital communication, most of today's mass media is wireless.
- Electronic signals have replaced wires, freeing people up to stay connected no matter where or when they want to communicate.

How the Communication Process Works

- Communication is the act of sending messages, ideas and opinions from one person to another.
- *Intra*personal communication means communication within one person.
- *Inter*personal communication means communication between two people.
- Mass communication is communication from one person or group of persons through a transmitting device (a medium) to large audiences or markets.
- By definition, mass communication is information that is made available to a large audience quickly.

What Are the Mass Media Industries?

- There are eight mass media businesses: books, newspapers, magazines, recordings, radio, movies, television and the Internet.
- Books were the first mass medium.
- The Internet is the newest mass medium.

Three Key Concepts to Remember

- Mass media are profit-centered businesses.
- Technological developments change the way mass media are delivered and consumed.
- Mass media both reflect and affect politics, society and culture.

Mass Media Are Profit-Centered Businesses

- All U.S. media are privately owned except the Public Broadcasting Service and National Public Radio, which survive on government support and private donations.
- Overall, American mass media ownership has been contracting rather than expanding, with fewer companies owning more aspects of the media business. This trend is called *concentration of ownership.*
- Concentration of ownership takes four forms: chains, broadcast networks, conglomerates and vertical integration.
- Above all, the major goal of the American mass media is to make money. Except for National Public Radio and the Public Broadcasting Service, all U.S. media operate primarily as profit-centered businesses.

Convergence Dominates the Media Business

- Media acquisitions in the U.S. have skyrocketed because most conglomerates today are publicly traded companies and because, beginning in 1980, the federal government deregulated the broadcast industry.
- The economic downturn that began in 2007 made publicly owned newspapers especially vulnerable to takeovers and acquisitions.
- The trend of mergers and acquisitions is expected to continue as changing technology expands the global market for media products.

Why Media Properties Converge

- U.S. media industries continue to prosper, but the share of profits is shifting among the different types of media industries.
- Supporters of concentrated ownership and convergence say a large company offers advantages that a small company can never afford; critics say concentrated ownership and convergence interfere with message pluralism.

Advertisers and Consumers Pay the Bills

- Most of the income the mass media industries collect comes from advertising.
- People who want to sell you products pay for most of the information and entertainment you receive through the American mass media.
- Consumers support the media indirectly by buying the products that advertisers sell.

Technology Changes Mass Media Delivery and Consumption

- The invention of phonetic writing in 1000 B.C. was considered the *first information communications revolution*.
- The invention of movable type in 1455 marked the *second information communications revolution*.
- The invention of digital computers in 1951 ushered in the *third information communications revolution*.
- The new world of mass media uses wireless communications technology, an intricate webbed network of many different types of communications systems.
- The development of communications technology directly affects the speed with which a society evolves.
- Storability, portability and accessibility of information are essential to today's concept of mass communication.

Media Take Advantage of Digital Delivery

- Today's information network includes the broadcast, cable, telephone, computer, software, satellite and consumer electronics industries.
- The traditional delivery system for information and entertainment is primarily a one-way system.
- The ability to talk back—to transmit as well as receive messages—makes the telephone interactive.
- Today's communications network is a two-way, interactive system.

How Today's Communications Network Operates

- The communications network needs content, two-way digital communication and digital storage.
- Cable companies, satellite services, telephone companies and cellular companies deliver services on the new communications network.
- Many Americans already have all the tools that a digital communications system requires—television, telephone, cellular, cable and satellite services and electronics.

- Information and entertainment that already have been produced, stored and digitized provided the first content for the communications network.
- Many motives shape the American mass media, including the desire to fulfill the public's need for information, to influence the country's governance, to disseminate the country's culture, to offer entertainment and to provide an outlet for creative expression.
- Media industries expand and contract in the marketplace to respond to the audience.

Mass Media Both Reflect and Affect Politics, Society and Culture

- The media are political, social and cultural institutions that both reflect and affect the society in which they operate.
- Multiplying sources of information and entertainment mean that, today, very few people share identical mass media environments.

Why You Should Understand Mass Media and Everyday Life

- In the United States, Europe and Asian countries that have encouraged technological advancements, communication changes are moving faster than ever before.
- For the media industries, this means increasing costs to replace old equipment. For consumers, this means a confusing array of products that need to be replaced soon after you buy them.
- The development of communications technology directly affects the speed with which a society and culture evolve.
- It has taken 5,500 years to achieve the capability for instant communication that we enjoy today.
- Forecasters predict that eventually all electronic devices will be connected in an Internet of Things.

Key Terms

These terms are defined in the margins throughout this chapter and appear in alphabetical order with definitions in the Glossary, which begins on page 361.

Critical Questions

1. Discuss the differences between one-way and two-way communication, and explain why two-way communication is important for the new communications network.

2. Identify the three communications revolutions and discuss how each one drastically changed the world's mass media.

3. Summarize the advantages and disadvantages of the concentration of ownership in today's mass media business.

4. In traditional media, advertising aimed at consumers pays for delivery of entertainment and information. How has digital delivery changed the way people pay for mass media?

5. What do technology forecasters mean when they talk about The Internet of Things? List and explain three advantages and disadvantages you can foresee if the Internet of Things becomes a reality.

Working the Web

This list includes both sites mentioned in the chapter as well as others to give you greater insight into mass media and everyday life.

AOL (formerly America Online)

aol.com

Originally part of AOL/Time Warner, AOL provides online digital content in partnership with The Huffington Post Media Group, as well as several other pay advertising platforms such as Adtech, Pictela and Studio Now.

CBS Corporation

cbscorporation.com

CBS operates in every field of media and entertainment, including CBS Radio, Showtime, Simon & Schuster Publishers, The CW, Pop, CBS Sports Network, CBS Television Studios, CBS Interactive and CBS Films.

Comcast Corporation

comcast.com

Comcast Corp. has two primary businesses—Comcast Cable and NBC Universal. Comcast provides cable, Internet and landline phone service throughout the United States under the Xfinity brand. NBC Universal operates news and basic cable networks, including the NBC and Telemundo broadcast networks, Universal Pictures and Universal Parks and Resorts.

Gannett Company

gannett.com

Gannett publishes 82 daily newspapers, including *USA Today*, and operates 46 television stations, G/O Digital (CareerBuilder.com and 120 online mobile applications), and Newsquest, a regional community news provider in the U.K.

News Corporation and 21st Century Fox

Formerly known as News Corporation (a combination of major newspaper publishers and the Fox media networks), in 2013 the company was split off into two companies, News Corporation and 21st Century Fox.

News Corporation

newscorp.com

News Corporation is comprised of Fox News Corp., News U.K., Dow Jones, *The New York Post*, Harper Collins Publishers, Amplify, News American Marketing, Storyful and Move.

21st Century Fox

21cf.com

21st Century Fox is made up of basic cable networks (Fox News, Fox Deportes and Fox Sports 1) filmed entertainment (20th Century Fox, Fox Searchlight and 20th Century Fox Television), and the SKY Satellite Network.

Sony Corporation of America (SCA)

sony.com

The U.S. subsidiary of Sony Corp. is located in New York City. A large manufacturer of audio, video and information technology products, SCA's primary businesses include Sony Electronics, Sony Pictures Entertainment, Sony Computer Entertainment America and Sony Music Entertainment.

Time Inc.

timeinc.com

Spun off from Time Warner, Inc. into a private publishing company in 2014, the company currently consists of both online and print versions of major magazine publications such as *People*, *Sports Illustrated*, *InStyle*, *Time*, *Real Simple*, *Entertainment Weekly* and *Fortune*.

Time Warner Inc.

timewarner.com

Time Warner Inc.'s primary businesses include cable and broadcast television networks and film and television entertainment companies (CNN, HBO, Cinemax and Warner Brothers). In 2014, Time Warner spun off its magazine division (including *Sports Illustrated* and *Time* magazines) into a separate company called Time Inc. (TimeInc.com).

Tribune Media Company and Tribune Publishing

Formerly known as The Tribune Company, Tribune was split into two companies in 2014.

Tribune Media

tribunemedia.com

Tribune Media is comprised of television and digital companies, including 42 television stations (including WGN America), Tribune Studios, Gracenote and WGN-Radio.

Tribune Publishing

tribpub.com

Tribune Publishing is now comprised of *The Chicago Tribune, The Los Angeles Times, The Orlando Sentinel, The Sun Sentinel* and *The Baltimore Sun.*

Twitter

twitter.com

Headquartered in San Francisco and claiming more than 500 million users, Twitter is an online social networking company that allows subscribers to send and receive 140-character messages or "tweets" from anywhere in the world via a cell phone.

Viacom Incorporated

viacom.com

Viacom Inc. has two large entertainment divisions—Viacom Media Networks and Paramount Pictures Corporation. Viacom Media Networks is comprised of MTV, Comedy Central, Nickelodeon and BET. Paramount Pictures includes Paramount Pictures, Paramount Vantage, Paramount Animation, Insurge Pictures, MTV Films and Nickelodeon Movies.

The Walt Disney Company

thewaltdisneycompany.com

The Walt Disney Company operates family entertainment and media companies under five different business operations: Media Networks (Disney/ABC Television Group and ESPN Inc.), Parks and Resorts, Walt Disney Studios, Disney Consumer Products and Disney Interactive.

YouTube

youtube.com

Owned and operated by Google Inc., YouTube allows people to watch videos online from around the world about any subject, including comedy, news and politics, pets and animals and sports. In early 2015, the company announced plans to launch a separate online channel just for children.

Impact/Action Videos are concise news features on various topics created exclusively for *Media/ Impact.* Find them in *Media/ Impact*'s MindTap at cengagebrain.com.

MindTap® Log on to MindTap for *Media/Impact* to access a variety of additional material—including learning objectives, chapter readings with highlighting and note-taking, **Impact/Action Videos**, activities, and comprehension quizzes—that will guide you through this chapter.

BOOKS
REARRANGING THE PAGE

02

Russell Westbrook of the Oklahoma City Thunder reads to children on February 23, 2015, at Martin Luther King Elementary in Oklahoma City, as part of the Russell Westbrook Why Not? Foundation's literacy initiative.

Layne Murdoch/NBAE via Getty Images

What's Ahead?

- Publishers Nurture Ideas and Try to Make a Profit
- How American Book Publishing Grew
- Cheaper Books Create a Mass Market
- Grove Press Tests Censorship
- Investors Buy Up Publishing Companies
- Book Publishing at Work
- Books Begin with Authors and Agents
- How Do Books Get Published?
- The Book Industry Has Three Major Markets
- Audiobooks and E-books Multiply the Audience
- Corporations Demand Higher Profits
- Small Presses Seek Specialized Audiences
- New Technologies Affect Production and Delivery
- Book Publishing Today Is a Competitive, Complex Business

"We're finding that you really have to get your head around a paradigm shift. Our digital library is stored in the cloud, so you don't have to come in to get a book."

—LAURA COLE, SPECIAL PROJECTS COORDINATOR AT BIBLIOTECH, THE NATION'S FIRST BOOKLESS PUBLIC LIBRARY, LOCATED IN SAN ANTONIO, TEXAS

"I'm not sure I can explain how to write a book," *said essayist and author E. B. White, who wrote* 19 books, including the popular children's book *Charlotte's Web.* "First you have to want to write one very much. Then, you have to know of something that you want to write about. Then, you have to begin. And, once you have started, you have to keep going. That's really all I know about how to write a book."

The process of writing a book today is much more complex than White suggests, and every year in the United States publishers produce about 200,000 book titles. This number includes revised editions of previously published books, but the majority of the book titles published today are new.

Publishers Nurture Ideas and Try to Make a Profit

The publishing industry always has been tugged by what publishing scholars Lewis A. Coser, Charles Kadushin and Walter W. Powell call "the culture and commerce of publishing"—the desire to preserve the country's intellectual ideas versus the desire to make money. But a publisher who doesn't consistently make a profit cannot continue to publish books.

Coser and his colleagues describe the four characteristics of book publishing in America:

1. The industry sells its products—like any commodity—in a market that, in contrast to that for many other products, is fickle and often uncertain.

2. The industry is decentralized among a number of sectors whose operations bear little resemblance to each other.

3. A mixture of modern mass media production methods and craftlike procedures characterizes these operations.

4. The industry remains perilously poised between the requirements and restraints of commerce and the responsibilities and obligations that it must bear as a prime guardian of the symbolic culture of the nation.

Many new owners of publishing houses try to bring some predictability to the market. Says Coser, "Publishers attempt to reduce . . . uncertainty . . . through concentrating on 'sure-fire' blockbusters, through large-scale promotion campaigns or through control over distribution, as in the marketing of paperbacks. In the end, however, publishers rely on sales estimates that may be as unreliable as weather forecasts in Maine."

How American Book Publishing Grew

Today, the book publishing industry divides responsibilities among many people. But when Americans first started publishing books, one person often did all the work.

Aboard the *Mayflower* in 1620, there were two dogs, 70 adults and only a few books, but the Pilgrims were very practical. They brought a map of Virginia, John Smith's *Description of New England* and their Bibles.

TimeFrame
1620–Today

AP Images/Sotheby's/Rex Features

1620 Imported books arrive in the colonies on the *Mayflower*.

✳ **1640** America's first book, *The Bay Psalm Book*, is printed at Cambridge, Mass.

1731 Benjamin Franklin creates the first lending library.

1776 Thomas Paine publishes the revolutionary pamphlet *Common Sense*.

1891 Congress passes the International Copyright Law of 1891, which requires publishing houses to pay royalties to all authors.

1900 Elementary education becomes compulsory, which means increased literacy and more demand for textbooks.

1926 Book-of-the-Month Club is founded, increasing the audience for books.

1939 Robert de Graff introduces Pocket Books, America's first series of paperback books.

1948 New American Library begins publishing serious fiction by and about African Americans.

1960 Publishing houses begin to consolidate, concentrating power in a few large corporations.

✳ **1970s** Book marketing changes significantly with the growth of retail bookstore chains.

1980s Publishers begin producing audiobooks of popular titles.

1990s Amazon.com begins doing business as an Internet retailer for books.

2000 Publishers launch e-books, electronic versions of paper books.

2007 Amazon introduces the Kindle e-reader tablet.

2010 Apple introduces the iPad, making books available as instant downloads.

2011 Chain book retailer Borders files for bankruptcy and eventually shuts down.

2014 Apple introduces the iPad 2, which holds 1,000 e-books.

✳ **TODAY** Most books are sold through Internet retailers. Chain bookstores and independent booksellers are struggling, but the book publishing industry has been revitalized with the introduction of e-books, which have rapidly expanded the market beyond traditional printed books.

Mark Mainz/Staff/Getty Images News/Getty Images

AP Images/Marcio Jose Sanchez

The first books in the United States were imports, brought by the new settlers or ordered from England after the settlers arrived. In 1638, the colonists set up a press at Cambridge, Mass., and in 1640 they printed America's first book: *The Bay Psalm Book* (see **Time-Frame**, p. 27, for a photograph of a rare copy of *The Bay Psalm Book*, officially titled *The Whole Book of Psalms*, which sold at auction in 2013 for $14.2 million). As the only book available, *The Bay Psalm Book* became an instant best-seller. There were only about 3,500 families in the colonies at the time, and the book's first printing of 1,750 sold out.

By 1680, Boston had 17 booksellers, but most of the books still came from England. Between 1682 and 1685, Boston's leading bookseller, John Usher, bought 3,421 books to sell. Among the books he ordered were 162 romance novels.

In 1731, Benjamin Franklin decided that Philadelphia needed a library. So he asked 50 subscribers to pay 40 shillings each to a library company. The company imported 84 books, which circulated among the subscribers. This circulating library was America's first.

The year after he established the circulating library, Franklin published *Poor Richard's Almanack*. Unlike most printers, who waited for someone to come to them with a manuscript, Franklin wrote his own books. The typical author sought a patron to pay for the book's printing and then sold the book at the print shop where it was published.

To expand readership, early publishers sold political pamphlets, novels, poetry and humor. In addition, three events of the 19th century ensured that the book publishing industry would prosper in the 20th century: the passage of the International Copyright Law, the creation of publishing houses and the establishment of compulsory education.

Political Pamphlets

The big seller of the 1700s was Thomas Paine's revolutionary pamphlet *Common Sense*, which argued for the colonies' independence from Great Britain. From January to March 1776, colonial presses published 100,000 copies of Paine's persuasive political argument—one copy for every 25 people in the colonies—a true best-seller. Throughout the Revolutionary War, Paine was America's best-read author.

Novels and Poetry

Political pamphlets became much less important once the new nation was established, and printers turned their

Mick Stevens/The New Yorker Collection/Cartoon Bank.com

"Let's say you want to write an award-winning short story—you just push this key, here . . . "

attention to other popular reading, especially fiction. Historians credit Benjamin Franklin with selling *Pamela* by Samuel Richardson in 1744, the first novel published in the United States, although it was a British import that first had appeared in England in 1740.

Because there was no international copyright law, colonial printers freely reprinted British novels like *Pamela* and sold them. It was cheaper than publishing American authors, who could demand royalties. (See **"International Copyright Law of 1891,"** p. 29.)

Like other media industries, book publishing always has faced moral criticism. Novels, for example, didn't start out with a good reputation. One critic said the novel "pollutes the imaginations." Women wrote one-third of all the early American novels, and women also bought most of them.

Especially popular after the Civil War and before the turn of the century were dime novels, America's earliest paperbacks. Dime novels often featured serial characters, like many of today's mystery novels. The stories and characters continued from one novel to the next. Most of them cost only a nickel, but some early paperbacks were as expensive as 25 cents.

Poetry generally has been difficult to sell, and it is correspondingly difficult for poets to get published. Literary scholar James D. Hart says that although poetry was never as popular as prose, the mid-1800s was "the great era of poetry. . . . It was more widely read in those years than it has been since."

Humor

Humor has been a durable category in book publishing since the days of humorist Mark Twain. Made famous by his short story "The Celebrated Jumping Frog of Calaveras County," Twain became a one-man publishing enterprise. One reason his books sold well was that he was the first American author to recognize the importance of advance publicity. Like most books, Twain's novels were sold door to door. Sales agents took advance orders before the books were published so the publisher could estimate how many to print. Before 1900, more than three-fourths of the popular books people bought were sold door to door.

International Copyright Law of 1891

Before 1891, publishers were legally required to pay royalties to American authors but not to foreign authors. This hurt American authors because books by American authors cost more to publish.

After the International Copyright Law of 1891, all authors—foreign and American—had to give permission for their works to be published. For the first time, American authors cost publishing houses the same amount as foreign authors. This motivated publishers to look for more American writers. In fact, after 1894, American writers published more novels in the United States than foreign writers did.

Publishing Houses

Many publishing houses that began in the late 18th century or during the 19th century continued into the 20th century. Nineteenth-century book publishing houses were just that—book publishing houses. They were nothing like today's multimedia corporations.

These pioneering companies housed all aspects of publishing under one roof: They sought out authors, reviewed and edited copy, printed and then sold the books.

Compulsory Education

By 1900, 31 states had passed compulsory education laws. This was important to book publishing because schools buy textbooks, and education creates more children who can read. Expanded public support for education also meant more money for libraries—more good news for the publishing industry.

Cheaper Books Create a Mass Market

The first quarter of the 20th century enabled still more publishing houses, such as Simon & Schuster and McGraw-Hill, to meet the public's needs. Publishers that specialized in paperbacks started in the 1930s and 1940s: Pocket Books (1939), Bantam Books (1946) and New American Library (1948). If you drop a product's price drastically, sales can explode. That's exactly what

happened to book publishing with the introduction of book clubs and paperbacks, beginning in the 1920s.

Book Clubs

Book clubs replaced door-to-door salespeople as a way to reach readers who otherwise wouldn't buy books. Book-of-the-Month Club was founded in 1926, and Literary Guild in 1927. By 1946, there were 50 book clubs in America, and the Book-of-the-Month Club was selling nearly 12 million copies a year.

Paperbacks

In 1939, Robert de Graff introduced America's first series of paperback best-sellers, called Pocket Books, which issued titles that had already succeeded as hardbound books. They were inexpensive (25 cents), and they fit in a pocket or a purse. Suddenly, a book could reach millions of people who had never owned a book before. Paperbacks democratized reading in America.

The books were so small, however, that people at first thought paperback books were shortened versions of the originals. So publishers printed messages to readers on the cover to assure them that the paperbacks were the "complete novel, as originally published" or "complete and unabridged."

More publishers joined Pocket Books to produce paperbacks: New American Library (NAL), Avon, Popular Library, Signet and Dell. NAL distinguished itself by being the first mass-market publisher willing to issue

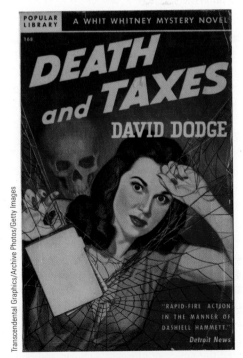

Transcendental Graphics/Archive Photos/Getty Images

When publishers first issued paperbacks in the 1930s, consumers thought the smaller books were abridged versions of the originals. So publishers often printed messages on the covers of paperbacks like *Death and Taxes* to assure readers that the books were "complete and unabridged."

serious books by and about African Americans—Richard Wright's *Native Son*, Lillian Smith's *Strange Fruit* and Ralph Ellison's *Invisible Man*. Signet's unexpected hit in the 1950s was J. D. Salinger's novel *Catcher in the Rye*, still popular today.

Grove Press Tests Censorship

Book publishers always have resisted any attempts by the government to limit freedom of expression. One of the first publishers to test those limits was Grove Press. In 1959, Grove published the sexually explicit *Lady Chatterley's Lover* by D. H. Lawrence (originally published in Italy in 1928); in 1961, the company published *Tropic of Cancer* by Henry Miller (originally published in Paris in 1934). Both books had been banned from the United States as obscene. The legal fees to defend Miller's book against charges of pornography cost Grove more than $250,000, but eventually the U.S. Supreme Court cleared the book in 1964.

The publisher again challenged conventional publishing in 1965, when it issued in hardback the controversial *Autobiography of Malcolm X*, the story of the leader of the African American nationalist movement, by Alex Haley, as told by Malcolm X. The book became a best-seller.

Investors Buy Up Publishing Companies

Forecasts for growing profits in book publishing in the 1960s made the industry attractive to corporations looking for new places to invest. Before the 1960s, the book publishing industry was composed mainly of independent companies whose only business was books. Then, rising school and college attendance from the post–World War II baby boom made some areas of publishing, especially textbooks, lucrative investments for media companies that had not published books before.

Beginning in the 1960s, publishing companies began to consolidate. Publishing expert John P. Dessauer says, "Publishing stocks, particularly those of educational companies, became glamour holdings. And conglomerates began to woo every independent publisher whose future promised to throw off even a modest share of the forecast earnings." Dessauer acknowledges that the new owners often brought a businesslike approach to an industry that was known for its lack of attention to making a profit.

But, according to Dessauer, another consequence of these large-scale acquisitions was that "in many cases they also placed the power of ultimate decision and policymaking in the hands of people unfamiliar with books, their peculiarities and the markets." The same pace of acquisitions continued through the end of the 20th century, and

today large media corporations own most of the major book publishing companies. (See **Illustration 2.1**, p. 32.)

In 2012, publishing companies Random House and Penguin merged into a new company called Penguin Random House, which became the fifth-largest book publishing company in the world, based in Germany. With the merger, Penguin Random House controls a 13 percent share of the global book market.

"Publishers are increasingly worried about the leverage wielded by Internet giants like Google, Apple and, especially, Amazon," reports *The New York Times*. "These companies have vast resources to invest in new technology, like digital sales platforms, and the size to let them negotiate better terms on prices." (See **Impact/Convergence**, "E-Book Restrictions Leave 'Buyers' with Few Rights," p. 31.)

Book Publishing at Work

When authors get together, often they tell stories about mistakes publishers have made—manuscripts that 100 publishers turned down that some bright-eyed editor eventually discovered and published. The books, of course, then become best-sellers. Some of the stories are true. But the best publishing decisions are made deliberately, to deliver an awaited book to an eager market. Successful publishing companies must consistently anticipate both their competitors and consumers.

Once books are written, they also must be printed, promoted and distributed in print and digital formats. This traditional publishing process takes at least a year from the time a project is signed by an editor until the book is published, so publishers are always working ahead. The classic publisher's question is, "Will someone pay $25 (or whatever the projected price of the book is) for this book 12 months after I sign the author?"

Books Begin with Authors and Agents

Publishers acquire books in many ways. Some authors submit manuscripts "over the transom," which means they send an unsolicited manuscript to a publishing house, hoping the publisher will be interested. However, most of the nation's larger publishers refuse to read unsolicited manuscripts and accept only books that agents submit.

Publishers pay authors a ***royalty*** for their work. A royalty amount is based on an established percentage of the

Royalty An amount the publisher pays an author, based on an established percentage of the book's price; royalties run anywhere from 6 to 15 percent.

IMPACT Convergence

E-Book Restrictions Leave "Buyers" with Few Rights

By Michael Hiltzik

There's a crass old joke about how you can never buy beer, just rent it. Who would think that the same joke applies to book buying in the digital age?

But that's the case. Many people who'll be unwrapping iPads, Amazon Kindles or Barnes & Noble (B&N) Nooks on [Christmas] morning and loading them with bestsellers or classics won't have any idea how limited their rights are as their books' "owners."

In fact, they won't be owners at all. They'll be licensees. Unlike the owners of a physical tome, they won't have the unlimited right to lend an e-book, give it away, resell it or leave it to their heirs. If it's bought for their iPad, they won't be able to read it on their Kindle. And if Amazon or the other sellers don't like what they've done with it, they can take it back, without warning.

All these restrictions "raise obvious questions about what 'ownership' is," observes Dan Gillmor, an expert on digital media at Arizona State University. "The companies that license stuff digitally have made it clear that you own nothing."

Typically, e-book buyers have no idea about these complexities. How could they? The rules and limitations are embodied in "terms of service" documents that Amazon, Apple, B&N and other sellers shroud in legalese and bury deep in their Web

E-books are a growing market for publishers, making books electronically available on mobile tablets such as the iPad and the Kindle. But consumers don't own an e-book like they own a physical book. Instead, publishers license consumers to use an e-book, and the publisher retains the rights to the book.

Matthew Horwood/Getty Images News/Getty Images

sites. That tells you how little they want you to know.

The rules are based, in turn, on the 1998 Digital Millennium Copyright Act, with which Congress hoped to balance the rights of copyright holders and content users.

Both camps have important rights to protect. Let's start with copyright owners.

In the non-digital world, copyright ends with the first sale of each copyrighted object. Under the "first sale" doctrine, once you buy a book, that physical book is yours to lend, give away, or resell.

In digital-dom, however, technology allows infinite copies to be made, with no loss of quality. Absent the usual restrictions, one could give away an e-book and still have it to read. Unrestricted transferability becomes a genuine threat to the livelihood of authors, artists, filmmakers, musicians.

So some limitation is sensible. The question is whether the balance has tipped too far in favor of the booksellers, at the consumers' expense. The answer is yes.

It should be a top priority for Congress to clear out the murk. The guiding principle must be that an e-book owner's rights and responsibilities parallel those of a book owner, and the same must go for authors, publishers and booksellers. Clarify these rules of e-book commerce, and the book market will reap the benefit. The power of electronic booksellers over publishers might be reduced, and consumers would know what they were buying—and would own what they bought. Leave the rules as vague as they are, and the victims will be authors, consumers and publishers.

IMPACT

Money

ILLUSTRATION 2.1

Book Publishing's Six Global Giants

Book publishing is an international business, and only one of the six leading companies (Reed Elsevier) has a corporate presence in the United States. The other five companies are based in Europe.

"The World's 56 Largest Book Publishers," June 27, 2014, publishersweekly.com.

1 Pearson
Parent Company:
Pearson
(UK)

3 Thomson-Reuters
Parent Company:
The Woodbridge Company
(Canada)

4 Wolters Kluwer
Parent Company:
Wolters Kluwer
(Netherlands)

2 Reed Elsevier
Parent Company:
Reed Elsevier
(UK, Netherlands, US)

5 Random House
Parent Company:
Bertelsmann AG
(Germany)

6 Hachette Livre
Parent Company:
Lagardère
(France)

---

book's price and may run anywhere from 6 to 15 percent of the cover price of the book. Some authors receive an **advance**, which is an amount the publisher pays the author before the book is published. Royalties the book earns once it is in print are charged against the advance payment, so the book first must sell enough copies to pay off the advance before the author gets additional money.

Agents who represent authors collect fees from the authors they represent. Typically, an agent's fee is 15 percent of the author's royalty. If a publisher prices a book at $25, for example, the author receives a maximum of $3.75 per book, depending on the author's agreement with the publisher; the agent then receives 56 cents of the author's $3.75, depending on the agent's agreement with the author.

How Do Books Get Published?

In most cases, books start with the *author*, who proposes a book to an acquisitions editor, usually with an outline and some sample chapters. Often an agent negotiates the contract for the book, but some authors negotiate their own contracts. Today the author is only one part of publishing a book. Departments at the publishing house called *acquisitions, media, design, production, manufacturing, marketing* and *fulfillment* all participate in the process. At a small publishing house, these jobs are divided among editors who are responsible for all the steps.

The *acquisitions editor* looks for potential authors and projects and works out an agreement with the author. The acquisitions editor's most important role is to be a liaison among the author, the publishing company and the book's audience. Acquisitions editors also may represent the company at book auctions and negotiate sales of **subsidiary rights**, which are the rights to market a book for other uses—to make a movie, for example, or to use the image of a character in the book on a toy.

The *media editor* works with the author to create digital materials to enhance the book. This could be simply an e-book version of the printed book or any other type of multimedia (such as archival photographs, slide shows or video). For textbooks, this might mean a Web site where students can take sample tests and download chapter outlines and instructors can access videos and exercises to use in the classroom.

The *designer* decides what a book will look like, inside and out. The designer chooses typefaces for the book,

---

Advance An amount the publisher pays the author before the book is published.

Subsidiary Rights The rights to market a book for other uses—to make a movie or to print a character from the book on T-shirts, for example.

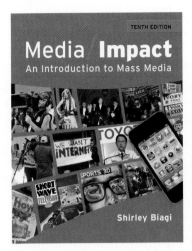
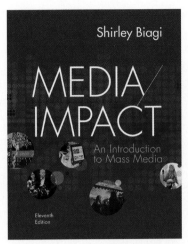

Book designers use digital technology to help them create the way a book looks inside and out. The cover is a vital part of the book's design. These covers for *Media/Impact's* 10th, 11th and 12th editions (*left to right*) show how the design has evolved since 2010.

determines how the pictures, boxes and headings will look, and decides where to use color. The designer also creates a concept—often more than one—for the book's cover. Designers also must help with the format for the e-book version of a text, which is different from the printed version.

The *production editor* manages all the steps that turn a manuscript into a book. After the manuscript comes in, the production editor sets up a schedule and makes sure that all the production work gets done on time.

The *manufacturing supervisor* buys the typesetting, paper and printing for the book. The book is sent outside the publishing company to be manufactured.

Marketing, an essential part of selling a book, is handled by several departments. *Advertising* designs ads for the book. *Promotion* sends the book to reviewers. Sales representatives visit bookstores and college campuses to tell book buyers and, in the case of textbooks, potential adopters about the book.

Fulfillment makes sure that the books get to the bookstores on time. This department watches inventory so that if the publisher's stock gets low, the publisher can order more books printed.

The Book Industry Has Three Major Markets

Today, adult and juvenile trade books account for almost half of the books people buy, and textbooks make up more than a third of all books sold. The number of new books and new editions has stabilized, but publishers are charging more for each book. Today, paperbacks and hardbacks cost about three times what they cost 30 years ago, while e-books typically cost less than hardback editions of new books but more than paperback editions.

Books fall into three major categories: adult and juvenile trade books, textbooks, and professional and scholarly books. Originally, many publishing houses were classified based on the type of publisher that produced the books. A textbook publisher produced only textbooks, for example. Today, one publishing house often produces several kinds of books—trade books and textbooks, for example—organized as separate divisions of the same company. (See **Illustration 2.2**, p. 34.)

Adult and Juvenile Trade Books

Usually sold through bookstores and to libraries, trade books are designed for the general public. These books include hardbound books and paperbound books for adults and children. Typical trade books include hardcover fiction, current nonfiction, biography, literary classics, cookbooks, travel books, art books and books on sports, music, poetry and drama. Many college classes use trade books as well as textbooks.

Juvenile trade books can be anything from picture books for children who can't read yet to novels for young adults. Included under trade books are mass-market paperbacks, such as detective series or romance novels. Many are reprints of hardcover books; others are only published as mass-market paperbacks.

Textbooks

Textbooks are published for elementary and secondary school students (called the "el-hi" market) as well as for college students. Most college texts are paid for by the students but are chosen by their professors.

Very little difference exists between some college texts and some trade books. Often the only real difference is that textbooks include what publishers call *apparatus*—for example, test questions and chapter summaries with

IMPACT

Money

ILLUSTRATION 2.2

How Do Book Publishers Make Their Money?

Most of the books people buy are adult and juvenile fiction and nonfiction trade books, but textbooks (kindergarten through 12th grade and college) account for a substantial percentage of the book market. Today, e-books account for 11 percent of the overall market.

"Book sales dipped in 2013," June 24, 2014, publishersweekly.com.

32%
Textbooks
(K-12 & college)

55%
Adult & Juvenile
Trade Books

13%
Professional &
Scholarly Books

11% of all book sales are e-books

extra assignments. A book that is used mainly in grammar school, high school or college classrooms, for example, with apparatus, is called a textbook.

Professional and Scholarly Books

University presses publish a small number of scholarly books every year and are defined solely by who publishes them: A university press book is one that a university publishes. Most university presses are nonprofit and are connected to a university, museum or research institution. These presses produce mainly scholarly materials in hardcover and softcover. Most scholarly books are sold through direct mail and in college bookstores.

Professional books are designed for a specific profession. Often these are reference books, such as an auto-repair manual or an encyclopedia of veterinary terms.

Audiobooks and E-books Multiply the Audience

Audiobooks

Since they were first introduced in the 1980s, **audiobooks** have been a small sales category for book publishers, aimed at people who would rather listen to a book than read it. Audiobooks can be abridged or complete versions of the originals.

Initially, book publishers produced literary classics and popular audiobooks on CDs, but now most audiobooks are sold as Internet downloads. Digital formats mean that consumers can download audiobooks from the Internet to be played on any device designed to play the files. The availability of audiobooks on mobile devices has revived interest in audiobooks because they are available so easily.

Electronic Books

Always looking for more income from the content they own, book publishers today are producing some books only as electronic books (***e-books***) as well as e-book versions of printed books. E-books can be downloaded and then read on an electronic tablet or even a mobile phone.

The introduction of e-books is a promising way for publishers to expand the market for their products. With the introduction of e-readers such as the Amazon Kindle and Apple iPad, e-books have become very popular. E-books now account for 11 percent of all book sales in the U.S.

According to Adobe software developer Russell Brady, "Two audiences that will benefit best are young people

Audiobooks Abridged or complete versions of classic books and popular new titles available on CDs and as Internet downloads.

E-books Electronic books.

IMPACT

Convergence

The First Bookless Library: BiblioTech Offers Only E-books

By Julianne Pepitone, CNN

BiblioTech is a new library in Texas, but you'd be forgiven for thinking otherwise. The library houses no physical books.

Staffers at San Antonio's BiblioTech say it's the first "bookless library." And in addition to its catalog of 10,000 e-books, this techy library also provides a digital lifeline to a low-income neighborhood that sorely needs it.

BiblioTech opened its doors Sept. 14, [2013] on the south side of San Antonio, a mostly Hispanic neighborhood where 40% of households don't have a computer and half lack broadband Internet service.

Although the library houses no printed books—and members can even skip the visit by checking out its e-books online—BiblioTech's staff says the library's physical presence is still key to its success.

"We're finding that you really have to get your head around a paradigm shift," said Laura Cole, BiblioTech's special projects coordinator. "Our digital library is stored in the cloud, so you don't have to come in to get a book. But we're a traditional library in that the building itself is an important community space."

That 4,800-square-foot space looks more like an Apple Store or a Google breakroom than a library. It's decked out with funky orange walls, a colorful play area for children complete with plush seats and glowing

AP Images/Eric Gay

A computer screen displays books available at BiblioTech, the nation's first all-digital public library in San Antonio, Texas.

AP Images/Eric Gay

Caroline Ramirez (*left*) and Sam Martinez use computers at the library to access digital materials, which are also available to library patrons online.

screens, plus loads of devices available for in-library use— 45 Apple iPads, 40 laptops and 48 desktop computers.

Members checking out one of the 10,000 e-books—provided through 3M's Cloud Library service—can borrow one of 600 stripped-down e-readers or 200 "enhanced" readers for children. Audiobooks and educational software are also available.

BiblioTech's efforts have attracted 7,000 members so far, and staffers relish sharing anecdotes about the people who walk through their doors.

Cole relayed a story about a young family's recent visit, during which the twentysomething father revealed that the regular e-readers were of no use to him; he couldn't read.

"One of our staff offered him a children's reader, which is enhanced with activities that help learn to read," Cole said. "He started

shaking, and his wife couldn't stop crying. It was a really profound experience for him. And this is why we worked to start something like BiblioTech."

The genesis of the idea came from Bexar County Judge Nelson Wolff, a self-described book fiend who felt libraries aren't evolving with technology. Wolff gathered about a half-dozen county employees, including Cole, to brainstorm ideas for a library that helped an underserved neighborhood in a truly modern way. Last October, the group began researching to find other libraries that had gone completely digital—but they couldn't find any.

"Not all libraries are going to be like us, and we understand that," Wolff said. "But we sure do hope it's going to drive them to do more to evolve. The world is changing, and libraries can't stay the same. Not if they want to stay relevant."

Julianne Pepitone, "The First Bookless Library: BiblioTech Offers Only E-books," *CNNMoney* (New York), October 8, 2013, cnn.com.

who loathe the idea of a library . . . and aging people who want the convenience of large type on demand, or freedom from lugging heavy hardcover tomes. We think that in the long term, e-book technology has a great future." (See **Impact/Convergence**, "The First Bookless Library: BiblioTech Offers Only E-books," p. 35.)

Most publishers now believe e-books are the only way the book publishing business can expand, so they're willing to absorb the huge costs of digital delivery and grapple with new copyright issues about who owns an e-book once it's downloaded.

Corporations Demand Higher Profits

Consolidation means the giants in today's publishing industry are demanding increasingly higher profits. The companies look for extra income in three ways: subsidiary and international rights, blockbuster books and chain and Internet marketing.

Subsidiary and International Rights

Publishers are especially interested in, and will pay more to acquire, books with the potential for subsidiary and international rights sales. The rights to make a video game or a movie version of a book, for example, are subsidiary rights.

In the 19th century, the number of copies of books that individual readers bought determined a book's profit. Today, profits also come from the sale of subsidiary rights to movie companies, book clubs, foreign publishers, paperback reprint houses, video game makers and e-book publishers. The same rights govern whether a character

in a book becomes a star on the front of a T-shirt or a video game or an e-book. For some publishing houses, subsidiary and international rights sales make the difference between making a profit and going out of business.

Blockbusters

Selling a lot of copies of one book is easier and cheaper than selling a few copies of many books. This is the concept behind publishers' eager search for **blockbuster** books. Publishers are attracted to best-selling authors because usually they are easy to market. Brand loyalty draws loyal readers to buy every book by a favorite author, so publishers can capitalize on an author's media visibility, which can help sell their books.

Following are some amounts that publishers recently paid for potential blockbusters:

▸ Little, Brown & Company reportedly signed a $5 million deal with TV comedian Tina Fey for a book called *Bossypants*, which was published in 2013 as a printed book and a Kindle e-book.

▸ In 2012, the 26-year-old writer and star of the HBO series *Girls*, Lena Dunham, received an advance of more than $3.5 million for an essay collection called *Not That Kind of Girl: A Young Woman Tells You What She's "Learned."*

▸ In December 2010, WikiLeaks founder Julian Assange received a $1.3 million advance for American and British rights to publish his memoirs.

Only the big publishing houses can afford such a bidding game. Some publishers have even developed computer models to suggest how high to bid for a book and still make a profit, but these high-priced properties still are a very small part of book publishing. The majority of editors and writers rarely get involved in an argument over seven-figure advances. Most authors would be pleased to see five-figure advances in a contract.

Many critics believe that what has been called a *blockbuster complex* among publishing houses hurts authors who aren't included in the bidding. One Harper & Row editor told *The Wall Street Journal* that seven-figure advances "divert money away from authors who really need it and center attention on commercial books instead of less commercial books that may nonetheless be better. God help poetry or criticism."

Publishers try to capitalize on an author's media visibility, which helps sell their books. U.S. Supreme Court Associate Justice Sonia Sotomayor signs copies of her book *My Beloved World* on January 28, 2013, during a promotional tour in San Francisco.

Justin Sullivan/staff/Getty Images News/Getty Images

Blockbuster A book that achieves outstanding financial success.

Chain Bookstores and Internet Retailers Compete

The most significant changes in book marketing in the past 40 years have been the growth of bookstore chains and the subsequent competition from Internet retailer Amazon.

Until 2010, the big chains, such as Borders and Barnes & Noble, accounted for more than half the bookstore sales of trade books. They brought mass-marketing techniques to the book industry, offering book buyers an environment that was less like the traditional cozy atmosphere of an independent bookstore and more like a department store.

"Blockbusters are going to be published anyway, but with a marginal book, like a volume of poetry, a chain's decision about whether to order it can sometimes determine whether the book is published," said Joan M. Ripley, a former president of the American Booksellers Association.

But in 2010, Barnes & Noble reported declining sales at its retail outlets, and in 2011 Borders filed for bankruptcy protection. Eventually all the Borders bookstores closed, leaving Barnes & Noble as the only U.S. chain bookstore. The reason? Internet booksellers, primarily Amazon, are rapidly stealing business from Barnes & Noble and independent booksellers.

Amazon has become a major factor in bookselling because the Internet retailer can buy in huge volume. The company buys books primarily from publishers that give it big discounts, so it can sell most books cheaper and carry a bigger inventory than retail bookstores. Even books that are published by smaller publishing houses can today easily reach online buyers through Amazon. For blockbusters and specialty books alike, the Internet retailer is an essential outlet.

Amazon also has been buying up smaller publishing companies to add titles to its Kindle book collection. In June 2012, Amazon bought Avalon Books, which publishes romances and mysteries. Books that are issued in a series and that are often read quickly—such as romances and mysteries—have been among the most popular titles on Kindle tablets.

Like the resistance to book clubs when they first were introduced, the skepticism among book publishers about chain bookstores, Internet retailers and e-books has changed into an understanding that these outlets can expand the market to people who didn't buy many books before. But the competitive pricing and the power over content that Internet retailers bring emphasizes what can happen when a few companies control the distribution of an industry's products, as they do in book publishing.

Small Presses Seek Specialized Audiences

The nation's large publishing houses (those with 100 or more employees) publish most of the books sold each year, but some of the nation's publishers are small operations with fewer than ten employees. These publishers are called *small presses*, and they counterbalance the corporate world of large advances and multimedia subsidiary rights.

Small presses do not have the budgets of the large houses, but their size means they can specialize in specific topics, such as the environment or bicycling, or in specific types of writing that are unattractive to large publishers, such as poetry.

Small presses are, by definition, alternative. Many of them are clustered in locations outside of the New York City orbit, such as Santa Fe, N. M., and Berkeley, Calif. Specialization and targeted marketing are the most important elements of small press success. However, because they have limited distribution capabilities, and because most of them don't have the money to invest in e-book production, many small presses today struggle to survive.

New Technologies Affect Production and Delivery

Technology is a major factor in all aspects of book publishing. Because books cost so much to publish, advances in technology can lower the cost of producing printed books, which benefits the industry. But the investment required to publish e-books has crowded out many smaller publishers that can't afford the new technology.

Internet book retailers such as Amazon, which offers lower prices and a larger inventory, threaten small booksellers like Book Passage, located in San Francisco's Ferry Building.

Courtesy of Shirley Biagi

"In preparation for landing, please turn off your books."

Ward Sutton/The New Yorker Collection/Cartoon Bank.com

Technological advances in the last 40 years have led to seven important changes in the way books are produced, distributed and promoted:

1. Because computers monitor inventories more closely, publishers can easily order new printings of books that are selling quickly so booksellers can keep the books in stock.

2. Book publishing is an on-screen industry. Publishers now receive most manuscripts from authors electronically via the Internet. Editors then send the books into production online. This means books can be formatted and printed anywhere, often overseas.

3. Electronic graphics make books more interesting, and many book publishers are using online content to produce expanded versions of traditional books and to add materials that enhance a book's marketability.

4. Publishers are using Web sites and social media to promote their books and to advertise blockbusters.

5. Large publishers are continuing to consolidate, and the number of small publishers is decreasing.

6. Many aspects of the publishing process, such as copyediting, photo research and design, are contracted to freelancers who work outside the publishing house. Because publishing can be done online, book projects can be managed from any location. This means that publishers have fewer in-house employees today and much of the work is contracted and sent overseas.

7. To expand the market for books, publishers are exploring all aspects of digital delivery for e-books so that books can be made available on all mobile devices as well as in printed form.

Book Publishing Today Is a Competitive, Complex Business

Because book publishing has been part of America's culture for so long, the contrast between its simple beginnings and its complicated future is especially striking. On August 2, 2010, book retailer Amazon.com announced that, for the first time, the company had sold more e-books in the previous three months than hardcover printed books—143 Kindle books for every 100 hardcovers.

In 2013, publishers sold 457 million e-books, according to the Association of American Publishers. Today e-books are even more portable than five years ago—an electronic tablet can hold 1,000 digital books in a space 9 inches square and 1/2 inch deep—smaller than a single copy of one hardback book. The accessibility of e-books—their storage size and reduced cost—makes schools and libraries a huge potential market.

Universal Images Group/Getty Images

An electronic tablet can store more than 1,000 books in a space 9 inches square and less than 1/2 inch deep. Elementary and high schools, as well as libraries, offer a huge potential market for e-books. In Wellsville, New York, a student works on an iPad alongside his traditional textbook.

"The real competition [at Amazon.com] is not . . . between the hardcover book and the e-book," Amazon executive Russ Grandinetti told *The New Yorker* magazine. "TV, movies, Web browsing, video games are all competing for people's valuable time. And if the book doesn't compete we think that over time the industry will suffer."

Book publishing, which had simple beginnings in America that still evoke romantic ideas about the way books were individually produced and sold, today has become a highly competitive, corporate media industry driven by digital delivery.

REVIEW, ANALYZE, INVESTIGATE

CHAPTER 2

Publishers Nurture Ideas and Try to Make a Profit

- U.S. book publishers produce about 200,000 book titles every year.
- Publishers have always been torn between the goal of preserving the country's intellectual ideas and the need to make money.
- Publishing houses try to limit uncertainty by publishing blockbusters and by spending money on promotional campaigns.

How American Book Publishing Grew

- Early publishers widened their audience by publishing political pamphlets, novels, poetry and humor.
- The International Copyright Law of 1891 expanded royalty protection to foreign writers, which also benefited American authors.
- The creation of publishing houses in the 19th and early 20th centuries centralized the process of producing books.
- The adoption of compulsory education throughout the U.S. was important for book publishing because schools buy textbooks, and education creates more people who can read.

Cheaper Books Create a Mass Market

- Beginning in the 1920s, publishers dropped prices and introduced book clubs and paperbacks.
- Early book clubs, such as Book-of-the-Month, expanded the market for books and widened the audience.
- The introduction of paperbacks that sold for as little as 25 cents meant that books could reach people who had never owned a book before.

Grove Press Tests Censorship

- Grove Press challenged book censorship by publishing *Lady Chatterley's Lover* in 1959 and *Tropic of Cancer* in 1961. Both books had been banned in the U.S. as obscene.
- The publication by Grove Press of *The Autobiography of Malcolm X* in 1965 was another challenge to censorship. The book became a best-seller.

Investors Buy Up Publishing Companies

- Before the 1960s, the book publishing industry was composed mainly of independent companies whose only business was books.
- Publishing company consolidation began in the 1960s, and this pattern of consolidation continues today.
- In 2012, Random House and Penguin merged into a new company called Penguin Random House, which became the fifth-largest book publisher in the world.

Book Publishing at Work

- Successful publishers consistently anticipate both their competitors and the market.
- The process of publishing a book usually takes at least 12 months from the time an author is signed until the book is published.

Books Begin with Authors and Agents

- Publishers acquire books in many ways. Some authors submit unsolicited manuscripts, hoping the publisher will be interested. However, many publishers refuse to read unsolicited manuscripts and accept only books that agents submit.
- Publishers pay authors a royalty for their work.
- Agents who represent authors collect fees from the authors they represent.

How Do Books Get Published?

- Book publishing requires an author, an acquisitions editor, a media editor, a designer, a production editor, a manufacturing supervisor, a marketing department and a fulfillment department.

- Small presses often operate with as few as ten employees.

The Book Industry Has Three Major Markets

- Books fall into three major categories: adult and juvenile trade books, textbooks and professional and scholarly books.

- Textbooks account for about one-third of book publishing income.

Audiobooks and E-books Multiply the Audience

- Audiobooks allow consumers to download and purchase book files on the Internet and listen to books on a mobile device.

- Electronic books (e-books) offer digital copies of thousands of titles instantly on an electronic tablet or even a mobile phone.

- The nation's first all-digital public library, called Biblio-Tech, opened in San Antonio, Texas, in 2013.

Corporations Demand Higher Profits

- Publishers are especially interested in books with subsidiary and international rights potential.

- To reduce their risks, many publishers look for blockbuster books (and best-selling authors) that they can sell through large-scale promotion campaigns.

- A chain bookstore, such as Barnes & Noble, and Internet retailers, such as Amazon, are big factors in book marketing.

- Barnes & Noble and Amazon can buy in huge volume, and often they buy books only from publishers that give them big discounts.

- Internet retailing has expanded the book market and has introduced competitive pricing.

- In 2011 Borders filed for bankruptcy protection and eventually all the Borders bookstores closed.

- In June 2012, Amazon bought Avalon Books, which publishes romances and mysteries.

- Books that are issued in a series and that are often read quickly—such as romances and mysteries—are among the most popular titles on Amazon's Kindle readers.

Small Presses Seek Specialized Audiences

- Small presses are, by definition, alternative.

- Many small presses exist outside the New York City orbit.

- Specialization and targeted marketing are important elements of small press success.

- Because they have limited distribution capabilities and don't have the money to invest in e-books, most small presses today are struggling to survive.

New Technologies Affect Production and Delivery

- Computers monitor inventories more closely.

- Publishers now receive and process manuscripts electronically via the Internet.

- Many aspects of the publishing process, such as copy-editing and photo research, are contracted to freelancers who work outside the publishing house, including overseas.

- Electronic graphics make books more interesting to look at, and many book publishers use Web sites to promote books and enhance the content.

- Large publishers are continuing to consolidate, and the number of small publishers is decreasing.

- To try to maintain and expand the market for books, publishers are exploring all aspects of electronic delivery for e-books so that books can be made available on all mobile devices as well as in printed form.

Book Publishing Today Is a Competitive, Complex Business

- On August 2, 2010, book retailer Amazon.com announced that, for the previous three months, the company had sold more e-books than hardcover printed books—143 Kindle books for every 100 hardcover books.

- In 2013, publishers sold 457 million e-books.

- Book publishing, which had simple beginnings in America that still evoke romantic ideas about the way books were produced and sold, today has become a highly competitive, corporate media industry driven by digital delivery.

Key Terms

These terms are defined in the margins throughout this chapter and appear in alphabetical order with definitions in the Glossary, which begins on page 361.

Critical Questions

1. Why was passage of the International Copyright Law of 1891 so important to American authors?

2. List five ways the economics of book publishing changed from Benjamin Franklin's day to today.

3. Will e-books totally replace print books? Why or why not?

4. Why are textbooks so important to the publishing industry?

5. What is the biggest challenge facing the book publishing industry today?

Working the Web

This list includes sites mentioned in the chapter and others to give you greater insight into the business of book publishing.

Amazon

amazon.com

Since this pioneer Internet bookseller started in 1995, Amazon has expanded its e-commerce offerings to include a wide variety of products in multiple categories, including movies, music and games, digital downloads and even groceries. Amazon.com operates sites internationally, including the United Kingdom, France, Japan, China, Canada and Germany.

American Booksellers Association (ABA)

bookweb.org

This national nonprofit trade association for independent booksellers exists to protect and promote the interests of its members—large and small independently owned bookstores. The ABA provides "advocacy, education, opportunities for peer interaction, support services and new business models." Its IndieBound program (evolved from Book Sense, indiebound.org) is a national marketing program to raise consumer awareness of the value of independent bookstores.

American Booksellers Foundation for Free Expression (ABFFE)

bookweb.org/abfe

Founded by the American Booksellers Association in 1990, ABFFE is "the bookseller's voice in the fight against censorship." The foundation opposes book banning and other restrictions on free speech, participates in legal cases about First Amendment rights and provides education on the importance of free expression to the public, press and public officials.

Association of American Publishers

publishers.org

This organization deals with broad issues concerning publishers, as well as specific concerns in particular industry segments. The organization follows and lobbies on behalf of publishers on issues including intellectual property rights; new technology; First Amendment rights; censorship and libel; funding for education and libraries; postal rates and regulations; and international copyright enforcement.

Barnes & Noble

barnesandnoble.com

Barnes & Noble uses mass-marketing techniques to sell books, DVDs, music and other merchandise. Barnesandnoble.com says it has 1 million titles available for immediate delivery, including used and out-of-print titles. The Web site features include online book clubs, B&N Review and B&N Studio, a video library with hundreds of webcasts where viewers can learn more about authors, musical artists and other book lovers.

Biblio

biblio.com

Biblio is an online marketplace for used, rare and out-of-print books and textbooks. The booksellers are located around the world, and the list of links to specialists is comprehensive (use the Bookstores tab and go to the Find Specialists link). Users can search 50 million used and rare books, browse by subject or author or browse collectible and rare books by featured category.

BookFinder

bookfinder.com

BookFinder.com is an e-commerce search engine for new, used, rare and out-of-print books and textbooks. It searches all the major online catalogs (such as Amazon.com and Barnes & Noble) and independent sources. Searches can be conducted in English, French, Dutch, Spanish, German and Italian. BookFinder's global network of book search engines includes JustBooks.de (Germany), JustBooks.co.uk (Britain) and JustBooks.fr (France).

IndieBound

indiebound.org

Evolved from the ABA's Book Sense program, IndieBound "rallies passionate readers around a celebration of independent stores and independent thinking." Independently owned ABA member bookstores are automatically part of the program and are encouraged to use the logos, spirit lines, posters, buttons, T-shirts and more provided by the ABA.

Pearson Education

pearson.com

Pearson is the largest educational publishing company in the world, with 40,000 employees in 80 countries. Pearson Education was established in 1998 when Pearson's parent company, Pearson PLC, purchased the Simon & Schuster education division from Viacom International and merged it with its education division, Addison-Wesley Longman. Pearson houses 45 educational print and online media companies, including Prentice Hall, Addison-Wesley, Longman, Penguin Readers, eCollege, BBC Active and *The Financial Times*. Pearson also owns a 47 percent share of the trade division of Penguin Random House.

Reed Elsevier

relxgroup.com

Owned by the RELX Group, Reed Elsevier is the second-largest publisher in the world, an English and Dutch publishing company headquartered in London and Amsterdam. The company was established in 1992 through a merger of Reed International, a British trade book and magazine publisher, and the Dutch science and medical publisher Elsevier. The company produces the leading medical journal, *Lancet*; the classic medical reference *Gray's Anatomy*; the primary legal reference service Lexis-Nexis; and the nurses' reference *Mosby's Index*.

Scholastic Corporation

scholastic.com

The world's largest publisher of children's books, Scholastic creates a variety of educational and entertainment materials and products for home and school use, distributing them through various channels including school-based book clubs and book fairs, retail stores, television networks and Scholastic.com.

Impact/Action Videos are concise news features on various topics created exclusively for *Media/Impact*. Find them in *Media/Impact*'s MindTap at cengagebrain.com.

MindTap® Log on to MindTap for *Media/Impact* to access a variety of additional material—including learning objectives, chapter readings with highlighting and note-taking, **Impact/Action Videos**, activities, and comprehension quizzes—that will guide you through this chapter.

NEWSPAPERS
MOBILIZING DELIVERY

03

BuzzFeed NEWS BUZZ LIFE

LoL · win · omg · cute · fail · wtf

News   Buzz   Life   Entertainment   Quizzes   Videos   More ⌄   f Like 4.6m

APPLE APP STORES SHUT DOWN BY MASSIVE SERVICE OUTAGE

DenyTunes

11 Animals Who Totally Didn't Do It, They Swear

PROMOTED BY
GEICO

What's The Best Thing About Having A Work BFF?

"Happy hour after work?" "Duh."

Jon-Michael Poff · a few minutes ago · respond

11 Things You Didn't Know Your Pet Does While You're Not Around

Well, perhaps you knew, but you didn't want to believe it! Keep an eye on your precious pet and all their antics with Skype.

PROMOTED BY
skype

This Is What Life In The Circus Is Like For Lions And Tigers

The decision to take elephants out of the Ringling Bros. Circus is an important step. But there is a long way to go to ensure that no animals are suffering for our entertainment.

Alana Massey · a few minutes ago · 22 responses

Can You Guess Which McDonald's Menu Item Is Higher In Calories?

Super Size Me.

Keijiro Abe · 15 minutes ago · 9 responses

29 Times Tumblr Saw Australia And Said Nope

Australia is batshit insane, and so is Tumblr.

Simon Crerar · a half hour ago · 188 responses

How To Make A Brief Appearance At A Really Crowded Party

For those nights you need to get away quickly.

BuzzFeedNEWS

Reports: Shooting At Lil Wayne's Miami Home

David Mack · respond

11 Military Members Presumed Dead After Helicopter Crashes In Florida

Francis Whittaker · 5 responses

Why The "Blurred Lines" Verdict Might Not Actually Mean Much For The Music Industry

Reggie Ugwu · 1 response

LoL · win · cute

Sign Up For The BuzzFeed Today

⚡ Trending

1
2
3   "I'M OKAY!"
4
5
6
7

Newspapers today face stiff competition from online news Web sites, such as BuzzFeed, which often feature celebrity and sensational news in an eye-catching format similar to early tabloids.

> "We're organizing ourselves to be a media company for the way people consume media today."
>
> —JONAH PERETTI, CO-FOUNDER AND CEO, BUZZFEED

In 1882, Harrison Gray Otis bought a 25 percent share of the Los Angeles Times *for $6,000. In 2000,* the Chandler family (Otis' descendants) sold Times Mirror Co., which included the *Los Angeles Times, Newsday, The Baltimore Sun* newspapers, the *Hartford Courant* and other media properties to Chicago-based Tribune Co. for $8.3 billion. Then in 2007, Chicago real estate tycoon Sam Zell paid $8.2 billion for the Tribune Company (including *Times Mirror* and the Tribune broadcast stations), less than the Tribune Company had paid for *Times Mirror* alone seven years earlier.

One year later, in December 2008, the Tribune Company filed for bankruptcy protection, citing the rapid decline in newspaper revenue. In 2014, the Tribune Company announced it was reorganizing into two companies. The Tribune Company now houses Tribune's 42 profitable TV stations, but the newspapers (which are still losing revenue) have been spun off into a separate company, Tribune Publishing. Tribune Publishing's uncertain future is an example of the precarious economics of the newspaper industry today.

Newspaper revenue is directly tied to the size of its audience because most newspaper income derives from advertising. Advertisers follow the audience, and the younger audience (especially for news) is abandoning newspapers and scattering in many directions, including digital news services such as BuzzFeed and social media sites such as Facebook—quite a different news environment than when the first colonial newspapers appeared in America more than three centuries ago.

First Mass Medium to Deliver News

The early colonial American newspapers were one-page sheets that consisted primarily of announcements of ship arrivals and departures and old news from Europe. For more than 300 years, from 1690 until the introduction of radio in 1920, newspapers were the *only* mass news medium available, competing to deliver news and information to an audience hungry for facts. In 1920, newspapers were the only way for large numbers of people to get the same news simultaneously. There was no competition, except among the newspapers themselves.

The invention of broadcasting in the mid-1920s changed newspapers' exclusive access to news because broadcasting offered quicker access to information. In the late 20th century, the expansion of the Internet challenged newspapers' delivery system again, and advertisers fled printed newspapers for an online audience. Yet, despite increasing competition for their audience, newspapers remain a significant source of information and news, and many newspapers are still profitable.

The nation's newspaper industry also historically has played an important role in defining society's concept of the role of an independent press, based on the belief that the press must remain independent from government control to fulfill its responsibility to protect the public interest. Concepts about what the public should know, when they should know it and who should decide what

TimeFrame
1690–Today

(Marvin Joseph / The Washington Post)

Post to be sold to Amazon's Jeff Bezos

Paul Farhi

The deal to sell the newspaper and its affiliated publications to the Amazon.com founder will end the Graham family's stewardship of one of America's leading news organizations after four generations.

1690 *Publick Occurrences*, America's first newspaper, is published.

1721 James Franklin publishes *The New England Courant*, the first newspaper to appear without the Crown's "Published by Authority" sanction.

1734 John Peter Zenger is charged with sedition. While he is in jail, his wife, Anna Zenger, continues to publish *The New York Weekly Journal*, making her America's first woman publisher.

1808 *El Misisipi*, America's first Spanish-language newspaper, begins publication in Georgia.

1827 John B. Russwurm and the Reverend Samuel Cornish launch *Freedom's Journal*, the nation's first newspaper directed specifically at an African American audience.

1828 Elias Boudinot (Galagina Oowati) launches the *Cherokee Phoenix*.

✳ **1831** In Boston, William Lloyd Garrison launches the abolitionist newspaper *The Liberator*.

1847 Frederick Douglass introduces the weekly *North Star*, considered America's most important African American pre–Civil War newspaper.

1848 Jane Grey Swisshelm publishes the first issue of the abolitionist newspaper the *Pittsburgh Saturday Visiter*, which also promotes women's rights.

1889 Ida B. Wells becomes part owner of the *Memphis Free Speech and Headlight* and begins her anti-lynching campaign.

1900 One-third of the nation's newspapers follow the popular trend toward yellow journalism.

✳ **1950** Newspaper readership begins to decline following the introduction of television.

1982 Gannett Co. creates *USA Today*, using a splashy format and color throughout the paper.

1990s Newspapers launch Internet editions to attract readers who have abandoned the printed product. Some newspapers launch Spanish-language editions.

2006 Internet technology entrepreneur Jonah Peretti launches BuzzFeed.

2009 More than 100 newspapers stop publishing. Tribune Company files for bankruptcy protection. Denver's *Rocky Mountain News* and the *Seattle Post-Intelligencer* close down.

2011 *The New York Times* begins charging for online content.

✳ **2013** Amazon founder and Internet entrepreneur Jeff Bezos buys *The Washington Post*.

TODAY The newspaper business is consolidating. To attract younger readers, newspapers have expanded their Internet editions, but they face stiff competition from Internet news and social networking sites.

the public needs to know developed in America during a time when newspapers were the main news source.

Publishers Fight for an Independent Press

The issue of government control of newspapers surfaced early in the history of the colonies. At first, newspapers were the mouthpieces of the British government, and news was subject to British approval. The British government subsidized many colonial newspapers, and publishers actually printed "Published by Authority" on the first page of the paper to demonstrate government approval.

The first colonial newspaper angered the local authorities so much that the newspaper issued only one edition. This newspaper, *Publick Occurrences*, which was published in Boston on September 25, 1690, often is identified as America's first newspaper.

The first and only edition of *Publick Occurrences* was just two pages, each page the size of a sheet of today's binder paper (then called a half-sheet), and was printed on three sides. Publisher Benjamin Harris left the fourth side blank so people could jot down the latest news before they gave the paper to friends. Harris made the mistake of reporting in his first issue that the French king was "in much trouble" for sleeping with his son's wife. The governor and council of the Massachusetts Bay Colony stopped the publication four days after the newspaper appeared.

The nation's first consecutively issued (published more than once) newspaper was *The Boston News-Letter*, which appeared in 1704. It was one half-sheet printed on two sides. In the first issue, editor John Campbell also reprinted the queen's latest speech, some maritime news and one advertisement telling people how to put an ad in his paper. Like many subsequent colonial publishers, Campbell reprinted several items from the London papers.

James Franklin's *New England Courant* Establishes an Independent Press Tradition

The next challenge to British control came in 1721 when James Franklin started his own newspaper in Boston. His *New England Courant* was the first American newspaper to appear without the crown's "Published by Authority" label. *Thus, James Franklin began the tradition of an independent press in this country.*

Benjamin Franklin Introduces Competition

In 1729, Benjamin Franklin, James' younger brother, moved to Philadelphia and bought the *Pennsylvania Gazette* to compete with the only other newspaper in town, the *American Weekly Mercury* published by Andrew Bradford. The *Pennsylvania Gazette* became the most influential and most financially successful of all the colonial newspapers. In the same print shop that printed the *Gazette*, Franklin published *Poor Richard's Almanack* in 1732, an annual book that sold about 10,000 copies a year for the next 25 years. *Benjamin Franklin proved that a printer could make money without government support.*

Truth Versus Libel: The Zenger Trial

In New York, John Peter Zenger started the *New York Weekly Journal* in 1733. The *Journal* continually attacked Governor William Cosby for incompetence, and on November 17, 1734, Zenger was arrested and jailed, charged with printing false and seditious writing. (**Seditious language** is language that authorities believe could incite rebellion against the government.) While Zenger was in jail, his wife, Anna, continued to print the paper, making Anna Zenger America's first woman publisher.

> **Seditious Language** Language that authorities believe could incite rebellion against the government.

Bettmann/Corbis

On November 17, 1734, John Peter Zenger, publisher of the *New York Weekly Journal*, was arrested and jailed, charged with printing false and seditious writing. While Zenger was in jail, his wife, Anna, continued to publish the paper, making her America's first woman publisher.

John Zenger's trial began on August 4, 1735, nine months after his arrest. His defense attorney argued that *truth was a defense against libel* and that if Zenger's words were true, they could not be libelous. (A **libelous** statement is a false statement that damages a person by questioning that person's character or reputation.)

The trial established a *landmark precedent for freedom of the press in America—the concept that truth is the best defense for libel*. If what someone publishes is true, the information cannot be considered libelous. (The issue of libel is explained further in **Chapter 14**.)

Women's Early Role as Publishers

Colonial women were not encouraged to work outside the home at all. Therefore, women who published newspapers during the colonial period are especially notable because so few women managed businesses early in the nation's history. Early colonial women printers, such as Anna Zenger, usually belonged to printing families that trained wives and daughters to work in the print shops. By the time the American Revolution began, at least 14 women had worked as printers in the colonies. One of these family-trained printers was Elizabeth Timothy.

Timothy became editor of the weekly *South Carolina Gazette* in Charleston when her husband, Lewis, died unexpectedly and their son, Peter, was only 13. Elizabeth Timothy published her first edition on January 4, 1737, under her son's name. Her first editorial appealed to the community to support the "poor afflicted widow and six small children." Mother and son ran the paper together until 1746, when Peter formally took over the business.

Birth of the Partisan Press

As dissatisfaction with British rule grew in the colonies, newspapers became political tools that fostered the debate that eventually led to the colonies' independence. By 1750, 14 weekly newspapers were being published in the colonies.

The Stamp Act

Opposition to the British Stamp Act in 1765 signaled the beginning of the revolutionary period. The Stamp Act taxed publishers a halfpenny for each issue that was a half-sheet or smaller and one penny for a full sheet. Each advertisement was taxed two shillings. All the colonial newspapers, even those loyal to the crown, fought the act.

Many newspapers threatened to stop publication, but only a few did. Instead, most editors published newspapers that mocked the tax. William Bradford III issued the famous tombstone edition of the *Pennsylvania Journal* on October 31, 1765. The front page, bordered in black, showed a skull and crossbones where the official stamp should have been.

The Stamp Act Congress met in New York in October 1765 and adopted the now-familiar slogan "No taxation without representation." Parliament, facing united opposition from all the colonial publishers, repealed the Stamp Act on March 18, 1766.

> **Libelous** A statement is libelous if it damages a person's character or reputation by exposing that person to public ridicule or contempt.

Furious colonists reacted to the Stamp Act in 1765 by throwing stamped documents onto a bonfire in Boston. Newspaper publishers threatened to stop publication but instead printed editions that mocked the tax. The Stamp Act was repealed a year later.

The Alien and Sedition Laws

During the early part of the country's history, journalists often used newspapers as a way to oppose the new government. The Alien and Sedition Laws, passed by Congress in 1798, were the federal government's first attempt to control its critics. Congress said that anyone who "shall write, print, or publish . . . false, scandalous and malicious writing or writings against the government of the United States, or either house of the Congress of the United States, or the President of the United States" could be fined up to $2,000 and jailed for two years.

Several journalists went to jail. A Boston publisher was jailed for libeling the Massachusetts legislature. A New York editor was fined $100 and jailed for four months. By 1800, the angry rhetoric had dissipated. The Alien and Sedition Laws expired after two years and were not renewed. However, *throughout American press history, the tradition of an independent press, established by James Franklin in 1721, continues to confront the government's desire to restrain criticism.*

Technology Helps Newspapers Reach New Readers

Technological advances of the 19th century—such as cheaper newsprint, mechanized printing and the telegraph—meant newspapers could reach a wider audience faster than before. Confined to eastern cities and highly educated urban audiences during the 1700s, newspaper publishers in the 1800s sought new readers—from the frontier, from among the nation's growing number of immigrants and from within the shrinking Native American population. This expansion resulted in three new developments for American newspapers: frontier journalism, ethnic newspapers and the alternative press.

Frontier Journalism

Gold, silver and adventure lured people to the West, and when the people arrived, they needed newspapers. The *Indiana Gazette*, the *Texas Gazette*, the *Oregon Spectator*, the *Weekly Arizonian* and Colorado's *Rocky Mountain News* met that need, aided by the telegraph, which moved news easily from coast to coast.

The wide-open land beckoned many journalists. The most celebrated journalist to chronicle the frontier was Samuel Clemens, who traveled to Nevada in 1861, prospecting for silver. Clemens didn't find any silver, but a year later Virginia City's *Territorial Enterprise*—the area's largest paper—hired him for $25 a week. Clemens first signed his name as Mark Twain on a humorous travel letter written for the *Enterprise*.

Frontier journalists learned to improvise. This press operation, assembled to publish the *New York Herald*, was set up in a field under a tree.

Ethnic and Native American Newspapers

English-language newspapers did not satisfy everyone's needs. In the first half of the 19th century, many newspapers sought to succeed by catering to ethnic and cultural interests. In the early 1800s, Spanish-speaking people in Georgia could read *El Misisipi*. Herman Ridder's German newspaper, *New Yorker Staats-Zeitung*, founded in 1845, was the most successful foreign-language newspaper in the United States. It formed the financial basis for the Knight Ridder chain, now part of the McClatchy Company.

People outside the mainstream of society, such as Spanish and German immigrants, used newspapers to create a sense of community and ethnic identity. In the 1800s, Native Americans who had been displaced by the settlers also felt a need to express their culture through a newspaper. As a non-mainstream group, they especially wanted to voice their complaints.

On February 21, 1828, the nation's first Native American newspaper appeared. Elias Boudinot, a Native American who had been educated at a Connecticut seminary, launched the *Cherokee Phoenix*, a weekly newspaper. Boudinot's native name was Galagina (The Buck) Oowati. (He took the name Elias Boudinot as a tribute to one of his early mentors.)

The Cherokee nation held exclusive control over the four-page paper, which was printed half in English and half in an 86-character alphabet that represented the Cherokee language. In August 1832, Boudinot resigned because of editorial differences with some of his partners, and the *Phoenix* published its last issue on May 31, 1834.

Dissident Voices Create the Early Alternative Press

Two strong social movements—emancipation and women's suffrage—brought new voices to the American press. This ***alternative press*** movement signaled the beginning of a significant American journalistic tradition. Newspapers became an outlet for the voices of social protest. (The alternative press also is called the ***dissident press***.)

Six early advocates for domestic change who used the press to advance their causes—the abolition of slavery and voting rights for women—were John B. Russwurm, the

Library of Congress Prints and Photographs Division

The Granger Collection, NYC

Elias Boudinot [Cherokee name: Galagina (The Buck) Oowati] (left) published the first Native American newspaper (right), the *Cherokee Phoenix*, from 1828 to 1832. The newspaper was published half in English and half in Cherokee.

Reverend Samuel Cornish, Frederick Douglass, William Lloyd Garrison, Jane Grey Swisshelm and Ida B. Wells.

In 1827, Russwurm and Cornish, who were African American, started *Freedom's Journal* in New York City with very little money. They launched their newspaper to respond to racist attacks in several local newspapers. *Freedom's Journal* lasted for two years and reached only a few readers, but it was the beginning of an African American press tradition that eventually created more than 2,700 newspapers, magazines and quarterly journals.

What often has been called the most important African American pre-Civil War newspaper was Frederick Douglass' weekly *North Star*. "Right is of no Sex—Truth is of no Color—God is the Father of us all, and we are all Brethren" read the masthead. Beginning in 1847, Douglass struggled to support the *North Star* by giving lectures. Eventually the newspaper reached 3,000 subscribers in the United States and abroad with its emancipation message.

In 1831, William Lloyd Garrison began publishing *The Liberator*, a weekly abolitionist paper in Boston. As a white man fighting slavery and advocating women's rights, Garrison was attacked by a mob in 1835 but survived when the Boston mayor jailed him for his own safety. Garrison continued to publish *The Liberator* for 30 years.

Alternative (Dissident) Press Media that present alternative viewpoints that challenge the mainstream press.

Frederick Douglass (left) established the weekly newspaper *North Star*, often called the most important African American pre–Civil War newspaper. William Lloyd Garrison (right), a Boston abolitionist, founded the New England Anti-Slavery Society and published *The Liberator*, another important abolitionist newspaper.

able to lower the price to a penny by filling the paper with advertising and by hiring children to sell the paper on street corners. In its four pages, this first successful penny paper reported local gossip and sensationalized police news and carried a page and a half of advertising.

Newsboys (and some newsgirls) paid 67 cents for 100 papers and had to sell them all each day to earn a profit because Day paid them no other wages. Even *The New York Times*, founded by Henry J. Raymond in 1851, was a **penny paper** when it began. The legacy of these early penny papers continues in today's celebrity news and crime reporting.

Like Douglass and Garrison, Ida B. Wells and Jane Grey Swisshelm campaigned for civil rights. Swisshelm's first byline appeared in 1844 in the *Spirit of Liberty*, published in Pittsburgh. Four years later, she began her own abolitionist publication, the *Pittsburgh Saturday Visiter*, which also promoted women's rights. (See **Impact/ Profile**, "Ida B. Wells Uses Her Pen to Fight 19th-Century Racism," p. 51.)

As a correspondent for Horace Greeley's *New York Tribune* in Washington, D.C., Swisshelm convinced Vice President Millard Fillmore to let her report from the Senate press gallery. The gallery had been open to male journalists for 55 years, and on May 21, 1850, Swisshelm became the first female journalist to sit in the gallery.

These pioneers—Russwurm, Cornish, Douglass, Garrison, Wells and Swisshelm—used newspapers to lobby for social change. Dissident newspapers offered a forum for protest and reform, which is an important cultural role for an independent press.

Newspapers Seek Mass Audiences and Big Profits

The voices of social protest reached a limited, committed audience, but most people could not afford to subscribe to a daily newspaper. Newspapers were sold by advance yearly subscription for $6 to $10 when most skilled workers earned less than $750 a year. Then, in 1833, Benjamin Day demonstrated that he could profitably appeal to a mass audience by dropping the price of a newspaper to a penny and selling the paper on the street every day.

Benjamin Day's *New York Sun* published sensational news and feature stories for the working class. He was

Benjamin Day's *New York Sun* published sensational news for the working class and dropped the price to a penny. He hired newsboys (and some newsgirls) to sell the papers on street corners. They paid 67 cents for 100 papers, hoping to sell all of them each day for a penny each. They received no other wages.

Profile

Ida B. Wells Uses Her Pen to Fight 19th-Century Racism

By Shirley Biagi

Ida B. Wells didn't start out to be a journalist, but the cause of emancipation drew her to the profession. Wells, who eventually became co-owner of the *Free Speech and Headlight* in Memphis, Tennessee, documented racism wherever she found it. She is known for her pioneering stand against the unjustified lynching of African Americans in the 1890s.

In 1878, both of Wells' parents and her infant sister died in a yellow fever epidemic, so 16-year-old Wells took responsibility for her six brothers and sisters, attended Rush College and then moved the family to Memphis, where she became a teacher.

A Baptist minister who was editor of the Negro Press Association hired Wells to write for his paper. She wrote under the pseudonym Iola.

In 1892, Wells wrote a story about three African American men who had been kidnapped from a Memphis jail and killed. "The city of Memphis

Michelle Duster holds a portrait of her great-grandmother, Ida B. Wells, a pioneering newspaper publisher and advocate for civil rights. Wells, part owner of the Memphis *Free Speech and Headlight*, wrote under the pseudonym Iola. Her struggle for social justice represents an important example of the role the dissident press played in American history.

AP Images/Charles Rex Arbogast

has demonstrated that neither character nor standing avails the Negro, if he dares to protect himself against the white man or become his rival," she wrote. "We are outnumbered and without arms." While in New York, she read in the local paper that a mob had sacked the *Free Speech* office.

Wells decided not to return to Memphis. She settled in Chicago, where she married a lawyer, Ferdinand Lee Barnett. Ida Wells-Barnett and her husband actively campaigned for African American rights in Chicago, and she continued to write until she died at age 69 in 1931.

Newspapers Dominate the Early 20th Century

For the first 30 years of the 20th century—before radio and television—newspapers dominated the country. Newspapers were the nation's single source of daily dialogue about politics and social issues. This also was the era of fierce competition among newspapers for readers.

Competition Breeds Sensationalism

In large cities such as New York, as many as ten newspapers competed for readers at once, so the publishers looked for new ways to capture an audience. Two New York publishers—Joseph Pulitzer and William Randolph Hearst—revived and refined the ***penny press*** sensationalism that had begun with Benjamin Day's *New York Sun*. Pulitzer and Hearst also proved that newspapers could

> **Penny Paper or Penny Press** A newspaper produced by dropping the price of each copy to a penny and supporting the production cost through advertising.

Bettmann/Corbis Bettmann/Corbis

The battle for New York readers between Joseph Pulitzer (left) and William Randolph Hearst (right) provoked the Spanish-American War and popularized the term *yellow journalism*.

reap enormous fortunes for their owners by promoting contests, manufacturing gossip and fabricating stories.

An ambitious man who knew how to grab his readers' interest, Joseph Pulitzer published the first newspaper comics and sponsored journalist Nellie Bly on an around-the-world steamship and railroad trip to try to beat the fictional record in the popular book *Around the World in 80 Days*. Bly finished the trip in 72 days, 6 hours and 11 minutes, and the stunt brought Pulitzer a massive boost in circulation. In San Francisco, young William Randolph Hearst, the new editor of the *San Francisco Examiner*, sent a reporter to cover Bly's arrival.

In 1887, Hearst had convinced his father, who owned the *San Francisco Examiner*, to let him run the paper. Hearst tagged the *Examiner* "The Monarch of the Dailies," added a lovelorn column and attacked several of his father's influential friends in the newspaper. He spent money wildly, buying talent from competing papers and staging showy promotions.

Yellow Journalism Is Born: Hearst's Role in the Spanish-American War

In New York, Hearst bought the *New York Journal*, hired Pulitzer's entire Sunday staff and cut the *Journal*'s price to a penny, so Pulitzer dropped his price to match it. Hearst bought a color press and printed color comics. Then he stole Pulitzer's popular comic "Hogan's Alley," which included a character named the Yellow Kid.

Hearst relished the battle, as the *Journal* screamed attention-grabbing crime headlines, such as "Thigh of the Body Found," and the paper offered $1,000 for information

that helped convict the murderer. Critics named this sensationalism ***yellow journalism*** after the Yellow Kid, a term that still is used to describe highly emotional, exaggerated or inaccurate reporting that emphasizes crime, sex and violence. By 1900, about one-third of the metropolitan dailies followed the trend toward yellow journalism.

Beginning in 1898, the Spanish-American War provided the battlefield for Pulitzer and Hearst to act out their newspaper war. For three years, the two newspapers unrelentingly overplayed events in the Cuban struggle for independence from Spain, each trying to beat the other with irresponsible, exaggerated stories, many of them invented.

The overplayed events that resulted from the sensational competition between Pulitzer and Hearst showed that newspapers could have a significant effect on political attitudes. The Spanish-American War began a few months after the sinking of the U.S. battleship *Maine* in Havana harbor, which killed 266 crew members. The cause of the explosion that sank the ship was never determined, but Pulitzer's and Hearst's newspapers blamed the Spanish.

Hearst dubbed the event "the *Journal*'s War," but in fact Hearst and Pulitzer shared responsibility because both men had inflamed the public unnecessarily about events in Cuba. *The serious consequences that resulted from their yellow journalism demonstrate the importance of press responsibility.*

Tabloid Journalism: Selling Sex and Violence

Sensationalism surfaced again in the tabloid journalism of the 1920s, also called jazz journalism. In 1919, the publishers of the *New York Daily News* sponsored a beauty contest to inaugurate the nation's first tabloid. A ***tabloid*** is a small-format newspaper, usually 11 inches by 14 inches, featuring illustrations and sensational stories.

The *Daily News* merged pictures and screaming headlines with reports about crime, sex and violence to

> **Yellow Journalism** News that emphasizes crime, sex and violence; also called jazz journalism and tabloid journalism.
>
> **Tabloid** A small-format newspaper that features large photographs and illustrations along with sensational stories.

This 1928 photo of Ruth Snyder's execution (left) in the *New York Daily News* exemplifies the screaming headlines of early tabloids that still populate today's *Daily News* (right) and Internet sites such as BuzzFeed. At the Snyder execution, a *Daily News* reporter strapped a small hidden camera to his leg and secretly snapped a picture of Snyder as she was executed.

exceed anything that had appeared before. It ran full-page pictures with short, punchy text. Love affairs soon became big news and so did murders. In the ultimate example of tabloid journalism, in 1928 a *Daily News* reporter strapped a camera to his ankle and took a picture of Ruth Snyder, who had conspired to kill her husband, as she was electrocuted at Sing Sing prison.

Snyder's picture covered the front page, with the caption, "This is perhaps the most remarkable exclusive picture in the history of criminology." Photojournalism had taken a sensational turn.

One of today's successors to the *Daily News'* splashy format is the online Web site BuzzFeed, featuring stories about sex, violence and celebrities. (See **Impact/Profile:** "BuzzFeed Co-Founder Jonah Peretti Wants to Take Its Content Far Beyond Lists," p. 58.)

Unionization Encourages Professionalism

The first half of the 20th century brought the widespread unionization of newspaper employees, which standardized wages at many of the nation's largest newspapers. Labor unions were first established at newspapers in 1800, and the International Typographical Union went national in the mid-1850s.

Other unions formed to represent production workers at newspapers, but reporters didn't have a union until 1934, when *New York World-Telegram* reporter Heywood

Broun called on his colleagues to organize. Broun became The Newspaper Guild's first president. Today, the Guild continues to cover employees at many of America's urban newspapers.

With the rise of unions, employee contracts, which once had been negotiated in private, became public agreements. In general, salaries for reporters at union newspapers rose, and this eventually led to a sense of professionalism, including codes of ethics for journalists. (For more information about journalistic ethics codes, see **Chapter 15**.)

Television Brings New Competition

The invention of television dramatically affected the newspaper industry. Before TV, newspaper publishers had to compete with only one other 20th-century news industry—radio. In the 1920s, when radio first became popular, for example, newspapers refused to carry advertising or time logs for the programs, but eventually newspapers conceded the space to radio.

In the 1950s, newspaper readership declined as TV became America's primary source for news and entertainment. The *Howdy Doody Show* celebrates its tenth anniversary in 1957.

In the 1950s, however, television posed a bigger threat: TV offered moving images of the news, along with live and filmed entertainment. The spread of television demonstrated how interrelated the media were. The newspaper industry gave up its position as the number one news medium and was forced to share the news audience with broadcasting. Eventually, television influenced both the look and the content of many newspapers.

Alternative Press Revives Voices of Protest

The social movements of the 1960s briefly revived one portion of the early newspaper industry—the alternative press. Like their 1800s predecessors in the abolition and emancipation movements, people who revived the alternative press in the 1960s believed the mainstream press was avoiding important issues, such as the anti–Vietnam War movement, the civil rights movement and the gay rights movement.

In 1964, as a way to pass along news about the antiwar movement, the *Los Angeles Free Press* became the first underground paper to publish regularly. The *Barb* in Berkeley, Calif.; *Kaleidoscope* in Chicago; and *Quicksilver Times* in Washington, D.C., soon followed. In 1965, Jim Michaels launched the nation's first gay newspaper, the Los Angeles *Advocate*. What the 1960s underground press proved already had been proven in the 19th century: In America, causes need a voice, and if those voices are not represented in the mainstream press, publications emerge to support alternative views.

Newspapers Expand and Contract

Since the 1970s, the overall number of newspapers has declined. Many afternoon papers died when TV took over the evening news. Other afternoon papers changed to morning papers. Then, newspaper publishers realized television could provide the news headlines, but newspapers could offer the background that television news could not.

Newspaper publishers also began to exploit the popularity of television personalities and expanded their entertainment, business and sports news. Eventually, advertisers realized that newspapers gave people the broader news that TV couldn't deliver. Also, viewers couldn't clip coupons out of their television sets or retrieve copies of yesterday's TV ads, so advertisers began to use newspapers to complement television ad campaigns. To try to match television's visual appeal, newspapers introduced advanced graphics and vivid color.

Jonathan Daniel/Staff/Getty Images Sport/Getty Images

Chicago Bulls mascot Benny reads the sports section at courtside. Today, newspapers are losing younger readers, and most cities have only one newspaper.

Today newspapers are facing declining readership, especially among young readers, and many major newspapers have announced staff cuts in an attempt to stay as profitable as they have been in the past. (See **Illustration 3.1**, "Percentage of Adults Who Say They Read a Newspaper Yesterday," p. 55.) To survive, most of today's dailies are part of a chain. Most cities have only one newspaper; some cities have no newspaper and must rely on other sources for news. "In 2009 and 2010, all the two-newspaper markets [became] one-newspaper markets," said Mike Simonton of Fitch Ratings, a company that analyzes the newspaper industry, "and you will start to see one-newspaper markets become no-newspaper markets."

Newspapers at Work

Many colonial publishers handled all the tasks of putting out a newspaper single-handedly, but today's typical newspaper operation is organized into two separate departments: the editorial side and the business side. The *editorial side* handles everything that you read in the paper—the news and feature stories, editorials, cartoons, photographs and online editions. The *business side* handles everything else—production, advertising, distribution and administration.

IMPACT Society

ILLUSTRATION 3.1

Percentage of Adults Who Say They Read a Newspaper Yesterday (Includes Internet and Mobile Phone Readers)

Adults between 18 and 34 today are much less likely to read a daily newspaper—even online—than mature adults (age 35 and above). Traditional newspapers are losing the younger audience to new Internet-only news services and social media.

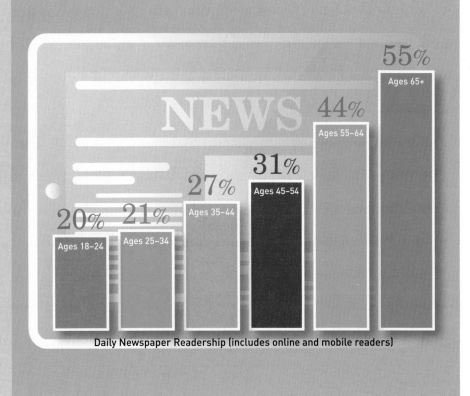

Daily Newspaper Readership (includes online and mobile readers)

"Newspapers: Readership by Age," *State of the News Media 2014*, Pew Research Center, journalism.org.

On the editorial side at a medium-size daily newspaper, different *editors*—a news editor, a sports editor, a features editor and a business editor, for example—handle different parts of the paper. The managing editor oversees these news departments. A copyeditor checks the reporters' stories before they are published, and a layout editor positions the stories. Opinion writers and editorial cartoonists usually work for an editorial page editor. The editorial department usually also manages all aspects of the newspaper's Internet editions. Editorial employees report to the *editor-in-chief* or the *publisher* or both.

A *business manager* and his or her staff run the business side of the paper: getting the paper out to subscribers, selling advertising and making sure the paper gets published every day. These people also ultimately report to the editor-in-chief or the publisher. Sometimes the publisher also owns the paper. If a corporation owns the paper, the publisher reports to its board of directors.

Almost all newspapers today run Web sites, and many newspapers have created New Media departments to introduce strong graphic and video elements to their Internet editions.

Newspapers also can add to their content without having to use their own reporters by buying content from **syndicates**, which are news agencies that sell articles for publication to several newspapers simultaneously. The first syndicated column was a fashion letter distributed in 1857. Syndicates mainly provide columnists, comics and editorial cartoons.

Most newspapers also subscribe to one or more news services, such as Associated Press, which provide articles from news bureaus around the world.

Technology Transforms Production

Since their colonial beginnings, newspapers have shown their ability to appeal to changing audiences, adapt to growing competition, continue to attract advertisers and adjust to rapidly changing technology. Today's digital

Syndicates News agencies that sell articles for publication to several newspapers simultaneously.

technology means that machines are doing work formerly done by people. For newspaper unions, this shift to technology has meant a consistent effort among newspaper owners to challenge union representation.

Before 1970, newspapers needed typographers to handset metal type, and labor unions represented most typographers. With the introduction of digital composition, newspaper management slowly moved to eliminate the typographers' jobs. The unions fought the transition, and many newspaper workers went on strike—notably at the *New York Daily News* in 1990, at the *San Francisco Chronicle* and *San Francisco Examiner* in 1994 and at the *Detroit News* in 1996, but newspaper production jobs continued their decline.

With the threat of new technologies eliminating even more jobs, newspaper unions are a much smaller factor in the newspaper business today. Union influence for reporters and production workers at some urban newspapers continues, but most employees at smaller newspapers are not unionized.

Consolidation Increases Chain Ownership

Because newspaper circulation is declining, large corporations have bought up many newspapers that once were family-owned. Instead of editors competing locally within a community, like Hearst battling Pulitzer, national chains now compete with one another.

Chain ownership doesn't necessarily mean that every newspaper in a chain speaks with the voice of the chain owner. Chains can supply money to improve a newspaper's printing plant and to add more reporters. But critics say chains often consolidate and limit readers' access to a wide range of information. (See **Chapter 1** for more discussion of media consolidation.)

Newspapers Fight to Retain Readers

Newspapers depend primarily on advertising for support. Subscriptions and newsstand sales account for only a small percentage of newspaper income, so newspaper companies must constantly try to figure out how to attract new readers.

In the 1980s, Gannett Co. introduced a new national newspaper, *USA Today*, designed with bold graphics and shorter stories. In the 1990s, other newspapers followed, adding more color and special editions, even expanding their comics to two pages and printing them in color.

In some cities with large Latino populations, English-language newspapers expanded by publishing Spanish-language editions, and existing Spanish-language newspapers found a wider audience among immigrants. In areas like Dallas-Fort Worth, for example, where about

"EXTRA! EXTRA! Internet is putting us out of business!"

a fifth of the population is Latino, newspaper companies see an ever-increasing audience with a desire for information in Spanish. *La Opinión*, in Los Angeles, is the Spanish-language paper with the largest circulation.

In the 1990s, newspapers added Internet editions, and today digital access for readers is an essential element of any newspaper business. (See **Illustration 3.2**, "Newspaper Readers Prefer the Printed Paper, But Mobile Access Is Increasing," p. 57.)

Still, beginning in the year 2000, many people—especially younger readers—stopped using the printed newspaper and migrated to the Internet for news from other sources. As a result, newspaper advertising revenue declined very quickly. Hundreds of newspapers shut down—more than 100 newspapers closed in the U.S. in the first 6 months of 2009. For example, Seattle lost Washington state's oldest newspaper, the *Seattle Post-Intelligencer*, and Denver lost the *Rocky Mountain News*.

National Newspapers Seek a Wider Audience

When the Gannett newspaper chain (which owns more newspapers than any other chain) created *USA Today*, the company was aiming at different readers than the nation's two other major newspapers, *The New York Times* and *The Wall Street Journal*. Gannett called *USA Today* "the nation's newspaper," and it found a large, overlooked audience who preferred shorter stories, more sports and feature news and splashy graphics.

IMPACT

Convergence

ILLUSTRATION 3.2

Newspaper Readers Prefer the Printed Paper, But Mobile Access Is Increasing

Most newspapers are available on many different platforms—print, Web and mobile access (smartphones and tablets). The majority of newspaper readers still use the newspaper in its printed format, but a growing number of newspaper users (29 percent) read their newspapers both online and in print.*

"Newspapers: Audience by Platform," *State of the News Media 2014*, Pew Research Center, journalism.org.

*Data total 99% because of rounding.

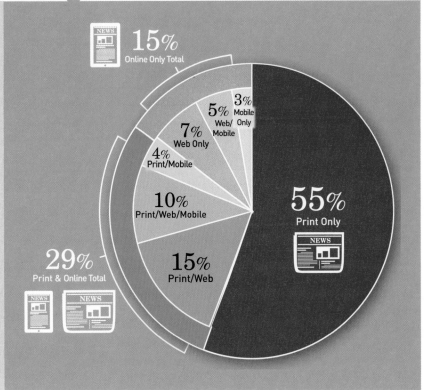

15%
Online Only Total

3%
Mobile
Only

5%
Web/
Mobile

7%
Web Only

4%
Print/Mobile

10%
Print/Web/Mobile

55%
Print Only

29%
Print & Online Total

15%
Print/Web

Today the three national papers each boast about a million daily readers in the U.S. for their print and Internet editions. *USA Today* concentrates on U.S. readers, but *The Journal* and *The Times* circulate widely overseas.

The Wall Street Journal publishes global editions in several different languages and is especially active in the Asian market. *The Times* publishes *The International New York Times* (originally the *International Herald Tribune*, see p. 348), an English-language daily covering global news throughout Europe. To compete with *The Journal*, in 2015 *The Times* announced plans to begin publishing a Chinese-language magazine in China.

Competition for readers became even more global in 2014 when the respected British newspaper *The Guardian* announced plans to challenge America's three national newspapers by aggressively marketing a U.S. edition called *Guardian US*.

Internet Editions Open Up New Markets

Today, newspapers available on-screen are an essential part of a reader-friendly strategy to maintain profitability. But Internet editions generate a lot less revenue than print editions because a print edition can carry much more advertising than an online version, and advertisers

still are willing to pay more for print ads than digital. Print editions also generate revenue from newsstand sales and subscriptions, but most Internet editions are available free.

In 2010, the results of a Pew Research Center survey showed that for the first time, more people (34 percent) went online for news than got their news from a newspaper (31 percent). Internet editions publish shorter highlights of the day's news, as well as special features that don't appear in the daily newspaper. Blogs offer subscribers the chance to share background information on specific topics, and other interactive features offer Internet links to lists and archived stories on related topics, plus current photos and video clips from breaking news events.

Recently, many newspapers have established a fee structure for Internet access (called a ***paywall***), which usually offers a sampling of the current stories free, for example, but requires a subscription to retrieve the full text of longer stories and for access to archives. Some newspapers offer free Internet access only to people who also subscribe to their daily print edition. *The Wall*

Paywall   A fee-for-access system set up by a newspaper to charge readers for Internet content.

Ige: Embrace change, risk

Ryan Kazmirzack - The Garden Island Posted: 5 hours ago

KAPAA — Gov. David Ige channeled his inner-engineer on Tuesday when he summed up his governing philosophy: "It's about execution: doing the ri...

Uluotopia sproutin'

Alden Alayvilla - The Garden Island Posted: 6 hours ago

PUHI — A Kauai Community College researcher is seven months into the first field experiment studying the potential of ulu (breadfruit) as a ma...

Courtesy of Shirley Biagi

Even small-town dailies, such as *The Garden Island*, published on the Hawaiian island of Kauai, offer Internet editions to boost their audience and attract advertising revenue. Online access means visitors from around the world can follow island news, boosting ad revenue.

Street Journal charges a subscription fee for access to its complete online edition, and in 2010 *The New York Times* began charging frequent users for content.

The biggest emerging competitors for news readers are Internet-only news sites called ***news aggregators***, technology-based companies, such as BuzzFeed, that produce very little original content. Instead, their writers scan the Internet for breaking news published by traditional news organizations and monitor social networks for public interest items posted by users. They then combine (aggregate) lists and shortened versions of the stories, add catchy headlines, and post the items on their own sponsored sites. The result is a news product that looks like a newspaper Web site but still depends heavily on borrowed content from traditional media organizations.

(See **Impact/Profile**: BuzzFeed Co-Founder Jonah Peretti Wants to Take Its Content Far Beyond Lists, p. 59.)

Today's Newspaper Audience Is a Moving Target

Although newspapers still hold power for advertisers, recent studies reveal that the future success of newspapers depends on retaining younger readers.

Newspaper publishers today also are forced to compete globally to maintain their audience because audiences attract advertisers—and profits. The average daily printed newspaper is about two-thirds advertising, and in some printed newspapers advertising runs as high as 80 percent. National advertisers (such as Procter & Gamble) buy much more television time than printed newspaper space, but small community businesses still need local newspapers to advertise their products and services.

Newspapers are racing to figure out how to remain profitable by chasing an audience that is constantly distracted by social media and the personal demands of their own lives. As the country's first mass medium for news, today's newspaper companies are no longer necessarily the first place people go for information, so newspapers are challenged to rediscover how they can fulfill their responsibility to keep the public informed and still stay profitable.

News aggregators such as BuzzFeed gather viral content from traditional news organizations and social networking sites, such as Facebook and Twitter, and post this borrowed content as news on their own sponsored sites.

News Aggregators Technology-based companies that primarily gather and re-format viral news content borrowed from traditional news organizations and social networks, then post the content as news on their own sponsored sites.

IMPACT *Profile*

BuzzFeed Co-Founder Jonah Peretti Wants to Take Its Content Far Beyond Lists

By Mike Isaac

Here are three completely crazy insights about BuzzFeed, the viral content start-up:

1. BuzzFeed is a Web traffic sensation that draws 150 million average monthly viewers.

2. Numbered lists, like this one, are what the site is most famous for and drive much of its audience.

3. BuzzFeed wants to be known for much, much more.

To help make that happen, BuzzFeed just closed a new $50 million investment from Andreessen Horowitz, a prominent venture capital firm in Silicon Valley. The investment values the company at about $850 million, according to a person with knowledge of the deal.

Now the question is whether BuzzFeed can maintain the agility and skills of a tech start-up while building the breadth of a large media company. "As we grow, how can we maintain a culture that can still be entrepreneurial?" said Jonah Peretti, the company's co-founder and chief executive.

BuzzFeed, which is based in New York, started in 2006 as a kind of laboratory for viral content—the kinds of highly shareable lists, videos and memes that pepper social media sites. But in recent years, the company has added more

Chang W. Lee/New York Times

The newspaper business today is facing challenges from online aggregators, such as BuzzFeed, which troll the Internet for stories and present them in a tabloid format. Jonah Peretti (left), co-founder of BuzzFeed, with Ben Smith, editor in chief, in the BuzzFeed newsroom in New York City.

traditional content, building a track record for delivering breaking news and deeply reported articles, and it has tried to marry its two halves in one site.

But what has really set BuzzFeed apart, Mr. Peretti said, is its grasp of technology. The company, which now has 550 employees, has been especially successful at distributing its lists and content through mobile devices and through social sites like Facebook and Twitter. Social media accounts for 75 percent of BuzzFeed's referral traffic, according to the company.

Still, the company faces the same problem that more traditional publications do—rates for traditional online advertising, on general interest sites like BuzzFeed, have dropped consistently from year to year. To keep up, sites must either perpetually increase traffic at a

steady clip, or innovate and move into new and potentially more lucrative areas like so-called native advertising and video.

This is not Mr. Peretti's first media enterprise, however. He was a co-founder, along with Arianna Huffington and the venture capitalist Kenneth Lerer, of *The Huffington Post*. That online media start-up, which relied heavily on showing up in Google search results for traffic, was sold to AOL in 2011 for $315 million.

The company also plans a fast expansion into international markets, already a major driver of the site's new-user growth, with plans to open offices in Japan, Germany, Mexico and India.

"We're organizing ourselves to be a media company for the way people consume media today," Mr. Peretti said.

Excerpted from Mike Isaac, "50 Million New Reasons BuzzFeed Wants to Take Its Content Far Beyond Lists," August 10, 2014, nytimes.com.

REVIEW, ANALYZE, INVESTIGATE

CHAPTER 3

First Mass Medium to Deliver News

- Between 1690 and 1920, newspapers were the only mass news medium.

- Newspapers are historically important in defining a society's concept of the importance of an independent press.

Publishers Fight for an Independent Press

- The issue of government control of newspapers surfaced early in colonial America, when the authorities stopped *Publick Occurrences* in 1690 after a single issue because the paper angered local officials.

- The tradition of an independent press in this country began when James Franklin published the first newspaper without the heading "Published by Authority."

- The John Peter Zenger case established an important legal precedent: If what a newspaper reports is true, the paper cannot successfully be sued for libel.

- By the time the American Revolution began, at least 14 women had worked as printers in the colonies.

- As dissatisfaction grew over British rule, newspapers became essential political tools in the effort to spread revolutionary ideas, including opposition to the British Stamp Act and the Alien and Sedition Laws.

Technology Helps Newspapers Reach New Readers

- The technological advances of the 19th century, such as cheaper newsprint, mechanized printing and the telegraph, meant that newspapers could reach a wider audience faster than ever before.

- In the 1800s, newspapers sought new readers—Native Americans, immigrants and those on the nation's frontiers.

- Elias Boudinot [Galagina (The Buck) Oowati] published the first issue of the nation's first Native American newspaper, the *Cherokee Phoenix*, on February 21, 1828.

- The abolition and women's suffrage campaigns fostered the first alternative press movements.

- Six early advocates for domestic change were John B. Russwurm, the Reverend Samuel Cornish, Frederick Douglass, William Lloyd Garrison, Jane Grey Swisshelm and Ida B. Wells.

Newspapers Seek Mass Audiences and Big Profits

- Penny papers made newspapers affordable for virtually every American.

- The penny press made newspapers available to the masses.

- The legacy of the penny press continues today in gossip columns and crime reporting.

Newspapers Dominate the Early 20th Century

- Newspapers were the nation's single source of daily dialogue about politics, culture and social issues.

- Intense competition bred yellow journalism.

Unionization Encourages Professionalism

- Unions standardized wages at many of the nation's largest newspapers.

- Unions raised wages and created a sense of professionalism.

Television Brings New Competition

- The introduction of television contributed to a decline in newspaper readership that began in the 1950s.

- Newspapers were forced to share their audience with broadcasting.

Alternative Press Revives Voices of Protest

- The social causes of the 1960s briefly revived the alternative press.

- People who supported the alternative press believed the mainstream press was avoiding important issues such as the anti–Vietnam War movement, the civil rights movement and the gay rights movement.

Newspapers Expand and Contract

- Since the 1970s, the overall number of newspapers has declined.

- To try to match TV's visual appeal, newspapers introduced advanced graphics and vivid color in the 1990s.

- Today newspaper audiences are still declining, especially among young readers.

Newspapers at Work

- Newspaper operations are divided into two areas: business and editorial.
- The editorial department usually also manages all aspects of the newspaper's Internet editions.
- Editorial employees report to the editor-in-chief or the publisher or both.
- Almost all newspapers today produce Internet editions to capture new audiences.
- Newspapers can also buy content from syndicates and news services.

Technology Transforms Production

- For newspaper unions, the shift to digital technology has brought a challenge to union representation.
- Before 1970, typographers handset metal type, and labor unions represented most typographers.
- The introduction of digital composition meant many typographers' jobs were eliminated.
- Some newspaper workers went on strike, but layoffs continued.
- Unions are a much smaller factor in the newspaper business today.

Consolidation Increases Chain Ownership

- Large corporations have bought up newspapers that once were family-owned.
- Instead of newspapers competing locally, national newspaper chains now compete with one another across the country.

Newspapers Fight to Retain Readers

- Newspapers depend primarily on advertising for support.
- Hundreds of newspapers have been shut down in the last ten years.
- More than 100 newspapers closed in the United States in the first six months of 2009.

National Newspapers Seek a Wider Audience

- The nation's three national newspapers are *USA Today*, *The New York Times* and *The Wall Street Journal*.

- Today the three national papers have about a million daily readers each.
- *The Wall Street Journal* publishes global editions in several different languages.
- *The Times* publishes *The International New York Times*.
- In 2014 the respected British newspaper *The Guardian* began aggressively marketing a U.S. edition of the paper called *Guardian US*.

Internet Editions Open Up New Markets

- Newspaper publishing companies first launched Internet editions in the late 1990s.
- Internet editions generate a lot less revenue than print editions.
- In 2010 for the first time, more people went online for news than got their news from a newspaper.
- Internet editions publish shorter news highlights plus many interactive features.
- Many newspapers are beginning to establish a fee structure for access called a *paywall*.
- The biggest emerging competitors for readers are Internet-only news sites called news aggregators.

Today's Newspaper Audience Is a Moving Target

- The future financial success of newspapers depends on their ability to appeal to a shifting audience and meet growing competition.
- Newspapers still hold power for advertisers, but recent studies reveal that younger readers are deserting the medium faster than any other group.
- In cities with large Latino populations, newspapers have introduced Spanish-language editions, and existing Spanish-language newspapers have expanded.
- The average daily newspaper is about two-thirds advertising.
- Newspapers are challenged to rediscover how they can fulfill their responsibility to keep the public well informed yet still stay profitable.

Key Terms

These terms are defined in the margins throughout this chapter and appear in alphabetical order with definitions in the Glossary, which begins on page 361.

Critical Questions

1. Describe the circumstances surrounding the John Peter Zenger decision. Which important precedent did the case set for the American mass media? Why is this precedent so important?

2. Describe the contributions of two early colonial American women publishers and two early alternative press publishers.

3. Describe the impact on American society of the competition that developed between the Hearst and Pulitzer newspaper empires. Describe the style of news coverage that characterized that competition. Give an example of sensationalized reporting from your experience.

4. Discuss the new national and global audiences newspapers are seeking to maintain their readership. How does broadening content to attract a global audience, for example, affect the nation's focus on events outside the U.S.?

5. Describe some of the Internet services newspapers offer and discuss how they make newspapers more accessible to readers. Do you read a newspaper online? How often? Do you use a news aggregator? Under which circumstances, if any, would you be willing to pay for online news content?

Working the Web

This list includes sites mentioned in the chapter and others to give you greater insight into the newspaper business.

American Society of News Editors (ASNE)

asne.org

Housed in the Reynolds School of Journalism at the University of Missouri, this professional organization for daily newspaper editors has committees and annual conventions that address such issues as the Freedom of Information Act, the role of newspapers in society, ethics and diversity—both in the workplace and in newspaper reporting. ASNE also is concerned about improving journalism training and education throughout the U.S.

BuzzFeed

buzzfeed.com

Founded in 2006 in New York City as an experimental media and entertainment Web site, BuzzFeed covers a wide array of topics, including politics, entertainment and finance. Most of its content is gathered and reproduced from traditional news organizations and social media, then organized in BuzzFeed's fast-moving, tabloid format. The site's writers produce some original reporting, but most of its content is borrowed. So far, BuzzFeed is supported primarily by investments from venture capital firms.

The Dallas Morning News

dallasnews.com

Owned by the Belo Corporation, the *Dallas Morning News* bills itself as the largest daily newspaper in the state of Texas.

Honolulu Star-Advertiser

staradvertiser.com

The flagship publication of Oahu Publications Inc. (OPI)—which is owned by Black Press Limited, a Canadian newspaper company—the *Honolulu Star-Advertiser* was formed in 2010, when OPI purchased the *Honolulu Advertiser* from the Gannett Corporation and merged it with the *Honolulu Star Bulletin*, making OPI the largest newspaper publisher in the state of Hawaii. Oahu Publications also publishes *The Garden Island* on Kauai.

La Opinión

Headquartered in Los Angeles, *La Opinión* is the largest Spanish-language newspaper in the country. *La Opinión* is owned by impreMedia, which also owns and publishes *El Diario*, *La Raza*, *El Mensajero*, *Rumbo* and *Vista*.

Los Angeles Times

latimes.com

First published in 1881 as the *Los Angeles Daily Times*, the *Los Angeles Times* is owned by Tribune Publishing. The *Times* has a well-established reputation for quality news and feature reporting and for its comprehensive coverage of entertainment industry news. Users can personalize their news pages around the content that interests them.

The Miami Herald

miamiherald.com

Considered the paper of record and South Florida's largest daily newspaper, the *Miami Herald* is owned by the

McClatchy Co. It has developed a reputation for its coverage of Caribbean and Latin American news for Miami's large Latino population. In 1946, the paper launched its international Clipper edition for Latin America, originally named for the Pan Am flying "clipper" seaplanes on which the paper was shipped.

The New York Times

nytimes.com

Long regarded as the nation's most credible and complete newspaper under the motto "All the News That's Fit to Print," *The New York Times*—known simply as *The Times*—still fiercely maintains its traditional "long-hand" journalism reporting format, in both the print and digital editions. *The Times* has won more than 100 Pulitzer Prizes, and was one of the first dailies in the U.S. to begin incorporating its own video news reporting service into its online site. It was also one of the first dailies in the country to begin charging a subscription access fee for its online content.

Newspaper Association of America (NAA)

naa.org

The NAA is the lobbying organization of the newspaper industry, with a membership that includes over 2,000 daily newspapers, non-dailies and Internet news providers in the U.S. and Canada. With the recent decline in print newspaper subscribers, the NAA uses its own nonprofit organization, the American Press Institute, to establish newspaper training and education initiatives throughout the country.

Topix

topix.net

Based in Palo Alto, Calif., Topix LLC is a privately held company with investment from Gannett Co., McClatchy Co. and Tribune Co. The customizable news Web site has more than 12 million subscribers that are interconnected with news and information from "74,000 sources to 450,000 news topics" throughout the country, according to the site. In 2012, Topix launched Politix, which allows readers to participate in on-site debates about current political topics.

The Washington Post

washingtonpost.com

Long known for uncovering and reporting the Watergate Scandal in 1972, *The Washington Post* was purchased by Amazon founder and chief executive Jeffrey Bezos for $250 million in 2013. *The Post* is the major daily newspaper of Washington, D.C., and the top newspaper of record for national political news.

Impact/Action Videos are concise news features on various topics created exclusively for *Media/Impact*. Find them in *Media/Impact*'s MindTap at cengagebrain.com.

MindTap® Log on to MindTap for *Media/Impact* to access a variety of additional material—including learning objectives, chapter readings with highlighting and note-taking, **Impact/Action Videos**, activities, and comprehension quizzes—that will guide you through this chapter.

MAGAZINES
CHASING THE AUDIENCE

Nancy Borowick/New York Times

Condé Nast, one of the nation's premier magazine publishers, produces 21 magazine "brands," including *Wired, Glamour, Vogue, The New Yorker* and *Vanity Fair.* In November 2014, Condé Nast moved into its new headquarters at 1 World Trade Center, New York City.

> ## "The print medium has to be innovative and reinvent itself."
>
> —MICHAEL A. CLINTON, PRESIDENT FOR MARKETING, HEARST MAGAZINES

By the early 1950s, magazine mogul Henry Luce's Time and Fortune were well established. He often traveled with his wife, Ambassador Clare Boothe Luce, and many of the people Henry Luce met overseas wanted to talk about sports instead of international politics.

"Luce knew nothing about sports," said *Los Angeles Times* sports columnist Jim Murray, who in the early 1950s was writing about sports for *Time* magazine. "But every place he'd go, all over the world, the conversation would veer to the World Cup or the British Open or whatever. He got fascinated and irritated, I guess, and finally said, 'Why this all-consuming interest in games?' We said, 'Well, that's the way the world is, Henry.' He said, 'Well, maybe we ought to start a sports magazine.'"

The result was *Sports Illustrated*, which, for more than 60 years, was ranked among the nation's most profitable magazine brands. In 2014, *Sports Illustrated*, along with all the other magazines once owned by the media giant Time Warner, was spun off into a separate company called Time Inc. The reason? Steeply declining advertising revenue at the company's magazines was affecting the profitability of the Time Warner corporation, so Time Warner separated the magazines from their corporate parent, claiming the magazines could be run better separately rather than attached to a massive media company. Adapting its magazines to the new digital environment proved too challenging for Time Warner.

When it began, *Sports Illustrated* was one of the first magazines to be successful by targeting a specific audience. Today, magazines, like newspapers, are being challenged to chase the audience and compete in a much more crowded field. Advertisers are still attracted to magazines because their readers are a more specific target: The articles in magazines are built around specialized audiences—skiers, hikers, new mothers, brides or race car enthusiasts, for instance—rather than the general, scattered audience for TV, for example.

To be successful today, magazines must give their readers information they can't find elsewhere and deliver that information where the readers are. This means that magazines, like all print media, are chasing today's mobile, digital audience.

Magazines Reflect Trends and Culture

Since their beginnings, magazines, more than any other medium, have reflected the surrounding culture and the characteristics of their society. As readers' needs and lifestyles change, so do magazines. The current trend toward specialty and online magazines, in response to the shrinking number of print magazine readers, is the latest development in this evolution.

Colonial Magazines Compete with Newspapers

In 1741, more than 50 years after the birth of the colonies' first newspaper, magazines entered the American media marketplace. Newspapers covered daily crises for local readers, but magazines could reach beyond the parochial concerns of small communities to carry their cultural, political and social ideas and help foster a national identity.

TimeFrame
1741–Today

Magazines Grow as a Specialized Medium That Targets Readers

1741 Benjamin Franklin and Andrew Bradford publish America's first magazines, *General Magazine* (Franklin) and *American Magazine* (Bradford).

1821 *The Saturday Evening Post* becomes the first magazine to reach a wide public audience.

1830 Louis A. Godey hires Sarah Josepha Hale as the first woman editor of a general circulation women's magazine, *Godey's Lady's Book*.

1865 *The Nation*, featuring political commentary, appears in Boston.

✳ **1887** Cyrus Curtis begins publishing *The Ladies' Home Journal*.

1893 Samuel A. McClure founds *McClure's Magazine*, featuring muckrakers Ida Tarbell and Lincoln Steffens.

1910 W. E. B. Du Bois and the National Association for the Advancement of Colored People (NAACP) start *The Crisis*.

1923 Henry Luce creates *Time*, the nation's first newsmagazine, then *Fortune* and *Life*, and eventually *Sports Illustrated*.

1925 Harold Ross introduces *The New Yorker*.

✳ **1945** John Johnson launches *Ebony* and then *Jet*.

1985 Advance Publications buys *The New Yorker* for more than $185 million, beginning the era of magazine industry consolidation.

1993 *Newsweek* launches an Internet edition.

1997 Dennis Publishing, which owns *Rolling Stone* magazine, launches *Maxim*, the most successful magazine launch in the last decade.

2000 Oprah Winfrey launches the lifestyle magazine *O, The Oprah Magazine*.

2005 *Slate* magazine grows popular as an Internet-only magazine, one of the first magazines to be issued exclusively online.

2009 Magazine publisher Condé Nast shuts down several formerly successful magazines, such as *Gourmet* and *Modern Bride*.

2010 Condé Nast launches mobile and tablet editions of its most popular printed magazines.

2012 *Newsweek* stops publishing a printed magazine and publishes only online.

2013 *Wired* magazine becomes the nation's most successful combined print and digital magazine, with 50 percent of its ad revenue derived online.

✳ **2014** *Ladies' Home Journal* stops regular publication after 130 years in print.

TODAY Large media companies publish most magazines, and some magazines are published only on the Internet. Magazine income continues to decline. The future of magazine brands depends on their ability to expand readership to a digital audience.

From the beginning, women have been magazines' best audience, and *Vogue* has adapted to attract an active female following.

The U.S. magazine industry began in 1741, in Philadelphia, when Benjamin Franklin and Andrew Bradford raced each other to become America's first magazine publisher. Franklin originated the idea of starting the first American magazine, but Bradford issued his *American Magazine* first, on February 13, 1741. Franklin's first issue of *General Magazine* came out three days later. Neither magazine lasted very long. Bradford published three issues, and Franklin published six, but their efforts initiated a rich tradition.

Because they didn't carry advertising, early magazines were expensive, and their circulations remained very small, limited to people who could afford them. Like colonial newspapers, early magazines primarily provided a means for political expression.

Magazines Travel Beyond Local Boundaries

Newspapers flooded the larger cities by the early 1800s, but they circulated only within each city's boundaries, so national news spread slowly. Colleges were limited to the wealthy because they cost too much to attend, and books were expensive. Magazines became America's only national medium to travel beyond local boundaries,

and subscribers depended on them for news, culture and entertainment.

The magazine that first reached a large public was *The Saturday Evening Post*, started in 1821. The early *Post*s cost a nickel each and were only four pages, with no illustrations. One-fourth of the magazine was advertising, and it was affordable.

Publishers Locate New Readers

Magazines like *The Saturday Evening Post* reached a wide readership with their general interest content, but many other audiences were available to 19th-century publishers, and they spent the century locating their readership. Four enduring topics that expanded the magazine audience in the 1800s were: women's issues, social crusades, literature and the arts and politics.

Women's Issues

Because women were a sizable potential audience, magazines were more open to female contributors than newspapers. A central figure in the history of women's magazines in America was Sarah Josepha Hale. In 1830, Louis A. Godey was the first publisher to capitalize on a female audience. Women, most of whom had not attended school, sought out *Godey's Lady's Book* and its gifted editor, Sarah Josepha Hale, for advice on morals, manners, literature, fashion, diet and taste.

When her husband died in 1822, Hale sought work to support herself and her five children. As the editor of *Godey's* for 40 years beginning in 1837, she actively supported higher education and property rights for women. By 1860, *Godey's* had 150,000 subscribers. Hale retired from the magazine when she was 89, a year before she died.

Social Crusades

Magazines also became important instruments for social change. *The Ladies' Home Journal* is credited with leading a crusade against dangerous medicines. Many of the ads in women's magazines in the 1800s were for patent medicines like Faber's Golden Female Pills ("successfully used by prominent ladies for female irregularities") and Ben-Yan, which promised to cure "all nervous debilities."

The Ladies' Home Journal was the first magazine to refuse patent medicine ads. Founded in 1887 by Cyrus Curtis, the *Journal* launched several crusades. It offered columns about women's issues, published popular fiction and even printed sheet music.

Journal editor Edward Bok began his crusade against patent medicines in 1892, after he learned that many of them contained more than 40 percent alcohol. Next, Bok revealed that a medicine sold to soothe noisy babies contained morphine. Other magazines joined the fight

AP Images

Hulton Archive/Archive Photos/Getty Images

Sarah Josepha Hale was the nation's first female editor of a major magazine. Beginning in 1837, she served as editor of *Godey's Lady's Book* for 40 years. She fervently supported access to higher education and property rights for women.

against fraudulent ads, and partly because of Bok's crusading investigations, Congress passed the Pure Food and Drug Act of 1906.

Fostering the Arts

In the mid-1800s, American magazines began to seek a literary audience by promoting the nation's writers. Two of today's most important literary magazines—*Harper's* and *The Atlantic*—began more than 150 years ago. *Harper's New Monthly Magazine*, known today as *Harper's*, first published in 1850.

The American literary showcase grew when *The Atlantic Monthly* appeared in 1857 in Boston. The magazine's purpose was "to inoculate the few who influence the many." That formula continues today, with *The Atlantic* and *Harper's* still publishing literary criticism and promoting political debate in print and digital editions.

Political Commentary

With more time (usually a month between issues) and space than newspapers had to reflect on the country's

problems, political magazines provided a forum for public debate by scholars and critical observers. Two of the nation's progressive political magazines that began in the 19th and early 20th centuries have endured: *The Nation* and *The Crisis*.

The Nation, founded by abolitionists in 1865, is the oldest continuously published opinion journal in the U.S., offering critical literary essays and arguments for progressive change. This weekly magazine has survived a succession of owners and financial hardships. It is published by a foundation, supported by benefactors and subscribers and publishes print and online editions. *The Nation* celebrated its 150th anniversary in 2015.

An important organization that needed a voice at the beginning of the century was the National Association for the Advancement of Colored People (NAACP). For 24 years, beginning in 1910, that voice was W. E. B. Du Bois, who founded and edited the organization's monthly magazine, *The Crisis*. Du Bois began *The Crisis* as the official monthly magazine of the NAACP. In *The Crisis*, he attacked discrimination against African American soldiers during World War I, exposed Ku Klux Klan activities and argued for African American voting and housing

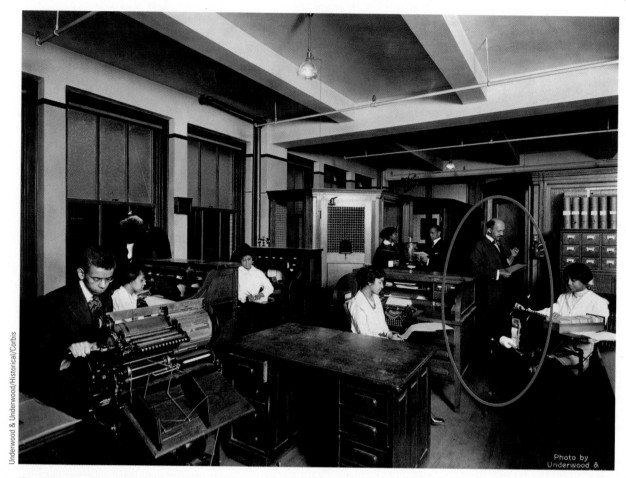

Underwood & Underwood/Historical/Corbis

The Crisis, founded by W. E. B. Du Bois in 1910 as the monthly magazine of the NAACP, continues to publish today as a quarterly. This photo, taken around 1910, shows workers in the magazine's offices. W. E. B. Du Bois is the man standing on the far right near the door.

rights. By 1919, circulation was more than 100,000. Today, *The Crisis* continues to publish quarterly.

Postal Act Helps Magazines Grow

Before Congress passed the Postal Act of 1879, newspapers traveled through the mail free while magazine publishers had to pay postage. The Postal Act gave magazines second-class mailing privileges and a cheap mailing rate. This meant quick, reasonably priced distribution for magazines, and today magazines still travel on a preferential postage rate.

Aided by lower mailing costs, the number of monthly magazines grew from 180 in 1860 to more than 1,800 by 1900. However, because magazines traveled through the mail, they became subject to government censorship. (See **Chapter 14**.)

McClure's Launches Investigative Journalism

Colorful, campaigning journalists began investigating big business just before the turn of the 20th century. These

writers became known as **_muckrakers_**. The strongest editor in the first 10 years of the 20th century was legendary magazine publisher Samuel S. McClure, who founded *McClure's Magazine* in 1893.

McClure and his magazine were very important to the Progressive era in American politics, which called for an end to the close relationship between government and big business. To reach a large readership, McClure priced his new monthly magazine at 15 cents per issue, while most other magazines sold for 25 or 35 cents. He hired writers such as Lincoln Steffens and Ida Tarbell to investigate corruption in government and big business. Ida Tarbell joined *McClure's* in 1894 as associate editor, and in 1904 she targeted the Standard Oil Co., the nation's biggest oil monopoly (See **Impact/**

Muckrakers   Investigative magazine journalists who targeted abuses by government and big business.

IMPACT

Profile

Muckraker Ida Tarbell Exposes Standard Oil's John D. Rockefeller

By Shirley Biagi

When John D. Rockefeller refused to talk with her, Ida Tarbell sat at the back of the room and watched him deliver a Sunday school sermon. In her autobiography, *All in the Day's Work*, written when she was 80, Tarbell described some of her experiences as she investigated Standard Oil:

The impression of power deepened when Mr. Rockefeller took off his coat and hat, put on a skullcap and took a seat commanding the entire room, his back to the wall. It was the head which riveted attention. It was big, great breadth from back to front, high broad forehead, big bumps behind the ears, not a shiny head but with a wet look. The skin was as fresh as that of any healthy man about us. The thin sharp nose was like a thorn. There were no lips; the mouth looked as if the teeth were all shut hard. Deep furrows ran down each side of the mouth from the nose. There were puffs under the little colorless eyes with creases running from them.

Wonder over the head was almost at once diverted to wonder over the man's uneasiness. His eyes were never quiet but darted from face to face, even peering around the jog at the audience close to the wall. . . .

My two hours' study of Mr. Rockefeller aroused a feeling I had not expected, which time has intensified. I was sorry for

In 1904 as a reporter for *McClure's Magazine*, muckraker Ida Tarbell targeted oil magnate John D. Rockefeller, who called her "that misguided woman."

Underwood & Underwood/Historical/Corbis

him. I know no companion so terrible as fear. Mr. Rockefeller, for all the conscious power written in face and voice and figure, was afraid, I told myself, afraid of his own kind.

Profile, "Muckraker Ida Tarbell Exposes Standard Oil's John D. Rockefeller," page 71.) Tarbell's 19-part series eventually became a two-volume book, *History of the Standard Oil Company*, which established Tarbell's reputation as a muckraker.

President Theodore Roosevelt coined the term *muckraker* in 1906 when he compared reformers like Tarbell and Steffens to the "Man with the Muckrake" who busily dredged up dirt in John Bunyan's book *Pilgrim's Progress*.

By 1910, many reforms sought by the muckrakers had been adopted, and this particular type of magazine journalism declined. The muckrakers are cited as America's original investigative reporters.

The New Yorker *and* Time *Succeed Differently*

Magazines in the first half of the 20th century matured and adapted to absorb the invention of radio and then television. As with magazines today, magazine publishers had two basic choices:

1. Publishers could seek a *definable, targeted loyal audience*, or

2. Publishers could seek a *broad, general readership*.

Harold Ross, founding editor of *The New Yorker*, and Henry Luce, who started Time Inc., best exemplify these two types of American publishers in the first half of the 20th century.

Harold Ross and *The New Yorker*

Harold Ross' *The New Yorker* magazine launched the wittiest group of writers that ever gathered around a table at New York's Algonquin Hotel. The "witcrackers," who met there regularly for lunch throughout the 1920s, included Heywood Broun, Robert Benchley, Dorothy Parker, Alexander Woollcott, James Thurber and Harpo Marx. Because they sat at a large round table in the dining room, the group came to be known as the Algonquin Round Table.

Harold Ross persuaded Raoul Fleischmann, whose family money came from the yeast company of the same name, to invest half a million dollars in *The New Yorker* before the magazine began making money in 1928, three years after its launch. Ross published some of the country's great commentary, fiction and humor, sprinkled with cartoons that gave *The New Yorker* its charm. Ross

Published since 1925, *The New Yorker* is one of the nation's most successful magazines and continues to be the primary showcase for American writers and artists. It is available in print and digital editions.

Chris Ware/The New Yorker

edited the magazine until he died in 1951, and William Shawn succeeded him.

After one owner—the Fleischmann family—and only two editors in 60 years, *The New Yorker* was sold in 1985 to Advance Publications, the parent company of one of the nation's largest magazine groups, Condé Nast. *The New Yorker* continues to be the primary showcase for contemporary American writers and artists. (Contemporary *New Yorker* cartoons appear throughout *Media/Impact*.)

Henry Luce's Empire: *Time*

Henry Luce is the singular giant of 20th-century magazine publishing. Unlike Harold Ross, who sought a sophisticated, wealthy audience, Luce wanted to reach the largest possible readership. Luce's first creation was *Time* magazine, which he founded in 1923 with his Yale classmate Briton Hadden. Luce and Hadden paid themselves $30 a week and recruited their friends to write for the magazine.

The first issue of *Time* covered the week's events in 28 pages, minus six pages of advertising—half an hour's reading. "It was of course not for people who really wanted to be informed," wrote Luce's biographer W. A. Swanberg. "It was for people willing to spend a half-hour to avoid being entirely uninformed." The brash news magazine became the foundation of Luce's media empire, which eventually also launched *Fortune*, *Life*, *Sports Illustrated*, *Money* and *People Weekly*. Eventually *Time* became a small part of the giant company Time Warner Inc., which includes television stations, movie studios, book publishing companies, HBO and CNN.

Luce's magazine fostered a *Life* magazine look-alike called *Ebony*, an African American magazine introduced in the 1940s by John H. Johnson. The Johnson chain also launched *Jet* magazine. At the beginning of the 21st century, *Ebony* and *Jet* had a combined readership of 3 million people. Johnson groomed his daughter, Linda Johnson Rice, to manage the company, a job Rice assumed in 2005 when her father died. In June 2014, *Jet* magazine became an online-only publication.

Specialized Magazines Take Over

In the 1950s, television began to offer Americans some of the same type of general interest features that magazines provided, and general interest magazines collapsed. Readers wanted specialized information they couldn't get from other sources. These new targeted magazines segmented the market, which meant each magazine attracted fewer readers.

Very few general interest magazines survive today. To be successful, a magazine must find a specific audience and then deliver specialized content for that audience, surrounded by the advertising to support it—*Motor Trend* carries ads for auto accessories, for example, and *Women's Health* carries ads for fitness gear and vitamin supplements. This is called *targeting an audience*, which magazines traditionally have been able to accomplish more effectively than any other advertising medium.

Companies Consolidate Ownership and Define Readership

In 1984, for the first time, the price paid for individual magazine companies and groups of magazines bought and sold in one year reached $1 billion. *U.S. News & World Report* sold for $100 million. *Billboard* sold for $40 million. Like other media industries, magazines were gathered together under large umbrella organizations. The elite magazine company Condé Nast, for example, today publishes 21 magazines each month.

As the audience becomes more segmented—in print and online—magazine publishers envision a time when they can deliver to each reader exactly what the reader wants to read.

Magazines Divide into Three Types

Today's magazines can be categorized into three types:

1. Consumer magazines
2. Trade, technical and professional magazines
3. Company magazines

You probably are most familiar with **consumer magazines** such as *People*, *Men's Health* and *Cosmopolitan*. In the magazine business, the term *consumer magazines* refers to all magazines sold by subscription or at newsstands, supermarkets, bookstores and online. As a group, consumer magazines make the most money because they have the most readers and carry the most advertising. (See **Illustration 4.1**, "Top 10 U.S. Consumer Printed Magazines," p. 74.)

People in a particular industry read **trade, technical and professional magazines** to learn

© Mike Baldwin / Cornered

Baldwin Mike/Cartoonstock.com

"'Have it all. Be an executive, community volunteer, a devoted wife and mother.' Good article. You should read this."

more about their businesses. *Veterinary Practice Management*, for example, is a trade magazine, published as "a business guide for small animal practitioners." Other examples of trade magazines are the *Columbia Journalism Review* (published by Columbia University) and *American Medical News* (published by the American Medical Association).

Company magazines are produced by businesses for their employees, customers and stockholders. These magazines usually don't carry advertising. Their main purpose is to promote the company. Chevron Corp., for instance, publishes a company magazine called *Chevron USA Odyssey*.

Consumer Magazines All magazines sold by subscription or at newsstands, supermarkets, bookstores and online.

Trade, Technical and Professional Magazines Magazines dedicated to a particular business or profession.

Company Magazines Magazines produced by businesses for their employees, customers and stockholders.

IMPACT

Money

ILLUSTRATION 4.1

Top 10 U.S. Consumer Printed Magazines

Magazines that target a female audience have always been the most successful type of magazine. Half the nation's top 10 printed magazines in 2014 were women's magazines (*Better Homes and Gardens, Good Housekeeping, Woman's Day, Family Circle* and *Ladies' Home Journal*, although the *Journal* stopped publishing in December 2014). *Game Informer Magazine* is the number two consumer printed magazine and the number one digital replica magazine (see **Illustration 4.2**).

Alliance for Audited Media, "Top 25 U.S. Consumer Magazines for June 2014," auditedmedia.com.

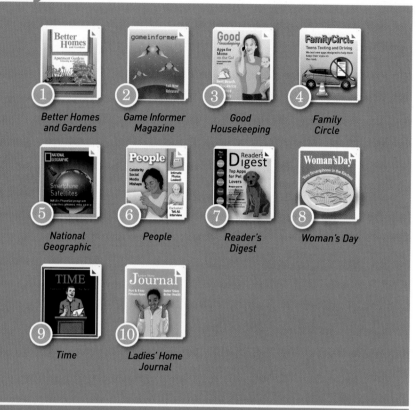

1 Better Homes and Gardens
2 Game Informer Magazine
3 Good Housekeeping
4 Family Circle
5 National Geographic
6 People
7 Reader's Digest
8 Woman's Day
9 Time
10 Ladies' Home Journal

ILLUSTRATION 4.2

Top 10 U.S. Digital Replica Magazines

A ***digital replica magazine*** is published in both print and digital (replica) versions. *Game Informer Magazine* is the only magazine popular with both print and digital readers. Four women's magazines (*Shape* and *Working Mother*, for example) are on the digital replica list, but with a totally different, younger readership than the audience for the most popular print magazines (*Good Housekeeping* and *Family Circle*). And there are two men's magazines (*Maxim* and *Men's Health*) on the digital list, but no men's magazines among the printed magazine top 10.

Alliance for Audited Media, "Top U.S. Consumer Magazines by Digital Replica Circulation," June 2014, auditedmedia.com.

1 Game Informer Magazine
2 Shape
3 Star Magazine
4 OK! Weekly
5 Working Mother
6 Maxim
7 National Geographic
8 Taste of Home
9 Men's Fitness
10 Cosmopolitan

Magazines at Work

Magazine employees work in one of five divisions:

1. Editorial

2. Circulation sales

3. Advertising sales

4. Manufacturing and distribution

5. Administration

The *editorial* department handles all the magazine's content, except the advertisements. Magazine editors work in this department, and they decide the subjects for each magazine issue, oversee the people who write the articles and schedule the articles for the printed and online magazine. Designers who determine the "look" of the magazine and the magazine's Web access site also are considered part of the editorial department, as well as the artists and photographers who provide illustrations and photographs.

The *circulation* department manages subscription information. Workers in this department enter new subscriptions and handle address changes and cancellations, for example, and often circulation is contracted out. The *advertising* department is responsible for finding advertisers for the magazine. Advertising employees often help the companies design their ads to be consistent with the magazine format.

Manufacturing and *distribution* departments manage the magazine's production and delivery to readers. This often includes contracting with an outside company to print the magazine and to manage the magazine on the Internet. Most magazine companies also contract with an outside distribution company rather than deliver the printed magazines themselves.

Administration, as in any media company, takes care of the organizational details—the paperwork of hiring, paying bills and managing the office, for example.

Because advertisers provide nearly half a magazine's income, tension often develops between a magazine's advertising staff and its editorial staff. The advertising staff may lobby the editor for favorable stories about potential advertisers, but the editor is responsible to the magazine's audience. The advertising department might argue to the editor, for example, that a local restaurant will not want to advertise in a magazine that publishes an unfavorable review of the restaurant. If the restaurant is a big advertiser, the editor must decide how best to maintain the magazine's integrity.

The Alliance for Audited Media (**AAM**), an independent agency of print media market research, verifies and publishes circulation figures for member magazines. Advertisers use AAM figures to help them decide which magazines will reach their audience. Circulation figures

Roz Chast/The New Yorker Collection/Cartoon Bank.Com

(how many readers each magazine has) determine how much the magazine can charge for its ads.

Putting the magazine together and selling it (circulation, advertising, administration, manufacturing and distribution) cost more than organizing the articles and photographs that appear in the magazine (editorial). Usually a managing editor coordinates all five departments.

The magazine editor's job is to keep the content interesting so people will want to read the magazine. Good magazine editors can create a distinctive, useful product by carefully choosing the best articles for the magazine's audience and ensuring the articles are well written and illustrated.

Full-time magazine staffers write many of the articles, such as a food editor who creates recipes or a columnist who writes commentary. Some magazines use articles by **freelancers**. Freelancers do not receive a salary from the

Digital Replica Magazines Magazines that are published in both printed and digital versions.

AAM Alliance for Audited Media (formerly Audit Bureau of Circulations); an independent agency of media market research that verifies and publishes circulation figures for member magazines.

Freelancers Writers who are not on the staff of a magazine but who are paid for each individual article published.

IMPACT

Convergence

ILLUSTRATION 4.3

Who Reads Digital Magazines?

The audience for digital magazines is evenly divided among men and women (compared to the audience for printed magazines, which skews toward female readers). The digital magazine audience also is younger (ages 18–44) than print magazine readers and better educated. These audience characteristics mean that digital magazine readers are a more desirable audience for advertisers.

Magazine Media Factbook 2014, The Association of Magazine Media, magazine.org.

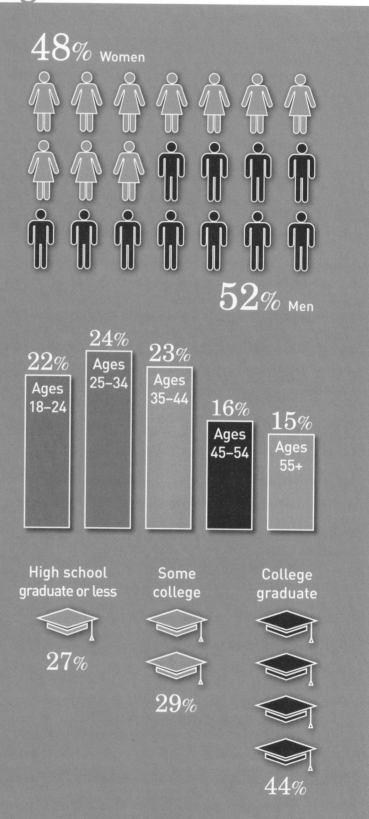

48% Women

52% Men

22% Ages 18–24
24% Ages 25–34
23% Ages 35–44
16% Ages 45–54
15% Ages 55+

High school graduate or less — 27%

Some college — 29%

College graduate — 44%

Throughout the 20th century, ads for consumer products like cigarettes, cars and food provided substantial revenue for magazines. Today, of course, most magazines refuse to carry cigarette advertising, but food and car ads are still a magazine staple. These magazine ads appeared in January 1950.

magazine; instead, they are paid for each article published in the magazine. Many freelancers write for several magazines simultaneously. Some freelancers specialize—just writing travel articles, for example. Other freelancers work just as the tradition of their name implies: They are versatile, and they can write about a variety of topics.

Magazines Compete for Readers in Crowded Markets

Today, trends in magazine publishing continue to reflect social and demographic changes, but magazines no longer play the cutting-edge social, political and cultural role they played in the past. Instead, most magazines are seeking a specific audience, and most magazines are competing for the same audience.

In 1990, for the first time, the number of magazines published in the United States stopped growing, and today the number is declining. Younger readers are less likely than their parents to read magazines. Men are more likely than women to read magazines online, yet women continue to be the single most lucrative audience for printed magazines.

An important part of the women's magazine market are ***point-of-purchase magazines*** like *Family Circle* and *Woman's Day*, sold mainly at the checkout stands in supermarkets. The female magazine audience is divided further with magazines like *Vogue, Glamour, Cosmopolitan, Women's Health, Savvy, Self* and *Essence.*

Readers Represent a Valuable Audience for Advertisers

The average magazine reader is a high school graduate, is married, owns a home and works full time. This is a very attractive audience for advertisers because magazine readers tend to be active consumers. Advertisers also like magazines because people often refer to an ad weeks after they first see it, and many readers subscribe to a magazine as much for the ads as for the articles. This, of course, also is very appealing to advertisers.

Point-of-Purchase Magazines   Magazines that consumers buy directly, not by subscription. They are sold mainly at checkout stands in supermarkets.

MPA   The Association of Magazine Media, originally the Magazine Publishers Association.

MPA—The Association of Magazine Media—estimates that people keep a magazine issue an average of 17 weeks and that each issue has at least 4 adult readers on average. This magazine sharing is called **pass-along readership**.

Advertisers can target their audiences better in magazines than in most other media because magazines can divide their audiences for advertisers by interests, age, education, geography, income and even ZIP code. This means that advertisers can promote special offers in separate portions of the country or market expensive products in regional issues of print magazines delivered to wealthy ZIP codes.

Most new magazines are small-scale efforts produced initially on the Internet and financed by loyal relatives or friends, but in 2000, television personality Oprah Winfrey launched a successful lifestyle magazine called *O, The Oprah Magazine*. She sold the magazine to the Hearst Corporation in 2012.

But Oprah's success was unusual. Today, only one in three new magazines will survive more than five years. The reason most magazines fail is that many new companies do not have the money to keep publishing long enough to refine their editorial content, sell advertisers on the idea and gather subscribers—in other words, until the magazine can make a profit.

Today, even well-established magazines are struggling to survive. In 2009, Condé Nast Publications shut down *Gourmet* and *Modern Bride*, which had been publishing for more than half a century. In 2014, Meredith Publishing, which owned *Ladies' Home Journal*, stopped publishing the magazine after 130 years in print.

All printed magazines are vulnerable to changing economic and even technology trends. Although magazines once were very inexpensive and advertising paid for most of the cost of production, publishers gradually have been charging more, even charging for digital content, to see if subscribers will be willing to pay for specific information. For example, some magazines like *The Economist* recently announced plans to charge for digital content separately, so a print subscriber who wants to read the digital magazine has to pay extra for a digital subscription. (See **Impact/Money**, "Digital Cracks 50 Percent of Ad Revenue at *Wired* Magazine," p. 79.)

Today's consumers are less willing to buy printed magazines when they believe they can find most of the information they want for free on the Internet. In 2009, when he announced that Condé Nast Publications was shutting down several popular magazines, CEO Chuck Townsend said, "In this economic climate it is important to narrow our focus to titles with the greatest prospects for long-term growth." Townsend's comment described the challenge facing the magazine industry as a whole—how to

David Paul Morris/Bloomberg/Getty Images

Magazines are expanding their readership by offering digital editions of the printed magazine. Next Issue Media offers unlimited Internet access to a large group of popular digital magazines for a monthly fee as low as $9.99.

maintain the audience that advertisers want and give readers content they can't find anywhere else.

Digital Editions Offer New Publishing Outlets

The way magazines do business in the future will be affected by technology as well as by the shifting economics of the industry. Digital editions offer magazine publishers a way to expand readership and give advertisers access to an expanded audience online.

As early as 1994, *Business Week* began offering its magazine online, including a feature that gave readers access to Internet conferences with editors and newsmakers and forums where readers could post messages related to topics covered in each issue. Most major consumer magazines today publish Internet editions.

The economics of Internet publishing also make it possible for someone to publish a magazine just online, dedicated to a fairly small audience, with none of the expense of mail distribution. Some large magazine publishing companies also have launched literary-political online magazines, such as *Salon.com* and *Slate*, which have attracted a very loyal Internet readership, in the tradition of the country's first political magazine, *The Nation*.

"There is clear demand for good content on mobile devices as evidenced by the amazing growth of e-books and the terrific response to the magazine apps launched

MPA The Association of Magazine Media, originally the Magazine Publishers Association.

Pass-Along Readership People who share a magazine with the original recipient.

IMPACT

Money

Digital Cracks 50 Percent of Ad Revenue at *Wired* Magazine

First for the Title Is an Encouraging Sign for the Industry

By Nat Ives

Digital contributed half of all ad revenue at *Wired* magazine in the final three months of 2012, a first for the title and an encouraging sign for an industry where most big brands still rely overwhelmingly on the difficult business of print. Across the year as a whole, digital ads comprised 45 percent of total ad sales at *Wired*, according to the magazine.

The Atlantic has ratcheted digital ad revenue to an even higher share of the total, saying today that digital delivered 59 percent of its ad revenue in 2012. But *Wired* has a larger print business, guaranteeing advertisers a paid and verified circulation of 800,000 last year and running 885 ad pages, according to the *Media Industry Newsletter*, compared with *The Atlantic*'s rate base of 450,000 and 463 ad pages.

Digital revenue for most magazines still runs at a significantly lower level.

Digital advertising contributed to about 10 percent of *Wired* ad revenue in 2006, when parent company Condé Nast bought Wired.com and reunited it with the magazine, according to Howard Mittman, VP-publisher at *Wired*.

"We spent a lot of time debating whether we were the best magazine with a Web site or the best Web site with a magazine," Mr. Mittman said. "And at the

Lester Cohen/Getty Images Entertainment/Getty Images

Wired magazine editor-in-chief Scott Dadich speaks at a digital design conference on September 30, 2014. *Wired* is the nation's most successful print and digital magazine, with 50 percent of its revenue coming from its digital "replica."

end of the day, I don't think we care. Hitting 50 percent is proof that there is a successful template inside of this industry that can be followed by others and that having a magazine doesn't necessarily need to be an analog anchor around your technological neck."

Wired ad pages declined 5.7 percent in 2012, according to the *Media Industry Newsletter*, but Mr. Mittman said digital's rise did not depend on a drop in print.

"Real-world print dollars were flat year over year," he said.

Roughly 90 percent of *Wired*'s digital ad revenue is coming from the traditional Web, he added. "The tablet is becoming a significant contributor to all this but, candidly, the bulk of this is coming from the Web site," Mr. Mittman said.

"Digital Cracks 50 Percent of Ad Revenue at Wired Magazine," January 3, 2013, adage.com.

on the iPad," according to Mark Edmiston, CEO for the digital travel publication *Nomads*. "We believe that there is even greater potential for content designed from the ground up for mobile rather than taking an existing format and converting it to mobile." (See **Illustration 4.3**, "Who Reads Digital Magazines?" p. 76.)

Magazines' Future Is Digital

Magazines complement other media yet have their own special benefits. Magazines' survival has always depended on their ability to adapt to new trends. To maintain and expand their audience and revenue, the magazine industry must maintain its print audience and seek new digital readers, who tend to be younger and better educated. "The print medium has to be innovative and reinvent itself," says Michael A. Clinton, publishing director and president for marketing at Hearst Magazines, New York.

In 2010, magazine giant Condé Nast announced plans to create tablet versions of some of its top magazines, such as *GQ*, *Vanity Fair* and *Wired*. "We feel confident enough that consumers will want our content in this new format that we are committing the resources necessary to be there," said Charles H. Townsend, president and chief executive of Condé Nast. "How large a revenue stream digitized content represents is an answer we hope to learn through this process." By 2013, *Wired* was the number one digital magazine in America.

REVIEW, ANALYZE, INVESTIGATE

CHAPTER 4

Magazines Reflect Trends and Culture

- Magazines mirror the society.
- Today, magazines target specific audiences.
- Internet editions expand magazines' traditional reach.

Colonial Magazines Compete with Newspapers

- American magazines began in 1741 when Andrew Bradford published *American Magazine* and Benjamin Franklin published *General Magazine*.
- Like colonial newspapers, early magazines provided a means for political expression.
- *The Saturday Evening Post*, first published in 1821, was the nation's first general interest magazine.
- Early magazines were expensive and had small circulations.

Magazines Travel Beyond Local Boundaries

- The Postal Act of 1879 encouraged the growth of magazines because it ensured quick, reasonably priced distribution for magazines. Today's magazines still travel on a preferential postal rate.
- *The Saturday Evening Post* was the first national magazine with a large circulation.

Publishers Locate New Readers

- Magazines widened their audience in the 1800s by catering to women, tackling social crusades, becoming a literary showcase for American writers and encouraging political debate.

- Sarah Josepha Hale, who edited *Godey's Lady's Book*, and Edward Bok, who edited *The Ladies' Home Journal*, were central figures in the development of early magazines in the United States that crusaded for reform.
- In 1910, W. E. B. Du Bois launched *The Crisis*, published for an African American audience.

McClure's Launches Investigative Journalism

- *McClure's Magazine* pioneered investigative reporting in the United States early in the 20th century. *McClure's* published the articles of Lincoln Steffens and Ida Tarbell.
- Early investigative magazine writers who exposed corruption in business and government were called *muckrakers*.

The New Yorker and *Time* Succeed Differently

- Magazines in the first half of the 20th century adapted to absorb the invention of radio and television. Some publishers sought a defined, targeted audience; others tried to attract the widest audience possible. *The New Yorker* and *Time* began as magazines that eventually became part of media empires.

Specialized Magazines Take Over

- Magazines in the second half of the 20th century survived by targeting readers' special interests.
- Specialization segments an audience for advertisers, making magazines the most specific buy an advertiser can make.

- Publishers can target their magazines by geography, age, education, income and interest group, as well as by ZIP code.

Companies Consolidate Ownership and Define Readership

- Magazines have consolidated into large groups just like other media.
- Magazine publishers envision a time when their readership will be even more specialized than today.

Magazines Divide into Three Types

- There are three types of magazines: consumer magazines; trade, technical and professional magazines; and company magazines.
- Consumer magazines make the most money because they have the most readers and carry the most advertising.

Magazines at Work

- Magazine employees work in one of five areas: editorial, circulation sales, advertising sales, manufacturing and distribution, and administration.
- The Alliance for Audited Media (formerly the Audit Bureau of Circulations) monitors and verifies readership.
- Advertisers provide nearly half a magazine's income.

Magazines Compete for Readers in Crowded Markets

- The number of magazines being published in the United States has been declining since 1990.
- Younger readers are less likely to read magazines.
- Women continue to be the single most lucrative audience for magazines.

Readers Represent a Valuable Audience for Advertisers

- Each issue of a magazine, according to the Magazine Publishers Association, has at least four adult readers on average, and people keep an issue an average of 17 weeks.
- Magazines can target readers for advertisers better than other media.

Digital Editions Offer New Publishing Outlets

- Many magazines have launched Internet editions to expand their readership.
- Today's digital technology means people can start an online magazine without the production and mailing expense of a printed publication.
- Some magazines, such as *Salon.com* and *Slate*, have been successful publishing only on the Internet.

Magazines' Future Is Digital

- Magazines complement other media.
- The audience for digital magazines is evenly divided among men and women (compared to the audience for printed magazines, which skews toward female readers).
- The digital magazine audience also is younger (ages 18–44) than print magazine readers and better educated.
- Men are a growing audience for online magazines.
- To maintain its audience and revenue, the magazine industry must expand its digital presence.

Key Terms

These terms are defined in the margins throughout this chapter and appear in alphabetical order with definitions in the Glossary, which begins on page 361.

AAM *75*
Company Magazines *73*
Consumer Magazines *73*

Digital Replica Magazines *75*
Freelancers *75*
MPA *78*

Muckrakers *70*
Pass-Along Readership *78*
Point-of-Purchase Magazines *77*

Trade, Technical and Professional Magazines *73*

Critical Questions

1. What important tradition in magazine journalism did Ida Tarbell and other muckrakers establish? Describe how Tarbell reported on Standard Oil Co. Why is her reporting significant?

2. Why do today's magazines target specialized audiences for readership? Give at least three specific examples of magazine advertisers targeting an audience and the reasons for each.

3. Discuss the role that magazines like *Ebony* and *Sports Illustrated*, targeted to a specific audience, contribute to American society.

4. If you started a magazine, what kind would you launch? How would you fund it? Who would read and advertise in it? Would you print it, publish only a digital version or publish both printed and replica editions? How would you ensure its success?

5. What impact are digital technologies having on the future of the magazine business? Consider the audience for magazines, the way in which magazines are delivered to their readers and the impact on advertisers and advertising.

Working the Web

This list includes sites mentioned in the chapter and others to give you greater insight into the magazine business.

AllYouCanRead.com

allyoucanread.com

Calling itself "the largest database of magazines and newspapers on the Internet," AllYouCanRead.com has listings for nearly 25,000 magazines, newspapers and news sites from more than 200 countries. Online visitors can read their favorite news sources online or subscribe to a magazine or a newspaper without ever leaving the site.

American Society of Journalists and Authors (ASJA)

asja.org

Founded in 1948 in New York City, the American Society of Journalists and Authors (ASJA) is a professional organization of "independent nonfiction" authors or freelance writers. With more than 1,100 members, ASJA offers a referral service as well as seminars and workshops where freelancers can interact and network with their peers.

The Cartoon Bank

cartoonbank.com

Visitors to this site can select from more than 120,000 cartoons that have been published in *The New Yorker* magazine. The cartoons are available for licensing and use by individuals and companies and are sold as framed prints.

Condé Nast Media Company

condenast.com

Saying it attracts "115 million consumers across its industry-leading print, digital and video brands," Condé Nast was established in 1909 when Condé Montrose Nast began publishing *Vogue* magazine. Today Condé Nast has a television broadcasting division and publishes several well-known magazines, including *The New Yorker, Vogue, Vanity Fair, Glamour, Brides, GQ, Architectural Digest and Wired*. In January 2015, Condé Nast launched 23 Stories, a "branded content" media company where marketers and advertisers will work directly with the editorial division of Condé Nast to create video ads that are integrated into existing broadcast and online advertising.

The New Yorker

newyorker.com

Established in 1925 as a weekly publication, *The New Yorker* is considered one of the top periodical publications in the

U.S. as well as internationally. *The New Yorker* is famous for its covers, which always contain an illustration depicting a scene relevant to a topical current event. The magazine has a rigorous fact checking and copyediting process and features both fiction and nonfiction on a wide array of subjects, including politics, popular culture and social issues.

Folio: The Magazine for Magazine Management

foliomag.com

Known as the "industry bible of magazine publishing," *Folio:* is an online and print magazine for professionals in all sectors of the magazine publishing industry. It is published six times a year with reports about industry trends and the latest concepts in sales and marketing.

Hearst Corporation

hearst.com

The Hearst Corporation owns 15 daily and weekly newspapers, including the *San Francisco Chronicle* and *Houston Chronicle*; magazines, including *Esquire, Car and Driver* and *O, The Oprah Magazine*; broadcast television stations, including WCVB-TV in Boston, KCRA-TV in Sacramento and WBAL Radio in Baltimore; and entertainment and syndication operations, including A&E Networks, King Features Syndicate and United Artists Media Group.

MPA—The Association of Magazine Media

magazine.org

Established in 1919, MPA (formerly the Magazine Publishers Association) represents 175 companies that publish more than 900 periodicals. Every October, the association hosts the Magazine Media Conference where media professionals discuss the future of the print and digital magazine industry. MPA is headquartered in New York City and has a lobbying office in Washington, D.C.

Salon

salon.com

Calling itself the first "major online media outlet," salon.com is news Web site based in San Francisco. Established in 1995, *Salon* offers a tabloid journalism approach to the coverage of "news, politics, entertainment, life, technology, business, sustainability and innovation."

Slate

slate.com

Slate is an online magazine created in 1996 by former *New Republic* editor Michael Kinsley and purchased in 2004 by The Washington Post Co. *Slate* is updated daily and is aimed at helping its readers "analyze and understand and interpret the world" through its coverage of news, politics, arts and culture.

Sports Illustrated
si.com

Known for its in-depth coverage of professional and amateur sports throughout the world, *Sports Illustrated* is a weekly sports magazine owned by Time Inc. that is published both in print and online. Its annual swimsuit edition has become so popular that a calendar, television show and video are released in conjunction with it.

Impact/Action Videos are concise news features on various topics created exclusively for *Media/Impact*. Find them in *Media/Impact*'s MindTap at cengagebrain.com.

MindTap®

Log on to MindTap for *Media/Impact* to access a variety of additional material—including learning objectives, chapter readings with highlighting and note-taking, **Impact/Action Videos**, activities, and comprehension quizzes—that will guide you through this chapter.

Stefano Buonamici/The New York Times

Artists' income from music sales is declining, which makes live concerts a crucial source of revenue. On June 1, 2014, 50,000 music lovers flocked to Primavera Sound in Barcelona, Spain, a five-day music festival featuring more than 300 artists.

> "The challenge is to get everyone to respect music again, to recognize its value."
>
> —RECORDING ARTIST JAY-Z AT THE 2015 LAUNCH OF TIDAL, AN ARTIST-OWNED SUBSCRIPTION STREAMING MUSIC SERVICE

For the first time in more than ten years, the music industry announced in 2013 that global sales had increased, instead of decreased, from the year before. "For years, the music industry's decline looked terminal, with record companies seemingly unable to come up with digital business models that could compete with the lure of online piracy," reported *The New York Times.* In 2012, however, "digital sales and other new sources of revenue grew significantly enough to offset the continuing decline in CD sales."

The sudden decline in music sales that began in 1999—primarily because of illegal downloading—meant that musicians could no longer rely on music sales to support their music. Concert performances that can draw huge audiences became a necessity, as the recording business struggled to find a financial model to sustain the industry. Ironically, the digital technology that led to the music industry's decline may now be its savior. "At the beginning of the digital revolution it was common to say that digital was killing music," Sony Music executive Edgar Berger told *The Times.* Now, he said, "digital is saving music."

Most of the music people listen to each year is categorized as popular music—rock, rap/hip-hop, urban,

Mark Metcalfe/HJPR/Getty Images Entertainment/Getty Images

More than half the music that people buy, and a majority of recording industry profits, comes from sales of contemporary artists such as One Direction, kicking off their 2015 World Tour in Sydney, Australia, on February 7, 2015.

country and pop—according to the **Recording Industry Association of America (RIAA)**. Other types of music—religious, classical, big band, jazz and children's

> **Recording Industry Association of America (RIAA)** Industry association that lobbies for the interests of the nation's major recording companies. Member companies account for 95 percent of all U.S. recording company sales.

TimeFrame
1877–Today

The Recording Industry Caters to a Young Audience

1877 Thomas Edison first demonstrates the phonograph.

1943 Ampex develops tape recorders, and Minnesota Mining and Manufacturing perfects plastic recording tape. Singer Bing Crosby is one of the first recording artists to use tape.

1947 Peter Goldmark develops the long-playing record.

1956 Stereophonic sound arrives.

✱ **1958** Motown, promoted as "Hitsville U.S.A.," introduces the Detroit Sound of African American artists, including The Supremes and Stevie Wonder, popularizing rock 'n' roll.

1979 Sony introduces the Walkman as a personal stereo, making music mobile.

1985 The recording industry begins to consolidate into six major international corporations. Only one of these companies is based in the U.S.

1999 MP3 technology, developed by Michael Robertson, makes it easy for consumers to download music files from the Internet.

✱ **2001** Apple introduces the iPod. Napster, which uses file-sharing software designed to download music on the Internet, shuts down after the Recording Industry Association of America (RIAA) sues for copyright infringement.

2003 Apple opens the online music store iTunes, offering legal music downloads for 99 cents per song.

2005 The U.S. Supreme Court says that the makers of file-sharing software can be sued for helping people violate recording industry copyright protections.

2007 RIAA sues online music consumer Jammie Thomas for copyright infringement, and a jury fines her $222,000 for sharing 24 songs.

2009 Virgin Music closes all of its U.S. Megastores, marking the end of large-store music retailing.

✱ **2012** The U.S. Justice Department shuts down international downloading site Megaupload, one of the Internet's largest offshore music and film file-sharing Web sites.

2013 The U.S. Supreme Court refuses to hear music downloader Jammie Thomas' file-sharing case, exhausting her appeals, and orders her to pay a $222,000 fine.

2015 Beyoncé and Jay-Z launch Tidal streaming service to challenge Spotify. Apple adds music streaming to its other music services.

TODAY Three major companies dominate the recording industry, which earns the majority of its revenue from digital music. The industry continues to fight copyright infringement and illegal Internet file-sharing. Industry income stabilizes. The iTunes online music store is the nation's dominant music retailer, but music streaming services are growing quickly as a music delivery system.

recordings—make up the rest, but most of the profits and losses in the recording business result from the mercurial fury of popular songs.

Of all the media industries, the recording industry is the most vulnerable to piracy and suffered the biggest losses as a result of digital technology. The recording industry also is at the center of recent debates over the protection of artistic copyright. In 2003, the Recording Industry Association of America sued 261 people for downloading music from the Internet, saying CD shipments dropped 15 percent from the year before. In 2009, a jury found one of the plaintiffs in the downloading case guilty of copyright infringement, and the case reached the U.S. Supreme Court in 2013. The Court found music downloader Jammie Thomas could be sued for copyright infringement, and she was fined $222,000.

But in 1877, when Thomas Edison first demonstrated his phonograph, who could foresee that the music business would become so complicated?

Edison Introduces His Talking Machine

Today's recording industry would not exist without Thomas Edison's invention, nearly 150 years ago, of what he called a *phonograph* (which means "sound writer"). In 1877, *Scientific American* reported Edison's first demonstration of his phonograph. Edison's chief mechanic had constructed the machine from an Edison sketch that came with a note reading, "Build this."

In 1887, Emile Berliner developed the gramophone, which replaced Edison's cylinder with flat discs. Berliner and Eldridge Johnson formed the Victor Talking Machine Company (later to become RCA Victor) and sold recordings of opera star Enrico Caruso. Edison and Victor proposed competing technologies as the standard for the industry, and eventually the Victor disc won. Early players required large horns to amplify the sound. Later the horn was housed in a cabinet below the actual player, which made the machine a large piece of furniture.

In 1925, Joseph Maxfield perfected the equipment to eliminate the tinny sound of early recordings. The first jukeboxes were manufactured in 1927 and brought music into restaurants and nightclubs.

By the end of World War II, 78 *rpm* (*r*evolutions *p*er *m*inute) records were standard. Each song was on a separate recording, and "albums" in today's sense did not exist. An album in the 1940s consisted of a bound set of ten envelopes about the size of a photo album. Each record, with one song recorded on each side, fit in one envelope. (This is how today's collected recordings got the title "album," even though they no longer are

AP Images

Today's recording industry would not exist without Thomas Edison's invention of the phonograph in 1877. Edison is shown in 1926 in New York.

assembled in this cumbersome way.) Each shellac, hard disc recording ran three minutes.

Peter Goldmark, working for Columbia Records (owned by CBS), changed that.

Goldmark Perfects Long-Playing Records

In 1947, engineer Peter Goldmark was listening with friends to Brahms' Second Piano Concerto played by pianist Vladimir Horowitz, led by the world-famous conductor Arturo Toscanini. The lengthy concerto had been recorded on 6 records, 12 sides.

Goldmark hated the interruptions in the concerto every time he had to turn a record over. He also winced at the 8 sound defects he detected. After several refinements, Peter Goldmark created the long-playing (***LP***) record, which could play for 23 minutes, but LPs were larger than 78 rpm records.

---

rpm Revolutions per minute.

LP Long-playing record.

Engineer Peter Goldmark (left) invented the long-playing record format. LPs could play for 23 minutes and offered better sound quality than 78-rpm records. Goldmark, Director of Engineering Research and Development for CBS, uses a microscope to check the quality of a long-playing record.

Paley Battles Sarnoff for Record Format

William Paley, who owned CBS radio and CBS records, realized he was taking a big risk by introducing LP records when most people didn't own a record player that could play the bigger 33 1/3 rpm discs. While the LP record was being developed, Paley decided to contact RCA executive David Sarnoff because RCA made record players. Paley tried to convince Sarnoff to form a partnership with CBS to manufacture LPs, but Sarnoff refused.

Stubbornly, Sarnoff introduced his own 7-inch, 45-rpm records in 1948. The 45s had a quarter-size hole in the middle, played one song on each side and required a different record player, which RCA started to manufacture. The 45s were a perfect size for jukeboxes, but record sales slowed as the public tried to figure out what was happening. Eventually Peter Goldmark and classical music conductor Arturo Toscanini convinced Sarnoff to manufacture LPs and include the 33 1/3 speed on RCA record players to accommodate classical-length recordings.

CBS, in turn, agreed to use 45s for its popular songs. Later, players were developed that could play all three speeds (33 1/3, 45 and 78 rpm). A limited number of jazz artists were recorded, but most of the available recorded music was big band music from artists like Tommy Dorsey,

Broadway show tunes and songs by popular singers like Frank Sinatra.

Hi-Fi and Stereo Rock In

In the 1950s, the introduction of rock 'n' roll redefined the concept of popular music. Contributing to the success of entertainers like Elvis Presley were the improvements in recorded sound quality that originated with the recording industry. First came *high fidelity*, developed by London Records, a subsidiary of Decca. Tape recorders grew out of German experiments with recorders during World War II.

Ampex Corp. built a high-quality tape recorder, and Minnesota Mining and Manufacturing (3M) perfected the plastic tape. The use of tape meant that recordings could be edited and refined, something that couldn't be done on discs. (See **Impact/Profile**, "Steve Martin, Lauryn Hill and Radiohead Archived by National Recording Registry," p. 90.)

Stereo arrived in 1956, and soon afterward came groups like The Supremes with the Motown sound, which featured the music of African American blues and rock 'n' roll artists. With an $800 loan from his family, songwriter Berry Gordy, 29, founded Motown studios in 1958 in a small, two-story house in Detroit. He named the label after Detroit's nickname, Mo(tor)town, and called the building "Hitsville U.S.A."

"Everything was makeshift," he told *Fortune* in 1999. "We used the bathroom as an echo chamber." In July 1988,

Berry Gordy founded Motown Records in 1958 and popularized the Detroit sound of singers like Stevie Wonder and The Supremes (bottom row, middle and right), pictured in 1965 with several other Motown artists.

IMPACT

Profile

In 2015, the recordings of Steve Martin (left), Lauryn Hill and Radiohead were added to the Library of Congress National Recording Registry. Every year the registry adds 25 recordings to be preserved as classic American music.

Steve Martin, Lauryn Hill and Radiohead Archived by National Recording Registry

By Michael O'Sullivan

The [2014] list of sound recordings selected by the Library of Congress for inclusion in its National Recording Registry reads like the world's most eclectic mix tape.

The 25 sound recordings just added to the registry run the gamut, from a turn-of-the-20th-century collection of over 600 wax cylinders featuring homemade recordings to the Doors' 1967 debut to Radiohead's 1997 masterpiece "OK Computer."

On the spoken-word side, comic Steve Martin [was] honored for his 1978 album "A Wild and Crazy Guy," [and] joins such comedy honorees as Abbott and Costello ("Who's on First?") and the novelty song "Rubber Duckie"—part of the album "Sesame Street: All-Time Platinum Favorites."

That's as it should be, says Mickey Hart, former Grateful Dead drummer and tireless evangelist for sonic diversity, who serves on the National Recording Preservation Board and was instrumental in its formation. Created by an act of Congress in 2000, the NRPB makes annual recommendations of recordings, chosen for their cultural, artistic and historical significance, to Librarian of Congress James H. Billington. Nominated recordings must be at least 10 years old.

Though often described as a world music expert, Hart bristles at that misnomer. "There's no such thing as 'world music,'" says Hart, who chatted by phone from his California studio. "If you're in the Philippines, back-porch music from the Adirondacks is world music. The Doors are world music, if you're from India."

The 71-year-old musician, whose practice these days consists of both his own compositions and the digital transcription of "endangered" music stored on

such unstable media as wax cylinders, knows firsthand how fragile those old artifacts can be. "I've watched some of these things disintegrate in front of my eyes, as I'm recording," he says, alluding to the "gremlins" that eat away at old media by the second. "I've seen a recording give its life, man, on the last play."

Among the 25 recordings selected for the 2014 National Recording Registry are: Vernacular Wax Cylinder Recordings at University of California at Santa Barbara Library (c. 1890–1910). Radio Coverage of President Franklin D. Roosevelt's Funeral, Arthur Godfrey, et al. (April 14, 1945). "The Doors" (album), Doors (1967). "A Wild and Crazy Guy" (album), Steve Martin (1978). "Sesame Street: All-Time Platinum Favorites" (album), various artists (1995). "OK Computer" (album), Radiohead (1997). "The Miseducation of Lauryn Hill" (album), Lauryn Hill (1998).

Excerpted from Michael O'Sullivan, "'Sesame Street,' Radiohead and Wax Cylinders Enter Library of Congress," March 25, 2015, washingtonpost.com.

Gordy sold Motown Records for $61 million. The Detroit house where Motown began is now a historical museum, and Motown Records is part of Universal Music Group.

During the same time that Berry Gordy was creating Motown, the Federal Communications Commission (FCC) approved "multiplex" radio broadcasts so that monaural (one source of sound) and stereo (two sound sources) could be heard on the same station. The development of condenser microphones also helped bring truer sound.

In the 1960s, miniaturization resulted from the transistor. Portable transistor radios that could be carried around meant that people could listen to radio wherever they wanted—on the beach, at the park, even in the shower. Eventually the market was overwhelmed with tape players smaller than a deck of playing cards. Quadraphonic (four-track) and eight-track tapes seemed ready to become the standard in the 1970s, but cassette tapes proved more adaptable and less expensive.

In 1979, Sony introduced the Walkman as a personal stereo. (The name Sony comes from the Latin *sonus* for "sound" and *sunny* for "optimism.") Walkmans were an ironic throwback to the early radio crystal sets, which also required earphones.

Then came compact discs (CDs), delivering crystal-clear sound, translating music into digital code on a 4.7-inch plastic and aluminum disc read by lasers. Discs lasted longer than records and cassettes, making CDs a much more practical format.

First introduced in the year 2000, CD players with a *CD recorder* (also known as a CD writer or CD burner) and computers with **CD-RW (Re-Writable) drives** meant consumers could copy music to a blank CD, play it and then re-record on the same disc. Recordable discs gained widespread acceptance quickly and made it even harder for the recording industry to police unauthorized use of copyrighted material.

The Apple iPod portable music player, first introduced in 2001, allowed users to store and play music downloads. Then in 2003, Apple launched iTunes, its online music store, charging 99 cents per song. By April 2008, the iTunes store had become the largest music retailer in the U.S., and by February 2010, according to Apple, customers had downloaded 10 billion songs.

The Apple iPhone, first sold in 2007, combined mobile phone technology with the capabilities of the iPod, expanding Apple's dominance in music retailing. Today, the iTunes online music store is the dominant consumer source for contemporary music.

Recently Spotify, Rhapsody and Pandora have begun to offer music streaming by subscription, and Apple launched its music streaming service in June 2015. These services pay a per-play fee to artists, but the artists complain they aren't being paid enough for their music. So

In 2015, a notable group of popular performers, including Kanye West (left), Jay-Z (right), Beyoncé and Madonna, launched Tidal, a subscription music streaming service co-owned by the musicians.

in 2015, a group of popular performers, including Jay-Z, Beyoncé, Madonna and Kanye West, announced a new company called Tidal, with a majority of the company owned by the artists, hoping to pay artists more for their work by managing the distribution themselves. "The challenge is to get everyone to respect music again, to recognize its value," Jay-Z said at Tidal's launch.

Recording Industry at Work

Recordings, like books, are supported primarily by direct purchases. But a recording company involves five separate levels of responsibility before the public hears a sound:

1. Artists and repertoire

2. Operations

3. Marketing and promotion

4. Distribution

5. Administration

Artists and repertoire (or A&R) functions like an editorial department in book publishing: It develops and coordinates talent. Employees of this division are the true talent scouts. They try to find new artists and constantly search for new songs to record.

Operations manages the technical aspects of the recording, overseeing the sound technicians, musicians, even the

> **CD-RW (Re-Writable) Drives** Computer drives that are used to read data and music encoded in digital form and can be used to record more than once.

people who copy the discs. This work centers on creating the master recording, from which all other recordings are made. Before stereophonic recording was developed in 1956, a recording session meant gathering all the musicians in one room, setting up a group of microphones and recording a song in one take. If the first take didn't work, the artists all had to stay together to do another, and then another.

It was common in the 1950s for a recording group to go through 50 takes before getting the right one. Today, artists on the same song—vocals, drums, bass, horns and guitars—can be recorded individually, and then the separate performances are mixed for the best sound. They don't have to be in the same room or even in the same country because digital sound can be mixed after each of the artists records his or her portion.

The producer, who works within the operations group, can be on the staff of a recording company or be a freelancer. Producers coordinate the artist with the music, the arrangement and the engineer.

Marketing and promotion decides the best way to sell the recording. These employees oversee the cover design and the copy on the cover (jacket or sleeve). They also organize giveaways to retailers and to reviewers to find an audience for their product. Marketing and promotion might decide that the artist should tour or that the group should produce and distribute a music video on YouTube. Recording companies also often use promoters to help guarantee radio play for their artists. This has led to abuses such as payola (see **Chapter 6**).

Distribution gets the recording into stores and online. There are two kinds of distributors: independents and branches. Independents contract separately with different companies to deliver their recordings. But independents, usually responsible for discovering music that is outside the mainstream, are disappearing as the big studios handle distribution through their own companies, called branches, which can offer retailers big discounts.

Administration, as in all industries, handles the bills. *Accounting* tracks sales and royalties. *Legal departments* handle wrangles over contracts.

All these steps are important in the creation of a recording, but if no one hears the music, no one will buy it. This makes *marketing* and *promotion* particularly important. Live concerts have become the best way for artists to promote their music. Many recording artists say that music sales alone don't make them any money and that the only way to make a living is to perform before a live audience.

Concerts Bring In Essential Revenue

Concerts have become high-profile showcases for technological innovation and provide an essential source of revenue for today's big bands, where ticket prices for top artists often reach $1,000 each. "While the recording industry frets about the financial impact of music trading over the Internet, innovative bands . . . are embracing the latest technologies to create spectacular live concerts and phantasmagoric festival experiences that are more like computer-controlled theme parks than like the rock festivals of yesteryear," reports *The New York Times*.

Richard Goodstone, a partner at Superfly Productions, told *The New York Times*, "The real difference between your normal rock festival . . . is that there's a lot of music, but now we're trying to make it a complete experience in terms of the activities that really interact with the patrons out there, so it's not just a one-element kind of event." Digital technology has become an important element of staging an artist's performance as well as selling the performer's music. (See **Illustration 5.1**, "How Does the Recording Industry Earn Money?," p. 93.)

Three Major Companies Dominate

Three companies dominate the global music business: Sony/BMG, Universal and Warner. In 2011, for the first time, half the music that consumers bought was digital. The main recording centers in the U.S. are Los Angeles, New York and Nashville, and many large cities have at least one recording studio to handle local productions.

The recording industry, primarily concentrated in large corporations, generally chooses to produce what has succeeded before. "Increasingly, the big record companies are concentrating their resources behind fewer acts," reports *The Wall Street Journal*, "believing that it is easier to succeed with a handful of blockbuster hits than with a slew of moderate sellers. One result is that fewer records are produced."

Most radio formats today depend on popular music, and these recordings depend on radio to succeed. The main measurement of what is popular comes from *Billboard*, the music industry's leading trade magazine. *Billboard* began printing a list of the most popular vaudeville songs and the best-selling sheet music in 1913. In 1940, the magazine began publishing a list of the country's top-selling records.

Today, *Billboard*—in print and online editions—offers more than two dozen charts that measure, for example, airplay and album sales for popular artists such as One Direction and Maroon 5. Radio, governed by ratings and what the public demands, tends to play proven artists, so new artists are likely to get more radio attention if their recordings make one of the *Billboard* lists. This radio play, in turn, increases the artists' popularity and promotes their music.

IMPACT

Money

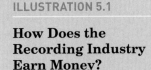

ILLUSTRATION 5.1

How Does the Recording Industry Earn Money?

Today the recording industry makes almost two-thirds of its revenue (64 percent) from digital units (such as downloads and streaming), compared to what the industry calls "physical" units, such as CDs. Digital streaming, which first became available in 2011, now accounts for 21 percent of total recording industry income.

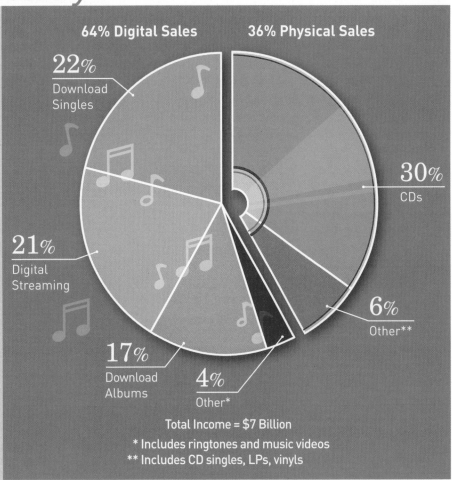

64% Digital Sales   36% Physical Sales

22%
Download Singles

30%
CDs

21%
Digital Streaming

6%
Other**

17%
Download Albums

4%
Other*

Total Income = $7 Billion
* Includes ringtones and music videos
** Includes CD singles, LPs, vinyls

"2014 Year-End Industry Shipment and Revenue Statistics," Recording Industry Association of America, riaa.com.

Music Sales and Licensing Drive Industry Income

Besides concert revenue, recording artists derive income from direct sales and music licensing.

Direct Sales

The promotional tour once was the only way a company sold recordings. But in the 1980s, music videos became a very visible form of promotion for an artist. This shift changed the industry's economics. Beyoncé, for example, is attractive to music companies because she is a recording artist who can perform well in videos.

Music Licensing: ASCAP Versus BMI

For the first 30 years of commercial radio, one reason broadcasters used live entertainment was to avoid paying royalties to the recording companies. Today, two licensing agencies handle the rights to play music for broadcast: the American Society of Composers,

Authors and Publishers (ASCAP) and Broadcast Music Inc. (BMI).

ASCAP, founded in 1914, was the first licensing organization. As noted in **Chapter 6**, ASCAP sued radio stations in the 1920s that were playing recorded music. Eventually some radio stations agreed to pay ASCAP royalties through a licensing agreement, which meant that each station that paid ASCAP's fee could play any music that ASCAP licensed.

Throughout the 1930s, many stations refused to pay ASCAP because they didn't have enough money. These stations agreed to explore the idea of forming a separate organization so they could license the music themselves.

In 1939, broadcasters came together to establish a fund to build their own music collection through ***BMI***.

ASCAP American Society of Composers, Authors and Publishers.

BMI Broadcast Music Inc.

ASCAP and BMI became competitors—ASCAP as a privately owned organization and BMI as an industry-approved cooperative. BMI used the same blanket licensing agreement, collecting payments from broadcasters and dividing royalties among its artists. ASCAP licensed the majority of older hits, but rhythm and blues and rock 'n' roll gravitated toward BMI.

Today broadcasters as well as subscription and streaming services must license artists through BMI and ASCAP. These services also must agree to play only licensed artists, which makes being heard more difficult for new talent. BMI and ASCAP, in turn, pay the authors, recording artists, producers and sometimes even the recording companies—whoever owns the rights to use the music. The royalty the artists receive is negotiated through whichever licensing agent they use. The rise of illegal file-sharing services, however, meant that consumers who downloaded free music didn't contribute to an artist's royalties. Internet piracy, beginning in the year 2000, is the main reason overall recording industry income has plummeted, leaving musicians to depend on finding other sources of revenue to support their music, such as concerts. (See **Illustration 5.2**, "Concert Audiences Drive Music Industry Profits," below.)

IMPACT

Society

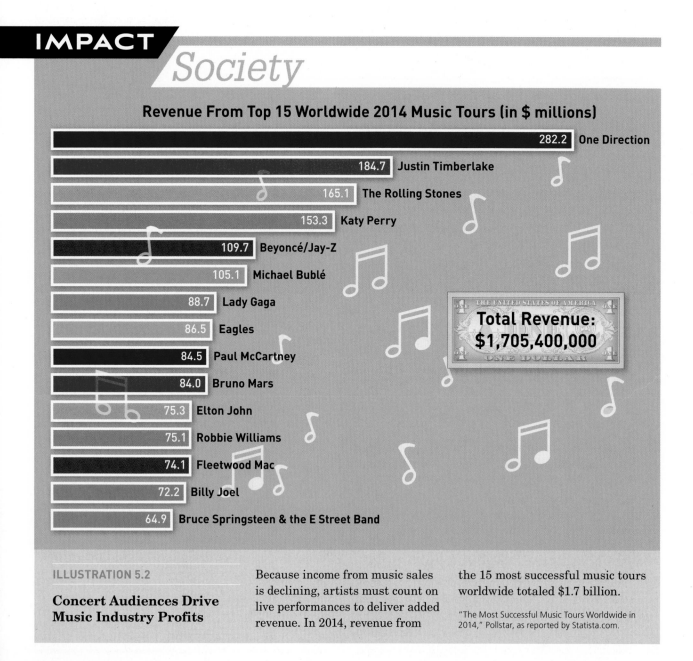

Revenue From Top 15 Worldwide 2014 Music Tours (in $ millions)

	Revenue
One Direction	282.2
Justin Timberlake	184.7
The Rolling Stones	165.1
Katy Perry	153.3
Beyoncé/Jay-Z	109.7
Michael Bublé	105.1
Lady Gaga	88.7
Eagles	86.5
Paul McCartney	84.5
Bruno Mars	84.0
Elton John	75.3
Robbie Williams	75.1
Fleetwood Mac	74.1
Billy Joel	72.2
Bruce Springsteen & the E Street Band	64.9

Total Revenue: $1,705,400,000

ILLUSTRATION 5.2

Concert Audiences Drive Music Industry Profits

Because income from music sales is declining, artists must count on live performances to deliver added revenue. In 2014, revenue from the 15 most successful music tours worldwide totaled $1.7 billion.

"The Most Successful Music Tours Worldwide in 2014," Pollstar, as reported by Statista.com.

Music Industry Fights to Protect Content

Since 1985, the recording industry has faced three challenges:

1. Attempts to control content through music labeling

2. Overseas music piracy

3. Protecting music copyrights from Internet file sharing

Music Content Labeling

In 1985, the Parents Music Resource Center (PMRC) called for recording companies to label their recordings for explicit content. The new group was made up primarily of the wives of several national political leaders, notably Susan Baker, wife of then-Treasury Secretary James A. Baker III, and Tipper Gore, wife of then-Senator Al Gore.

Claiming that recordings come under the umbrella of consumer protection, the PMRC approached the National Association of Broadcasters and the Federal Communications Commission with their complaints. "After equating rock music with the evils of 'broken homes' and 'abusive parents,' and labeling it a 'contributing factor' in teen pregnancy and suicide, they single[d] out Madonna, Michael Jackson, Mötley Crüe, Prince, Sheena Easton, Twisted Sister and Cyndi Lauper for their 'destructive influence' on children," reported journalism law professor Louis P. Sheinfeld.

The result was that, beginning in January 1986, the RIAA, whose member companies accounted for 95 percent of U.S. recording sales, officially urged its members either to provide a warning label or to print lyrics on albums with potentially offensive content. Like the movie industry when it adopted its own ratings system (see **Chapter 7**), the recording industry favored self-regulation rather than government intervention.

Overseas Music Piracy

Overseas pirates who copy prerecorded music that is then sold in the United States cost the recording industry a lot of money. RIAA says pirates control 18 percent of album sales, and this represents $1 billion a year in lost income.

Besides the lost revenue, counterfeit copies can easily fool consumers and usually are inferior quality recordings that don't truly represent the artist's music. This is a continuing battle for the music industry because many countries where the counterfeit copying takes place do not have agreements with the United States to force them to honor U.S. copyrights and prosecute the pirates.

Internet File Sharing

Portable MP3 players—electronic devices that allow users to download music to a computer chip–based player—were introduced in 1999. Using software-sharing program available at a Web site called Napster.com skyrocketed into popularity. With the program, computer users could download music over the Internet for free, called *file sharing*. Then, using MP3 technology (which provides high-quality sound and requires very little computer storage space), users could keep and use the music. RIAA immediately sued Napster, claiming violation of copyright.

In April 2000, the heavy-metal rock group Metallica sued Napster for copyright infringement. Rapper Dr. Dre filed suit two weeks later. In July 2000, an appeals court ordered Napster to shut down the site, and Napster finally ceased its file sharing in 2001.

Recording Industry Association Sues Downloaders

In 2003, Apple opened its online iTunes Music Store, offering legal downloads for 99 cents per song. Still, people continued to download free music, aided by new free online music services such as Kazaa and Grokster. So in 2003,

© Mike Baldwin / Cornered

"Don't interrupt – he's downloading another song."

Baldwin, Mike/Cartoon Stock.com

File Sharing The distribution of copyrighted material on the Internet. *Illegal* file sharing is distribution of copyrighted material *without* the copyright owner's permission.

In 2003, the Recording Industry Association of America sued 261 individual music downloaders in the U.S., in an attempt to stop music piracy. Protestors demonstrate in 2005 in front of the U.S. Supreme Court. The Court eventually decided that file-sharing software providers could be held liable for copyright infringement.

RIAA sued 261 individual music downloaders across the U.S., intensifying its efforts to stop music piracy. On average, each defendant had shared 1,000 songs each.

Copyright laws allowed the industry to seek $750 to $150,000 for each violation, and eventually the issue headed to the U.S. Supreme Court.

U.S. Supreme Court Rules Against Illegal File Sharing

In June 2005, the U.S. Supreme Court announced a decision that shut down many free music software providers. In *MGM Studios v. Grokster*, the Court said the makers of Grokster, which allowed Internet users to browse freely and copy songs from each other, could be sued for their role in helping people violate recording industry copyright protections.

This Supreme Court decision gave the recording companies the legal ammunition they needed, and the services quickly closed.

Music Industry Wins Legal Action Against Downloader

In 2007, a federal jury ruled that a Minnesota woman, Jammie Thomas, was liable for copyright infringement because she had shared music online. The jury imposed a $222,000 penalty against Thomas—$9,250 in damages for each of the 24 songs she

allegedly downloaded. In September 2008, the judge set aside the original verdict and ordered a retrial.

The verdict represented the first time a federal jury had imposed a legal fine on someone for music piracy. Bringing the charges against Thomas were Capitol Records, the Universal Music Group, Sony BMG Entertainment and the Warner Music Group. According to evidence presented at the Thomas trial, the downloads were linked to a Kazaa account user name that belonged to Thomas. Thomas denied she had a Kazaa account.

In late 2008, RIAA announced that it was dropping the legal actions it had initiated against about 35,000 other people for music downloading, but RIAA continued to pursue the Thomas case. Eventually the case reached the U.S. Supreme Court. On March 18, 2013, the Court let the original $222,000 judgment against Thomas stand.

U.S. Justice Department Targets Megaupload

Aware of the ongoing damage to recording company income, RIAA joined an international crackdown on overseas companies that sell pirated music in the U.S. In one of the biggest copyright cases in U.S. history, in March 2012 the U.S. Justice Department announced the arrest in Auckland, New Zealand, of the co-founders of the well-known international file-sharing site Megaupload.

Megaupload's co-founders, including a man named Kim Dotcom (formerly known as Kim Schmitz), were

Megaupload co-founder Kim Dotcom (formerly known as Kim Schmitz) was arrested in Auckland, New Zealand, in 2012 and charged with violating U.S. copyright law by illegally downloading and distributing U.S. music and movies through the Megaupload Web site. He and six other men who were arrested fought extradition, but in 2015 one of the men pleaded guilty to copyright infringement and agreed to cooperate with U.S. authorities.

charged with music and movie copyright infringement, among other violations of U.S. law. The Web site was shut down, and the Justice Department seized $50 million in assets. Seven men eventually were indicted in the case. The men denied they had acted illegally and fought extradition to the U.S., but they remained under indictment.

On February 13, 2015, one of the men who had been indicted, an Estonian computer programmer named Andrus Nomm, pleaded guilty in a U.S. federal court in Virginia to conspiracy to commit copyright infringement. He agreed to serve one year and one day in prison and to cooperate with U.S. prosecutors. He also acknowledged as part of his plea agreement that he and the other men knew that the Megaupload site contained copyright-infringing materials and that many of the files he reviewed contained the FBI's anti-piracy warning. In 2015, Kim Dotcom remained in New Zealand, facing extradition to the U.S..

Digital Technology Transforms Delivery

Music company executives originally thought that the way to protect their music was to develop digital technology that would make free downloads impossible. Yet despite aggressive attempts by RIAA and the U.S. Justice Department to stop music file sharing, it is still widespread.

No industry can survive for long on such a rapid loss of income. So the recording companies have no choice but to pursue copyright infringement wherever they find it. Licensed music is governed by national and international copyright law, and the recording industry continues to aggressively pursue all the legal remedies available to curtail illegal music downloads in the United States and reduce piracy, especially overseas. The industry, of course, also encourages all legal music download services, such as iTunes, and subscription sites, such as Spotify, Pandora and Rhapsody, along with new streaming music services announced in 2015, Tidal and Apple Streaming.

Some streaming services are free (supported by advertising), and some charge a monthly fee for access to an almost unlimited selection of music. Others offer the option of free or subscription music. In 2014, RIAA reported that revenue from subscription music services grew to a new high of nearly $2 billion, with 7 million users.

Internet Brings New Obstacles and New Audiences

Because of the Internet, music today is shared globally, which is a huge benefit for artists and consumers. (See **Impact/Global**, "Primavera Sound Sets the Stage for Music Festivals Worldwide," p. 98.) Yet the Internet also makes music piracy so easy that many people consider it a harmless act, and the economic implications for recording artists are substantial.

Music artists today can find a bigger audience than Thomas Edison ever could have imagined—through music downloads and subscription services, but the music business cannot escape the challenges of the Internet. Recording companies and music artists must learn how to produce music consumers want to buy, delivered in a format and/or through services that can financially sustain the industry.

When Edison demonstrated his phonograph for the editors of *Scientific American* in 1877, the magazine reported that "Mr. Thomas Edison recently came into this office, placed a little machine on our desk, turned a crank, and the machine inquired as to our health, asked how we liked the phonograph, informed us that it was very well, and bid us a cordial good night. These remarks were not only perfectly audible to ourselves, but to a dozen or more persons gathered around."

None of the discoveries by Edison's successors has been a new invention, only refinements. Berliner flattened the cylinder; Goldmark and Sarnoff slowed down the speed; hi-fi, stereo and quadraphonic sound increased

Harley Schwadron/Cartoonstock.com

"WHEN I GROW UP, I PLAN TO MAJOR IN MUSIC DOWNLOADING AND DIGITIZING."

IMPACT

Global

Primavera Sound Sets the Stage for Music Festivals Worldwide

By Melena Ryzik

Stephano Buonamici/New York Times

Primavera in Barcelona, Spain, has become one of the world's most successful concert venues, featuring more than 300 bands from around the world during five days in June every year.

BARCELONA, Spain— Caetano Veloso, the bossa nova elder statesman, was holding court here on Saturday evening, floating his baritone voice and easy guitar over an amphitheater audience that swayed and sang along as he offered a slightly raunchy paean to his native Brazilian sounds.

A few dozen feet away, on another stage, Earl Sweatshirt, the young California rapper and member of the Odd Future hip-hop clan, was doing his own conducting. "Make some noise," he instructed his audience, growling, "if you're ready to go to hell for, like, three minutes." The polyglot crowd spit back his rhymes, profanities included, with enthusiasm.

It was the final big night of Primavera Sound, an expansive music showcase here that has gradually become one of the top tickets of the European festival season and a template for promoters worldwide. In [five days in 2014], some 50,000 people a day saw nearly 300 acts—electronica to soul to postpunk—in concerts that stretched from afternoon to sunrise.

The international lineup featured arena stars like Nine Inch Nails and up-and-comers like FKA Twigs on a dozen stages. The audience traveled from across Europe and, increasingly, North America. Walking through the grounds was a mini-United Nations of fandom, reflecting a global music industry and an orderly Euro youth culture, an acknowledgment that taste can translate across borders.

About 40 percent of the attendees are from abroad, said Pablo Soler, a founder and director of the festival, which also offers free park shows and other programming for the city.

The mystique of Primavera has expanded alongside its scale and booking prowess, which started with small clubs and European acts. Now the festival has a reputation for scouting bands early—the future dance-punk stars LCD Soundsystem performed on the strength of a few singles—and cajoling reunion gigs out of seminal retirees like Pulp, Slowdive and the Pixies. It's "one of those shows that reminds us why we love playing live," said David Lovering, the Pixies drummer.

"Year after year, their booking blows me away," said Lauren Beck, the director of music programming for the Northside Festival in Brooklyn. "It's probably the only festival where you're going to see Slint, Slowdive, Speedy Ortiz and Spoon listed next to each other on posters," she added in an email.

In a display of egalitarianism, Primavera lists artists alphabetically, rather than headliner-first. Organizers also take care not to overcrowd spaces and are sure to indulge their performers with a choice of equipment and snacks. Wine is served in real glasses.

It's "a relative sanctuary for music fans," said Chris Kaskie, president of Pitchfork, whose festivals in Chicago and Paris were partly modeled on the rarefied Primavera experience. "The fact that you get to do that while on the Mediterranean, well, game over."

Excerpted from Melena Ryzik, "Showcasing Music Till the Sun Comes Up: Primavera Sound Sets the Stage for Music Festivals Worldwide," June 1, 2014, nytimes.com.

the fidelity; cassettes, compact discs, digital recorders and MP3 players refined the sound further. File-sharing software, music downloading and music streaming services allow people to share music globally. And while advances in technology have dramatically improved the quality of recordings, they also have made free copying possible, robbing the recording companies and musicians of substantial income.

Still, the basic foundation of the recording industry today is the same as it was for Thomas Edison in 1877.

Reflecting on the movie version of Edison's life, Robert Metz describes the development of the phonograph: An Edison employee was tinkering with "a makeshift device consisting of a rotating piece of metal with a pointed piece of metal scratching its surface. The device was full of sound and fury—and signified a great deal. . . . And thus, supposedly through idle play, came the first permanent 'record' of ephemeral sound. By any measure, it was an invention of genius."

REVIEW, ANALYZE, INVESTIGATE

CHAPTER 5

Edison Introduces His Talking Machine

- Thomas Edison first demonstrated his phonograph in 1877.
- Emile Berliner developed the gramophone in 1887.
- Berliner and Eldridge Johnson formed the Victor Talking Machine Company (later RCA Victor) to sell recordings.
- Joseph Maxfield perfected recording equipment to eliminate the tinny sound.
- The first standard records were 78 rpm.

Goldmark Perfects Long-Playing Records

- Peter Goldmark, working for CBS' William S. Paley, developed the long-playing (LP) record (33 1/3 rpm).
- The first long-playing records played for 23 minutes and were larger than 78s.

Paley Battles Sarnoff for Record Format

- David Sarnoff's staff at RCA developed the 45 rpm record.
- Eventually record players that could play all the different speeds—33 1/3 rpm, 45 rpm and 78 rpm— were sold.

Hi-Fi and Stereo Rock In

- Rock 'n' roll redefined the concept of popular music.
- Recording industry efforts to improve recorded sound quality contributed to the success of rock 'n' roll entertainers like The Supremes.
- The introduction of transistor radios in the '60s and the Walkman in the late '70s made music personal and portable.

- CD-RWs, compact discs that could record as well as play, meant consumers could create their own CDs.
- The Apple iPod music player, first introduced in 2001, allowed users to store and play music downloads.
- Apple launched iTunes, its online music store, in 2003, charging 99 cents per song and providing legal music downloads.
- The Apple iPhone, introduced in 2007, combined mobile phone technology with the capabilities of the iPod, expanding Apple's dominance in music retailing.
- Today, Apple's iTunes store has become the primary consumer source for downloading contemporary music.

Recording Industry at Work

- A recording company is divided into artists and repertoire, operations, marketing and promotion, distribution and administration.
- Music sales alone don't generate enough revenue to support most music groups, who must rely on concert revenue to enhance their income.

Concerts Bring In Essential Revenue

- Concerts require high-tech innovation.
- Concert ticket sales are an essential source of revenue for large bands.

Three Major Companies Dominate

- Three large corporations dominate the recording industry.
- Recording companies sell more than 2 billion recordings a year.
- Radio depends on popular music to succeed.

Music Sales and Licensing Drive Industry Income

- The recording industry collects income from direct sales, music licensing, music videos, music downloads and streaming.
- Two licensing agencies—ASCAP and BMI—handle the rights to play music for broadcast.

Music Industry Fights to Protect Content

- Since 1985, the music industry has faced three important challenges: attempts to control music content through labeling, overseas piracy and copyright protection for Internet file sharing.
- The recording industry responded to threats of government regulation of music lyrics by adopting its own standards for music labeling.
- MP3 digital technology, perfected in 1999, allowed consumers to download and store good-quality music directly from the Internet.
- Music-sharing company Napster was sued in 1999 for copyright infringement by RIAA and shut down in 2001.
- Consumers continued to use music-sharing sites such as Kazaa and Grokster, even though the downloaded songs were covered by copyright.

Recording Industry Association Sues Downloaders

- In 2003, the Recording Industry Association of America sued 261 individual music downloaders, hoping to stop the flow of free music on the Internet, but people continued to download.
- The lawsuits included specific names of people who had downloaded music.

U.S. Supreme Court Rules Against Illegal File Sharing

- In June 2005, the U.S. Supreme Court in *MGM Studios v. Grokster* ruled that the makers of Grokster, which allowed Internet users to browse freely and copy songs from each other, could be sued for helping people violate recording industry copyright protections.
- *MGM Studios v. Grokster* ruling gave the recording industry the legal standing it needed to try to stop illegal file sharing.

Music Industry Wins Legal Action Against Downloader

- In 2007, a federal jury imposed a penalty for file sharing of $222,000 against Jammie Thomas—the first time a federal jury had imposed a legal fine on someone for music piracy.
- The Thomas case eventually reached the U.S. Supreme Court, and on March 18, 2013, the Court let the original $222,000 judgment against Thomas stand.

U.S. Justice Department Targets Megaupload

- In March 2012, the U.S. Justice Department announced the arrest in Auckland, New Zealand, of the co-founders of the well-known international file-sharing site Megaupload, including Kim Dotcom (formerly known as Kim Schmitz).
- Kim Dotcom and six other men eventually were charged with music and movie copyright infringement, and Megaupload was shut down. The men denied they had acted illegally and fought extradition but remained under indictment.
- On February 13, 2015, one of the men who had been indicted pleaded guilty to copyright infringement in a U.S. federal court and agreed to cooperate with authorities. Kim Dotcom remained in New Zealand, facing extradition.
- The recording companies have no choice but to pursue copyright infringement wherever they find it.

Digital Technology Transforms Delivery

- Licensed music is governed by national and international copyright law, so the recording industry aggressively pursues all legal remedies available to curtail illegal music downloads in the United States and reduce piracy, especially overseas.
- The industry also encourages all legal music download services, such as iTunes, and subscription sites, such as Spotify, Pandora, Rhapsody and Tidal.

Internet Brings New Obstacles and New Audiences

- Because of the Internet, music can be shared globally.
- The Internet also makes music piracy so easy that many people consider it a harmless act, but the economic implications for recording artists are substantial.
- Music artists today can find a bigger audience than Thomas Edison ever could have imagined—through legal music downloads, concerts, streaming and subscription services.
- Recording companies and music artists must learn how to produce music that consumers want to buy, delivered in a format and/or through a service that can financially sustain the industry.

Key Terms

These terms are defined in the margins throughout this chapter and appear in alphabetical order with definitions in the Glossary, which begins on page 361.

ASCAP *93*

BMI *93*

CD-RW (Re-Writable) Drives *91*

File Sharing *95*

LP *88*

Recording Industry Association of America (RIAA) *86*

RPM *88*

Critical Questions

1. Describe the competition between William Paley's 33 1/3 records and David Sarnoff's 45s. How was that battle resolved? What does that battle tell you about the role that technology plays in the media industries?

2. Why are the recording industry and the radio industry so interdependent?

3. Give a brief history of Motown. Why was the company so important in the history of the music industry?

4. Discuss the response of the music recording industry to file sharing, and evaluate the extent to which it has been successful in protecting recording artists and recording companies. Do you believe the various U.S. court decisions covering music copyright infringement will stop illegal file sharing? Explain.

5. How have recent developments in digital technologies affected the music recording and performance industries financially? Discuss.

Working the Web

This list includes sites mentioned in the chapter and others to give you greater insight into the recording business.

American Top 40 (AT40) with Ryan Seacrest

at40.com

Hosted by Ryan Seacrest, America's Top 40 is the longest-running popular music weekend countdown radio show. AT40 offers music news, artist pictures and podcasts, plus user contests and blogs.

AOL Radio (formerly AOL Music)

aolradio.slacker.com

Still a division within AOL Inc., AOL Radio is an online free and subscription radio service that is now operated in partnership with Slacker Radio. Free access is available to more than 200 programmed radio stations. For a monthly fee, subscribers can download music to listen to on-demand on their computers and mobile phones.

Apple.com/iTunes

apple.com/itunes

Originally developed and known as SoundJam MP, Apple changed the name to iTunes when it acquired the company in 2000. Today, iTunes offers users on almost any media platform the ability to stream or download music, movies, television shows and podcasts and even listen to online radio through its iTunes program.

Billboard and Billboard Business

billboard.com

billboard.com/biz

Launched as Billboardonline in 1995, Billboard.com is essentially the online version of *Billboard Magazine*—the music industry bible—but with some obvious interactive differences. Billboard.com offers users playable music samples from best-selling music albums and singles, music videos, news articles and blogs on music artists, as well as the latest trends and fashions in the music industry. Billboard.biz, the companion Web site, offers breaking news about the music, television and film industries.

Pandora Radio

pandora.com

Available only in the U.S., Australia and New Zealand, Pandora offers a free and subscription-based online music "recommendation" streaming service—although only a small portion of listeners use the subscription service. Listeners select and can vote for the type of music they prefer, which Pandora tracks and uses to decide what types of music to offer. With its own channel now on YouTube, Pandora is owned and operated by Pandora Media Inc.

Recording Industry Association of America (RIAA)

riaa.com

As the trade group representing U.S. music companies, RIAA protects intellectual property rights and First Amendment rights globally, conducts consumer and technical research and monitors governmental regulations and policies. It also certifies the Gold, Platinum, Multiplatinum and Diamond sales of music recordings as well as Los Premios De Oro y Latino, an award celebrating Latin music sales.

Rhapsody Inc.

rhapsody.com

With offices in Seattle, San Francisco, New York and Frankfurt, Germany, Rhapsody is a subscription-only music streaming service where users can stream and download more than 32 million songs from edited and predetermined playlists.

SoundCloud

soundcloud.com

SoundCloud is a social media digital platform where users can create and share music via Twitter, Tumblr, Facebook and Foursquare. Recording and uploading sounds to SoundCloud lets people share them privately with their friends or publicly through blogs, sites and social networks.

Universal Music Group (UMG)

universalmusic.com

Universal Music Group has worldwide operations for recorded music, music publishing and music merchandising in North America, Europe, Asia and Latin America. UMG owns well-known and top-selling recording labels, including EMI, Interscope Geffen A & M, Universal Motown and Nashville groups, plus Universal Music Latino.

Impact/Action Videos are concise news features on various topics created exclusively for *Media/Impact*. Find them in *Media/Impact*'s MindTap at cengagebrain.com.

MindTap®

Log on to MindTap for *Media/Impact* to access a variety of additional material—including learning objectives, chapter readings with highlighting and note-taking, **Impact/Action Videos**, activities, and comprehension quizzes—that will guide you through this chapter.

RADIO
RIDING NEW WAVES

06

Bryan Steffy/Getty Images

iHeartRadio is an Internet radio service that streams stations owned by iHeartRadio Inc. (formerly Clear Channel) throughout the U.S. iHeartRadio sponsored a music celebration at the 2015 Consumer Electronics Show in Las Vegas.

What's Ahead?

- Radio Sounds Are Everywhere
- Radio Takes a Technological Leap
- Broadcasting Is Born
- Federal Government Regulates the Airwaves
- Radio Audience Expands Quickly
- Radio Grows into a Powerful Force

- "The War of the Worlds" Challenges Radio's Credibility
- Radio Networks Expand
- Radio Adapts to Television
- Radio at Work
- Congress Creates National Public Radio
- Portability and Immediacy Help Radio Survive
- Telecommunications Act of 1996 Overhauls Radio

- Are Radio Ratings Accurate?
- Radio Depends on Ready-Made Formats
- Audience Divides into Smaller Segments
- Competition Revives Payola
- Digital Audio Delivers Internet and Satellite Radio
- Streaming Splits Radio Industry Income

> "Our ultimate goal is to help artists across the spectrum build and maintain their careers."
>
> —TIM WESTERGREN, FOUNDER, PANDORA RADIO

Today, the nation's collective memory and impressions about events that happened in the first half of the 20th century are directly tied to radio. Newspapers offered next-day reports and occasional extras, and magazines offered long-term analysis. But radio gave listeners an immediate news record at a time when world events demanded attention. Radio also gave people entertainment, including sports, big bands, Jack Benny, George Burns and Gracie Allen, Abbott and Costello and Bob Hope.

Radio transformed national politics by transmitting the sounds of public debate, as well as the words, to the audience. Radio also expanded Americans' access to popular as well as classical culture. Opera played on the same dial as slapstick comedy; drama and music shared the airwaves with sports—all supported by advertising.

Radio Sounds Are Everywhere

The legacy of news and music remains on radio today, but the medium that once was the center of attention in everyone's front room has moved to the bedroom, the office, the car and the mobile phone. Radio can wake you up and put you to sleep. Radio goes with you when you run on the trail or sit on the beach. Internet radio even follows you to your desk at work. Consider these industry statistics about radio today:

- 99 percent of America's homes have radios.

- 95 percent of America's cars have radios, and radio reaches 3 out of 5 adults in their cars at least once a week.

- 70 percent of the nation's cars are equipped to receive SiriusXM satellite radio, and 30 percent of all cars sold in 2015 are equipped with Pandora Internet radio.

- 40 percent of Americans listen to the radio each day sometime between 6 a.m. and midnight.

- Weekly Internet radio listening is at an all-time high—39 percent of the U.S. population.

Although radio is more accessible today, what you hear is not the same as what your great-grandparents heard. Advertisers, who once sought radio as the only broadcast access to an audience, have many more places to put their ads. For audiences, radio has become an accessory rather than a necessity. No one envisioned radio's place in today's media mix when radio's pioneers began tinkering just before the turn of the 20th century. All these pioneers wanted to do was figure out how to send sounds along a wire.

Radio Takes a Technological Leap

Today we are so accustomed to sending and receiving messages instantaneously that it is hard to imagine a time when information took more than a week to travel from place to place. In the early 1800s, stagecoaches had to travel 44 hours to bring news from New York City to Washington, D.C. In 1860, the Pony Express took 10 and a half days to go from St. Joseph, Missouri, to San Francisco.

TimeFrame
1899–Today

Digital Technology and Standardized Programming Chase the Audience

1899 Guglielmo Marconi introduces his wireless radio to the United States with a report of the America's Cup race.

1906–1907 Reginald Aubrey Fessenden transmits the first voice and music broadcast. Lee de Forest introduces the Audion tube.

1920 Station KDKA in Pittsburgh goes on the air, the nation's first commercial radio station.

1934 Congress establishes the Federal Communications Commission to regulate broadcasting.

1936 Edwin H. Armstrong licenses frequency modulation (FM).

1938 *Mercury Theatre on the Air* broadcasts "The War of the Worlds," demonstrating how quickly broadcast misinformation can cause a public panic.

✱ **1948** The first transistor radios are sold, making radio portable and expanding radio's reach to audiences outside the home and the car.

1959 Gordon McLendon introduces format radio at KABL in San Francisco.

1960 The Manhattan grand jury indicts disc jockey Alan Freed for payola.

1970 National Public Radio (NPR) goes on the air. By design, public radio is created as an alternative to commercial radio.

1996 Congress passes the Telecommunications Act of 1996, which encourages unprecedented consolidation in the radio industry.

2001 Sirius Satellite Radio and XM Radio begin offering digital satellite radio service.

2005 The New York Attorney General charges that payola still is pervasive in the radio industry.
Radio broadcasters form the HD Digital Radio Alliance to promote HD radio.
Internet radio pioneer Tim Westergren launches Internet radio service Pandora to offer free and subscription music online.

✱ **2008** Satellite radio companies XM and Sirius merge to become SiriusXM.
The Nielsen Company, which provides ratings for television, launches a radio ratings service, ending Arbitron's monopoly on radio ratings.

2009 Pandora Internet radio reaches a royalty-fee agreement with a group representing artists and record labels, which frees Pandora to legally expand its Internet radio services.

2012 Nielsen buys Arbitron, consolidating radio ratings into one company.

✱ **2015** Pandora Radio is installed in 30 percent of all new cars sold in the U.S.

TODAY The broadcast radio industry is concentrated primarily in large groups of stations that use standardized formats, and faces strong competition from satellite and Internet radio. Most broadcast radio stations have a presence on the Internet. Radio broadcasters are competing with Internet radio entrepreneurs for the audience.

Technological advances brought rapid changes in how quickly information could move throughout the country. First came the invention of the telegraph and the telephone, which depended on electrical lines to deliver their messages, and then wireless telegraphy, which delivers radio signals through the air.

In 1835, Samuel F. B. Morse first demonstrated his electromagnetic telegraph system in America. In 1843, Congress gave him $30,000 to string four telegraph lines along the Baltimore & Ohio Railroad right of way from Baltimore to Washington, D.C. Morse sent the first official message—"What hath God wrought?"—from Baltimore to Washington, D.C., on May 24, 1844.

Telegraph lines followed the railroads, and for more than 30 years Americans depended on Morse's coded messages printed on tape, sent from one railroad station to another. On March 10, 1876, *Alexander Graham Bell* sent a message by his new invention, the telephone, to his associate Thomas A. Watson in an adjoining room of their Boston laboratory: "Mr. Watson, come here. I want you." Both Morse's telegraph and Bell's telephone used wires to carry messages.

Then in Germany in 1887, the physicist *Heinrich Hertz* began experimenting with radio waves, which became known as Hertzian waves—the first discovery in a series of refinements that eventually led to the development of radio broadcasting.

In many parts of the world today, radio is a necessity. In March 2015, a Nigerian man listens to the results of his country's election.

Pius Utomi Ekpei/AFP/Getty Images

Broadcasting Is Born

Broadcasting was truly a revolutionary media development. Imagine a society in which the only way you can hear music or enjoy a comedy is at a live performance or by listening to tinny noises on a record machine. The only way you can hear a speech is to be in the audience. Movies show action but no sound.

Without the inventions of broadcasting's early pioneers such as Heinrich Hertz, you could still be living without the sounds of media that you have come to take for granted. Four pioneers besides Hertz are credited with advancing early radio broadcasting in America: Guglielmo Marconi, Reginald Aubrey Fessenden, Lee de Forest and David Sarnoff.

Wireless Breakthrough: Guglielmo Marconi

Twenty-year-old Guglielmo Marconi, the son of wealthy Italian parents, used the results of three discoveries by Morse, Bell and Hertz to expand his idea that messages should be able to travel across space without a wire. Marconi became obsessed, refusing food and working at home in his locked upstairs room. Soon Marconi was able to ring a bell across the room or downstairs without using a wire. Eventually he was able to broadcast over a distance of 9 miles. "The calm of my life ended then," Marconi said later.

The *New York Herald* invited Marconi to the United States to report the America's Cup race in October 1899. Marconi reported "by wireless!" American businesspeople, intrigued by the military potential of Marconi's invention, invested $10 million to form American Marconi.

To experiment with the new discovery, amateur radio operators created radio clubs. Two experimenters, Reginald Aubrey Fessenden and Lee de Forest, advanced Marconi's discovery to expand radio's popularity.

Experimental Broadcasts: Reginald Aubrey Fessenden

Reginald Aubrey Fessenden, a Canadian, began wireless experiments in the U.S. in 1900 when he set up his National Electric Signaling Company to attempt to send voices by radio waves. On Christmas Eve 1906, "ship wireless operators over a wide area of the Atlantic . . . were startled to hear a woman singing, then a violin playing, then a man reading passages from Luke. It was considered uncanny; wireless rooms were soon crowded with the curious," wrote broadcast historian Erik Barnouw.

The noises were coming from Fessenden's experimental station at Brant Rock, Massachusetts. Fessenden's 1906 experiment is considered the world's first voice and music broadcast.

Detecting Radio Waves: Lee de Forest

Lee de Forest called himself the father of radio because in 1907 he perfected a glass bulb called the Audion that could detect radio waves. "Unwittingly then," wrote de Forest, "had I discovered an invisible Empire of the Air." Besides being an inventor, de Forest was a good promoter.

He began what he called "broadcasts" from New York and then from the Eiffel Tower.

In 1910, de Forest broadcast Enrico Caruso singing at the Metropolitan Opera House. Later his mother broadcast an appeal to give women the vote. Gradually, the Audion became the technical foundation of modern broadcasting.

A Household Utility: David Sarnoff

In 1912, 21-year-old wireless operator David Sarnoff relayed news from Nantucket Island, in Massachusetts, that he had received a distress call from the *Titanic* on his Marconi wireless. Four years later, when Sarnoff was working for the Marconi Company in New York, he wrote a visionary memo that predicted radio's future, but originally his ideas were widely ignored.

"I have in mind a plan of development which would make radio a household utility. The idea is to bring music into the home by wireless," Sarnoff wrote. Eventually, as commercial manager and then president of RCA, Sarnoff watched his early vision for radio come true, and RCA became the nation's primary radio distributor.

Federal Government Regulates the Airwaves

The federal government decided to regulate broadcasting almost as soon as it was invented. This decision to regulate separated the broadcast media, which are regulated by the federal government, from print media, which are not regulated directly by any federal government agency.

As amateurs competed with the military for the airwaves, Congress passed the Radio Act of 1912 to license people who wanted to broadcast or receive messages. The federal government decided to license people to transmit signals because there only were a certain number of frequencies available. Many amateurs, trying to send signals on the same frequency, were knocking each other off the air, so the government intervened to try to keep the operators out of each other's way.

Then, during World War I, the federal government ordered all amateurs off the air and took control of all privately owned stations, and the military took over radio broadcasting. After the war, the federal government lifted the freeze, and the Navy argued that the military should maintain the monopoly over the airwaves that it had enjoyed during the war.

Government Approves Commercial Broadcasting

Faced with strong arguments by the amateurs who wanted to return to the airwaves, Congress decided against a Navy monopoly. Instead, the government sanctioned a private monopoly formed by General Electric, Westinghouse, AT&T, Western Electric Company and United Fruit Company. General Electric (GE) bought out American Marconi and its patents, and in 1919, these five sympathetic interests pooled the patents they controlled to form Radio Corporation of America (RCA).

David Sarnoff became RCA's general manager in 1921. Because of this early monopoly, RCA dominated radio development for many years, but eventually smaller operations formed all over the country as radio fever spread nationwide.

Experimental Stations Multiply

A plaque placed on a building in San Jose, California, in 1959 celebrates the 1909 founding of the experimental station FN: "On this site in 1909, Charles D. Herrold founded a voice radio station which opened the door to electronic mass communication. He conceived the idea of 'broadcasting' to the public, and his station, the world's first, has now served Northern California for half a century." Today, KCBS is based in San Francisco.

Various other stations claim they were among the earliest radio pioneers. Station 9XM broadcast music and weather reports from Madison, Wis.; 6ADZ broadcast concerts from Hollywood, Calif.; 4XD sent phonograph music from a chicken coop in Charlotte, N.C.; and 8MK in Detroit, operated by *Detroit News* publisher William E. Scripps, transmitted election returns.

These stations were run by amateur radio operators who broadcast messages to each other and their friends but not to the public; nevertheless, they are early examples of broadcast entrepreneurs. They were tinkerers, fascinated with an invention that could carry sounds through the air. One of these tinkerers, Frank Conrad, is credited with creating the beginnings of the nation's first *commercial* radio station.

KDKA Launches Commercial Broadcasting

An ad in the September 29, 1920, *Pittsburgh Sun* changed broadcasting from an exclusive hobby to an easy-to-use medium available to everyone. The ad described a 20-minute evening concert broadcast from the home of Frank Conrad, a "wireless enthusiast" who worked for Westinghouse.

Conrad often broadcast concerts from his garage on his station, 8XK, but his boss at Westinghouse, Harry P. Davis, had an idea: Why not improve the broadcasts so more people would want to buy radios? Davis talked Conrad into setting up a more powerful transmitter at the Westinghouse plant by November 2, 1920, so Conrad could broadcast election returns.

On October 27, 1920, using the powers of the 1912 Radio Act, the U.S. Department of Commerce licensed

The nation's first commercial radio station, KDKA in Pittsburgh, went on the air in 1920. A group of musicians, including Stanley Turrentine on saxophone, Tommy Turrentine on trumpet and Willie Love on saxophone, offered live music on KDKA in 1943.

station KDKA as the nation's first *commercial* radio station. The broadcast began at 8 p.m. on November 2, 1920, and continued past midnight, reporting that Warren G. Harding was the nation's next president. KDKA immediately began a daily one-hour evening schedule, broadcasting from 8:30 to 9:30 p.m.

Radio Audience Expands Quickly

The crude KDKA broadcasts proved that regular programming could attract a loyal audience. KDKA was just the beginning of what eventually became radio networks. The radio craze led almost immediately to a period of rapid expansion as entrepreneurs and advertisers began to grasp the new medium's potential. Almost as quickly, government was compelled to step in to expand its regulation of radio broadcasting.

Radio's potential as a moneymaker for its owners fueled competition for the airwaves. Three important developments for radio's future were the

1. Blanket licensing agreement

2. Decision that radio would accept commercial sponsors

3. Radio Act of 1927

Blanket Licensing

At first, stations played phonograph records; then they invited artists to perform live in their studios. Some of the nation's best talent sought the publicity that radio could give them, but eventually the performers asked to be paid.

In 1923, the American Society of Composers, Authors and Publishers (**ASCAP**) sued several stations for payment. ASCAP claimed that if radio aired ASCAP-licensed music, people would buy less sheet music, cheating ASCAP members out of royalties. Station owners argued that playing the songs on their stations publicized the sheet music, which meant ASCAP members would make more money.

Eventually the stations agreed to pay royalties to ASCAP through a ***blanket licensing agreement***, which meant the stations paid ASCAP an annual $250 fee. In exchange, the stations could use all ASCAP-licensed music on the air. (ASCAP licenses its music to stations the same way today, but the annual fee, of course, is considerably higher.) Eventually another licensing organization, Broadcast Music Inc., or ***BMI***, also would collect broadcast royalties.

Commercial Sponsorship

Once station owners agreed to pay for their programs, they had to figure out where they would get the money. AT&T had the answer with an idea pioneered at its station WEAF in New York. WEAF started selling advertising time to sponsors. Its first sponsored program cost the advertiser $100 to sponsor a 10-minute program.

The success of commercial sponsorship as a way to support radio settled the issue of who would pay the cost of airing the programs. Advertisers paid for programs through their advertising; the American public paid for the programs indirectly by supporting the advertisers who supported radio.

Federal Radio Commission

As more stations began to crowd the air, their signals interfered with one another. With only so many good radio frequencies available, the provisions of the Radio Act of 1912 began to seem inadequate. Congress passed the Radio Act of 1927, which formed the Federal Radio Commission under the jurisdiction of the Department of

ASCAP American Society of Composers, Authors and Publishers.

Blanket Licensing Agreement An arrangement whereby radio stations become authorized to use recorded music for broadcast by paying a fee.

BMI Broadcast Music Inc., a cooperative music licensing organization.

Commerce. The president appointed the commission's members, with Senate approval.

The shortage of air space required that broadcasting in the United States operate under a type of government regulation unknown to newspaper and magazine publishers. The federal government licensed the stations for three years, and the commission mandated that the stations operate "*as a public convenience, interest or necessity requires.*"

The commission, created to protect the stations by allocating frequencies, also became the license holder. The stations could operate only with the government's approval, and the stations needed commission approval to be sold or transferred. The Radio Act of 1927, including the concept that broadcasters must operate in the "*public convenience, interest or necessity,*" became the foundation for all broadcast regulation in the United States.

In 1934, Congress established the Federal Communications Commission (***FCC***) to regulate the expanding wireless medium, making the FCC a separate agency of government and no longer a part of the Department of Commerce. ***It is important to remember that the commission's original purpose was to allocate the broadcast spectrum so station broadcast signals would not interfere with one another. The FCC was not originally envisioned to oversee broadcast content.***

The FCC began work on July 11, 1934, composed of seven commissioners appointed by the president and approved by the Senate. This same basic structure and purpose govern the commission's actions today, but now there are only five commissioners. The establishment of the FCC in 1934 also set the precedent for the later regulation of television.

Radio Grows into a Powerful Force

Most radio stations mixed entertainment, culture and public service, and together they created a new kind of collective national experience. In the 1930s and 1940s, radio became a powerful cultural and political force and gave millions of people a new, inexpensive source of information and entertainment (see **Illustration 6.1**, "Where Do People Listen to the Radio?," p. 110).

The commercialization of American broadcasting also gave advertisers access to this audience at home. Radio's massive group of listeners sat enraptured with sponsored programming of many types: comedy, music, serials, sports, drama and news. Eventually, all these types of programming migrated to television.

"The War of the Worlds" Challenges Radio's Credibility

On Halloween Eve, October 30, 1938, the *Mercury Theatre on the Air* broadcast a play based on the H. G. Wells novel *The War of the Worlds*. The live 8 p.m. broadcast played opposite the very popular Edgar Bergen program on NBC, and the *Mercury Theatre* broadcast rarely had even 4 percent of the audience. Very few people heard the announcement at the beginning of the program that the *Mercury Theatre* was performing a version of the Wells story.

The program began with the announcer introducing some band music. A second voice then said, "Ladies and gentlemen, we interrupt our program of dance music to bring you a special bulletin. At 20 minutes before 8 o'clock Central Time, Professor Farrell of Mount Jennings Observatory, Chicago, reports observing several explosions of incandescent gas occurring at regular intervals on the planet Mars."

Buyenlarge/Archive Photos/Getty Images

Radio in the 1930s and 1940s became a powerful cultural and political force, offering people an inexpensive source of news and entertainment. In 1930, the new magazine *Radio News* featured "1001 Radio Questions and Answers."

FCC   Federal Communications Commission.

IMPACT

Society

ILLUSTRATION 6.1

Where Do People Listen to the Radio?

Adults tune in to the radio more at work and in the car than they do at home. Advertisers, such as car dealers, use this demographic information to help target radio audiences with their messages.

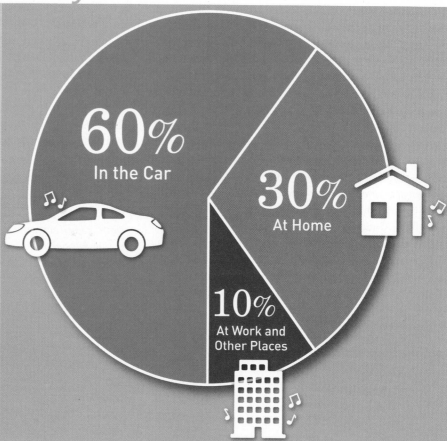

60%
In the Car

30%
At Home

10%
At Work and Other Places

Radio Advertising Bureau, rab.com.

The fear created by Orson Welles' "The War of the Worlds" broadcast in 1938 demonstrated how easily unsubstantiated information could be misinterpreted on the radio. Orson Welles (center, in the light-colored suit) met with reporters on October 31, 1938, to answer questions about the broadcast.

More dance music followed and then more bulletins about a meteor, with the startling news that 1,500 people near Princeton, New Jersey, had died when the meteor hit the town. Then the announcer said it was not a meteor but a spaceship carrying Martians armed with death rays.

Two professors from the Princeton geology department actually set out to locate the "meteors." In Newark, New Jersey, more than 20 families rushed out of their homes, covering their faces with wet handkerchiefs to protect them from the "gas." After a burst of horrified calls, CBS began repeating the announcement that the program was just a radio drama, but the damage had been done.

The episode demonstrated how easily alarming information could be innocently misinterpreted, especially because the listeners had no other source than radio to check the reliability of what they were hearing. Radio listeners truly were a captive audience.

Radio Networks Expand

The formation of radio networks as a source of programming and revenue is a crucial development in the history of American radio. A ***network*** is a collection of stations (radio or television) that offers programs, usually simultaneously, throughout the country, during designated times.

As the radio networks stretched across the U.S. they provided a dependable source of programming. Most stations found it easier to affiliate with a network and receive and distribute network programming than to develop local programs.

David Sarnoff (left), who began his broadcast career as a wireless operator, eventually became president of RCA. William S. Paley (right), who launched CBS radio, often battled with Sarnoff. The continuing competition between Sarnoff and Paley shaped the early development of American radio and TV broadcasting.

David Sarnoff Launches NBC

NBC grew out of the government's original agreement with RCA. RCA, GE and Westinghouse formed the National Broadcasting Company in 1926. By January 1927, NBC, headed by David Sarnoff, had formed two networks: the Red network (fed from WEAF in New York) and the Blue network (originating from station WJZ in Newark).

Station engineers drew the planned hookups of the two networks with red and blue colored pencils, which is how the networks got their names. RCA faced criticism about its broad control over the airwaves because it continued to be the world's largest distributor of radios, which were made by Westinghouse and General Electric.

William S. Paley Starts CBS

Twenty-six-year-old William S. Paley, heir to a tobacco fortune, bought the financially struggling Columbia Phonograph Company in 1929. He changed the name to Columbia Broadcasting System, and put his CBS network on the air with 25 stations. Programming originated from WABC in New York. Paley became the nemesis of NBC, then controlled by David Sarnoff, and this early competition between Sarnoff and Paley shaped the development of American broadcasting.

Edward Noble Buys ABC

In 1941, the FCC ordered RCA to divest itself of one of its networks. In 1943, RCA sold NBC-Blue to Edward J. Noble (who had made his fortune as head of the company that produced LifeSavers candy). Noble paid $8 million for the network that became the American Broadcasting Company (ABC), giving the country a three-network radio system (which later became the basis for the nation's three-network TV system).

Radio Adapts to Television

Radio networks prospered from the 1940s to the 1980s, when NBC sold its radio network, and CBS and ABC devoted more attention to their TV holdings. When television initially was launched in the 1940s, it seemed it would cause the death of radio. As soon as television proved itself, advertisers abandoned radio, said comedian Fred Allen, "like the bones at a barbecue."

The entertainers fled to television, too—original radio talents such as Bob Hope, Milton Berle and Jackie Gleason soon dropped their radio programs and moved to TV. Public affairs programs like *Meet the Press* made the move from radio to TV, as did Edward R. Murrow's radio news program, *Hear It Now*, which on television became *See It Now*.

> **Network** A collection of radio or TV stations that offers programs, usually simultaneously, throughout the country during designated program times.

Five developments in the 1940s, 1950s and 1960s transformed the medium of radio as well as guaranteed radio's survival alongside television:

1. The FM radio frequency was accepted by the public.

2. Disc jockeys hosted music shows.

3. People started using clock, car and transistor radios.

4. Radio formats streamlined broadcasts.

5. The payola scandals focused on broadcast ethics.

Inventor Edwin H. Armstrong Pioneers FM

After working for more than a decade to eliminate static from radio broadcasts, engineer Edwin H. Armstrong applied to the FCC in 1936 to broadcast using his new technique, frequency modulation (FM). Because of the way FM signals travel through the air, FM offered truer transmission than AM (amplitude modulation) with much less static. Armstrong faced difficult opposition from David Sarnoff at RCA, who originally had been an Armstrong sponsor.

The FCC received 150 applications for FM licenses in 1939 but then froze licensing during World War II. After the war, Armstrong again faced Sarnoff, but this time Armstrong lost. RCA was using Armstrong's frequency modulation in its TV and FM sets but refused to pay Armstrong royalties, so Armstrong sued RCA.

RCA fought Armstrong for 20 years, saying that RCA had been among the early developers of FM and citing RCA's sponsorship of Armstrong's initial experiments. In 1953, Armstrong became ill and suffered a stroke, then committed suicide. RCA quickly settled the suit with Armstrong's widow for $1 million. Eventually FM became the spectrum of choice for music lovers, far surpassing the broadcast quality of AM.

Licensed Recordings Launch Disc Jockeys

Early radio station owners avoided playing records because they would have had to pay ASCAP royalties. The FCC also required stations that played records to remind their audiences every half hour that the audience was listening to recorded music, not a live orchestra. This discouraged record spinning.

In 1935, newscaster Martin Block at New York's independent station WNEW began playing records in between his newscasts, and then he started a program called *Make Believe Ballroom*. He is generally considered America's first disc jockey. In 1940, the FCC ruled that once stations bought a record, they could play it on the air whenever they liked, without the announcements every half hour.

Bettmann/Corbis

Edwin H. Armstrong's invention of FM made radio signals clearer. For nearly 20 years, Armstrong battled RCA's David Sarnoff for royalties for his invention. Disheartened by the legal battle, Armstrong committed suicide, but his widow eventually won the royalty payments. In 1923, Armstrong shows off one of his inventions—a very bulky portable radio in a suitcase—on the beach.

To counteract ASCAP's insistence on royalties, broadcasters formed a cooperative music-licensing organization called Broadcast Music Inc. Most rhythm and blues, country and rock 'n' roll artists eventually signed with BMI, which charged stations less for recording artists than ASCAP did. This inexpensive source of music also created a new type of media personality—the disc jockey.

Clock, Car and Transistor Radios Make Radio a Necessary Accessory

Clock and car radios helped ensure radio's survival by making it an everyday accessory. Transistor radios, first sold in 1948 for $40, were more reliable and cheaper than tube radios. Clock radios, introduced in the 1950s, woke people up and caused them to rely on radio for the first news of the day.

William Lear, who also designed the Lear jet, invented the car radio in 1928. Early car radios were enormous,

Drivers have always been an important radio audience. William Lear invented the first car radio in 1928. By 1945, 9 million cars in the United States had radios. Shown here are (top) a 1941 Cadillac dashboard with a luxury push-button radio and (bottom) a 2015 Tesla dashboard, which connects through a touchscreen tablet.

with spotty reception, but the technology that was developed during World War II helped refine them.

In 1946, 9 million cars had car radios. By 1963, the number was 50 million. A radio station owner coined the term ***drive-time audiences*** to describe people who listened in their cars on the way to work from 6 to 9 a.m. and on the way home from 4 to 7 p.m. (Today 99 percent of America's cars have radios.)

Gordon McLendon Introduces Format Radio

How would the stations know which mix of records to use and who would play them? The answer came from Gordon McLendon, the father of format radio. At KLIF in Dallas, McLendon combined music and news in a predictable

rotation of 20-minute segments, and eventually KLIF grew very popular. Next he refined the music by creating the Top-40 format.

Top 40 played the top-selling hits continually, interrupted only by a disc jockey or a newscast. By 1959, McLendon launched the beautiful-music format at KABL in San Francisco. In 1964, he created a 24-hour news format for Chicago's WNUS, using three news vans with "telesigns" that showed news on the roofs in lights as the vans drove around town.

Formats meant stations could share standardized programs instead of producing programs individually. Eventually, formatted programming spread, which made network programming and the networks themselves less important to individual stations.

Payola Scandals Highlight Broadcast Ethics

The rise of rock 'n' roll coincided with the development of transistor and portable radios, which meant radio played a central role in the rock revolution. "Rock and radio were made for each other. The relationship between record companies and radio stations became mutually beneficial. By providing the latest hits, record companies kept stations' operating costs low. The stations, in turn, provided the record companies with the equivalent of free advertising," wrote radio historian David MacFarland.

Eventually this relationship proved too close. On February 8, 1960, Congress began hearings into charges that disc jockeys and program directors had accepted cash to play specific recordings on the air. To describe this practice, the term ***payola*** was coined from the combination of *pay* and *Victrola* (the name of a popular early record player).

In May 1960, the Manhattan grand jury charged eight men with commercial bribery for accepting more than $100,000 in payoffs for playing records. The most

Drive-Time Audiences People who listen to the radio in their cars during 6 to 9 a.m. and 4 to 7 p.m.

Payola The practice of accepting payment to play specific recordings on the air.

prominent among them was Alan Freed, who had worked in Cleveland (where he was credited with coining the term *rock 'n' roll*) and at New York's WABC.

In February 1962, Freed pleaded guilty to 2 counts of accepting payoffs, paid a $300 fine and received 6 months of probation. Then he was found guilty of income tax evasion. He died in 1965 while awaiting trial, at age 43. In September 1960, Congress amended the Federal Communications Act to prohibit the payment of cash or gifts in exchange for airplay; nevertheless, the issue of payola surfaced again in 2005 and resulted in stiff fines in 2007.

Radio at Work

A Columbia University report, commissioned by NBC in 1954, defined radio's role after television. "Radio was the one medium that could accompany almost every type of activity. . . . Where radio once had been a leisure-time 'reward' after a day's work, television was now occupying that role. Radio had come to be viewed less as a treat than as a kind of 'companion' to some other activity." Like magazines, radio survived in part because the medium adapted to fill different needs for its audience.

Today, about 10,800 broadcast radio stations are on the air in the United States, evenly divided between FM and AM. Network programming plays a much smaller role than when radio began because most stations play just music and don't need network programming to survive. National Public Radio is the only major public network. Many commercial stations today use *program services*, which provide satellite as well as formatted programming.

Most stations are part of a *group*, which means that a company owns more than one station in more than one broadcast market. Some stations are part of a combination AM/FM (*a combo*), which means that a company owns both AM and FM stations in the same market. A few stations remain family-owned, single operations that run just like any other small business.

The management structure at a radio station usually includes a general manager, a program manager, account executives, the traffic department, production department, engineering department and administration.

The *general manager* runs the radio station. The *program manager* oversees what goes on the air, including the news programs, the station's format and any on-air people. Salespeople, who are called *account executives*, sell the advertising for programs.

The *traffic department* schedules the commercials, makes sure they run correctly and bills the clients. The *production department* helps with local programming, if there is any, and produces local commercials for the station. *Engineering* keeps the station on the air. *Administration* pays the bills, answers the phones and orders the paper clips. A small station requires five employees, or fewer, to handle all these jobs.

Congress Creates National Public Radio

The Public Broadcasting Act of 1967 created the Corporation for Public Broadcasting and included funding for public radio and TV stations. National Public Radio launched a national program on FM in 1970, but many radios still didn't have an FM dial. Most public stations—owned by colleges and universities and staffed by volunteers—were staffed irregularly.

Then NPR started the program *All Things Considered* for the evening drive-time and in 1979 launched *Morning Edition*. Today, *Morning Edition* and *All Things Considered* have a very loyal audience for their long interviews on topical issues and international reports. By design, public radio is an alternative to commercial radio. Today, NPR still receives some public funding, but it depends primarily on private donations to survive.

We've got 9 seconds. Explain your life's research on the business cycle and how it applies to the current economy.

Doug Pike/Cartoon Stock

Portability and Immediacy Help Radio Survive

Instead of dying after the spread of television, radio managed to thrive by adapting to an audience that sought the portability and immediacy that radio offers. Nothing can beat radio for quick news bulletins or the latest hits. Radio also delivers a targeted audience much better than television because the radio station you prefer defines you to an advertiser much better than the television station you watch.

In the 1990s, the advertising potential for an intimate medium like radio attracted entrepreneurs who had never owned a station and group owners who wanted to expand their holdings. When you listen to the radio in your car or through earphones while you jog, for instance, radio is not competing with any other medium for your attention. Advertisers like this exclusive access to an audience. Three important issues for people in broadcast radio today are

1. Deregulation
2. Ratings
3. Formats

Jennifer Pottheiser/NBAE/Getty Images

Live sports and sports talk remain popular radio formats. In May 2013, Heather Cox of ESPN interviewed basketball player Kevin Love about being drafted by the Minnesota Timberwolves. Love now plays for the Cleveland Cavaliers.

Telecommunications Act of 1996 Overhauls Radio

The Telecommunications Act of 1996 was the first major overhaul of broadcast regulation since the Federal Communications Commission was established in 1934. Today the legacy of the act is that commercial radio is regulated much less than it was in the 1970s. This is called a government policy of *deregulation*.

Before the 1996 act passed, the FCC limited the number of radio stations that one company could own nationwide. The Telecommunications Act removed these limits, and in each local market the number of stations that one owner can hold depends on the size of the market. (For a complete discussion of the Telecommunications Act, see **Chapter 14**.)

The Telecommunications Act also allows *cross-ownership*, which means that companies can own radio and TV stations in the same market and broadcast and cable outlets in the same market. As soon as the act passed in February 1996, radio station sales began to soar.

Today several radio corporations each own hundreds of broadcast stations. Supporters of the changes say this makes broadcast radio more competitive because these larger companies can give the stations better financial support than small, single owners. Opponents point out that consolidation in the radio industry leads to less program variety for consumers and too much power for companies that own large numbers of radio stations nationwide.

Are Radio Ratings Accurate?

Radio station owners depend on ratings to set advertising rates, and the stations with the most listeners command the highest ad rates. Originally, a company called Arbitron gathered ratings for the radio business. To find out what radio stations people were listening to, Arbitron requested that selected listeners complete and return diaries the company sent them.

Arbitron often was criticized because minorities, non-English-speaking listeners and people ages 18 to 24 didn't return the diaries in the same proportion as other people that Arbitron surveyed. The critics contended that Arbitron's ratings hurt rock and urban formats, such as rap/hip-hop and Spanish-language programming, while aiding the contemporary and news/talk/information formats, whose audiences are older and more responsive to the diaries. Arbitron acknowledged the problems and tried filling out diaries for people over the phone and adding bilingual interviewers.

Deregulation Government action that reduces restrictions on the business operations of an industry.

Cross-Ownership The practice of one company owning radio and TV stations in the same broadcast market.

Still, questions persisted. In November 2008, the Nielsen Company, which provides ratings for TV, launched a radio ratings service in direct competition with Arbitron. Then in 2012, Nielsen bought Arbitron, eliminating its competitor. This made Nielsen the only company in the United States that provides ratings information for radio.

Radio Depends on Ready-Made Formats

Today's broadcast radio station owners, looking for an audience, can use one of several ready-made formats. By adjusting their formats, radio managers test the markets until they find a formula that works to deliver their target audience to advertisers. (See **Illustration 6.2**, "Which Radio Formats Are Most Popular?" below.)

If you were a radio station manager today, and you wanted to program your station, you could choose from several popular formats.

COUNTRY. The Grand Ole Opry first broadcast country music on WSM in Nashville in 1925. This radio format is aimed at 25- to 45-year-olds in urban as well as rural areas.

NEWS/TALK/INFORMATION/SPORTS. A station with this format devotes most of its airtime to different types of talk shows, which can include call-in features,

IMPACT

Money

15% Country
12% News/Talk
8% Pop Contemporary
7% Adult Contemporary
6% Classic Hits
5% Classic Rock
5% Hot Adult Contemporary
4% Urban Adult Contemporary
3% Rhythmic Contemporary
3% Sports
32% Other*

Home   Navigation   Audio   Phone

* Includes Contemporary Christian, Spanish Contemporary, Adult Hits, 80's Hits, Alternative, All News, Classical and Oldies.

ILLUSTRATION 6.2

Which Radio Formats Are Most Popular?

The most popular radio formats are country, news/talk, contemporary, classic hits and sports. Radio station owners use pre-packaged formats to attract a specific audience for advertisers—truck dealers might choose a country station, for example.

Radio Advertising Bureau Format Analysis, rab.com, 2014.

where listeners question on-the-air guests. Its typical audience is 35 years old and older. It is difficult for a small radio station to survive on news alone, so most of these stations are in big cities because of the continuing source of news stories. The news/talk category also includes live sports broadcasts, which are very popular because radio is a convenient way to follow live sports.

SPANISH. In the 1990s, Spanish-language stations were the fastest-growing radio format in urban areas, as radio owners targeted the nation's expanding Latino population, but the number of Spanish-language formats recently stabilized. Spanish-language radio usually features news, music and talk. Many Spanish-language stations are AM stations that recently have been converted from less-profitable formats.

ADULT CONTEMPORARY. This program format includes adult rock and light rock music from the 1970s to today and aims to reach 25- to 40-year-olds in all types of markets.

CONTEMPORARY HITS/TOP 40. Playing songs on *Billboard*'s current hits list, a Top-40 station closely follows trends among listeners, especially teenagers.

The most popular radio formats are country music, news/talk and pop contemporary music. However, although news/talk radio is very popular in Los Angeles, the most-listened-to radio station in the L.A. area is a Spanish-language station. Its popularity in an area with an expanding Latino population shows how cultural changes in urban areas can affect the economics of local radio.

Stations also can divide traditional formats into subcategories: Adult Contemporary has split further into classic rock and classic hits; some Spanish-language stations play only love songs. The use of prepackaged program formats means that a station can specialize its programming simply by what it chooses to play.

Most stations operate without any disc jockeys or limit personality programming to morning and evening drive-time. At these stations, engineers and announcers carry the programming. Today, radio networks, which once dominated radio programming, mainly exist to provide national news to their affiliates.

Station managers can program their own stations, mixing local news, music and announcements. Stations also can get programming from satellite program services. Satellites make program distribution easier, and satellite networks provide original, up-to-date programming without a large local staff.

Audience Divides into Smaller Segments

Another significant trend in radio is the move toward more segmentation of the audience, similar to the targeting of audiences in the magazine industry. Identifying a specific audience segment and programming for it is called ***narrowcasting***.

"With narrowcasting, advertising efficiency goes way up as overall costs go down. . . . We are approaching the unstated goal of all radio programmers: to create a station aimed so perfectly that the listener will no longer have to wait, ever, for the song that he wants to hear," says radio historian Eric Zorn.

Competition Revives Payola

As radio technology grows more complex and companies test new formats and different program delivery systems, the competition for your ear expands the choices that advertisers can make to reach you. However, as the competition among stations intensifies, some stations look for profits from a familiar but unethical source.

In 2005, New York's Attorney General Eliot Spitzer announced he was investigating the four major music companies to examine their practice of paying independent promoters to influence which songs the stations played on the air. The practice often was criticized as a way for stations to get around laws prohibiting payola that date from the 1960s. Some record labels paid individual stations as much as $100,000 to help promote their songs, Spitzer said. Other companies gave the stations luxury travel for station employees or gifts to use in station giveaways.

"To disguise a payoff to a radio programmer at KHTS in San Diego, Epic Records called a flat-screen television a 'contest giveaway,'" reported *The New York Times*. "Epic . . . used the same gambit in delivering a laptop computer to the program director of WRHT in Greenville, N.C.—who also received PlayStation 2 games and an out-of-town trip with his girlfriend."

After more payoffs like these were uncovered, Sony agreed to a $10 million settlement and fired the top promotion executive at its Epic label. Radio executives at some of the other corporations said they already had stopped paying independent promoters, but the attorney general said, "This is not a pretty picture; what we see is that payola is pervasive." In 2007, the stations agreed to pay an additional $12.5 million to the Federal Communications Commission to settle the complaints.

Narrowcasting   Segmenting the radio audience.

Digital Audio Delivers Internet and Satellite Radio

A recent technology known as **digital audio broadcast** (DAB) eliminates all the static and hiss of current broadcast signals and means infinite program choices for consumers as all digital radio signals share the same delivery system. Today digital stations send their digital signals over the Internet as well as over the air.

SATELLITE RADIO. Today **satellite radio** offers more than 140 channels of varied music and talk, with limited advertising on some stations and no advertising on others. For a subscription fee, two companies—Sirius Satellite Radio (based in New York) and XM (based in Washington)—began offering the service in 2001.

Satellite radio service required a special satellite radio receiver. In 2002, General Motors began offering satellite radios as a factory-installed option on some models. Ford and Daimler-Chrysler began offering the feature in 2003. New-car buyers bundled the subscription fee with their automobile financing.

> **Digital Audio Broadcast** A new form of audio transmission that eliminates all static and makes more program choices possible.
>
> **Satellite Radio** Radio transmission by satellite, with or without advertising, available by subscription.

IMPACT

Convergence

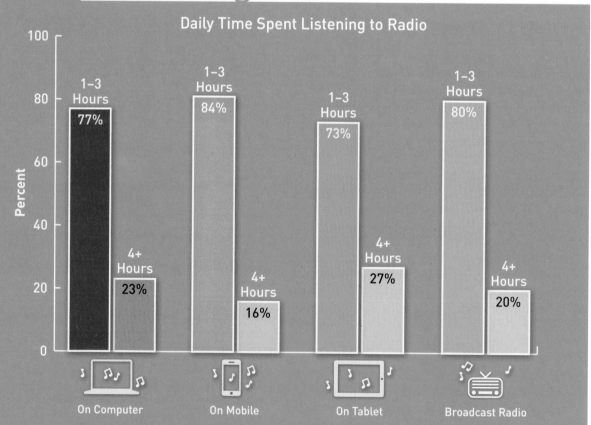

Daily Time Spent Listening to Radio

On Computer: 1–3 Hours 77%, 4+ Hours 23%
On Mobile: 1–3 Hours 84%, 4+ Hours 16%
On Tablet: 1–3 Hours 73%, 4+ Hours 27%
Broadcast Radio: 1–3 Hours 80%, 4+ Hours 20%

ILLUSTRATION 6.3

Radio Listening Goes Digital and Mobile

A radio station's audience originally was limited to the reach of the station's broadcast tower. Today Internet radio means a station's reach is global, so that a station in California can reach a listener in New York, for example, or Paris. And streaming radio, such as Pandora and iHeartRadio, now is available across all digital devices. According to industry estimates, regular radio listeners access radio through a variety of delivery systems.

"Digital Audio Usage Trends: A Highly Engaged Listenership," Internet Advertising Bureau, Radio Advertising Bureau, Parks Associates White Paper, rab.com.

IMPACT

Convergence

Pandora Radio Opens Listener Data to Let Musicians Target Fans

Bloomberg News

Pandora, the world's largest Internet radio service, is giving musicians free access to the data it stores about their biggest fans.

Pandora already uses the listener data for advertising purposes. It has helped political candidates decide where to advertise for the upcoming election.

Starting [on October 22, 2014], the more than 125,000 artists on Pandora will be able to view detailed information about their songs' popularity, breakdowns of the audience based on age and gender, and a map that shows where listeners are located. The data can be used to plan tours and set lists and better target fans, Pandora said in a blog post.

"We hope to make the day in and day out easier for artists by eliminating the guesswork," Pandora founder Tim Westergren wrote on the blog. "Our ultimate goal is to help artists across the spectrum build and maintain their careers."

Bloomberg/Getty Images

In 2014, Pandora Internet Radio announced that the radio service will be interactive so artists can track their songs' popularity. By 2015, car manufacturers offered Pandora's streaming service in 30 percent of the nation's new cars.

Pandora, which has more than 76 million active users, has amassed a trove of information over the past nine years. It wants to use that data to improve its contentious relationship with the music industry, which has long sought more money from the Oakland, California-based company.

The company has reached agreements to license music from rights management groups BMG and Merlin, which collect fees on behalf of artists. The company said in those deals it would share its data with musicians.

With the Artist Marketing Platform, musicians can log in and find out how many people are listening to their songs, how many people have created a new station based on a song and how many listeners they have in total.

The data can help artists decide where to stop on a tour, decide what songs to play and pick their next single, Mr. Westergren wrote.

"Pandora Opens Listener Data to Let Musicians Target Fans," *Bloomberg News*, October 22, 2014, adage.com.

By 2005, XM boasted 4 million subscribers, and in 2008, the Justice Department approved the merger of XM and Sirius, which became SiriusXM. Today, about 70 percent of the nation's cars are equipped to receive satellite radio.

INTERNET RADIO. The majority of U.S. radio stations today send their programming over the Internet. The Internet offers unlimited possibilities for radio to be distributed free beyond the bounds of a local radio audience, and people in the United States can easily hear overseas stations, such as the **BBC** (British Broadcasting Corporation), as well as stations based in the United States but outside their local area. (See **Illustration 6.3, Impact/Convergence**: "Radio Listening Goes Digital and Mobile," p. 118.)

BBC   British Broadcasting Corporation.

10/8

AFTER LISTENING TO NPR, THIS JELLY DONUT TASTES MORE LIKE A MULTI-GRAIN BAGEL.

STAHLER

©Jeff Stahler/Distributed by Universal Uclick for UFS via CartoonStock.com

Jeff Stahler/CartoonStock

The streaming Internet radio service Pandora, launched in 2005, allows users to select the programs and music they want to hear, free and by subscription. In 2015, Pandora moved into cars and is now available in 30 percent of new cars sold in the U.S.

Other streaming services, such as Rhapsody and Spotify, have followed, and in 2013 Apple launched iTunes Radio. iHeart Radio also delivers programming from the group of broadcast stations owned by iHeart Radio Inc. (formerly Clear Channel) on the Internet, which gives listeners access to live local radio broadcast programming, including commercials and announcers. Each service has a different revenue model. Some are available free and supported by advertising; others require subscriptions.

Streaming Splits Radio Industry Income

The more stations and digital radio services (such as satellite and Internet radio) that are available for customers,

the harder every station and delivery service must compete for advertising. This means less revenue for each station because each station's potential audience becomes smaller.

Streaming Internet radio changes the entire revenue equation for the radio industry. Consumers can pay subscription fees to hear radio on satellite—some without commercials—and go to the Internet for access to new free channels they couldn't hear before, offering listener-specific programming and interactivity. (See **Impact/ Convergence**, "Pandora Radio Opens Listener Data to Let Musicians Target Fans," p. 119.)

Meanwhile, broadcast radio is trying to stay afloat using the same commercial model that has served the industry for nearly 100 years. In 2005, commercial radio introduced the concept of **HD radio**, hybrid digital technology that improves sound quality and also makes it possible for radio stations to transmit real-time, text-based information services along with their programming. HD radio can display song titles and artists' names, weather, news and traffic alerts as a digital readout accompanying the audio programming.

Because there has been very little consumer demand, the conversion to HD has been slow. However, by contrast, in September 2014, Pandora Radio announced that its Internet streaming service is now available in 30 percent of all new cars being built.

In the 1930s, radio learned how to compete with newspapers. In the 1950s, radio learned how to compete with television. Beginning in 2000, satellite and then Internet radio challenged the supremacy of broadcast radio as an advertising medium.

Convergence means that broadcast, satellite and Internet radio are available to consumers simultaneously wherever they listen—outdoors or indoors, in the car, at home or at the office. The choices consumers make over the next ten years about how they want to receive radio programming ultimately will determine whether the competition for listeners will lead to expansion or contraction of the radio business.

> **HD Radio** Hybrid digital technology that improves sound quality and makes it possible for radio stations to transmit real-time text messaging along with their programming.

REVIEW, ANALYZE, INVESTIGATE

CHAPTER 6

Radio Sounds Are Everywhere

- Radio transformed national politics and expanded Americans' access to popular, as well as classical, culture.
- Radio is a commercial medium, supported almost entirely by advertising.

Radio Takes a Technological Leap

- Radio history began with Samuel F. B. Morse's invention of the telegraph, first demonstrated in 1835.
- Alexander Graham Bell invented the telephone, demonstrated in 1876, and Heinrich Hertz first described radio waves in 1887.

Broadcasting Is Born

- Guglielmo Marconi's promotion of wireless radio wave transmission began in 1899 with the America's Cup race.
- Reginald Fessenden advanced wireless technology, but Lee de Forest called himself the father of radio because he invented the Audion tube to detect radio waves.
- David Sarnoff and William S. Paley made radio broadcasting a viable business in the U.S.

Federal Government Regulates the Airwaves

- The federal government intervened to regulate broadcasting almost as soon as it was invented.
- Early regulation separated the broadcast media from the print media, which are not regulated directly by the federal government.

Radio Audience Expands Quickly

- Three important developments for commercial radio were blanket licensing, commercial sponsorship and the Radio Act of 1927.
- Blanket licensing meant that radio owners could use recorded music inexpensively.
- Commercial sponsorship established the practice of advertisers underwriting the cost of American broadcasting.
- The Radio Act of 1927 established the concept that the government would regulate broadcasting "as a public convenience, interest or necessity requires."

- The Radio Act of 1927 is the foundation for all broadcast regulation in the United States, including the establishment of the Federal Communications Commission (FCC) in 1934.

Radio Grows into a Powerful Force

- In the 1930s, radio programming expanded to include comedy, music, serials, drama and news.
- Radio also indirectly created a collective national experience that had not existed before.
- Commercials gave advertisers access to an audience at home.

"The War of the Worlds" Challenges Radio's Credibility

- On Halloween Eve, October 30, 1938, *Mercury Theatre on the Air* broadcast "The War of the Worlds," a fictional radio drama that sounded to some listeners like a legitimate newscast and featured Martians landing in New Jersey.
- The "War of the Worlds" broadcast demonstrated the vulnerability of a captive broadcast audience.

Radio Networks Expand

- Originally, the three radio networks (NBC, CBS and ABC) provided most radio programming. Today, most stations use a variety of sources to program themselves.
- David Sarnoff launched NBC radio in 1927, William S. Paley started CBS radio in 1929 and Edward Noble bought NBC-Blue, which became ABC, in 1941.

Radio Adapts to Television

- Edwin H. Armstrong is responsible for the invention of FM radio. Today, FM stations are three times as popular as AM stations.
- Disc jockeys hosted music shows.
- Clock, car and transistor radios expanded radio's audience, but the role of radio changed with the advent of TV, which meant radio had to compete with visual entertainment and TV news.
- Gordon McLendon launched format radio in 1959.
- In the 1960s, Congress uncovered the unethical practice of payola in the radio industry. Recording companies were paying station disc jockeys to play their songs on the air.

Radio at Work

- Radio is a portable medium that can accompany almost every activity.
- Today the 10,800 broadcast radio stations in the United States are about evenly divided between AM and FM.
- There is one major public network, NPR. Most commercial stations are part of a group or a combo and use program services instead of doing original programming.
- The management structure at a radio station includes a general manager; a program manager; account executives; the traffic, production and engineering departments; and administration.

Congress Creates National Public Radio

- The federal government began funding National Public Radio in 1967, and NPR began broadcasting national programming in 1970.
- Today, NPR programs such as *Morning Edition* and *All Things Considered* still attract a very loyal audience, and public radio depends on private donations to survive.

Portability and Immediacy Help Radio Survive

- Radio is the best medium for quick news bulletins and the latest hits.
- Because it is an intimate medium, radio delivers a targeted audience to advertisers much better than TV.
- Radio is also portable—you can listen to it in your car and take it with you anywhere.

Telecommunications Act of 1996 Overhauls Radio

- The Telecommunications Act of 1996 was the first major overhaul of broadcast regulation since the FCC was established in 1934.
- The act removed the limit on the number of stations one company can own, and in each local market the number of stations one owner can hold depends on the size of the market.

Are Radio Ratings Accurate?

- Arbitron historically had been the primary ratings service for radio.
- Stations use ratings to set their rates for advertising.
- In November 2008, the Nielsen Company launched a radio ratings service in direct competition with Arbitron.

- In 2012, Nielsen bought Arbitron, leaving the broadcast industry with a single ratings service for radio and TV.

Radio Depends on Ready-Made Formats

- Formats systematize radio broadcasts.
- Stations use formats to target a specific type of radio listener and define the audience for advertisers.
- The most popular radio formats are country music and news/talk/sports.

Audience Divides into Smaller Segments

- A significant trend in radio today is the move toward more segmentation of the audience, similar to the division of audiences in the magazine industry.
- Identifying a specific audience segment and programming for it is called *narrowcasting*.

Competition Revives Payola

- Payola resurfaced in 2005 when New York's attorney general charged that the four major recording companies paid private promoters to get their songs on the air.
- Sony paid $10 million to settle the charges against it, and in 2007 the radio stations paid the FCC an additional $12.5 million.

Digital Audio Delivers Internet and Satellite Radio

- Digital audio broadcast, Internet radio and satellite radio mean more program choices for listeners.
- Today the majority of U.S. radio stations deliver programming over the Internet.
- Streaming Internet radio services, including Pandora, launched in 2005, and iHeart Radio offer radio programming free and by subscription.

Streaming Splits Radio Industry Income

- The addition of new sources for radio programming, such as satellite and Internet radio, are changing the economics of radio today.
- In 2005, commercial radio introduced the concept of HD radio, but there has been limited demand for it.
- Pandora announced in 2015 that 30 percent of all new cars were equipped to deliver Pandora Internet radio.

Key Terms

These terms are defined in the margins throughout this chapter and appear in alphabetical order with definitions in the Glossary, which begins on page 361.

Critical Questions

1. How did the Radio Act of 1912 set a precedent for American broadcasting?

2. How did the following developments in radio affect the industry? Why is each of them so important?

   a. Blanket licensing

   b. Commercial sponsorship

   c. Establishment of networks

   d. Format radio

3. Discuss the "War of the Worlds" broadcast and its effects upon its audience. How did it change people's perceptions of radio?

4. Discuss the ethics issues involved in the payola scandals.

5. List and explain three challenges facing the radio business today. If you were an Internet entrepreneur today, would you invest in radio? Why?

Working the Web

This list includes sites mentioned in the chapter and others to give you greater insight into the radio business.

The Broadcast Archive
oldradio.com

This is a site for radio historians, with an emphasis on radio technology. The site includes an archive of manuals and schematics, as well as historical narratives and biographies of people who worked in early broadcasting.

Canadian Broadcasting Corporation (CBC) Radio-Canada
cbc.ca/radio

The radio division of Canada's national public broadcasting system, the CBC was created in 1936 in response to concern about the growing U.S. influence in radio. Now encompassing television and new media services, the CBC has a mandate to provide a wide range of programming that is predominantly and distinctively Canadian. The Web site provides live radio streams from CBC Radio One (news and talk) and Radio 2 (jazz, blues and classical music), as well as program schedules, podcasts and forums. It also has links to CBC Radio 3 (rock, pop, hip-hop, electronica and alt-country music) and Sirius XM.

CBS Radio
cbsradio.com

As one of the largest U.S. major-market radio operators, CBS provides broadcast, digital and on-demand radio. In addition to operating 130 radio stations, it is home to more than 2 dozen professional sports franchises.

Friday Morning Quarterback (FMQB)
fmqb.com

Recently celebrating 40 years of serving the music and radio industries, FMQB is the self-proclaimed "premier destination

for music and radio industry professionals." The production division is renowned for its one-hour National Radio Series that features major artists premiering new music. FMQB features breaking radio industry and music news, a voice talent vault, music available for airplay, ratings and job information and industry links.

Inside Radio
insideradio.com

This radio industry publication features industry news, ratings and classifieds. *Inside Radio* also publishes *Who Owns What* (a weekly update on station ownership), *Radio Journal* (featuring FCC updates and technical news) and *The Radio Book* (a directory of radio stations in the United States and Canada).

National Public Radio
npr.org

NPR distributes and produces noncommercial news, talk and entertainment programs. Its more than 860 independently operated local stations mix national and local programming to fit the needs of their communities. Audio archives are available for a growing number of nationally produced shows.

Radio Advertising Bureau (RAB)
rab.com

The goal of the RAB, the promotional arm of the commercial radio industry, is to increase the use of radio advertising and develop the skills of radio marketing representatives.

Radio Lovers
radiolovers.com

Radiolovers.com offers hundreds of vintage radio shows online for free. Its goal is to bring the world of Old Time Radio to a new generation of listeners. Users can browse by show genre or search by title. The site includes a disclaimer stating that the creators believe all show copyrights have expired or never existed and that they will remove any recording that is shown to violate a copyright.

SiriusXM

siriusxm.com

SiriusXM offers 140 channels of satellite radio, including commercial-free music as well as sports, news and talk shows. Radios must be SiriusXM-ready to receive the SiriusXM signal, but the company also offers programming to mobile devices such as cell phones and tablets through the Internet.

TuneIn

tunein.com

TuneIn allows users to listen to music, sports and news on over 70,000 radio stations around the world via its Web site. Listeners can access more than 2 million programs, including podcasts, concerts and interviews.

Impact/Action Videos are concise news features on various topics created exclusively for *Media/Impact*. Find them in *Media/Impact*'s MindTap at cengagebrain.com.

MindTap® Log on to MindTap for *Media/Impact* to access a variety of additional material—including learning objectives, chapter readings with high-lighting and note-taking, **Impact/Action Videos**, activities, and comprehension quizzes—that will guide you through this chapter.

MOVIES
DIGITIZING DREAMS

Chad Ress/The New York Times/Redux

Although many American movies today are produced overseas, visitors still flock to Hollywood to be near their favorite stars—even if it's just to stand on a cement star in the sidewalk showcasing the star's name.

What's Ahead?

- Movies Mirror the Culture
- Inventors Capture Motion on Film
- Filmmakers Turn Novelty into Art
- Studio System and Independent Moviemakers Flourish
- Movies Become Big Business
- Big Five Studios Dominate
- Labor Unions Organize Movie Workers
- Movies Glitter During the Golden Age
- Congress and the Courts Change Hollywood
- Movies Lose Their
- Audience to Television
- Movies and Money Today
- Movies at Work
- Digital Technology Drives the Business
- Emerging Markets and Mergers Bring New Opportunities

"Some pictures make a lot of money, and a lot of pictures make no money."

—DAVID V. PICKER, MOVIE ANALYST

The movie industry has been called "an industry based on dreams" because it is a business founded on an imaginative, creative medium. Because the publicity surrounding movie celebrities captures a great deal of attention, it would be easy to assume the movie industry is one of the most profitable media businesses. So it often surprises people to learn that most movies lose money because movies are expensive to make and only a few movies each year become blockbusters.

Movies and movie stars thrive on public attention because the size of the audience has a direct effect on whether a movie succeeds. Investors, therefore, often favor "bankable" talent that brings fans to a movie, rather than new, untested talent. But even movies featuring established talent often fail. Every movie is a gamble because no one in the movie industry can accurately predict which movies will make a profit.

Movies Mirror the Culture

Perhaps more than any other medium, movies mirror the society that creates them. Some movies offer an underlying political message. Other movies reflect changing social values. Still other movies are just good entertainment. And all movies need an audience to succeed.

Like other media industries, the movie business has had to adapt to changing technology. Before the invention of television, movies were the nation's primary form of visual entertainment. The current use of special effects and 3-D is one way the movie industry tries to compete with television for your attention and dollars. But special effects and 3-D don't fit most movies, and they are very expensive. Today, as always, filmmakers are constantly

searching for that special blend of a good story and the right cast to grab an audience's attention.

Inventors Capture Motion on Film

Movies were invented at a time when American industry welcomed any new gadget, and inventors wildly sought patents for appliances and electrical devices. The motion picture camera and projector were two of the Industrial Revolution's early gadgets.

Early Inventors Nurture the Movie Industry

Movies were not the invention of one person. First, a device to photograph moving objects had to be invented, followed by a device to project those pictures. This process involved six people: Étienne-Jules Marey, Eadweard Muybridge, Thomas Edison, William K. L. Dickson and Auguste and Louis Lumière.

Marey and Muybridge

Étienne-Jules Marey, a scientist working in Paris, sought to record an animal's movement by individual actions— one at a time—to compare one animal to another. He charted a horse's movements on graphs and published the information in a book, *Animal Mechanism*.

Unknown to Marey, photographer Eadweard Muybridge was hired by railroad millionaire and horse breeder Leland Stanford to settle a $25,000 bet. Stanford had bet that during a gallop, all four of a horse's feet simultaneously leave the ground. In 1877, Muybridge and Stanford built a special track in Palo Alto, Calif., with 12 cameras

TimeFrame
1877–Today

Eadweard Muybridge/Corbis

1877 Eadweard Muybridge catches motion on film when he uses 12 cameras to photograph a horse's movements for Leland Stanford in Palo Alto, Calif.

1915 Director D. W. Griffith introduces the concept of the movie spectacular with *The Birth of a Nation*.

1916 Brothers Noble and George Johnson launch Lincoln Films, the first company to produce movies called "race films," serious narrative movies for African American audiences.

1919 Oscar Micheaux releases *Within Our Gates*, a response to D. W. Griffith's controversial, anti-black epic *The Birth of a Nation*.

1927 *The Jazz Singer*, the first feature-length motion picture with sound, opens in New York City.

1928 Walt Disney releases *Steamboat Willie* as the "first animated sound cartoon."

1930 The Motion Picture Producers and Distributors Association adopts a production code to control movie content.

1947 The House Un-American Activities Committee calls The Hollywood Ten to testify.

1948 The U.S. Supreme Court breaks up the large studios' control of Hollywood by deciding in the case of *United States v. Paramount Pictures, Inc., et al.* that the studios are a monopoly.

1966 The Motion Picture Association of America introduces a voluntary content-ratings system for the movies.

1994 Steven Spielberg, Jeffrey Katzenberg and David Geffen launch DreamWorks SKG, the first independent American movie studio created since United Artists.

2001 To attempt to stop movie piracy, the Motion Picture Association of America challenges the availability of recordable DVD technology, but eventually DVD-Rs reach the marketplace.

2006 DreamWorks is sold to Viacom Inc., leaving the United States without a major independent movie studio.

2011 3-D movies begin to generate higher revenue for the industry.

2013 Disney buys Lucasfilm, including all rights to the Star Wars series, for $40.5 billion.

2015 Netflix announces that it has more than 60 million subscribers, more than 40 million of them in the U.S.

Today Movie theaters collect about 1 billion tickets a year, but more people see movies on video and by streaming than in theaters. 3-D movies lose their luster, but the market for American movies continues to grow overseas.

DreamWorks Animation SKG

AP Images/Paul Sakuma

STAR WARS™

DIGITAL MOVIE COLLECTION

AP Images/Uncredited

Eadweard Muybridge/Time & Life Pictures/Getty Images

This series of images photographed by Eadweard Muybridge showed that a horse's hooves all leave the ground at a full gallop. They were produced to win a $25,000 bet, but eventually the photographic method Muybridge used led to the development of the first motion picture camera.

inside. Edison named this device the *kinetoscope.* On April 11, 1894, America's first kinetoscope parlor opened in New York City. For 25 cents, people could see 10 different 90-second black-and-white films, including *Trapeze, Horse Shoeing, Wrestlers* and *Roosters.*

Auguste and Louis Lumière

In France, the Lumière brothers, Auguste and Louis, developed an improved camera and a projector that could show film on a large screen. The first public Lumière showing was on December 28, 1895: 10 short subjects with such riveting titles as *Lunch Hour at the Lumière Factory,* which showed workers leaving the building, and *Arrival of a Train at a Station.* Admission was 1 franc, and the Lumières collected 35 francs.

precisely placed to take pictures of a horse as it moved around the track. The horse tripped a series of equidistant wires as it ran, which in turn tripped the cameras' shutters. Stanford won his $25,000—one photograph showed that all four of the horse's feet did leave the ground—and the photographic series provided an excellent study of motion.

Muybridge expanded to 24 cameras, photographed other animals and then took pictures of people moving. He traveled throughout Europe showing his photographs. Eventually, Muybridge and Marey met. In 1882, Marey perfected a photographic gun camera that could take 12 photographs on one plate—the first motion picture camera.

Thomas Edison

Thomas Edison bought some of Muybridge's pictures in 1888 and showed them to his assistant, William K. L. Dickson. Edison then met with Marey in Europe, where Marey had invented a projector that showed pictures on a continuous strip of film, but the filmstrip moved unevenly across the projector lens, so the pictures jumped.

William K. L. Dickson

Back in America, Dickson perforated the edges of the film so that, as the film moved through the camera, sprockets inside the camera grabbed the perforations and locked the film in place, minimizing the jumps.

Dickson looped the strip over a lamp and a magnifying lens in a box 2 feet wide and 4 feet tall. The box stood on the floor with a peephole in the top so people could look

Edison Launches American Movies

Four months after the Lumière premiere in France, Edison organized the first American motion picture premiere with an improved camera developed by independent inventor Thomas Armat. Edison dubbed the new machine the *Vitascope,* and America's first public showing of the motion picture was on April 23, 1896, at Koster and Bial's theater in New York. Edison sat in a box seat, and Armat ran the projector from the balcony.

At first, movies were a sideshow. Penny-arcade owners showed movies behind a black screen at the rear of the arcade for an extra nickel. But soon the movies were more popular than the rest of the attractions, and the arcades were renamed *nickel*odeons. In 1900, there were more than 600 nickelodeons in New York City, with more than 300,000 daily admissions. Each show lasted about 20 minutes. The programs ran from noon until late evening, and many theaters blared music outside to bring in business.

By 1907, Edison had contracted with most of the nation's movie producers, as well as the Lumière brothers and the innovative French producer Georges Méliès, to provide movies for the theaters. Licensed Edison theaters used licensed Edison projectors and rented Edison's licensed movies, many of which Edison produced at his own studio. The important exception to Edison's licensing plan was his rival, the American Mutoscope and Biograph Company, commonly called Biograph.

Biograph manufactured a better motion picture camera than Edison's, and Edison was losing business. In 1908, Biograph signed an agreement with Edison, forming the

Motion Picture Patents Company (MPPC), which standardized movie cameras.

Filmmakers Turn Novelty into Art

All the early films were black-and-white silent movies. Sound did not come to the movies until the 1920s, and color experiments did not begin until the 1930s. Two innovative filmmakers are credited with turning the novelty of movies into art: Georges Méliès and Edwin S. Porter.

Georges Méliès

French filmmaker Georges Méliès added fantasy to the movies. Before Méliès, moviemakers photographed theatrical scenes or events from everyday life. But Méliès, who had been a magician and a caricaturist before he became a filmmaker, used camera tricks to make people disappear and reappear and to make characters grow and then shrink.

His 1902 film, *A Trip to the Moon*, was the first outerspace movie adventure, complete with fantasy creatures. When his films, which became known as *trick films*, were shown in the United States, American moviemakers stole his ideas.

Georges Méliès created fanciful creatures for his 1902 film, *A Trip to the Moon*, introducing fantasy to motion pictures. In a scene from the movie, an explorer lands on the moon landscape, hitting the moon in the eye.

Edwin S. Porter

Edison hired projectionist/electrician Edwin S. Porter in 1899, and in the next decade Porter became America's most important filmmaker. Until Porter, most American films were trick films or short documentary-style movies that showed newsworthy events (although some filmmakers used sultry subjects in movies such as *Pajama Girl* and *Corset Girl* to cater to men, who were the movies' biggest customers). In 1903, Porter produced *The Great Train Robbery*, an action movie with bandits attacking a speeding train.

Instead of using a single location like most other moviemakers, Porter shot 12 different scenes. He also introduced the use of dissolves between shots, instead of abrupt splices. Porter's film techniques—action and changing locations—foreshadowed the classic storytelling tradition of American movies.

Studio System and Independent Moviemakers Flourish

None of the actors in the early movies received screen credit, but then fans began to write letters addressed to "The Biograph Girl," who was Biograph star Florence Lawrence. In 1909, Carl Laemmle formed an independent production company, stole Lawrence from Biograph and gave her screen credit. She became America's first movie star.

Biograph was the first company to make movies using the studio system. The *studio system* meant that a studio hired a stable of stars and production people who were paid a regular salary. These people signed contracts with that studio and could not work for any other studio without their employer's permission.

In 1910, Laemmle lured Mary Pickford away from Biograph by doubling her salary. He discovered, says film scholar Robert Sklar, "that stars sold pictures as nothing else could. As long as theaters changed their programs daily—and the practice persisted in neighborhood theaters and small towns until the early 1920s—building up audience recognition of star names was almost the only effective form of audience publicity." (Mary Pickford became one of the most influential women in early Hollywood and helped finance the independent studio United Artists. See page 131.)

The *star system*, which promoted popular movie personalities to lure audiences, was nurtured by the independents. This helped broaden the movies' appeal beyond their original working-class audience. Movie houses began

---

Studio System An early method of hiring a stable of salaried stars and production people under exclusive contracts to a specific studio.

Star System Promoting popular movie personalities to lure audiences.

to open in the suburbs, and from 1908 to 1914, movie attendance doubled.

In 1915, the first real titan of the silent movies, director D. W. Griffith, introduced the concept of spectacular entertainment. Most early movies were two reels long, 25 minutes. Griffith expanded his movies to four reels and longer, pioneering the feature-length film. In his best-known epic, *The Birth of a Nation* (1915), the Southern-born Griffith presented a controversial view of the Civil War and Reconstruction, portraying racial stereotypes and touching on the subject of sexual intermingling of the races. The movie's cost—about $110,000—was five times more than any American film before that time.

With *The Birth of a Nation* and his subsequent epics, Griffith showed the potential that movies had as a mass medium that could gather large audiences. He also proved that people would pay more than a nickel or a dime to see a motion picture.

In 1916, brothers Noble and George Johnson launched the Lincoln Motion Picture Company, the first company to produce serious narrative movies for African American audiences, called "race films," which paved the way for African American film stars Paul Robeson and Josephine Baker.

Moviemakers like the Johnson brothers and Oscar Micheaux proved that movies produced for specialized audiences could succeed. From 1910 to 1950, filmmakers produced more than 500 movies directed at African American audiences. (See **Impact/Profile**, "Lighting Up a Black Screen: Early 'Race Films' Pioneered the Art of Breaking Stereotypes," p. 131.)

By the 1920s, movies clearly had arrived as a popular, viable mass medium, moving from the crowded nickelodeon to respectability.

Movies Become Big Business

The movie business was changing quickly. Five important events in the 1920s transformed the movie industry:

1. The move to California

2. The adoption of block booking

3. The formation of United Artists

4. The industry's efforts at self-regulation

5. The introduction of sound

Studios Move to Hollywood

During the first decade of the 20th century, the major movie companies were based in New York, the stage theater capital. Film companies sometimes traveled to Florida or Cuba to chase the sunshine because it was easier to build sets outdoors to take advantage of the light, but soon they found a new home in California.

In 1903, Harry Chandler, who owned the *Los Angeles Times*, also owned a lot of Los Angeles real estate. He and his friends courted the movie business, offering cheap land; moderate, predictable weather; and inexpensive labor. Soon the moviemakers moved to a place called "Hollywood."

Distributors Insist on Block Booking

People who owned theater chains then decided to make movies, and moviemakers discovered they could make more money if they owned theaters, so production companies built theaters to show their own pictures. The connection between production, distribution and exhibition grew, led by Paramount's Adolph Zukor, who devised a system called *block booking*.

Block booking meant a company, such as Paramount, would sign up one of its licensed theaters for as many as 104 pictures at a time. The movie package contained a few "name" pictures with stars, but the majority of the movies in the block were lightweight features with no stars. Because movie bills changed twice a week, the exhibitors were desperate for something to put on the screen. Often, without knowing which movies they were getting in the block, exhibitors accepted the package and paid the distributor's price.

United Artists Champions the Independents

In 1919, the nation's five biggest movie names—cowboy star William S. Hart, Mary Pickford, Charlie Chaplin, Douglas Fairbanks and D. W. Griffith—rebelled against the strict studio system of distribution and formed their own studio. Eventually Hart withdrew from the agreement, but the remaining partners formed a company called United Artists (UA). They eliminated block booking and became a distributor for independently produced pictures, including their own.

In its first six years, UA delivered many movies that today still are considered classics, including *The Mark of Zorro*, *The Three Musketeers*, *Robin Hood* and *The Gold Rush*. These movies succeeded even though UA worked outside the traditional studio system, proving that it was possible to distribute films to audiences without using a major studio.

Block Booking The practice of requiring theaters to take a package of movies instead of showing the movies individually.

IMPACT

Profile

Lighting Up a Black Screen: Early "Race Films" Pioneered the Art of Breaking Stereotypes

By Teresa Moore

The halcyon age for African Americans on the big screen was the period between 1910 and 1950 when blacks—and some whites— produced more than 500 "race movies," showcasing all-black casts in a variety of genres, including Westerns, mysteries, romances and melodramas.

In the naturally sepia-toned world of race movies, African Americans could—and did—do just about anything.

Lena Horne shone as the *Bronze Venus*. Crooner Herb Jeffries was the *Bronze Buckaroo*. There were black millionaires and black detectives, black sweethearts and socialites. Black heroines who swooned—tender, wilting ladies who never swept a broom or donned a do-rag. Black heroes who could be gentle and genteel, tough and smart. Black villains of both genders, out to separate black damsels and grandees from their virtue or fortune.

Race movies were so called because they were made for black Southern audiences barred from white-owned theaters. The films were shown either in the black-owned movie palaces of the urban North and Midwest or in "midnight rambles"—special midnight-to-2 a.m. screenings in rented halls or segregated theaters of the South.

Under segregation, the moviemakers created an onscreen

Oscar Micheaux (center) was a pioneering African American filmmaker who produced "race movies," showing all–African American casts in a variety of roles. Micheaux's *Within Our Gates* was designed to counter the racism in D. W. Griffith's epic *The Birth of a Nation*.

The New York Public Library/Art Resource, NY

world that not only reflected the accomplishments of the rising black middle class but also transformed reality into a realm where race was no impediment to love, power or success. . . .

The leading directors and producers—Oscar Micheaux and the brother team of Noble and George Johnson—wanted to uplift African Americans. Besides presenting black images more appealing to black audiences, they also offered black perspectives on racial injustice.

"In some ways these filmmakers were more free because they were making the movies for themselves," said Michael Thompson, a professor of African American history at Stanford. In *Within Our Gates*, Micheaux's filmic response to

D. W. Griffith's controversial, anti-black epic *The Birth of a Nation*, a white man tries to rape a young black woman—stopping only when he recognizes her as his illegitimate daughter.

According to *Midnight Ramble*, Bestor Cram and Pearl Bowser's 1994 documentary on the black film industry, that industry developed alongside—and initially in reaction against—the white film industry. Virtually shut out of Hollywood, where a handful of black actors were usually cast as Indians and in various "ethnic" or "exotic" roles while whites in blackface cavorted onscreen, African Americans formed their own production companies, making hundreds of features and shorts.

(Left) Mary Pickford, D. W. Griffith, Charlie Chaplin and Douglas Fairbanks (left to right) founded United Artists in 1919. (Right) In 1994, (left to right) Jeffrey Katzenberg, Steven Spielberg and David Geffen launched DreamWorks SKG, the first major independent movie studio created in the U.S. since United Artists. In 2006, the media conglomerate Viacom bought DreamWorks Animation, leaving the United States without a major independent studio (although Spielberg retained a partnership in the live-film division called DreamWorks SKG).

Moviemakers Use Self-Regulation to Respond to Scandals

In the 1920s, the movie industry faced two new crises: scandals involving movie stars and criticism that movie content was growing too provocative. As a result, the moviemakers decided to regulate themselves.

The star scandals began when comedian Roscoe "Fatty" Arbuckle hosted a marathon party in San Francisco over Labor Day weekend in 1921. As the party was ending, model Virginia Rappe was rushed to the hospital with stomach pains. She died at the hospital, and Arbuckle was charged with murder. Eventually the cause of death was listed as peritonitis from a ruptured bladder, and the murder charge was reduced to manslaughter. After three trials, two of which resulted in hung juries, Arbuckle was acquitted.

Then director William Desmond Taylor was found murdered in his home. Mabel Normand, a friend of Arbuckle's, was identified as the last person to see Taylor alive. Eventually Normand was cleared, but then it was revealed that "Taylor" was not the director's real name, and there were suggestions he was involved in the drug business. Hollywood's moguls and businesspeople were shocked. The Catholic Legion of Decency announced a movie boycott. Quick to protect themselves, Los Angeles business leaders met and decided that Hollywood should police itself.

Los Angeles Times owner Harry Chandler worked with movie leaders to bring in Will Hays, a former postmaster general and Republican Party chairman, to respond to these and other scandals in the movie business. Hays' job was to lead a moral refurbishing of the industry. In March 1922, Hays became the first president of the Motion Picture Producers and Distributors Association (MPPDA), at a salary of $100,000 a year. A month later, even though Arbuckle

had been acquitted, Hays suspended all of Fatty Arbuckle's films, ruining Arbuckle's career.

Besides overseeing the stars' personal behavior, Hays decided that his office also should oversee movie content. The MPPDA, referred to as the Hays Office, wrote a code of conduct to govern the industry. In 1930, the MPPDA adopted a production code, which began with three general principles:

1. No picture shall be produced which will lower the moral standards of those who see it. Hence the sympathy of the audience shall never be thrown to the side of crime, wrongdoing, evil or sin.

2. Correct standards of life, subject only to the requirements of drama and entertainment, shall be presented.

3. Law, natural or human, shall not be ridiculed, nor shall sympathy be created for its violation.

The code then divided its rules into 12 categories of wrongdoing, including

▶ Murder: "The technique of murder must be presented in a way that will not inspire imitation."

▶ Sex: "Excessive and lustful kissing, lustful embraces, suggestive postures and gestures are not to be shown."

▶ Obscenity: "Obscenity in word, gesture, reference, song, joke, or by suggestion (even when likely to be understood only by part of the audience) is forbidden."

▶ Costumes: "Dancing costumes intended to permit undue exposure or indecent movements in the dance are forbidden."

An acceptable movie displayed a seal of approval in the titles at the beginning of the picture. Producers balked at the interference, but most of them, afraid of censorship from outside the industry, complied with the monitoring.

Although standards have relaxed, the practice of self-regulation of content still operates in the motion picture industry today in the form of the movie ratings system.

New Technology Brings the Talkies

By the mid-1920s, silent movies were an established part of American entertainment, but technology soon pushed the industry into an even more vibrant era—the era of the talkies. MPPDA President Will Hays was the first person to appear on screen in the public premiere of talking pictures on August 6, 1926, in New York City. Warner Bros. and Western Electric had developed the movie sound experiment, which consisted of seven short subjects, called *The Vitaphone Preludes*.

The Warner brothers—Sam, Harry, Jack and Albert—were ambitious, upstart businessmen who beat their competitors to sound movies. On October 6, 1927, *The Jazz Singer*, starring Al Jolson, opened at Warners' Theatre in New York and was the first feature-length motion picture with sound. The movie was not an all-talkie but instead contained two sections with synchronized sound.

" IS IT ANY GOOD ? "

Jorodo/cartoonstock

The success of *The Jazz Singer* convinced Warners competitors to change over to sound. By July 1, 1930, 22 percent of theaters still showed silent films. By 1933, less than 1 percent of the movies shown in theaters were silents.

Big Five Studios Dominate

In the 1930s, the Big Five—Warner Bros., Metro-Goldwyn-Mayer, Paramount, RKO and Twentieth Century Fox—dominated the movie business, collecting more than two-thirds of the nation's box office receipts. United Artists remained solely a distribution company for independent producers.

The Big Five all were vertically integrated: They produced movies, distributed them worldwide and owned theater chains, which guaranteed their pictures a showing. The studios maintained stables of stars, directors, producers, writers and technical staff. Film scholar Tino Balio calls the studios at this point in their history a "mature oligopoly"—a group of companies with so much control over an industry that any change in one of the companies directly affected the future of the industry.

In the 1930s, Walt Disney was the only major successful Hollywood newcomer. He had released *Steamboat Willie* as "the first animated sound cartoon" in 1928. Disney was 26 years old, and he had sold his car to finance the cartoon's soundtrack. After some more short-animated-feature successes, Disney announced in 1934 that his studio would produce its first feature-length animated film, *Snow White and the Seven Dwarfs*. The film eventually cost Disney $2.25 million, more than MGM usually spent on a good musical. *Snow White* premiered December 21, 1937, at the Cathay Circle Theater in Hollywood and became an instant hit, the foundation for Disney's movie empire.

Box office receipts sagged in the 1930s as the Depression settled into every aspect of America's economy. Facing bankruptcy, several theaters tried to buoy their profits by adding bingo games and cut-rate admissions. The one innovation that survived the 1930s was the double feature: two movies for the price of one.

Labor Unions Organize Movie Workers

The Depression introduced another factor into motion picture budgets: labor unions. Before the 1930s, most aspects of the movie business were not governed by union agreements. But in 1937, the National Labor Relations Board held an election that designated the Screen Actors Guild to bargain for wages, working conditions and overtime.

The Screen Writers Guild was certified in 1938 and the Screen Directors Guild soon afterward. Unionization limited the studios' power over the people who worked for them, and by the late 1930s all the major studios had

Bettmann/Corbis

The late 1930s and early 1940s have been called the Golden Age of Movies. On December 1, 1939, Carole Lombard and Clark Gable arrive at Loew's Grand Theater in Atlanta for the premiere of *Gone with the Wind*, an MGM hit.

signed union agreements. Union agreements also introduced professionalism into the movie business. Then the Depression ended, and the studios once again prospered.

Movies Glitter During the Golden Age

With glamorous stars and exciting screenplays, supported by an eager pool of gifted directors, producers and technical talent, plus an insatiable audience, the movie industry reached its apex in the late 1930s and early 1940s. The most successful studio in Hollywood was MGM, which attracted the best writers, directors and actors. MGM capitalized on its star lineup with movies such as *The Great Ziegfeld*, *The Wizard of Oz* and *Gone with the Wind*.

Not only did *Gone with the Wind*'s phenomenal success demonstrate the epic stories that movies could tell, but the movie also was a technological breakthrough, with its magnificent use of color. The movie business was so profitable that even MGM's dominance didn't scare away the competition. Many other studios, such as RKO, created enduring stars, such as Fred Astaire and Ginger Rogers, in films with light plots but stunning dance production numbers.

Congress and the Courts Change Hollywood

Before television arrived throughout the country in 1948, two other events of the late 1940s helped

reverse the prosperous movie bonanza that began in the mid-1930s:

1. The hearings of the House Un-American Activities Committee (HUAC)

2. The 1948 antitrust decision of the U.S. Supreme Court in *United States v. Paramount Pictures, Inc., et al.*

The House Un-American Activities Committee

In October 1947, America was entering the Cold War, an era in which many public officials, government employees and private citizens seemed preoccupied with the threat of Communism and people identified as "subversives." The House of Representatives Committee on Un-American Activities, chaired by J. Parnell Thomas, summoned ten "unfriendly" witnesses from Hollywood to testify about their Communist connections. (Unfriendly witnesses were people the committee classified as having participated at some time in the past in "un-American activities." This usually meant that the witness had been a member of a left-wing organization in the decade before World War II.) These eight screenwriters and two directors came to be known as the Hollywood Ten.

The Ten's original strategy was to appear before the committee as a group and avoid answering the direct

AP Images/Ed Widdis

The Hollywood Ten, targeted in 1947 by the House Un-American Activities Committee, eventually went to jail for refusing to answer questions before the committee about their political beliefs. On June 8, 1950, about 500 people at the Los Angeles Airport showed support for Hollywood Ten screenwriter Dalton Trumbo (third from right, wearing glasses). Trumbo was leaving for Washington, D.C., to begin serving a jail term for contempt of Congress.

question "Are you now or have you ever been a member of the Communist Party?" Instead, the Ten tried to make statements that questioned the committee's authority to challenge their political beliefs. In a rancorous series of hearings, the committee rejected the Ten's testimony, and the witnesses found themselves facing trial for contempt. All of them were sentenced to jail, and some were fined. By the end of November 1947, all the Hollywood Ten had lost their jobs. Many more movie people would follow.

In an article for the *Hollywood Review*, Hollywood Ten member Adrian Scott reported that 214 movie employees eventually were **blacklisted**, which means that many studio owners refused to hire people who were suspected of taking part in "subversive" activities. The movie people who were not hired because of their political beliefs included 106 writers, 36 actors and 11 directors. This effectively gutted Hollywood of some of its best talent.

United States v. Paramount Pictures, Inc., et al.

The U.S. Justice Department began an antitrust suit against the studios in 1938. In 1940, the studios came to an agreement with the government, while admitting no guilt. They agreed to

1. Limit block booking to five films.
2. Stop **blind booking** (the practice of renting films to exhibitors without letting them see the films first).
3. Stop requiring theaters to rent short films as a condition of acquiring features.
4. Stop buying theaters.

After this agreement, the Justice Department dropped its suit with the stipulation that the department could reinstitute the suit again at any time.

By 1944, the government still was unhappy with studio control over the theaters, so it reactivated the suit. In 1948, *United States v. Paramount Pictures, Inc., et al.* reached the Supreme Court. Associate Justice William O. Douglas argued that although the 5 major studios—Paramount, Warner Bros., MGM-Loew's, RKO and Twentieth Century Fox—owned only 17 percent of all theaters in the United States, these studios held a *monopoly* over first-run exhibition in the large cities. The Supreme Court decided against Paramount, and by 1954 the 5 studios had given up ownership or control of all their theaters. Production and exhibition were now split; vertical integration was crumbling.

When the movie companies abandoned the exhibition business, banks grew reluctant to finance film projects because the companies could not guarantee an audience—on paper. Soon the studios decided to leave the production business to independents and became primarily distributors of other people's pictures. The result was the end of the studio system.

Movies Lose Their Audience to Television

In the 1950 Paramount movie *Sunset Boulevard*, aging silent screen star Norma Desmond (played by Gloria Swanson) romances an ambitious young screenwriter (played by William Holden) by promising him Hollywood connections.

> "You're Norma Desmond. You used to be in silent pictures. You used to be big," says the screenwriter.
>
> "I am big," says Desmond. "It's the pictures that got small."

Desmond could have been talking about the movie business itself, which got much smaller after 1948, when television began to offer home-delivered entertainment nationwide. The House hearings and the consent decrees in the *Paramount* case telegraphed change in the movie business, but television truly transformed Hollywood forever. In the 1950s, the number of television sets people owned grew by 400 percent, while the number of people who went to the movies fell by 45 percent.

Theaters tried to make up for the loss by raising their admission prices, but more than 4,000 theaters closed between 1946 and 1956. Attendance has leveled off or risen briefly a few times since the 1950s, but the trend of declining movie attendance continues today. The movie industry has tried several methods to counteract this downward trend.

Stunned by television's popularity, the movie business tried technological gimmicks in the 1950s to lure its audience back. First came 3-D movies, using special effects to create the illusion of three-dimensional action. To watch special effects like rocks flying off the screen, people had to wear special plastic glasses. The novelty was fun at first, but the 3-D movie plots were weak, and most people didn't come back to see a second 3-D movie.

Wide-Screen and 3-D Movies

Next came Cinerama, CinemaScope, VistaVision and Panavision—wide-screen color movies with stereophonic

---

Blacklisting   Studio owners' refusal to hire someone who was suspected of taking part in subversive activities.

Blind Booking   The practice of renting films to exhibitors without letting them see the films first.

In the 1950s, the movie business used technological gimmicks, such as very primitive 3-D, to try to compete with television. In 2011, faced with declining audiences because of the Internet and streaming, the movie studios launched an updated version of 3-D, but 3-D movies proved too expensive to produce, so the fad again began to fade.

sound. All these techniques tried to give the audience a "you are there" feeling that they couldn't get from television, but eventually these specialty movies proved too expensive.

Changes in Censorship

On May 26, 1952, the Supreme Court announced in *Burstyn v. Wilson* that motion pictures were "a significant medium for the communication of ideas," designed "to entertain as well as to inform." The effect of this decision was to protect movies under the First Amendment, which meant fewer legal restrictions on what movies could show.

In 1953, Otto Preminger challenged the movies' self-regulating agency, the Production Code Administration (PCA). United Artists agreed to release Preminger's movie *The Moon Is Blue*, even though the PCA denied the movie a certificate of approval because it contained such risqué words as *virgin* and *mistress*. Then, in 1956, United Artists released Preminger's *Man with the Golden Arm*, a film about drug addiction, and the PCA restrictions were forever broken.

Encouraged by the *Burstyn* decision and the United Artists test, moviemakers tried sex and violence to lure audiences away from television. In the 1950s, Marilyn Monroe and Jayne Mansfield offered generously proportioned examples of the new trend. Foreign films also became popular because some of them offered explicit dialogue and love scenes.

Spectaculars

One by one, the studio moguls retired, and they were replaced by a new generation of moviemakers. This second generation "inherited a situation where fewer and fewer pictures were being made, and fewer still made

money," says film historian Robert Sklar, "but those that captured the box office earned enormous sums. It was as if the rules of baseball had been changed so that the only hit that mattered was a home run."

Spectaculars like *The Sound of Music* (1965) and *The Godfather* (1971) and its sequels rewarded the rush for big money. But then a few majestic flops taught the studios that nothing demolishes a studio's profits like one big movie bomb.

In the 1960s, moviemakers tried to compete with television by producing spectaculars, such as *The Sound of Music*. On March 10, 1965, *The Sound of Music* star Julie Andrews (center) appeared with several cast members at the film's premiere in Hollywood. The film, still being shown today around the world, celebrated its 50th anniversary in 2015.

Movie Ratings

In 1966, Jack Valenti, former adviser to President Lyndon Johnson, became president of the Motion Picture Producers Association (MPPA) and renamed it the Motion Picture Association of America (MPAA). The MPAA protects the business interests of movie companies by lobbying Congress about issues that are important to the movie business, such as freedom from government censorship. One of Valenti's first acts was to respond to continuing public criticism about shocking movie content. (Valenti ran the MPAA until his retirement in 2004.)

The MPAA began a rating system of self-regulation modeled on Great Britain's: G for general audiences, M (later changed to PG) for mature audiences, R for restricted (people under 17 admitted only with an adult), and X for no one under 18 admitted. The PG-13 rating—special parental guidance advised for children younger than 13—was added, and the X rating was changed to NC-17. Standards for the R rating have eased since the ratings system began, further blurring the effectiveness of the ratings system for the public.

Movies and Money Today

In today's system of moviemaking, each of the major studios (such as Disney, Viacom/Paramount and Sony Pictures Entertainment) usually makes fewer than 20 movies a year. The rest come from independent producers, with production, investment, distribution and exhibition each handled by different companies. Most of these independently produced movies are distributed by one of the large studios.

In an attempt to counteract the strong influence of the traditional movie studios, Steven Spielberg, Jeffrey Katzenberg and David Geffen launched a company called DreamWorks SKG (their initials—S, K, G) in 1994. DreamWorks was the first major independent movie studio created in America since United Artists was formed in 1919. The company survived as an independent studio for 12 years, but in 2006 DreamWorks was sold to Viacom, leaving the United States without a major independent movie studio.

In 2004, the animation division, DreamWorks Animation, was spun off as a publicly traded company, with Katzenberg as CEO. Viacom/Paramount kept the live-action portion of the studio. Geffen left the live-action studio in 2008, and in 2009, Spielberg, with two partners, bought back the live-action part of the original studio from Paramount.

So today there is DreamWorks Animation, a publicly traded company that produces only animated features, and Spielberg and his partners own DreamWorks Studios to produce live-action movies, such as *War Horse* (2011) and *Lincoln* (2012).

Movies are created by one group (the writers and producers), funded by another group (the investors), sold by a third group (the distributors) and shown by a fourth group (the exhibitors). No other mass media industry is so fragmented.

Ticket Prices Rise and Ticket Sales Drop

In 1946, the movies' best year, American theaters collected more than 4 billion tickets. Today, as more people watch more movies on video and by streaming, the number of theater admissions has dropped to about 1 billion. Exhibitors believe that if they raise their admission prices much more, ticket sales will fall further. This is why exhibitors charge so much for refreshments, which account for 10 to 20 percent of their income. (See **Illustration 7.1**, "Global Box Office Drives Movie Industry Profits," and **Illustration 7.2**, "Asia/Pacific and Latin America Are Fastest-Growing Movie Markets," p. 138.)

The average cost to make a movie today is more than $100 million, but an average is just that—many movies cost less, and a few movies cost a lot more. Even if a movie is a big box office success, a movie is a financial success only when it brings in more money than it costs to make.

The movie studios claim they lose money on *most* of the pictures they underwrite. Producers claim that, by hiding behind complicated financing schemes, the studios are able to keep exorbitant profits on the movies they distribute, which raises the cost of making movies for producers.

Movie finance is an important part of the movie business today because movies, like other media industries, are part of publicly owned corporations, where loyalty to stockholders comes first. Studios tend to choose safer projects and seek proven audience-pleasing ideas rather than take risks.

One way the movie industry collects predictable income is to make movies for television. Half the movies produced every year are made for television and underwritten by the TV networks. Video sales and movie streaming also bring reliable revenues, an important factor in movie funding called ***ancillary rights***.

Ancillary Rights Fund Projects

In 1950, a movie ticket cost about 50 cents. Today you can see a film for less than 50 cents a person if you pick up a Redbox movie for $1.50 and invite five friends to join you.

The explosion of video rentals and sales since the VCR was first marketed in 1976 has had a powerful effect on

Ancillary Rights Marketing opportunities related to a movie, in addition to direct income from the movie itself.

IMPACT

Money

ILLUSTRATION 7.1

Global Box Office Drives Movie Industry Profits

Since 2009, movie box office receipts overseas have increased 33 percent, while the U.S./Canadian box office has remained virtually unchanged. This trend highlights why overseas markets have become such an important source of revenue for U.S. filmmakers.

"Theatrical Markets Statistics 2013," Motion Picture Association of America Inc., mpaa.com.

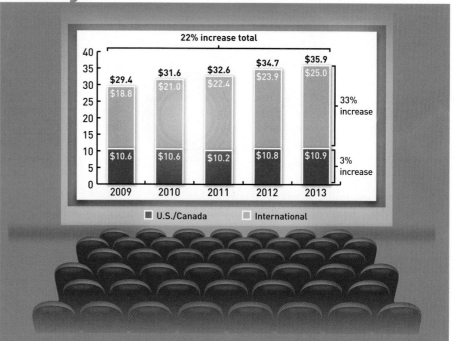

IMPACT

Global

ILLUSTRATION 7.2

Asia/Pacific and Latin America Are Fastest-Growing Movie Markets

Movies are a global business. From 2009 to 2013, box office receipts in Europe, the Middle East and Africa grew 10 percent, but revenue in the Asia/Pacific region grew 55 percent, and the Latin American market increased 78 percent. Today the Asia/Pacific market is bigger than Europe, the Middle East and Africa combined.

"Theatrical Markets Statistics 2013," Motion Picture Association of America Inc., mpaa.com. (*Note:* International box office totals include money generated by U.S.-made movies exhibited overseas and overseas movies exhibited in the U.S.)

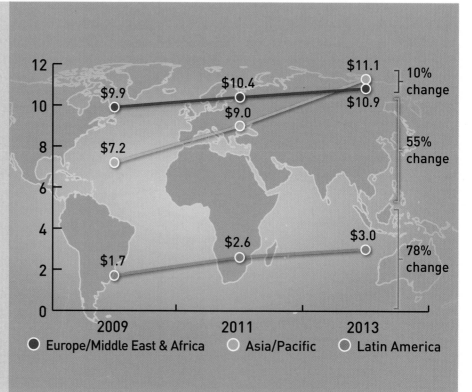

how the movie business operates today. The sale of movies on video and movie streaming are part of the ancillary rights market, which means marketing opportunities that are related to a movie (such as video games), in addition to direct income from theater ticket sales for the movie itself.

"Some pictures make a lot of money," says movie analyst David V. Picker, "and a lot of pictures make no money." But the fact is that the large studios usually make a respectable overall return on their investment each year because earnings are not just dependent on ticket sales alone. In 2013, the U.S. movie industry reported income of $10.9 billion.

Before a theatrical movie starts shooting, the investors want some assurances that they'll make their money back. Moviemakers use the sale of ancillary rights to add to investors' return on their investment. Ancillary rights include

▶ Subscription television rights

▶ Network television rights

▶ Syndication rights (sales to independent TV stations)

▶ Airline rights for in-flight movies

▶ Military rights (to show films on military bases)

▶ College rights (to show films on college campuses)

▶ Song rights for soundtrack albums

▶ Book publishing rights (for original screenplays that can be rewritten and sold as books)

▶ DVD reproduction rights

▶ Product placement

▶ Video game rights

▶ Internet downloads and streaming rights

Movies are commercialized in the sense that sometimes they are tied to products, which is another way of advertising a movie. A movie that can be exploited as a package of ancillary rights, with commercial appeal, is much more attractive to investors than a movie with limited potential.

Often the only choice for a filmmaker who wants to make a film without substantial ancillary-rights potential is to settle for a low budget. Once the film is made, the independent filmmaker must then find a way to distribute the movie. This severely limits the number of independent films that make it to the box office.

Movies at Work

Today the center of the movie industry is movie production. Independent companies produce most of the movies that are distributed by the major studios and exhibited at your local theater under agreements with individual studios. Although these production companies work independently, and each company is organized differently, jobs in movie production fall mainly into the following categories:

1. Screenwriters

2. Producers

3. Directors

4. Actors

5. Technical production

6. Marketing and administration

Every movie begins with a story idea, and these ideas come from *screenwriters*. Screenwriters work independently, marketing their story ideas through agents, who promote their clients' scripts to the studios and to independent producers.

Typically, *producers* are the people who help gather the funding to create a movie project. Financing can come from banks or from investors who want to back a specific movie. Sometimes producers or actors help finance the movies they make in exchange for a percentage of the profits.

Star Wars is the most enduring and successful movie project ever produced, generating unprecedented income for the movies' creator, George Lucas. In 2012, Lucas sold Disney all rights to the *Star Wars* series for $40.5 billion and Disney plans to release *Star Wars: The Force Awakens* in December 2015. On September 4, 2015, 3-year-old Nashira Higdon shows that she is number one in line on "Force Friday" for the new *Star Wars* toys at the Disney Store at Tysons Corner in McLean, Virginia.

The Washington Post/Getty Images

AND COULD I HAVE A SMALL DIET SODA PLEASE?

Ralph Hagen/Cartoonstock

1. Production

2. Distribution

3. Exhibition

Production

Smaller, portable cameras mean a camera operator can move more easily through a crowd. Digital video means that filmmakers can shoot more scenes at night and in dark places with less artificial lighting. Directors digitally record scenes as they shoot them and immediately play back the scene to be sure they have the shot they want. Technology also offers exciting special effects possibilities.

The ability to digitize color also means the images in movies can be intensified, adjusted and totally transformed after the movie is shot, in a way that was impossible even 20 years ago.

Distribution

Reproducing copies of films to send to theaters and guaranteeing their arrival is one of the costliest aspects of moviemaking. Many distribution companies already send their movies by satellite-to-satellite dishes on top of each theater and directly to consumers' homes. Live performances, such as a music concert or a major sports event, already are available by satellite at many local theaters, and some first-run movies can be sent directly to your home the same day they're released in the theater.

The theater industry is replacing the traditional film projector, invented more than 100 years ago, with

Once the funding for the story is in place, a *director* organizes all the tasks necessary to turn the script into a movie. The director works with the producer to manage the movie's budget.

Obviously, *actors* are important to any movie project. Sometimes the producer and director approach particular stars for a project even before they seek funding, to attract interest from the investors and to help assure the investors that the movie will have some box office appeal.

Technical production includes all the people who actually create the movie—camera operators, set designers, film editors, script supervisors and costumers, for example. Once the movie is finished, the *marketing* people seek publicity for the project. They also design a plan to advertise and promote the movie to the public.

As in any media industry, people who work in *administration* help keep all the records necessary to pay salaries and track the employees' expenses, as well as keep track of the paperwork involved in organizing any business.

Digital Technology Drives the Business

New digital technologies affect three aspects of today's movie business:

Matthew Pasant/Flickr Vision/Getty Images

Movie streaming on mobile devices is transforming movie distribution. In November 2012, a child watches the 82-year-old Disney movie *Steamboat Willie* on her iPad.

digital projectors, which can show movies that are sent by satellite or recorded on optical discs. Most of the nation's larger theaters have converted to digital projection, but the price of the conversion can be prohibitive for small, independent film houses. Digitized movies are cheaper to distribute and can be shown on more screens or removed quickly, depending on audience demand.

Also, as video technology grew faster and more accessible, established movie studios and independent moviemakers devised a whole new distribution system, based on digitized movies delivered directly to consumers via streaming on the Internet. In 2008, Apple iTunes launched online movie rentals, and in 2015, Netflix announced that it had more than 60 million subscribers for its streaming and movies-on-demand services, more than 40 million of them in the U.S.

Exhibition

To draw people back into theaters, New Line Cinema and DreamWorks began developing a new digital version of 3-D technology similar to what theaters tried in the 1950s. *Avatar*, released late in 2009, was the first big 3-D hit, and Disney followed with a 3-D version of *Toy Story 3*. At first, higher ticket prices for 3-D features helped increase profitability but, as with 3-D's initial launch in the 1950s, the novelty faded, and recently movie studios have been unwilling to underwrite new 3-D projects.

American motion pictures are one of America's strongest exports, and income from foreign sales accounts for more than one-third of the movie industry's profits. "If Hollywood has learned anything the past few years," says *Business Week*, "it's that the whole world is hungry for the latest it has to offer." International ticket sales reached $25 billion in 2013, primarily driven by rapid growth in Asia and Latin America.

Merging Media Production

In 1993, the Federal Communications Commission voted to allow the TV networks to produce and syndicate their own programs. This opened the door for TV networks to enter the movie business. Today, people in the television business are buying pieces of the movie business, and people in the movie business want to align themselves with television companies.

The result today is consolidated companies that finance movies, make movies and show those movies on their own television stations, on video and on the Internet. By controlling all aspects of the business, a company can have a better chance to collect a profit on the movies it makes.

Sound familiar? The studios held this type of controlling interest in their movies before the courts dismantled the studio system with the 1948 consent decrees (see "*United States v. Paramount Pictures, Inc., et al.*," p. 135). Today's major studios are trying to become again what they once were: a mature oligopoly in the business of dreams.

Emerging Markets and Mergers Bring New Opportunities

Today's movie industry is undergoing two major changes. One recent trend in the movie business is global ownership and global marketing. The second trend is the merging of the movie industry with the television industry.

Global Influence

Overseas companies own two of the major studios (Sony owns Sony Pictures Entertainment and Rupert Murdoch's News Corporation owns Twentieth Century Fox). Foreign ownership gives these companies easier access to overseas markets.

Kevin Winter/Getty Images

The international market for American films accounts for more than one-third of movie industry profits. On March 1, 2015, *Cinderella* star Lily James appeared at the movie's premiere in Los Angeles, but the movie actually opened in Germany and England a month before it was shown in the U.S.

Hollywood Takes a Roman Holiday . . . Again

By Jim Yardley

ROME—Inside the Cinecittà film studios, originally built by Mussolini in part to produce fascist propaganda, a catapult is parked beside Soundstage 13. Not far away, craftsmen touch up chariots. The props are for the remake of the 1959 swords-and-sandals epic, *Ben-Hur*, which is consuming much of the vast studio lot, if not all of it.

Five soundstages are being used to film the Ben Stiller comedy *Zoolander 2*. And crews for the James Bond thriller *Spectre* used the studio in March [2015] while shooting scenes around Rome.

The recent arrival of Hollywood is in part because Rome is one of the most visually alluring and historically resonant cities in the world. But it is also about money. Having watched different countries use financial incentives to attract lucrative Hollywood productions, Italy's Ministry of Culture has sweetened the tax credits provided to foreign movie companies.

The glory days of Hollywood filmmaking in Rome came during the 1950s and 1960s—the so-called era of Hollywood on the Tiber. To many Americans, the defining film was *Roman Holiday* (1953), which depicted Audrey Hepburn and Gregory Peck riding a scooter around Rome. But the big-budget productions were the historical blockbusters

Daniel Craig, star of the new James Bond movie *Spectre*, shoots a scene in central Rome on February 23, 2015. Moviemakers, who used Rome as a backdrop for many movies in the 1950s and 1960s, have returned because of financial incentives offered by the Italian government.

Tiziana Fabi/Getty Images

including *Quo Vadis* (1951) and *Ben-Hur*.

The biggest, *Cleopatra* (1963), became what was then the most expensive movie in history, with huge cost overruns that almost bankrupted 20th Century Fox. The two stars, Elizabeth Taylor and Richard Burton, had a torrid affair that provided fodder for gossip magazines around the world.

Antonio Monda, a film professor at New York University, said the Hollywood-Rome connection gradually diminished in the 1960s for different reasons, including Italian hiring quotas for crews. Foreign films still came to Italy, but countries such as Bulgaria, Romania and the Czech Republic gradually began offering low-cost alternatives.

[A] policy was initiated last year [that] allows each production

company to claim a tax rebate of up to €10 million on expenses incurred in Italy, meaning big-budget films produced by more than one company receive bigger savings.

Productions like the remake of *Ben-Hur* are estimated to spend up to €50 million during production in Rome alone. Last year, Italy generated €167 million from 53 foreign films being shot in the country, according to the Ministry of Culture.

Out at Cinecittà, a small museum chronicles the era of Hollywood on the Tiber and the Spaghetti Westerns that were filmed in Italy in the mid-1960s and that made a star of Clint Eastwood. "Rome has always been a center of cinematography," said [Giuseppe] Basso of Cinecittà, "and must be."

Excerpted from Jim Yardley, "Hollywood Takes a Roman Holiday . . . Again," April 6, 2015, nytimes.com.

REVIEW, ANALYZE, INVESTIGATE

CHAPTER 7

Movies Mirror the Culture

- Before the invention of TV, movies were the nation's primary form of entertainment.
- Like other industries, the movie business has had to adapt to changing technology.

Inventors Capture Motion on Film

- Eadweard Muybridge and Thomas Edison contributed the most to the creation of movies in America. Muybridge demonstrated how to photograph motion, and an Edison employee, William K. L. Dickson, developed a projector, the kinetoscope.
- Auguste and Louis Lumière developed an improved camera and a projector to show film on a large screen.
- Edison also organized the Motion Picture Patents Company to control movie distribution.

Filmmakers Turn Novelty into Art

- French filmmaker Georges Méliès envisioned movies as a medium of fantasy.
- Edwin S. Porter assembled scenes to tell a story.

Studio System and Independent Moviemakers Flourish

- Biograph became the first studio to make movies using what was called the studio system.
- The studio system put the studio's stars under exclusive contract, and the contract could not be broken without an employer's permission.
- The star system promoted popular movie personalities to lure audiences.
- D. W. Griffith mastered the full-length movie. Griffith's best-known movie is a controversial view of the Civil War, *The Birth of a Nation*.
- From 1910 to 1950, filmmakers like Noble and George Johnson and Oscar Micheaux produced movies specifically directed at African American audiences, called "race films."

Movies Become Big Business

- The movie studios moved from New York to Hollywood, where the climate was more favorable.
- The practice of block booking, led by Adolph Zukor, obligated movie houses to accept several movies at once, usually without previewing them first.

- The formation of United Artists by Mary Pickford, Charlie Chaplin, Douglas Fairbanks and D. W. Griffith was a rebellion against the big studios.
- UA distributed films for independent filmmakers.
- In the 1920s, the movie industry faced two crises: scandals involving movie stars and criticism that movie content was growing too explicit.
- The movie industry responded to the scandals and criticism about content by forming the Motion Picture Producers and Distributors Association under the direction of Will Hays.
- In 1930, the MPPDA adopted a production code, which created rules that governed movie content.
- Although standards have relaxed, the practice of self-regulation of content continues today.
- *The Jazz Singer*, the first feature-length motion picture with sound, premiered in New York City on October 6, 1927.

Big Five Studios Dominate

- As the studio system developed, the five largest Hollywood studios were able to control production, distribution and exhibition.
- In 1937, Walt Disney premiered the first feature-length animated film, *Snow White and the Seven Dwarfs*.
- Box office receipts sagged during the Depression, so theaters introduced the double feature—two movies for the price of one.

Labor Unions Organize Movie Workers

- In the 1930s, labor unions challenged studio control and won some concessions.
- Union agreements limited the studios' power over their employees.

Movies Glitter During the Golden Age

- The movies' golden age was the 1930s and 1940s, supported by the studio system and an eager audience.
- The most successful Hollywood studio was MGM, which concentrated on blockbuster movies such as *The Wizard of Oz* and *Gone with the Wind*.

Congress and the Courts Change Hollywood

- Three factors caused Hollywood's crash in the 1950s: the House Un-American Activities Committee hearings, the U.S. Justice Department's antitrust action against the studios and television.

- At least 214 movie employees eventually were blacklisted as a result of the hearings of the House Un-American Activities Committee (HUAC).
- In 1948, the U.S. Supreme Court decision in *United States v. Paramount Pictures Inc., et al.* ended the studio system.

Movies Lose Their Audience to Television

- People abandoned the movies for television, and the trend of declining movie attendance continues today.
- Hollywood tried to lure audiences back to the movies in the 1950s with technological gimmicks, sultry starlets and spectaculars, but the rewards were temporary.
- Movie ratings were originally a response to criticism about immoral movie content, but the standards for these ratings have become blurred.

Movies and Money Today

- DreamWorks SKG, launched in 1994 by Steven Spielberg, Jeffrey Katzenberg and David Geffen, was the first major independent movie studio created in the United States since United Artists was formed in 1919. In 2006, DreamWorks was sold to Viacom, leaving the United States without a major independent movie studio.
- Today the number of moviegoers continues to decline, although DVD sales and streaming, as well as video game development, add to movie industry income.
- Most movies are funded in part by ancillary rights sales.
- The median cost to make a movie today is more than $100 million.
- Most movies are sold as packages, with all their potential media outlets underwriting the movie before it goes into production. This makes independent filmmaking difficult.

Movies at Work

- Movie production is the heart of the movie industry today.

- Screenwriters begin the moviemaking process; other jobs include producer, director, actor, technical production, marketing and administration.

Digital Technology Drives the Business

- New digital technologies affect production, distribution and exhibition of movies.
- Independent moviemakers can use computers to create movies inexpensively and distribute them on the Internet.
- Distribution companies send movies by satellite to satellite dishes on top of theaters and directly to consumers' homes.
- In 2008, Apple made first-run movie downloads available on its iTunes Web site for $2.99 each.
- In 2015, Netflix announced that it had more than 60 million subscribers for its streaming and video-on-demand services, more than 40 million of them in the U.S.
- New 3-D technology initially added to industry income, but recently movie studios have been unwilling to invest in new 3D projects.

Emerging Markets and Mergers Bring New Opportunities

- In 1993, the Federal Communications Commission voted to allow the TV networks to produce and syndicate their own programs. This opened the door for TV networks to enter the movie business.
- Overseas companies own two of the major studios.
- Foreign ownership gives these companies easier access to overseas markets.
- Overseas sales of American movies account for more than one-third of movie industry income.
- The movie and television industries have aligned themselves more closely to control all aspects of moviemaking.

Key Terms

These terms are defined in the margins throughout this chapter and appear in alphabetical order with definitions in the Glossary, which begins on page 361.

Ancillary Rights *137*

Blacklisting *135*

Blind Booking *135*

Block Booking *130*

Star System *129*

Studio System *129*

Critical Questions

1. What were "race movies"? Discuss the ways in which these films changed the perspective of African Americans portrayed in the films and for their audiences.

2. What were the effects of the practices of block booking and blind booking on the movie industry? How and why did these practices end?

3. Why do you believe the Hollywood Ten became a target of the House Un-American Activities Committee? Could the same thing happen today? Why? Explain.

4. Describe how today's digital technologies are changing moviemaking, distribution and exhibition.

5. In which areas of the world are moviegoing audiences growing the fastest? What role do international markets play in the movie business today? Explain.

Working the Web

This list includes sites mentioned in the chapter and others to give you greater insight into the movie business.

Academy of Motion Picture Arts and Sciences

oscars.org

Established in 1927 with legendary actor Douglas Fairbanks as its first president, the Academy of Motion Picture Arts and Sciences is the home of the Academy Awards, more commonly known as the Oscars. This is an honorary association of over 7,000 motion picture professionals. The Academy works to advance the arts and sciences of motion pictures, recognizing outstanding achievement and promoting technical research of methods and equipment.

DEG Digital Entertainment Group

degonline.org

DEG is a nonprofit trade consortium of more than 56 companies, ranging from major motion picture studios to consumer electronics manufacturers, retailers and ancillary businesses that support the home entertainment industry. DEG's primary goal is to explore opportunities in digital technologies and represent all aspects of the home entertainment industry. Members include DreamWorks Animation, DirectTV, Warner Brothers Home Entertainment and Samsung Electronics.

Directors Guild of America

dga.org

The Directors Guild of America is a labor organization that represents the creative and economic rights of directors and members of the directorial team working in film, television, commercials, documentaries, news, sports and new media. The DGA is governed by an elected National Board of Directors and has offices in Los Angeles, New York and Chicago.

Internet Movie Database (IMDb)

imdb.com

Owned by Amazon.com, IMDb started in 1990 as a hobby project by an international group of movie and TV fans. Today, IMDb is "the world's most popular and authoritative source for movie, TV and celebrity content." IMDb offers a searchable database of more than 100 million data items, including more than 2 million movies, TV and entertainment programs and listings for more than 4 million cast and crew members.

Lucasfilm

lucasfilm.com

This film and entertainment company founded by George Lucas in 1971 has produced such hits as *American Graffiti* and the *Star Wars* and *Indiana Jones* series. In addition to motion picture and television production, the company's businesses include Industrial Light & Magic (visual effects), Skywalker Sound and LucasArts (video games).

Motion Picture Association of America (MPAA) and Motion Picture Association (MPA)

mpaa.org

Founded in 1922, the MPAA is the primary advocate for the motion picture, home video and television industries. The MPAA and its international counterpart the MPA are responsible for the movie ratings and work to protect copyrights and stem piracy of filmed works in more than 30 countries around the world.

Netflix

netflix.com

Founded in 1997 and headquartered in Los Gatos, Calif., Netflix lays claim to being "the world's leading Internet television network with over 57 million members in nearly 50 countries enjoying more than two billion hours of TV shows and movies per month." Subscribers can watch original series, documentaries and feature films as much as they want, anytime, anywhere, on nearly any Internet-connected screen. Members can play, pause and resume watching, all without commercials.

Screenwriters Federation of America (SFA)

screenwritersfederation.org

Formerly the Screenwriters Guild of America, the SFA's goals are to educate screenwriters about their craft and about the entertainment business. The SFA works to create a network for screenwriters and to administer standards for marketing scripts.

Sundance Institute

sundance.org

This nonprofit organization dedicates itself to discovering and developing independent moviemakers. Founder Robert Redford began hosting labs in 1981 where emerging filmmakers could work with leading writers and directors to develop their original projects. The Institute is now an internationally recognized independent artist resource and the host of the annual Sundance Film Festival.

Warner Bros.

warnerbros.com

Initially founded by the four Warner brothers as a silent-film distributor in 1903, today the company is headquartered on 142 acres in Burbank, Calif., and has a 160-acre studio lot in the United Kingdom. The company is now a division of Time Warner Inc. and includes Castle Rock Entertainment, New Line Cinema, Warner Brothers Home Entertainment, Warner Brothers Television Group, Warner Brothers Animation and DC Comics and Entertainment.

Impact/Action Videos are concise news features on various topics created exclusively for *Media/Impact*. Find them in *Media/Impact*'s MindTap at cengagebrain.com.

MindTap® Log on to MindTap for *Media/Impact* to access a variety of additional material—including learning objectives, chapter readings with highlighting and note-taking, **Impact/Action Videos**, activities, and comprehension quizzes—that will guide you through this chapter.

CBS Photo Archive/Getty Images

Traditional TV networks, such as NBC, CBS and ABC, depend on successful comedy series, such as *The Big Bang Theory*, to attract a loyal audience for advertisers. But today new program suppliers, including Netflix and Amazon, are challenging the networks by providing subscription shows that stream on the Web without commercials.

What's Ahead?

- Television Transforms Daily Life
- TV Delivers an Audience to Advertisers
- *Visual Radio* Becomes *Television*
- Television Outpaces Radio
- Quiz Shows Bring Ethics Scandals
- Ratings Target the Audience
- Newton Minow Criticizes TV as a "Vast Wasteland"
- Public Television Finds an Audience
- Satellites Make Transatlantic TV and Live Broadcasts Possible
- Television Changes National and Global Politics
- Mergers Affect Station Ownership
- TV Promotes Professional Sports
- Critics Challenge the Accuracy of TV Ratings
- Cable and Satellite Expand Delivery
- Television at Work
- Audiences Drive TV Programming
- Digital Technology Broadens TV's Focus
- Streaming TV Brings a New Vision

"We've had 80 years of linear TV, and it's been amazing. The next 20 years will be this transformation from linear TV to Internet TV."

—REED HASTINGS, CEO, NETFLIX

"Television is the pervasive American pastime," *wrote media critic Jeff Greenfield in 1987.* "Cutting through geographic, ethnic, class and cultural diversity, it is the single binding thread of this country, the one experience that touches young and old, rich and poor, learned and illiterate. A country too big for homogeneity, filled by people from all over the globe, without any set of core values, America never had a central unifying bond. Now we do. Now it is possible to answer the question, 'What does America do?' We watch television."

Forty years later, we still watch television, but where we watch television has changed. We still watch TV at home, but TV programs also have moved to the Internet, which makes current shows—as well as an endless archive of classic programs your parents watched—available on many different types of screens wherever and whenever you want to see them.

On average, American viewers watch television 31 hours a week, according to The Nielsen Company, which monitors television usage for advertisers. (See **Illustration 8.1**, "How Much Time Do People Spend Each Week Watching Traditional TV and Internet Video?" p. 150.) Even though you may not watch TV this much, the percentage of people in the United States who watch television more than you (especially people 50 and older) counterbalances your viewing time, which makes TV viewers a very lucrative market for advertisers.

Television Transforms Daily Life

It's not surprising that the effects of such a pervasive medium have attracted so much attention from parents, educators, social scientists, religious leaders, public officials and anyone else who wants to understand society's habits and values. TV has been blamed for everything from declines in literacy to rises in violent crime to the trivialization of national politics. Every once in a while it is praised, too, for giving viewers instant access to world events and uniting audiences in times of national crisis.

An industry with this much presence in American life is bound to affect the way we live. Someone who is watching television is not doing other things: playing basketball, visiting a museum or looking through a telescope at the planets, for instance. Television can, however, bring you to a museum you might never visit or to a basketball game you cannot attend or to the surface of a planet you can only see through a telescope.

Television technology, by adding pictures to the sounds of radio, truly transformed Americans' living and learning patterns. The word *television*, which once meant programs delivered by antennas through over-the-air signals, now means a *television screen*, where several different types of delivery systems bring viewers a diversity of programs.

The programs Americans watch today are delivered by antennas, cables, satellites and the Internet and appear on many different types of screens. As a viewer, you probably don't really care how the programs arrive.

TimeFrame
1884–Today

Television Is the Nation's Primary Medium for News and Entertainment

CBS Photo Archive/Getty Images

Andrew H. Walker/Getty Images

Kevin Schafer/Getty Images

1884 In Germany, Paul Nipkow patents the Nipkow disk, which forms the basis for TV's development through the 1920s.

1907 The word television first appears in the June 1907 issue of *Scientific American*.

1939 NBC's David Sarnoff debuts television at the World's Fair in New York City. President Franklin D. Roosevelt, broadcasting from the fair, is the first U.S. president to appear on TV.

✳ **1947** NBC and CBS begin broadcasting television news.

1951 CBS launches *I Love Lucy*, a situation comedy, which becomes TV's most durable type of entertainment program.

1962 *Telstar I* sends the first transatlantic satellite broadcast.

✳ **1963** Public television begins broadcasting as National Educational Television. Network television provides nonstop coverage of the assassination and funeral of President John F. Kennedy.

1973 The television networks present live broadcasts of the Watergate hearings.

1979 Ted Turner starts Cable News Network. CNN's global reach gives the U.S. audience instant access to news about international events.

1983 More than 120 million people tune in for the final episode of *M*A*S*H*, the highest-rated program ever.

1987 TV broadcasts the Iran-Contra hearings.

1993 More than 80 million people tune in for the final episode of *Cheers*.

2001 TV news offers nonstop, ad-free coverage of the terrorist attacks at the World Trade Center, at the Pentagon, and in rural Pennsylvania.

2003 TV broadcasts live news coverage of the Iraq War.

2006 Congress mandates that TV broadcasters switch totally to digital high-definition signals by February 17, 2009.

2008 More than 70 million people watch President Barack Obama's election night victory on TV on November 4, a record audience for a presidential election night.

2009 The U.S. changes to a national high-definition television transmission standard (HDTV).

2010 Television manufacturers introduce 3-D television.

✳ **2012** Netflix offers original programming via video streaming.

✳ **2014** Sesame Street celebrates its 45th anniversary.

Today HDTV is the standard for broadcast TV. TV programming is delivered by over-the-air broadcast, cable, satellite and Internet streaming.

IMPACT

Society

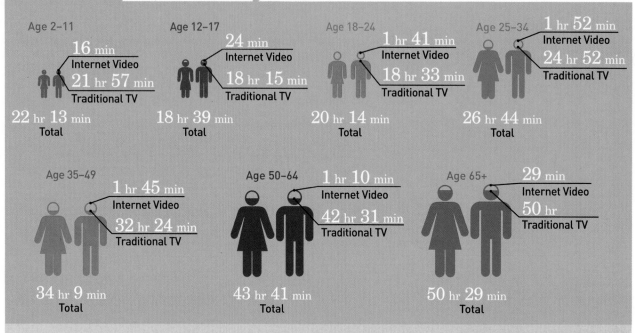

Age 2–11
16 min Internet Video
21 hr 57 min Traditional TV
22 hr 13 min Total

Age 12–17
24 min Internet Video
18 hr 15 min Traditional TV
18 hr 39 min Total

Age 18–24
1 hr 41 min Internet Video
18 hr 33 min Traditional TV
20 hr 14 min Total

Age 25–34
1 hr 52 min Internet Video
24 hr 52 min Traditional TV
26 hr 44 min Total

Age 35–49
1 hr 45 min Internet Video
32 hr 24 min Traditional TV
34 hr 9 min Total

Age 50–64
1 hr 10 min Internet Video
42 hr 31 min Traditional TV
43 hr 41 min Total

Age 65+
29 min Internet Video
50 hr Traditional TV
50 hr 29 min Total

ILLUSTRATION 8.1

How Much Time Do People Spend Each Week Watching Traditional TV and Internet Video?

Americans spend an average of 31 hours a week watching traditional TV and video on the Internet. However, people who are 50 and over spend about twice as much time watching traditional TV as younger viewers (18–49). And younger viewers (18–49) spend more time than older viewers (50+) watching video on the Internet.

"The Total Audience Report Q4 2014," nielsen.com.

"Apparently they hand out awards for something called 'television.'"

Tom Toro/The New Yorker Collection/Cartoon Bank.com

What you do know is that television gives you access to all types of news and entertainment—drama, comedy, sports, news, game shows and talk shows. You can see many types of people—murderers, public officials, foreign leaders, reporters, soldiers, entertainers, athletes, detectives and doctors. The television screen is truly, as scholar Erik Barnouw observed, a "tube of plenty."

About 1,700 television stations operate in the United States. Three out of four of these are commercial stations, and the others are noncommercial stations. About half the commercial stations are affiliated with a network.

"The most common misconception most people have about television concerns its product," media critic Jeff Greenfield observed. "To the viewer, the product is the programming. To the television executive, the product is the audience. Strictly speaking, television networks and stations do not make any money by producing a program that audiences want to watch. The money comes from selling advertisers the right to broadcast a message to that audience. The programs exist to capture the biggest possible audiences."

TV Delivers an Audience to Advertisers

To understand why we get the programming we do, it is important to remember that *commercial television exists primarily as an advertising medium.* Programming surrounds the advertising, but it is the advertising that is being delivered to the audience. Commercial television, from its inception, was created to deliver audiences to advertisers.

Because television can deliver a larger audience faster than other mass media, television can charge higher rates than any other medium for its advertising—which makes TV stations rich investments. During a widely watched TV program like the 2015 Super Bowl (with an estimated audience of half the U.S. population and an even larger audience worldwide), a 30-second ad can cost as much as $4.5 million. Today, even the smallest independent television station is a multimillion-dollar operation. However, the television era began much more humbly, and with very little excitement, around the turn of the 20th century.

Visual Radio Becomes Television

The word *television* first appeared in the June 1907 issue of *Scientific American.* Before then, experiments in image transmission had been called "visual wireless," "visual radio" and "electric vision." Alexander Graham Bell's telephone and Samuel F. B. Morse's telegraph contributed to the idea of sending electrical impulses over long distances.

The first major technological discovery to suggest that pictures also could travel was the *Nipkow disk.* Twenty-four-year-old *Paul Nipkow* patented the Nipkow disk, which he called the "electrical telescope," in Germany in 1884. This disk, which formed the basis for television's development through the 1920s, was about the size of a phonograph record, perforated with a spiral of tiny holes.

Also crucial in television's (and radio's) development were *Guglielmo Marconi* and *Lee de Forest* (see chapter 6). Marconi eliminated sound's dependence on wires and put sound on airwaves. De Forest contributed the Audion

In 1939, RCA's David Sarnoff introduced TV at the 1939 New York World's Fair. Other manufacturers, including Emerson, followed, and television soon became an essential part of daily life. This ad offers a TV, phonograph and radio all in one console.

tube, which amplified radio waves so that people could hear the sound clearly.

In 1927, Secretary of Commerce Herbert Hoover appeared on a 2-inch screen by wire in an experimental AT&T broadcast. On September 11, 1928, General Electric broadcast the first dramatic production, "The Queen's Messenger"—the sound came over station WGY, in Schenectady, N.Y., and the picture came from experimental television station W2XAD. All the pictures were close-ups, and their quality could best be described as primitive.

Two researchers, one working for a company and one working alone, brought television into the electronic age. Then the same man who was responsible for radio's popularity, RCA's David Sarnoff, became television's biggest promoter.

The three U.S. television networks began producing and distributing commercial programs in the late 1940s. This TV studio crew is producing a commercial in the 1950s.

Vladimir Zworykin was working for Westinghouse when he developed an all-electronic system to transform a visual image into an electronic signal that traveled through the air. When the signal reached the television receiver, the signal was transformed again into a visual image for the viewer.

Philo T. Farnsworth, working alone in California, developed the cathode ray tube (which he called a dissector tube). Farnsworth's cathode ray tube used an electronic scanner to reproduce the electronic image much more clearly than Nipkow's earlier mechanical scanning device. In 1930, 24-year-old Farnsworth patented his electronic scanner.

NBC television's commercial debut was at the 1939 World's Fair in New York City at the Hall of Television. On April 30, 1939, President Franklin D. Roosevelt formally opened the fair and became the first president to appear on television. Sarnoff also spoke, and RCA displayed its 5-inch and 9-inch sets, priced from $199.50 to $600 (equivalent to $3,389 to $10,192 in today's dollars)—a very expensive family purchase.

NBC and CBS were the original TV networks. A *network* is a collection of radio or television stations that offers programs, usually simultaneously, throughout the country, during designated program times.

In 1943, ABC, the third major network, grew out of NBC's old Blue network. ABC labored from its earliest days to equal the other two networks but didn't have as many affiliates as NBC and CBS. The two leading networks already had secured the more powerful, well-established broadcast outlets for themselves. David Sarnoff and William Paley controlled the network game.

Television Outpaces Radio

By 1945, 10 television stations were on the air in the United States. According to media historian Eric Barnouw, "By the late 1940s, television began its conquest of America. In 1949, the year began with radio drawing 81 percent of all broadcast audiences. By the year's end, television was grabbing 41 percent of the broadcast market. When audiences began experiencing the heady thrill of actually seeing as well as hearing events as they occurred, the superiority of television was established beyond doubt."

Black-and-white television replaced radio so quickly as the nation's major advertising medium that it would be easy to believe television erupted suddenly in a surprise move to kill radio. But remember that the two major corporate executives who developed television—Sarnoff and Paley—also held the country's largest interest in radio. They used their profits from radio to develop television, foreseeing that television eventually would expand their audience and their income.

News with Pictures

Broadcast news, pioneered by radio, adapted awkwardly at first to the new broadcast medium—television. According to David Brinkley, a broadcast news pioneer who began at NBC, "When television came along in about 1947–1948, the big time newsmen of that day—H. V. Kaltenborn, Lowell Thomas—did not want to do television. It was a lot of work, they weren't used to it, they were doing very well in radio, making lots of money. They didn't want to fool with it. So I was told to do it by the news manager. I was a young kid and, as I say, the older, more established people didn't want to do it. Somebody had to."

In 1947, CBS launched *Television News with Douglas Edwards*, and NBC broadcast *Camel News Caravan* (sponsored by Camel cigarettes) with John Cameron Swayze (see **Chapter 12**). Eventually, David Brinkley joined Swayze for NBC's 15-minute national newscast. He recalled, "The first broadcasts were extremely primitive by today's standards. It was mainly just sitting at a desk and talking. We didn't have any pictures at first. Later we began to get a little simple news film, but it wasn't much.

Network A collection of radio or TV stations that offers programs, usually simultaneously, throughout the country, during designated program times.

Dragnet (top), a 1950s series set in Los Angeles and starring Jack Webb, is an early example of one of the most enduring types of prime-time TV programming—the detective drama. Today's *Blue Bloods*, set in New York, starring Donnie Wahlberg and Marissa Ramirez, continues TV's original detective format.

The talk show is a very profitable TV program format. CBS announced in 2015 that Stephen Colbert (left) would succeed current *Late Night* host David Letterman (right), shown together in 2015 on *The Kennedy Center Honors*. *The Tonight Show*, which has been on the air since 1954, is TV's longest-running late night talk show.

"In the beginning, people would call after a program and say in tones of amazement that they had seen you. 'I'm out here in Bethesda, and the picture's wonderful,'" Brinkley said. "They weren't interested in anything you said. They were just interested in the fact that you had been on their screen in their house."

At first, network TV news reached only the East Coast because there was no national hookup to deliver television across the country. By 1948, AT&T's coaxial cable linked Philadelphia with New York City and Washington, D.C. The 1948 political conventions were held in Philadelphia and broadcast to 13 eastern states. When the 1952 conventions were broadcast, AT&T's national coaxial hookups joined 108 stations across the country.

CBS had developed a strong group of radio reporters during World War II, and by 1950 many of them had moved to the new medium. CBS News also made a practice, more than the other networks, of using the same reporters for radio and television news. The major early news figure at CBS was Edward R. Murrow, who, along with David Brinkley at NBC, created the early standards for broadcast news. (See **Impact/Profile**, "Edward R. Murrow (1908–1965) Sets the Standard for Broadcast News," p. 154.)

Public affairs programs like Murrow's *See It Now* continued to grow along with network news, and in 1956 NBC teamed David Brinkley with Chet Huntley to cover the political conventions. The chemistry worked, and after the convention, NBC put Huntley and Brinkley together to do the evening news, *The Huntley-Brinkley Report*. Brinkley often called himself "the other side of the hyphen."

Entertainment Programming

Early television entertainment also was the same as radio with pictures: It offered variety shows, situation comedies, drama, Westerns, detective stories, Hollywood movies, soap operas and quiz shows. The only type of show television offered that radio did not (besides movies, of course) was the talk show. (However, radio eventually created call-in programs, radio's version of the TV talk show.)

IMPACT

Profile

Edward R. Murrow (1908–1965) Sets the Standard for Broadcast News

By Theodore H. White

Note: Edward R. Murrow had established a reputation for excellence as a CBS radio news broadcaster when he migrated to television news in 1951. In this profile, veteran journalist Theodore H. White outlines Murrow's broadcast career and its impact on television audiences.

It is so difficult to recapture the real Ed Murrow from the haze that now shrouds the mythical Ed Murrow of history.

Where other men may baffle friends with the infinite complexity of their natures, Ed was baffling otherwise. He was so straightforward, he would completely baffle the writers who now unravel the neuroses of today's demigods of television. When Ed was angry, he bristled; when he gave friendship, it came without withholding.

He could walk with prime ministers and movie stars, GIs and generals, as natural in rumpled GI suntans as in his diplomatic homburg. But jaunty or somber, to those of us who knew him he was just plain old Ed. In his shabby office at CBS cluttered with awards, you could loosen your necktie, put your feet up and yarn away. The dark, overhanging eyebrows would arch as he

In the 1950s, Edward R. Murrow established a very high standard for TV news. Murrow is shown here in the 1950s on the CBS set.

punctured pretension with a jab, the mouth would twist quizzically as he questioned. And then there were his poker games, as Ed sat master of the table, a cigarette dangling always from his lips—he smoked 60 or 70 a day—and called the bets.

Then—I can hear him now—there was the voice. Ed's deep and rhythmic voice was compelling, not only for its range, halfway between bass and baritone, but for the words that rolled from it. He wrote for the ear—with a cadence of pauses and clipped, full sentences. His was an aural art but, in Ed, the art was natural—his inner ear composed a picture and, long before TV, the imagination of his listeners caught

the sound and made with it their own picture.

We remember the voice. But there was so much more to Ed. He had not only a sense of the news but a sense of how the news fit into history. And this sense of the relation of news to history is what, in retrospect, made him the great pioneer of television journalism. . . .

He is very large now, for it was he who set the news system of television on its tracks, holding it, and his descendants, to the sense of history that give it still, in the schlock-storm of today, its sense of honor. Of Ed Murrow it may be said that he made all of us who clung to him, and cling to his memory still, feel larger than we really were.

Excerpted from "When He Used the Power of TV, He Could Rouse Thunder," *TV Guide* 34, no. 3 (Jan. 18, 1986), pages 13–14. Reprinted by permission of Heyden White Rostow and David F. White.

VARIETY SHOWS. The best radio stars jumped to the new medium. Three big variety show successes were Milton Berle's *Texaco Star Theater, The Admiral Broadway Revue* (later *Your Show of Shows*) with Imogene Coca and Sid Caesar and Ed Sullivan's *Toast of the Town* (later *The Ed Sullivan Show*). These weekly shows featured comedy sketches and appearances by popular entertainers. *The Ed Sullivan Show*, for example, is where most Americans got their first glimpse of Elvis Presley and the Beatles. All of the shows were done live.

The time slot in which these programs were broadcast, 7 to 11 p.m., is known as ***prime time***. Prime time simply means that more people watch television during this period than any other, so advertising during this period costs more. Berle's 8 p.m. program on Tuesday nights often gathered 85 percent of the audience. *Texaco Star Theater* became so popular that one Laundromat installed a TV set and advertised, "Watch Berle while your clothes twirl."

SITUATION COMEDIES. Along with drama, the ***situation comedy*** (sitcom) proved to be one of TV's most durable types of programs. The situation comedy established a regular set of characters in either a home or work situation. *I Love Lucy*, starring Lucille Ball and Desi Arnaz, originated from Los Angeles because the actors wanted to live on the West Coast. In 1951, Ball began a career as a weekly performer on CBS that lasted for 23 years.

In 1960, CBS launched *The Andy Griffith Show*, which followed the adventures of widower and Mayberry sheriff Andy Taylor, who was raising his young son. It ran for eight seasons and is still shown today on the TV Land cable television network. *Modern Family* and *The Big Bang Theory* are examples of current situation comedy successes.

DRAMA. *The Loretta Young Show* offered noontime drama—broadcast live—every day in the 1950s. *The Hallmark Hall of Fame* established a tradition for high-quality, live dramatic presentations. For many years, TV dramas were limited to one- or two-hour programs. But in the 1970s, encouraged by the success of Alex Haley's *Roots,* which dramatized Haley's search for the story of his African ancestry, television began to broadcast as many as 14 hours of a single drama over several nights. Today, the series *The Good Wife* is an example of a popular prime-time drama.

WESTERNS. TV went Western in 1954, when Jack Warner of Warner Bros. signed an agreement with ABC to provide the network with a program called *Cheyenne*. The outspoken Warner had openly criticized TV's effect on the movie business, but when ABC asked Warner to produce programs for them, Warner Bros. became the first movie company to realize that the studios could profit from television. Westerns are the only early TV format that isn't popular today.

DETECTIVE SHOWS. *Dragnet*, starring Jack Webb as Sergeant Friday, was an early TV detective series, starting in 1951 and running for eight seasons. The detective genre became a TV staple: *Dragnet's* successors today are programs like *Blue Bloods*.

MOVIES. The movie industry initially resisted the competition from TV, but then it realized there was money to be made in selling old movies to TV. In 1957, RKO sold 740 pre-1948 movies to television for $25 million. The other studios followed. Through various distribution agreements, movie reruns and movies produced specifically for television were added to television's program lineup.

SOAP OPERAS. Borrowed from radio serials, soap operas filled morning television programming. Today, game shows and reruns are more popular choices, but some soaps still survive. Soap operas (*telenovelas*) also are an important element of today's Spanish-language television.

TALK SHOWS. Sylvester "Pat" Weaver (actress Sigourney Weaver's father) created and produced television's single original contribution to programming: the talk show. Weaver's *Tonight Show* (originally *Jerry Lester's Broadway Open House*) first appeared in 1954. Through a succession of hosts from Lester to Steve Allen to Jack Paar to Johnny Carson to Jay Leno, Conan O'Brien and Jimmy Fallon, *The Tonight Show* has lasted longer than any other talk show on television. Another modern-day successor of the late-night talk show format is, of course, *Late Night with David Letterman*. Letterman was replaced in 2015 by comedian Stephen Colbert.

QUIZ SHOWS. In the mid-1950s, all three TV networks introduced quiz shows, on which contestants competed with each other for big-money prizes. Soon, the quiz shows were mired in controversy because of charges that the contestants had been given answers.

Quiz Shows Bring Ethics Scandals

Sponsored by Revlon, CBS's *The $64,000 Question* premiered June 7, 1955. Contestants answered questions from a glass "isolation booth." Successful contestants returned in succeeding weeks to increase their winnings, and Revlon advertised its Living Lipstick. By September, the program was drawing 85 percent of the audience, and Revlon had to substitute an ad for another product because its factory supply of Living Lipstick had completely sold out.

As the most popular quiz show on early television, *The $64,000 Question* engendered imitation: *Treasure Hunt, Giant Step* and *Twenty-One*. Winnings grew beyond the $64,000 limit; Charles Van Doren won $129,000 on

---

Prime Time The TV time period from 7 to 11 p.m. when more people watch TV than at any other time.

Situation Comedy A TV program that establishes a regular cast of characters typically in a home or work situation. Also called a sitcom.

Bettmann/Corbis

Charles Van Doren won $129,000 on the quiz show *Twenty-One*, facing contestant Herb Stempel. Contestants appeared in isolation booths (where Van Doren is shown in this sequence of four photos), allegedly to keep them from hearing answers from the audience. When they later admitted that the show's producers fed them the answers beforehand, Van Doren and Stempel became central figures in the 1950s quiz show ethics scandals. Their story was dramatized in the 1994 movie *Quiz Show*.

Twenty-One. In the fall of 1955, CBS replaced Murrow's *See It Now* with a quiz program.

Sponsors produced many network quiz shows like *The $64,000 Question* for the networks, and these programs usually carried the sponsor's name. In the 1958–1959 quiz show scandals, Revlon was implicated when a congressional subcommittee investigated charges that the quiz shows were rigged to enhance the ratings. Charles Van Doren admitted before the subcommittee that *Twenty-One*'s producer had fed him the answers. Staff members from other quiz shows confirmed Van Doren's testimony.

The quiz show scandals caused the networks to reexamine the relationship between advertisers and programs. Before the scandals, advertisers and their agencies produced one-quarter to one-third of network programming. As a result of the quiz show scandals, the networks turned to other sources, such as independent producers, for their programming.

By the late 1960s, advertisers provided less than 3 percent of network programming, and soon advertisers provided no network shows. The networks programmed themselves. They also used reruns of newly acquired studio movies to replace the quiz shows, but quiz shows resurfaced in 1983 with *Wheel of Fortune* and, in the 1990s, *Who Wants to Be a Millionaire?*

Ratings Target the Audience

After the quiz show scandals, the networks were criticized for being motivated only by ratings. Ratings give sponsors information about the audience they're reaching with their advertising—what advertisers are getting for their money.

By the late 1950s, The Nielsen Company dominated the television ratings business. The national Nielsen ratings describe the audience to advertisers; based on the Nielsens, advertisers pay for the commercial time to reach the audiences they want.

Today, Nielsen provides two types of numbers, known as rating and share. The ***rating*** is a percentage of the total number of households with television sets. If there are 95 million homes with TV sets, for example, the rating shows the percentage of those sets that were tuned in to a specific program. The share (an abbreviation for share-of-audience)

> **Rating** The percentage of the total number of households *with TV sets* tuned to a particular program.

AP Images

Live sports events are among the most profitable types of TV programming today because of their high audience ratings. In 2015, CBS Sports broadcast The Masters from Augusta, Ga., when Jordan Spieth, 21, became one of the event's youngest winners.

IMPACT

Money

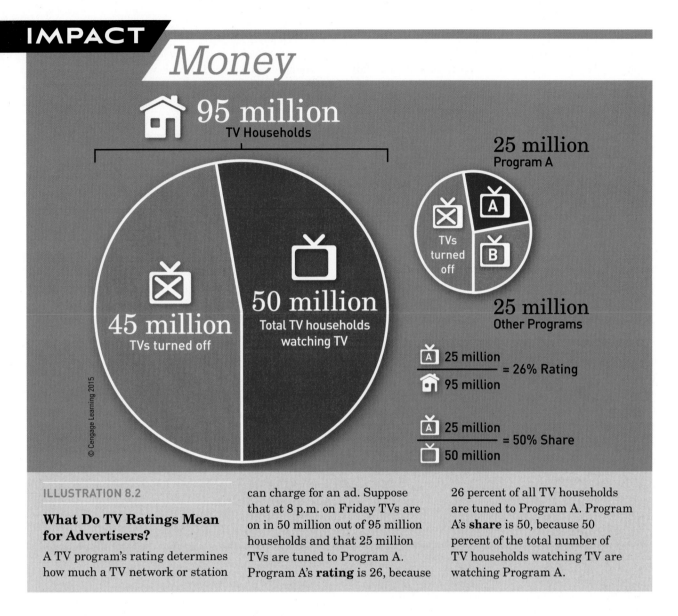

🏠 **95 million**
TV Households

45 million
TVs turned off

50 million
Total TV households
watching TV

25 million
Program A

TVs
turned
off

25 million
Other Programs

$$\frac{\text{A } 25 \text{ million}}{\text{🏠 } 95 \text{ million}} = 26\% \text{ Rating}$$

$$\frac{\text{A } 25 \text{ million}}{\text{📺 } 50 \text{ million}} = 50\% \text{ Share}$$

© Cengage Learning 2015

ILLUSTRATION 8.2

What Do TV Ratings Mean for Advertisers?

A TV program's rating determines how much a TV network or station can charge for an ad. Suppose that at 8 p.m. on Friday TVs are on in 50 million out of 95 million households and that 25 million TVs are tuned to Program A. Program A's **rating** is 26, because 26 percent of all TV households are tuned to Program A. Program A's **share** is 50, because 50 percent of the total number of TV households watching TV are watching Program A.

compares the audience for one show with the audience for another. **Share** means the percentage of the audience with TV sets turned on that is watching each program.

For example, if TV sets in 50 million homes were turned on at 8 p.m. on Friday night, and 25 million homes were tuned to Program A, that program would have a rating of 26 (25 million divided by 95 million, expressed as a percentage) and a share of 50. (See **Illustration 8.2**, "What Do TV Ratings Mean for Advertisers?" above.)

The most concentrated ratings periods for local stations are "sweeps" months—February, May and November. (Ratings are taken in July, too, but the numbers are not considered accurate because so many people are on vacation.) The sweeps provide an estimate of the local TV audience, and advertisers use that information when they decide where to place their commercials.

Sweeps are the months when the ratings services gather their most important ratings, so the networks and local stations often use these important months to showcase their best programs. This is when you are most likely to see a new one-hour episode of a popular series, for example, or a lavishly produced special.

Today's Nielsen ratings work essentially the same as they did in the 1950s, except that the Nielsens now deliver very specific information on *demographics*—age, occupation and income, for instance—and Nielsen can deliver daily ratings information to any client willing to pay for it.

> **Share** The percentage of the audience *with TV sets turned on* that is watching a particular program.
>
> **Sweeps** The months when TV ratings services gather their most important ratings—February, May and November.
>
> **Demographics** Data about consumers' characteristics, such as age, occupation and income level.

In 2007, The Nielsen Company expanded its tracking service to count people who watch TV outside the home, in places like bars, restaurants, airports, offices and retail stores. Nielsen then announced in 2013 that it would also track mobile viewing. "Nielsen has a mandate to follow the video wherever it goes," said Sara Erichson, executive vice president for client services at Nielsen Media Research North America.

Advertisers use this ratings information to target their most likely consumers. Nike shoes might create a new advertising campaign for the Super Bowl, for instance, and Nielsen could tell Nike, judging from previous Super Bowls, the projected demographics of the people who watch the game.

A major flaw in the ratings system today, critics contend, is the way the broadcast community religiously follows and uses ratings to determine programming, producing what has succeeded before rather than introducing new ideas.

Newton Minow Criticizes TV as a "Vast Wasteland"

The 1950s were a trial period for television, as the networks and advertisers tested audience interest in various types of programming. Captured by the miracle that television offered, at first audiences seemed insatiable; they watched almost anything that TV delivered. But in the 1960s, audiences became more discriminating and began to question how well the medium of television was serving the public.

Once it established itself throughout the country, television needed a public conscience. That public conscience was Newton Minow. An unassuming soothsayer, Minow was named chairman of the Federal Communications Commission in 1961 by newly elected President John F. Kennedy. On May 9, 1961, speaking to the National Association of Broadcasters in his first public address since his appointment, Minow told broadcast executives what he believed were the broadcasters' responsibilities to the public. According to Minow, in his book *Equal Time*, he told the broadcasters:

Your license lets you use the public's airwaves as trustees for 180 million Americans. The public is your beneficiary. If you want to stay on as trustees, you must deliver a decent return to the public—not only to your stockholders. . . .

Your industry possesses the most powerful voice in America. It has an inescapable duty to make that voice ring with intelligence and with leadership. In a few years this exciting industry has grown from a novelty to an instrument of overwhelming impact on the American people. It should be making ready for the kind of leadership that newspapers and magazines assumed years ago, to make our people aware of their world.

Ours has been called the jet age, the atomic age, the space age. It is also, I submit, the television age. And just as history will decide whether the leaders of today's world employed the atom to destroy the world or rebuild it for mankind's benefit, so will history decide whether today's broadcasters employed their powerful voice to enrich the people or debase them.

Minow then asked his audience of broadcast station owners and managers to watch their own programs. He said that they would find a "vast wasteland," a phrase that resurfaces today during any critical discussion of television.

Public Television Finds an Audience

The concept of educational television has been alive since the 1950s, when a few noncommercial stations succeeded in regularly presenting public service programs without advertisements, but the shows were low budget.

The educational network NET (National Educational Television) emerged in 1963 to provide some national programming (about ten hours a week), sponsored mainly by foundations, with some federal support. Then in 1967, the Ford Foundation agreed to help pay for several hours of live evening programming.

Also in 1967, the Carnegie Commission on Educational Television released its report *Public Television: A Program for Action*, which included a proposal to create the Corporation for Public Broadcasting (CPB). CPB would collect money from many sources—including the enhanced federal funds the Carnegie report suggested—and disburse the money to the stations.

Slaven Vlasic/Getty Images

PBS began broadcasting as National Educational Television in 1963. Today *PBS Newshour* provides an hour-long evening news broadcast, featuring Judy Woodruff, as an alternative to the traditional TV network evening news. PBS receives some government funding but relies mainly on private donations and corporate sponsors.

In 1962, technicians work on the *Telstar I* communications satellite, which enabled the first transatlantic satellite broadcast. Today's modern satellites, the successors to *Telstar I*, make television delivery systems like DirecTV possible.

President Lyndon Johnson's administration and several foundations added money to CPB's budget. The Public Broadcasting Service (PBS) was created to distribute programs. The extra money underwrote the creation of programs like *Sesame Street* and *The French Chef. PBS Newshour* became a weeknight staple. PBS also began to buy successful British television programs, which were broadcast on *Masterpiece Theatre.* PBS programs actually started to show up in the ratings.

In 1995, members of Congress called for the "privatization" of public television, with the idea that eventually PBS would become completely self-sustaining. Today, the CPB, which oversees public television, still receives funding from the federal government. Local funding supplements this government underwriting, but within the past 10 years, public donations to public television have been declining. This decline in funding has led public broadcasters to seek underwriting from more corporate donors, but companies accustomed to advertising on commercial networks are reluctant to advertise on a network that commonly attracts less than 3 percent of the national audience.

For the first time, public television began to pay attention to ratings. This attention to an audience of consumers means the pressure is building on public television executives to make each program profitable.

The FCC began liberalizing its rules for commercial announcements on public television in 1981. Now, corporate sponsors often make announcements, including graphics and video, at the beginning and the end of PBS-produced programs. The announcements often look the same as advertisements on commercial television. Critics of this commercialization of public television are calling for more government funding, but Congress seems unwilling

to expand its underwriting. Public television is continuing to reinvent itself to try to stay relevant to today's audience.

Satellites Make Transatlantic TV and Live Broadcasts Possible

On July 10, 1962, *Telstar I* sent the first transatlantic satellite broadcast. Before *Telstar,* copper cable linked the continents, film footage from overseas traveled only by plane and in most homes a long-distance telephone call was a special event. Today, *Telstar*'s descendants orbit at a distance of more than 22,000 miles. A single modern communication satellite can carry more than 30,000 telephone calls and 3 television channels. (Modern satellites make program services like CNN and satellite systems like DirecTV possible.)

By 1965, all three networks were broadcasting in color. Television demonstrated its technological sophistication in December 1968 with its live broadcast from the *Apollo* spacecraft while the spacecraft circled the moon, and seven months later television showed Neil Armstrong stepping onto the moon.

Television Changes National and Global Politics

Just as radio was first an entertainment medium and then expanded to cover important news events, television first established itself with entertainment and then developed a serious news presence. Franklin D. Roosevelt had been the first president to understand and use radio, and John F. Kennedy became the country's first television president. Some of Kennedy's predecessors had appeared on television, but he instinctively knew how to *use* television to promote his agenda.

Observers attributed Kennedy's 1960 presidential victory partly to his success in the televised presidential debates with Richard Nixon. Kennedy also was the first president to hold live televised news conferences. In July 1962, he oversaw the launch of the first communications satellite, *Telstar I.* One year later news organizations used that same satellite technology to broadcast live coverage of the news events following President Kennedy's assassination on November 22, 1963.

Television received credit for uniting the nation with its news coverage of the Kennedy assassination, but it also was blamed for dividing it. President Lyndon Johnson, beleaguered by an unpopular war in Vietnam, used television to make an announcement to the nation in 1968 that he would not run for a second term.

Boston Globe/Getty Images

Originally a very small part of television programming, television news today gives audiences access to 24-hour coverage of global events, such as the Boston blizzard on February 15, 2015.

Johnson's successor, President Richard Nixon, had always been uncomfortable with the press. The Nixon administration often attacked the press for presenting perspectives on world affairs that the administration did not like. Upset with the messages being presented, the Nixon administration battled the messenger, sparking a bitter public debate about the role of a free press (especially television) in a democratic society.

Ironically, television's next live marathon broadcast chronicled the ongoing investigation of the Nixon presidency—Watergate. The Watergate scandal began when burglars broke into the offices of the Democratic Party's national headquarters in the Watergate complex in Washington, D.C., on June 17, 1972. Some of the burglars had ties to President Nixon's reelection committee as well as to other questionable activities originating in the White House.

In the months following the break-in, the president and his assistants sought to squelch the resulting investigation. Although Nixon denied knowledge of the break-in and the cover-up, the U.S. Senate hearings about the scandal, televised live across the country, created a national sensation. (See also **Chapter 12**.) Eventually, faced with the prospect of impeachment, Nixon announced his resignation—on television—on August 8, 1974.

In 1987, television repeated its marathon coverage of an important national investigation with the Iran-Contra hearings, a congressional investigation of the Reagan administration's role in illegally selling weapons to Iran and using the money to secretly finance Nicaraguan rebels, called contras.

Television news has matured from its early beginnings as a 15-minute newscast to today's 24-hour international coverage of global events. On September 11, 2001, U.S. TV network news offered nonstop coverage of the terrorist events at New York's World Trade Center, at the Pentagon and in rural Pennsylvania. Two years later, TV networks brought viewers even closer to events when TV reporters and photographers sent live battlefield images and stories during the Iraq War.

And in February 2015, news coverage of devastatingly cold weather on the nation's East Coast brought residents' shared hardship to a worldwide audience. National events instantly become global events because of TV's immediate international reach.

Mergers Affect Station Ownership

The Telecommunications Act of 1996 (see **Chapter 14**) used a station's potential audience to measure ownership limits. The Act allowed one company to own TV stations that reach up to 35 percent of the nation's homes. Broadcasters also are no longer required, as they once were, to hold onto a station for 3 years before selling it. Today, stations may be sold as soon as they are purchased.

In 1999, the Federal Communications Commission (FCC) adopted new regulations that allow media companies to own two TV stations in one market, as long as eight separately owned TV stations continue to operate in that market after the merger. The rules said the four top-rated stations in one market cannot be combined under the same ownership, but a station that is among the four top-rated stations can combine with one that is not in the top four.

In 2003, the FCC relaxed ownership rules even further, leaving few restrictions on network ownership. As with radio, fewer companies are putting together larger and larger groups of TV stations. Today, most local TV stations are not owned by local companies, as they once were. Television is *concentrating* ownership, but it is also *shifting* ownership, as stations are bought and sold at an unprecedented rate. This has introduced instability and change to an industry that until 1980 witnessed very few ownership turnovers.

TV Promotes Professional Sports

Sports is one of TV's most profitable types of television programming because most sports events are broadcast live, and viewers tend to watch the entire program, including commercials. In 1964, CBS paid $28 *million* for television rights to the 1964–1965 National Football League (NFL) games. In 1990, the networks paid $3.6 **billion** to broadcast NFL football.

In 2012, ESPN (owned by the Walt Disney Company) spent $5.6 billion for an 8-year contract to carry Major League Baseball on ESPN as well as for radio, international and digital rights to the games. In 2014, NBC Universal paid $7.75 billion for broadcast rights to the six Olympic games from 2022 to 2032.

Television licensing fees fund most of the cost of organized sports today. Televised sports have become spectacularly complex entertainment packages, turning professional and college athletes as well as sports commentators into media stars. The expansion of sports programming beyond the networks to cable channels such as ESPN means even more sports programming choices for viewers and big payoffs for American sports teams.

Critics Challenge the Accuracy of TV Ratings

People meters, first used in 1987 by The Nielsen Company to record television viewing, gathered data through a 4-inch-by-10-inch box that sat on the television set in metered homes. People meters monitored the nation's Nielsen families (about 4,000 of them, which Nielsen says are a cross section of American viewers), and the results of these recorded viewing patterns became the ratings system that is the basis for television advertising rates.

Nielsen family members each pushed an assigned button in the set-top box when they began to watch television. The system's central computer, linked to the home by telephone lines, correlated each viewer's number with information about that person stored in its memory.

Network ratings plunged after people meters were introduced as a ratings system, and the networks complained that the people meters underestimated specific audiences, especially African Americans and Latinos.

Nielsen recently changed to a more sophisticated measurement system that electronically monitors traditional as well as mobile audiences, but criticism of the ratings' accuracy persists. Still, Nielsen remains the only company in the United States that offers TV audience measurement.

Cable and Satellite Expand Delivery

Today's cable giants, ESPN (Entertainment and Sports Programming Network) and CNN, are descendants of America's first cable TV system, which was established in Pennsylvania and Oregon to bring TV signals to rural areas that couldn't receive an over-the-air signal. Soon, this community antenna television (*CATV*) system spread to remote areas all over the country where TV reception was poor.

By 1970, there were 2,500 CATV systems in the United States, and commercial broadcasters were getting

William Haefeli The New Yorker Collection/The Cartoon Bank

"We're all together watching television, but we're not all watching television together."

nervous about what they called "wired TV." Cable operators were required by the FCC to carry all local broadcast programming, and programs often were duplicated on several channels. The FCC also limited the programs that cable could carry. One FCC ruling, for example, said that movies on cable had to be at least 10 years old.

Believing that cable should be able to offer its own programming, Home Box Office (owned by Time Warner) started operating in Manhattan in 1972, offering a modest set of programs. Ted Turner's Turner Network Television (TNT) first relayed programs by satellite in 1976, and in 1979 Turner started Cable News Network (CNN). Today, more than 125 different program services, ranging from sports on ESPN to 1930s and 1940s movies on American Movie Classics (AMC), are available to cable subscribers.

In 1982, the FCC authorized direct broadcast satellite (*DBS*), making direct satellite-to-home satellite transmission possible. In 1994, a company called DirecTV began offering services directly to the home by satellite for a monthly fee that is about the same as cable. Cable and satellite program delivery systems now are collectively called *subscription television* services.

CATV   Community antenna television or cable television.

DBS   Direct broadcast satellite.

Subscription Television   A new term used to describe consumer services delivered by cable and satellite program delivery.

Cable and satellite programming, which divides viewers into smaller segments than the networks, makes it easier for advertisers to target a specific audience. Programs such the award-winning *Mad Men* series, for example, which ran for eight seasons on AMC, made the once-obscure channel very successful because of the upscale audience the program attracted.

Today, the number of satellite and cable subscribers has stopped growing because of the cost to subscribe and because many popular cable and satellite programs are available on the Internet.

Some consumers have abandoned cable, satellite and even antenna program delivery altogether and instead watch TV solely through Internet streaming. In 2013, The Nielsen Company began tracking this trend, labeling people in this group "*Zero TV consumers*." Nielsen reported there were 5 million Zero TV households in 2013, up from 2 million in 2007.

"The Zero TV segment is increasingly important because the number of people signing up for traditional TV service has slowed to a standstill," reports *The New York Times*. "Nielsen's study suggests that this new group may have left traditional TV for good. While three-quarters actually have a physical TV set, only 18 percent are interested in hooking it up through a traditional pay TV subscription."

Television at Work

A typical television station has eight departments:

1. Sales

2. Programming (which includes news as well as entertainment)

3. Production

4. Engineering

5. Traffic

6. Promotion

7. Public affairs

8. Administration

People in the *sales* department sell the commercial slots for the programs. Advertising is divided into national and local sales. Advertising agencies, usually based on the East Coast, buy national ads for the products they handle. An ad agency may buy time on a network for the Ford Motor Company, for instance, for a TV ad that will run simultaneously all over the country.

But local Ford dealers, who want you to shop at their showroom, buy their ads directly from the local station. These ads are called local (or spot) ads. For these sales, salespeople (called account executives) at each station

negotiate packages of ads based on their station's advertising rates. These rates are a direct reflection of the station's position in the ratings.

The *programming* department selects the shows that you will see and develops the station's schedule. Network-owned stations, usually located in big cities (KNBC in Los Angeles, for example), are called **O & Os**, which stands for "owned and operated." O & Os automatically carry network programming. **Affiliates** are stations that carry network programming but are not owned by the networks. The networks pay affiliates to carry their programming, for which the networks sell most of the ads and keep the money. An affiliate is allowed to insert into the network programming a specific number of local ads, for which the affiliate keeps the income.

Because affiliates can make money on network programming and don't have to pay for it, many stations choose to affiliate themselves with a network. When they aren't running what the network provides, affiliates run their own programs and keep all the advertising money they collect from them.

Some of the nation's commercial TV stations operate as independents. Independent stations must buy and program all their own shows, but independents also keep all the money they make on advertising. Independents run some individually produced programs and old movies, but most of their programming consists of reruns such as *Frasier* and *Everybody Loves Raymond* that once ran on the networks. Independents buy these reruns from program services called **syndicators**.

Local news usually makes up the largest percentage of a station's locally produced programming. In some large markets, such as Los Angeles, local nightly news programs run as long as two hours.

The *production* department manages the programs the station creates in-house. This department also produces local commercials for the station. The *engineering* department makes sure all the technical aspects of a broadcast operation are working: antennas, transmitters, cameras and any other broadcast equipment. The *traffic* department

Zero TV Consumers People who do not use a traditional TV set to watch programs via antenna, cable or satellite, but instead access TV programs through video streaming on the Internet.

O & Os TV stations that are owned and operated by the networks.

Affiliates Stations that use network programming but are owned by companies other than the networks.

Syndicators Services that sell programming to broadcast stations and cable.

The live broadcast of President Obama's election night victory on November 4, 2008, captured 70 million viewers, a record number for a presidential election night.

integrates the advertising with the programming, making sure that all the ads that are sold are aired when they're supposed to be. Traffic also handles billing for the ads.

The *promotion* department advertises the station—on the station itself, on billboards, on radio and in the local newspaper. These people also create contests to keep the station visible in the community. The *public affairs* department helps organize public events, such as a fun run to raise money for the local hospital. *Administration* handles the paperwork for the station—paychecks and expense accounts, for example.

Audiences Drive TV Programming

Today's most-watched television programs are situation comedies and sports. Super Bowls generally grab about half the homes in the United States. More than 120 million people tuned in for the final episode of the situation comedy *M*A*S*H* in 1983, making it the highest-rated television program ever. In 1993, the final episode of the sitcom *Cheers* garnered

an audience of 80 million, and today network comedies like *The Big Bang Theory* continue to lead in TV audience ratings.

In 2008, the surprise ratings leader was President-elect Barack Obama. More than 70 million people watched his election victory the night of November 4, 2008, a record number of viewers for a presidential election night.

Two developments promise to affect the television industry over the next decade: the shrinking role of the networks and the demand for more diverse programming to attract new audiences.

The Networks' Shrinking Role

Advertisers always have provided the economic support for television, so in 1986 the networks were disturbed to see the first decline in advertising revenues in 15 years. New and continuing developments—such as cable, satellite broadcast, DVDs, streaming—have turned the television set into a smorgasbord of choices. Audiences—and advertisers—began to desert the networks, and network ratings declined as a result.

Today, because there are so many sources of TV programming available, even the most popular shows attract a relatively small percentage of the overall audience.

The networks' share of the audience for the evening news also is shrinking. The story is familiar, paralleling the decline in radio listening in the late 1940s when television first replaced radio and then television began competing with itself. Today more stations and more sources of programming mean the TV networks must expand their audience beyond the traditional prime-time evening time slot to stay profitable.

Online retailer Amazon Studios produced a new streaming Web series called *Transparent*, which premiered in Los Angeles on September 15, 2014.

Demand for Diverse Programming

During the summer of 2005, Univision, the nation's largest Spanish-language network, drew more prime-time viewers in the 18–34 age group than any of the traditional broadcast networks—NBC, CBS, ABC and Fox. This was the first time Spanish-language TV had beaten the networks for this lucrative young audience. The main draw was *telenovelas*, or Spanish-language soap operas.

This Spanish-language lead in prime time had been building for several years, as the nation's Latino population increased. According to *The New York Times*, "Market researchers say that Latinos—no matter their age or dominant language—tend to tune in to Spanish-language television for two main staples: newscasts, because networks like Univision cover Latino issues and Latin America with more breadth and resources than English-language networks, and telenovelas, which function like a kind of cultural touchstone.

"Whether you're U.S.-born and you're introduced to it by a parent or grandparent or whether you're foreign-born and you grew up with it, it's the kind of thing that's inherent in the culture," multicultural marketing consultant Derene Allen told *The Times*. As traditional audiences shrink, and advertisers try to find new ways to sell their products, Spanish-language TV is emerging as one promising audience market.

Video programs produced solely for Internet distribution also offer a new avenue to target audiences with edgier, timely subjects. In 2014, for example, online retailer Amazon launched Fire TV, an electronic device with access to Amazon's extensive video library, including a new streaming Web series produced by Amazon Studios called *Transparent*. The show explores a family headed by Maura Pfefferman (played by Jeffrey Tambor), who is in the midst of changing his identity from male to female. For his portrayal, Tambor won a Golden Globe in 2015, an acknowledgment that Web TV programming could compete for viewers with traditional TV.

Digital Technology Broadens TV's Focus

When technological developments move like a rocket, as they have in the past decade, program delivery becomes easier and less expensive. New technologies have brought more competition.

Ethan Miller/Getty Images

At the 2015 Consumer Electronics Show, manufacturers promote a curved-screen, 65-inch 4K TV, called ultrahigh-definition.

Several new delivery systems and products have been developed to bring more choices to consumers than ever before—from the size of the screen to the clarity of the picture—and to change further the way people use television.

Digital Video Recorders

Digital video recorders (**DVRs**), available since the 1990s, download programming from any program service (including the broadcast networks and satellite and cable programmers). This allows viewers to decide what they want to watch and when, a practice called *time-shifting*, which makes consumers' viewing habits much more difficult for advertisers to track accurately.

High-Definition Television, 3-D and 4K Screens

A traditional television picture scans 525 lines across the screen. *High-definition television (HDTV)* scans at least 1,125 lines. CBS first demonstrated HDTV in the U.S. in 1982. HDTV, which offers a wider, sharper digital picture and better sound, requires more spectrum space than conventional television signals.

DVR   Digital video recorders.

Time-Shifting   Recording a television program on a DVR to watch at a more convenient time.

High-Definition Television (HDTV)   The industry standard for digital television transmission as of 2009; it provides a picture with a clearer resolution than earlier TV sets.

IMPACT

Convergence

Netflix Is Betting Its Future on Exclusive Programming

By Emily Steel

LOS GATOS, Calif.—It is April 9 [2015] just before midnight in the war room of Netflix's headquarters here, where the smell of popcorn fills the air and a team of engineers, social media experts and other specialists starts counting down the seconds until the new *Daredevil* superhero series goes live on the streaming service.

At the stroke of 12, applause breaks out in the room. Flutes of Champagne are passed around as the Netflix team checks that the series is available for binge watching across devices in more than 50 countries around the world.

Daredevil is the 17th Netflix original series to make its debut [in 2015], representing a bold bet by the company to significantly increase its investment in exclusive programming. The company is planning 320 hours of original programming in 2015, about three times what it offered [in 2014].

Reed Hastings, Netflix's chief executive, is a connoisseur of them all. Hastings wants to position the company as the entertainment world undergoes a digital revolution.

Traditionally, television networks needed to stand for something to carve out an audience, he said, whereas the Internet allows brands to mean different things to different people because the service can be personalized for individual viewers. "We want the original content to be as broad as human experience."

The emphasis on original content is an extension of Netflix's long-term view that the Internet is replacing television, that apps are replacing channels and that screens are proliferating, Mr. Hastings said.

"We've had 80 years of linear TV, and it's been amazing, and in its day the fax machine was amazing," he said. "The next 20 years will be this transformation from linear TV to Internet TV."

But some analysts have expressed concern about the company's long-term prospects for more growth in the United States. Netflix also faces a new wave of intense competition in the U.S. as a number of tech and media companies introduce streaming services. That includes HBO, which recently started HBO Now, which does not require a cable or satellite subscription.

Reed Hastings, Netflix's CEO, says the company plans to compete with HBO by producing original series available primarily by video streaming on the Web.

AP Images/Bernd von Jutrczenka

Mr. Hastings said that he welcomed the new streaming entrants. Rather than a competitive threat, they represent the realization of the benefits of on-demand streaming television that allows people to watch shows on their own schedule and on the devices of their choosing, he said.

"It will be like the Yankees and the Red Sox," Mr. Hastings said. "I predict HBO will do the best creative work of their lives in the next 10 years because they are on war footing. They haven't really had a challenge for a long time, and now they do. It's going to spur us both on to incredible work."

Excerpted from Emily Steel, "Netflix Is Betting Its Future on Exclusive Programming," April 19, 2015, nytimes.com.

Digital TV also makes it easier for manufacturers to combine the functions of TV and the functions of a computer in the same piece of equipment. HDTV became the national industry standard in 2009.

In 2010, major television manufacturers started selling 3-D TVs, and several programmers announced plans to create 3-D shows to feed the new market, but by 2015 interest in 3-D had faded, just like interest in 3-D movies.

In 2014, hoping that consumers could be convinced to upgrade to an even better picture than HDTV, manufacturers introduced 4K screens, which offer a picture with twice the resolution as HDTV. The new sets are called ultrahigh-definition TVs, but only programs produced in 4K can be viewed in the ultrahigh-definition format.

Streaming TV Brings a New Vision

Forecasts for the future of television parallel the forecasts for radio—a menu board of hundreds of programs and services available to viewers at the touch of a remote-control button. In the 1990s, regional telephone companies (abbreviated as *telcos*) rushed to merge with cable TV companies to form giant telecommunications delivery systems.

To try to maintain their audience dominance, the TV networks have invested heavily in satellite TV and Internet program services to develop the capability to deliver programs to screens as small as a cell phone, and these new financial powerhouses can spend large sums of money for research to reach the audiences they want.

In 2006, when Congress passed a law that required TV broadcasters to switch totally to digital signals by 2009, only about 60 percent of U.S. households were capable of receiving a digital TV signal, according to the Consumer Electronics Association. Today, digital television is the new national standard. Television audiences seem to welcome most new technologies, even seek them out. (See **Impact/Convergence**, "Netflix Is Betting Its Future on Exclusive Programming," p. 165.)

Digital technology makes high-quality television images available on screens as large as a wall and as small as a cell phone. HDTV and ultrahigh-definition TVs offer movie-quality pictures and CD-quality sound. Internet delivery offers programming that's mobile and can follow you wherever and whenever you want it.

And new players are entering the game. In 2012, Netflix offered a new original series, *House of Cards*, through its video streaming service, and in 2014 Amazon Studios announced it had signed several pilot TV programs for Internet distribution. In 2015, Netflix launched its 17th original series, with plans to produce 320 hours of original programming.

The definition of what we call "television" and "television program" is exploding. Lanny Smoot, an executive at Bell Communications Research, calls the future of television a *telepresence*. "This," he says, "is a wave that is not possible to stop."

Telcos An abbreviation for "telephone companies."

REVIEW, ANALYZE, INVESTIGATE

CHAPTER 8

Television Transforms Daily Life

- The word *television*, which once meant programs delivered by antennas through over-the-air signals, today means a *television screen*, where a variety of delivery systems bring viewers a diversity of programs.

- Many groups are concerned that, because of its pervasiveness, television influences the nation's values, habits and behavior.

- About 1,700 television stations operate in the United States. Three out of four of these are commercial stations and about half of U.S. stations are affiliated with a network.

TV Delivers an Audience to Advertisers

- More than any other media industry today, commercial television exists primarily as an advertising medium.

- A 30-second ad during Super Bowl 2015 cost an advertiser as much as $4.5 million.

Visual Radio Becomes *Television*

- Guglielmo Marconi put sound on airwaves. Lee de Forest invented the Audion tube. Vladimir Zworykin turned an electronic signal into a visual image. Philo T. Farnsworth added the electronic scanner.

- The rivalry between David Sarnoff (RCA) and William S. Paley (CBS) is central to the early history of television.
- The ABC network was formed when the Federal Communications Commission (FCC) ordered David Sarnoff to sell one of his two networks (Red and Blue). The Blue network became ABC.

Television Outpaces Radio

- The first television news broadcasts were primitive compared to today's broadcasts. Television news, like radio news, developed its own standard of excellence, led by news pioneers Edward R. Murrow and David Brinkley.
- Most television entertainment programming was derived from radio.
- The only type of program that didn't come from radio was the talk show, which appeared on television first and then moved to radio. The situation comedy proved to be one of television's most durable types of programming.

Quiz Shows Bring Ethics Scandals

- A congressional investigation revealed that several 1950s TV quiz shows were rigged to enhance their ratings.
- The 1950s quiz show scandals caused the networks to eliminate advertiser-produced programming.
- Charles Van Doren, who admitted that he cheated, was a central figure in the quiz show scandals.

Ratings Target the Audience

- The Nielsen ratings determine the price that TV advertisers pay to air their commercials.
- TV audiences are measured as ratings and shares.

Newton Minow Criticizes TV as a "Vast Wasteland"

- In the 1960s, audiences grew more discriminating and began to question how well the medium of television was serving the public.
- An influential person who outlined TV's responsibility to its audience was then-FCC Chairman Newton Minow, who coined the phrase "vast wasteland" to describe television.

Public Television Finds an Audience

- National Educational Television (NET) is the predecessor of today's Corporation for Public Broadcasting (CPB).
- In 1981, the FCC loosened the rules for commercials on public television.

Satellites Make Transatlantic TV and Live Broadcasts Possible

- In 1962, *Telstar I* sent the first transatlantic satellite broadcast.
- Modern satellites make CNN and DirecTV possible.

Television Changes National and Global Politics

- In the 1960s, television drew criticism for the way it was perceived to influence politics and the dialogue about national issues.
- Television broadcast nonstop coverage of the Watergate hearings, President Nixon's resignation and investigations of the Iran-Contra scandal.
- In 2001, U.S. TV network news offered nonstop coverage of the terrorist attacks at New York's World Trade Center, at the Pentagon and in rural Pennsylvania.
- In 2003, the TV networks brought viewers even closer to events when TV reporters and photographers sent live battlefield images and stories during the Iraq War.
- In 2015, TV showed people around the world events surrounding the record-setting Boston blizzard.
- National events become global events because of TV's instant international reach.

Mergers Affect Station Ownership

- Deregulation, with relaxed ownership rules, means that instability, mergers and change have become major characteristics of the television industry.
- Today, most local TV stations are not owned by local companies, as they once were.

TV Promotes Professional Sports

- TV licensing fees fund most of the cost of the nation's college and professional sports.
- The expansion of sports programming beyond the networks to cable channels such as ESPN means bigger payoffs for American sports teams.

Critics Challenge the Accuracy of TV Ratings

- Network ratings plunged after The Nielsen Company introduced people meters as a ratings system.
- TV networks also must compete with the huge variety of program options vying for consumers' attention.
- Nielsen recently changed to a more sophisticated measurement system that monitors both traditional and mobile TV audiences, but criticism persists.

Cable and Satellite Expand Delivery

- Today's cable giants ESPN (Entertainment and Sports Programming Network) and CNN are descendants of America's first cable TV system, established in Pennsylvania and Oregon to bring TV signals to rural areas.
- This community antenna television (*CATV*) system spread to remote areas nationwide where TV reception was poor.
- By 1970, there were 2,500 CATV systems in the U.S.
- In 1982, the FCC authorized direct broadcast satellite (*DBS*), making direct satellite-to-home broadcasts possible.
- In 1994, DirecTV began offering satellite services to the home.

- Cable and satellite program delivery systems now are collectively called *subscription television* services.

- Today, the number of satellite and cable subscribers has stopped growing.

- Some consumers, labeled Zero TV households, have abandoned cable, satellite and even antenna program delivery altogether and instead watch TV solely through Web streaming.

Television at Work

- A typical TV station has eight departments: sales, programming, production, engineering, traffic, promotion, public affairs and administration.

- Many TV stations are affiliated with a network.

Audiences Drive TV Programming

- The most-watched TV programs are situation comedies and sports.

- Spanish-language networks draw increasing numbers of prime-time viewers.

- Amazon Studios produced the original streaming Web show *Transparent* in 2014. The show's star, Jeffrey Tambor, won a Golden Globe for his performance in its first year, an acknowledgment that Web TV programs could compete with traditional TV.

Digital Technology Broadens TV's Focus

- Several technological developments have changed the way programs are delivered to consumers, including digital video recorders, high-definition television and the Internet.

- HDTV offers better pictures, clearer sound and a flatter screen than traditional TV and became the national industry standard in 2009.

- Digital TV makes it easier for manufacturers to combine the functions of TV and the functions of a computer in the same TV set.

- In 2010, major television manufacturers started selling 3-D TVs, but by 2015 consumer interest in 3-D had faded.

- In 2015, trying to stimulate sales, TV manufacturers introduced 4K TV, offering a picture with twice the resolution of HDTV, called ultrahigh resolution.

Streaming TV Brings a New Vision

- Cable, satellite and Internet program services have developed the capability to deliver programs to screens as small as a cell phone.

- In 2012, Netflix offered a new original series, *House of Cards*, through its video streaming service, and in 2014 Amazon Studios announced it had signed several pilot TV programs for Internet distribution.

Key Terms

These terms are defined in the margins throughout this chapter and appear in alphabetical order with definitions in the Glossary, which begins on page 361.

Critical Questions

1. Explain what media observer Jeff Greenfield means when he says, "To the television executive, the product [of television] is the audience."

2. How did the quiz show scandals of the 1950s affect the relationship between advertisers and the networks? Is the relationship between advertisers and the networks different or the same today? Explain.

3. Discuss the economic challenges facing public broadcasting and the various sources of funding on which individual public broadcast stations as well as CPB and PBS rely. How has public broadcasting responded to these challenges?

4. Explain the role of the Nielsen ratings in television, including such factors as ratings accuracy, advertisers' dependence on ratings, the effect of ratings on programming and the emergence of the Zero TV household.

5. Describe three ways that new technologies (such as Internet video streaming) affect the future of the television industry.

Working the Web

This list includes sites mentioned in the chapter and others to give you greater insight into the television business.

CBS Television

cbs.com

Originally known as the Columbia Broadcasting Network, CBS Television is the national commercial television broadcast network owned by the CBS Corporation. It provides entertainment, sports and news programming from the national network level to local CBS television stations throughout the U.S. as well as programming that can be accessed online.

Disney/ABC Television Group

disneyabcpress.com

Disney/ABC Television Group is comprised of The Walt Disney Company's entertainment and news television properties, owned television stations group and radio business. This includes ABC Studios, the ABC Owned Television Stations Group, and the ABC Television Network, which provides entertainment, news and kids programming to viewers via affiliated stations across the U.S.

HBO (Home Box Office)

hbo.com

HBO is the pay television programming division of Time Warner Inc. It offers programming via HBO and Cinemax to more than 127 million viewers throughout the world. In 2015, HBO introduced HBO Now, a stand-alone subscription-based service that offers streaming access to all of its programming.

Interactive Advertising Bureau (IAB)

iab.net

Established in 1996 and headquartered in New York City, the IAB is composed of more than 650 media and technology companies that are "responsible for selling 86 percent of online advertising in the United States." The IAB lobbies on behalf of these companies in Washington, D.C., and around the country, making recommendations on standards and practices as well as conducting its own research on the interactive advertising industry.

National Association of Broadcasters (NAB)

nab.org

The National Association of Broadcasters is the "voice for the nation's radio and television broadcasters." As the trade association for over-the-air broadcasters, the NAB advances the interests of its members in federal government, industry and public affairs. NAB is the chief lobbying advocate for broadcasters in Washington, D.C., also coordinating with the lobbying efforts of broadcast associations in the capitals of all 50 states.

National Cable & Telecommunications Association (NCTA)

ncta.com

NCTA is the principal trade association for the U.S. cable industry, representing cable operators serving more than 90 percent of the nation's cable television households and more than 200 cable program networks. The cable industry is the nation's largest broadband provider of high-speed Internet access, serving more than 51 million customers. Cable companies also provide digital telephone service to more than 27 million American consumers.

NBC

nbc.com

A division of NBC Universal, NBC is a national commercial broadcast television network. NBC provides entertainment, sports and news programming from the national network level to local NBC television stations throughout the U.S. as well as programming that can be accessed online.

Nielsen Media Research

nielsen.com

Nielsen Media Research (NMR), once one of the largest media research companies in the world, began as a division of AC Nielsen, a marketing research firm. The Nielsen TV ratings have been produced in the U.S. since the 1950s and statistically measure which programs are watched by different segments of the population. Today, NMR also provides radio broadcast ratings. The results of these ratings are used to set the advertising rates for commercials broadcast on U.S. radio and TV stations as well as some digital media companies.

Parental Guide

parentalguide.org

Primarily an online shopping Web site for young families, Parental Guide also provides a resource for parents and caregivers seeking information on the voluntary parental guideline systems in place for television, movies, video games and recorded music.

Public Broadcasting Service (PBS)

pbs.org

With more than 350 publicly funded, noncommercial TV stations throughout the U.S., PBS reaches nearly 103 million viewers per week through on-air broadcasts and 33 million viewers of programming and content online. PBS.org includes a program search, TV schedules and links to online-featured programming on topics such as History, Culture & Society and News & Public Affairs. PBS Kids Online (pbskids.org) provides educational entertainment for children as well as a comprehensive resource section for parents and teachers.

Television Bureau of Advertising (TVB)
tvb.org

TVB is the not-for-profit trade association of America's commercial broadcast television industry. Its members include television broadcast groups, advertising sales reps, syndica-tors, international broadcasters, associate members and almost 700 individual television stations. TVB actively promotes local media marketing solutions for television stations.

TV.com
tv.com

This fan-run site includes information about programs, episodes, actors, lines and trivia for TV shows from the 1940s to today. It has a wide variety of online forums sorted by show genre as well as news, celebrity photos, downloads and podcasts.

Impact/Action Videos are concise news features on various topics created exclusively for *Media/Impact*. Find them in *Media/Impact*'s MindTap at cengagebrain.com.

MindTap® Log on to MindTap for *Media/Impact* to access a variety of additional material—including learning objectives, chapter readings with highlighting and note-taking, **Impact/Action Videos**, activities, and comprehension quizzes—that will guide you through this chapter.

TINA FINEBERG/The New York Times

Columbia University law professor Tim Wu, who coined the term *net neutrality*, argues that the federal government should guarantee equal Internet access for everyone through law and regulation.

What's Ahead?

- Digital Communication Transforms Media
- Digital Media Support Convergence
- 20th-Century Discoveries Made Internet Possible
- Web Opens to Unlimited Access
- What Happens to Old Media?
- Transformation Takes 30 Years
- Web Access Leaves Some People Behind
- Internet Combines Commerce, Information and Entertainment
- Mobile Media Chase the Audience
- Social Networks Grow Globally
- Government Attempts to Coordinate and Control the Net
- Protection Sought for Intellectual Property Rights
- FCC Promotes Internet Neutrality
- Storage, Competing Systems and Security Bring Challenges
- Disruptive Technologies Revolutionize Old Concepts
- Consumers Intersect with Technology

> "The FCC's Open Internet rules protect and maintain open, uninhibited access to legal online content without broadband Internet access providers being allowed to block, impair, or establish fast/slow lanes to lawful content."
>
> —FEDERAL COMMUNICATIONS COMMISSION, FEBRUARY 26, 2015

"Today's world has become so wired together, so flattened, that you can't avoid seeing just where you stand on the planet—just where the caravan is and just how far ahead or behind you are," says *New York Times* columnist Thomas L. Friedman. The main reason for today's flattened planet, of course, is the Internet. Within the last 30 years, the emergence of the Internet as an interactive delivery system has transformed the structure and the economics of the media business in the United States and throughout the world.

Before the 1970s, media were defined by the systems that delivered them. Paper delivered the print media—newspapers, magazines and books. Antennas carried broadcast signals—radio and television. Movies required film, and music traveled on round discs. These traditional media each were specifically connected to their own method of delivery and organized into different types of companies—newspaper, magazine and book publishers; recording and movie studios; and radio and TV stations.

Digital Communication Transforms Media

Today, the Internet delivers all types of media—print, broadcast, audio and video—using a single delivery system without barriers. You can receive all types of media just about anywhere you want, delivered by many different types of companies, carried on invisible electronic

signals. The Internet has caused the emergence of new media products and new competition in the media business that were impossible to foresee when the Internet first emerged as a place for consumers in 1978. Originally the Internet was designed by a group of scientists who were simply hoping to share information.

The Internet combines millions of computer networks sending and receiving data from all over the world—competing interests joined by a common purpose but no common owner. "No government or commercial entity owns the Net or directly profits from its operation," notes information designer Roger Fidler. "It has no president, chief executive officer or central headquarters."

In its global size and absence of central control, the Internet is completely different from traditional media. Originally developed to help researchers, scientists and educators communicate, the Internet has "evolved in a way no one planned or expected," says Fidler. "It is the relationships among people that have shaped the medium."

The term ***digital media*** describes all forms of communications media that combine text, pictures, sound

---

Digital Media All emerging communications media that combine text, graphics, sound and video using computer technology.

TimeFrame
1978–Today

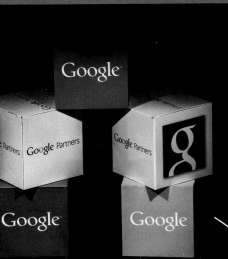

1978 Nicholas Negroponte at MIT first uses the term *convergence* to describe the intersection of the media industries.

✱ **1984** Apple launches the Macintosh personal computer.

1988 Less than one-half of 1 percent of U.S. households are online.

1989 Tim Berners-Lee develops the first browser and programming languages that allow people to share all types of information online.

1992 Neil Papworth, a software programmer in England, sends the first text message.

1994 Marc Andreessen and his colleagues at the University of Illinois introduce the Mosaic browser.

1995 David Filo and Jerry Yang launch Yahoo! as a search engine company.

1996 Internet advertising reaches $200 million. Congress passes the Communications Decency Act.

1998 One in four U.S. households is online. Congress passes the Digital Millennium Copyright Act. Larry Page and Sergey Brin launch Google.

1999 The Recording Industry Association of America (RIAA) sues Internet file-sharing company Napster for copyright infringement.

2000 The number of Internet businesses explodes.

2001 File-sharing company Napster shuts down. The number of Internet startups begins to shrink, and many existing companies close.

2003 RIAA and the Motion Picture Association of America announce campaigns to aggressively fight online piracy.

2004 Mark Zuckerberg launches Facebook as a social networking site.

2005 File-sharing company Grokster shuts down, settling a landmark intellectual property case.

2006 Internet advertising reaches $17 billion.

2007 Apple introduces the iPhone.

✱ **2008** Google celebrates its tenth anniversary.

2010 Apple introduces the iPad and the iPhone 4.

2011 Apple launches iCloud. Apple's App Store reaches 25 billion downloads. Twitter hits 100 million users. Apple CEO Steve Jobs dies.

2012 Facebook has 1 billion monthly users.

2013 President Obama signs an executive order promoting cybersecurity.

✱ **2015** The Federal Communications Commission approves net neutrality, guaranteeing equal access to the Internet.

TODAY Four out of five American adults use the Internet. Fifty-two percent of online adults use two or more social media sites. Businesses spend more than $51 billion a year for Internet advertising.

and video using computer technology. Digital media read, write and store data electronically in numerical form—using numbers to code the data (text, pictures, sound and video). Because all digital media use the same numbered codes, digital media are ***compatible***, which means they can function well with one another to exchange and integrate text, pictures, sound and video. This compatibility is the main reason digital media are growing so fast. Because of its rapid growth, digital communications has become the central factor affecting the development of today's mass media industries.

Rather than the one-way communication of traditional media, communication on today's compatible digital networks means someone can receive and send information simultaneously, without barriers. Digital networks "free individuals from the shackles of corporate bureaucracy and geography and allow them to collaborate and exchange ideas with the best colleague anywhere in the world," said futurist George Gilder. "Computer networks give every hacker the creative potential of a factory tycoon of the industrial [turn-of-the-century] era and the communications power of a TV magnate of the broadcasting era."

In an interconnected digital world, the speed and convenience of the network redefines the mass media industries and erases all previous notions of how mass communications should work. Today's media are constantly evolving. Digital media forms "do not arise spontaneously and independently from old media," says media scholar Roger Fidler. Digital media are related and connected to old media. Fidler says today's media are members of an interdependent system, with "similarities and relationships that exist among past, present and emerging forms."

Digital media are similar to traditional media yet different in ways that make them distinct from their predecessors. Because of the interdependence of today's mass media, all the media industries are transforming simultaneously.

Digital Media Support Convergence

In 1978, Nicholas Negroponte at the Massachusetts Institute of Technology was the first to identify a theory called ***convergence***. This theory gave a name to the process by which the various media industries in the late 1970s were beginning to intersect, and MIT was among the first places to foresee and identify this trend. (See **Illustration 9.1**, "The Evolution of Today's Convergence: 1978 to 2016," p. 175.)

The media industries not only were combining economically, as media companies began to buy and sell each other, but the technology of the industries also was merging, according to MIT. This convergence meant that eventually the products the media companies produced began to interact with each other.

Negroponte also said that the combination of the traditional media industries with the computer industry would create a new type of communication.

To identify what was happening to the media industries, Negroponte created two models to show the position of the media industries in 1978 and his projected vision for those industries in the year 2000. He listed three segments of the media business: (1) print and

The Internet offers people mobile media access just about wherever and whenever they want it, including in their cars. Because of the distractions it causes, many states have made texting while driving illegal.

Tony Avelar/The Christian Science Monitor/Getty Images

Compatible Media that can function well with one another to exchange and integrate text, pictures, sound and video.

Convergence The melding of the communications, computer and electronics industries.

IMPACT

Convergence

The year **1978**

The year **2000**

The year **2016**

© Cengage Learning 2015

ILLUSTRATION 9.1

The Evolution of Today's Convergence: 1978 to 2016

The diagram on the left displays the alignment of the mass media industries

in 1978, showing each media industry with very little overlapping territory. The middle diagram shows what MIT's Nicholas Negroponte predicted would happen by 2000, with the three types of industries—broadcast/ motion pictures, printing/publishing and computers—merging further.

The 2016 diagram shows what convergence looks like today. Because of digital computing technology, all three media segments have completely intersected. Printing/publishing and broadcast/ motion picture products are available to consumers across all types of media devices.

---

publishing, (2) broadcast and motion pictures and (3) the computer industry.

The first diagram in Negroponte's model displays the alignment of the media industries in 1978, which shows them with a small amount of integrated territory. In the second diagram, which shows Negroponte's predictions for the year 2000, the three segments of the media industries completely overlap. Negroponte's forecast was a very accurate prediction, and it helped establish the framework for today's thinking about the Internet.

This early economic and technological convergence in the media industries is the most important reason for the development of today's digital media. By the year 2000, every media industry was equally well positioned to take advantage of new developments, and today every media industry benefits from convergence.

20th-Century Discoveries Made Internet Possible

Several technological developments were necessary for people to be able to share text, graphics, audio and video online. These developments made the creation of the World

Wide Web possible. The person most responsible for the World Wide Web is Tim Berners-Lee, a British native with an Oxford degree in physics. Working in 1989 in Geneva, Switzerland, at the CERN physics laboratory, Berners-Lee created several new programming languages.

One of these new computer-programming languages was ***HTML*** (hypertext markup language). Hypertext transfer protocol (***HTTP***) allowed people to create and send text, graphics and video information electronically and to set up electronic connections (called ***links***) from one source of information to another. These developments were very important in the Web's early days, and today people who use the Internet don't even need to know the programming language that made the Web possible.

HTML   Hypertext markup language.

HTTP   Hypertext transfer protocol.

Links   Electronic connections from one source of information to another.

British computer scientist Tim Berners-Lee invented the World Wide Web and gave the Web its name. Berners-Lee gives a presentation at the Palace of Westminster, London, on February 5, 2015.

After he invented the language and mechanisms that would allow people to share all kinds of information electronically, Berners-Lee gave this invention its name—the World Wide Web. "The original goal was working together with others," says Berners-Lee. "The Web was supposed to be a creative tool, an expressive tool." Berners-Lee also created the first *browser*, which allows people to search electronically among many documents to find what they want.

Today, Berners-Lee still is involved in the Web's development, as founder of the World Wide Web Foundation, which promotes access to the Web throughout the world. "When you think about how the Web is today and dream about how it might be, you must, as always, consider both technology and people," says Berners-Lee. "Future technology should be smarter and more powerful, of course. But you cannot ethically turn your attention to developing it without also listening to those people who don't use the Web at all, or who could use it if only it were different in some way. The Web has been largely designed by the developed world for the developed world. But it must be much more inclusive in order to be of great value to us all."

Marc Andreessen and his colleagues at the University of Illinois further defined the browser, and in 1994 they introduced software called Mosaic, which allowed people to put text and pictures in the same online document. Some of the successors to Mosaic are Safari, Mozilla, Google Chrome, Firefox and Internet Explorer, which are among the most widely used commercial browsers.

Another level of help for Web access is the *search engine*. This tool locates information in computer databases. Two familiar search engines are Google and Yahoo! These systems turn your typed request for information into digital bits that then search for what you want and return the information to you. Yahoo!, founded in 1995 as a search engine company, today makes money through subscriptions, advertising and classified ads and employs more than 8,000 people around the world. Google Inc., which has more than 50,000 employees, celebrated its 15th anniversary in 2013. Launched by entrepreneurs Larry Page and Sergey Brin in 1998 with four computers and $100,000, Google Inc. is now worth more than $370 billion.

To encourage people to use their systems, both Berners-Lee and Andreessen placed their discoveries in the *public domain*, which means that anyone with a computer and a modem can download them from the Internet and use them for free. *This culture of free information access, coupled with a creative, chaotic lack of direction, still permeates the Web today.*

The process of putting documents on the Web drew its terminology from print, the original mass medium. That's why placing something on the Web is called *publishing*, and the publication begins with a *home page*, the front door to the site—the place that welcomes the user and explains how the site works. However, even though Web sites are similar to published documents in the way they work, what is created on the Web has few of the legal limitations or protections that apply to other published documents. (See **Chapter 14**.)

Web Opens to Unlimited Access

Once Tim Berners-Lee had created the tools for access so that all types of text and video images could become available on the Web, it was left to anyone who could use the tools to create whatever they wanted and make it available to anyone who wanted it.

"Nobody ever designed the Web," says Canadian sociologist Craig McKie, who maintains his own Web site. "There are no rules, no laws. The Web also exists without

Browser   Software that allows people to display and interact with information on Web pages.

Search Engine   The tool used to locate information in a computer database.

Public Domain   Publications, products and processes that are not protected by copyright and thus are available free to the public.

Publishing   Placing items on the Web.

Home Page   The first page of a Web site, which welcomes the user.

Companies are using today's emerging technologies to create new products like the Apple Watch, introduced in 2015, which they hope the public will embrace.

Media and computer entrepreneurs try to capitalize on fast-moving developments to be the first to deliver new creative products that large numbers of people will want to use, and society struggles to adjust to the access to communication that new products create.

There are many parallels between the development of the Internet and the early history of traditional media, such as movies. Like traditional media, today's emerging technologies are being used to try to create new popular products that the public will crave.

In the early 1900s, when movies first were introduced as flickering images on a small screen, the moving images were something consumers hadn't seen before, but many people thought the silent movies were just a passing fad (see **Chapter 7**). The inventions Thomas Edison and his colleagues introduced at the time made the movies technologically possible, but the movies also needed creative minds like director D. W. Griffith and stars like Mary Pickford to create epic stories that people wanted to see. When new inventions brought sound to the movies, the success of the new medium was unstoppable.

This combination of technological development, creative expression and consumer demand was crucial for the movies' enduring prosperity. The same collision of economics, technology and creativity that drove the early days of the movie industry is behind today's race to develop digital media.

national boundaries." Any type of information—video, audio, graphics and text—can travel virtually instantly to and from anyone who has a computer and access to the Internet anywhere in the world.

Universal access, limited only by the available technology, is what gives the Web the feeling and look of what has been called "anarchy"—a place without rules. The Web is a new medium, but its growth as a true *mass medium* for people seeking information and entertainment is limited only by digital technology and economics. Large media companies have huge amounts of money available to bankroll new technologies. These companies also have a shared interest in seeing their investments succeed. So convergence is continuing at a very rapid pace, which is the main reason new digital media products are being introduced so quickly.

Some of the digital media products that flood the marketplace succeed; many do not. However, the potential reward if consumers adopt a digital media product is so large that all types of media companies are willing to take the risks associated with developing new products. For consumers, this means an array of products bombarding the marketplace simultaneously, such as the Apple Watch.

When newer forms of media emerge, older media systems evolve and adapt. However, discarded electronic gear like this pile of old computers and TV sets in Philadelphia poses a challenge for recyclers.

What Happens to Old Media?

How does the development of digital media affect older, traditional media? Some scholars have predicted, for example, that print media are dead, yet book sales continue to be steady, and publishers have developed e-books to take advantage of the digital form. The history of the evolution of media shows that the introduction of a new medium or a new delivery system does not mean the end of the old. The continuous expansion of the media industries during the 20th century demonstrates this evolution.

When television was introduced, for example, radio did not disappear. Instead, radio adapted to its new place in the media mix, delivering music, news and talk. Today, radio exists alongside television. Movies, which also were threatened by the introduction of television, responded by delivering more spectacular and more explicit entertainment than people could see on television, and today movies still play an important role in the business of media.

"When newer forms of communication media emerge, the older forms usually do not die—they continue to evolve and adapt," says Roger Fidler. The different media compete for the public's attention and jockey for positions of dominance, but no medium disappears. Instead, each medium contributes to the development of its successors. Together, all media that now exist will contribute to media forms that are yet to be invented.

Transformation Takes 30 Years

Just how quickly consumers adopt new technologies is predictable, according to Paul Saffo, former director of the Institute for the Future in Menlo Park, Calif. Saffo theorizes that for the past five centuries the pace of change has always been 30 years, or about three decades, from the introduction of a new technology to its complete adoption by the culture.

Saffo calls his theory the **30-year rule**, which he divides into 3 stages, with each stage lasting about 10 years. In the first stage, he says, there is "lots of excitement, lots of puzzlement, not a lot of penetration." In the second stage, there is "lots of flux, penetration of the product into society is beginning." In the third stage, the reaction to the technology is, "Oh, so what? Just a standard technology and everybody has it." By Saffo's standard, American society is in the third stage of acceptance of online technology. Widespread consumer use of

AP Images/John Shearer

Even though Internet access is everywhere in America, 21 percent of the U.S. population still has never gone online. The gap between people who use the Internet and people who don't is called the *digital divide*. *Furious 7* star Dwayne Johnson takes a "selfie" on a mobile phone with fans at the film's premiere in Los Angeles on April 1, 2015.

the Internet started to grow beginning in 1988, when less than one-half of 1 percent of the U.S. population was on the Internet. Today, 79 percent of the U.S. population is online.

Saffo's description of the third decade of acceptance coincides with the adaptability of today's media marketplace. New media are more familiar, and people seem better able to incorporate combinations of new and existing media technologies. The digital technological transformation is a commonly accepted part of everyday life.

Web Access Leaves Some People Behind

The initial sign of the expansion of the Internet to consumer and educational users in the first decade of change—the early 1990s—was the adoption by businesses and private users of electronic mail, or *e-mail*, technology. With a computer, a modem and a telephone line, just about anyone could learn how to communicate electronically online.

"The driving force for achieving large subscriber gains is the incorporation of the Internet by consumers as part of their routine," according to Veronis Suhler

30-Year Rule Developed by Paul Saffo, the theory that it takes about 30 years for a new technology to be completely adopted within a culture.

E-mail Mail that is delivered electronically over the Internet.

Stevenson, a media research company. "The Internet has become a tool that allows users to economize on what has become their scarcest resource—time. Virtually all of the leading Internet applications allow users to accomplish tasks more quickly than they can through alternative means."

E-mail and text messaging at school, work or home still are how most people first experience communicating in an electronic environment. Just as telephone answering machines in the 1970s changed voice communication by allowing people to send and receive messages on their own time schedule, e-mail and text messaging allow people to communicate and receive information at their convenience.

E-mail and text messaging are easy-to-use, text-based systems, which means that people type in messages on a keyboard, which is a familiar tool. Familiarity and convenience are very important in the adoption of new technologies because people's fear of something they don't understand and misunderstandings about how new technologies work can keep them from changing their established habits.

Yet, according to the Pew Internet and American Life Project, one out of five American adults says he or she has never used the Internet or e-mail and does not live in an Internet-connected household. Some people don't use the Internet because they can't afford it or they're afraid to try it or they don't have access. People living with a disability also are less likely to go online. This gap between people who have Internet access and those who don't is called the ***digital divide***.

Pew calls these people "truly disconnected adults"—typically people who have less than a high school education, are over 65, or live in a rural area. "If they needed to get information from a Web site or other online source, they probably could not easily do so," says Susannah Fox, associate director of the Pew Internet Project.

Pew says that the main reason adults give for not going online is that "they don't think the Internet is relevant to them. Most have never used the Internet before, and don't have anyone in their household who does."

For children, the great equalizer is public education. Access to computers in the classroom guarantees they will be comfortable with the technology as they grow up. Mature adults and rural populations without access to the technology can be disadvantaged unless government institutions, such as public libraries, close the gap.

Courtesy of Shirley Biagi

The Internet offers consumers access to a worldwide array of products and services, which has changed the way many people shop and plan their travel. The Web site airbnb.com, for example, allows travelers to connect with people who want to rent out extra rooms in their homes for vacation stays all over the world.

Internet Combines Commerce, Information and Entertainment

What makes the Web as a mass medium different from traditional media is its capacity to combine commerce with access to information and entertainment. Not only can people buy products on the Web, but they can also learn new things and enjoy themselves.

Most people use an Internet service provider (***ISP***, also called an Internet access provider), such as a telephone, satellite or cable company, to organize and deliver Internet information and entertainment. Today, a major source of Web income is the money people pay their ISP to connect to the Web. There are three other potential sources of income on the Web: commerce (connecting sellers with potential buyers), advertising and content.

Commerce

"Millions of Internet users are forsaking yard sales and the local dump for the prospect of selling their

> **Digital Divide** The gap between people who have Internet access and those who do not.
>
> **ISP** Internet service provider, also called an Internet access provider.

hand-me-downs and unwanted gear online," according to a report by the Pew Internet and American Life Project. "About one in six Internet-using adults have sold something online." This recent success of the Internet as a way for people to buy and sell things is only one example of the Internet's potential as a marketplace.

The most resilient commercial Internet operation is Amazon. It began as a place where people could buy media products such as books, CDs and DVDs, but today consumers also can shop on Amazon for just about anything—clothes, cosmetics, cars and sports equipment, for example—often at discount prices from individuals as well as large retailers, such as Target. Amazon has grown into a vast international Internet department store.

Small retailers and individuals also can use the Web to sell products directly, without setting up a store or spending a lot of money on expensive advertising, on *eBay*, a Web site that began about 25 years ago as a place where individual sellers offered products—mostly collectibles—in an online auction atmosphere.

Today, eBay is another vast marketplace where individuals sell collectibles, but eBay also promotes direct consumer-to-consumer sales for products as varied as cars, houses, even used jeans. Most individual sellers on the site do not have retail stores. Their only outlet is eBay, yet the Internet gives eBay sellers access to buyers all over the world.

Convenience, reliability and affordability sustain both these Web sites as successful commercial ventures— two

examples of new types of businesses that thrive because of the Internet.

Advertising

When television was introduced to the public in the late 1940s, people assumed from the beginning that it would be a commercial medium—that is, advertisers who bought the commercials surrounding the programs would pay for the programming. This concept of using advertising to underwrite TV programs was a natural evolution from radio, where commercials also paid for the programming.

Advertisers follow the audience, so as consumers have migrated to the Web, advertisers have tried to figure out how to follow them. Advertising is the second potential source of income on the Web.

Most commercial Web sites now carry some form of advertising. These appear as banners across the top of the Web site or run as borders alongside the site's pages. But just as in traditional media, advertising can crowd out the original message and turn away consumers, and entrepreneurs continue to test the market to develop new Web advertising structures and designs that will pay the bills. (See **Illustration 9.2**, "How Much Do Businesses Spend Annually to Advertise on the Internet?," p. 181.)

Because the Web is such a targeted medium—the seller can gather a lot of information about the buyer— the Web holds better potential for monitoring consumers' buying habits than traditional methods of advertising. Ultimately, Web advertisers hope to "achieve the merchandiser's dream—targeting an audience far more precisely than it can with either newspapers or television by advertising a product only on sites that draw people likely to be interested in that product," says media critic David Shaw, with "nearly instantaneous electronic feedback on whether their ads are effective: How many people saw the ad? How many 'clicked' on it and went on to a more detailed presentation? How many bought the product right then, online?"

Internet "tracking" offers advertisers information about their audiences. Commercial sites offer advertisers information about how many "hits" the sites receive— how many times people look at the site and how much time they spend. This information-gathering is so sophisticated that the data can even show an advertiser which specific user bought which specific products that were advertised on a specific site.

Companies also have developed "ad robots" that allow a business to, in effect, eavesdrop on chat room conversations while the user is online. If someone mentions a car problem online, for example, the robot recognizes the pattern of words in the discussion and sends the person an ad for the car repair shop.

Always looking for new ways to target specific audiences, advertising agencies also offer services such as

© John McPherson/Distributed by Universal Uclick via CartoonStock.com

DEB'S YARN SHOP

THAT? THAT'S A STORE, HON. IN THE OLDEN DAYS PEOPLE WOULD BUY THINGS IN STORES INSTEAD OF ONLINE.

In the year 2030.

John McPherson/Cartoonbank.com

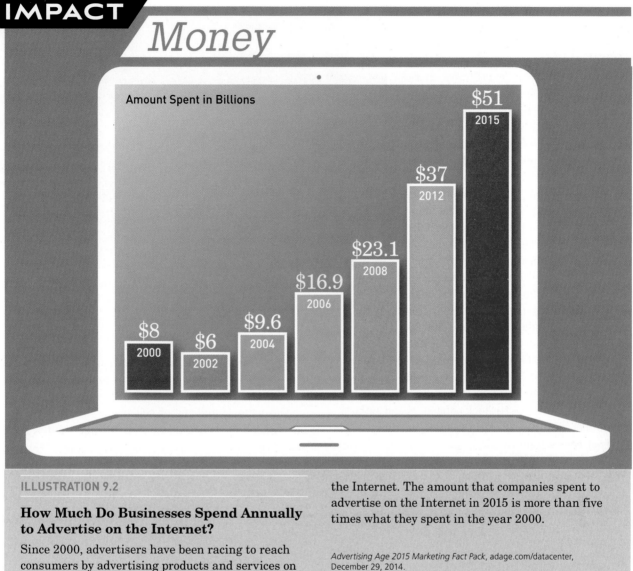

IMPACT

Money

Amount Spent in Billions

$8 — 2000
$6 — 2002
$9.6 — 2004
$16.9 — 2006
$23.1 — 2008
$37 — 2012
$51 — 2015

ILLUSTRATION 9.2

How Much Do Businesses Spend Annually to Advertise on the Internet?

Since 2000, advertisers have been racing to reach consumers by advertising products and services on the Internet. The amount that companies spent to advertise on the Internet in 2015 is more than five times what they spent in the year 2000.

Advertising Age 2015 Marketing Fact Pack, adage.com/datacenter, December 29, 2014.

search marketing, which means placing client ads next to consumers' Internet search results so that when someone starts a search for SUVs, for example, the SUV car manufacturer's ad immediately appears on the screen next to the user's search results. Appearing within the SUV ad, of course, is a link to a Web site where the user can customize and order a car. By connecting consumers directly to advertisers, search marketers say, they can better trace and document the connection between Internet ads and their audiences, something many advertisers are demanding before they invest in the Internet audience.

Ad robots and search marketing are just two examples of the refined tools advertisers have developed to more accurately track and target the Internet consumer.

Content

The culture of the Web began with the idea that content would be available free, so it has taken a long time for consumers to embrace the idea that they should pay for media content on the Web.

Slate, the online literary magazine, tried to start charging subscribers in 1997, but then decided against it. Editor Michael Kinsley said, "It would be better to establish a brand name with wide readership first." *Slate* celebrated its 20th anniversary in 2015 and still does not charge subscribers.

Some explicit Web sites charge for access, and some news and information sites, such as *The Wall Street Journal*, charge subscribers an annual fee for access to archived online content older than seven days—beyond

> **Search Marketing** Positioning Internet advertising prominently next to consumers' related online search results.

what's available free on the main *Journal* news site. *The New York Times* began charging for access to its site in 2011. Other sites, such as the sports network ESPN, give away some information and then charge for "premium" services. Internet gamemakers, who offer video games on the Web, charge by the hour or use a tiered pricing structure—free, basic and premium.

In 2003, consumers showed they were willing to pay for music downloads when Apple founder Steve Jobs introduced iTunes, a music service for subscribers that allows people to download popular songs for a fee. Less than a year after its launch, iTunes celebrated its one-billionth music download.

In 2010, when Apple introduced the iPad, an electronic tablet offering many more functions than its predecessor from Amazon (the Kindle), Apple sold 500,000 iPads in the first week. Tablet devices offer another mobile outlet for purchased media, such as books, newspapers and magazines. Downloads of a currently popular book sell for about $5 to $15, bringing a new source of revenue for book publishers and authors.

Another major source of revenue generated by the Internet comes from the development and sale of video games. The video game industry is a hybrid that combines equipment (such as Xbox and PlayStation), software and Internet downloads. According to the Entertainment Software Association, computer and video gaming generated nearly $60 billion worldwide in 2014. The average game player is 30 years old and has been playing video games for 12 years. (See **Impact/Global**, "Can Video Games Be a Force for Good?," p. 183.)

Originally appealing to younger consumers, with war games for young adults and animated products for children, today's video game companies recently broadened their audience significantly by producing nonviolent kinetic games. "The industry is saying we care about hard-core fans, but we have to go after the wide audience," says Brian Crescente, editor in chief of gaming Web site Kotaku. The shift is also economic—a way to escape the industry's reputation for exploiting violence by producing only "shooter" games and to avoid government attempts to control video game content and distribution.

Mobile Media Chase the Audience

Internet receivers have grown smaller and smaller, and retailers have expanded their ads to mobile phones and tablets. Much like radio broadcasters who followed radio

ullstein bild/Getty Images

Web developers cater to mobile media users because they are such a big audience. Consumers shop at a Vodafone mobile media store in Munich, Germany.

listeners from their homes into their cars when car radios were invented, Web site businesses are chasing today's mobile consumers.

The nation's millions of cell phone and tablet users make mobile media consumers an inviting target. Consumers use mobile media to send text messages, take pictures, search the Internet and buy products. This makes smartphones and other mobile media devices extremely attractive media markets. (See **Illustration 9.3**, "How and Where Do People Use Mobile Media?," p. 184.)

Mobile media content has restrictions—content must be audible and clearly visible in the smaller viewing space of a cell phone or tablet screen. News and sports bulletins, short video clips and social media are perfectly suited for this media environment.

All four of the major TV networks and most subscription channels now offer most of their entertainment programs and news video online, on demand, for computer, cell phone and tablet viewing.

Social Networks Grow Globally

A **social network** is an Internet community where people share information, ideas, personal messages, photographs, audio and video. Mobile applications (**apps**)

> **Social Network**   An Internet community where users share information, ideas, personal messages, photographs, audio and video.
>
> **App**   Mobile application.

IMPACT / *Global*

Can Video Games Be a Force for Good?

By Edward Helmore

A decade ago Asi Burak developed a video game designed to encourage opposing parties in the Israel-Palestine dispute over land to better understand—even empathize with—each other's point of view. That conflict may be no closer to a resolution, but the concept that interactive games can be used for more than mere entertainment, even as a tool for positive change, is looking like the next big thing in online gaming.

[In April 2014] Burak's 11th annual Games for Change Festival [joined] forces with New York's prestigious Tribeca Film Festival in an effort to give video games greater recognition and counter the stereotype that this £39bn global industry can specialize only in war games, urban chaos and medieval fantasy.

"People understand that games are powerful, but they're also scared of this power," says Burak. "We need to change the perception that all games are shallow, violent and childish, because they are not."

Statistics show that gaming has outgrown its reputation as an activity for children and teenagers. The average age of players is now 30, 10 years older than it was a decade ago.

There are games for women in their 30s, and games for seniors to combat declines in mental function.

Collectively, the world now spends one billion hours every

Miles Willis/Getty Images

Some video game developers are trying to counteract the stereotype that all video games are shallow, violent exercises. Child gamers participate in a *Minecraft* tournament in Ascot, England, on August 9, 2014. *Minecraft* has been cited as a creative, nonviolent alternative video game for children.

day playing video games—up more than 50% in three years. Meanwhile, the average young person racks up 10,000 hours playing video games by the age of 21, only slightly less than the time they spend in secondary education.

"People see the negative side and they talk about addiction, but there are many games on the positive side," says Burak. Games such as *Minecraft*, he adds, are "amazingly creative experiences and far more engaging than watching TV."

Many of the new studies claim a wide variety of benefits from gaming, including improved attention, higher creativity and improved ability to manage difficult emotions, such as fear and anger.

The technology poses as many questions as it answers. If virtual-reality games connect us to the real world, what does that say about our

lack of connection? Are video games a source of "real" happiness? Do the positive emotions contribute to real wellbeing, or are these feelings also virtual?

Philosopher Bernard Suits, author of *The Grasshopper: Games, Life and Utopia*, claims that, if we ever create a perfect society, games will be the only reason to go on living. We would have to play, or else have no purpose in our lives, Suits argues, because they can bring a sense of service and collective meaning.

Like real-world reality, there is no single virtual reality, says Burak. It's an open debate. Some want to use virtual reality for behavioral change; some to make political statements.

But, speaking personally, he adds: "I would like to see more design purpose and effort going towards creating empathy."

Excerpted from Edward Helmore, "Ethical Gaming: Can Video Games Be a Force for Good?" April 12, 2014, theguardian.com.

IMPACT

Society

Where People Use Mobile Media

Waiting for something — **83%**

Lying in bed — **81%**

Watching TV — **61%**

Commuting — **57%**

Spending time with family — **51%**

At social gatherings — **46%**

Shopping — **43%**

In the bathroom — **27%**

In a meeting or class — **25%**

How People Use Mobile Media

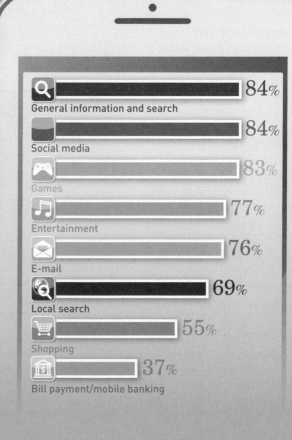

General information and search — **84%**

Social media — **84%**

Games — **83%**

Entertainment — **77%**

E-mail — **76%**

Local search — **69%**

Shopping — **55%**

Bill payment/mobile banking — **37%**

ILLUSTRATION 9.3

How and Where Do People Use Mobile Media?

Mobile media is the fastest-growing area of consumer media use. **Consumers spend more** time using mobile phones (97 minutes) than watching TV (81 minutes), and 61 percent of mobile Web users engage in mobile activities *while* watching TV, according to InMobi, a mobile advertising company.

"Wave 3: Global Mobile Media Consumption: A 'New Wave' Takes Shape," February 2014, www.info.inmobi.com; "5 Ways Mobile Devices Have Changed the Way Americans Consume Media," August 16, 2012, www.info.inmobi.com.

---

make social network connections, such as Facebook, available to anyone with a mobile phone, anywhere in the world.

Social networks enable anyone who wants to create a podcast or a blog or a personal Web space to share information and ideas and, most often, to stay in touch with friends and family.

PODCASTS. Podcasting is the distribution of an audio or video file online. Individuals can easily use the Internet to create and share *podcasts*, and many news organizations, such as *PBS* and *The New York Times*, frequently add podcasts to their Web sites as a way to expand coverage.

There also are podcast networks that feature several shows on the same feed, similar to a radio station.

> **Podcast** An audio or video file made available on the Internet for anyone to download, often by subscription.

Consumers can download podcasts and listen to them whenever and wherever they want, which also makes podcasts an easy way to reach a mobile audience.

BLOGS. By one estimate, 80,000 new blog sites are launched daily. The blog search engine Technorati tracks 29 million blog sites. A *blog* (short for Web log) is an online discussion group where people can post comments about a topic in a running conversation with each other.

Many news sites post live blogs to cover breaking news events. When Hurricane Sandy hit the East Coast in October 2012, several newspapers began blogs that invited people involved in the storm to contribute photos and news from their affected areas, as events were happening.

The text of the blog runs in reverse chronological order, with the most recent comments posted at the top of the blog so people can read through the previous postings for background on the topic, or they can start reading what follows after they join the group. Typically blogs do not carry advertising and are created as a way to enhance other content on the Web.

Blogs also have become frequent sources of information for news organizations seeking public reaction to ongoing events. The 2004 presidential election was the first time bloggers actually were accredited as part of the presidential press corps, indicating the importance of the bloggers' role as commentators on topical issues.

SOCIAL MEDIA SITES. In its report *Why Americans Use Social Media*, the Pew Internet and American Life Project said that 91 percent of adults use social media sites to stay in touch with current friends. Facebook and Pinterest are among the most popular social media networks, but several competitors have emerged, such as Pinterest and LinkedIn. In 2012, Facebook reported the Web site had reached 1 billion monthly users. (See **Illustration 9.4**, "Why Do People Use Social Media?" and **Illustration 9.5**, "Which Social Media Sites Are Most Popular?," p. 186).

Users create a personal page, a short blog for personal messages, plus they can add photos and video. Some sites, such as Facebook, are ad-supported; subscription fees for upgrades support others, such as LinkedIn.

Podcasts, blogs and social media sites are the latest ways the media business has expanded its audience. It's important to remember that, in the history of the media business, advertisers always have followed consumers. To be successful, Internet providers know they must attract customers to be able to capitalize on the advertising potential the audience brings with it.

Government Attempts to Coordinate and Control the Net

The federal government has attempted to coordinate and regulate the Internet in the same way government traditionally coordinated and regulated the broadcast media in its early days. However, the U.S. government has learned the hard way that it can exercise only limited control over the Internet, especially its content.

In 1994, in its first attempt to coordinate the growing presence of the Internet, the U.S. Congress named the effort to coordinate the nation's various senders, channels and receivers in the United States the National Information Infrastructure (**NII**). This congressional intervention in the structure of the Internet was based on the history of radio and TV in the United States, which the government had regulated since the 1920s.

Three principles guided the creation of the nation's telecommunications structure, Congress said:

1. Private industry, not the government, would build the digital network.

2. Programmers and information providers would be guaranteed access to the digital network to promote a diversity of consumer choices.

3. Steps would be taken to ensure universal service so that the digital network did not result in a society of information "haves" and "have-nots."

Then two years later, in its first attempt to control Internet content, Congress passed the Telecommunications Act of 1996. Included in that legislation was the Communications Decency Act (**CDA**), which outlined content that would be forbidden on the Internet. As soon as the act passed, civil liberties organizations challenged the law, and in 1997 the U.S. Supreme Court upheld the concept that the U.S. government could not control Internet content.

Although the U.S. government has retreated from its attempts to control Internet content, central governments in many countries control Internet access through ownership and/or regulation of the utilities that carry Web signals. Government control affects the free flow of information globally and, in turn, affects Internet users in the U.S. Any government interference with Internet traffic can result in periodic or permanent blocks on users' Web access and poses security concerns for global Internet providers, such as Google Inc., based in the U.S. In December 2014, for example, the Chinese government

---

Blog   Short for Web log. A running Internet discussion group, where items are posted in reverse chronological order. Blogs usually focus on a specific topic.

NII   National Information Infrastructure.

CDA   Communications Decency Act.

IMPACT

Society

ILLUSTRATION 9.4

Why Do People Use Social Media?

Most adults use social media to stay in touch with friends and family, but there are several other reasons people visit sites such as Facebook, Twitter and LinkedIn. People use social media to:

91% Stay in touch with current friends

87% Stay in touch with family members

86% Connect with old friends with whom they've lost touch

49% Connect with others with shared hobbies or interests

43% Make new friends

25% Read comments by celebrities, athletes or politicians

16% Find potential romantic or dating partners

Pew Internet and American Life Project, www.pewinternet.org.

ILLUSTRATION 9.5

Which Social Media Sites Are Most Popular?

Today 52 percent of online adults use two or more social media sites. Facebook is the most popular social media site, but Instagram is more popular among young adults ages 18–29. Here is the overall percentage of American adults who use the following sites:

Facebook **58%**
LinkedIn **23%**
Pinterest **22%**
Instagram **21%**
Twitter **19%**

Pew Research Center, "Social Media Update 2014," January 9, 2015.

allegedly blocked Google Inc.'s e-mail service within the country. (See **Impact/Global**, "Chinese Access to Gmail Cut, Regulators Blamed," p. 188.)

Protection Sought for Intellectual Property Rights

Money is the main reason the federal government continues to be involved in the global development of the Internet—to protect the commercial value of Internet products. Digitized bits, once they are widely available, can be easily stolen and reproduced for profit, which can mean billions of dollars in lost revenue for companies and individuals who produce media content and the tax dollars that generates. Writers, moviemakers, singers, TV producers, Web site developers and other creative people who provide content for the media industries are especially concerned about their ideas being reproduced in several different formats, with no payment for their property.

This issue, the protection of what are called **intellectual property rights**, is a crucial part of the U.S. government's interest in the design of the Internet as a communications network. To protect online content, various copyright holders have used court challenges to establish their legal ownership, but some groups still are trying to avoid detection by keeping their online activities hidden from government scrutiny.

With access to copyrighted digital content, someone could capture video from a Disney movie sent over the Internet and join sections of that video with comedy bits from an episode of *Saturday Night Live*, putting the two casts together in a newly digitized program, for example. Once this content is captured and stored, it would be available to anyone who wants to use it.

The protection of content is one of the dilemmas created by digitized files that can be transmitted to anyone's storage system over an international network. The creative people who contribute this content, and the people who produce and own these programs, are demanding laws and regulations structured to protect intellectual property rights.

The issue of who owns existing copyrighted material, such as recordings and movies, is particularly complex on a medium like the Internet with global access and few international controls. In 1998, Congress passed the Digital Millennium Copyright Act (**DMCA**) to make it illegal to share copyrighted material on the Internet. (For more information about the DMCA, see **Chapter 14**.) Using this law and provisions of existing copyright law,

John Klossner The New Yorker Collection/The Cartoon Bank

industries with a big stake in content ownership have sued to stop people from sharing copyrighted content on the Internet.

The Recording Industry Association of America (**RIAA**) and the Motion Picture Association of America (**MPAA**) have been especially aggressive in seeking to prosecute people who make copyrighted content available on the Web. In 1999, RIAA sued Napster, a company that provided a music-swapping service on the Internet. In 2001, after several appeals, the courts found that Napster was liable for "vicarious copyright infringement." Napster eventually shut down and then reopened as a subscription music service that pays royalties to companies that own rights to music available on the site.

In 2001, the MPAA sued to stop publication of the digital code that allows a person to copy DVDs and place copies of movies on the Internet. The court agreed with the MPAA, saying that even if people possess the code but don't use it, they are committing piracy. This was an important legal precedent for content sharing on the Web and has led to more corporate attempts to seek wider protections over copyrighted content.

In 2003, Apple launched iTunes, a service that charges a fee to download songs legally. iTunes was created to respond to the various court actions since 1999 and designed to end

---

Intellectual Property Rights The legal right of ownership of ideas and content published in any medium.

DMCA Digital Millennium Copyright Act.

RIAA Recording Industry Association of America.

MPAA Motion Picture Association of America.

IMPACT

Global

Chinese Access to Gmail Cut, Regulators Blamed

By Didi Tang, The Associated Press
December 30, 2014, 2:17 a.m.

BEIJING (AP)—Chinese access to Google Inc.'s email service has been blocked amid government efforts to limit or possibly ban access to the U.S. company's services, which are popular among Chinese seeking to avoid government monitoring.

Data from Google's Transparency Report show online traffic from China to Gmail fell precipitously on Friday [December 25, 2014] and dropped to nearly zero on Saturday [December 26, 2014], although there was a tiny pickup on Monday [December 28, 2014].

Taj Meadows, a spokesman for Google Asia Pacific, said Google has checked its email service and "there's nothing technically wrong on our end."

In a Tuesday [December 29, 2014] editorial, the Chinese Communist Party-run *Global Times* newspaper raised the possibility, without confirmation, that the government had cut access to Gmail.

"If the China side indeed blocked Gmail, the decision must have been prompted by newly emerged security reasons," the editorial read. "If that is the case, Gmail users need to accept the reality of Gmail being suspended in China. But we hope it is not the case."

Earl Zmijewski, vice president of data analytics at U.S.-based Internet analysis firm Dyn Research, said his tests showed that China's

AP Images/Mark Schiefelbein

A security guard walks by a Google, china, display booth at the Global Mobile Internet Conference in Beijing, China, on April 29, 2015. For three days beginning on December 25, 2014, the Chinese government allegedly cut off Internet service for its Google mail customers, blocking access to the Web. Periodic interruptions in Internet service are fairly common in countries where access to the Web is subject to government censorship.

government had blocked Google IP addresses in Hong Kong used by people on the mainland to access Gmail services.

Calls to the government regulator, the China Internet Information Office, were unanswered Monday [December 28, 2014]. Foreign Ministry spokeswoman Hua Chunying said she did not know about any blockage.

U.S. State Department spokesman Jeff Rathke said in a statement that the development was troubling.

"We continue to be concerned by efforts in China to undermine freedom of expression, including on the Internet, and we believe Chinese authorities' censorship of the media and of certain Web sites is incompatible with China's aspirations to build a modern

information-based economy and society," he said.

Google closed its mainland China search engine in 2009, saying it would no longer cooperate with the country's censors. That followed hacking attacks traced to China aimed at stealing the company's operating code and breaking into email accounts.

Since then, access to Google services has been periodically limited or blocked, possibly in an effort to pressure Chinese users into abandoning Google products and shifting to services from domestic companies willing to cooperate with the government.

Google products are popular among Chinese young people and activists who do not want their email communications to be monitored or intercepted by the Chinese government.

illegal *file sharing*, which means downloading files placed on the Internet by another person, not necessarily the original copyright holder.

In 2005, the music-file-sharing network Grokster shut down after reaching a settlement with the movie and music industries about online piracy. And in 2010, a federal judge ordered the major remaining music-file-sharing service, LimeWire, to shut down its Web site.

In February 2013, the *Copyright Alert System (CAS)* in the United States was activated to warn consumers who try to download copyrighted material. Internet companies AT&T, Cablevision, Comcast, Verizon and Time Warner Cable created the system, which notifies offenders when they try to download a copyrighted file. Administered by the Center for Copyright Administration, the system tracks illegal downloaders and, after six warnings, the Internet service provider, such as Comcast, can block the offender's account. (For more information about file sharing, copyright and the U.S. Supreme Court's view of the Internet, see **Chapters 5** and **14**.)

Mark Wilson/Getty Images

On February 26, 2015, the Federal Communications Commission voted 3-2 in favor of Open Internet rules, or *net neutrality*, which means Internet providers must deliver "open, uninhibited access to legal content" for all their customers. FCC Chairman Tom Wheeler (center) announces the vote with commissioners Mignon Clyburn (left) and Jessica Rosenworcel, who voted with him.

FCC Promotes Internet Neutrality

On February 26, 2015, the Federal Communications Commission (FCC) outlined Open Internet rules for Internet service providers that require them to keep their networks open and available to carry all legal content from all carriers. These provisions, often referred to as Internet neutrality (or *net neutrality*), generally mean that telecommunications companies, such as AT&T and Verizon, must maintain an open network. They cannot restrict access by other providers to their network nor can they limit the type or delivery of content they carry. There are three basic Open Internet rules, as defined by the FCC:

1. No Blocking: Broadband providers may not block access to legal content, applications, services, or non-harmful devices.

2. No Throttling: Broadband providers may not impair or degrade lawful Internet traffic on the basis of content, applications, services, or non-harmful devices.

3. No Paid Prioritization: Broadband providers may not favor some lawful Internet traffic over other lawful

traffic in exchange for consideration of any kind—in other words, no "fast lanes." This rule also bans ISPs from prioritizing content and services of their affiliates.

For consumers, these rules mean, for example, that manufacturers such as Apple cannot require iPhone users to sign up exclusively with AT&T and that people with iPhones and tablets may use any carrier they choose. The rules also mean that a telecommunications company cannot give priority to a high-volume business (Amazon, for example) to deliver its signal at a faster rate than a low-volume customer. All digital signals will travel at the same rate.

The FCC's Open Internet rules place the Internet under regulations that govern the Internet as a utility. In making the announcement about the Open Internet rules, the FCC said the rules "protect and maintain open,

File Sharing The peer-to-peer distribution of copyrighted material on the Internet without the copyright owner's permission.

Copyright Alert System (CAS) A government-mandated warning to alert consumers who try to download copyrighted material.

Net Neutrality Rules for Internet service providers that require them to keep their networks open and available to carry all legal content. Under these rules, providers cannot restrict access to their network by other providers nor can they limit the type or delivery of content they carry.

uninhibited access to legal online content without broadband Internet access providers being allowed to block, impair, or establish fast/slow lanes to lawful content." (See **Chapter 14** for more information about FCC regulation of the Internet.)

Storage, Competing Systems and Security Bring Challenges

International government support for net neutrality is an important issue for the future health of the Internet. The system faces at least three other major challenges: storage capacity, competing delivery systems and system security.

Storage Capacity

The main technological advance that makes today's communications network possible is that electronic systems transform text, audio and video communication into the same type of digital file.

Digital systems theoretically should be compatible, but many places in the world and many media systems have not yet totally converted to the technology that efficient digital delivery requires.

For example, digital delivery requires a huge amount of electronic storage space. To eliminate the need for so much storage, researchers developed a process called *data compression*. A copy of a major movie contains about 100 billion bytes of data. Compression squeezes the content down to about 4 billion bytes.

Data compression makes it much easier for a movie program service to keep movies available for use on demand. This helps make the movie affordable to deliver and usable for customers.

Once the data are compressed, the company that delivers the service also must store the data. The next step in the process is equipment that grabs a movie the consumer has selected from a storage area and delivers it to the customer on request. This transfer equipment is called a *server* because it serves thousands of programs to millions of subscribers, on demand, all at the same time.

A recent innovation in data storage is called *cloud computing*, which allows one business to rent remote use of another company's computer space, operating "in the cloud." In 2011, Apple launched iCloud. Other large companies that can handle massive amounts of data over an online network, like Microsoft and Google, now provide cloud computing to businesses all over the world.

The latest innovation in data storage is cloud computing. This allows one company to use another company's computer system, transferring information through the Internet to a "cloud"—the second company's secure online network. Video games can be played on the cloud and no longer require separate equipment, such as the Sony PlayStation 4 (PS4) consoles being used at the Tokyo Game Show in Chiba, Japan, on September 18, 2014.

Bloomberg/Getty Images

Online video game and gambling sites, media producers and software designers as well as video program providers (TV and cable networks) also are big consumers of cloud computing services.

Data streaming is the most familiar use of cloud computing. With video and audio data streaming, you can begin to play back a file without first completely downloading it. For example, you can start a movie on your laptop and immediately begin watching the film. While you are watching the movie, the file is being downloaded and stored on your computer. With a fast Internet connection, you can even stream live audio and video. Common streaming software brands are Real Audio and QuickTime.

Warehouses called *data farms* house the equipment that feeds the world's digital appetite. Often placed

---

Data Compression The process of squeezing digital content into a smaller electronic space.

Server The equipment that delivers programs from their source to the programs' subscribers.

Cloud Computing The remote use by one business of another company's computer space, operating "in the cloud."

Data Streaming A common type of cloud computing that allows the user to play back an audio or video file without first completely downloading it.

Data Farms Locations that house data centers for the servers that process data flowing over the Internet.

in remote, rural areas, tens of thousands of data centers throughout the world house millions of massive servers that process the data flowing over the Internet. According to *The New York Times*, these digital warehouses "use about 30 billion watts of electricity, roughly equivalent to the output of 30 nuclear power plants."

The U.S. contains about a third of these data centers, and many of them are running on local power grids, backed up by generators and lead-acid batteries in the case of a power failure. A basic necessity for the Internet's future will be the ability to maintain an efficient energy grid to feed the system's growing data storage needs.

Bloomberg/Getty Images

The transition to global digital delivery faces many barriers, including competition between existing media systems and new technologies. Until all global systems are compatible, digital delivery remains a mix of old and new. At the INTX Internet and Television Expo in Chicago on May 6, 2015, attendees explore the benefits of Comcast's Xfinity X1 Platform.

Competing Delivery Systems

Today's global communications system is a mixture of old and new technologies. The current delivery system is a combination of coaxial cable, copper wire, fiber optics and cellular and satellite technology. Before the new communications network will be complete, new technology must replace old technology throughout the system. Some broadcasters, for example, still send signals over the airwaves with the same technology they have used since the 1930s, when broadcasting was first introduced. This technology is called *analog*.

Analog technology is very cumbersome because an analog signal needs a lot of space to travel on the airwaves. However, because analog signals travel through the air by transmitters, consumers can receive them free with just an antenna.

At least 10 million homes in the United States still receive only over-the-air analog broadcasts. They do not subscribe to cable or satellite. And although the federal government mandated that TV stations in large cities digitize their signals by 2009, today some smaller stations still have not completed the costly transition to digital.

Cable companies eliminated the need for antennas by using coaxial cable, buried underground or strung from telephone poles, but some coaxial cable systems still use analog technology. Cable operators capture programming, such as HBO, from satellite systems, then gather analog broadcast signals from their local TV stations and deliver this programming to the consumer using a combination of coaxial cable, copper wire and optical fiber.

Optical fiber is composed of microscopic strands of glass that transmit messages in digitized "bits"—zeroes and ones. Each fiber-optic strand carries 250,000 times as much information as one copper wire. A fiber-optics communication system is very efficient because fiber can carry digitized information easily and quickly from one place to another.

Satellite services use digital signals to carry their programming. Programs that are delivered to a home satellite dish follow a wireless electronic journey from the program source through one of the many telecommunications satellites hovering around the globe. Satellite delivery, however, still requires a telephone connection to bring the programs and the menus for the programs to a home receiver.

Telephone companies have converted almost all their major communications delivery systems from coaxial cable and copper wire to fiber optics and cellular technology. However, the incompatibility between analog and digital technology means that any remaining analog signals must be converted first to digital signals so they can

Analog In mass communications, a type of technology used in broadcasting, whereby video or audio information is sent as continuous signals through the air on specific airwave frequencies.

travel smoothly everywhere. Conversion is very expensive.

Digital technology is the most efficient method of delivery, but making the same system available throughout the world with a standardized delivery system is very complex. Each competing system wants to control the entire delivery system because control of the delivery system means billions of dollars in revenue for whichever system consumers eventually adopt.

System Security

With all these different media delivery systems and services available, consumers, industry and government must be able to use them securely. Telephone companies already have a complex system that matches people with the calls they make and carries conversations and texts on secure lines all over the world. To be effective, security for digital communications on the Internet must be at least as safe as current telephone communications.

Commercial operations, such as banks and retailers, have developed secure systems for transferring transaction records on the Internet. To protect consumers' banking records, banks use digital codes and dedicated transmission lines to secure the transactions from Internet hackers. Software companies have developed reasonably reliable systems to ensure that the personal records and content contained in interactive transactions are safe. An entirely new industry has evolved dedicated to the issue of Internet data security.

However, on January 30, 2013, *The New York Times* announced that Chinese hackers had infiltrated its computer systems and obtained passwords for its reporters and other employees. "The attacks appear to be part of a broader computer espionage campaign against American news media companies that have reported on Chinese leaders and corporations," said *The Times*. Officials of the Chinese government denied the charges.

Less than a week later, Twitter reported that hackers had victimized about 250,000 of its accounts, including accounts for President Barack Obama, Vice President Joe Biden and House Speaker John Boehner. On February 12, 2013, President Obama signed an executive order to promote cybersecurity, which encourages the government and private companies to share information about data breaches that threaten national security.

Saul Loeb/Getty Images

On February 12, 2013, President Obama signed an executive order to promote cybersecurity. On January 13, 2015, at the nation's National Cybersecurity and Communications Integration Center in Arlington, Va., agents monitor digital communications.

The rules that individual nations develop to govern the security of this complex global communications network will have a profound impact on individuals, businesses, governments and the media industries.

Disruptive Technologies Revolutionize Old Concepts

The Internet affects consumers daily—how people shop, get their news, study, manage their money and, especially, socialize with friends and family. For businesses, global information is instantly available to most companies simultaneously, making communication much easier but inviting more intense competition.

For the media industries, the Internet places every element of the media business in transition. Today, owners and managers of the companies that make up the media industries are deciding daily how to invest in equipment, employees, research and development to protect current income while trying to ensure their companies adapt to the Internet's evolving demands.

Some digital entrepreneurs succeed, some create transitional products that will, in turn, spark new products, and many new ideas fail. Until the digital media landscape is clearer, however, it is important to follow ongoing developments because no one can predict exactly where digital media are headed. Five ongoing developments to watch that could affect the future of Internet media are: touch technology, massive open online courses (MOOCs), Open Intellectual Property, newsgathering drones and 3-D printing.

Touch Technology

Touch technology uses computing power to digitally enhance the five senses—touch, sight, hearing, taste and smell. Researchers at IBM and other companies are developing a system of cognitive computing, which uses artificial intelligence and advanced speech recognition to make a computer capable of learning.

Scientists say eventually you will be able to simulate the sensation of touch through your cell phone, for example. So when you look at a display of silk sheets on Amazon, you will be able to feel the fabric by touching your cell phone screen. And when an ad for pizza appears on your laptop, it will awaken your taste buds with digital sensors, sending the aroma of tomatoes and cheese and garlic.

Bloomberg/Getty Images

In 2015, CNN announced that it would begin testing camera drones, like this Phantom 2 quadcopter, to help cover news events.

Massive Open Online Courses

Massive open online courses **(MOOCs)** create huge online virtual classrooms, available to anyone with an Internet connection. Initially the courses have been offered free through established universities such as Princeton, Columbia and Duke. Typically the courses do not carry academic credit, but the idea is that eventually Internet classes will create a massive virtual university where students can sign up and receive credit for university-approved classes offered anywhere in the world via the Internet.

Three emerging companies, Coursera, edX and Udacity, are promoting MOOCs as an answer to the shortage of classes and increased tuition facing today's students. But there are critics and several unsolved problems. So far MOOCs have a very high dropout rate—nine out of ten students who enroll leave before the class is over. And how can one teacher effectively give grades to thousands of students or verify that the students who are enrolled are the students taking the tests or that they are, in fact, learning the material?

Still, some educators and entrepreneurs are investing in the idea that, for some college courses, a virtual classroom may offer a more efficient, cost-effective alternative to the traditional teacher-student classroom experience.

Open Intellectual Property

Open Intellectual Property is a term used to describe an Internet location where registered users collaborate to create, review and update information on a shared site, commonly known as a **wiki**. The term *wiki* derives from a Hawaiian word that means "fast." The best-known wiki is *Wikipedia*, an online encyclopedia where registered contributors post additions and changes to any entry.

Open Intellectual Property technology records the original material plus the material that contributors add and subtract over time. Wikis have great potential to gather wide-ranging contributions worldwide from all the experts on one subject, for example, but there are very few internal safeguards to guarantee that material placed on the site is secure, accurate or reliable.

Camera Drones for News Reporting

In 2015, CNN signed an agreement with the Federal Aviation Administration (FAA) to begin testing camera drones for use in newsgathering. CNN and the Georgia Institute of Technology announced a joint effort to study how to operate unstaffed aerial vehicles (**UAVs**, commonly called *drones*) to help cover news events.

So far, the FAA has severely limited the use of UAVs for any commercial purpose, but camera drones offer the potential for news organizations to photograph breaking news events, such as earthquakes or fires, that are

---

Touch Technology   Uses computing power to digitally enhance the five senses—touch, sight, hearing, taste and smell.

MOOCs   Massive open online courses.

Wiki   An Internet location where registered users collaborate to create, review and share information on a shared site.

UAV   Unstaffed aerial vehicle, commonly called a *drone*.

inaccessible from the ground. The FAA has the authority to regulate national airspace, so any newsgathering UAVs used in the U.S. would have to be licensed by the FAA.

3-D Printing

Pioneered by the movie industry in the 1950s, 3-D photographic technology has been adapted by today's moviemakers who can use a new technology called 3-D printing to create special effects characters more efficiently. *3-D printing* uses a large commercial printer, similar to the original small Inkjet printers, and liquid plastic rather than ink to fabricate ("print") individual, custom-designed pieces of equipment based on computer-generated designs.

For example, in *The Hobbit: An Unexpected Journey*, 3-D printers fabricated animatronic pieces of the goblins that appeared in the movie, such as facial muscles, lips and tongues. These props normally would take weeks to design and fabricate individually by hand, but 3-D printing meant the props were designed and manufactured ("printed") in days. 3-D printing holds real potential for the video production business.

Consumers Intersect with Technology

The future of digital media is bound only by the needs of consumers and the imaginations of media developers, as diverse as the people who are online today and going online tomorrow. The new media universe could become a purer reflection of the real universe than any medium yet created, with unprecedented potential, like all mass media, to both reflect and direct the culture.

"The Internet is still in its infancy, and its potential is enormous," writes media critic David Shaw. The Internet, says Shaw, could "revolutionize human communication even more dramatically than Johann Gutenberg's first printing press did more than 500 years ago."

> **3-D Printing** A process that uses a large commercial printer and liquid plastic to fabricate individual, custom-designed pieces of equipment based on computer-generated designs.

REVIEW, ANALYZE, INVESTIGATE

CHAPTER 9

Digital Communication Transforms Media

- The emergence of the Internet within the last 40 years has transformed the structure and economics of the U.S. media business.
- The Internet today offers people wireless access to information just about wherever and whenever they want it.
- The Internet delivers all types of media using a single delivery system.
- The Internet is a combination of millions of computer networks sending and receiving data from all over the world.
- In its global size and absence of central control, the Internet is completely different from traditional media.

Digital Media Support Convergence

- Nicholas Negroponte at the Massachusetts Institute of Technology was the first person to identify the theory of convergence.

- The theory of convergence helped shape today's thinking about the Internet.
- Every media industry benefits from convergence.

20th-Century Discoveries Made Internet Possible

- The person most responsible for creating the World Wide Web is Tim Berners-Lee, who created the first browser and gave the World Wide Web its name.
- Marc Andreessen at the University of Illinois created Mosaic, which allowed people to put text and pictures in the same online document.
- Both Andreessen and Berners-Lee placed their creations in the public domain, which meant that anyone with a computer and a modem could download them free.
- A culture of free information access, coupled with a creative, chaotic lack of direction, still permeates the Web today.

Web Opens to Unlimited Access

- Universal access, limited only by the available technology, is what gives the Web the feeling and look of what has been called "anarchy"—a place without rules.
- Today's media companies have a shared interest in seeing their investments in new technologies succeed.

What Happens to Old Media?

- The introduction of a new medium such as the Internet does not mean the end of the old.
- Older media forms continue to evolve and adapt to the new media environment.

Transformation Takes 30 Years

- Paul Saffo says the pace of change has consistently been about 30 years from the introduction of a new technology to its complete adoption by the culture.
- By Saffo's standard—the 30-year rule—American society is beginning to enter the third stage of acceptance, where the majority of the population has adapted to the new technology.

Web Access Leaves Some People Behind

- About 21 percent of Americans still do not go online—because they can't afford it, they're afraid of it or they don't have access.
- The gap between people who have online access and those who do not is called the *digital divide*.

Internet Combines Commerce, Information and Entertainment

- A major source of Web income is the money people pay their Internet service provider.
- Three other potential sources of income on the Web are commerce, advertising and content.
- Most commercial Web sites now carry some form of advertising.
- Tablet devices, such as the iPad, offer another outlet for purchased media.
- Another source of revenue generated by the Internet comes from the development and sale of video games.
- The video game industry is a hybrid that combines equipment (such as Xbox and PlayStation), software and Internet streaming.
- The global video game industry generated $60 billion in 2014.
- Consumers worldwide spend 1 billion hours every day playing video games.
- The average young person has spent 10,000 hours playing video games by the time he or she reaches age 21.
- The average video game player is 30 years old and has been playing games for 12 years.

- Internet tracking tells advertisers about the audience's behavior.

Mobile Media Chase the Audience

- The latest targets for expanding Internet media use are mobile media—smartphones and tablets.
- Mobile media content must be audible and viewable in the small viewing space of a cell phone or tablet screen. News, sports bulletins and audio and video clips are perfectly suited for a mobile media environment.
- All four of the major TV networks and most subscription channels offer their entertainment and news programs online.

Social Networks Grow Globally

- A social network is an Internet community where people can share information, ideas, personal messages, photographs, audio and video.
- Two-thirds of adults who go online use social media sites.
- In 2014, Facebook and LinkedIn were among the most popular social media networks, but Instagram is more popular among young adults ages 18–29.
- Today, 52 percent of online adults use 2 or more social media sites.

Government Attempts to Coordinate and Control the Net

- The federal government has attempted to coordinate and regulate the Internet, but the U.S. government can exercise no control over legal Internet content.
- In 1994, the U.S. Congress named the effort to coordinate the nation's various senders, channels and receivers the National Information Infrastructure (NII).
- In 1997, the U.S. Supreme Court upheld the concept that the U.S. government could not control Internet content.
- In many countries, such as China, the government controls Internet access, which can result in periodic or permanent blocks on Web access and security concerns for Internet providers such as Google.

Protection Sought for Intellectual Property Rights

- Legal protections for digital content are called *intellectual property rights*.
- In 1998, Congress passed the Digital Millennium Copyright Act to make it illegal to share copyrighted material on the Internet.
- The Recording Industry Association of America and the Motion Picture Association of America have aggressively pursued copyright infringement.
- In 2003, Apple introduced iTunes, which allows people to download music legally.

- In 2005, the free music-file-sharing network Grokster shut down after reaching a settlement with the movie and music industries about online piracy.

- In 2010, a federal judge ordered the major remaining music-file-sharing service, LimeWire, to shut down its Web site.

- In February 2013, the Copyright Alert System (CAS) in the United States was activated to warn consumers who are trying to download copyrighted material.

FCC Promotes Internet Neutrality

- On February 26, 2015, the Federal Communications Commission (FCC) outlined Open Internet rules for Internet service providers that require them to keep their networks open and available to carry all legal content from all carriers.

- There are three basic Open Internet FCC rules: (1) no blocking, (2) no throttling, and (3) no paid prioritization.

Storage, Competing Systems and Security Bring Challenges

- Researchers have developed a process called *data compression*, which collapses the size of data files so they are easier to download.

- A recent innovation in data storage is called *cloud computing*, which allows one business to rent remote use of another company's computer space, operating "in the cloud."

- Data streaming is the most familiar use of cloud computing.

- Today's communications system is a mixture of analog and digital technologies.

- At least 10 million homes in the United States still receive only over-the-air broadcasts. They do not subscribe to cable or satellite.

- On January 30, 2013, *The New York Times* announced that Chinese hackers had infiltrated its computer systems and obtained passwords for its reporters and other employees. Officials of the Chinese government denied the charges.

- Less than a week later, Twitter reported that hackers had victimized about 250,000 of its accounts, including accounts for President Barack Obama, Vice President Joe Biden and House Speaker John Boehner.

- On February 12, 2013, President Obama signed an executive order to promote cybersecurity.

- The rules that individual nations develop to govern the Internet will have a profound impact on individuals, businesses, government and the media industries.

Disruptive Technologies Revolutionize Old Concepts

- The Internet means that every element of the mass media industries is in transition.

- Five developments with the potential to affect the future of Internet media are: touch technology, massive open online courses (MOOCs), Open Intellectual Property, camera drones for newsgathering and 3-D printing.

Consumers Intersect with Technology

- The future of digital media is bound only by the needs of consumers and the imagination of media developers.

- The new media universe has unprecedented potential to both reflect and direct the culture.

Key Terms

These terms are defined in the margins throughout this chapter and appear in alphabetical order with definitions in the Glossary, which begins on page 361.

Critical Questions

1. Explain the concept of the digital divide as outlined in this chapter. Why does the digital divide exist? How can the digital divide be eliminated?

2. Why does the Web show remarkable potential for revenue growth? Be specific.

3. What role do video games play in online commerce? What are video game developers doing to counteract their image as providers of violent, shallow content? What do you think of their arguments?

4. Discuss the role of the U.S. government in regulating activity on the Internet. Identify areas in which the government has been successful in regulating the Internet, as well as areas in which it has failed.

5. What communications role do social networks play in today's society? What role do social media play in your life? Explain.

Working the Web

This list includes sites mentioned in this chapter and others to give you greater insight into the Internet media industries.

Apple Inc.

apple.com

The home page of Apple, this site's sections include Apple Store, iPod, iTunes, iPhone, iPad, Mac computers, Apple Watch and software, plus Support. Apple.com Worldwide allows users to shop internationally from the U.S. to Africa, Asia, Europe and Latin America.

CNET

cnet.com

A CBS Interactive site, CNET distributes programming through its Internet television network, CNET Video and its podcast and blog networks. In addition, CNET currently has region-specific and language-specific editions in the UK, Australia, China, France, Germany, Japan and Korea, as well as CNET en Español.

Digital Content Next (formerly the Online Publishers Association)

onlinepub.org

Digital Content Next represents online digital content providers to the advertising community, the press, the government and the public. Members agree to abide by standards of quality and credibility.

Electronic Frontier Foundation (EFF)

eff.org

The Electronic Frontier Foundation is a nonprofit organization that works to protect online user privacy as the requirement for technology becomes a more integral part of everyday life. EFF seeks to accomplish this through litigation, policy analysis, grassroots activism and participation in technology development.

Facebook

facebook.com

With over 1.5 billion users worldwide, Facebook is an online social networking service headquartered in Menlo Park, Calif. Registered users can create a profile, join common groups of interest, add friends, exchange messages, post status updates and photos, share videos and receive notifications when an update and/or a response to something is posted online.

Institute of Electrical and Electronics Engineers (IEEE)

ieee.org

IEEE (pronounced "Eye-triple-E") is "the world's largest professional association dedicated to advancing technological innovation and advancement for the benefit of humanity." The organization's members come from a variety of professions, including computing, sustainable energy systems, aerospace, robotics, communications and health care. Research is presented in clear, accessible language to help readers understand and appreciate the world of computing.

Journal of Electronic Publishing (JEP)

journalofelectronicpublishing.org

JEP is a forum for research and discussion of electronic publishing and the impact of electronic publishing practices. Established in 1995, it recognizes the significant changes in print communication and the growing role of digital communication in transmitting published information. Journal articles present innovative ideas, best practices and progressive thinking about all aspects of publishing, authorship and readership.

MIT Media Lab Project

media.mit.edu

A multidisciplinary research laboratory at the Massachusetts Institute of Technology, the media lab explores how people can use computers to improve their lives. Faculty members, research staff and students at the lab work in research groups on projects that range from digital approaches for treating neurological disorders to stackable, electric cars for sustainable cities to advanced imaging technologies that can see around a corner.

Pew Internet, Science and Technology Project

pewinternet.org

Solely supported by the privately held Pew Charitable Trust, the Pew Internet, Science and Technology Project explores the effects of the Internet on various aspects of life. Information available on the site includes reports, presentations, data sets and current trends in technology.

Pinterest

pinterest.com

Billed as "a place to discover ideas for all your projects and interests, hand-picked by people like you," Pinterest is a photo-sharing website. New users are required to register before accessing the site. Once online, individuals are free to share just about anything they wish, from thoughts, photos and videos to illustrations, personal concepts and ideas, by "pinning" items to their "board" or user site.

Reddit

reddit.com

Reddit is a content-sharing, open Web site to which users can send photos, ideas for discussion or current news stories via their reddit communities. Reddit claims more than 169 million monthly visitors. Users vote "up" or "down" on topics suggested by contributors. "Hotter" topics get discussed and draw comments; "cooler" topics usually are dropped. Site users call themselves "redditors."

Skype

skype.com

Skype users can do voice calls or video chats from their computers, tablets and mobile devices via the Internet to other devices or telephones or smartphones. Users also can send instant text and video messages, exchange files and images and create conference calls. Most of the service is free, but users are required to use "Skype Credit" or a subscription to call landline or mobile numbers.

The Verge

theverge.com

The Verge delivers information about the latest technology trends and products as well as content and information from a variety of locations around the world, including North and South America, Europe and Asia.

Vine

vine.com

Users can watch, create and share short, looping videos— anytime, anywhere—through videos or "Vines" worldwide via their computer or smartphone.

Impact/Action Videos are concise news features on various topics created exclusively for *Media/Impact*. Find them in *Media/Impact*'s MindTap at cengagebrain.com.

MindTap® Log on to MindTap for *Media/Impact* to access a variety of additional material—including learning objectives, chapter readings with high-lighting and note-taking, **Impact/Action Videos**, activities, and comprehension quizzes—that will guide you through this chapter.

ADVERTISING
CATCHING CONSUMERS

10

YOUR ADVERTISEMENT COULD BE HERE!
like our billboard since...1914
844-465-3515
billboardatwrigley@gmail.com

www.WRIGLEYROOFTOPS.com

www.SKYBOX ON SHEFFIELD.c

o.com

EAMUS CATULI!   ACO669106

SKYBOX ON SHEFFIELD.com
3627

AP Images/Charles Rex Arbogast

Advertising is an essential yet controversial factor in the growth of American businesses. An advertising billboard stands out high above a worker as he removes snow from Chicago's Wrigley Field on March 2, 2015, in time for opening day.

"Interactive advertising revenue is on a strong upward trajectory. Marketers across all advertising categories are increasing their investment in digital media."

—SHERRILL MANE, INTERNET ADVERTISING BUREAU

American consumers pay for most of their media (newspapers, magazines, radio and television) by watching, listening to and reading advertisements. The American Marketing Association defines advertising as "any paid form of non-personal presentation and promotion of ideas, goods or services by an identified sponsor."

You pay directly for books, movies and recordings, although these media use advertising to sell their products. But the broadcast programs you want to hear and see, the articles you want to read and the Internet sites you use every day are filled with advertisements placed by companies that want to sell you products. In 2014, U.S. businesses spent $181 billion—$567 per person—to advertise their products to American consumers, more than any other country in the world. (See **Illustration 10.1**, "In Which Countries Do Marketers Spend the Most *per Person* for Advertising?" p. 201.)

Advertising Supports Mass Media

Advertising is not a mass medium. Advertising carries the messages that come to you from the people who pay for the American mass media. Advertising is at least 3,000 years old. In 1200 B.C., the Phoenicians painted messages on stones near paths where people often walked. In the 6th century B.C., ships that came into port with products on board sent criers around town with signboards to announce their arrival.

In the 13th century A.D., the British began requiring trademarks to protect buyers and to identify the makers of quality products. The first printed advertisement was prepared by printer William Caxton in England in 1478 to sell one of his books.

Advertising became part of the American experience even before the settlers arrived. "Never was there a more outrageous or more unscrupulous or more ill-informed advertising campaign than that by which the promoters for the American colonies brought settlers here," writes historian Daniel J. Boorstin. "Brochures published in England in the 17th century, some even earlier, were full of hopeful overstatements, half-truths, and downright lies, along with some facts which nowadays surely would

Bucella/Cartoonstock.com

"To tell you the truth, I don't think the average consumer will notice. Run with it."

IMPACT

Global

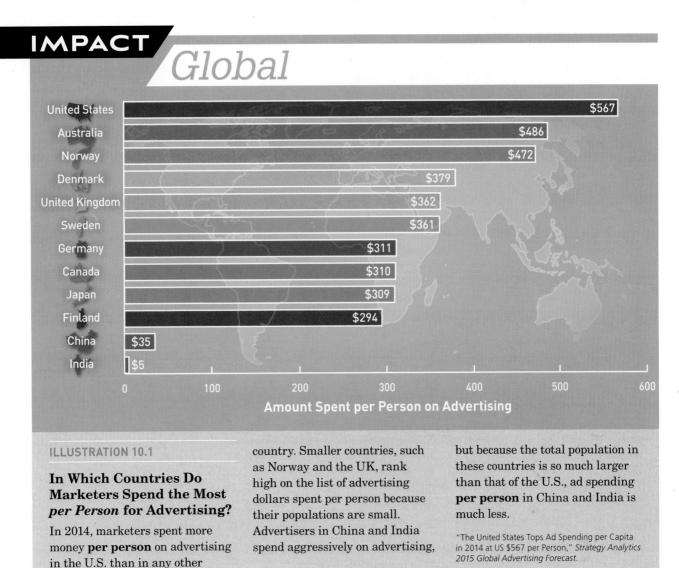

Country	Amount
United States	$567
Australia	$486
Norway	$472
Denmark	$379
United Kingdom	$362
Sweden	$361
Germany	$311
Canada	$310
Japan	$309
Finland	$294
China	$35
India	$5

Amount Spent per Person on Advertising

ILLUSTRATION 10.1

In Which Countries Do Marketers Spend the Most *per Person* for Advertising?

In 2014, marketers spent more money **per person** on advertising in the U.S. than in any other country. Smaller countries, such as Norway and the UK, rank high on the list of advertising dollars spent per person because their populations are small. Advertisers in China and India spend aggressively on advertising, but because the total population in these countries is so much larger than that of the U.S., ad spending **per person** in China and India is much less.

"The United States Tops Ad Spending per Capita in 2014 at US $567 per Person," *Strategy Analytics 2015 Global Advertising Forecast.*

be the basis for a restraining order from the Federal Trade Commission (FTC). Gold and silver, fountains of youth, plenty of fish, venison without limit, all these were promised, and of course some of them were found."

Advertising in Newspapers

The nation's first newspaper ad appeared in *The Boston News-Letter*'s first issue in 1704 when the newspaper's editor included an ad for his own newspaper. The penny press of the 1800s counted on advertising to underwrite its costs.

In 1833, the *New York Sun* candidly said in its first issue: "The object of this paper is to lay before the public, at a price within the means of everyone, all the news of the day and at the same time afford an advantageous medium for advertising." Three years later, the *Philadelphia Public Ledger* reported that "advertising is our revenue, and in a paper involving so many expenses as a penny paper, and especially our own, the only source of revenue."

Because they were so dependent on advertisers, newspapers in the 1800s accepted any ads they could get. Eventually, customers complained, especially about the patent medicines that advertised cures for every imaginable disease and often delivered unwelcome hangovers. (Many of these medicines contained mostly alcohol.)

Products like Anti-Corpulence pills claimed they would help someone lose 15 pounds a month: "They cause no sickness, contain no poison and never fail." Dr. T. Felix Couraud's Oriental Cream guaranteed it would "remove tan, pimples, freckles, moth patches, rash and skin diseases and every blemish on beauty."

The newspaper publishers' response to complaints was to develop an open advertising policy, which meant newspapers would accept advertising from anyone who paid for it. This allowed the publishers to continue accepting the ads and then criticize the ads on their editorial pages. The *Public Ledger* described its policy this way: "Our advertising columns are open to the 'public, the whole public, and nothing but the public.' We admit any advertisement of any thing or any opinion, from any persons who will pay the price, excepting what is forbidden by the laws of the land, or what, in the opinion of all, is offensive to decency and morals."

But some editors did move their ads, which had been mingled with the copy, to a separate section. Advertising historian Stephen Fox says:

> Advertising was considered an embarrassment . . . the wastrel relative, the unruly servant kept backstairs and never allowed into the front parlor. . . . A firm risked its credit rating by advertising; banks might take it as a confession of financial weakness.

> Everyone deplored advertising. Nobody—advertiser, agent or medium—took responsibility for it. The advertiser only served as an errand boy, passing the advertiser's message along to the publisher: the medium printed it, but surely would not question

the right of free speech by making a judgment on the veracity of the advertiser.

Advertising in Magazines

Until the 1880s, magazines remained wary of advertising, but Cyrus H. K. Curtis, who founded *The Ladies' Home Journal* in 1887, promoted advertising as the way for magazines to succeed.

Once when he was asked what made him successful, he answered, "Advertising. That's what made me whatever I am. . . . I use up my days trying to find men who can write an effective advertisement." When Curtis hired Edward Bok as editor, Bok began a campaign against patent medicine ads and joined *Collier's* and the American Medical Association to seek government restraints. Congress created the Federal Trade Commission (FTC) in 1914, and part of its job was to monitor deceptive advertising. The FTC continues to be the major government watchdog over advertising (see "Federal Government Regulates Advertisers," p. 212).

Advertising on Radio

WEAF in New York broadcast its first advertisement in 1922, selling apartments in New Jersey. B. F. Goodrich, Palmolive and Eveready commercials followed. In September 1928, the Lucky Strike Dance Orchestra premiered on NBC, and Lucky Strike sales went up 47 percent. More cigarette companies moved to radio, and Camel cigarettes sponsored weekly, then daily, programs.

Sir Walter Raleigh cigarettes sponsored the Sir Walter Raleigh Revue. In one hour, the sponsor squeezed in 70 references to the product, according to Stephen Fox in *The Mirror Makers: A History of American Advertising and Its Creators*. "The theme song ('rally round Sir Walter Raleigh') introduced the Raleigh Revue in the Raleigh Theater with the Raleigh Orchestra and the Raleigh Rovers; then would follow the adventures of Sir Walter in Virginia and at Queen Elizabeth's court, with ample mention of his cigarettes and smoking tobacco," according to Fox. In 1938, for the first time, radio collected more money from advertising than magazines did.

Advertising on Television

Television began as an advertising medium. Never questioning how television would be financed, the TV networks assumed they would attract commercial support. They were right. In 1949, television advertising totaled $12.3 million. One year later, the total was $40.8 million. In 1951, advertisers spent $128 million on television. In 2014, TV advertising revenue in the U.S. totaled **$78 billion**.

Bloomberg/Getty Images

The U.S. advertising industry collected $181 billion in 2014. Procter & Gamble, maker of many familiar products (including Duracell batteries, Pampers diapers, Gillette blades and Crest toothpaste), spends more money on advertising in the U.S. than any other company.

Gary Leonard/Historical/Corbis

In the 1950s, many advertisers shifted their marketing dollars from radio to television. This 1950s Nabisco billboard in Los Angeles promotes the fact that Oreos are now advertised on TV.

In a practice adopted from radio, television programs usually carried **direct sponsorship**. Many shows, such as *Camel News Caravan*, carried the sponsor's name in the title and advertised just one product (Camel cigarettes). Advertising agencies became television's programmers. "Given one advertiser and a show title often bearing its name, viewers associated a favorite show with its sponsor and—because of a 'gratitude factor'—would buy the products," writes Fox.

Alfred Hitchcock became legendary for leading into his show's commercials with wry remarks about the sponsor: "Oh dear, I see the actors won't be ready for another 60 seconds. However, thanks to our sponsor's remarkable foresight, we have a message that will fill in here nicely." But Hitchcock's sarcasm was the exception, and the television industry today relies heavily on advertising support.

Advertising on the Internet

Advertisers flocked to major Internet sites when they were first launched. They expected quick returns, as consumer use of the Internet skyrocketed. At first, advertisers primarily used banner advertising, which meant their advertising messages scrolled across a Web site or appeared in a box on the site.

Internet sites also tried **pop-up** advertisements, which meant an ad popped up either behind a Web site screen when someone left the site or on top of the Web site home page when someone first visited. Advertisers quickly learned, however, that no matter how they packaged the message, advertising on an Internet site didn't necessarily bring increased sales for their products.

What advertisers call the **click-through rate** (the percentage of people who see an advertising message on an Internet site and actually click through to learn more) is less than 1 percent. This is a very disappointing return, especially because Web site advertising can be expensive. By 2015, Internet ad spending reached $51 billion. Advertisers today are still trying to figure out the magic formula to reach consumers on the Internet, and they're willing to spend a lot of money to try to find out what works.

Ford, BMW, Coca-Cola and Absolut Vodka created "advertainments" on their Web sites—short movies (2 to 11 minutes) featuring lots of action and familiar movie stars. Many marketers are using **viral marketing** to try to reach younger audiences. Viral marketing means creating an online message that is so entertaining or interesting that consumers pass it along through social media, such as Facebook and Twitter, and by e-mail links. The message becomes an online "virus" that promotes a product without the expense of a paid commercial.

These new approaches are meant to make Internet advertisements seem less like advertisements—further blurring the line between information, entertainment and advertising. (See **Impact/Profile**, "The Advertising Networker: Sir Martin Sorrell of WPP," p. 204.)

Ads Share Three Characteristics

The word *advertise* originally meant to take note or to consider. By the 1700s, the word's meaning had changed. *To advertise* meant "to persuade." "If we consider democracy not just a political system," says Daniel J. Boorstin, "but as

---

Direct Sponsorship   A program that carries an advertiser's name in the program title.

Pop-Up   An advertisement on a Web site that appears on the screen either behind a Web page when someone leaves the site or on top of the Web site home page when someone first visits.

Click-Through Rate   The percentage of people who see an advertising message on an Internet site and actually click through to learn more.

Viral Marketing   Creating an online message that is entertaining enough to get consumers to pass it on over the Internet like a virus.

IMPACT

Profile

The Advertising Networker: Sir Martin Sorrell of WPP

By Andrew Hill, Financial Times

When chief executives meet in Sir Martin Sorrell's absence, they sometimes deliberately email him simultaneously to test how quickly he replies and to whom. The chief executive of WPP, the world's largest advertising agency by revenue, is rarely offline, whether at a private dinner, a conference or a board meeting, his thumbs flashing terse replies back to contacts, colleagues, customers and the media. His rapid reaction time is legendary, triggering the occasional rumour (which Sorrell denies) that he has a team of assistants responding under his name.

Philip Lader, WPP's chairman and former US ambassador to Britain, recalls sitting behind Sorrell at the Wimbledon finals. When the match was over, Lader's wife whispered: "Did he ever look up from the BlackBerry?" These days, the response is as likely to come from his iPhone 6. But while Sorrell says he still loves his two BlackBerrys (one on a US network, one on a British network), he also carries something much more precious: a "letter of wishes" from his father, Jack, dated a year before his death in 1989. "It's a very deep letter," says Sorrell, one which contains the message that "no matter how dark the clouds are, [you must] have no fear."

That advice has stood Sorrell in good stead. Through a combination of prolific deal-

Sir Martin Sorrell, 71, CEO of London-based WPP, the world's largest advertising agency, appears on Fox Business Network in New York on May 15, 2015.

making, relentless communication, near-constant travel and tireless promotion of himself and his company, Sorrell has turned a small maker of wire baskets—Wire & Plastic Products—into a vast marketing, media and communications conglomerate, with a stock market valuation of more than £20bn [$31 billion US]. After 30 years, WPP now embraces some of the best-known names in marketing, advertising and public relations, including Ogilvy & Mather, J Walter Thompson and Burson-Marsteller.

In the process, Sorrell has become one of the best-connected executives in the world. Sorrell has won the sometimes-reluctant respect of rivals and the admiration of peers for turning advertising and marketing from a creative cottage industry into an efficient and global money machine.

The WPP chief executive turned 70 on Valentine's Day [2014] and everyone agrees he is likely to cling to his position, even if it means dying in harness. How long does Sorrell himself think he can continue?

"I will carry on as long as I can or as long as people will have me. At some point in time people will cart you off to the glue factory," Sorrell says, in an interview just before his birthday. "I enjoy it....When you start something—you start an idea, you start a company—it's something that you live and breathe."

The advertising magnate is a voluble, engaging but elusive subject. Sitting at the boardroom table in WPP's London mews headquarters, he deftly diverts more personal lines of questioning into a dead end of well-polished stories. The time he tried to call Eddie George, former governor of the Bank of England (the switchboard, having heard his explanation of what WPP was, put him through to the marketing department). The meeting he will have the next day—in California—with Sheryl Sandberg of Facebook. His energy and deep interest are evident; his age—seemingly irrelevant.

Excerpted from Andrew Hill, "The Networker: Martin Sorrell of WPP," *FT Magazine*, ft.com, March 13, 2015.

a set of institutions which do aim to make everything available to everybody, it would not be an overstatement to describe advertising as the characteristic rhetoric of democracy."

Boorstin says that advertising in America shares three characteristics: repetition, style and ubiquity.

Repetition

In 1851, when Robert Bonner bought the *New York Ledger,* he wanted to advertise his newspaper in the competing *New York Herald,* owned by James Gordon Bennett. Bennett limited all his advertisers to the same type size, so Bonner paid for an entire page of the *Herald,* across which he repeated the message "Bring home the *New York Ledger* tonight." This is an early example of advertising's widespread practice of repeating a simple message for effect.

An Advertising Style

At first, advertising adopted a plain, direct style. Advertising pioneer Claude Hopkins, says Boorstin, claimed: "Brilliant writing has no place in advertising. A unique style takes attention from the subject. . . . One should be natural and simple . . . [I]n fishing for buyers, as in fishing for bass, one should not reveal the hook." The plain-talk tradition is a foundation of what advertisers call modern advertising. But advertising today often adopts a style of hyperbole, making large claims for products. Boorstin calls this "tall-talk."

The tall-talk ad is in the P. T. Barnum tradition of advertising. Barnum was a carnival barker and later impresario who lured customers to his circus acts with fantastic claims. You may recognize this approach in some of the furniture and car ads on television, as an announcer screams at you that you have only a few days left until all the chairs or all the cars will be gone.

Both plain talk and tall-talk combine, Boorstin says, to create advertising's new myth. "This is the world of the neither true nor false—of the statement that 60 percent of the physicians who expressed a choice said that our brand of aspirin would be more effective in curing a simple headache than any other brand. . . . It is not untrue, and yet, in its connotation it is not exactly true."

Ubiquity

In America, advertising is everywhere. Advertisers are always looking for new places to catch consumers' attention.

In the U.S., advertising is everywhere—it is *ubiquitous.* Surrounded by palm trees, a Coca-Cola ad sprouts above the right field bleachers at Dodger Stadium in Los Angeles.

Ads appear on shopping carts, on video screens at sports stadiums, atop parking meters. Says Daniel Boorstin, "The ubiquity of advertising is, of course, just another effect of our uninhibited efforts to use all the media to get all sorts of information to everybody everywhere. Since the places to be filled are everywhere, the amount of advertising is not determined by the needs of advertising, but by the opportunities for advertising, which become unlimited."

In some cases, this ubiquity works to advertising's disadvantage. Many advertisers shy away from radio and TV because the ads are grouped so closely together. In 1986, in an attempt to attract more advertisers, TV began selling the "split-30" ad, which fits two 15-second ads into a 30-second spot. Even 10-second ads are available. Wherever these shorter commercials are sold, the station runs twice or three times as many ads for different products, crowding the commercial time even more. Too many ads that run together make it hard for one ad to grab consumers' attention.

Ads Compete for Your Attention

To sell the products, advertisers must catch your eye or your ear or your heart (preferably all three). A study by the Harvard Graduate School of Business Administration reported that the average American is exposed to at least 500 ads a day.

With so many ads competing for your attention, the advertiser must first get you to read, listen to or watch one ad instead of another. "The immediate goal of advertising [is to] tug at our psychological shirt sleeves and slow us down long enough for a word or two about whatever is being sold," says humanities and human sciences professor Jib Fowles in *Mass Advertising as Social Forecast*. Research shows there are at least 15 common ways ads appeal to consumers.

15 Ways Ads Appeal to Consumers

You make your buying decisions based on several sources of information besides advertising: friends, family and your own experience, for example. To influence your choices, the advertising message must appeal to you for some reason as you sift through the ads to make judgments and choose products.

Fowles enumerated 15 appeals, which he calls an "inventory of human motives," that advertisers commonly use in their commercials:

1. Need for sex. Surprisingly, Fowles found that only 2 percent of the television ads he surveyed used this appeal. It may be too blatant, he concluded, and often detracts from the product.

Advertisers use at least 15 different types of appeals to attract consumers. This 1935 ad shows Santa Claus promoting Lucky Strike cigarettes. Which of the 15 ad appeals listed by Jib Fowles does this ad use?

2. Need for affiliation. The largest number of ads uses this approach: You are looking for friendship. Advertisers can also use this negatively, to make you worry that you'll lose friends if you don't use a certain product.

3. Need to nurture. Every time you see a puppy or a kitten or a child, the appeal is to your maternal or paternal instincts.

4. Need for guidance. A father or mother figure can appeal to your desire for someone to care for you, so you won't have to worry. Betty Crocker is a good example.

5. Need to aggress. We all have had a desire to get even, and some ads give you this satisfaction.

6. Need to achieve. The ability to accomplish something difficult and succeed identifies the product with winning. Sports figures as spokespersons project this image.

7. Need to dominate. The power we lack is what we can look for in a commercial: "Master the possibilities."

8. Need for prominence. We want to be admired and respected, to have high social status. Luxury car ads and ads for diamond rings offer this potential.

9. Need for attention. We want people to notice us; we want to be looked at. Cosmetics are a natural for this approach.

10. Need for autonomy. Within a crowded environment, we want to be singled out, to be "a breed apart." This can also be used negatively: You may be too ordinary without a particular product.

11. Need to escape. Flight is very appealing; you can imagine adventures you cannot have. The idea of escape is pleasurable.

12. Need to feel safe. To be free from threats, to be secure is the appeal of many insurance and bank ads.

13. Need for aesthetic sensations. Beauty attracts us, and classic art or dance makes us feel creative, enhanced.

14. Need to satisfy curiosity. Facts support our belief that information is quantifiable, and numbers and diagrams make our choices seem scientific.

15. Physiological needs. Fowles defines sex (item 1) as a biological need, and so he classifies our need to sleep, eat and drink as physiological. Advertisements for juicy pizza are especially appealing late at night.

Marketers Use Demographics

Advertisers target their messages to an audience according to the audience's needs. But an advertiser also seeks to determine the audience's characteristics. This analysis of observable audience characteristics is called *demographics*.

Demographics are composed of data about a target audience's gender, age, income level, marital status, geographic location and occupation. These data are observable because they are available to advertising agencies through census data and other sources. Advertising agencies use demographic audience analysis to help advertisers target their messages.

A motorcycle dealer certainly wouldn't want to advertise on a baby products Web site, for example; a candy manufacturer probably wouldn't profit from advertising in a diet and exercise magazine. Advertising agencies try to match a client's product to a thoroughly defined audience so each advertising dollar is well spent, such as matching an upscale bank with well-educated high earners.

Defining the audience is very important because the goal of advertising is to market a product to people who have the desire for the product and the ability to buy it. Audience analysis tells an advertiser whether there are enough people who can be targeted for a product to make the advertising worthwhile.

Advertising Feeds Consumerism

According to Louis C. Kaufman, author of *Essentials of Advertising*, critics of advertising make three main arguments:

1. Advertising adds to the cost of products. Critics of advertising maintain that advertising, like everything that is part of manufacturing a product, is a cost. Ultimately, the consumer pays for the cost of advertising. But the industry argues that advertising helps make more goods and services available to the consumer and that the resulting competition keeps prices lower.

2. Advertising causes people to buy products they do not need. Says media scholar Michael Schudson,

Bloomberg/Getty Images

Critics of advertising claim that it causes consumers to buy products they don't need. The advertising industry contends the ultimate test of any product is the marketplace. A woman walks in front of several ads for the luxury brand Gucci in Tokyo, Japan.

Most blame advertising for the sale of specific consumer goods, notably luxury goods (designer jeans), frivolous goods (pet rocks), dangerous goods (cigarettes), shoddy goods (some toys for children), expensive goods that do not differ at all from cheap goods (non-generic over-the-counter drugs), marginally differentiated products that do not differ significantly from one another (laundry soaps), and wasteful goods (various un-ecological throw-away convenience goods).

3. The advertising industry contends the ultimate test of any product is the marketplace and that advertising may stimulate consumers to try a new product or a new brand, but consumers will not continue to buy an unsatisfying product.

4. Advertising reduces competition and thereby fosters monopolies. Critics point to the rising cost of advertising, especially on television, which limits which companies can afford to launch a new product or a new campaign. The industry argues that advertising is still a very inexpensive way to let people know about new products.

"The cost of launching a nationwide advertising campaign may be formidable," writes Louis C. Kaufman, "but the cost of supporting larger, nationwide sales forces for mass-marketed goods would be greater still."

Demographics Data about consumers' characteristics, such as age, gender, income level, marital status, geographic location and occupation.

Does advertising work? According to Schudson, "Apologists are wrong that advertising is simply information that makes the market work more efficiently—but so too are the critics of advertising who believe in its overwhelming power to deceive and to deflect human minds to its ends."

"Evaluating its impact," Kaufman says, "is more difficult than these simplicities of apology and critique will acknowledge."

Advertising at Work

Several worldwide advertising agencies are based in the United States, but many advertising agencies are small local and regional operations. (See **Illustration 10.2**, "Top 10 Global Advertising Agencies," below.) Advertising agencies buy time and space for the companies they represent. For this, they usually earn a commission (commonly 15 percent). Many agencies also produce television and radio commercials, plus build and maintain Internet sites for their clients.

Depending on the size of the agency, the company may be divided into as many as six departments:

1. Marketing research

2. Media selection

3. Creative activity

4. Account management

5. Administration

6. Public relations

Marketing research examines the product's potential, where it will be sold and who will buy the product. Agency researchers may survey the market themselves or contract with an outside market research company to evaluate potential buyers.

IMPACT

Money

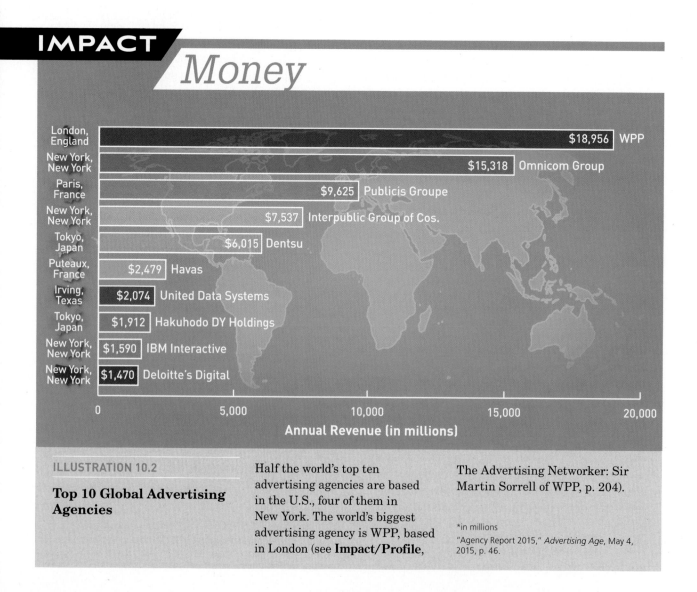

Location	Agency	Annual Revenue (in millions)
London, England	WPP	$18,956
New York, New York	Omnicom Group	$15,318
Paris, France	Publicis Groupe	$9,625
New York, New York	Interpublic Group of Cos.	$7,537
Tokyo, Japan	Dentsu	$6,015
Puteaux, France	Havas	$2,479
Irving, Texas	United Data Systems	$2,074
Tokyo, Japan	Hakuhodo DY Holdings	$1,912
New York, New York	IBM Interactive	$1,590
New York, New York	Deloitte's Digital	$1,470

Annual Revenue (in millions)

ILLUSTRATION 10.2

Top 10 Global Advertising Agencies

Half the world's top ten advertising agencies are based in the U.S., four of them in New York. The world's biggest advertising agency is WPP, based in London (see **Impact/Profile**, The Advertising Networker: Sir Martin Sorrell of WPP, p. 204).

*in millions
"Agency Report 2015," *Advertising Age*, May 4, 2015, p. 46.

Media selection suggests the best combination of buys for a client—television, newspapers, magazines, billboards and/or Internet.

Creative activity thinks up the ads. The "creatives" write the copy for TV, radio, print and Internet. They design the graphic art, and often they produce the commercials. They also verify that the ad has run as often as it was scheduled to run.

Account management is the liaison between the agency and the client. Account executives handle client complaints and suggestions and manage the company team assigned to the account.

Administration pays the bills, including all the tabs for the account executives' lunches with clients. *Public relations* planning is an extra service that some agencies offer for companies that don't have a separate public relations office.

All these departments work together on an ad campaign. An ***advertising campaign*** is a planned advertising effort, coordinated for a specific time period. A campaign can last anywhere from a month to a year, and the objective is a coordinated strategy to sell a product or a service.

Typically, the company assigns the account executive a team of people from the different departments to handle the account. The account executive answers to the people who control the agency, usually a board of directors. The members of the campaign team coordinate all types of advertising—print and broadcast, for example—to make sure they share consistent content. After establishing a budget based on the client's needs, the campaign team creates a slogan, recommends a strategy for the best exposure for the client, approves the design of print and broadcast commercials and then places the ads with the media outlets.

Half of the world's biggest advertising agencies are based in New York. In part, this is by tradition because New York has always been a base for advertising companies. They also have access to a larger pool of talent and facilities such as video production studios, but today Internet technology enables greater flexibility for agencies to work from many different, even remote, cities.

Mass Media Industries Depend on Advertising

The advertising business and the media industries are interdependent—that is, what happens in the advertising business directly affects the media industries. The advertising business also is very dependent on the nation's economic health.

If the national economy expands, the advertising business and the media industries prosper. If the nation's economy falls into a recession, advertisers typically reduce their ad budgets, which eventually may lead to a

Mike Hewitt/Getty Images

TV sports programs are a big draw for advertisers. In 2015, the Women's Tennis Association (WTA) signed a 10-year agreement for $535 million for broadcast rights to all games on the WTA tour. In Rome, Italy, Maria Sharapova displays the trophy for her WTA women's singles win at the Internazionali BNL d'Italia on May 17, 2015.

decline in advertising revenue for the agencies and for the media industries where the agencies place their ads. During a downturn, advertisers also may change their advertising strategies—choosing the Internet over television, for example, because the Internet is much less expensive.

The advertising industry today, therefore, must be very sensitive to economic and media trends. The success of an ad agency is best measured by the results an ad campaign brings. The agency must analyze the benefits of different types of advertising—broadcast, print, Internet—and recommend the most efficient combinations for its clients. (See **Illustration 10.3**, "Top 10 Advertisers in the United States," p. 210.)

> **Advertising Campaign**   A planned advertising effort, coordinated for a specific time period.

IMPACT

Society

ILLUSTRATION 10.3

Top 10 Advertisers in the United States

Auto manufacturers, such as General Motors, Ford, Toyota and Fiat Chrysler, always have spent a lot of money to advertise their products to American consumers. Telecommunications companies, such as AT&T (2), Comcast (4) and Verizon (6), spend nearly as much as or more than General Motors (which ranks 3) on U.S. advertising. Only three of the top ten U.S. advertisers are companies based outside the U.S.

2015 Advertising Age Marketing Fact Pack, December 29, 2014.

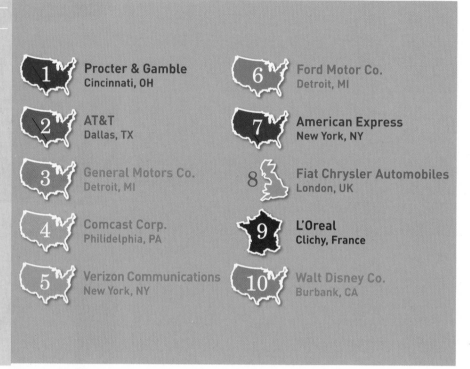

1 Procter & Gamble
Cincinnati, OH

2 AT&T
Dallas, TX

3 General Motors Co.
Detroit, MI

4 Comcast Corp.
Philidelphia, PA

5 Verizon Communications
New York, NY

6 Ford Motor Co.
Detroit, MI

7 American Express
New York, NY

8 Fiat Chrysler Automobiles
London, UK

9 L'Oreal
Clichy, France

10 Walt Disney Co.
Burbank, CA

Commercials on Television

Even though the cost seems exorbitant, sponsors continue to line up to appear on network television. "Advertisers must use television on whatever terms they can get it, for television is the most potent merchandising vehicle ever devised," writes TV producer Bob Shanks in his book *The Cool Fire: How to Make It in Television.* Shanks is talking about national advertisers who buy network time—companies whose products can be advertised to the entire country at once.

Advertising minutes within every network prime-time hour are divided into 10-, 15- and 30-second ads. If an advertiser wants to reach the broad national market, television is an expensive choice because the cost for a 30-second commercial on the highest-rated network sitcom, such as *The Big Bang Theory*, is $345,000. The price tag for a 30-second commercial reaches $4.5 million for a widely watched program such as the Super Bowl, but many other sports attract large audiences for advertisers. In 2015, for instance, the Women's Tennis Association (WTA) signed the biggest single commercial contract in the history of women's sports—$535 million over ten years for broadcast rights to every game in the WTA tour. (See **Impact/Money**, "What It Costs," p. 214.)

National advertising on TV network programs is bought by national advertising agencies, which handle the country's biggest advertisers—Procter & Gamble and McDonald's, for example. These companies usually have in-house advertising and public relations departments, but most of the advertising strategy and production of commercials for these companies is handled by the agencies. National agencies buy advertising space based on a careful formula, calculated on a cost-per-thousand (**CPM**) basis—the cost of an ad per 1,000 people reached (M is the Roman numeral for 1,000).

Making a TV commercial for national broadcast is more expensive per minute than making a television program because each company wants its ads to be different from the rest. The price to create a TV commercial can run more than $1 million a minute. That may be why, as one producer said, "the commercials are the best things on TV." Network television commercials certainly are the most visible type of advertising, but not everyone needs the reach of network television. The goal of well-placed advertising is to deliver the best results to the

CPM Cost per thousand, the cost of an ad per 1,000 people reached. (M is the Roman numeral for 1,000.)

client for the lowest cost, and this may mean looking to other media.

Using Print and Radio

Different types of media deliver different types of audiences. Advertising agencies may buy time and space on local radio and in newspapers and magazines to target a specific audience by demographics: age, education, gender and income. A radio station with a rock format delivers a different audience than an easy-listening station does. *The New York Times* delivers a different reader than the *Honolulu Advertiser. Sports Illustrated* targets a different group than *Vogue.*

Language also can be a targeting factor. Some agencies use Spanish-language media to target Latino consumers, for example, on a Spanish-language radio station or in a Spanish-language newspaper.

With newspaper and magazine circulation declining, and over-the-air radio audiences migrating to satellite radio or listening to their iPods, Internet advertising is quickly becoming the fastest growing avenue for advertisers to reach consumers.

Internet Delivers Display, Search and Social Networks

The Internet offers the largest potential audience, but consumers also can quickly click past ads on the Web so advertisers have become clever at placing Internet ads within and around the sites themselves. Internet ads run as banners that appear at the top of the page or alongside the copy.

Another successful method of access to consumers through the Internet is *search advertising*, often called simply *search.* Advertisers pay Internet companies fees to list and/or link their company's site domain name to a specific search word or phrase. If a consumer searches for "Car Insurance," for example, the next screen will show information about car insurance, and the sides and top of the screen also might show ads for cars at the local dealership. Search advertising accounts for nearly half of all Internet advertising revenue today, according to the Internet Advertising Bureau, which divides search advertising into four types:

1. Paid listings: Places links at the top or side of the screen next to search results.

2. Contextual search: Places text links in the article based on the context of the content.

3. Paid inclusion: Guarantees that a search engine indexes a marketer's URL, so that when someone searches for something, the marketer's URL shows up.

4. Site optimization: Fixes a site so search engines can more easily index the site.

Social networks such as Facebook and YouTube offer even more marketing outlets. An ad campaign today can include a presence on Facebook, a YouTube video promoting the product or a carefully orchestrated Twitter campaign to take advantage of timely marketing moments.

Branded content has become another way that advertisers can promote products—by using either the Internet or traditional media. Also called *content marketing* and *branded entertainment*, branded content is a program or story that mimics regular commercial programming or standard journalism but is custom-produced by an advertiser to promote a specific product. The content may or may not be labeled as advertising, and, in most cases, the consumer may be unaware a product is being advertised. In one campaign for Jaguar Land Rover, for example, in a

Marty Bucella, CartoonStock.com

"I don't know what it means, but sales have skyrocketed since I put the 'i' in front of it."

series called *Travel Channel's Road to the Unexpected*, a Travel Channel host drives a Land Rover on adventures in Bolivia, Britain, Jamaica and Quebec.

"Interactive advertising revenue is on a strong upward trajectory," according to Sherrill Mane of the Internet Advertising Bureau. "Nearly all types of ad formats are showing positive movement and marketers across all advertising categories, most notably consumer packaged goods and pharmaceuticals, are increasing their investment in digital media."

Media Compete Fiercely for Clients

The competition among the media industries for advertisers is fierce:

▸ A study commissioned by the American Newspaper Publishers Association reveals that only one in five prime-time adult viewers could remember the last ad they had seen on television.

▸ Print advertisers claim that because viewers can so easily change channels and skip the ads, TV commercials are an unreliable way to deliver an audience.

▸ "Radio is the medium working women don't have to make time for," boasts the Radio Advertising Bureau (RAB). Whereas working women spend 15 percent of their daily media time reading a newspaper, they spend half of their media time with radio, says the RAB.

▸ The Internet Advertising Bureau says that mobile advertising is growing faster than any other type of marketing.

Advertising agencies gather demographic information provided by Nielsen for broadcast and the Internet and by the Alliance for Audited Media for print; the audience is converted into numbers. Based on these numbers, agencies advise advertisers about how to best reach buyers for their products, for example, by advertising regionally or online.

For example, Danielle's Health and Fitness Salon, a small local business, does not need to advertise on the *Tonight Show* or in *The New York Times*. Danielle and other local business owners may need to reach only their local communities. Businesses larger than the fitness salon, such as a car dealer or a furniture store, could buy local TV or radio time but also establish an Internet site to attract buyers from outside the geographic area.

A local advertising agency can design a campaign, produce the ad and place the ad just as the national agencies do, but on a much smaller scale. Many small companies design and place their own ads directly with local media. To attract customers, local media also help companies design their ads. Newspapers, for example, will help a small advertiser prepare an ad using ready-made art.

A radio or television station may include the services of an announcer or access to a studio in the price for a series of spot ads. Broadcast stations sometimes trade ads for services offered by the advertiser—dinner for two at the local restaurant in return for two spot ads, for example. Then the station gives the dinners away as a promotion for a local program.

The Internet has added another dimension for small, local companies. With Internet access, you can sell your local product from Boise, Idaho, anywhere in the world. Many small companies design their own Web sites, or hire a Web site designer, bypassing an ad agency altogether. They also can list their products on a consumer Web site such as eBay or Etsy or place a product demonstration on a social networking site such as YouTube.

Federal Government Regulates Advertisers

Government protection for consumers dates back to the beginning of the 20th century when Congress passed the Pure Food and Drug Act in 1906, mainly as a protection against patent medicine ads that magazines were running (see **Chapter 4**). The advertising industry itself has adopted advertising standards, and in some cases the media have established their own codes.

Government oversight is the main deterrent against deceptive advertising. This responsibility is shared by

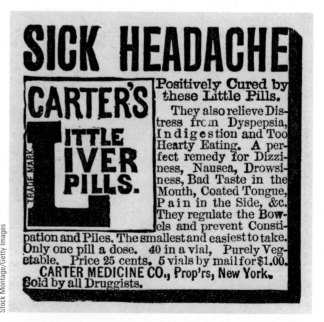

Stock Montage/Getty Images

In 1906, the U.S. Congress passed the Pure Food and Drug Act, primarily to protect consumers against patent medicine ads like this one for Carter's Little Liver Pills, which promises to cure a variety of ailments, including dizziness, nausea, pain in the side and bad taste in the mouth.

Advertisers in the United States are subject to FTC and FDA regulation. Based on an FTC complaint against POM Wonderful beverage, the U.S. Supreme Court ruled in 2014 that beverage companies can be sued if their product labels would "mislead and trick consumers."

several government agencies: the Federal Trade Commission, the Food and Drug Administration and the Federal Communications Commission.

Federal Trade Commission

The mission of the Federal Trade Commission, established in 1914, is "to prevent business practices that are anticompetitive or deceptive or unfair to consumers; to enhance informed consumer choice and public understanding of the competitive process; and to accomplish this without unduly burdening legitimate business activity." If the FTC determines an ad is deceptive, the commission can order the advertiser to stop or revise the campaign.

The commission also can require corrective advertising to counteract the deception. In 2012, an administrative law judge issued a cease-and-desist order against the company that produced POM Wonderful juice, which the company advertised as offering health benefits that could treat, prevent or reduce the risks of heart disease and prostate cancer.

The order was based on a complaint filed by the FTC in 2010. The judge's order said the company "shall not make any representation, in any manner, expressly or by implication, including through the use of a product name, endorsement, depiction, illustration, trademark or trade name, about the health benefits, performance or efficacy of any covered product."

In a subsequent hearing on the case, the U.S. Supreme Court ruled unanimously in 2014 that beverage companies can be sued if their product label would "mislead and trick consumers."

The Federal Trade Commission and the Bureau of Alcohol, Tobacco and Firearms (BATF) regulate the spirits industry, but neither agency has the authority to ban hard liquor ads on television. Although beer and wine advertisements have appeared on TV for decades, the TV networks traditionally did not advertise hard liquor, operating under a voluntary Code of Good Practice. In 1996, some liquor companies challenged the voluntary ban by placing ads on local television.

Seagram's, the first company to question the ban, advertised Crown Royal whiskey on a local TV station in Texas. "We believe distilled spirits should have the same access to electronic media, just the same way beer and wine do," said Arthur Shapiro, executive vice president in charge of marketing and strategy for Seagram's in the United States.

Because hard liquor advertising means a great deal of revenue, the TV networks did not resist, and hard liquor ads on TV are now quite common.

Food and Drug Administration

The Food and Drug Administration (FDA) oversees claims that appear on food labels or packaging. If the FDA finds a label is deceptive, the agency can require the advertiser to stop distributing products with that label. In the case against POM Wonderful, for example, the FTC said the company had made health benefit claims on its labels that had not been reviewed by the Food and Drug Administration, and on that basis the government filed a claim against the company.

Federal Communications Commission and Other Agencies

The Federal Communications Commission (FCC) enforces rules that govern the broadcast media. The FCC's jurisdiction over the broadcast industry gives the commission indirect control over broadcast advertising. In the past, the FCC has ruled against demonstrations of products that were misleading and against commercials the FCC decided were tasteless, but the FTC and the FDA are the primary enforcement agencies for advertising regulation. Other government agencies, such as the Environmental Protection Agency and the Consumer Product Safety Commission, also can question the content of advertisements.

Advertising agencies have formed the National Advertising Review Board (NARB) to hear complaints against advertisers. This effort at self-regulation among advertising agencies parallels that of some media industries, such as the movie industry's ratings code and the recording industry's record labeling for lyrics.

IMPACT

Money

What It Costs: Ad Prices From TV's Biggest Buys to the Smallest Screens

$400,000

The average outlay for a commercial during the fifth season of AMC's *The Walking Dead*, making it the costliest scripted series on TV. The Oct. 12, 2014, season premiere drew 17.3 million viewers; the March 29 [2015] season finale, 15.8 million.

$750,000

The amount Snapchat demands per "Brand Story" ad, a branded post (or "snap") that appears within the app's "Stories" feed. Snapchat doesn't disclose user numbers.

$35

The cost for a thousand impressions on Hulu for standard, run-of-site, in-stream video ads, with a minimum requirement of two ads per campaign.

$615,000

The cost of 30 seconds of ad time in the championship game of the 2015 NCAA Men's Division I Basketball Tournament on CBS. That's up from $1.49 million in 2014. [In 2014] the championship game averaged 21.2 million viewers, down from 23.4 million in 2013.

$112,000

The average cost for 30 seconds of commercial time in prime time broadcast TV [in 2014]. That's up from $110,000 in 2013.

$344,827

The average cost of a 30-second commercial during *The Big Bang Theory* on CBS, the most expensive comedy on TV. *Big*

To advertise for four weeks on the largest digital billboard in New York's Times Square costs $2.5 million. The billboard, owned by Clear Channel, is eight stories tall and runs for a complete city block, between W. 45th and W. 46th Streets.

Richard Perry/The New York Times

Bang averaged 16.7 million viewers [in 2015].

$50,000

The cost of one full-color ad on the front page of *The New York Times*. To appear on the *Times*' front page, though, marketers must commit to a certain frequency, such as front-page ads every Tuesday for six months; the total cost of running frequent page-one ads would likely top $1 million.

$615,000

The price of a 30-second sliver of airtime during Fox's Sunday afternoon NFL package. [The 2014] season's eight-game slate averaged 26.6 million viewers and a 15.5 household rating, making it TV's most-watched and highest-rated program.

$20

The cost of a thousand impressions for a sponsored photo on Instagram, down from $40 in 2013 when Instagram first rolled out ads.

Instagram says more than 300 million people around the world check out the photo-sharing app each month. Instagram's minimum ad spend is $200,000.

$2.5 million

The cost of four weeks on Times Square's biggest billboard, Clear Channel's eight-story sign on Broadway from West 45th Street to West 46th Street.

$237,406

The cost of a back-cover ad on *Vogue*, which claims a total readership of 12.7 million.

$675,000

The daily rate for YouTube's universal video masthead ad, which runs across YouTube's Web site and apps. YouTube attracted 210.4 million people to its desktop and mobile Web sites in January [2015].

$8 to $10

The average cost of a thousand impressions for a sponsored product on Buzzfeed.

Excerpted from "What It Costs," *Advertising Age*, April 6, 2015, p. 14.

Global Marketing Delivers New Audiences

When U.S. products seek international markets, and international products want to reach American consumers, the marketers' job is to design appealing campaigns to reach those consumers. Global industries often also use American advertising agencies to help them sell products in the United States. American agencies today collect nearly half of the *world's* revenue from advertising.

International advertising campaigns are becoming more common for global brands, such as Ikea and Coca-Cola, and this has meant the creation of international advertising markets. Cable News Network (CNN), for example, sells advertising on CNN worldwide, so that any company in any nation with CNN's service can advertise its product to a worldwide audience. Overall, billings outside the United States are commanding an increasing share of U.S. advertising agencies' business.

The most important factor for the global advertising market is emerging technology. The widespread use of the Internet creates new outlets, and new pricing, as the advertising community adapts to meet ever-changing digital media marketplace. (See **Impact/Money**, "What It Costs," p. 214.)

Another factor in the future of advertising is shifting demographic patterns. As the ethnicity, education and wealth of global consumers shift, marketing programs have to adapt quickly to reach target-specific audiences. Advertisers must find new ways to encourage product loyalty when the competition for customers extends beyond national borders. Amazon, for example, faces wide-ranging competition from Chinese online global retailer Alibaba.

The challenges for the advertising business are as great as the challenges for the media industries. The advertising industry will do what it has always done to adapt—follow the audience. The challenge for the advertising business is how to efficiently and effectively match today's audiences with the product messages the media industries deliver.

AP Images/IKEA/REX Shutterstock

International marketing campaigns are becoming more common for global products. On May 28, 2015, Swedish retailer Ikea opened a Breakfast in Bed Café in London to introduce British consumers to the unfamiliar concept of eating breakfast in bed (and promoting Ikea products at the same time).

REVIEW, ANALYZE, INVESTIGATE

CHAPTER 10

Advertising Supports Mass Media

- Advertising carries the messages that come to you from the sponsors who pay for the American media.
- In 2014, U.S. businesses spent a total of $181 billion to advertise their products to consumers—$567 per person, more than any other country in the world.

- As early as 1200 B.C., the Phoenicians painted messages on stones to advertise.
- In the 6th century B.C., ship captains sent criers around to announce that their ships were in port.
- In the 13th century A.D., the British began requiring trademarks to protect buyers.

- In 1704, newspapers were the first medium to use advertising. Magazines, radio, television and the Internet followed in the 19th and 20th centuries.

- Advertisers flocked to major Internet sites when they first were established. They expected quick returns as consumer use of the Internet skyrocketed. Advertisers quickly learned, however, that no matter how they packaged the message, advertising on an Internet site doesn't necessarily bring increased sales.

- What advertisers call the *click-through rate* (the percentage of people who see an advertising message and actually click through to learn more) is less than 1 percent.

- In 2015, Internet ad spending reached $51 billion.

- Viral marketing is a form of advertising that involves creating an online message that consumers pass on—an online "word of mouth."

- Advertisers today are still trying to figure out the magic formula to reach consumers on the Internet. New approaches are meant to make advertisements seem less like advertisements—further blurring the line between information, entertainment and advertising.

Ads Share Three Characteristics

- Daniel Boorstin says that advertising in America shares three characteristics: repetition, an advertising style and ubiquity.

- The sheer number of ads sometimes works to advertisers' disadvantage because they can crowd each other so much that no individual ad stands out in consumers' minds.

Ads Compete for Your Attention

- To influence consumers, an advertising message must appeal to them for some reason.

- Advertising can catch your attention, according to Jib Fowles, in 15 ways, including playing on your need to nurture, the need for attention and the need for escape.

Marketers Use Demographics

- Advertisers target their messages according to an audience's characteristics.

- Demographics are composed of data about a target audience's gender, age, income level, marital status, geographic location and occupation.

Advertising Feeds Consumerism

- Advertising provokes three main criticisms: It adds to the cost of products, it causes people to buy products they do not need and it reduces competition and thereby fosters monopolies.

- Because the audience is increasingly fragmented, advertisers have used other tactics—from the Internet to viral marketing.

Advertising at Work

- Many advertising agencies are small, local operations.

- Depending on the size of the company, an advertising agency may be divided into as many as six departments: marketing research, media selection, creative activity, account management, administration and public relations.

Mass Media Industries Depend on Advertising

- The advertising business and the media industries are interdependent—what happens in the advertising business directly affects the media industries.

- The advertising business is very dependent on the nation's economic health.

- The price for a 30-second commercial on TV's highest-rated sitcom, *The Big Bang Theory*, is $345,000. The price tag for a 30-second commercial can reach $4.5 million for a widely watched program such as the Super Bowl.

- The cost to create a TV commercial can run more than $1 million a minute.

- Different types of media deliver different types of audiences.

Internet Delivers Display, Search and Social Networks

- The most successful Internet access to consumers today is *search advertising*, often called simply *search*.

- There are four types of search advertising: paid listings, contextual search, paid inclusion and site optimization.

- Advertising agencies have learned to use social media to their advantage.

- Advertisers also use *branded content*, a program or story that mimics regular commercial programming or standard journalism but that is custom-produced by an advertiser to promote a specific product.

Media Compete Fiercely for Clients

- Advertising is divided into national and local categories.

- The media compete with each other for the advertising dollar, and some media are better than others for particular products.

Federal Government Regulates Advertisers

- Government protection for consumers dates back to the beginning of the 20th century.

- Protection for consumers from misleading advertising comes from government regulation (the Federal Trade Commission, Food and Drug Administration and Federal Communications Commission, for example), and from advertising industry self-regulatory groups (National Advertising Review Board, for example).

- In 1996, the distilled spirits industry challenged the 30-year-old industry-wide voluntary ban on hard liquor advertising on TV. The liquor industry placed the ads on local TV stations, and hard liquor ads are now common-place on television.

- Neither the Federal Trade Commission nor the Bureau of Alcohol, Tobacco and Firearms, which regulate the spirits industry, has the power to stop liquor ads from appearing on TV.

- Based on an FTC complaint, in 2012 an administrative law judge issued a cease-and-desist order against the company that produced POM Wonderful beverage.

- In a subsequent ruling in 2014, based on the POM Wonderful complaint, the U.S. Supreme Court said that companies can be sued for false advertising if their product labels would "mislead and trick consumers."

Global Marketing Delivers New Audiences

- The future of advertising will parallel the development of international markets, the refinement and expansion of new media technologies (especially the Internet) and changing demographics.

- Today's advertising agencies use sophisticated technology to track demographics to help deliver the audience the advertiser wants.

- International marketing is becoming more common for global brands, such as Coca-Cola and Ikea, and this means the creation of international advertising campaigns.

Key Terms

These terms are defined in the margins throughout this chapter and appear in alphabetical order with definitions in the Glossary, which begins on page 361.

Advertising Campaign *209*	Content Marketing *211*	Direct Sponsorship *203*	Search Advertising *211*
Branded Content *211*	CPM *210*	Pop-Up *203*	Viral Marketing *203*
Branded Entertainment *211*	Demographics *207*	RTM *211*	
Click-Through Rate *203*			

Critical Questions

1. Why is advertising not a medium? What role does advertising play in the mass media?

2. What are the three main arguments given by advertising's critics and by its supporters?

3. What are the benefits to an advertiser of TV instead of print? Of radio instead of TV? Of the Internet instead of broadcast and print? What are the differences in cost for the different media?

4. Discuss 3 of Jib Fowles' 15 psychological appeals for advertising in some detail, and present an example of an ad that demonstrates each of the 3 appeals you discuss.

5. Discuss government regulation and industry self-regulation of advertising. Which government agencies are involved in advertising regulation? Do you think government regulation or industry self-regulation is more effective at protecting consumer interests? Explain.

Working the Web

This list includes sites mentioned in the chapter and others to give you greater insight into the advertising business.

Adrants

adrants.com

Adrants provides marketing and advertising news with a "no-holds barred with an attitude" commentary on the state of the advertising and media industries. Adrants covers topics such as emerging advertising trends and the effects of demographic shifts on advertising strategies in the industry.

Advertising Age

adage.com

One of the advertising industry's leading sources of news, information and analysis, *Advertising Age* produces more than 15 original rankings each year, including the 100 Leading National Advertisers and 100 Leading Media Companies lists, the Digital A-List, and the annual Agency Report.

Advertising Council

adcouncil.org

Established in 1942, the nonprofit Ad Council originated and created the very first public service announcement (PSA). Today, the Ad Council is the leading producer of PSAs in the U.S. The Ad Council has sponsored such familiar campaigns as "Friends Don't Let Friends Drive Drunk" and Smokey Bear's "Only You Can Prevent Forest Fires." Its clients are both nonprofit and governmental organizations.

American Advertising Federation (AAF)

aaf.org

Boasting 40,000 professional members and 6,500 collegiate student members at 200 U.S. colleges and universities, AAF is the oldest national advertising trade association in the country. AAF educates members about the latest trends in the industry, honors advertising excellence, promotes diversity in advertising and "applies the communication skills of its members to help solve community concerns."

American Association of Advertising Agencies

aaaa.org

Commonly referred to in the advertising industry as the 4A's, the American Association of Advertising Agencies was jointly founded in 1917 by 111 ad agencies. The management-oriented trade association provides research, media advice and information and benefit programs for its members.

American Marketing Association (AMA)

ama.org

Originally created in 1937, the AMA is a marketing association for individuals and organizations involved in the practice, teaching and study of marketing. AMA members are connected to a network of marketers in academics, research and practice. The association's Web site offers marketing data, articles, case studies, best practices and an online employment application.

Association of Hispanic Advertising Agencies (AHAA)

ahaa.org

The AHAA is the only national trade association in the U.S. for the Hispanic marketing, communications and media industry. Its primary objective is "to bring Hispanic inspiration and innovation to every marketer in the U.S." AHAA represents 45,000 marketing, research and media executives.

Clio Awards

clioawards.com

Since 1959, the Clio Awards have recognized creative achievements in the advertising industry throughout the world. Gold, Silver and Bronze Clio Awards are presented to category winners in advertising, sports, fashion, music, entertainment and health care. In Greek mythology, Clio was "the muse of history and the recorder of great deeds."

Federal Trade Commission (FTC)

ftc.gov

The FTC is the only U.S. government agency with consumer protection and competition jurisdiction in all areas of the American economy. In 1938, Congress granted the FTC broad prohibition powers against "unfair and deceptive acts or practices." Since then, the commission also has been directed to administer a wide variety of other consumer protection laws, including the Telemarketing Sales Rule, the Pay-Per-Call Rule and the Equal Credit Opportunity Act. In 1975, Congress gave the FTC the authority to adopt industry-wide trade regulations.

Forrester Research

forrester.com

Forrester Research is a research and advisory firm that provides information about the current and future impact of technology. It annually surveys more than 500,000 consumers and business leaders throughout the world. Forrester has five research centers in Cambridge, Mass. New York; San Francisco; Washington, D.C.; and Dallas.

Interactive Advertising Bureau (IAB)

iab.net

The Interactive Advertising Bureau is an advertising business trade organization that develops industry standards, conducts research and provides legal support for the online advertising industry. It is made up of 650 media and technology companies and recommends standards and practices regarding interactive advertising.

MediaPost Communications

mediapost.com

An integrated publishing and content company, MediaPost is the leading advertising and media Internet site for news, events, directories and a social network to help its more than 100,000 members plan and buy both traditional and online advertising. The site's media directory includes information on a wide array of electronic, traditional and marketing publications, stations and networks.

Impact/Action Videos are concise news features on various topics created exclusively for *Media/Impact*. Find them in *Media/Impact*'s MindTap at cengagebrain.com.

MindTap® Log on to MindTap for *Media/Impact* to access a variety of additional material—including learning objectives, chapter readings with highlighting and note-taking, **Impact/Action Videos**, activities, and comprehension quizzes—that will guide you through this chapter.

PUBLIC RELATIONS
PROMOTING IDEAS

11

Courtesy of The San Diego Union-Tribune

Public relations people help promote nonprofit fundraising events such as the Rock 'n' Roll San Diego Marathon. More than 20,000 people participated in the May 31, 2015, event, which raises money for lymphoma and leukemia research.

What's Ahead?

- PR Helps Shape Public Opinion
- PR Pioneer Issues *Declaration of Principles*
- Government Recruits PR Professionals
- Women Join PR Firms
- Professionals Promote Ethics Codes

- Public Relations at Work
- PR Agencies Respond to Social Media
- PR Companies Monitor Brands
- Ad Agencies and Public Relations Firms Merge
- Variety of Clients Use Public Relations

- Public Relations Organizations Offer Many Services
- Publicity Means Free Media
- Public Relations Grows Globally

> "A really great visual can cross language and cultural barriers and be instantly relatable."
>
> —JANET TYLER, AIRFOIL PUBLIC RELATIONS, CO-CEO

You may think today's cash rebates from car dealers are relatively new, but in 1914, Henry Ford announced that if he sold 300,000 Model Ts that year, each customer would receive a rebate. When the company reached its goal, Ford returned $50 to each buyer. This was good business. It also was good public relations. Like Henry Ford, public relations people today work to create favorable images—for corporations, public officials, products, schools and nonprofit organizations.

There are three ways to encourage people to do what you want them to do: power, patronage and persuasion. Power involves ruling by law, but it also can mean ruling by peer pressure—someone does something because his or her friends do. Patronage is a polite term for bribery—paying someone with favors or money to do what you want. The third method—persuasion—is the approach of public relations. **Persuasion** is the act of using argument or reasoning to induce someone to do something.

Like advertising, the public relations business is not a mass medium. The public relations business is a media support industry. In the classic definition, **public relations** involves creating an understanding for, or goodwill toward, a company, a person or a product.

Barbara Smaller The New Yorker Collection/The Cartoon Bank

"It's not a completely blind date—he sent me some promotional material."

throughout the Roman Empire to enhance his image. Since then, many political leaders have ordered heroic images of themselves printed on coins and stamps.

Modern public relations can be traced to the beginning of the 20th century. Journalists were an important reason for the eventual emergence of the public relations profession.

PR Helps Shape Public Opinion

One of the first political leaders to realize the importance of public relations was Augustus Caesar, who in the 1st century commissioned statues of himself to be erected

> **Persuasion** The act of using argument or reasoning to induce someone to do something.
>
> **Public Relations** Creating understanding for, or goodwill toward, a company, a person or a product.

Before 1900, businesses believed they could work alongside the press, or even ignore it. Many stories that appeared in the press promoted companies that bought advertising. Then the Industrial Revolution arrived, and some industrialists exploited workers, collecting enormous profits. Just before the turn of the 20th century, Ida Tarbell and Lincoln Steffens began to make businesspeople uncomfortable, writing stories for magazines like *McClure's* about the unprofessional practices of companies such as Standard Oil (see **Chapter 4**, p. 70).

According to *This Is PR: The Realities of Public Relations*, "No longer could the railroads butter up the press by giving free passes to reporters. No longer would the public buy whitewashed statements like that of coal industrialist George F. Baer, who in 1902 told labor to put their trust in 'the Christian men whom God in His infinite wisdom has given control of the property interests of the country.'"

President Theodore Roosevelt fed public sentiment—public opinion—against the abuses of industry when he started his antitrust campaigns. According to *Effective Public Relations*, "With the growth of mass-circulation newspapers, Roosevelt's canny ability to dominate the front pages demonstrated a new-found power for those with causes to promote.

"He had a keen sense of news and knew how to stage a story so that it would get maximum attention. His skill forced those he fought to develop similar means. He fully exploited the news media as a new and powerful tool of presidential leadership, and he remade the laws and the presidency in the process." Roosevelt used his skills at swaying public opinion to gain support for his antitrust policies.

is not a secret press bureau. All our work is done in the open. We aim to supply news. . . . In brief, our plan is, frankly and openly, on behalf of business concerns and public institutions, to supply to the press and public of the United States prompt and accurate information concerning subjects which it is of value and interest to the public to know about."

Lee and Parker dissolved their firm in 1908, when Lee went to work as a publicity agent for the Pennsylvania Railroad. Eventually, John D. Rockefeller hired Lee to counteract the negative publicity that began with Tarbell's investigation of Standard Oil. (Lee worked for the Rockefellers until he died in 1934.)

The idea of in-house corporate public relations grew as the Chicago Edison Company and American Telephone & Telegraph began promotional programs. The University of Pennsylvania and the University of Wisconsin opened publicity bureaus in 1904, and the YMCA of Washington, D.C., hired a full-time publicist to oversee fundraising in 1905—the first time someone hired a publicist to do fundraising.

Government Recruits PR Professionals

During World War I (1914–1918), the U.S. government set up the Committee on Public Information, organized by former newspaper reporter George Creel, blurring the line between propaganda and publicity. Creel recruited journalists, editors, artists and teachers to raise money

PR Pioneer Issues Declaration of Principles

The first publicity firm was called The Publicity Bureau and opened in Boston in 1900 to head off growing public criticism of the railroad companies. The best-known early practitioner of public relations was Ivy Lee, who began his PR career by opening an office in New York with George F. Parker.

Lee and Parker represented coal magnate George F. Baer when coal workers went on strike. A former newspaper reporter, Lee issued a *Declaration of Principles* that he mailed to newspaper city editors. This declaration became a manifesto for early public relations companies to follow.

Reacting to criticism that The Publicity Bureau worked secretly to promote the railroads, Lee wrote in 1906 in *American Magazine*, "This [the firm of Lee & Parker]

In what was the largest public relations drive of its time, the Office of War Information promoted the role of the United States in World War II. Today, the federal government is the largest employer of public relations people.

for Liberty Bonds and to promote the nation's participation in the war. One of the people who worked for Creel was Edward L. Bernays. Both Bernays and Ivy Lee have been called the father of public relations.

In 1923, Bernays wrote the first book on public relations, *Crystallizing Public Opinion*, and taught the first course on the subject. Bernays was interested in mass psychology—how to influence the opinions of large groups of people. Procter & Gamble, General Motors and the American Tobacco Company were among his clients. "Public relations," Bernays wrote in 1955, "is the attempt, by information, persuasion and adjustment, to engineer public support for an activity, cause, movement or institution."

In 1985, still practicing his craft, Bernays further defined public relations as "giving a client ethical advice, based on research of the public, that will win the social goals upon which the client depends for his livelihood." (Bernays died in 1995 at the age of 103.)

To sell the New Deal in the 1930s, Franklin D. Roosevelt used every tactic he knew. Comfortable with the press and the public alike and advised by PR expert Louis McHenry Howe, FDR "projected an image of self-confidence and happiness—just what the American public wanted to believe in. He talked to them on the radio. He smiled for the cameras. He was mentioned in popular songs. He even allowed himself to be one of the main characters in a Rodgers and Hart musical comedy (played by George M. Cohan, America's favorite Yankee Doodle Dandy)," according to *This Is PR*.

To gain support for the nation's entry into World War II (1939–1945), the federal government mounted the largest public relations drive in its history, centered at the Office of War Information, led by former newscaster Elmer Davis. After the war, the public relations business boomed along with the postwar economy.

Women Join PR Firms

Doris E. Fleischman became one of the first women in public relations when she joined her husband, Edward L. Bernays, in his PR firm. Fleischman became an equal partner with Bernays in their public relations business. An early advocate of public relations as a profession for women, in 1931 Fleischman wrote, "One finds women working side by side with men in forming the traditions and rules that will govern the profession of the future."

Two other women who were public relations pioneers were Leone Baxter and Anne Williams Wheaton. Baxter and her husband, Clem Whitaker, formed San Francisco's Baxter and Whitaker—the first public relations agency to specialize in political campaigns. In 1957, President Dwight Eisenhower appointed Anne Williams Wheaton as his associate press secretary.

Professionals Promote Ethics Codes

In the 1930s, the requirements to work in public relations were loose, and many people who said they worked in public relations were press agents who often used tricks to get attention for their clients. Henry Rogers, co-founder of what was then the world's largest entertainment PR firm, Rogers & Cowan (based in Beverly Hills), admitted that in 1939 he created a "best-dressed" contest to promote little-known actress Rita Hayworth.

There was no contest, but Rogers dubbed Hayworth the winner of this fictional event. *Look* magazine gave Hayworth a ten-page spread. "Press agents, and that's what we were, would dream up all sorts of phony stories," he said. "Journalists knew they were phony but printed them because they looked good in print."

During the 1950s, the question of ethics in public relations arose publicly when Byoir and Associates, hired by a railroad company to counteract the expansion of trucking, was charged with creating "front" organizations to speak out against the trucking industry. In court, Byoir's agency argued they were exercising free speech. In 1961, the U.S.

Bettmann/Corbis

Doris Fleischman, a public relations pioneer, began her career in the 1920s. Fleischman was an early advocate of public relations as a profession for women. Fleischman and her husband, Edward L. Bernays (*right*), were equal partners in their public relations business.

Supreme Court upheld Byoir's right to represent a client even if the presentation was dishonest, but this left the ethical issue of honesty in public relations unresolved.

The Public Relations Society of America (PRSA) established its first code of ethics in 1954 and expanded that code in 1959 with a *Declaration of Principles*. That ethics code still exists today to guide the business of public relations. (Excerpts from the PRSA code are in **Chapter 15**.) PR professionals continue to argue among themselves about the differences between the profession's beginnings as press agentry (which often meant fabricating stories) and the concept of ethically representing a client's business, as Edward L. Bernays described.

Public relations grew throughout the 1960s and 1970s with the encouragement of television, the federal government and corporate America. In 1961, for example, the federal government had about 1,000 people working as writer-editors and public affairs specialists. Today, *the federal government is the nation's largest single employer of public information people.* ("Public information" is the name given to the job of government public relations.)

Public Relations at Work

Public relations is an industry of specialties. The most familiar public relations areas are financial public relations, product public relations and crisis public relations, but there are many other specialty areas.

Financial Public Relations

People in financial public relations provide information primarily to business reporters. "Business editors like a PR staff that can provide access to top management," wrote James K. Gentry in the *Washington Journalism Review*, "that knows its company well or can find needed information quickly, that demonstrates ethics and honesty and that knows and accepts the difference between news and fluff." Gentry then listed comments gathered from editors about what he believed made a bad PR operation:

▶ "Companies that think they can hide the truth from the public or believe it's none of the public's business."

▶ "I despise it when a PR person intercepts our calls to a news source but then isn't capable of answering our questions."

▶ "When they hire an outside PR firm to handle the job."

▶ "The 'no-comment' attitude. When they have little or no interest in going beyond the press release."

▶ "People who either get in the way of you doing your job, complain too much or are no help at all."

Product Public Relations

Product PR uses public relations techniques to sell products and services. Many companies have learned that seeking publicity for a product often is less expensive than advertising. Public relations "is booming partly because of price," reports *The Wall Street Journal*. A PR budget of $1 million for a corporate client is considered huge, whereas an ad budget that size is considered tiny.

Public relations often works better than advertising. For example, the Wieden & Kennedy agency in Seattle contracted Bigger Than Life, Inc., which makes large inflatables, to manufacture a 21-story pair of Nike tennis shoes. The company attached the shoes to the Westin Copley Place Hotel during the Boston Marathon and to the Westin Hotel in downtown Cincinnati during the March of Dimes walkathon. Pictures of the shoes appeared in *The New York Times*, *The Cincinnati Enquirer* and newspapers as far away as Japan. Wieden & Kennedy estimated that buying the same advertising would have cost $7 million.

Another example of product public relations is the M&M-sponsored #MakeMlaugh campaign in 2015, which used M&M spokescandies Yellow and Red, who joined a 24-hour danceathon to help combat poverty. For every laugh someone sent to the #MakeMlaugh hashtag, M&M's donated $1 to charity.

AP Images/Donald Traill

Companies often combine product promotion with charity benefits, such as the appearance of M&M Red and Yellow with Nick Cannon of "America's Got Talent" in the 24-hour danceathon on Red Nose Day. The marathon was sponsored by organizations that work to combat childhood poverty.

Crisis Public Relations

This aspect of public relations goes back as far as Edward Bernays responding to the charges against Standard Oil. The term *crisis public relations* (sometimes called **crisis communication**) describes the response to a public relations emergency facing a company because of an unexpected event that could seriously hurt the company's reputation.

ODWALLA. In October 1996, beverage maker Odwalla Inc. faced a public relations crisis when *E. coli* bacteria was traced to unpasteurized apple juice that had been sold by the natural juice company. The death of a 16-month-old girl in Colorado and more than 50 cases of severe illness were eventually traced to the bacteria. Odwalla, the leading manufacturer of unpasteurized juices, had made its reputation on natural, unfiltered products. But as soon as Odwalla detected the bacteria, the company announced an immediate recall of 13 products in the 7 western states and British Columbia.

Then the company worked with the Food and Drug Administration to scour the Odwalla processing facilities, which were found to be free of the bacteria. The company continued the investigation, including the processors who supplied fruit for the juice. One month after the outbreak, Odwalla took out full-page ads in several newspapers, an "open letter" to its customers, thanking them for their support and offering sympathy for people diagnosed with *E. coli*–related illnesses after drinking Odwalla juices. The Odwalla case is often used as an example of effective crisis public relations.

TOYOTA AND BP PLC. The year 2010 offered two classic corporate crisis public relations challenges—Toyota Motor Corp. and BP PLC (formerly called British Petroleum). Toyota and BP "exacerbated their woes by either declining to fess up promptly, casting blame elsewhere or striking adversarial postures with the public, the government and the news media," wrote Peter S. Goodman in *The New York Times*.

In January 2010, Toyota recalled more than 2 million vehicles for accelerator flaws, a potentially huge public relations blow to its reputation for vehicle quality. The accelerator problems were linked to at least 51 deaths. There were reports that Toyota had known about the gas pedal defect much earlier but did not admit the problem publicly until the National Highway Traffic Safety Administration (NHTSA) issued a public alert.

Then, after the NHTSA disclosure, Toyota hired a public relations firm to try to contain the damage to its reputation by posting comments to counteract negative posts on social networking sites. Still, critics charged the public relations effort came too late.

"Toyota blew it," communications expert Brad Burns told *The New York Times*. "It's been the proverbial death by a thousand cuts. They knew they had problems long ago, whether it was a mechanical issue or operator error, but they knew they had an issue they had to deal with. And rather than put public safety over profits, they appear

Akio Toyoda, president of Toyota Motor Corp., speaks at a press conference in Tokyo on March 6, 2013. Toyota used crisis communication—including social media monitoring—to try to overcome the public relations problems created by the massive vehicle recall for accelerator flaws linked to at least 51 deaths. In July 2013, Toyota agreed to a $1.6 billion settlement.

Bloomberg/Getty Images

to have listened to the product liability lawyers and they totally lost it. It's brand damage."

In July 2013 Toyota agreed to pay $1.6 billion to settle a class-action lawsuit for allegations about sudden acceleration in its vehicles.

On April 20, 2010, the British Petroleum Deepwater Horizon drilling platform exploded in the Gulf of Mexico, the biggest oil spill in the gulf's history. Eleven people died, four were critically injured, and millions of gallons of oil spilled into the gulf.

"It [BP] was one of the worst PR approaches that I've seen in my 56 years of business," said public relations expert Howard Rubinstein. "They tried to be opaque. They had every excuse in the book. Right away they should have accepted responsibility and recognized what a disaster they faced. They basically thought they could spin their way out of catastrophe. It doesn't work that way." In 2013, BP agreed to a $4 billion criminal settlement over the Gulf oil spill, and in 2015, BP agreed to pay an additional $18.7 billion environmental fine to the U.S. government and 7 states, the largest amount ever collected for environmental damages.

JAPAN MCDONALD'S. In the fall of 2014, Japan McDonald's faced a consumer public relations crisis when customers reported several different types of foreign material in their food. Initially, Japan McDonald's officials suggested the company was the victim of possible product tampering,

> **Crisis Communication** A timely public relations response to a critical situation that could cause damage to a company's reputation.

but they eventually issued a public apology several months later. The company then announced a mobile phone app for customers to report problems, but the delayed public relations response seriously damaged consumer trust in McDonald's products. In April 2015, Japan McDonald's announced it was closing more than 131 stores and projected a revenue loss of $318 million. (See **Impact/Global**: "McDonald's Launches Customer Complaint App in Japan," p. 226.)

These four examples—Odwalla, Toyota, British Petroleum and McDonald's—illustrate the importance of effective crisis public relations.

PR Agencies Respond to Social Media

Because of its ability to deliver information quickly and directly, the Internet offers many benefits for public relations companies. Public relations people, in fact, often are very much involved in creating and modifying Web sites for their clients—creating a public face. News releases, product announcements and company profiles can be made available online, to be captured on demand by the press, stockholders, supporters and anyone else who is interested. But managing an Internet presence also can be risky because it is interactive, and public responses to posts on the sites are immediate.

In 2012, YouTube played a significant role in a public relations crisis for the cancer research charity Susan G. Komen for the Cure. On January 31, 2012, The Associated Press broke the story that Komen was eliminating most of its funding for Planned Parenthood. Within 48 hours, supporters flooded the Internet with negative comments and started a "Defund Komen" campaign. (See **Impact/Money**, "Susan G. Komen Foundation Discovers the Price of Poor Public Relations," p. 229.)

PR Companies Monitor Brands

The Internet also brings hazards for companies' brand reputation. Disgruntled customers, pranksters and competitors can create their own sites to immediately challenge and even undermine a client's site. "In the pre-Internet days we used to say that a satisfied customer will tell one or two prospects but a dissatisfied customer will tell 10 or more," wrote G. A. "Andy" Marken, a public relations adviser, in *Public Relations Quarterly*. "With the Internet and the Web those same dissatisfied customers can tell millions of people . . . and they're doing it every day around the globe."

Marken says these attacks, which he calls ***cybersmears***, include anti-Disney and anti-McDonald's sites, as well as chat rooms, discussion groups and online forums. In 2013, for example, hackers broke into the Burger King site and posted a message that said McDonald's had bought Burger King.

To counter these negative messages, many businesses and organizations hire public relations firms to continuously monitor the Internet and alert their clients when negative information appears so the client can decide the best way to counter the information.

"It's a tedious task but any organization that isn't monitoring Internet traffic and Web activity could find itself in serious trouble," says Marken. "Companies and agencies spend hundreds and thousands of dollars on audio, video and print clipping services to analyze how their messages are being picked up, interpreted and used by the conventional media. They spend little or no time finding out what people are saying in real-time in cyberspace about them. . . . What you don't hear can hurt you . . . and it could be fatal."

By using public relations techniques, such as monitoring Internet social media like Facebook and Twitter for negative comments about the company, public relations people often play a central role in trying to protect their clients from unfavorable publicity.

Ad Agencies and Public Relations Firms Merge

More than 150,000 people in the United States work in public relations, and about 4,000 firms throughout the nation offer PR-related services. The largest public relations firms employ more than 1,000 people. Several major corporations have 100 to 400 public relations specialists, but most public relations firms have fewer than 4 employees. (See **Impact/Money, Illustration 11.1**, "Top 10 Worldwide Public Relations Agencies" and **Illustration 11.2**, "Top 10 U.S. Public Relations Agencies," p. 227.)

Public relations people often deal with advertising agencies as part of their job, and because PR and advertising are so interrelated, several large public relations firms have joined several large advertising agencies. For example, the London firm WPP Group PLC owns more than 250 public relations, advertising and marketing companies.

Combined agencies can offer both public relations and advertising services to their clients in one place. The difference between public relations and advertising at the nation's largest agencies can be difficult to discern. Advertising is an aspect of marketing that aims to sell products. People in advertising usually *aren't* involved in a company's policy making. They implement the company's policies after company executives decide how to sell a product, a corporate image or an idea.

Cybersmears Negative information organized and presented on the Internet as continuing attacks against a corporation.

IMPACT
Global

McDonald's Launches Customer Complaint App in Japan

New Smartphone App for "Feelings, Opinions and Requests" Aimed at Turning the Tide on a Year of Public Relations Mistakes

McDonald's Japan is to launch a new smartphone app for customer complaints as it looks to turn the page on a series of scares including the discovery of a human tooth in some fries.

The move comes with in-country sales sliding, profits plunging and the burger giant's reputation in Japan badly dented.

"We will introduce a new smartphone app customers can use to post their feelings, opinions and requests, aiming at strengthening our ability to listen to customers' voices," McDonald's Japan Holdings, the parent company, said in a statement issued [March 11, 2015].

The firm also said it was reviewing its procedures for dealing with suspected cases of product tampering and will draft new rules on communication with customers.

The chain came in for heavy media criticism for its handling of incidents over the past year in which unexpected objects were discovered in food.

A human tooth was found in some French fries sold at an Osaka outlet last year, the firm admitted in January, although

On February 5, 2015, Japan McDonald's company officials bow in apology for reported food safety problems with its products in the fall of 2014. The delayed public relations response damaged the company's credibility with consumers, causing a large drop in revenue.

it said it did not know how the contamination had occurred.

McDonald's said there were no employees missing a tooth at the outlet and it believed there was a very low possibility of contamination at the US factory that had shipped the chips.

Two days later, a Japanese woman claimed to have discovered what was later identified as "dental material" in a McDonald's hamburger from northernmost Hokkaido in September [2014].

Japanese media reported several other cases of contamination, including a piece of metal in a pancake.

The problems marked another public relations setback for a firm still struggling to recover from

a scandal last summer when a Chinese supplier was found to be mixing out-of-date meat with fresh product.

Then late last year the company had to airlift an emergency supply of French fries from the US after a chip shortage resulted in rationing at restaurants across Japan.

In February, the firm said it had lost a worse-than-expected 21.8bn yen ($186m) for 2014—against a year-earlier profit and recording its first loss in 11 years. Nationwide sales in January [2015] were down 39 percent on year.

McDonald's Japan [in March 2015] announced the appointment of a new chairman and chief operating officer.

Excerpted from Agence France-Presse, "McDonald's Launches Customer Complaint App in Japan," March 11, 2015, theguardian.com.

AP Images/Reiri Kurihara

Money

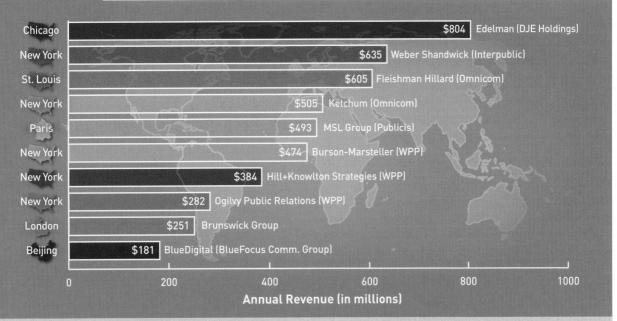

Annual Revenue (in millions)

Chicago	Edelman (DJE Holdings)	$804
New York	Weber Shandwick (Interpublic)	$635
St. Louis	Fleishman Hillard (Omnicom)	$605
New York	Ketchum (Omnicom)	$505
Paris	MSL Group (Publicis)	$493
New York	Burson-Marsteller (WPP)	$474
New York	Hill+Knowlton Strategies (WPP)	$384
New York	Ogilvy Public Relations (WPP)	$282
London	Brunswick Group	$251
Beijing	BlueDigital (BlueFocus Comm. Group)	$181

ILLUSTRATION 11.1

Top 10 Worldwide Public Relations Agencies

Seven of the top ten worldwide public relations agencies are based in the U.S., and nine of them are owned by large advertising agencies (listed in parentheses).

The Agency Issue, *Advertising Age*, May 4, 2015, p. 51.

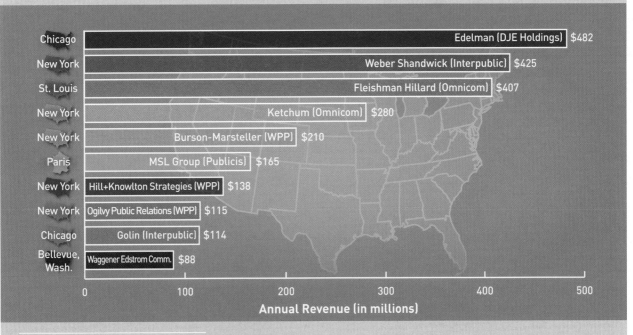

Annual Revenue (in millions)

Chicago	Edelman (DJE Holdings)	$482
New York	Weber Shandwick (Interpublic)	$425
St. Louis	Fleishman Hillard (Omnicom)	$407
New York	Ketchum (Omnicom)	$280
New York	Burson-Marsteller (WPP)	$210
Paris	MSL Group (Publicis)	$165
New York	Hill+Knowlton Strategies (WPP)	$138
New York	Ogilvy Public Relations (WPP)	$115
Chicago	Golin (Interpublic)	$114
Bellevue, Wash.	Waggener Edstrom Comm.	$88

ILLUSTRATION 11.2

Top 10 U.S. Public Relations Agencies

Five of the nation's top ten public relations agencies are based in New York, and nine of them are owned by large advertising agencies (listed in parentheses).

Note that Edelman is the number one agency in the U.S. and in the world.

The Agency Issue, *Advertising Age*, May 4, 2015, p. 51.

Public relations people, in comparison, usually *are* involved in policy. A PR person often contributes to decisions about how a company will deal with the public, the press and its own employees.

Variety of Clients Use Public Relations

Public relations people work for several types of clients, including governments, educational institutions, nonprofit organizations, industry, athletic teams, entertainment companies and international businesses.

Government

The federal government is the nation's largest single employer of public information people. State and local governments also hire people to handle PR. Related to government are PR people who work for political candidates and for lobbying organizations. Media consultants also are involved in political PR. These people counsel candidates and officeholders about how they should present themselves to the public through the media.

Education

Universities, colleges and school districts often hire public relations people to promote these educational institutions and to handle press attention from the consequences of hazardous on-campus events and other decisions that educators make.

Nonprofit Organizations

Nonprofit organizations include hospitals, churches, museums and charitable organizations. Public relations for nonprofit organizations is growing especially fast as different charities compete with each other to attract wealthy donors. (See **Impact/Money**, "Susan G. Komen Foundation Discovers the Price of Poor Public Relations," p. 229.)

Industry

Chicago Edison's early use of promotion was one type of industry PR. Many industries are government-regulated, so this often means that the industry PR person works with government agencies on government-related issues that affect the industry, such as utility rate increases or energy conservation programs.

Business

This is the best-known area of public relations. Large companies keep an in-house staff of public relations people, and these companies also often hire outside PR firms to help on special projects. Product publicity is one of the fastest-growing aspects of business-related public relations.

Within many large businesses are people who handle corporate PR, sometimes called financial PR. They prepare annual reports and gather financial data on the company for use by the press. They also may be assigned directly to the executives of a corporation to help establish policy about the corporation's public image. Many companies also sponsor charity events to increase their visibility in the community.

Athletic Teams and Entertainment Organizations

A professional sports team needs someone to travel with it and handle the press requests that inevitably come at each stop. Sports information people also are responsible for the coaches', the owner's and the team's relationship with the fans. College and university sports departments also hire public relations people to handle inquiries from the public and the press. Professional athletic teams sponsor public relations events such as the National Basketball Association's Green Week.

As described earlier, in 1939 Henry Rogers learned how to use press agentry to gather publicity for actress Rita Hayworth. Today, entertainment public relations agencies promote movies and handle celebrities and well-known athletes who appear on the lecture circuit.

International

As the nation's consumer market broadens, more attention is being given to developing business in other countries. This means more opportunities in international PR.

Luis Sinco Copyright © 2013. Los Angeles Times. Reprinted with Permission.

Public relations often involves organizing events like CicLAvia in Venice, Calif., near Los Angeles, which encourages residents to abandon their cars for a day. About 100,000 people travel the roads along a 15-mile route by foot, skateboard and bike. No cars allowed.

IMPACT

Money

Susan G. Komen Foundation Discovers the Price of Poor Public Relations

By Michael Hiltzik

The Susan G. Komen Breast Cancer Foundation committed one of the great PR faux pas of the decade in January 2012, when it summarily cut off funding to Planned Parenthood in what appeared to be a bow to anti-abortion crusaders.

Now, with its release of its latest financial statements, the cost of that decision can be measured: It's more than $77 million, or fully 22 percent of the foundation's income.

That's how much less the Dallas-based foundation collected in contributions, sponsorships and entry fees for its sponsored races in the fiscal year ended March 31, 2013, compared with the previous year. In the most recent fiscal year Komen booked $270 million; the year before that, Komen booked $348 million.

Komen officials are candid in attributing much of last year's sharp decline to the Planned Parenthood controversy, though they also point to the general economic slump. Participation in the group's signature Race for the Cure events is also down.

The foundation's decision to cease funding Planned Parenthood was a huge blunder. Komen officials said at the time that they had merely tightened grant eligibility rules to exclude groups under investigation by government authorities— Planned Parenthood was the target of a ginned-up

A group of women protested outside the Susan G. Komen Breast Cancer Foundation headquarters in Dallas on February 7, 2012, after the Komen group announced it was eliminating most of its funding for Planned Parenthood, creating a public relations challenge for the nonprofit organization.

"investigation" by anti-abortion Republicans in the House.

The decision by the nation's leading breast cancer charity to defund the nation's leading provider of health services to women sparked a predictable uproar, and Komen reversed the decision after only three days.

But the damage was immediate and, plainly, lasting. There were indications that the original decision had been driven by Karen Handel, the organization's vice president for public policy, who had joined Komen after losing a race for governor of Georgia on an anti-abortion platform. She resigned from Komen days after the reversal.

The affair led to more public scrutiny of the foundation's own record. It transpired, for instance, that while the foundation depicted itself as devoted chiefly to research for a breast cancer cure, it spent

only about 20 percent of its donations on research; the biggest expenditure category was public education, at more than 50 percent. Critics questioned whether "education" really should be such a heavy priority in a field where research issues remain important.

Since the controversy, the foundation has struggled to regain the nearly unquestioned public support it once had. Its founder, Nancy Brinker, a prominent figure in the Texas GOP who says she founded the organization after her sister Susan Komen succumbed to breast cancer, has stepped down as CEO.

The organization hopes that time is erasing the black mark left by its foray into abortion politics. People "tend to say, 'OK, we were mad about that but we're not mad anymore,'" a spokesman told the Associated Press last week. But so far, time hasn't been on Komen's side.

Excerpted from Michael Hiltzik, "Susan G. Komen Foundation Discovers the Price of Playing Politics," latimes.com, January 8, 2014.

Two U.S. firms, Hill+Knowlton and Burson-Marsteller, are among the most active global public relations firms.

Public Relations Organizations Offer Many Services

Responsibilities of PR people include writing, editing, media relations and Internet site management, special events, public speaking, production tasks, research, programming and counseling, training and management.

▶ Writing: Writing news releases, newsletters, correspondence, reports, speeches, booklet texts, radio and TV copy, film scripts, trade paper and magazine articles, institutional advertisements, product information and technical materials and developing Web site content.

▶ Editing: Editing special publications, employee newsletters, shareholder reports and other communications for employees and for the public.

▶ Media Relations, Placement and Internet Services: Contacting news media, magazines, Sunday supplements, freelance writers and trade publications with the intent of getting them to publish or broadcast news and features about or originated by clients; responding to media requests for information or spokespersons; charting Web site activity and monitoring social media for comments about clients.

▶ Special Events: Arranging and managing press conferences, convention exhibits, open houses, anniversary celebrations, fundraising events, special observances, contests and award programs.

▶ Public Speaking: Appearing before groups and arranging platforms for others before appropriate audiences by managing a speaker's bureau.

▶ Production Tasks: Creating art, photography and layout for brochures, booklets, reports, institutional advertisements and periodicals; recording and editing audio, video and Internet materials.

▶ Research: Gathering data to help an organization plan programs; monitoring the effectiveness of public relations programs. This fast-growing area of public relations includes focus groups to test message concepts; research to target specific audiences; surveys of a company's reputation for use in improving the company's image; surveys to determine employee and public attitudes; and shareholder surveys to improve relations with investors.

S Harris/Cartoon Stock

"FIRST OF ALL WE WANT OUR NAME CHANGED FROM 'COCKROACH' TO 'COMPANION BEETLE'."

▶ Programming and Counseling: Establishing a program for effective public relations within the company.

▶ Training: Working with executives and other people within the organization to prepare them to deal with the media.

▶ Management: Overseeing the costs of running the public relations program; paying the bills.

Publicity Means Free Media

Public relations work often means finding ways to attract the attention of the press. Seymour Topping, former managing editor of *The New York Times*, said, "PR people do influence the news, but really more in a functional manner rather than in terms of giving new editorial direction. We get hundreds of press releases every day in each of our departments. We screen them very carefully for legitimate news, and very often there are legitimate news stories. Quite a lot of our business stories originate from press releases. It's impossible for us to cover all of these organizations ourselves."

People in public relations can provide **publicity**, which creates events and presents information so the press and the public will pay attention. Publicity and advertising differ: An advertising message is *paid for*; publicity is *free*. Advertising is a *controlled* use of media because the person or company that places the ad governs the message and where it will appear. Publicity is considered an *uncontrolled* use of the media because the public relations person provides

> **Publicity** Uncontrolled free use of media by a public relations firm to create events and present information to capture press and public attention.

Public relations today aims for a global audience. The London Zoo regularly creates public relations events and posts photos on the Internet to attract public attention. On February 4, 2015, the zoo invited the press to attend the first birthday of its Sumatran tiger triplets.

AP Images/KGC-42/Star Max/Ipx

information to the press but has no control over how the information will appear—the press presents the story.

"We know how the media work," says David Resnicow of the PR firm Ruder Finn & Rotman, "and we make judgments on that, providing access to events as it becomes necessary." It is precisely because people in the media and people in PR know how each other work that they debate about the role of public relations and the news.

Public Relations Grows Globally

Clever ways to attract attention are trademarks of today's successful public relations professional. Like advertising, the future of public relations is tied closely to the future of the media industries. The basic structure of the business will not change, but public relations practitioners find themselves facing the same challenges as people in the advertising business.

Growing international markets mean that many U.S. public relations firms have expanded overseas and that overseas companies seek help from American companies when faced with international marketing challenges. Global communications mean that public relations agencies often work internationally on some projects, and the agencies have to adjust to the cultural differences that global exposure brings.

"To be successful they need an education on how our market works, what is reputation and how do you build it and who are the people they need to know to have 'permission to operate' in both a formal and informal sense," according to Margery Kraus, global CEO of the independent agency APCO. "Many of these companies also have

to overcome the fact that they are from countries that are misunderstood or feared by the U.S., such as Russia and China."

New technologies, especially the Internet, mean more ways to deliver public relations messages and to monitor public relations efforts globally.

The Council of Public Relations Firms, an industry group, cited the top five issues facing the public relations industry today:

1. The industry will need to deal with content overload. "A piece of content doesn't carry the same weight that it did before and doesn't have the same impact," says Steve Rubel, executive vice president for global strategies and insights at Edelman.

2. Brands will get increasingly visual. "A really great visual can cross language and cultural barriers and be instantly relatable," says Janet Tyler, co-CEO of Airfoil.

3. Real-time marketing will take off. "We need not just make marketing plans for four months down the road, but to draft off what real people are talking about right now," says Jeff Beringer, executive director and global practice leader–digital at GolinHarris.

4. Business-to-business marketing will move to embrace social media. Sam Ford, director of digital strategy for Peppercomm, says his agency provides "content support" for its clients. "Our job is to help them get more active in social media and stay on top of the trends."

5. As the social media space matures, consumer and marketer behavior will change. "People are settling into the right behaviors for them and their connections, and to some degree user behaviors online have plateaued," says Mike Manual, senior vice president of Voce Communications. Manual says not every social network is right for every company, and companies might see that Facebook or Twitter is a useful place for them, but not both.

Internet technology has streamlined delivery of print, audio and video, giving public relations agencies the same access to distributing information globally to news organizations that the news organizations themselves possess. As in the advertising industry, shifting demographic patterns also mean growing potential markets and challenges for public relations services around the world.

REVIEW, ANALYZE, INVESTIGATE

CHAPTER 11

PR Helps Shape Public Opinion

- There are three ways to encourage people to do what you want them to do: power, patronage and persuasion.
- Public relations people use persuasion to form public opinion about their clients.
- Modern public relations emerged at the beginning of the 20th century as a way for business to respond to the muck-rakers and to Theodore Roosevelt's antitrust campaign.
- President Roosevelt successfully used public relations to influence public opinion.

PR Pioneer Issues *Declaration of Principles*

- The first U.S. publicity firm, called The Publicity Bureau, opened in Boston in 1900.
- The best-known practitioner of early public relations was Ivy Lee, who wrote a *Declaration of Principles* to respond to the secret publicity activities of The Publicity Bureau.
- The Chicago Edison Company and American Telephone & Telegraph were the first companies to begin in-house promotional programs.

Government Recruits PR Professionals

- Both Edward L. Bernays and Ivy Lee have been called the father of public relations.
- The Committee on Public Information, headed by George Creel, promoted the war effort during World War I.
- The Office of War Information, headed by newscaster Elmer Davis, promoted the country's efforts during World War II.
- Edward L. Bernays wrote the first book on public relations, *Crystallizing Public Opinion*.
- Franklin Roosevelt, assisted by public relations expert Louis McHenry Howe, successfully used public relations to promote the New Deal.

Women Join PR Firms

- Among the pioneering women in the public relations business were Doris E. Fleischman, Leone Baxter and Anne Williams Wheaton.
- Doris Fleischman and Edward L. Bernays were equal partners in their public relations firm.
- Doris Fleischman was an early advocate of public relations as a career for women.

Professionals Promote Ethics Codes

- The Public Relations Society established the profession's first code of ethics in 1954.
- Public relations expanded quickly in the 1960s and 1970s to accommodate television, the federal government and corporate America.

- The federal government is the largest single employer of public relations ("public information") people.

Public Relations at Work

- Three of the most common public relations specialties are financial public relations, product public relations and crisis public relations.
- Crisis public relations successfully repaired the public image of Odwalla Inc.
- Public relations experts criticized Toyota Motor Corp., BP PLC and Japan McDonald's for the way they handled their public relations crises.

PR Agencies Respond to Social Media

- Negative PR can spread very quickly on the Web, where anyone is free to post damaging comments about a company, organization or product.
- In 2012, YouTube was a significant factor in a public relations crisis for the cancer research charity Susan G. Komen Breast Cancer Foundation.

PR Companies Monitor Brands

- Public relations companies play an important role in protecting brand names.
- On March 18, 2013, hackers attacked the Burger King site and posted messages, including one that said Burger King had been sold to a competitor.
- Companies and agencies must be continually vigilant to monitor how their messages are being used and interpreted on the Internet.

Ad Agencies and Public Relations Firms Merge

- Today, more than 150,000 people work in public relations nationwide and about 4,000 firms in the U.S. offer PR-related services.
- Because PR and advertising are so interrelated, public relations people and advertising agencies often work together in the same company to offer advertising and marketing communications services.

Variety of Clients Use Public Relations

- Public relations people work in government, education, nonprofit agencies, industry, business, athletic teams, entertainment companies and international business.

Public Relations Organizations Offer Many Services

- Responsibilities of PR people include writing, Web site development, editing, media relations and placement,

Internet monitoring, special events, public speaking, production tasks, research, programming and counseling, training and management.

Publicity Means Free Media

- The main difference between advertising and public relations is that advertising messages are controlled, and public relations messages are uncontrolled.

- Public relations people create publicity, which is considered an uncontrolled use of media.

Public Relations Grows Globally

- New technologies, especially the Internet, mean new ways to deliver public relations messages.

- Satellite technology has streamlined print, audio and video delivery, giving PR the same access to information distribution as news organizations.

- Global communications mean many public relations agencies work internationally on some projects and must adjust to cultural differences that global exposure brings.

- Growing international markets mean that many U.S. public relations firms have expanded overseas.

- The Council of Public Relations Firms, an industry group, identified the top five challenges facing the industry: (1) The industry will need to deal with content overload. (2) Brands will get increasingly visual. (3) Real-time marketing will take off. (4) Business-to-business marketing will move to embrace social media. (5) As the social media space matures, consumer and marketer behavior will change.

- Shifting demographic patterns mean growing potential markets and challenges for public relations services.

Key Terms

These terms are defined in the margins throughout this chapter and appear in alphabetical order with definitions in the Glossary, which begins on page 361.

Crisis Communication *224*

Cybersmears *225*

Persuasion *220*

Publicity *230*

Public Relations *220*

Critical Questions

1. How did each of the following people contribute to the development of public relations?

   a. Ivy Lee and George F. Parker

   b. Edward L. Bernays

   c. Doris E. Fleischman

2. Explain in some detail how the Office of War Information contributed to positive public relations for World War II.

3. When is it necessary for a company to apply crisis public relations techniques? Give an example from the public relations crises that developed at Toyota, BP, Susan G. Komen and Japan McDonald's.

4. Describe the ways that advertising and public relations are different. Describe the ways they are similar.

5. Describe one or more examples of how negative information on the Internet can create challenges for public relations practitioners.

Working the Web

This list includes sites mentioned in the chapter and others to give you greater insight into the public relations business.

All About Public Relations

aboutpublicrelations.net

All About Public Relations provides information and links to PR jobs, careers and internships as well as press release and ad campaign data analysis services. Subject links include a *How to PR Toolkit*, a *PR Desk Reference Guide* and an online guide for public relations campaigns and strategies.

Center for Media and Democracy (CMD)

prwatch.org

"Investigating and exposing the undue influence of corporations and front groups on public policy," CMD is a nonprofit, nonpartisan organization that promotes media literacy and citizen journalism. Located in Madison, Wis., CMD "educates the public and aids grassroots action about policies affecting people's lives—their rights and the health of our democracy." CMD publishes *PR Watch*, a quarterly publication dedicated to investigative reporting on the PR industry; *Latest News*, a web-based daily report on PR campaigns and media spin; and SourceWatch, an online collaborative encyclopedia of people, groups and issues that shape the public agenda.

Chartered Institute of Public Relations (CIPR)

cipr.co.uk

The Chartered Institute of Public Relations (CIPR) is a professional organization for British public relations professionals. CIPR provides training and events, a professional development program, PR policy and research, and a PR careers board. Its members sign an enforced code of conduct.

Institute for Public Relations (IPR)

instituteforpr.com

The Institute for Public Relations (IPR) is an independent non-profit foundation "dedicated to the science beneath the art of public relations." IPR sponsors and disseminates scientific research about public relations and sponsors the Commission on Public Relations Measurement and Evaluation, which establishes standards and methods for PR research and issues best-practices white papers.

International Public Relations Association (IPRA)

ipra.org

Formally established in London in 1955, IPRA is a nonprofit organization for public relations executives throughout the world. It has established a specific set of ethical global industry standards and practices for the public relations industry. In 2001, it launched and continues to maintain the Campaign for Media Transparency—a global effort designed to reduce "the incidence of unethical and sometimes illegal practices in the relationships between public relations professionals and the media."

Online Public Relations

online-pr.com

Online Public Relations was developed and is maintained by James L. Horton, a PR executive and educator who specializes in less expensive, technology-based public relations methods for corporations. The site has a list of media, reference and PR resources and contains many links to reliable sources categorized by subject and alphabetically indexed.

PR Newswire

prnewswire.com

PR Newswire provides specialized multimedia platforms, including electronic and video content distribution, targeting, measurement, translation and broadcast services for government, associations, labor and nonprofit organizations throughout the world. PR Newswire's site provides content and access to a professional community, user tracking, and multimedia and multicultural public relations services.

PRWeb

prweb.com

PRWeb is a direct-to-consumer news release Web site service maintained by global media company Cision. Clients can create a free account, access the site's search engine optimization tools and upload a press release for online distribution.

PR Week

prweek.com/us

"Required reading for all public relations professionals," *PR Week* is published by Haymarket Media. *PR Week* provides timely news, reviews and profiles plus information about the most current techniques used by the public relations industry. As the companion Web site for the magazine, prweek.com/us offers a searchable archive of editorials, news, features, industry research and special reports.

Public Relations Society of America (PRSA)

prsa.org

With more than 22,000 members worldwide, PRSA was established in 1947 and is organized into more than 110 chapters. Representing for-profit and not-for-profit organizations from areas including business and industry, government, health and education, its primary objectives are to advance the standards of the public relations industry.

Public Relations Student Society of America (PRSSA)

prssa.prsa.org

An organization for students founded by the Public Relations Society of America, PRSSA's goal is to help students become aware of current theories and procedures of the public relations industry. PRSSA has more than 11,000 members at over 300 chapters on college campuses throughout the U.S., Argentina, Colombia and Peru.

Impact/Action Videos are concise news features on various topics created exclusively for *Media/Impact*. Find them in *Media/Impact*'s MindTap at cengagebrain.com.

MindTap® Log on to MindTap for *Media/Impact* to access a variety of additional material—including learning objectives, chapter readings with highlighting and note-taking, **Impact/Action Videos**, activities, and comprehension quizzes—that will guide you through this chapter.

NEWS AND INFORMATION
STAYING CONNECTED

Spencer Platt/Getty Images

U.S. Attorney General Loretta Lynch faces the press in New York to announce the arrests of several FIFA (Fédération Internationale de Football Association) officials on May 27, 2015.

What's Ahead?

> "Seventy percent of young adults said their social media feeds include a mix of viewpoints, increasing their chances of reading a wider array of content."
>
> —TOM ROSENSTIEL, EXECUTIVE DIRECTOR, AMERICAN PRESS INSTITUTE

Because the First Amendment to the U.S. Constitution prescribes freedom of the press, it is important to understand the development of news reporting in this country. Today's news delivery is the result of a tug of war between audiences as they define the types of news they want and the news media that try to deliver it. (See **Impact/Convergence**: "Young Adults Want News Every Day, Survey Shows," p. 237.)

Publick Occurrences, the nation's first newspaper, published only one issue in 1690 before the authorities shut it down. The nation's first *consecutively issued* newspaper (published more than once) was *The Boston News-Letter*, which appeared in 1704. In the first issue, editor John Campbell reprinted the queen's latest speech, some maritime news and one advertisement telling people how to put an ad in his paper.

From 1704 until the Civil War, newspapers spread throughout New England and the South and across the frontier. The invention of the telegraph, in 1844, meant news that once took weeks to reach publication could be transmitted in minutes.

Early News Organizations Cooperate to Gather News

In 1848, 6 newspapers in New York City decided to share the cost of gathering foreign news by telegraph from Boston. Henry J. Raymond, who subsequently founded *The New York Times*, drew up the agreement among the papers to pay $100 for 3,000 words of telegraph news.

Valery Hache/Getty Images

Today the public's appetite for news means there are more news outlets gathering more types of news than ever before. Actor Sean Penn jogs past reporters at the Cannes Film Festival in Cannes, France, on May 14, 2015.

Convergence

Young Adults Want News Every Day, Survey Shows

By Associated Press

Young adults have a reputation for being connected to one another and disconnected from the news, but a survey found that mobile devices and social networking are keeping them more engaged with the broader world than previously thought.

They want news, they say, though they don't always aggressively seek it out—perhaps simply happening upon it on a friend's online feed. And they want it daily.

The survey of Americans ages 18 to 34 found that two-thirds of respondents said they consume news online regularly, often on a social networking site. Of those, 40 percent do so several times a day, according to the poll conducted by The Associated Press-NORC Center for Public Affairs Research and the American Press Institute.

It's been a slowly building trend in news consumption that experts say is trickling up to older generations—and that young people say helps them stay current, even if they never read an actual newspaper or watch the evening news on TV.

Among other things, the respondents of the survey said their consumption of news and information on various devices was most often sparked by an interest in civic issues, for social reasons, including discussing a topic with friends,

Marilu Rodriguez checks a news Web site on her smartphone before boarding a train home from work in Chicago. Rodriguez, like two-thirds of 18- to 34-year-olds polled in a recent survey, consumes news online regularly, often on social networking sites.

AP Images/M. Spencer Green

or because they just find it enjoyable.

The survey found young adults generally get harder news from more traditional news sites and "softer" lifestyle news from social networks, Facebook being the overwhelming favorite.

That's generally how it works for Marilu Rodriguez, a 29-year-old from suburban Chicago, who participated in a focus group that accompanied the survey. She recalls how, as a child, the TV news would come on at her house after her family had watched the latest episode of their favorite telenovela, a Spanish-language soap opera. "It was a family thing to watch the news," Rodriguez says.

Now her smartphone is her most frequent portal to the world, as she

surfs social networking and news sites, often on her train ride to and from work as a coordinator for a nonprofit organization in downtown Chicago. Like many in the survey, she gets a lot of her news through a "diverse mix of friends" on those social networking sites.

Still, only 39 percent of the survey's respondents said they actively seek out news, while 60 percent said they mostly "bump into" that type of content as they do other things on Facebook and other sites.

Tom Rosenstiel, executive director of the American Press Institute, noted that 70 percent of young adults surveyed said their social media feeds include a mix of viewpoints, increasing their chances of reading a wider array of content.

Note: The survey of 1,046 young adults was conducted from Jan. 5 to Feb. 2, 2015, by the Media Insight Project, a partnership between the AP-NORC Center and the American Press Institute, which funded the study.

Excerpted from Associated Press, "Staying Current: Young Adults Want News Every Day, Survey Shows," March 17, 2015.

Soon known as the New York Associated Press, this organization was the country's first **cooperative news gathering** association.

Being a cooperative meant the member organizations shared the cost of getting the news, domestic and foreign, returning any profits to the members. Today's Associated Press (AP) is the result of this early partnership. United Press, founded in 1884 to compete with AP, devised a different way of sharing information. United Press, which eventually became United Press International (UPI), was established not as a cooperative but as a privately owned, for-profit wire service. (Today wire services are called news services.)

Because news services now use digital delivery instead of the original telegraph machines, cooperative and for-profit news gathering is virtually instantaneous. Most American newspapers and broadcast news operations subscribe to at least one news service, such as AP. Many other news services send stories and broadcasts worldwide: Agence France-Presse (France), Reuters (Great Britain), ITAR-TASS (Russia), Agenzia Nazionale Stampa Associata (ANSA; Italy), Deutsche Presse-Agentur (Germany) and Xinhua (China).

The news services especially help small newspapers and broadcast stations that can't afford overseas correspondents. Large dailies with their own reporters around the world still rely on news services when they can't get to a story quickly. UPI has had several owners and has very few subscribers. Associated Press is the nation's primary news service, constantly feeding stories to newspapers, broadcast outlets and Internet news services. AP remains a cooperative, as it was when it began in New York, and employs broadcast as well as print reporters all over the world.

Some newspaper organizations in the United States—*The New York Times, The Washington Post* and the *Chicago Tribune*—also run their own news services. Subscribers publish each other's news service stories. For many newspapers, news service stories provide information at a relatively low cost because the subscribing newspaper doesn't need as many staff reporters to cover the news.

Civil War Brings Accreditation and Photojournalism

In the 1860s, interest in the emotional issues of the Civil War sent many reporters to the battlefront. Hundreds of correspondents roamed freely among the soldiers, reporting for

Mathew B Brady/Bettmann/Corbis

Mathew Brady's photojournalism during the Civil War created a standard for future photojournalists to follow—using photo images to help capture a story's realism. In 1864, Brady photographed members of the 1st Connecticut Artillery at Fort Brady.

the North and the South. Two important results of Civil War reporting were the accreditation of reporters and the introduction of photographs to enhance written reports.

Government Accredits Journalists

The issue of government interests versus press freedom surfaced early in the Civil War. In 1861, Union General Winfield Scott prohibited telegraph companies from transmitting military information because he was afraid some stories would help the South. At the Battle of Bull Run in 1861, *New York Times* editor Henry J. Raymond, reporting the war from the front, mistakenly telegraphed a story that said the North had won.

When Raymond followed up with the correct story, military censors blocked the news, arguing the information should be kept secret. Then Union General William T. Sherman ordered *New York Herald* correspondent Thomas E. Knox arrested and held as a spy for sending sensitive military information.

President Lincoln intervened to reach a compromise that would balance the needs of the press with the needs of the nation through a process called **accreditation**.

> **Cooperative News Gathering** Member news organizations that share the expense of getting the news.
>
> **Accreditation** The process by which the government certifies members of the press to cover government-related news events.

Photojournalist Margaret Bourke-White photographed stories for *Fortune* and *Time* magazines, establishing a 20th-century standard for photojournalism. Bourke-White, dressed in high-altitude flying gear, poses in front of a U.S. Army Flying Fortress aircraft in February 1943. Bourke-White covered World War II and the Korean War as a photojournalist.

This meant that the federal government certified members of the press to cover the war. Accredited journalists were required to carry press passes issued by the military. The practice of accreditation continues today as the government's method of certifying war-reporting journalists. This concept of accreditation—that a journalist is someone who could be credentialed—served to add to a sense of professionalism among journalists.

Photojournalism Is Born

Also at the Battle of Bull Run was photographer Mathew Brady, who convinced President Lincoln that a complete photographic record of the war should be made. Until the Civil War, photography had been confined primarily to studio portraits because of the cumbersome equipment and slow chemical processing. Brady photographed the battles of Antietam and Fredericksburg and sent photographic teams to other battles.

Newspapers did not yet have a method to reproduce the photographs, but Brady's pictures were published in magazines, making Brady the nation's first news photographer. His 3,500 photographs demonstrated the practicality and effectiveness of using images to help report a news story, although newspaper photographs did not become widely used until the early 1900s.

The marriage of images and text to tell a better story than either text or photographs could tell alone formed the beginnings of today's concept of *photojournalism*. It was photojournalism that made *Life* magazine, founded by *Time*'s Henry Luce, such a success and created stars out of gifted photographers like Margaret Bourke-White. The perfect image to accompany the words—the best photojournalism—has become an essential part of any good news story.

Tabloid News Takes Over

The beginning of the 20th century brought the expansion of newspapers—New York City once had more than ten daily newspapers— and intensified competition. The introduction of the penny papers meant newspapers had to grab a bigger audience to survive. And, as described in **Chapter 3**, the race for readers ushered in yellow journalism—featuring stories about grisly crimes and illicit sex, often illustrated with large, startling photographs. Substantial newspapers, covering important stories, were being published all over the country, but today people still think first about tabloid journalism when they think about this period in newspaper history.

In the 1930s, people began to turn to radio for instant news headlines and information. Newspapers still flourished, but where they once had an exclusive corner on news, now they shared their audiences with radio. When World War II began, both radio and newspapers were in place to bring home expanded news of the war.

Newsreels Bring Distant Events to American Moviegoers

Beginning at the turn of the 20th century and lasting until television took over news coverage, movie newsreels showed audiences distant locations and newsworthy events. Produced by companies including British Pathé (from 1900 until 1970) and Fox Movietone News (between 1919 and 1960), newsreels were shown in movie theaters to audiences hungry for the pictures that radio couldn't provide. Newsreels and news features, such as *March of Time*, were usually no longer than ten minutes, with running commentary by a narrator, updated every week.

Photojournalism   Using photographs to accompany text to capture a news story.

Before TV news, newsreels and news features were very popular with movie audiences. Shown in movie theaters before the main feature, newsreels, such as Movietone News, brought viewers closer to distant locations and newsworthy events. On March 8, 1933, President Franklin D. Roosevelt gives his first press conference as president, in Washington, D.C.

Because it took time to assemble the stories and develop the film, newsreel footage usually reached audiences a week or more after the events took place. Movietone News, produced by Fox, offered the most popular newsreel in the United States, with more than 1,000 camera operators who roamed the globe to cover the news each day.

Besides serious news stories, such as President Franklin Delano Roosevelt speaking to a national audience, newsreel photographers captured Hollywood celebrities, scoured exotic travel locations and produced sports and feature stories. Another newsreel company, All-American News, produced newsreels directed at African American audiences; often these were shown before feature movies in addition to, or instead of, Movietone newsreels.

Newsreels offered an important realistic glimpse at worldwide news and information events that audiences couldn't get anywhere else.

Newspapers and Radio Personalize World War II

The most honored print journalist during World War II was Ernie Pyle, who worked for the Scripps Howard news organization. His reporting, which focused on the people who were fighting the war rather than battles and casualty counts, reached deep into the emotions of Americans who were stateside waiting for word from the front. (See **Impact/Profile**, "Ernie Pyle: The War Correspondent Who Hated War," p. 241.)

Radio is the news medium that began to shine during World War II because radio news broadcasts meant that, for the first time, people could hear the action as it was happening. Imagine the date is September 8, 1940. World War II has begun its second year in Europe. You don't have a television set. You are sitting at home in the United States, listening to your radio.

CBS announces a special bulletin from journalist Edward R. Murrow, reporting the first bombing of London: 626 bombers have pounded the city, leaving more than 1,000 people dead and 2,000 people injured. You and your family listen intently in your living room as Murrow describes "men with white scarves around their necks instead of collars . . . dull-eyed, empty-faced women. . . . Most of them carried little cheap cardboard suitcases and sometimes bulging paper shopping bags. That was all they had left. . . .

"A row of automobiles with stretchers racked on the roofs like skis, standing outside of bombed buildings. A

During World War II, radio became the most immediate way for people to learn about current events. Radio broadcaster Howard K. Smith reports from Moscow, Russia, on October 1, 1943. U.S. war reporters, like Smith and Ernie Pyle, wore military uniforms when they were working.

IMPACT

Profile

Ernie Pyle: The War Correspondent Who Hated War

By Dan Thomasson

Note: Ernie Pyle worked for Scripps Howard. Dan Thomasson, the editor of Scripps Howard News Service, wrote this reflection on Pyle's work to accompany a collection of Pyle's dispatches that was published in 1986. Pyle, 45, was killed while covering a battle on Ie Shima, Japan, on April 18, 1945.

The other day while going through some old files in our library, I came upon a yellowed and tattered dispatch.

It made me cry.

It was about the death of a Capt. Waskow during the Italian campaign of 1944. And it probably is the most powerful treatise on war and death and the human spirit I have ever read.

I took it out and had it treated and framed and I hung it in the office in a prominent position where now and then one of the younger reporters will come by and read it and try to hide the inevitable tear.

The man who wrote it, Ernest Taylor Pyle, is but a memory as distant as

PFC Murray/Historical/Corbis

War correspondent Ernie Pyle (1900–1945), the most honored journalist in the United States, died during the last days of World War II. Pyle (*center, standing with foot on the hill*) visits with a soldier on Okinawa, Ryukyu Islands, in 1945.

the war he covered so eloquently and ultimately died in.

But unlike so many who perished beside him, Pyle's contribution to what Studs Terkel calls "the last good war" remains with us in his work—thousands of words that will forever memorialize brave men and debunk the "glory" of war.

The column that says it best perhaps is the one drafted for the end of the fighting in Europe. It was found in his pocket by the foot soldiers who had risked their lives to retrieve his body on the Japanese island of Ie Shima in 1945:

"Dead men by mass production—in one country after another—month after month and year after year. Dead men in winter and dead men in summer.

"Dead men in such familiar promiscuity that they become monotonous.

"Dead men in such infinity that you come almost to hate them."

. . . When I was a kid starting out in this business, the trade magazines were full of job-seeking ads by those who claimed they could "write like Ernie Pyle." This was 10 years after his death and he was still everyone's model.

From "Why They Still Write Ernie Pyle Books," *Honolulu Advertiser*, June 20, 1986, page A-1. Reprinted by permission of Scripps Howard News Service.

man pinned under wreckage where a broken gas main sears his arms and face. . . .

". . . the courage of the people, the flash and roar of the guns rolling down streets . . . the stench of air-raid shelters in the poor districts."

This was radio news reporting at its best. For 26 years, from 1921 until the advent of television news in 1947, radio reporters like Murrow painted pictures with words. (For more information about Murrow's career in television, see **Chapter 8**.)

During the first half of the 20th century, radio reporters described Prohibition and its repeal, the stock market crash, the Depression, the election of Franklin D. Roosevelt, the New Deal, the bombings of London and Pearl Harbor, the Normandy invasion, Roosevelt's funeral and the signing of the armistice that ended World War II.

Most radio stations maintained their own radio news departments, until the advent of format radio. Today, very few radio stations maintain full-time news departments, and radio stations with news formats tend to be concentrated in the nation's big cities. Still, the heritage of colorful, exciting radio news created the foundation for TV news, which began to blossom in the 1950s.

TV News Enters Its Golden Age

The first network TV newscasts in the 1950s lasted only 15 minutes, but by the 1960s, TV network evening news had expanded to half an hour—the same amount of time the networks dedicate to national news today. Radio news stars like Edward R. Murrow moved from radio to television, and eventually the TV networks created large news departments with bureaus and correspondents spread throughout the United States and overseas.

What has been called the Golden Age of Television News was the decade that began in 1961, with President John F. Kennedy's inauguration. The Kennedy family was very photogenic, and they invited press coverage. Kennedy's victory as president, in fact, has been credited to his on-camera presence during the Kennedy-Nixon debates in 1960. So it was fitting that Kennedy would be the first president to play Cold War brinkmanship on television, when TV news grew to become a part of politics, not just a chronicler of political events.

TV and the Cold War

President Kennedy asked all three networks to clear him time on Monday, October 22, 1962, at 7 p.m. Eastern time.

The president had learned that missile sites were being built in Cuba with Russian help. Kennedy used television to deliver his ultimatum to dismantle the missile bases.

"Using the word *nuclear* 11 times, Kennedy drew a panorama of devastation enveloping the whole hemisphere," according to media historian Eric Barnouw. "The moves that had made such things possible, said Kennedy, could not be accepted by the United States 'if our courage and our commitments are ever to be trusted again by either friend or foe.'"

Kennedy admonished Russian Premier Nikita Khrushchev and urged him to stop the ships the Soviet Union was sending to Cuba to help build the missile sites. Faced with such a visible challenge, the Soviet Union turned its ships around in the Atlantic and sent conciliatory messages in order to reach a settlement. The Cuban missile crisis was in fact a carefully constructed live television drama, in which Kennedy performed well.

TV News as a Window on the World

In 1963, television news was forced into an unexpected role as it conveyed a sense of collective national grief following President Kennedy's assassination. For four days beginning at 1:30 p.m. Eastern time on Friday, November 22, 1963, the country witnessed the aftermath of the assassination of the president. At 2:38 p.m., Vice President

AP Images/Uncredited

Television news provided a sense of collective national experience covering the events that followed the assassination of President Kennedy. On November 25, 1963, an NBC camera records the funeral procession. Network news broadcasts during the events surrounding the Kennedy assassination have been called the finest four days of television news.

Lyndon Johnson was sworn in as president on television.

On Saturday, TV viewers watched the world's diplomats arrive for Kennedy's funeral. On Sunday, viewers watched the first murder ever broadcast live on television, as Jack Ruby killed assassination suspect Lee Harvey Oswald. Then, on Monday, November 25, 1963, came the president's funeral.

As many as nine out of ten television sets were turned on during the marathon events surrounding the president's funeral. The networks canceled all commercials. "Some television employees had slept as little as six hours in three nights," wrote media historian Eric Barnouw. "They went on, almost welcoming the absorption in the task at hand." The network news broadcasts during the events surrounding the Kennedy assassination were called the finest four days of television news. Television had become the nation's "window on the world," wrote Barnouw. "The view it offered seemed to be *the* world. They trusted its validity and completeness."

TV News Changes the Nation's Identity

In the late 1960s and early 1970s, television played a defining role in two very important stories—the war in Vietnam and the Watergate hearings.

Vietnam Coverage Exposes Reality

The longest-running protest program in the nation's history began appearing on television news as anti–Vietnam War marchers showed up on camera daily in the late 1960s. During live coverage of the Chicago Democratic Convention in 1968, demonstrators faced police in a march toward the convention hall. Television covered the resulting violence, which caused injuries to hundreds of protesters and to 21 reporters and photographers.

"When the war in Vietnam began to escalate in 1965," wrote TV critic Jeff Greenfield, "it was the television networks, covering the war with few official restrictions, that brought to American homes pictures of the

On March 29, 1973, news cameras recorded the last U.S. serviceman to leave Vietnam, Army Chief Master Sergeant Max Bielke. Graphic TV coverage of the Vietnam War shook American viewers as no previous war coverage had. It also gave them an appetite for live news coverage—instant information about events as they were happening.

face of war that had never been shown before: not friendly troops welcomed by the populace, but troops setting fire to villages with cigarette lighters; troops cutting off the ears of dead combat foes; allies spending American tax money for personal gain."

Candid reporting from the war itself shook viewers as previous war reporting never had, but it also gave Americans an appetite for news and for live news coverage—instant information about events as they were happening.

Through live coverage of the Senate Judiciary Committee's Watergate hearings from May to August 1973, TV viewers got a close look inside the Nixon presidency as committee members examined evidence against the president. Nixon resigned in 1974.

Watergate Hearings Reveal Politics at Work

In 1973, live television news took another leap with the continuous broadcast of the U.S. Senate's Watergate hearings to investigate allegedly illegal activities of the Republican Committee to Re-elect the President (CREEP). A parade of government witnesses and political appointees fascinated viewers with descriptions of the inner workings of the Nixon presidency.

According to media scholars Christopher Sterling and John Kittross, "Running from May through August 1973, and chaired by North Carolina's crusty Sam Ervin, these hearings were a fascinating live exposition of the political process in America, and were 'must' television watching as a parade of witnesses told—or evaded telling—what they knew of the broad conspiracy to assure the reelection of Nixon and then to cover up the conspiracy itself." For more than a year the political drama continued to unfold on television's nightly news.

Ultimately, the Judiciary Committee of the House of Representatives began a televised debate on whether to impeach the president. For the first time in its history, the nation faced the prospect of seeing a president brought to trial live on national television. On August 8, 1974, President Nixon brought the crisis to an end by announcing his resignation—on television.

TV News Expands and Contracts

Because viewers were hungry for news and wanted to watch it, local TV news operations expanded—some stations offering as much as two hours of local news plus the national news broadcasts. Throughout the 1970s and 1980s, networks and local news departments expanded. Then came broadcast deregulation in the 1980s. The networks were sold and consolidated, and local stations, many of which had been locally owned, became pieces of larger corporations.

In 1980, Ted Turner founded Cable News Network (CNN), which offered round-the-clock news on cable. CNN established overseas bureaus and the concept that all-news-all-the-time would grab an audience. Audiences responded, and CNN became an alternative to network news, often the first place audiences turned whenever there was a crucial international story that required constant updating.

In general, however, in the 1990s, the American public read fewer newspapers and watched less news on

During the Iraq War, the Pentagon embedded more than 600 reporters with American troops. On May 1, 2004, embedded reporter Kevin Sites (*left*) of NBC and photographer Sung Su Cho of *Time* magazine ride in the back of a U.S. Marines vehicle in Fallujah, Iraq.

Scott Peterson/Getty Images

television. Network and local TV news audiences declined. News departments began to shrink. Soon, another medium replaced the public's seemingly insatiable need for instant news and information—the Internet.

Iraq War Produces "Embedded" Reporters

Since the Vietnam War, access to battlefield locations has been a battle between the press' aggressive need-to-know and the military's need-to-keep-secret. In 2003, military press relations took a new turn when the United States declared war on Iraq.

Before the battles began, the U.S. military announced a plan to *embed* more than 600 reporters with American troops. Embedding offered the reporters access to the frontlines but also kept them within the military's control. Still, it was a reversal of past Pentagon policy makers, who often had sought to keep the press far from military operations.

CNN and the major television networks offered non-stop coverage in the early days of the war, and people watched. "A lot of people have been surprised at the access and cooperation we've had in the field," said Tony

> **Embed** A term used to describe the placement of journalists who were allowed to cover the Iraq War on the frontlines, supervised by the U.S. military.

Maddox, senior vice president Europe, Middle East and Africa for CNN International. "It's produced some remarkable images."

Reality Shows and Advertorials Blur the Line

TV reality shows, such as *Undercover Boss*, blur the distinction between what is news and what is re-created drama. These shows use interviews and cover live action in a documentary style that imitates news stories. Reality shows, or docudramas, make it difficult for an audience to distinguish between packaged entertainment and spontaneous events.

Infomercials—programs that pretend to give viewers information but that are really advertisements for the sponsors' products—also are making it harder to discern what is reporting and what is advertising. The line between news and entertainment on television becomes even trickier when advertisers produce programs that look like news but are really advertisements. Paid advertising supplements in newspapers and magazines—called **advertorials**—also blur the line between news content and advertising. Although these supplements usually are labeled as advertising, they often look similar to the regular news pages.

This merging of news with entertainment and advertising, as well as the entertaining graphics and the light-hearted presentation style of most local TV newscasts, makes it more difficult for viewers and readers to separate fact from fiction, reality from reenactment, and news from advertising. The result may be a decline in the audience's trust in the news media to deliver accurate information. This makes it important that so-called pseudo-news be properly labeled so it doesn't mislead the public.

Internet Transforms News Delivery

The immediacy of the Internet brought several changes to the news business. News became more personalized, and the Internet began to replace broadcast news because it is more immediate. The Internet also changed how journalists work because often they are required to deliver several different types of stories simultaneously for print, broadcast and Internet.

According to the most recent study from the Pew Research Center, Internet news is attracting a large segment of the national audience. At the same time, many people are losing the news habit, according to the study. They pay attention to the news only when

"Let me answer your question by saying that you're being really aggressive, and it's totally freaking me out."

David Sipress The New Yorker Collection/The Cartoon Bank

something important happens, and many watch broadcast news with the remote control nearby to skip uninteresting stories and move on to something they would rather watch. Today, the Internet is a nonstop news and information machine. Half of all U.S. adults now have a mobile connection to the Web through either a smartphone or tablet. (See **Illustration 12.1**, "Top 10 Digital-Only News Sites," and **Illustration 12.2**, "The Growing Market for Mobile News in the United States," p. 246.)

Anyone with access to the Internet can choose the sources and subjects to investigate. Yahoo! News, with a significant number of online subscribers, compiles headlines from television and print news outlets—photos and stories from major news organizations—as well as updated headline stories from news magazines like *Time* and *Bloomberg Businessweek*. For specialty information, and for more background, you can visit any corporation's, association's or nonprofit organization's Web site.

You can choose what to look for and also *when* you look. The Internet is available on your schedule—independent of any TV network or local broadcast time schedule. News rotates through CNN Headline News (HLN) on

> **Advertorial** Paid advertising supplements in newspapers and magazines that often look similar to the regular news pages.

IMPACT
Society

ILLUSTRATION 12.1

Top 10 Digital-Only News Sites

The audience for news is swiftly migrating from newspapers and TV to the Internet. Although some of the news sites people visit originate with traditional news organizations (like ABC News and *USA Today*), Internet-only news sites began as online sources and were never part of a traditional news group. Many are drawing audiences away from traditional news sites. According to the Pew Research Center, the top 10 digital-only news sites are:

"Digital News—Audience Fact Sheet," *State of the News Media 2015*, April 29, 2015, journalism.org.

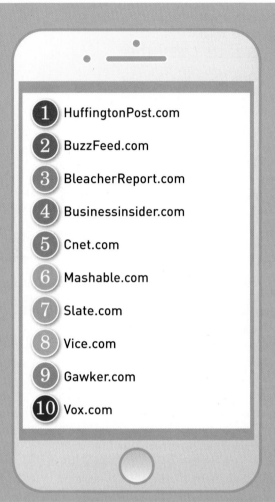

1. HuffingtonPost.com
2. BuzzFeed.com
3. BleacherReport.com
4. Businessinsider.com
5. Cnet.com
6. Mashable.com
7. Slate.com
8. Vice.com
9. Gawker.com
10. Vox.com

ILLUSTRATION 12.2

The Growing Market for Mobile News in the United States

More people get their news on mobile devices (tablets and smartphones) than on their desktop or laptop computers, according to the Pew Research Center, which called this group "the mobile majority."

journalism.org/analysis_report/future-mobile-news

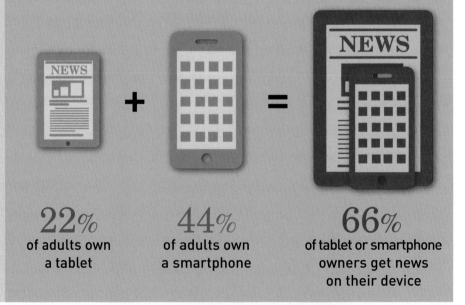

22%
of adults own a tablet

44%
of adults own a smartphone

66%
of tablet or smartphone owners get news on their device

television in short segments, but you can check your computer or your cell phone and find just about anything you want to know—sports scores, the weather, international headlines—whenever you want it, and you control how much time you spend with each story.

The Internet, unlike any other form of news and information delivery, is completely self-directed—targeted to individual needs and not connected to a specific time of day or night. The Internet also is the place where people can get all the news in one location that they previously had to gather from several sources.

Today, one of four Americans lists the Internet as a main source of news (compared to just 15 percent in 2000), and 44 percent say they receive news reports from the Internet at least once a week, according to the Pew Center. At the same time, network evening television news viewership for the major TV networks is stabilizing, while the audience for cable news (such as CNN) is eroding.

Two other important findings of the Pew news analysis were:

▶ Large numbers of Americans younger than age 30 turn to the Internet for news, but people of all ages read the news online.

▶ Thirty-three percent of people younger than age 30 go online for news every day, but so do 27 percent of people in their 40s and 25 percent of people in their 50s.

Information Access Creates a News Evolution

This evolution in people's news habits has taken more than a century and required several technological innovations. From print to radio to television to the Internet, as each new system of delivery emerged, the old systems still stayed in place. This means that today there's more news available from more news sources, delivered through more systems than ever before.

People can select the types of information they want, when they want it, creating personal news, and the news business is becoming even more competitive and harder to define. Consumers now have many sources—local, national and international plus the enormous variety of resources available on the Internet, including social media sites—where they can look for what they want to know and then immediately share with friends.

Getty Images

News organizations increasingly hire "all-platform journalists"— reporters who shoot video and write articles for the Internet and broadcast simultaneously. Working on a dangerous assignment in Mogadishu, Somalia, multi-platform journalist Abdukadir Hassan Abdirahman shoots video, wearing a pistol around his neck for protection.

Social Media Spread the News

According to the Pew Research Center, the audience for news has never been stronger, and social networks are beginning to play a growing role in the news landscape, connecting audiences to the current events through social media. The report cited several trends that affect how people get their news today, including

1. Half of Facebook users get news on the site even though they did not go there looking for news. And the Facebook users who get news at the highest rates are 18- to 29-year-olds.

2. Half the people who watch online videos watch news videos, and young users constitute the greatest portion of these viewers.

3. Half of social network users share or repost news stories, while nearly as many discuss news issues or events on social network sites.

4. Roughly one in ten social network users has posted news videos that the user took.

5. Eleven percent of all online news consumers have submitted their own content (including videos, photos, articles or opinion pieces) to news Web sites or blogs.

6. On social sites and even many of the new digital-only sites, news is mixed in with all other kinds of content—people bump into news when they are doing other things.

Reuters/Eric Thayer

Ignoring the sign, journalists gather around a newsmaker. Agenda-setting often occurs when a group of journalists, reporting the same story, present a similar view of events.

Journalists at Work

The audience for news is rapidly shifting (away from print news sources, such as newspapers and magazines, and toward video delivery sources, such as TV and Internet sites). With so many sources of news available, the audience for news is becoming further segmented into smaller shares.

In a practical sense, this means lower revenues for each news media organization, and advertising rates that are based on audience size. Fewer readers, listeners or viewers means less money to hire people to write and report the news. This has led to the need for a new kind of versatile reporter—one who can produce all types of news stories—the *"all-platform journalist."*

These reporters must be able to write the story and take photographs as well as produce video. In 2008, CNN began assigning "digital journalists" to ten cities in the United States to report local stories. These journalists report live, using laptops and cell phone cameras. "We are harnessing technology that enables us to be anywhere and be live from anywhere," said Nancy Lane, senior vice president for newsgathering for CNN/U.S. "It completely changes how we can report."

"Today, as they confront new competition on the Web, television networks are increasingly embracing portable—and inexpensive—methods of production," reports *The New York Times*. "A new breed of reporter, sometimes called a 'one-man band,' has become the new norm. Though the style of reporting has existed for years, it is being adopted more widely as these reporters act as their own producer, cameraman and editor, and sometimes even transmit live video."

Journalists Channel the Public's Attention

News organizations often are criticized for presenting a consistently shared view of the news. Often news values are shaped by the way news organizations are structured and the routines they follow. The press in America, in general, doesn't tell people what to think but does tell people what and whom to think *about*. This is called **agenda-setting**. Agenda-setting works in two ways: the flow of information from one news organization to another and the flow of information from news organizations to their audiences.

In agenda-setting, the stories that appear in the nation's widely circulated print media provide ideas to the other media. For example, a widely circulated print media outlet, such as *The New York Times*, can identify specific stories as important by giving them in-depth attention, and this may set the news agenda on specific national issues for other news organizations to follow.

Another type of agenda-setting occurs when a group of journalists, reporting the same story individually, presents a similar picture of the event, rather than differing interpretations of the event. This is called **consensus journalism**.

The emergence of the Internet as a news source means that people now have more places to look for news—even overseas—which means more viewpoints on stories are available. This puts a bigger burden on the news consumer to seek out and verify the most reliable sources of information, as a way to gain a wider perspective on each day's events.

How the Public Perceives the Press

It has not been shown in any comprehensive study of news gathering that journalists with liberal or conservative values insert their personal ideology directly into

All-Platform Journalists Broadcast journalists who act as their own producer, cameraperson and editor, and sometimes even transmit live video.

Agenda-Setting The belief that journalists don't tell you *what* to think but do tell you *what and whom to think about*.

Consensus Journalism The tendency among many journalists covering the same event to report similar conclusions about the event.

their reporting or that the audience unquestioningly accepts one point of view.

But the assumption that journalists' personal beliefs directly influence their professional performance is common. Although the job of columnists and editorial writers is to present a certain point of view, the majority of journalists view themselves as detached observers of events. According to media scholar Herbert J. Gans:

> Journalists, like everyone else, have values, [and] the two that matter most in the newsroom are getting the story and getting it better and faster than their prime competitors—both among their colleagues and at rival news media. Personal political beliefs are left at home, not only because journalists are trained to be objective and detached, but also because their credibility and their paychecks depend on their remaining detached.

Some press critics, in fact, argue that journalists most often present establishment viewpoints and are unlikely to challenge prevailing political and social values. The pressure to come up with instant analyses of news events also may lead to conformity in reporting—an unwillingness to think independently.

Credibility Draws the Audience

Overall, the growing trust in Internet news sources and their expanding popularity as information sources may be connected. As Internet news sources gain credibility, the news audience will follow, and the audience is global. Credibility, of course, is the basis of all good journalism.

"But the weather looks great for the rest of the week."

Frank Cotham The New Yorker Collection/The Cartoon Bank

This is a familiar pattern: In the nation's news history, newspaper readers added radio and newsreels, and then moved to television for news. Today's news audiences still have access to traditional news sources, but they've expanded their search for news and information to the Internet. The Internet combines all the news sources anyone could want in one place on the news consumer's own timetable, a trend that has been called a "digital tide."

REVIEW, ANALYZE, INVESTIGATE

CHAPTER 12

Early News Organizations Cooperate to Gather News

- The nation's first consecutively issued newspaper (published more than once) was the *Boston News-Letter*, which appeared in 1704.
- The invention of the telegraph in 1844 meant news that once took weeks to reach publication could be transmitted in minutes.
- In 1848, six newspapers in New York City formed the New York Associated Press, the first cooperative news-gathering association.

- Today, most American newspapers and broadcast news operations subscribe to at least one news service, such as Associated Press (AP).
- Some U.S. newspaper organizations also run their own news services, which allow subscribers to publish each other's stories for a fee.

Civil War Brings Accreditation and Photojournalism

- In 1861, during the Civil War, President Lincoln introduced the practice of accreditation for journalists.

- During the Civil War, Mathew Brady introduced the concept of photojournalism—using images to help capture a story.

Tabloid News Takes Over

- The competition for newspaper readers spawned yellow journalism—stories about grisly crimes and illicit sex, often accompanied by large, startling photographs.

- In the 1930s, newspapers began to share the audience for news with radio.

Newsreels Bring Distant Events to American Moviegoers

- Produced by companies including British Pathé (from 1900 until 1970) and Fox Movietone News (between 1919 and 1960), newsreels were shown in movie theaters to audiences hungry for the pictures that radio couldn't provide. Audiences also watched news features such as *March of Time*.

- Newsreel footage usually took a week or more from the time it was shot to when audiences saw it.

Newspapers and Radio Personalize World War II

- In the 1930s, people began to turn to radio for instant news headlines and information.

- In the 1930s and 1940s, most radio stations maintained their own news departments until the advent of format radio.

- Journalist Ernie Pyle gave World War II the human touch because he wrote stories about the soldiers' lives, not troop movements.

- Very few radio stations today maintain full-time news departments, and radio stations with news formats tend to be concentrated in the nation's big cities.

TV News Enters Its Golden Age

- What has been called the Golden Age of Television News was the decade that began in 1961, with President John F. Kennedy's inauguration.

- In 1962, in what was called the Cuban missile crisis, President Kennedy used live television to deliver his ultimatum to Soviet leader Nikita Khrushchev, urging him to stop sending ships to Cuba to help build missile sites. Faced with this ultimatum, the Soviet Union turned its ships around.

- Television became a window on the world with its coverage of events in the days following the assassination of President Kennedy.

TV News Changes the Nation's Identity

- Coverage of the war in Vietnam gave Americans an appetite for live television news.

- The Watergate hearings showed viewers the inner workings of national politics.

TV News Expands and Contracts

- Ted Turner founded CNN in 1980, offering round-the-clock news on cable.

- The 1980s brought broadcast deregulation and consolidation of the TV networks.

- In the 1990s, in general, the American public read fewer newspapers and watched less news on television.

Iraq War Produces "Embedded" Reporters

- Before the war in Iraq began in 2003, the U.S. military announced a plan to embed more than 600 reporters with American troops.

- Embedding offered the reporters access to the frontlines but also kept them within the military's control.

Reality Shows and Advertorials Blur the Line

- Reality TV shows tend to blur the line between entertainment and news.

- TV infomercials and advertising supplements called "advertorials" in newspapers and magazines make it harder for readers to differentiate between news content and advertising.

- The merging of news with entertainment and advertising makes it more difficult for viewers to separate facts from fiction.

Internet Transforms News Delivery

- The Internet, unlike any other form of news and information delivery, is completely self-directed news and information—targeted to individual needs.

- A recent American Press Institute/Associated Press study revealed that young adults consume some news online regularly.

- Today, one in four Americans lists the Internet as a main source of news.

Information Access Creates a News Evolution

- The immediacy of news on the Internet means people can personalize the news.

- Half of all U.S. adults now have a mobile connection to the Web through either a smartphone or tablet.

Social Media Spread the News

- Social media connect audiences to news sources.

- Half of Facebook users get news on the site even though they did not go there looking for news.

- Facebook users who get news at the highest rates are 18- to 29-year-olds.

- Half the people who watch online videos watch news videos.

- Half of social network users share or repost news stories.

- Roughly one in ten social network users has posted news videos that the user took.

- Eleven percent of all online news consumers have submitted their own content to news sites or blogs.

- People bump into news when they are doing other things.

Journalists at Work

- The audience for news is shifting and in some cases—especially print—is declining.

- With so many sources of news available, news organizations must each be satisfied with a smaller piece of the audience.

- Smaller audiences mean lower revenues for media with advertising rates based on audience share.

- In today's media business, many reporters must work as "all-platform journalists."

Journalists Channel the Public's Attention

- The press in America doesn't tell you what to think. It does tell you what and whom to think about. This is called agenda-setting.

- Consensus journalism occurs when a group of journalists, reporting the same story individually, presents a similar picture of the event rather than differing interpretations.

How the Public Perceives the Press

- It has not been shown in any comprehensive study of news gathering that journalists with liberal or conservative values insert their personal ideology directly into their reporting.

- Some press critics argue that journalists most often present establishment viewpoints and are unlikely to challenge prevailing political and social values.

Credibility Draws the Audience

- The growing trust in Internet news sources may be related to the Internet's increasing popularity as a source of news.

- If Internet news can maintain its believability, the majority of the news audience may gravitate to the Internet.

Key Terms

These terms are defined in the margins throughout this chapter and appear in alphabetical order with definitions in the Glossary, which begins on page 361.

Accreditation *238*

Advertorial *245*

Agenda-Setting *248*

All-Platform Journalists *248*

Consensus Journalism *248*

Cooperative News Gathering *238*

Embed *244*

Photojournalism *239*

Critical Questions

1. List two specific ways in which news coverage changed during the Civil War.

2. List and explain three ways the Internet has changed consumers' news habits.

3. How have changes in the way news is delivered affected how journalists do their jobs?

4. Discuss three news trends that have emerged from people's use of social media.

5. What is the relationship between mobile media and news delivery? Explain.

Working the Web

This list includes sites mentioned in the chapter and others to give you greater insight into professional news media organizations.

Association for Education in Journalism and Mass Communication (AEJMC)

aejmc.org

Founded in 1912 by Willard Grosvenor Bleyer and formerly known as the American Association of Teachers of Journalism, AEJMC is a nonprofit organization comprised of more than 3,700 educators, students and media professionals around the world. It is the oldest and largest alliance of journalism and mass communication administrators at the collegiate level. AEJMC works to encourage high curriculum standards in the classroom as well as in the selection of research subjects and methods.

American Journalism Historians Association (AJHA)

ajha.wildapricot.org

Established in 1981, AJHA, through its annual convention, regional meetings, committees, publications, speakers and awards, works to emphasize the importance of journalism history "and apply this knowledge to the advancement of society."

American Society of Journalists and Authors (ASJA)

asja.org

Founded in 1948, ASJA is the nation's professional organization for independent nonfiction writers. The association has more than 1,100 members who are freelance writers of articles, trade books and various other forms of nonfiction. ASJA ensures all of its members maintain high ethical standards and supports the right for freelancers to control the publication and financial profitability of their works.

Center for Investigative Reporting (CIR)

revealnews.org

CIR was founded in 1977 with a focus on consistently shining "a bright light on injustice and protect[ing] the most vulnerable in our society." CIR is based in San Francisco and its Reveal Web site houses investigative print stories as well as television and radio programming and podcasts.

Committee to Protect Journalists (CPJ)

cpj.org

CPJ works to ensure the "free flow of news and commentary by taking action wherever journalists are attacked, imprisoned, killed, kidnapped, threatened, censored or harassed." The CPJ site has resources journalists worldwide can access for emergency assistance for themselves and their families; a listing of journalists who have been killed annually and since 1992; streaming audio and video news and analysis of instances in which journalists have faced or are currently facing dangerous circumstances throughout the world; and listings of CPJ's advocacy campaigns, scholarships and public support programs.

Cyberjournalist.net

cyberjournalist.net

This news and resource site was established and is maintained by former digital media executive Jonathon Dube. Cyberjournalist.net focuses on how the convergence of traditional and contemporary technologies is changing the methods and practices of the news media. Included on the site are sections on the Future of Media, Innovation and Social Media.

Fox Movietone News

foxnews.com/on-air/movietone-news/index.html

This site houses an archive of the Fox Movietone News reels that ran in movie theaters from 1927 to 1963. Movietone video clips on topics such as sports, Hollywood, World War II and a variety of important historical events are available on the site.

Investigative Reporters and Editors (IRE)

ire.org

This organization, dedicated to improving the quality of investigative reporting, provides educational services to reporters and editors and works to maintain high professional investigative journalism standards. The site features news and publications with examples of investigative reporting and suggested story ideas, information on conferences and workshops hosted by IRE, and job and resource centers for members as well as a link to the National Institute for Computer-Assisted Reporting (NICAR) and DocumentCloud.

National Association of Black Journalists (NABJ)

nabj.org

Celebrating 40 years as the organization promoting the interests of African American media professionals, educators and students throughout the U.S., NABJ offers online access to and information on task forces maintained by the association regarding digital journalists and visual, sports, print and broadcast journalism. Additional resources include online versions of the association's monthly publication, the *NABJ Journal*, as well as the *NABJ Style Guide* and Career Center.

National Association of Hispanic Journalists (NAHJ)

nahj.org

NAHJ is the largest Latino media professional organization in the U.S. Established in 1984, NAHJ's mission "is to increase the number of Latinos in the newsrooms" and to work toward "fair and accurate representation of Latinos in news media." The site includes information on NAHJ conferences as well as the association's scholarships and awards.

National Lesbian and Gay Journalists Association (NLGJA), also known as the Association of Lesbian, Gay, Bisexual and Transgender (LGBT) Journalists

nlgja.org

Founded in 1990 by Roy Aarons, NLGJA is an organization of "journalists, media professionals, educators and students working from within the news industry to foster fair and accurate coverage of LGBT issues." The NLGJA site provides information about professional development for its members; local NLGJA chapters, at-large chapters and student chapters; the LGBT Stylebook and Journalists Toolbox; the Rapid Response Task Force; and Connect—the association's student training project.

Native American Journalists Association (NAJA)

naja.com

NAJA is the media professional organization that represents Native American journalists through "programs and actions designed to enrich journalism and promote Native cultures." Recognizing Native Americans as "distinct peoples based on tradition and culture," NAJA is committed to increasing the representation of Native journalists in mainstream media. The site contains information on the association's annual conference, scholarships and awards, as well as resources regarding "Mascots and Media," the Native Health News Alliance and the NAJA legal hotline.

Online News Association (ONA)

journalists.org

ONA's more than 2,200 members are producers, content editors, news directors, reporters, bloggers, technologists, designers and academics "who are creating and refining the online medium at breakneck speed." ONA offers webinars and in-person workshops with and for those who produce news for all of the current media digital delivery systems and platforms. In addition, ONA offers a variety of awards, fellowships, grants and scholarships.

Pew Research Center: Journalism and Media

journalism.org

This nonpartisan research organization within the Pew Research Center think tank uses empirical methods to evaluate and study the performance of the press. Its goal is to help journalists and consumers develop a better understanding of what the press is delivering. Features of the site include Journalism Resources—with links to organizations, schools and career information and the Pew Research database—and the project's annual report, *State of the News Media*.

Pew Research Center: U.S. Politics and Policy

people-press.org

An independent, nonpartisan public policy analysis organization within the Pew Research Center think tank, the Pew Research Center for U.S. Politics and Policy studies attitudes toward the press, politics and public policy issues. The organization's site has Survey Reports by the Center on a variety of current media issues and demographics as well as findings of polls sponsored by various media organizations.

Poynter Institute

poynter.org

Founded in 1975 by *St. Petersburg Times* publisher Norman Poynter and formerly known as the Modern Media Institute,

the Poynter Institute is a unique school where former and current journalists from around the world come to explore best practices and work to improve their skills as members of the "21st Century media." The Poynter Institute is housed near the University of South Florida, St. Petersburg campus and maintains its controlling ownership interest in the *Tampa Bay Times*, Florida's largest daily newspaper.

Talking Points Memo (TPM)

talkingpointsmemo.com

The flagship blog of TPM Media, LLC, Talking Points Memo is a digital U.S. news and politics publication with an obvious and unapologetic liberal perspective. Founded by Josh Marshall, now the TPM editor and publisher, Talking Points is based in New York City and maintains a bureau office in Washington, D.C.

UNITY: Journalists for Diversity

unityjournalists.org

This alliance of four national associations—Asian American Journalists Association, National Association of Black Journalists, National Association of Hispanic Journalists and the Native American Journalists Association—advocates news coverage about people of color and challenges organizations at all levels to reflect the nation's diversity. Its goals include raising awareness and participation of the media industry in understanding diverse cultures, increasing and broadening news coverage focused on people of color and dispelling racial and ethnic stereotypes and myths.

Vanderbilt Television News Archive

tvnews.vanderbilt.edu

"The world's most extensive and complete archive of television news" holds network evening news broadcasts from ABC, CBS and NBC from 1968 to the present, as well as an hour of daily news programs from CNN (beginning in 1995) and Fox News (beginning in 2004). DVD duplications of entire broadcasts as well as compilation videotapes of individual news stories may be borrowed for a fee.

Impact/Action Videos are concise news features on various topics created exclusively for *Media/Impact*. Find them in *Media/Impact*'s MindTap at cengagebrain.com.

MindTap®

Log on to MindTap for *Media/Impact* to access a variety of additional material—including learning objectives, chapter readings with highlighting and note-taking, **Impact/Action Videos**, activities, and comprehension quizzes—that will guide you through this chapter.

AP Images/David Goldman

Mass media effects research focuses on the relationship between the mass media and social movements, such as the campaign against gun violence. On June 20, 2015, marchers demonstrate in front of the Daughters of the Confederacy Building in memory of nine victims who died in a shooting at the Emanuel AME Church in Charleston, S.C.

What's Ahead?

- Early Mass Media Studies Assess Impact
- Scholars Look for Patterns
- How TV Affects Children's Behavior
- Do the Mass Media Cause Violence?
- National Political Campaigns Depend on Mass Media
- Cost of Political Advertising Skyrockets
- Voters and Campaigns Use the Internet and Social Media
- Mass Media Reflect Social Values
- Mass Media Slow to Reflect Ethnic Diversity
- Mass Media Face Gay, Lesbian and Transgender Issues
- How to Analyze Media Effects

> "Younger voters tend to be not just consumers of news and current events but conduits as well—sending out e-mailed links and videos to friends and their social networks."
>
> —BRIAN STELTER, POLITICAL ANALYST, *THE NEW YORK TIMES*

Researchers at the Southern Illinois University School of Medicine have identified a new psychiatric condition they have dubbed "celebrity worship syndrome." This affliction is an unhealthy interest in the rich and famous. People who admire celebrities often want to be just like them, even though some celebrities set examples that aren't very positive. Celebrity worship is just one example of the effect of mass media on our lives.

Today, scholars understand that the media have different effects on different types of people with differing results, and generalizations about the media's effects are easy to make but difficult to prove. "We do not fully understand at present what the media system is doing to individual behavior, much less to American culture," according to media scholars William L. Rivers and Wilbur Schramm. "The media cannot simply be seen as stenciling images on a blank mind. That is too superficial a view of the communication process."

Early Mass Media Studies Assess Impact

The concept that the media have different effects on different types of people is relatively new. Early media observers were certain that a one-to-one relationship existed between what people read, heard and saw and what people did with that information. They also believed that the effects were the same for everyone.

The magic bullet theory, discussed later in the chapter (see "The Payne Fund Studies," p. 257) and sometimes called the hypodermic needle theory, alleged that ideas

from the media were in direct causal relation to behavior. The theory held that the media could inject ideas into people the way liquids are injected through a needle. This early distrust of the media still pervades many people's thinking today, although the theory has been disproved.

Mass media research, like other social science research, is based on a continuum of thought, with each new study advancing slightly the knowledge from the studies that have come before. This is what has happened to the magic bullet theory. Eventually, the beliefs that audiences absorbed media messages uncritically and that all people reacted the same to each message were proven untrue. Research disclosed that analyzing media effects is a very complex task.

Some media research had been done before television use became widespread in the mid-1950s, but TV prompted scholars to take a closer look at media's effects. Two scholars made particularly provocative assertions about how the media influence people's lives: David M. Potter and Marshall McLuhan.

David Potter, a historian, arrived at just the right moment—when the public and the scholarly community were anxiously trying to analyze media's effects on society. In his book *People of Plenty*, published in 1954, Potter first articulated the idea that American society is a consumer society driven primarily by advertising and the images advertising promotes.

Potter asserted that American advertising is rooted in American abundance: "Advertising is not badly needed in an economy of scarcity, because total demand is usually equal to or in excess of total supply, and every producer can normally sell as much as he produces. . . . It is when potential supply outstrips demand—that is,

Chevy puts the purr in performance!

The dashing new Corvette (left) and the Bel Air Sport Coupe.

Fotosearch/Getty Images

In *People of Plenty*, David Potter first identified the idea that America is a consumer society driven primarily by marketing and the images advertising promotes, such as the modern family portrayed in this ad, a 1957 Chevrolet Bel Air for her and a Chevrolet Corvette for him. The cars are shown parked in front of a modern ranch-style house with a two-car garage, a luxury at the time.

when abundance prevails—that advertising begins to fulfill a really essential economic function."

Potter also warned about the dangers of advertising: "Advertising has in its dynamics no motivation to seek the improvement of the individual or to impart qualities of social usefulness. . . . It has no social goals and no social responsibility for what it does with its influence." Potter's perspective was important in shaping the critical view of modern advertising. *People of Plenty* is still in print today.

Scholars Look for Patterns

Like Potter, Canadian author and educator Marshall McLuhan arrived at just the right moment. In the 1960s, McLuhan piqued the public's interest with his phrase "The medium is the message," which he later parodied in the title of his book *The Medium Is the Massage*. One of his conclusions was that the widespread use of television was a landmark in the history of the world, "retribalizing" society and creating a "global village" of people who use media to communicate.

McLuhan suggested that electronic media messages are inherently different from print messages—to watch information on TV is different from reading the same information in a newspaper. McLuhan never offered systematic proof for his ideas, and some people criticized him as a charlatan, but his concepts still are debated widely.

Scholars who analyze the media today look for patterns in media effects, predictable results and statistical evidence to document how the media affect us. Precisely because the media are ubiquitous, studies of their effects on American society are far from conclusive. In this chapter, you will learn about some of the major studies and some of the recent assertions about the role that the media play in our lives.

Mass media research today includes mass media effects research and mass media content analysis. **Mass media effects research** tries to analyze how people use the information they receive from the media—whether political advertising changes people's voting behavior, for example. **Mass media content analysis** examines what is presented by the media—how many children's programs portray violent behavior, for example. Sometimes these two types of analysis (effects research and content analysis) are combined in an attempt to evaluate the effect of a specific type of content on a specific audience.

The Payne Fund Studies

The prestigious Payne Fund sponsored the first major study of media in 1929. It contained 12 reports on media effects. One of these studies concentrated on the effects of movies on children. In his interviews, researcher Herbert Blumer simply asked teenagers what they remembered about the movies they had seen as children. Using this unsystematic approach, he reported that the teenagers had been greatly influenced by the movies because they *said* they had been greatly influenced.

Blumer's conclusion and other conclusions of the Payne Fund studies about the media's direct, one-to-one effect on people were accepted without question, mainly because these were the first major studies of

Mass Media Effects Research An attempt to analyze how people use the information they receive from the media.

Mass Media Content Analysis An attempt to analyze how mass media programming influences behavior.

IMPACT

Society

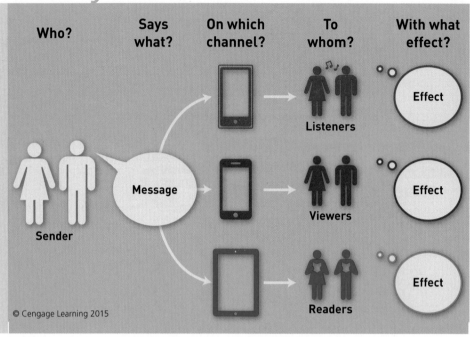

© Cengage Learning 2015

ILLUSTRATION 13.1

Lasswell's Model Asks Five Questions

The Lasswell model analyzes the communication process by asking five questions: Who? Says what? On which channel? To whom? With what effect?

media effects, and the results were widely reported. The Payne Fund studies were the source of the ***magic bullet theory***, the belief that media messages directly and measurably affect people's behavior.

The Payne Fund studies also contributed ammunition for the Motion Picture Producers and Distributors Association production code, adopted in 1930, which regulated movie content.

The Cantril Study

The Martians who landed in New Jersey in the Mercury Theatre "War of the Worlds" broadcast of October 30, 1939 (see **Chapter 6,** "'The War of the Worlds' Challenges Radio's Credibility," p. 109), sparked the next major study of media effects, conducted by Hadley Cantril at Princeton University. The results of the Cantril study contradicted the findings of the Payne Fund studies and disputed the magic bullet theory.

Cantril wanted to find out why certain people believed the Mercury Theatre broadcast and others did not. After interviewing 135 people, Cantril concluded that high critical-thinking ability was the key. Better-educated people were much more likely to decide the broadcast was a fake. This finding might seem to be self-evident today, but the importance of the Cantril study is that it differentiated among listeners: People with different personality characteristics interpreted the broadcast differently.

The Lasswell Model

In 1948, political scientist Harold D. Lasswell designed a model to describe the process of communication that is still used today. Lasswell said the communication process could be analyzed by answering the five questions shown in **Illustration 13.1**.

Lasswell said you could analyze the process of communication by determining who the sender is and what the sender says. Next, you must identify which channel—or method—of communication the sender used. Then you must examine the audience and define the effect on that audience. Because Lasswell described the communication process so succinctly, most communications research still focuses on his five original questions.

How TV Affects Children's Behavior

The 1950s were a time of adjustment to the new medium of television, which at first was a novelty and then became a necessity. Since 1960, four of the major studies of the effects of television have focused on children.

> **Magic Bullet Theory** The assertion that media messages directly and measurably affect people's behavior.

Television in the Lives of Children

Published in 1961, by Wilbur Schramm, Jack Lyle and Edwin Parker, *Television in the Lives of Our Children* was the first major study of the effects of television on children. Researchers interviewed 6,000 children and 1,500 parents, as well as teachers and school officials.

Schramm and his associates reported that children were exposed to television more than to any other mass medium. On average, 5-year-old children watched television two hours every weekday. TV viewing time reached three hours by the time these children were 8 years old. In a finding that often was subsequently cited, Schramm said that from the ages of 3 to 16, children spent more time in front of the television set than they spent in school.

Children used television for fantasy, diversion and instruction, Schramm said. Children who had troubled relationships with their parents and children who were classified as aggressive were more likely to turn to television for fantasy, but Schramm could find no serious problems related to television viewing. Schramm also found, in support of Cantril, that different children showed different effects.

Television and Social Behavior

Television and Social Behavior, a study of the effects of television, was funded by $1 million appropriated by Congress in 1969, after the violent decade of the 1960s. The U.S. Department of Health, Education and Welfare, which sponsored the study, appointed a distinguished panel of social scientists to undertake the research.

The study's major findings, published in six volumes in 1971, concerned the effects of television violence on children. A content analysis of one week of prime-time programming, conducted by George Gerbner of the University of Pennsylvania, reported that eight out of ten prime-time shows contained violence.

Television and Social Behavior did not make a direct connection between TV programming and violent behavior, however. The report said there was a "tentative" indication that television viewing caused aggressive behavior. According to the study, TV violence affected only *some* children who were already classified as aggressive children and *only* in some environments.

Even though the report avoided a direct statement about violent behavior in children as a result of television viewing, the U.S. surgeon general called for immediate action against violence on television. The television industry dismissed the results as inconclusive.

The Early Window

Several studies since 1971 have suggested that television violence causes aggression among children. In their 1988 book *The Early Window: Effects of Television on Children and Youth*, psychologists Robert M. Liebert and Joyce Sprafkin urged caution in drawing broad conclusions about the subject:

> Studies using various methods have supported the proposition that TV violence can induce aggressive and/or antisocial behavior in children. Whether the effect will hold only for the most susceptible individuals (e.g., boys from disadvantaged homes) or whether it will hold for a wider range of youngsters obviously depends in part upon the measure being used. . . . The occurrence of serious violent or criminal acts results from several forces at once. Researchers have said that TV violence is *a* cause of aggressiveness, not that it is *the* cause of aggressiveness. There is no one, single cause of any social behavior.

Still, criticism of television's effects on children's behavior persists, especially the effects of advertising.

Television Advertising to Children

The effects of advertising on adults have been analyzed widely, but in 1979 the advertising of children's products became an object of serious government attention with the Federal Trade Commission's release of the 340-page report *Television Advertising to Children*. The report, based on a two-year study, was designed to document the dangers of advertising sugar-based products to children, but embedded in the report was some provocative information about children's advertising.

Children are an especially vulnerable audience, said the FTC. The report concluded:

1. The average child sees 20,000 commercials a year, or about 3 hours of TV advertising a week.

2. Many children regard advertising as just another form of programming and do not distinguish between programs and ads.

3. Televised advertising for any product to children who do not understand the intent of the commercial is unfair and deceptive.

The report called for a ban on advertising to very young children, a ban on sugared products in advertising directed to children younger than age 12, and a requirement for counter-ads with dental and nutritional information to balance ads for sugared products.

The FTC report and subsequent research about children's advertising suggest that younger children pay more attention to television advertising than older children. But by sixth grade, children adopt what has been called a "global distrust" of advertising.

Alberto E. Rodriguez/Getty Images

Children are an especially vulnerable mass media audience because they tend to pay more attention to the TV ads that surround the programs. On June 2, 2015, the Disney Channel launched the second season of *Girl Meets World*, with advertising aimed at a young audience.

Linking TV to School Performance

There have been many studies about children and television, such as the National Institute of Mental Health (NIMH) report. In 1981, a California study suggested a link between television viewing and poor school performance.

The California Assessment Program (CAP), which tests academic achievement, included a new question: "On a typical weekday, about how many hours do you watch TV?" The students were given a choice ranging from 0 to 6 or more hours. An analysis of the answers to that question from more than 10,000 sixth graders was matched with the children's scores on the achievement test.

The results suggested a consistent relationship between viewing time and achievement. Students who said they watched a lot of television scored lower in reading, writing and mathematics than students who didn't watch any television. The average scores for students who said they viewed six or more hours of television a day were six to eight points lower than for those children who said they watched less than a half-hour of television a day.

In 2010, new research further attempted to define whether children are poor students because they watch a lot of television or whether children who watch a lot of television are poor students for other reasons. Canadian researchers released a study in the May 2010 issue of the journal *Pediatrics and Adolescent Medicine* that linked a decline in classroom engagement with early television viewing. The study, *Prospective Associations Between Early Childhood Television Exposure and Academic, Psychosocial, and Physical Well-being by Middle Childhood,* followed the TV viewing habits of 1,314 toddlers until they entered fourth grade.

From their analysis of the data, the researchers concluded that children who watched a lot of TV in their early years were less likely to perform well when they reached the fourth grade. The researchers noted that there were "long term risks associated with higher levels of [TV] exposure."

In 2011, a study conducted by Common Sense Media, a San Francisco nonprofit group, reported that children younger than 8 years old spend more time using media than ever, and more than half of these children have access to a mobile device like a smartphone or a tablet. Still, according to the study, TV accounts for the largest amount of screen time.

"The report also documents for the first time an emerging 'app gap' in which affluent children are likely to use mobile educational games while those in low-income families are the most likely to have televisions in their rooms," reported *The New York Times*.

This new aspect of the effects of the digital divide (see **Chapter 9**)—the difference in media access between disadvantaged families and the rest of the nation—merits further study.

Do the Mass Media Cause Violence?

The search for a possible direct link between violent behavior and violence in the mass media has existed for more than 30 years. The first major modern study, *Television and Behavior: Ten Years of Scientific Progress and Implications for the Eighties*, published in 1982 by the National Institute for Mental Health, compiled information from 2,500 individual studies of television. According to NIMH, three findings of these 2,500 studies, taken together, were that:

1. A direct correlation exists between televised violence and aggressive behavior, yet there is no way to predict who will be affected and why.

2. Heavy television viewers are more fearful, less trusting and more apprehensive than light viewers.

3. Children who watch what the report called "pro social" programs (programs that are socially constructive, such as *Sesame Street* and *SpongeBob*) are more likely to act responsibly.

Most of the latest studies of the mass media's role have continued to reinforce the concept that different people in different environments react to mass media differently.

In 1994, cable operators and network broadcasters agreed to use an independent monitor to review programming for violent content. The agreement came after Congress held hearings on the subject in 1993 and threatened to introduce regulations to curb violence if the industry didn't police itself. The agreement also called for the development of violence ratings for TV programming and endorsed a v-chip—*v* for "violence"—technology that would be built into a television set to allow parents to block programs rated as violent.

The monitoring is qualitative rather than quantitative, which means the programs are examined for content, not just for incidents of violence. The Telecommunications Act of 1996 established a television ratings code for TV content, which standardized the labels.

Then in 2011, the U.S. Supreme Court ruled 7-2 against a California law that would have restricted the sale and rental of violent video games to minors. After the decision, the Entertainment Software Association, which represents video and computer game makers, voluntarily created a ratings system.

The court ruling and industry ratings systems continue the tradition of media self-regulation in the U.S. That is, the video game, broadcast, recording and movie media industries have responded—often reluctantly—to congressional pressure to restrict access to media content by monitoring themselves rather than invite government content regulation.

Chris Ferguson, a professor at Texas A&M International, says that recent research about the effects of videogame violence has been "quite inconsistent." In a 2012 article for the *Journal of Psychiatric Research*, Ferguson and his co-authors looked at 165 video game players over three years and reported that they could not directly link young people who played violent video games to youth aggression or dating violence. The researchers said that "depression, antisocial personality traits, exposure to family violence and peer influences" were the best way to predict aggression-related behavior.

Other researchers argue that, while it is impossible to directly link gun violence to video games, there could still be some connection. Professor Brad Bushman, of The Ohio State University, in dissenting comments to the 2011 U.S. Supreme Court decision, noted that the

David McNew/Getty Images

The relationship between violence portrayed in video games and violent behavior in American society continues to spark debate. On June 15, 2015, Ubisoft Quebec Creative Director Marc-Alexas Cole announces the release of the company's latest version of *Assassin's Creed Syndicate* at the annual Electronic Entertainment Expo in Los Angeles.

connection between violent video games and gun violence "shouldn't be dismissed as a trivial cause either."

National Political Campaigns Depend on Mass Media

The mass media have transformed politics in ways that could never have been imagined when President Franklin D. Roosevelt introduced what were called Fireside Chats in 1933. Roosevelt was the first president to use the media effectively to stimulate public support.

The newest technology introduced during FDR's era—radio—gave him immediate access to a national audience. Roosevelt's media skill became an essential element in promoting his economic programs. Today, politics and the media seem irreversibly dependent on each other, one of the legacies of Roosevelt's presidency.

The Fireside Chats

In March 1933, just after he was inaugurated, FDR looked for a way to avoid a financial panic after he announced that he was closing the nation's banks. For a week, the country cooled off while Congress scrambled for a solution. On the Sunday night eight days after his inauguration, Roosevelt used radio to calm the nation's anxiety before the banks began to reopen on Monday. FDR went down to the basement of the White House to give his first Fireside Chat. There was a fireplace in the basement, but no fire was burning. The president could not find his script, so he borrowed a mimeographed copy from a reporter.

In his first address to the nation as president, FDR gave a banking lesson to his audience of 60 million people: "I want to talk for a few minutes with the people of the United States about banking. . . . First of all, let me state the simple fact that when you deposit money in a bank, the bank does not put the money into a safe deposit vault. It invests your money in many different forms." When he finished, he turned to people in the room and asked, "Was I all right?" America had its first media president, an elected leader talking directly to the people through the media.

Roosevelt's chats are cited as a legendary example of mass media politics, yet he gave only 8 Fireside Chats in his first term of office. His other meetings with the press also enhanced his reputation for press access: In 13 years in office, he held more than 900 press conferences.

The People's Choice

The first major study of the influence of mass media on politics was *The People's Choice*, undertaken precisely because FDR seemed to be such a good media politician. This comprehensive examination of voter behavior in the 1940 presidential election was quite systematic.

Researchers Paul Lazarsfeld, Bernard Berelson and Hazel Gaudet followed 3,000 people in rural Erie County, Ohio, from May to November 1940 to determine what influenced the way these people voted for president. The researchers tracked how people's minds changed over the 6-month period and then attempted to determine why. (It is important to remember this study was undertaken before television.)

Radio had become the prevailing medium for political advertising beginning in 1932, when the two parties spent more money for radio time than for any other campaign item. What effect, the researchers wanted to know, did the media have on people's choosing one candidate over another? The results were provocative.

Lazarsfeld and his colleagues found that only 8 percent of the voters in the study were actually *converted* by the media. The majority of voters (53 percent) were *reinforced* in their beliefs by the media, and 14 percent were *activated* to vote. Mixed effects or no effects were shown by the remaining 25 percent of the people.

Lazarsfeld said opinion leaders, who got their information from the media, shared this information with their friends. The study concluded that instead of changing people's beliefs, the media primarily activate people to vote and reinforce already held opinions. *The People's Choice* also made the following findings:

▶ Family and friends have more effect on people's decisions than the media.

In 1932, Paul Lazarsfeld and his colleagues studied people's voting habits to attempt to document the media's effect on their decisions. In 1942, Lazarsfeld (right) worked with Dr. Frank Stanton (left, future president of the CBS network) on an audience analysis machine. Viewers pressed a button on the Lazarsfeld-Stanton Program Analyzer when they saw a program they liked, and the machine printed out the results. The machine never gained widespread use.

CBS Photo Archive/Getty Images

▶ The media have different effects on different people, reinforcing Cantril's findings.

▶ A major source of information about candidates is other people.

The finding that opinion leaders often provide and shape information for the general population was a bonus—the researchers hadn't set out specifically to learn this. This transmission of information and ideas from mass media to opinion leaders and then to friends and acquaintances is called the ***two-step flow*** of communication.

The Unseeing Eye

In 1976, a second study of the media and presidential elections, called *The Unseeing Eye: The Myth of Television Power in National Elections*, revealed findings that paralleled those of *The People's Choice*.

With a grant from the National Science Foundation, Thomas E. Patterson and Robert D. McClure supervised interviews with 2,707 people from early September to just before Election Day in the November 1972 race between George McGovern and Richard Nixon. The study did not discuss political media events, but it did analyze television campaign news and political advertising.

> **Two-Step Flow** The transmission of information and ideas from mass media to opinion leaders and then to friends.

The researchers concluded that although political advertising influenced 16 percent of the people they interviewed, only 7 percent were manipulated by political ads. The researchers defined people who were *influenced* as those who decided to vote for a candidate based mostly on what they knew and only slightly on what the ads told them. The 7 percent of the people in the survey who were *manipulated*, according to Patterson and McClure, were people who cited political advertising as a major factor in their choices. Patterson and McClure concluded that political advertising on TV has little effect on most people:

> By projecting their political biases . . . people see in candidates' commercials pretty much what they want to see. Ads sponsored by the candidate who shares their politics get a good response. They like what he has to say. And they like him. Ads sponsored by the opposing candidate are viewed negatively. They object to what he says. And they object to him.

Even though political ads affect a minority of people, it is important to remember that in some elections the difference of a few percentage points can decide the outcome. Political advertising is designed to sway these swing voters. This is why political advertising continues to play such an important campaign role.

Election Campaigns on Television

So far, no convincing systematic evidence has shown that the mass media change the voting behavior of *large* groups of people. Yet, since John F. Kennedy debated Richard Nixon during the 1960 presidential campaign, many people deeply feel that the media—television in particular—have changed elections and electoral politics.

The series of debates between Kennedy and Nixon in 1960 were the first televised debates of presidential candidates in American history. Kennedy's performance in the debates often is credited for his narrow victory in the election. In his book *Presidents and the Press*, media scholar Joseph C. Spear wrote:

> As the panel began asking questions, Nixon tended to go on the defensive, answering Kennedy point by point and ignoring his huge audience beyond the camera.
>
> Kennedy, by contrast, appeared rested, calm, informed, cocksure. Whatever the question, he aimed his answer at the millions of Americans viewing the program in their living rooms.
>
> It was an unmitigated disaster for Nixon. In the second, third and fourth debates, he managed to recover somewhat from his initial poor performance, but it was too late. Surveys showed that an overwhelming percentage of the television audience had judged Kennedy the victor.

AP Photos

The series of TV debates in 1960 between Senator John F. Kennedy (left) and Vice President Richard Nixon (right) were the first widely televised debates of presidential candidates. Kennedy's debate performance often is credited for his narrow victory in the election. The two are shown shaking hands at their fourth and final debate on October 21, 1960.

One legacy of Kennedy's television victory was that national political campaigns came to depend almost entirely on TV to promote presidential candidates, and televised presidential debates became a staple of every presidential election.

Television is a very efficient way to reach large numbers of people quickly, but campaigning on television also distances the candidates from direct public contact. Instead of meeting the public in person to promote and debate issues, candidates can isolate themselves from public scrutiny by using television ads to portray their views.

Cost of Political Advertising Skyrockets

Television advertising also is very expensive. The cost of national and statewide campaigns—especially since the year 2000—has skyrocketed. Presidential, gubernatorial, congressional and senatorial candidates typically devote 40 to 60 percent of their campaign budgets to advertising.

Many candidates run in metropolitan areas like Los Angeles, where the media markets are much larger than their districts. Television advertising in large markets reaches a bigger audience than the candidates need, so they also use direct mail and the Internet. But a candidate running for Congress in Des Moines, Iowa, might use mainly local television ads because the entire district is included in the local TV station's coverage area. Historian James David Barber describes the public's role in politics:

> Particularly since television has brought national politics within arm's length of nearly every American, the great majority probably has at least some experience of the quadrennial passing parade. But millions vote their old memories and habits and interests, interpreting new perceptions that strike their senses to coincide with their prejudices and impulses.
>
> At the other end of the participation spectrum are those compulsive readers of *The New York Times* who delve into every twitch and turn of the contest. Floating in between are large numbers of Americans who pick up on the election's major events and personalities, following with mild but open interest the dominant developments.
>
> Insofar as the campaign makes a difference, it is this great central chunk of The People who swing the choice. They respond to what they see and hear. They are interested but not obsessed. They edit out the minor blips of change and wait for the campaign to gather force around a critical concern. They reach their conclusions on the basis of a widely shared common experience. It is through that middling throng of the population that the pulse of politics beats most powerfully, synchronizing to its insistent rhythm the varied vibrations of discrete events.

The rising cost of running for public office can exclude people without the means to raise huge sums of money. Since 1972, when political campaigns first began widespread use of television advertising, presidential campaign expenditures have skyrocketed from less than $2 *million*

WE WANT TO WARN YOU THAT THE CANDIDATE'S COMMENTS HAVE YET TO BE SPUN, SO YOU MAY HAVE TO FORMULATE YOUR OWN OPINION.

BREAKING POLITICAL NEWS

Dave Carpenter/Cartoon Stock

in 1972 to $6 *billion* in 2012. (See **Illustration 13.2,** "TV Political Campaign Spending in Presidential Elections, 1972–2012," p. 265.) Most of this money went to pay for TV and Internet advertising.

Today the mass media are an essential part of American politics, changing the behavior of politicians as well as the electorate, which raises important questions about the role of the nation's mass media in governance and the conduct of elections.

Voters and Campaigns Use the Internet and Social Media

The year 2004 was the first presidential election year when the Internet began to play a role in national politics, as citizen blogs became an outlet for political debate, and bloggers covered the presidential campaigns along with members of the established press corps.

The New York Times noted in 2004, "Democrats and Republicans are sharply increasing their use of e-mail, interactive Web sites, candidate and party blogs and text messaging to raise money, organize get-out-the-vote efforts and assemble crowds for rallies. The Internet, they say, appears to be far more efficient, and less costly, than the traditional tools of politics, notably door knocking and telephone banks."

The Pew Research Center reported that 75 million Americans used the Internet for political news during the 2004 presidential election. "The effect of the Internet on politics will be every bit as transformational as television was," Republican national chairman Ken Mehlman told *The Times.* "If you want to get your message out, the old way of paying someone to make a TV ad is insufficient: You need your message out through the Internet, through e-mail, through talk radio."

Political consultants also experimented with political podcasts that featured daily downloaded messages from candidates and viral marketing videos supporting the candidates. Supporters passed along the video messages through e-mail to their friends—an online chain of free Internet political messaging that reached young voters more directly than traditional advertising.

By 2008, the Internet had become a central force in national politics. "The 2008 race for the White House fundamentally upended the way presidential campaigns are fought in the United States," wrote Adam Nagourney of *The New York Times.* "It has rewritten the rules on how to reach voters, raise money, organize supporters, manage the news media, track and mold public opinion, and wage—and withstand—political attacks, including many carried by blogs that did not exist four years ago."

According to Mark McKinnon, a senior adviser to President George W. Bush's 2000 and 2004 campaigns,

IMPACT

Money

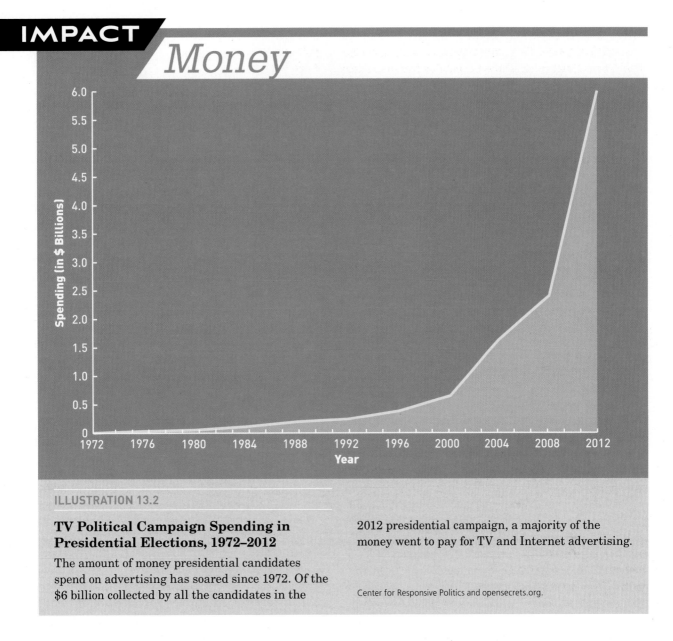

ILLUSTRATION 13.2

TV Political Campaign Spending in Presidential Elections, 1972–2012

The amount of money presidential candidates spend on advertising has soared since 1972. Of the $6 billion collected by all the candidates in the 2012 presidential campaign, a majority of the money went to pay for TV and Internet advertising.

Center for Responsive Politics and opensecrets.org.

the year 2008 was when "campaigns leveraged the Internet in ways never imagined. The year we went to warp speed. The year the paradigm got turned upside down and truly became bottom up instead of top down." The Obama campaign especially used the Internet and social media, such as YouTube, as well as cell-phone text messaging. The Internet connection also helped the campaign raise record amounts of money.

Also in 2008, many younger voters sought alternative sources of information about the campaigns such as *The Daily Show* with Jon Stewart, and they shared blogs, video clips and online discussions through Facebook and YouTube, social media sites that were not a large factor in the 2004 election.

"According to interviews and recent surveys, younger voters tend to be not just consumers of news and current events but conduits as well—sending out e-mailed links and videos to friends and their social networks. And in turn, they rely on friends and online connections for news to come to them," reported political writer Brian Stelter. "In essence, they are replacing the professional filter—reading *The Washington Post*, clicking on CNN.com—with a social one.

"Young people also identify online discussions with friends and videos as important sources of election information," wrote Stelter. "The habits suggest that younger readers find themselves going straight to the source, bypassing the context and analysis that seasoned journalists provide."

However, even though Internet political marketing may reach large groups of people quickly and efficiently, there is no clear understanding yet of how—or

Steve Starr/Corbis News/Corbis

During the 2012 election, most political campaigns used the Internet to spread their messages, but they still relied on TV for the majority of their advertising. Students at the University of Denver watch the first 2012 presidential debate on an outside TV screen, two blocks away from where the actual debate took place on campus. The debate drew 67.2 million TV viewers.

Silencing Opposing Viewpoints

Political scientist Elisabeth Noelle-Neumann has asserted that because journalists in all media tend to concentrate on the same major news stories, the audience is assailed on many sides by similar information. Together, the media present the consensus; journalists reflect the prevailing climate of opinion.

As this consensus spreads, people with divergent views, says Noelle-Neumann, may be less likely to voice disagreement with the prevailing point of view. Thus, because of a *"spiral of silence,"* the media gain more influence because opponents of the consensus tend to remain silent. The implication for future research will be to ask whether the media neutralize dissent and create a pattern of social and cultural conformity.

if—Internet political messages can be used to change people's minds. In the 2012 election, most political campaigns used the Internet to spread their messages, but they still relied on television for the majority of their advertising, and expenditures on Internet advertising remained very small.

The total amount spent by presidential candidates for the 2012 elections reached $6 billion, more than twice what the candidates spent in 2008. "Advertising veterans say the stakes are too high to experiment with a medium that, despite its ability to monitor the browsing habits of consumers, might not be effective," reported the *Los Angeles Times*. So, political campaigns are still spending more money on the controlled messages that TV advertising provides rather than the uncontrolled environment of the Internet. However, in the 2012 election, 47 percent of voters said they turned to the Internet for campaign news. (See **Illustration 13.3**, "Number of Voters Who Follow Political Figures on Social Media Increasing," and **Illustration 13.4**, "Voters Follow Political Figures on Social Media to Stay Current, Connected and Informed," p. 267.)

Mass Media Reflect Social Values

Because media research is a continuing process, new ideas will emerge in the next decade from today's ideas and studies. Several provocative recent analyses have extended the boundaries of media research.

Losing a Sense of Place

In his book *No Sense of Place*, published in 1985, Joshua Meyrowitz provided new insight into television's possible effects on society. In the past, says Meyrowitz:

> Parents did not know what their children knew, and children did not know what their parents knew they knew. Similarly, a person of one sex could never be certain of what a member of the other sex knew. . . . Television undermines such behavioral distinctions because it encompasses children and adults, men and women and all other social groups in a single informational sphere or environment. Not only does it provide similar information to everyone, but, even more significant, it provides it publicly and often simultaneously.

This sharing of information, says Meyrowitz, means that subjects that rarely were discussed between men and women, for instance, or between children and adults, have become part of the public dialogue.

A second result of television viewing is the blurred distinction between childhood and adulthood, says Meyrowitz. When print dominated the society as a medium, children's access to adult information was limited. The only way to learn about "adult" concepts was to read about them, so

---

Spiral of Silence The belief that people with divergent views may be reluctant to challenge the consensus of opinion offered by the media.

IMPACT

Convergence

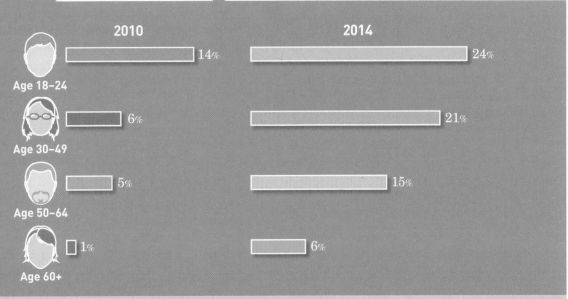

	2010	2014
Age 18–24	14%	24%
Age 30–49	6%	21%
Age 50–64	5%	15%
Age 60+	1%	6%

ILLUSTRATION 13.3

Number of Voters Who Follow Political Figures on Social Media Is Increasing

A survey conducted in 2014 by The Pew Research Center revealed a large increase in the number of voters—especially 30- to 49-year-olds and 50- to 64-year-olds—who follow public figures on social media.

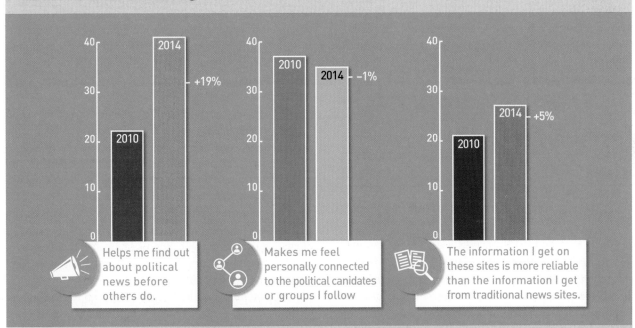

Helps me find out about political news before others do.

Makes me feel personally connected to the political canidates or groups I follow

The information I get on these sites is more reliable than the information I get from traditional news sites.

ILLUSTRATION 13.4

Voters Follow Political Figures on Social Media to Stay Current, Connected and Informed

The main reason people follow public figures on social media is to stay current and learn about political news before others, but social media also make people feel more connected and informed about politics.

Pew Research Center, "Cell Phones, Social Media and Campaign 2014," October 11, 2014. http://www.pewinternet.org/2014/11/03/

typically children were not exposed to adult ideas or problems, and taboo topics remained hidden from children.

In a video world, however, any topic that can be portrayed in pictures on television challenges the boundaries that print places around information. This, says Meyrowitz, causes an early loss of the naïveté of childhood:

> Television removes barriers that once divided people of different ages and reading abilities into different social situations. The widespread use of television is equivalent to a broad social decision to allow young children to be present at wars and funerals, courtships and seductions, criminal plots and cocktail parties. . . . Television thrusts children into a complex adult world, and it provides the impetus for children to ask the meanings of actions and words they would not yet have heard or read about without television.

Meyrowitz concedes that movies offered similar information to children before television, but he says that the pervasiveness of television today makes its effects more widespread.

Complicating recent mass media effect studies is the massive increase in the variety and number of available media sources.

Stereotyping

Journalists often use shorthand labels to characterize ethnic and other groups. As early as 1922, in his book *Public Opinion*, political journalist Walter Lippmann first identified the tendency of journalists to generalize about other people based on fixed ideas:

> When we speak of the mind of a group of people, of the French mind, the militarist mind . . . we are liable to serious confusion unless we agree to separate the instinctive equipment from the stereotypes, the patterns, the formulae which play so decisive a part in building up the mental world to which the native character is adapted and responds. . . . Failure to make this distinction accounts for oceans of loose talk about collective minds, national souls and race psychology.

The image of women portrayed by the media has been the subject of a significant number of contemporary studies. Media researchers who study the stereotyping of women point to past and current media portrayals showing very few women in professional roles or as strong, major characters. (See **Impact/Profile**: "Barbie Can Be a Computer Engineer . . . but Only with the Help of a Man," p. 269.)

The media's overall portrayal of women in mass culture is slowly improving, but in her book *Loving with a Vengeance: Mass-Produced Fantasies for Women*, Tania Modleski says that the portrayal in popular fiction of women in submissive roles goes back to 1740, with the British novel *Pamela*, which was published in America by Benjamin Franklin in 1744. Modleski analyzed the historical content of gothic novels, Harlequin romances and soap operas:

> In Harlequin Romances, the need of women to find meaning and pleasure in activities that are not wholly male-centered such as work or artistic creation is generally scoffed at.
>
> Soap operas also undercut, though in subtler fashion, the idea that a woman might obtain satisfaction from these activities [work or artistic creation]. . . . Indeed, patriarchal myths and institutions are . . . wholeheartedly embraced, although the anxieties and tensions they give rise to may be said to provoke the need for the texts in the first place.

The implication of Modleski's research is that women who read romance novels will believe they should act like the women in the novels they read. A stereotype that has existed since 1740 still shows up in today's mass media, often in advertising campaigns directed at women.

Mass Media Slow to Reflect Ethnic Diversity

Beginning in the year 2000, the U.S. census allowed Americans to use more than one racial category to describe themselves, and the categories have been changed to reflect America's changing face. In the past, people were forced to choose one category from among the following: Black, White, Asian or Pacific Islander, American Indian or Alaska Native, or "Other—specify in writing."

In the 2010 census, 9 million people chose more than one race, a change of about 32 percent since 2000. People who identify with more than one group also were able to check more than one description—African American and American Indian, for example. All government forms are required to use the new categories.

This new census method allows people to identify themselves to the government and shows the evolving social landscape of the U.S. population. Yet the American media have been very slow to acknowledge the nation's rapidly changing population.

Specific media outlets, such as African American and Latino newspapers, magazines and Internet sites, cater to specific audiences. But the mainstream media, especially daily newspapers and the TV networks, traditionally have represented the interests of the mainstream culture. Historically, scores of media studies have documented stereotypical representation and a lack of representation of people of color in all areas of the culture, even though the potential audience for ethnic media is very large.

IMPACT

Profile

Barbie Can Be a Computer Engineer . . . but Only with the Help of a Man

I'll need Steven and Brian's help to turn this into a real game!' laughs computer programmer Barbie in her new book

By Aisha Gani

Breaking away from her pink heels, pink ball gown and oversized pink hairbrush, Barbie—the fashion doll manufactured by Mattel—now has a range of gender-stereotype-breaking books. In the "I can be" series, we learn that Barbie can be president, a sports star and a computer engineer . . . except in the latter case she needs the help of a man.

Pamela Ribon, a writer at Walt Disney animation studios, this week pointed out the sexism on her blog when she picked up the *Barbie: I Can Be a Computer Engineer* children's book, published by Random House US.

In a book intended to inspire young girls, Barbie the programmer, who wears a pink heart-shaped USB drive around her neck, needs help to reboot her computer. And one passage from the book reveals that this computer engineer cannot even code:

At breakfast one morning, Barbie is already hard at work on her laptop.

"What are you doing, Barbie?" asks Skipper.

"I'm designing a game that shows kids how computers work," explains Barbie. "You can make a robot puppy do cute tricks by matching up colored blocks!"

"Your robot puppy is so sweet," says Skipper. "Can I play your game?"

"I'm only creating the design ideas," Barbie says, laughing. "I'll need Steven and Brian's help to turn it into a real game!"

The reviews on Amazon, the online shopping site, have not been complimentary.

Although the mass media's stereotyping of women has improved in recent years, in 2015 Random House issued a new series of "I Can Be" books showing Barbie in nontraditional roles. Still, the book's text suggested that Barbie was incapable of doing the job without a man's help, furthering a gender stereotype.

Bloomberg/Getty Images

Aisha Gani, "Barbie can be a computer engineer . . . but only with the help of a man," theguardian.com, November 19, 2014.

Media scholar Carolyn Martindale, for example, in a content analysis of *The New York Times* from 1934 to 1994, found that most nonwhite groups were visible "only in glimpses." According to Martindale, "The mainstream press in the U.S. has presented minorities as outside, rather than a part of, American society."

After examining 374 episodes of 96 prime-time series on ABC, CBS, NBC, Fox, WB and UPN, the Center for Media and Public Affairs for the National Council of La Raza concluded that only 2 percent of prime-time characters during the 1994–1995 season were Latinos, and most of the roles played by those characters were minor. The study, *Don't Blink: Hispanics in Television Entertainment*, also revealed that although Latino characters were portrayed more positively than they had been in the past, they were most likely to be shown as poor or working class. (See **Impact/Society**: "Hollywood Still Stereotypes Native Americans," p.270.)

IMPACT / *Society*

Hollywood Still Stereotypes Native Americans

By Esther J. Cepeda

It's hard to get upset at Adam Sandler for inanity, recklessness or disrespect. He's never promised anything more than to be a jester for our amusement, a few hours at a time.

This is why it's almost beside the point to mention Sandler in a discussion about whether his upcoming Netflix film, *The Ridiculous Six*, stands as a turning point for the portrayal of American Indians in Hollywood.

The film, which Netflix describes as "a broad satire of Western movies and the stereotypes they popularized, featuring a diverse cast that is not only part of—but in on— the joke," had bits in it so repulsive, such as crude and vulgar "Indian" names, as well as disgusting uses of Native-themed props, that several American Indian actors quit the production.

According to the Associated Press, nine Native American actors and a Native American consultant walked off the set last week after producers told the group to leave if they felt offended because there would be no script changes.

It's difficult to explain how hard this must have been for these actors. They walked away from the job's pay and risk being blacklisted in Hollywood.

Plus, these actors had to have known they were going to get it from all sides. And so they have.

Actor Bonifacio Gurule told an Albuquerque TV station that the majority of Native Americans stayed and that those who exited should "lighten up. . . . It's a comedy, not a documentary."

Navajo Nation President Ben Shelly was bashed after issuing a statement that said, in part, "Our Native American culture and tradition is no joking matter. I applaud these Navajo actors for their courage and conviction to walk off the set in protest. . . . Native people have dealt with negative stereotypes on film for too long."

Which brings us to the question of whether this small insurrection was a game-changer, or whether hurtful portrayals of Native Americans will continue to be the norm in Hollywood.

So far, *Rolling Stone* reports, a producer promised the cast that a disclaimer at the end of the movie would reiterate that Sandler's movie is not an accurate portrayal of Native American culture.

Understatement of the year.

The truth is that the 500-nation Native American culture is richly diverse—with different customs and beliefs—and will never be accurately portrayed in the media until American Indians are integral parts of the production and creative teams that tell stories about individuals, not a monolithic people.

There will probably always be ridiculous portrayals, but for some, this felt like a precedent.

Maybe this will make filmmakers think twice next time. Or maybe inspire more Native American actors to start creating and promoting their own content.

This would be a start.

In April 2015, nine Native American actors walked off the set of an Adam Sandler movie being produced by Netflix to protest the negative stereotypes portrayed in the film. Actor Bonifacio Gurule dismissed the criticism and said the actors should "lighten up. It's a comedy."

Vera Anderson/WireImage

Excerpted from Esther J. Cepeda, "Hollywood Still Stereotypes Native Americans," *Washington Post* as published on sfgate.com, April 30, 2015.

Based on a comprehensive analysis of the nation's newspapers, a 56-page *News Watch* report issued at a convention of the nation's African American, Asian, Latino and Native American journalists concluded that "the mainstream media's coverage of people of color is riddled with old stereotypes, offensive terminology, biased reporting and a myopic interpretation of American society."

To counteract stereotyping, the Center for Integration and Improvement of Journalism at San Francisco State University (which sponsored the study) offered the following Tips for Journalists:

▶ Apply consistent guidelines when identifying people of race. Are the terms considered offensive? Ask individual sources how they wish to be identified.

▶ Only refer to people's ethnic or racial background when it is relevant.

▶ When deciding whether to mention someone's race, ask yourself: Is ethnic/racial identification needed? Is it important to the context of the story?

▶ Consult a supervisor if you are unsure of the offensiveness or relevance of a racial or ethnic term.

▶ Use sensitivity when describing rites and cultural events. Avoid inappropriate comparisons. For example, Kwanzaa is not "African American Christmas."

▶ Be specific when using ethnic or racial identification of individuals. Referring to someone as Filipino American is preferred to calling that person Asian. The latter term is better applied to a group.

The issue of accurate reflection by mass media of a diverse society invites analysis as the face of America grows more complex every day.

Mass Media Face Gay, Lesbian and Transgender Issues

In 1993, newspapers confronted an editorial dilemma when cartoonist Lynn Johnston, who draws the very popular syndicated strip *For Better or For Worse*, decided to reveal that Lawrence, one of the teenagers in the comic strip, was gay. Most newspapers published the strip, but 19 newspapers canceled their contracts for the comic, which was carried by Universal Press Syndicate of Kansas City.

One newspaper editor who refused to carry the strip explained, "We are a conservative newspaper in a conservative town." Another editor said he "felt the sequence condoned homosexuality 'almost to the point of advocacy.'" Responding to criticism that, by revealing Lawrence's sexual preference, she was advocating homosexuality, Johnston said, "You know, that's like advocating left-handedness. Gayness is simply something that exists. My strip is a reality strip, real situations, real

crises, real people." One newspaper executive at a paper that carried the strip wrote, "It seems to me that what we're talking about here isn't the rightness or wrongness of homosexuality. It is about tolerance."

An understanding of the media portrayals of Americans' diverse lifestyles on television grabbed attention in 1997, when the program *Ellen* portrayed two women exchanging a romantic kiss. (Although promoted as the nation's first female television kiss, the first televised romantic lesbian relationship actually had been portrayed on the TV program *L.A. Law* in 1991.)

Same-sex relationship issues remained primarily a subject for the nation's lesbian and gay newspapers and magazines, although in 1996, *The New Yorker* ran a controversial cover that portrayed two men kissing on a Manhattan sidewalk. Bringing the issue to a mainstream audience, as the *Ellen* television program did, presented a dilemma for the TV networks because, when notified beforehand

Marc Stamas/Getty Images

In 2012, Marvel Comics announced that its first openly gay hero, Northstar, would marry his longtime boyfriend, Kyle. Northstar had revealed that he is gay in 1992, one of the first comic characters to do so. A poster showing Kyle and Northstar decorates a commemorative gay marriage ceremony on June 20, 2012, in New York City.

about the content of the program, some local TV stations refused to show the episode. The reluctance of mainstream television to portray alternative relationships was as much a reflection of the networks trying to protect their economic interests as it was a reflection of the nation's social values.

By 2003, society's strong reactions to the portrayals of gay people on television seemed to have subsided when Bravo introduced its series *Queer Eye for the Straight Guy*. The title itself would have been shocking just a few years earlier, but audiences seemed ready for programming that featured gay men offering advice about fashion, home decor, cuisine and culture. Television programming traditionally has been slow to adapt to changing social standards, trailing the culture's ability to accommodate its evolving diversity.

More than ten years after the comic strip *For Better or Worse* revealed that one of its characters was gay, veteran cartoonist Dan Piraro confronted the issue of gay parenting. A Piraro cartoon drawn in 2005 appeared in newspapers in two different versions. One version showed a doctor outside a surgery room talking to a man, saying, "Your husband is in the recovery room. You could go back and see him if you like, but our government-sanctioned bigotry forbids it."

Piraro's editor at King Features Syndicate, saying he had received complaints about Piraro's liberal bias, asked Piraro to draw a second version with the doctor talking to a man and saying, "She's going to be just fine—she's quite a fighter. The anesthesiologist has a black eye and I think she may have cracked my ribs."

Different papers chose which version to run, but some subscribers noticed the difference. "Not wishing to lose my voice entirely, I thought it was wise to send in a replacement caption for the same picture," Piraro said.

In 2012, Marvel Comics announced a wedding for its first openly gay hero, Northstar, and his longtime boyfriend, Kyle. In 1992, Northstar had become one of the first comic characters to reveal that he is gay. "The Marvel Universe has always reflected the world outside your window, so we strike to make sure our characters, relationships and stories are grounded in that reality," said Axel Alonso, Marvel's editor-in-chief.

Liza Donnelly The New Yorker Collection/The Cartoon Bank

"I don't see liking trucks as a boy thing.
I see it as a liking-trucks thing."

How to Analyze Media Effects

Scholars once thought the effects of media were easy to measure, as a direct relationship between mass media messages and the effects of those messages. Contemporary scholars now know that the relationship between mass media and their audiences is complex.

Communications scholar Neil Postman poses some questions to ask about mass media's relationship to political and social issues:

▶ What are the main psychic effects of each [media] form?

▶ What is the main relation between information and reason?

▶ What redefinitions of important cultural meanings do new sources, speeds, contexts and forms of information require?

▶ How do different forms of information persuade?

▶ Is a newspaper's "public" different from television's "public"?

▶ How do different information forms dictate the type of content that is expressed?

These questions should be discussed, says Postman, because "no medium is excessively dangerous if its users understand what its dangers are. . . . This is an instance in which the asking of the questions is sufficient. To ask is to break the spell."

REVIEW, ANALYZE, INVESTIGATE

CHAPTER 13

Early Mass Media Studies Assess Impact

- Media scholars look for patterns in the effects of media rather than for anecdotal evidence.
- David Potter, in *People of Plenty*, described the United States as a consumer society driven by advertising.

Scholars Look for Patterns

- Canadian scholar Marshall McLuhan introduced the term *global village* to describe the way media bring people together through shared experience.
- The magic bullet theory, developed in the 1929 Payne Fund studies, asserted that media content has a direct causal relationship to behavior and that mass media affects everyone in the same way.
- Challenging the magic bullet theory, Hadley Cantril found that better-educated people listening to "The War of the Worlds" were much more likely to detect that the radio broadcast was fiction. Today, scholars believe the media have different effects on different people.
- In 1948, political scientist Harold D. Lasswell described the process of analyzing communication as answering five questions: Who? Says what? On which channel? To whom? With what effect?

How TV Affects Children's Behavior

- In 1961, Wilbur Schramm and his associates revealed that children used TV for fantasy, diversion and instruction. Aggressive children were more likely to turn to TV for fantasy, said Schramm, but he could find no serious problems related to TV viewing.
- The 1971 report to Congress, *Television and Social Behavior*, made a faint causal connection between TV violence and children's violent behavior, but the report said that only some children were affected, and these children already had been classified as aggressive.
- Several recent studies have suggested that TV violence causes aggression among children. Researchers caution, however, that TV violence is not *the* cause of aggressiveness, but only *a* cause of aggressiveness.
- The Federal Trade Commission report *Television Advertising to Children* said that children see 20,000 commercials a year and that younger children are much more likely to pay attention to TV advertising than older ones.
- A study by the California Assessment Program of children's TV viewing habits seems to support the idea that children who watch a lot of TV do not perform as well in school as children who watch less television.

- A 2011 study by Common Sense Media reports that children younger than 8 years of age spend more time than ever using media, and more than half of these children have access to a mobile device.

Do the Mass Media Cause Violence?

- The summary study by the National Institute of Mental Health in 1982 asserted that a direct connection exists between televised violence and aggressive behavior, but there is no way to predict who will be affected and why.
- Most of the latest studies of the media's role have continued to reinforce the concept that different people in different environments react to the media differently.
- In 1994, cable operators and network broadcasters agreed to use an independent monitor to review programming for violent content.
- The agreement called for the development of violence ratings for TV programming and endorsed a v-chip—*v* for "violence"—technology that eventually was required for all television sets to allow parents to block programs rated as violent.
- The Telecommunications Act of 1996 established a television ratings code for content.
- The Entertainment Software Association, which represents video and computer game makers, also has voluntarily created a ratings system.
- In 2011, the U.S. Supreme Court ruled against a California law that would have restricted the sale and rental of violent video games to minors.
- These ratings systems continue a tradition of media self-regulation.

National Political Campaigns Depend on Mass Media

- Media politics began in 1933 with President Franklin Roosevelt's Fireside Chats. John F. Kennedy broadened the tradition when he and Richard Nixon appeared in the nation's first televised debate of presidential candidates, in 1960.
- The first major study of politics and the media, *The People's Choice*, concluded that only 8 percent of the voters in the study were actually converted by media coverage of the 1940 campaign.
- The 1976 study *The Unseeing Eye* revealed that only 7 percent of the people in the study were manipulated by TV ads. The researchers concluded that political advertising has little effect on most people.

- Television is a very efficient way to reach large numbers of people quickly, but campaigning through television also distances the candidates from direct public contact.

Cost of Political Advertising Skyrockets

- The rising cost of national political campaigns is directly connected to the expense of television advertising.
- Opinion leaders shape political views, a transmission of ideas that is called the *two-step flow* of communication.
- TV political advertising affects only a small percentage of people, but just a few percentage points decide many elections.
- Political spending by presidential candidates in 2012 totaled $6 billion.
- In most political contests, television advertising accounts for more than half of campaign spending, which means healthy earnings for local TV stations.

Voters and Campaigns Use the Internet and Social Media

- The 2004 presidential election was the first election where the Internet began to play a role in national politics.
- During the 2004 presidential election, 75 million people used the Internet to find political news.
- Candidates use Web sites, e-mail, blogs, podcasts and social-networking sites such as MySpace, Facebook and YouTube to reach the public.
- By 2008, the Internet had become a central force in national politics, although there is no clear understanding yet of how—or if—the Internet affects voters' decisions.

Mass Media Reflect Social Values

- Elisabeth Noelle-Neumann has asserted that due to what she calls a "spiral of silence" supporting the consensus point of view, the media have more influence because opponents of the consensus tend to remain silent.
- Joshua Meyrowitz says that television viewing blurs the distinction between childhood and adulthood.
- Walter Lippmann first identified the tendency of journalists to generalize about groups of people and create stereotypes.
- Scholar Tania Modleski says the media's inaccurate portrayals of women are not new but began in 1740 with the publication of *Pamela*, the nation's first published novel.
- In 2014, Random House published a series of "I Can Be" books meant to show the character Barbie as a professional woman, yet the books continued to promote stereotypes.

Mass Media Slow to Reflect Ethnic Diversity

- In the 2010 census, 9 million people identified themselves as a member of more than one race.
- The mainstream media, especially daily newspapers and the TV networks, have traditionally represented the interests of the mainstream culture.
- A study of *The New York Times* from 1934 to 1994 found that most nonwhite groups were visible "only in glimpses."
- A study by the National Council of La Raza concluded that only 2 percent of prime-time characters during the 1994–1995 TV season were Latinos, and most of the roles played by those characters were minor.
- In 2015, nine Native American actors walked off the set of an Adam Sandler movie, produced by Netflix, because they said the film promoted negative stereotypes.
- To avoid ethnic stereotyping, journalists should refer to people's ethnic or racial background only when it is relevant, use sensitivity when describing rites and cultural events and be specific when identifying someone's race or ethnicity, asking the person how he or she would like to be identified.

Mass Media Face Gay, Lesbian and Transgender Issues

- The lesbian character on the TV program *Ellen* and the gay character Lawrence in the cartoon strip *For Better or For Worse* focused attention on media portrayals of gender issues in the 1990s.
- By 2003, the strong reactions to the portrayals of gay people on television seemed to have subsided when Fox Television introduced its series *Queer Eye for the Straight Guy*.
- The experience of the cartoonist Dan Piraro in 2005 is a reminder that same-sex issues still are sensitive topics for media. At the insistence of his editor, Piraro provided two captions for the same cartoon, one that reflected a male-female couple and one that showed a male-male married couple.
- In 2012, Marvel Comics announced a wedding for its first openly gay hero, Northstar, and his longtime boyfriend, Kyle.

How to Analyze Media Effects

- The relationship between media and their audiences is complex.
- Communications scholar Neil Postman says that scholars should continue to analyze the media's effects so people will not just accept what they see without question.

Key Terms

These terms are defined in the margins throughout this chapter and appear in alphabetical order with definitions in the Glossary, which begins on page 361.

Critical Questions

1. How did each of the following people contribute to media effects research?

    a. David M. Potter
    b. Marshall McLuhan
    c. Harold D. Lasswell
    d. George Gerbner

2. Describe three studies involving children and TV and discuss the results. Why are children often the subject of media effects research?

3. Discuss your understanding of the role that American mass media play in political campaigns today. Include a discussion of how today's voters use mass media to follow public affairs issues.

4. List and describe the effects of the Internet on American politics.

5. How fairly do you believe women, African Americans, Latinos, Native Americans and other ethnic groups are portrayed in American mass media today? How fairly do you believe gay, lesbian and transgender issues are represented in today's mass media? Give three specific examples.

Working the Web

This list includes sites mentioned in the chapter and others to give you greater insight into social and political media issues research.

Benton Foundation

benton.org

William Benton, publisher of the *Encyclopedia Britannica* and a U.S. senator, established the Benton Foundation "to ensure that media and telecommunications serve the public interest and enhance our democracy." The foundation site offers a weekly roundup of news headlines from across the country and a Daily Digital Blog on current communications policy issues, as well as a listing of the issues the foundation monitors.

Center on Media and Child Health (CMCH)

cmch.tv

Dedicated to "understanding and responding to the effects of media on the physical, mental and social health of children through research, production and education," the center is located at Children's Hospital Boston. The CMCH Database of Research catalogs current research on the relationship of media exposure to health-risk behaviors. Site visitors can access a number of child health care resources for parents, including Ask the Mediatrician—questions from parents about child health care and the media that are answered by CMCH founder, pediatrician Michael Rich; the Clinician Toolkit, the center's e-newsletter; a database of the center's research; issue briefs and tip sheets for parents.

C-SPAN

c-span.org

Started in 1979 by the cable industry as a public affairs cable network, C-SPAN (Cable Satellite Public Affairs Network) is available to over 100 million American households. C-SPAN's three channels and FM radio programming on WCSP in Washington, D.C., offer a wide array of around-the-clock commercial-free television and radio public affairs programming featuring all branches of the U.S. federal government. C-SPAN programming includes live committee and floor sessions of the U.S. Congress and government agency hearings mixed in with live sessions from the Canadian, Australian and British parliaments as well as live speeches and regular interview programs about current national political issues. The C-SPAN Web site offers additional archived programming of past-aired shows and podcasts that are available to stream or download.

Joan Shorenstein Center on Media, Politics and Public Policy (Harvard University)

shorensteincenter.org

The center "analyzes the power of media, in all its forms, and its impact on public policy and politics." The research center is based at the John F. Kennedy School of Government at Harvard University. Site users can access "must read" articles about media and politics and download documents, including books written by center faculty, staff and associates; newsletters from the center; and a variety of reports, papers and case studies. The center offers fellowships, internships and scholarships for students.

MediaSmarts

mediasmarts.ca

Established in 1994 by the Canadian Radio-television and Telecommunications Commission as part of a television violence initiative, MediaSmarts is the online site maintained by Canada's Centre for Digital and Media Literacy. MediaSmarts promotes media and technology education for families, parents and children by producing online programs and resources through partnerships with other Canadian and international organizations. The site offers a Digital and Media Literacy section, including information on body image, gender representation, cyberbullying and cybersecurity. There also are links to teacher resources and a blog covering a wide variety of topics such as alcohol marketing, cell phones and texting, media literacy, digital health and digital citizenry.

Media Effects Research Lab (MERL) at Penn State University

http://comm.psu.edu/research/centers/medialab

This research facility is housed in the College of Communications at Penn State University. MERL conducts experiments in two subject areas: (a) Traditional Media—the effects of television entertainment and video games; and (b) New Media—the effects of online media and communications technology. Educator resources as well as research abstracts and publications are available at the site on a wide variety of subjects, including Facebook sharing, Web site engagement and the psychology of "click here."

Moorland-Spingarn Research Center (MSRC) at Howard University

library.howard.edu/MSRC

MSRC is one of the largest and oldest repositories for "documentation of the history and culture of people of African descent in Africa, the Americas and other parts of the world." This site includes a link to the archives of the center's electronic journal (HUArchivesNet). Additional links to the Library Division and the Manuscript Division offer brief descriptions and samples of the center's holdings.

National Journal

nationaljournal.com

National Journal Group offers nonpartisan publications "for people who have a professional interest in politics, policy and government." Web site users can access online content from *National Journal Magazine, National Journal Daily, National Journal Hotline,* and *The Almanac of American Politics* as well as links to Atlantic Media publications, including *The Atlantic, Citylab, Wire, Government Executive* and *Quartz.*

National Press Club

press.org

Known as the "place where news happens," the National Press Club is a private organization for more than 3,500 journalism and communication professionals. More than 250,000 people attend more than 2,000 events annually at the Press Club facility in Washington, D.C., including the prestigious Washington Correspondents Dinner. The National Press Club Institute provides training, classes, panel discussions and professional development activities for media professionals. Visitors to the site can access resources on freedom of the press, photos, video and podcasts from events held at the Press Club.

Nieman Foundation for Journalism at Harvard University

nieman.harvard.edu

With a stated mission to "promote and elevate the standards of journalism," the foundation has been in operation since 1938, offering academic fellowships to more than 1,400 journalists from 100 countries to spend 12 weeks teaching at Harvard University. Resources at the site include Nieman Lab (focused on the future of news and innovation), *Nieman Reports* (which explores contemporary journalism's challenges) and Nieman Storyboard (which offers examples of narrative journalism).

University of Iowa Department of Communication Studies: Political Communication and Campaigns

clas.uiowa.edu/commstudies/political-communication-campaigns

This resource site provides links to articles and Web sites related to politics and political advertising from political media consulting firms.

Washington Center for Politics and Journalism

wcpj.org

The center is a nonprofit organization that offers seminars and classes to train future political reporters about politics from the perspective of political practitioners and political reporters. Students from 50 participating universities throughout the U.S. are nominated to study at the center. Students chosen for a Politics and Journalism Semester class are assigned to a major Washington news bureau, working full-time. The center's Web site has a complete listing of donors, links to political journalism publications (such as politico.com) and streaming video of speakers and courses taught at the center from the most recent class term.

Impact/Action Videos are concise news features on various topics created exclusively for *Media/Impact*. Find them in *Media/Impact*'s MindTap at cengagebrain.com.

MindTap® Log on to MindTap for *Media/Impact* to access a variety of additional material—including learning objectives, chapter readings with highlighting and note-taking, **Impact/Action Videos**, activities, and comprehension quizzes—that will guide you through this chapter.

LAW AND REGULATION
REFORMING THE RULES

The Washington Post/Getty Images

The U.S. Constitution establishes the right of free
expression. Reporting on court actions is an important part
of the press' public responsibility. On May 15, 2014, advocates
for Internet neutrality demonstrate in front of the Federal
Communications Commission building in Washington, D.C.

What's Ahead?

- U.S. Constitution Sets Free Press Precedent
- Government Tries to Restrict Free Expression
- Prior Restraint Rarely Used
- Government Manages War Coverage
- WikiLeaks Challenges Government Secrecy
- USA PATRIOT Act Meets Public Resistance
- What Is the Standard for Obscenity?

- Libel Law Outlines the Media's Public Responsibility
- Invasion of Privacy Defined Four Ways
- Debate Continues over Fair Trial, Courtroom Access and Shield Laws
- FCC Regulates Broadcast and Cable
- Telecommunications Act of 1996 Changes the Marketplace
- Deregulation Unleashes the Media

- TV Industry Agrees to Ratings and the V-Chip
- Congress Attempts to Control Access to Indecent Content
- Intellectual Property Rights Affirmed
- FCC Adopts Open Internet Rules
- Courts and Regulators Govern Advertising and PR
- Law Must Balance Rights and Responsibilities

"America's broadband networks must be fast, fair and open."

—FEDERAL COMMUNICATIONS COMMISSION, ANNOUNCING OPEN INTERNET RULES ON FEBRUARY 26, 2015

According to the precedent-setting New York Times v. Sullivan case, which helped define press freedom in 1964, the U.S. media's role is to encourage "uninhibited, robust and wide-open" debate.

"Even though absolute press freedom may sometimes have to accommodate itself to other high constitutional values, the repeal or modification of the First Amendment seems unlikely," wrote *New York Times* columnist Tom Wicker. "If the true freedom of the press is to decide for itself what to publish and when to publish it, the true responsibility of the press must be to assert and defend that freedom."

The mass media in America are businesses operating to make a profit, but these businesses enjoy a special trust protected by the U.S. Constitution. The legal and regulatory issues the mass media face today are attempts by the government, the public and the mass media industries to balance the nation's legal rights and public responsibilities, as envisioned in the First Amendment.

U.S. Constitution Sets Free Press Precedent

All legal interpretations of the press's responsibilities attempt to determine exactly what the Framers of the U.S. Constitution meant when they included the First Amendment in the Bill of Rights in 1791. The First Amendment established the concept that the press should operate freely:

Congress shall make no law respecting an establishment of religion, or prohibiting the free exercise thereof; or abridging the freedom of speech, or of the press; or the right of the people peaceably to assemble, and to petition the Government for a redress of grievances.

In his book *Emergence of a Free Press*, Leonard W. Levy explains his interpretation of the First Amendment:

By freedom of the press the Framers meant a right to engage in rasping, corrosive and offensive discussions on all topics of public interest. . . . The press had become the tribune of the people by sitting in judgment on the conduct of public officials. A free press meant the press as the Fourth Estate, [as] . . . an informal or extra-constitutional fourth branch that functioned as part of the intricate system of checks and balances that exposed public mismanagement and kept power fragmented, manageable and accountable.

While efforts to interpret the Framers' meaning continue, along with challenges and rebuttals to existing laws and regulations, the discussion of the restrictions and laws covering free expression today can be divided into six categories: (1) federal government restrictions, (2) prior restraint, (3) censorship, (4) libel, (5) privacy and (6) right of access.

Government Tries to Restrict Free Expression

At least four times in U.S. history before 1964, the federal government felt threatened enough by press freedom to attempt to control access to information. These four notable attempts to limit how the mass media operate were the Alien and Sedition Laws of 1798, the Espionage Act of 1918, the Smith Act of 1940 and the Cold War congressional investigations of suspected Communists in the late 1940s and early 1950s. All four challenges were attempts by the government to control free speech.

The Alien and Sedition Laws of 1798

Under the provisions of the Alien and Sedition Laws of 1798, 15 people were indicted, 11 people were tried, and 10 were found guilty. The Alien and Sedition Laws set a fine of up to $2,000 (more than $50,000 in today's dollars) and a sentence of up to 2 years in jail for anyone who was found guilty of speaking, writing or publishing "false, scandalous and malicious writing or writings" against the government, Congress or the president.

The laws expired in 1801, and when Thomas Jefferson became president that year, he pardoned everyone who had been found guilty under the laws.

The Espionage Act of 1918

Although Henry Raymond had challenged censorship of Civil War reporting (see **Chapter 12**), journalists and the general population during the Civil War accepted government control of information. But during World War I, Congress passed the Espionage Act of 1918.

Not all Americans supported U.S. entry into the war. To stop public criticism, the Espionage Act made it a crime to say or write anything that could be viewed as helping the enemy. Under the act, 877 people were convicted. Many, but not all, of them were pardoned when the war ended.

The most notable person cited under the Espionage Act of 1918 was labor organizer and Socialist Party presidential candidate Eugene V. Debs, who was sentenced to two concurrent ten-year terms for giving a public speech against the war. At his trial, Debs said, "I have been accused of obstructing the war. I admit it. Gentlemen, I abhor war. I would oppose the war if I stood alone." Debs was released from prison by a presidential order in 1921.

PhotoQuest/Getty Images

Eugene V. Debs was the most notable person convicted of violating the Espionage Act of 1918. He was jailed for speaking publicly against World War I. He was released from prison by a presidential order in 1921.

The Smith Act of 1940

During World War II, Congress passed the Smith Act of 1940, which placed some restrictions on free speech. Only a few people were cited under it, but reporters were required to submit their stories for government censorship before publication.

President Franklin D. Roosevelt created the Office of Censorship, which worked out a voluntary Code of Wartime Practices with the press. The code spelled out the types of information the press should not report about the war, such as troop and ship movements, and the military retained power to censor all overseas war reporting.

The Office of Censorship also issued the Code of Wartime Practices for American Broadcasters, which were guidelines for news broadcasts and commentaries. (See **Impact/Society**, "Excerpts from the 1943 Code of Wartime Practices for American Broadcasters," p. 280.) The federal government exercised its power over broadcasters because it licensed broadcast outlets.

HUAC and the Permanent Subcommittee on Investigations

The fourth major challenge to the First Amendment protection of free speech came in the late 1940s and early 1950s, culminating with actions of the House Un-American Activities Committee (**HUAC**) against

HUAC House Un-American Activities Committee.

IMPACT

Society

Excerpts from the 1943 Code of Wartime Practices for American Broadcasters

Note: During World War II, the Office of War Information tried to control what was broadcast from the United States. Following are some of the voluntary rules radio broadcasters were expected to follow.

News Broadcasts and Commentaries

It is requested that news in any of the following classifications be kept off the air unless made available for broadcast by appropriate authority or specifically cleared by the Office of Censorship.

▶ Weather—Weather forecasts other than those officially released by the Weather Bureau.

▶ Armed forces—Types and movements of United States Army, Navy, and Marine Corps units, within or without continental United States.

Programs

▶ Request programs—No telephoned or telegraphed requests for musical selections should be accepted. No requests for musical selections made by word-of-mouth

Under provisions of the 1943 Code of Wartime Practices for American Broadcasters, all live radio programs—including this 1944 radio show featuring singers (*left to right*) Dinah Shore, Frank Sinatra and Bing Crosby—were subject to on-air censorship.

at the origin of broadcast, whether studio or remote, should be honored.

▶ Quiz programs—Any program which permits the public accessibility to an open microphone is dangerous and should be carefully supervised. Because of the nature of quiz programs, in which the public is not only permitted access to the microphone but encouraged to speak into it, the danger of usurpation by the enemy is enhanced.

Foreign Language Broadcasts

▶ Personnel—The Office of Censorship, by direction of the president, is charged with the

responsibility of removing from the air all those engaged in foreign language broadcasting who, in the judgment of appointed authorities in the Office of Censorship, endanger the war effort of the United Nations by their connections, direct or indirect, with the medium.

▶ Scripts—Station managements are requested to require all persons who broadcast in a foreign language to submit to the management in advance of broadcast complete scripts or transcriptions of such material.

Excerpted from U.S. Government Office of Censorship, *Code of Wartime Practices for American Broadcasters*. Washington, DC: Government Printing Office, 1943, pages 1–8.

Gene Lester/Getty Images

Senator Joseph R. McCarthy (at the easel) explains his theory of Communism during the Army-McCarthy hearings in 1954. Army counsel Joseph N. Welch, who was defending people who were declared subversive by McCarthy, is seated at the table. News reports and Edward R. Murrow's exposure of McCarthy's investigative excesses eventually triggered public criticism of McCarthy's tactics, and his Senate colleagues censured him.

Katharine Graham (*right*), publisher of *The Washington Post*, and Executive Editor Ben Bradlee celebrate the U.S. Supreme Court's 6-3 decision on June 30, 1971, to allow publication of the Pentagon Papers.

the Hollywood Ten (see **Chapter 7**) and the Senate's Permanent Subcommittee on Investigations, presided over by Senator Joseph R. McCarthy.

These congressional committees set a tone of aggressive Communist hunting. After television broadcasts in 1954 of McCarthy's investigation of Communist influence in the Army and other reports eventually exposed his excesses, McCarthy's Senate colleagues censured him by a vote of 67 to 22. But while the hearings were under way, they established a restrictive atmosphere that challenged the public's right to free expression.

Prior Restraint Rarely Used

Prior restraint means government censoring of information before the information is published or broadcast. The Framers of the Constitution clearly opposed prior restraint by law. However, in 1931, the U.S. Supreme Court established the circumstances under which prior restraint could be justified.

Near v. Minnesota

J. M. Near published the weekly *Saturday Press*, which printed the names of people who were violating the nation's Prohibition laws. Minnesota authorities obtained a court order forbidding publication of *Saturday Press*, but the U.S. Supreme Court overturned the state's action.

In *Near v. Minnesota* in 1931, the Court condemned prior restraint, although it acknowledged that the government could limit information about troop movements during war and could control obscenity. The Court also

said "the security of community life may be protected against incitements to acts of violence and the overthrow of orderly government."

Saturday Press had not violated any of these prohibitions, so the Minnesota court's order was lifted. But future attempts to stop other publications were based on the *Near v. Minnesota* decision, making it a landmark case.

In two important instances since *Near* (the Pentagon Papers and *United States v. The Progressive*), courts were asked to bar publication of information to protect national security.

The Pentagon Papers

On June 13, 1971, *The New York Times* published the first installment of what became known as the Pentagon Papers—excerpts from a document titled *History of U.S. Decision-Making Process on Vietnam Policy*. The Pentagon Papers detailed decisions that were made about U.S. involvement in Vietnam starting in the 1940s.

The documents were labeled top secret, but they were given to *The Times* by one of the report's authors, Daniel Ellsberg, a consultant to the Defense Department and the White House. Ellsberg said that he believed the papers had been improperly classified and that the public should have the information.

After the first three installments were published in *The Times*, Justice Department attorneys obtained a

> **Prior Restraint** Government censorship of information before the information is published or broadcast.

restraining order against the paper, which stopped publication of the installments for 2 weeks while *The Times* appealed the case. While the case was being decided, *The Washington Post* began publishing the papers, and *The Post* also was stopped, but only until the U.S. Supreme Court decided the *Times* case. On June 30, 1971, in a 6-3 decision, the Court agreed that the newspapers should be permitted to publish the Pentagon Papers.

In *New York Times Co. v. United States*, the Court said the government did not prove that prior restraint was necessary. *The Times* and *The Post* then printed the papers, but the court action had delayed publication of the information for two weeks. This was the first time in the nation's history that the federal government had stopped a newspaper from publishing specific information.

Legal fees cost *The Post* and *The Times* more than $270,000 (equivalent to $1.6 million today). Forty years later, on June 13, 2011, the U.S. government publicly released the complete set of documents once known as the Pentagon Papers.

The *Progressive* Case

The next instance of prior restraint happened in 1979, when editors of *The Progressive* magazine announced that they planned to publish an article by Howard Morland about how to make a hydrogen bomb. The author said the article was based on information from public documents and interviews with government employees. The Department of Justice brought suit in Wisconsin, where the magazine was published, and received a restraining order to stop the information from being printed (*United States v. The Progressive*). *The Progressive* did not publish the article as planned.

Before the case could reach the U.S. Supreme Court, a Wisconsin newspaper published a letter from a man named Charles Hansen that contained much of the same information as the Morland article. Hansen sent eight copies of the letter to other newspapers, and the *Chicago Tribune* also published the letter, saying that none of the information was proprietary. Six months after the original restraining order, *The Progressive* published the article.

Government Manages War Coverage

The U.S. government historically has tried to control its image during wartime. Four recent examples of government press management occurred in Grenada, the Gulf War, Afghanistan and Iraq.

In 2009, the U.S. government eased previous restrictions on press access during the Gulf War when, with the family's consent, it allowed reporters to photograph caskets of fatally injured soldiers that were being returned home.

Restricting Press Access in Grenada

In an incident in 1983 that never reached the courts but that was a type of prior restraint, the Reagan administration kept reporters away from the Caribbean island of Grenada, where the administration had launched a military offensive. A press blackout began at 11 p.m. on October 24, 1983.

The administration didn't officially bar the press from covering the invasion on October 25, but the Pentagon refused to transport accredited reporters and turned back press yachts and airplanes that attempted to enter the war zone. About a dozen print journalists and photographers were able to get in anyway, but no television crews were allowed.

More than 400 journalists from 170 news organizations around the world who couldn't get to Grenada were left on Barbados, waiting for the news to get to them. Charles Lachman of the *New York Post* flew to Barbados and then to St. Vincent. Then he and some other reporters paid $6,000 to charter a boat to Grenada. They arrived 5 days after the invasion and discovered that a hospital had been a casualty of the military action, information the military had tried to keep from being reported.

News Blackouts and Press Pools During the Gulf War

In the 1990s, the Gulf War posed another tough battleground for the rights of reporters versus the rights of the military to restrict access. On Saturday, February 23, 1991, when the ground assault began about three weeks into the Gulf War, the Defense Department announced the first 24-hour news blackout in U.S. military history. Press organizations protested the ban, but the military argued that modern communications technology necessitated the blackout.

Subsequent Pentagon rules for war coverage, reached in cooperation with journalists, imposed stricter limits on reporting in the Persian Gulf than in any previous U.S. war. Reporters were required to travel in small "pools," escorted by public affairs officers, and every story the pool produced was subject to military censorship. This system, called **pool reporting**, was created to respond to reporters' complaints about news blackouts during the Grenada incident.

An unprecedented number of journalists—1,300 in Saudi Arabia alone—posed a challenge for military press officers. In a commentary protesting the restrictions, *The New Yorker* magazine said, "The rules, it is clear, enable the Pentagon to promote coverage of subjects and events

Pool Reporting An arrangement that places reporters in small, government-supervised groups to cover an event.

that it wishes publicized and to prevent reporting that might cast it, or the war, in a bad light." Yet, in a *Los Angeles Times* poll of nearly 2,000 people 2 weeks after the fighting started, 79 percent approved of the Pentagon's restrictions, and 57 percent favored even further limits.

War in Afghanistan

During the early days of the war in Afghanistan—especially in the months immediately following the September 11, 2001, terrorist attacks in the United States—the military carefully controlled press access to information, citing national security. The military used press pools and provided its own video footage of troop landings, produced by the military's combat film teams.

"In World War II, accredited journalists from leading news organizations were on the front lines to give the public an independent description of what was happening," reported *The New York Times*. "In the new war on terrorism, journalists have had limited access to many of the United States forces that are carrying out the war. . . . The media's access to American military operations is far more limited than in recent conflicts."

"Embedded" Reporters During Iraq War

Beginning in 2003, during the Iraq War, the U.S. government adopted a system called *embedding*, which meant that members of the press traveled with the military, but the press's movements were restricted and managed by their military units.

Embedding was a reaction to the press's limited access in Afghanistan, but many journalists said they still had restricted access to the real action in Iraq. However, the coverage left the impression with the public that the press was giving the whole story, when in fact the press had access to only a very restricted view. (For more about embedded reporters, see **Chapter 12**.)

Photographs of War Fatalities

During the Iraq War, the George W. Bush administration (2001–2009) banned the media from covering the arrival of war fatalities as they were returned to America, saying the administration wanted to protect the families' privacy. Critics of the ban said that the government was trying to hide the consequences of war from public view. In 2009, the Obama administration lifted the ban, and the press now is allowed access to photograph the return of fatally wounded soldiers, with family permission.

PAUL J. RICHARDS/Getty Images

Members of the U.S. Army Honor Guard carry the casket of Spc. Ryan M. Lumley, from Lakeland, Fla., who died in combat in Afghanistan. The George W. Bush administration's (2001–2009) ban on press coverage of fatally wounded U.S. soldiers was lifted in 2009 by the Obama administration, and allowed coverage with the family's permission. This transfer of Lumley's casket occurred at Dover Air Force Base, Del., on December 5, 2011.

Today, the federal government still requires the accreditation of war zone reporters (see **Chapter 12**), but the U.S. military and the press operate under a less restrictive, more accommodating arrangement.

WikiLeaks Challenges Government Secrecy

Founded in 2006 by Australian Julian Assange, WikiLeaks is a whistle-blowing organization devoted to uncovering government secrets and publishing them on its Web site. Beginning in 2010, WikiLeaks began releasing classified U.S. diplomatic documents, including military information and State Department communications.

In late July 2010, WikiLeaks posted tens of thousands of confidential military documents about the wars in Iraq and Afghanistan. "The battlefield consequences of the release of these documents are potentially severe and dangerous for our troops, our allies and Afghan partners, and may well damage our relationships and reputation in that key part of world," Defense Secretary Robert M. Gates told Pentagon reporters.

On November 28, 2010, *The New York Times* began publishing a series of articles based on a new release of State Department documents. "Some 250,000 individual cables, the daily traffic between the State Department and more than 270 American diplomatic outposts around the world were made available to *The Times* by a source who insisted on anonymity," reported *The Times* in an explanatory front page Note to Readers that accompanied the first article.

FABRICE COFFRINI/Getty Images

On May 23, 2015, WikiLeaks founder Julian Assange appears in a video transmitted from the Ecuadorian Embassy in London, England, where he was granted political asylum. Despite U.S. government objections, WikiLeaks had posted more than 700,000 confidential State Department documents on its Web site as of December 28, 2010, and since then has continued to release restricted documents on the Web.

The Times acknowledged that WikiLeaks originally obtained the documents but did not directly cite WikiLeaks as *The Times'* source. "As daunting as it is to publish such material over official objections, it would be presumptuous to conclude that Americans have no right to know what is being done in their name," *The Times* explained.

Outraged at the leaks, several countries called for Assange's arrest. For months, he eluded authorities by traveling to various European countries. He eventually turned himself in to British authorities on December 7, 2010. According to *The New York Times*, as of December 28, 2010, WikiLeaks had posted 391,832 secret documents on the Iraq war, 77,000 classified Pentagon documents on the Afghan conflict and 250,000 State Department cables.

In July 2010, the U.S. military charged Pfc. Bradley Manning, an intelligence analyst, with downloading large amounts of classified information from a computer at a military base in Iraq and sharing the information with WikiLeaks. In February 2013, Manning pleaded guilty to 10 of the charges against him. On July 30, 2013, a military judge found Manning not guilty of "aiding the enemy," but found him guilty of 20 other charges, including 6 violations of the Espionage Act. On August 21, 2013, Manning was sentenced to 35 years in prison.

On February 23, 2011, a British court ordered that Assange be extradited to Sweden for charges unrelated to the WikiLeaks case. He appealed and the case is pending. Assange currently is living inside the Ecuadorian Embassy in London, where he has been granted political asylum. The U.S. government has not filed any charges against Assange for his role in publishing secret U.S.

documents on the Internet. WikiLeaks continues to release restricted documents on its Web site.

When should the government be able to prevent military information from reaching the public? When should the press be granted access? The Supreme Court has never specifically addressed these questions, and the U.S. press and news organizations remain vulnerable to fluctuating military restrictions.

USA PATRIOT Act Meets Public Resistance

In 2001, a few weeks after the terrorist attacks on the World Trade Center in New York City, Congress passed the USA PATRIOT Act (an abbreviation for *U*niting and *S*trengthening *A*merica by *P*roviding *A*ppropriate *T*ools *R*equired to *I*ntercept and *O*bstruct *T*errorism), designed to give the U.S. government broad powers to track, detain and interrogate people who were deemed a threat to the country.

Among the provisions of the act was Section 215, which allows the Federal Bureau of Investigation (FBI) to obtain "business records." These could include public library records, such as computer log-ins and lists of books people check out, although the act did not specifically mention libraries.

The American Library Association (ALA) said librarians would cooperate with a government investigation, but only if they received a search warrant. The librarians said the PATRIOT Act allowed officials to seize anything they wanted without a search warrant, which librarians said would inhibit the use of public libraries—a clear limit on free expression.

Some libraries posted signs warning patrons that federal authorities might review their records; others systematically shredded patrons' sign-in sheets to use library computers. The ALA went on record opposing unwarranted government access to library records. The American Civil Liberties Union (ACLU) sued in several cities nationwide to keep library records private, and in 2004 a Los Angeles federal judge ruled that parts of the PATRIOT Act were unconstitutional violations of the First and Fifth Amendments to the U.S. Constitution.

In 2005, the FBI demanded library records from Library Connection, a nonprofit library group in Bridgeport, Conn., saying the agency needed the information as part of a terrorism investigation under the PATRIOT Act. The ACLU challenged the request in court, saying the request was unconstitutional. Eventually the FBI withdrew its request.

In March 2006, Congress reauthorized the act for another four years, including Section 215. Opponents, including the ALA, vowed to renew their challenges to the most aggressive provisions of the act, especially Section 215, to stop what they said was an intrusion into important American civil liberties.

In 2007, a federal judge in New York struck down provisions of the PATRIOT Act that had authorized the government to issue so-called National Security Letters (**NSLs**), compelling businesses (such as Internet service providers, telephone companies and public libraries) to release customer information without a judge's order or grand jury subpoena.

U.S. District Judge Victor Marrero said using the PATRIOT Act, even as rewritten and reauthorized in 2006, to obtain customer information without court authorization "offends the fundamental constitutional principles of checks and balances and separation of powers." President Obama signed a four-year extension of the act on May 30, 2011.

When the act again came up for renewal in 2015, the ALA and civil liberties organizations lobbied fervently against the bulk collection of consumer information by the National Security Agency (NSA). The USA PATRIOT Act was renamed the USA Freedom Act when President Obama signed it on June 2, 2015, and new provisions of the act curtailed the government's bulk data collection program. This eliminated the threat that libraries and telecommunications companies would be required to disclose customers' information to the government without a court order.

"Unless people feel free to investigate and read, and now, look at Web sites . . . they cannot truly be good citizens and they cannot oversee the government," said Emily Sheketoff, head of the ALA's Washington, D.C., office.

What Is the Standard for Obscenity?

Different media industries historically have reacted differently to threats of **censorship**, the practice of suppressing material that is considered morally, politically or otherwise objectionable. Most threats of censorship concern matters of morality.

According to the American Library Association, the top three reasons critics try to challenge content are:

1. The material is considered "sexually explicit."

2. The material contains "offensive language."

3. The material is "unsuited to an age group."

CALL 1-800-JUSTICE FOR ALL YOUR LEGAL NEEDS

Michael Crawford The New Yorker Collection/The Cartoon Bank

In the U.S., censorship almost always occurs after the fact. Once the material is printed or displayed, the courts can be asked to review the content for obscenity.

To avoid ongoing government scrutiny, the motion picture and recording industries have accepted some form of self-regulation (ratings systems) to avoid government intervention. The electronic media are governed by laws in the federal criminal code against broadcast obscenity, and the federal Cable Act of 1984 bars obscenity on cable TV.

Print media, including book publishers, have been the most vigorous defenders of the right to publish. The print media were the earliest mass media to be threatened with censorship, beginning with the philosopher Plato, who suggested in 387 B.C. that Homer's *Odyssey* be censored for immature readers.

Government efforts to censor free expression happen on the local and federal levels.

Local Efforts

More than 2,000 years after Homer's *Odyssey* was threatened with censorship, Boston officials banned the sale of the April 1926 issue of H. L. Mencken's magazine *The American Mercury*. The local Watch and Ward Society had denounced a fictional story in the magazine as "salacious." The story featured "Hatrack," a prostitute whose clientele included members of various religious congregations who visited her after church.

NSL National Security Letter.

Censorship The practice of suppressing material that is considered morally, politically or otherwise objectionable.

In Boston, surrounded by his supporters, Mencken sold a copy of the magazine at a prearranged time to a member of the Watch and Ward. The chief of the Boston Vice Squad arrested Mencken and marched him to jail, where he spent the night before going to court the next morning. "Mencken passed an uneasy night," says Mencken's biographer Carl Bode, "knowing that he could be found guilty and perhaps even be imprisoned. . . . Returning to court he listened to Judge Parmenter's decision: 'I find that no offense has been committed and therefore dismiss the complaint.'"

Mencken spent $20,000 (the equivalent of $270,000 today) defending *The Mercury*, but according to Bode, "the net gain for both *The Mercury* and Mencken was great. *The Mercury* became the salient American magazine and Mencken the international symbol of freedom of speech." Mencken was defending his magazine against local censorship. Until 1957, censorship in America remained a local issue because the U.S. Supreme Court had not considered a national censorship case.

U.S. Supreme Court Writes Obscenity Criteria

Censorship still primarily is a local issue, and two landmark Supreme Court cases—*Roth v. United States* and *Miller v. California*—established the major criteria for local censorship.

ROTH V. UNITED STATES. This 1957 decision involved two separate cases. Samuel Roth was found guilty in New York of sending obscenity through the mail, and David S. Alberts was found guilty of selling obscene books in Beverly Hills. (The case carries Roth's name because his name appeared first when the cases were combined for review.) The U.S. Supreme Court upheld the guilty verdict and, according to legal scholar Ralph Holsinger, established several precedents:

▸ The First Amendment does not protect obscenity.

▸ Obscenity is defined as material "utterly without redeeming social importance."

▸ Sex and obscenity are not synonymous. Obscene material is material that appeals to "prurient [obsessively sexual] interest."

▸ A test of obscenity is "whether to the average person, applying contemporary community standards, the dominant theme of the material taken as a whole appeals to prurient interest." (This last description of obscenity has become known as the **Roth test**.)

MILLER V. CALIFORNIA. In the late 1960s, a California court found Marvin Miller guilty of sending obscene, unsolicited advertising material through the mail. The case reached the U.S. Supreme Court in 1973. The decision described which materials a state could censor and set a three-part test for obscenity.

According to the Supreme Court, states may censor material that meets this three-part local test for obscenity. The local court, according to legal scholar Ralph Holsinger, must determine:

1. Whether "the average person, applying contemporary community standards," would find that the work, taken as a whole, appeals to prurient interest.

2. Whether the work depicts or describes, in a patently offensive way, sexual conduct specifically defined by the applicable state law.

3. Whether the work, taken as a whole, lacks serious *L*iterary, *A*rtistic, *P*olitical or *S*cientific value—often called the **LAPS test**.

The *Roth* and *Miller* cases together established a standard for obscenity, leaving the decision in specific obscenity challenges to local courts. The result is that widely different standards exist in different parts of the country because local juries and elected officials are free to decide what they consider offensive in their communities. Books and magazines that are available to young readers in some states may be unavailable in other states. (See **Impact/Society**, "2014 Top 10 Most Frequently Challenged Books," p. 289.)

School Boards as Censors

Many censorship cases begin at schools and local government boards, where parents' groups protest books, magazines and films that are available to students, such as these examples:

▸ In 2014, a school district in Riverside, Calif., banned the popular novel *The Fault in Our Stars* from its middle school library after one parent objected to its portrayal of death, illness and sex.

▸ A school district in Little Rock, Ark., removed Harry Potter books from its library because the school board claimed the tales of wizards and spells could harm schoolchildren.

▸ A school board in Minnesota banned four books, including *Are You There, God? It's Me, Margaret* by Judy Blume, a very popular young adult author.

> **Roth Test**   A standard court test for obscenity, named for one of the defendants in an obscenity case.
>
> **LAPS Test**   A yardstick for local obscenity judgments, which evaluates an artistic work's literary, artistic, political or scientific value.

▶ The state of Alabama ordered 45 textbooks pulled from the shelves after a federal judge said the books promoted "secular humanism."

The ALA fiercely opposes any attempt to censor or restrict access to information. Since 1990, the ALA and several other organizations have sponsored Banned Books Week to bring public attention to the issue of censorship. "Censorship has no place in a free society," said ALA President Camila Alire. "Part of living in a democracy means respecting each other's differences and the right of all people to choose for themselves what they and their families read."

Most reported book challenges take place in schools and in public libraries, according to the ALA. These challenges usually are reversed when appealed, but while the specific issues are being decided, the books, magazines and videos are unavailable, and censorship efforts continue nationwide. (See **Impact/Profile**: "John Green's *The Fault in Our Stars* is Banned, Then Returned to Riverside, California, Classrooms," p. 288 and **Impact/Society: Illustration 14.1**, "2014 Top 10 Most Frequently Challenged Books" pp. 288–289.)

The *Hazelwood* Case

In 1988, the U.S. Supreme Court for the first time gave public school officials considerable freedom to limit what appears in student publications. The case, *Hazelwood v. Kuhlmeier*, became known as the *Hazelwood* case because the issues originated at Hazelwood High School in Hazelwood, Mo.

The high school paper, funded mostly from the school budget, was published as part of a journalism class. The principal at Hazelwood regularly reviewed the school paper before it was published, and in this case he deleted two articles the student staff had written. One deleted article was about student pregnancy and included interviews with three students who had become pregnant while attending school.

Although the article used pseudonyms instead of the students' names, the principal said he believed the anonymity of the students was not sufficiently protected. He also believed the girls' discussion of their use or nonuse of birth control was inappropriate for a school publication. By a vote of 5 to 3, the U.S. Supreme Court agreed.

The *Washington Post*, however, editorialized against the decision. "Even teenagers," the *Post* editorial said, "should be allowed to publish criticism, raise uncomfortable questions and spur debate on subjects such as pregnancy, AIDS and drug abuse that are too often a very real aspect of high school culture today."

The Hazelwood principal's action drew the attention of the *St. Louis Post-Dispatch*, which published the censored articles, bringing them a much wider audience than the students at Hazelwood High.

Many states subsequently have adopted legislation to protect student newspapers from similar censorship. The Supreme Court decision is significant, however, because it has changed the way local officials in some states monitor school publications.

Libel Law Outlines the Media's Public Responsibility

"Americans have increasingly begun to seek the refuge and vindication of litigation," writes legal scholar Rodney A. Smolla in his book *Suing the Press*. "Words published by the media no longer roll over us without penetrating; instead, they sink in through the skin and work inner damage, and a consensus appears to be emerging that this psychic damage is serious and must be paid for."

Three cases demonstrate how the mass media become targets of litigation:

1. In 1983, entertainer Carol Burnett sued the *National Enquirer* for $10 million for implying in an article that she was drinking too much and acting rude in a Washington, D.C., restaurant.

2. In 1989, entertainer Wayne Newton was awarded $19.2 million in damages after he sued NBC-TV for a story that linked him to organized crime.

3. In September 2010, Republican U.S. Senate candidate Jeff Greene, a Florida real estate developer who lost the Democratic primary, sued the *St. Petersburg Times* and *The Miami Herald* for $500 million, saying the newspapers' stories were part of "a coordinated and agreed upon plan to assassinate Greene's character."

These three cases involve the law of *libel*, a legal restraint on press freedom in the U.S. (A libelous statement is one that unjustifiably exposes someone to ridicule or contempt.) The cases clearly indicate the mass media's legal vulnerability to charges of participating in and/or provoking irresponsible, damaging behavior.

How can the country accommodate both the First Amendment concept of a free press and the right of the nation's citizens to keep their reputations from being unnecessarily damaged?

> **Libel** A false statement that damages a person's character or reputation by exposing that person to public ridicule or contempt.

IMPACT

Profile

John Green's *The Fault in Our Stars* is Banned, then Returned to Riverside, California, Classrooms

By Shirley Biagi

On September 22, 2014, the Riverside, California, Unified School District voted 6 to 1 to ban the international bestseller by John Green, *The Fault in Our Stars*, from the district's middle schools. The board banned the book, about two young adults who are dying of cancer, after one parent complained about sex and crude language. The book remained available in the district's high schools.

In voting for the ban, board member Tom Hunt read a 32-line passage from the book that described the pair's sexual relationship. Then Hunt commented, "This is two young people who are facing death. This is not appropriate for middle school."

According to *Time* magazine, when a fan asked author John Green to respond to news of the ban, he said, "I guess I am both happy and sad. I am happy because apparently young people in Riverside, California, will never witness or experience mortality since they won't be reading my book, which is great for them. But I am also sad because I was really hoping I would be able to introduce the idea that human beings die to the children of Riverside, California, and thereby crush their dreams of immortality."

After national publicity about the ban, the board voted 3-2 three months later to return the book to middle school library shelves. Praising the board's December action, Riverside's local newspaper, *The Press-Enterprise*, published an editorial on December 11, 2014 that concluded, "The idea that government officials ought to have a say in what books children have access to is concerning. What a young person chooses to read should more appropriately be determined by the youth and their parents or guardians. For public institutions to moralize by committee or decree is an inappropriate exercise of government power."

AP Images/Matt Sayles

John Green, author of the international bestseller *The Fault in Our Stars*, whose book was banned by the Riverside (California) Unified School District in 2014 and then reinstated.

Sullivan Case Establishes a Libel Landmark

Modern interpretation of the free speech protections of the First Amendment began in 1964 with the landmark *New York Times v. Sullivan* case in which the U.S. Supreme Court began a process that continues today to define how the press should operate in a free society. Many of today's arguments about the free press's role in a libel case derive from this decision.

The *Sullivan* case began in early 1960 in Alabama, where civil rights leader Dr. Martin Luther King, Jr., was arrested for perjury on his income tax form (a charge of which he was eventually acquitted). The Committee to Defend Martin Luther King bought a full-page ad in the March 29, 1960, *New York Times* that included statements about harassment of King by public officials and the police. The ad included a plea for money to support civil rights causes. Several notable people were listed in the ad as supporters, including singer Harry Belafonte, actor Sidney Poitier and former First Lady Eleanor Roosevelt.

IMPACT

Society

ILLUSTRATION 14.1

2014 Top 10 Most Frequently Challenged Books

Each year, the American Library Association's Office for Intellectual Freedom compiles a list of the top ten most frequently challenged books in order to inform the public about censorship in libraries and schools. The ALA condemns censorship and works to ensure free access to information.

A challenge is defined as a formal, written complaint filed with a library or school requesting that materials be removed because of content or appropriateness. The number of challenges reflects only incidents reported. We estimate that for every reported challenge, four or five remain unreported. Therefore, we do not claim comprehensiveness in recording challenges.

American Library Association, ala.org

Chris Felver/Getty Images

Sherman Alexie is the author of *The Absolutely True Diary of a Part-Time Indian*, 2014's most frequently challenged book. Alexie recounts his experiences as a 14-year-old who left the Spokane Reservation, where he grew up, to attend a local high school 22 miles away.

The Absolutely True Diary of a Part-Time Indian by Sherman Alexie

1

And Tango Makes Three by Peter Parnell and Justin Richardson

2

Persepolis by Marjane Satrapi

3

The Bluest Eye by Toni Morrison

4

It's Perfectly Normal by Robie Harris

5

Saga by Brian Vaughan and Fiona Staples

6

The Kite Runner by Khaled Hosseini

7

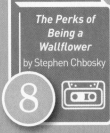

The Perks of Being a Wallflower by Stephen Chbosky

8

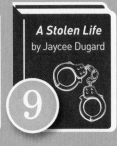

A Stolen Life by Jaycee Dugard

9

Drama by Raina Telgmeier

10

L. B. Sullivan, who supervised the police and fire departments as commissioner of public affairs in Montgomery, Ala., demanded a retraction from *The Times* regarding the statements about King's harassment, even though he had not been named in the ad. *The Times* refused, and Sullivan sued *The Times* for libel in Montgomery County, where 35 copies of the March 29, 1960, *Times* had been distributed for sale. The trial in Montgomery County lasted three days, beginning on November 1, 1960. The jury found *The Times* guilty and awarded Sullivan $500,000.

Eventually, the case reached the U.S. Supreme Court. In deciding the suit, the Court said that although *The Times* might have been negligent because it did not spot some misstatements of fact that appeared in the ad, *The Times* did not deliberately lie—it did not act with what the Court called *actual malice*.

In the U.S., legal interpretation of free-speech protections of the First Amendment began with the landmark *New York Times v. Sullivan* case. L. B. Sullivan (*second from right*) appears in November 1960 with his attorneys. Although Sullivan's libel suit was successful in Alabama, the U.S. Supreme Court decided in 1964 that he had failed to prove malice on the part of *The New York Times*.

To prove libel of a public official, the official must show that the defendant published information with *knowledge of its falsity* or out of *reckless disregard* for whether it was true or false, the Court concluded. The *Sullivan* decision thus became the standard for subsequent libel suits: Public officials in a libel case must prove actual malice.

Redefining the *Sullivan* Decision

Three important cases further defined the *Sullivan* decision.

GERTZ V. ROBERT WELCH INC. The 1974 decision in *Gertz v. Robert Welch Inc.* established the concept that the expression of opinions is a necessary part of public debate, and so an opinion—an editorial or a restaurant review, for example—cannot be considered libelous. The *Gertz* case also expanded the definition of public *official* to public *figure*. Today, the difference between public figures and private figures is very important in libel suits.

People who are defined as *private citizens* by a court must show only that the libelous information is false and that the journalist or news organization acted negligently in presenting the information. *Public figures*, however, must show not only that the libelous information is false but also that the information was published with actual malice—that the journalist or the news organization knew the information was untrue or deliberately overlooked facts that would have proved the published information was untrue.

HERBERT V. LANDO. The 1979 decision in *Herbert v. Lando* established the concept that because a public figure suing for libel must prove actual malice, the public figure can use the discovery process (the process by which potential witnesses are questioned under oath before the trial to help define the issues to be resolved at the trial) to determine a reporter's state of mind in preparing the story.

Because of this decision, reporters are sometimes asked in a libel suit to identify their sources and give up their notes and the tapes of the interviews they conducted to write their stories. Reporters usually refuse and, as a result, may face legal sanctions.

MASSON V. NEW YORKER MAGAZINE. In 1991, the U.S. Supreme Court reinstated a $10 million libel suit brought against *The New Yorker* magazine by psychoanalyst Jeffrey M. Masson. Masson charged that author Janet Malcolm libeled him in two articles in *The New Yorker* and in a book when she deliberately misquoted him. Malcolm contended the quotations she used were recorded or were written in her notes.

Malcolm wrote, for example, that Masson said, "I was like an intellectual gigolo." However, this exact phrase was not in the transcript of her interview. Masson contended that he never used the phrase. Issues in the case included whether quoted material must be verbatim and whether a journalist can change grammar and syntax. When the case was heard again in 1994, the Court found that Malcolm had changed Masson's words but that the changes did not libel Masson. The *Masson* case is an

This paper only prints the truth or the closest thing to it that doesn't get us sued for libel.

Patrick Rolands/Cartoon Stock

important example of the Court's attempts to define the limits of libel.

Charges and Defenses for Libel

To prove libel, someone must show that:

▸ The statement was communicated to a third party.

▸ People who read or saw the statement would be able to identify the person, even if that person was not actually named.

▸ The statement injured the person's reputation or income or caused mental anguish.

▸ The journalist or the print or broadcast organization is at fault.

Members of the press and press organizations that are faced with a libel suit can use three defenses: (1) truth, (2) privilege and (3) fair comment.

TRUTH. The first and best defense against libel, of course, is that the information is true. True information, although sometimes damaging, cannot be considered libelous. Publishing true information, however, can still be an invasion of privacy, as explained later in this chapter. Furthermore, truth is a successful defense only if truth is proved to the satisfaction of a judge or jury.

PRIVILEGE. The press is free to report what is discussed during legislative and court proceedings, even though the information presented in the proceedings by witnesses and others may be untrue or damaging. This is called ***qualified privilege***.

FAIR COMMENT. The courts also have carefully protected the press's freedom to present opinions. Because opinions cannot be proved true or false, the press is free to comment on public issues and to praise a play or criticize a movie, for example.

Legal Outcomes Reflect Mixed Results

The outcomes of the three cases listed at the beginning of this discussion of libel law (on p. 287) were the following:

1. The jury in the Carol Burnett case originally awarded her $1.6 million, but the amount was reduced to $150,000 on appeal.

2. The jury awarded Wayne Newton $19.2 million in 1989. NBC appealed the case, and in 1990 the courts overturned the award, ruling there was not enough evidence to prove actual malice, but NBC's legal costs were in the millions of dollars.

3. The Jeff Greene case was dismissed. In responding to the charges, the editor of the *St. Petersburg Times* said, "It is our firm opinion that the allegations in this lawsuit are preposterous. We believe Jeff Greene is a sore loser and he's trying to blame the newspapers because he can't accept the verdict of the voters." The Greene case could be considered an example of a ***SLAPP*** suit—*s*trategic *l*awsuit *a*gainst *p*ublic *p*articipation. (See "Internet Comments Bring SLAPP Suits," p. 292.)

In two of the three cases, the courts faulted members of the media for their reporting methods, but neither members of the press nor the media companies were found legally responsible. All three cases show that journalists and media organizations must always be diligent about their responsibilities, and there are serious financial and professional consequences for news organizations that forget to act responsibly and heed the law.

Most successful libel judgments eventually are reversed or reduced when they are appealed. Often the major cost of a libel suit is the defense lawyers' fees. Large media organizations carry libel insurance, but a small newspaper, magazine or book publisher, broadcast station or Internet site may not be able to afford the insurance or the legal costs.

> **Qualified Privilege** The freedom of the press to report what is discussed during legislative and court proceedings.
>
> **SLAPP** Strategic lawsuit against public participation.

Internet Comments Bring SLAPP Suits

Bloggers and other Internet users who post critical comments on sites like Facebook, Twitter and Yelp may find themselves the target of what lawyers call a SLAPP. This is a common tactic of businesses and government officials because suing someone for defamation can intimidate the person with the prospect of an expensive court battle against a well-financed opponent.

Today, the Internet makes a person's critical comments available instantly, and some companies and public officials are threatening libel suits against their critics. There are 27 states with anti-SLAPP laws, which may require that the person who brings the suit pay the combined legal costs if the suit is dismissed.

Federal anti-SLAPP legislation, which would make protections uniform across the country, continues to be debated in Congress. "Just as petition and free speech rights are so important that they require specific constitutional protections, they are also important enough to justify uniform national protections against SLAPPs," said Mark Goldowitz, director of the California Anti-SLAPP Project.

Invasion of Privacy Defined Four Ways

The public seems to think invasion of privacy is one of the mass media's worst faults. However, libel suits are much more common in the United States than suits about invasion of privacy. Because there is no U.S. Supreme Court decision covering privacy like *The New York Times v. Sullivan* covers libel, each state has its own privacy protections for citizens and its own restrictions on how reporters can get the news and what can be published.

Privacy is an ethical issue as well as a legal one. (See **Chapter 15** for a discussion of the ethics of privacy.) Generally, the law says the media can be guilty of invasion of privacy in four ways:

1. By intruding on a person's physical or mental solitude.

2. By publishing or disclosing embarrassing personal facts.

3. By giving someone publicity that places the person in a false light.

4. By using someone's name or likeness for commercial benefit.

If they are successful, people who initiate privacy cases can be awarded monetary damages to compensate them for the wrongdoing. However, very few invasion of privacy cases succeed.

Physical or Mental Solitude

The courts in most states have recognized that a person has a right not to be pursued by the news media unnecessarily. A reporter can photograph or question someone on a public street or at a public event, but a person's home and office are private. For this reason, many photographers request that someone who is photographed in a private situation sign a release form, designating how the photograph can be used.

One notable case establishing this right of privacy is *Galella v. Onassis*. Jacqueline Onassis, widow of President John F. Kennedy, charged that Ron Galella, a freelance photographer, was pursuing her unnecessarily. He had used a telephoto lens to photograph her on private property, and he had pursued her children at private schools. In 1973, Galella was ordered to stay 25 feet away from Onassis and 30 feet away from her children.

Embarrassing Personal Facts

The personal facts the media use to report a story should be newsworthy, according to the courts. If a public official is caught traveling with her boyfriend on taxpayers' money while her husband stays at home, information about the boyfriend is essential to the story. If the public official is reported to have contracted AIDS from her boyfriend, the information probably is not relevant to the story and could be protected under this provision of privacy law.

In reality, however, public officials enjoy few legal protections from reporting about their private lives. Information available from public records, such as court proceedings, is not considered private, and if the public official's husband testifies in court about his wife's disease, for example, the information could be reported.

False Light

A writer who portrays someone in a fictional version of actual events should be especially conscious of ***false light*** litigation. People who believe that what a writer or photographer *implies* about them is incorrect (even if the portrayal is flattering) can bring a false-light suit.

The best-known false-light suit is the first, *Time Inc. v. Hill*. In 1955, *Life* magazine published a story about a Broadway play, *The Desperate Hours*, which portrayed someone taking a hostage. The play's author said he based it on several real-life incidents. One of these involved the Hill family, a husband and wife and their five children who

> **False Light** The charge that what was implied in a story about someone is incorrect.

had been taken hostage in their Philadelphia home by three escaped convicts. The Hills told police the convicts had treated them courteously, but the Hills were frightened by the events and eventually moved to Connecticut.

When *Life* decided to do a story about the play, the cast went to the Hills' old home, where *Life* photographed the actors in scenes from the play—one son being roughed up by the convicts and a daughter biting a convict's hand. None of these incidents had happened to the Hills, but *Life* published the photographs along with a review of the play.

The Hills sued Time Inc., which owned *Life* magazine, for false-light invasion of privacy and won $75,000, which eventually was reduced to $30,000. When the case went to the U.S. Supreme Court, the Court refused to uphold the decision, saying the Hills must prove *actual malice*. The Hills dropped the case, but the establishment of actual malice as a requirement in false-light cases was important.

In 1974, in *Cantrell v. Forest City Publishing Co.*, the U.S. Supreme Court held that a reporter for the Cleveland *Plain Dealer* had wrongly portrayed the widow of an Ohio man who was killed when a bridge collapsed. The story talked about the woman as if the reporter had interviewed her, although he had only interviewed her children. She was awarded $60,000 in her false-light suit, and the U.S. Supreme Court upheld the verdict.

Only a few false-light cases have been successful, but the lesson for the press is that portraying events and people truthfully avoids the problem altogether.

Right of Publicity

This facet of privacy law is especially important in the advertising and public relations industries. A portable toilet seems a strange fixture to use to establish a point of law, but a case brought by former *Tonight Show* host Johnny Carson demonstrates how the right of publicity protects someone's name from being used to make money without that person's permission.

In *Carson v. Here's Johnny Portable Toilets*, Carson charged, in 1983, that a Michigan manufacturer of portable toilets misappropriated Carson's name to sell the toilets. The manufacturer named his new line Here's Johnny Portable Toilets and advertised them with the phrase "The World's Foremost Commodian." Carson said that he did not want to be associated with the product and that since he had begun hosting *The Tonight Show* in 1957 he had been introduced with the phrase "Here's Johnny." The court agreed that "Here's Johnny" violated Carson's right of publicity.

The right of publicity can apply to a person's picture on a poster or name in an advertisement. In some cases, this right is covered even after the person dies, so the members of the immediate family of a well-known entertainer, for example, are the only people who can authorize the use of the entertainer's name or likeness.

Bartnicki v. Vopper

In an important recent case for the press, *Bartnicki v. Vopper*, the U.S. Supreme Court in 2001 reaffirmed the media's right to broadcast information and to comment on that information, no matter how the information was obtained.

The case resulted from a cell phone conversation between Pennsylvania teachers' union negotiator Gloria Bartnicki and Anthony Kane, the union's president. The union was in the middle of negotiating a teachers' contract. During the conversation (which was intercepted and recorded without Bartnicki's or Kane's knowledge), Kane is heard to say that if the school board didn't increase its offer, "We're going to have to go to their homes . . . to blow off their front porches."

A local activist gave the recording to radio station WILK-AM, and talk-show host Fred Vopper (who used the on-air name Fred Williams) aired the recording. Bartnicki and Kane sued Vopper under the federal wiretap law, which provides civil damages and criminal prosecution for someone who disseminates information that is illegally intercepted. The case pitted the public's right to know versus the erosion of personal privacy by new technologies.

U.S. Supreme Court Justice John Paul Stevens wrote the opinion for the 6-3 majority that "a stranger's illegal conduct does not suffice to remove the First Amendment shield from speech about a matter of public concern." In this decision, the Court again reaffirmed the press's right to report information in the public interest.

Debate Continues over Fair Trial, Courtroom Access and Shield Laws

The answers to three other questions that bear on press freedoms and individual rights remain discretionary for the courts:

1. When does media coverage influence a jury so much that a defendant's right to a fair trial is jeopardized?

2. How much access should the media be granted during a trial?

3. Should journalists be required to reveal information they obtained in confidence while reporting a story if a court decides that information is necessary to the judicial process?

Fair Trial

The best-known decision affecting prejudicial press coverage of criminal cases is *Sheppard v. Maxwell*. In 1954, Dr. Samuel Sheppard of Cleveland was sentenced to life imprisonment for murdering his wife. His conviction followed reams of newspaper stories, many of which proclaimed his guilt before the jury decided the case. The jurors, who went home each evening, were told by the judge not to read newspapers or pay attention to broadcast reports, but no one monitored what the jurors did.

Twelve years later, lawyer F. Lee Bailey took Sheppard's trial to the U.S. Supreme Court, where the conviction was overturned on the premise that Sheppard had been a victim of a biased jury. In writing the decision, Justice Tom C. Clark prescribed several remedies. He said that the reporters should have been limited to certain areas in the courtroom, that the news media should not have been allowed to interview the witnesses and that the court should have forbidden statements outside the courtroom.

AP Images/Uncredited

Whether to allow cameras in the courtroom is a state-by-state decision. Cameras were barred during the 2015 trial of James Holmes, who was charged with killing 12 people and injuring 58 in a movie theatre in Aurora, Colo. However, cameras were allowed to show the trial's final arguments on July 14, 2015. (Holmes is on the far left in the white shirt. On the screen is a picture of the youngest shooting victim, Veronica Moser-Sullivan.)

Courtroom Access

The outcome of the *Sheppard* case led to many courtroom experiments with restrictions on the press. The most widespread practices were restraining (gag) orders and closed proceedings. With a gag order, the judge limits what the press may report. Closed proceedings excluded the press from the courtroom. But since 1980, several court cases have overturned most of these limitations. Today the press is rarely excluded completely from courtroom proceedings, and the exclusion lasts only as long as it takes the news organization to appeal to a higher court for access.

Although print reporters usually gain access, the presence of cameras in the courtroom is a sticky issue between judges (who want to avoid the cameras' disruption) and broadcast news people (who want to photograph what is going on). The U.S. Supreme Court, for example, never allows cameras.

In some high-profile cases, cameras have been allowed to record complete trials. In 1994, for example, Court TV broadcast the entire murder trial of former football star O. J. Simpson. In 2015, cameras were barred from the trial of James Holmes, who was charged with killing 12 people and injuring 58 at a theater in Aurora, Colo. But cameras were allowed to photograph closing arguments on July 14, 2015. (See **Illustration 14.2**, "Cameras in the Courtroom: A State-by-State Guide.")

Whether to allow cameras in the courtroom is a state-by-state decision. Some states allow cameras during civil but not criminal trials. Other states try to limit access altogether. The U.S. courts and the press are not yet completely comfortable partners.

Shield Laws

Traditionally, U.S. courts have been reluctant to compel journalists to reveal information they gather from confidential sources as part of their reporting on stories. In 1972, in *Branzburg v. Hayes*, the U.S. Supreme Court ruled for the first time that journalists do not have a constitutional privilege to refuse to testify but that there was "merit in leaving state legislatures free, within First Amendment limits, to fashion their own standards."

According to the Congressional Research Service, "31 states and the District of Columbia have recognized a journalist's privilege through enactment of press '***shield laws***,' which protect the relationship between reporters, their source, and sometimes, the information that may be communicated in that relationship." This means, for example, that reporters in California, Alaska and Colorado have state shield law protection, but reporters in

Shield Laws Laws that protect journalists from revealing their sources and the information that is communicated between journalists and their sources in a journalistic relationship.

IMPACT

Society

ILLUSTRATION 14.2

Cameras in the Courtroom: A State-by-State Guide

Most states allow at least some camera access to courtroom proceedings. The U.S. Supreme Court does not allow cameras.

Radio-Television Digital News Association, rtdna.org/pages/media_items/cameras-in-the-court-a-state-by-state-guide55.php

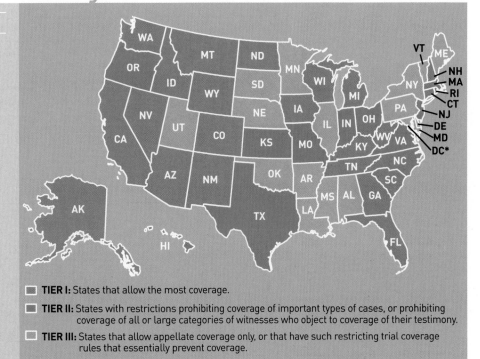

☐ **TIER I:** States that allow the most coverage.

☐ **TIER II:** States with restrictions prohibiting coverage of important types of cases, or prohibiting coverage of all or large categories of witnesses who object to coverage of their testimony.

☐ **TIER III:** States that allow appellate coverage only, or that have such restricting trial coverage rules that essentially prevent coverage.

*The District of Columbia is the only jurisdiction that prohibits trial and appellate coverage entirely.

Texas, South Dakota and Connecticut do not. Occasionally members of Congress have introduced legislation to create a federal shield law to protect journalists on a national level, but Congress has never seriously considered the issue. This leaves journalists at the mercy of individual state shield laws.

FCC Regulates Broadcast and Cable

People who work in the American mass media are expected to abide by the country's legal framework. The print media are not regulated specifically by any government agency, but regulation of broadcast and Internet media comes from government agencies that oversee aspects of the media business.

The largest single area of regulation comes from the Federal Communications Commission (FCC), which oversees broadcast and Internet providers. Other regulating agencies, such as the Federal Trade Commission, scrutinize specific areas related to the media, such as advertising.

Since 1927, the rationale for broadcast regulation has been that the airwaves belong to the public and that broadcasters are trustees operating in the public interest.

The history of U.S. broadcast regulation can be traced to government's early attempt to organize the airwaves. The FCC, based in Washington, D.C., now has five commissioners who are appointed by the president and approved by the U.S. Senate. Each commissioner serves a five-year term, and the president appoints the chairperson.

FCC regulation touches many aspects of broadcast and Internet operations. Because U.S. broadcast stations must be licensed by the FCC to operate, the federal government exercises more direct control over broadcast and Internet media than over the print media. And like the print media, broadcasters also must operate under the nation's laws covering libel, obscenity and the right of privacy.

Telecommunications Act of 1996 Changes the Marketplace

On February 8, 1996, President Clinton signed the Telecommunications Act of 1996, the most far-reaching reform in U.S. government regulation of mass media since the creation of the FCC in 1934. The act affects all aspects of the media industries, especially broadcast, cable, telephone and the Internet. The act is transforming the nation's media industries.

Justin Sullivan/Getty Images

The Telecommunications Act of 1996 removed many regulations governing the services telecommunications companies provide. A telecommunications company can now offer Internet, telephone and satellite TV together, called a "bundle," for power users. A worker climbs a cellular communications tower in Oakland, California, on March 6, 2014.

When Congress created the FCC in 1934, the agency was charged with ensuring that broadcasters operated in the "public interest, convenience and necessity." The Telecommunications Act, however, is an extension of the philosophy of deregulation—that free competition, with less government regulation, eventually improves consumers' choices, lowers costs and encourages investment in new technologies.

This philosophy of open competition governs the media industries in the 21st century. The strategies of providing multiple services and targeting select users are two examples of the effects of the act today.

Goal: To Sell Consumers "The Bundle"

"It's War!" declared *The Wall Street Journal* on September 16, 1996. The battlefield was telecommunications, and the goal was the **bundle**. In telecommunications, this term describes the combination of services the media industries now offer. After the 1996 Telecommunications Act passed, large companies began delivering a combination of telecommunications services that they think consumers want. The *Journal* reported:

> Thanks to a combination of deregulation and new technologies, war has broken out in the communications market. Everybody has joined the fray— long-distance telephone giants, the regional [local telephone] Bell companies and the cable-TV operators, the satellite outfits, the fledgling digital wireless phone firms and the Internet service providers. Even your old-fashioned power company.

And they all want the same thing: to invade one another's markets and sell you one another's products and services. In short, they want to sell you The Bundle. Your long-distance telephone company, such as AT&T or Verizon, wants to become your local telephone company, your satellite TV company, your cable company and your Internet service provider.

Targeting the Power User

This bundling of services means that you can pay one monthly bill for several types of media services to a single company, which, of course, dramatically increases that company's portion of media revenue. "The goal for these companies is twofold," says Richard Siber, a wireless analyst for Andersen Consulting in Boston. "One is locking in a customer for life and providing one-stop shopping. And the other is revenue maximization, getting you to use their products more and more."

BusinessWeek magazine called this intense competition for customers a "telescramble." The primary target is the so-called power user, someone who uses a lot of media at home or in business.

The Telecommunications Act of 1996 created this battlefield for consumers' attention with huge financial incentives for the winners. The economic future of every media company in the country has, in some way, been affected by this battle.

Deregulation Unleashes the Media

The major provisions of the Telecommunications Act affect telecommunications, broadcast and cable. The Communications Decency Act, which was part of the Telecommunications Act, attempted to regulate access to cable and television programming and monitor the content of computer networks, including the Internet.

Bundle   The combination of telecommunications services that the media industries can offer consumers.

Created a Goal of Universal Service

The Telecommunications Act of 1996 established, for the first time, a goal of universal service—meaning that, as a matter of public policy, everyone in the U.S. should be guaranteed access to affordable telecommunications services.

The FCC's responsibility is to decide what exactly constitutes universal service, and whether Internet access is part of that service guarantee, to improve the economies of rural areas as well as major cities.

Deregulated Free Media

The Telecommunications Act of 1996 also continued a policy of deregulation of commercial radio and TV ownership that began in the 1980s. Radio and over-the-air broadcast TV are viewed as "free media."

Unlike cable stations and satellite companies, which require extra equipment and charge consumers for their services, over-the-air broadcasting is available to anyone with a radio or television—and 99 percent of U.S. households have a TV set. Over-the-air broadcasting offers the largest potential audience for free media.

Relaxed Ownership and Licensing Rules

The FCC licenses every radio and TV station in the country and, before the act passed, the renewal process was very complicated. TV stations were required to renew their licenses every five years and radio stations every seven. The act relaxed the renewal requirements and extended the renewal period for both radio and TV to eight years.

Previously, broadcast companies were allowed to own only 12 television stations. The act eliminated the limits on the number of TV stations one company may own and instead used a station's potential audience to measure ownership limits. The act said existing television networks (such as NBC and ABC) can begin new networks, but they cannot buy an existing network. NBC cannot buy ABC, for example, but NBC could begin a second network of its own, such as NBC2.

Before the act passed, radio broadcasters were allowed to own 20 AM or 20 FM radio stations nationwide. The act removed the limit on the number of radio stations a company may own, and in each market, the number of stations that one owner can hold depends on the size of the market.

The act also allows **broadcast cross-ownership**. This means that companies may own TV and radio stations in the same broadcast market as well as broadcast and cable outlets in the same area.

In 2003, the FCC made it even easier to own more TV stations, and today one company is allowed to own TV stations that reach 35 percent of the U.S. population. The broadcast industry continues to lobby to reduce the limitation or remove it completely.

In 2002, the FCC began considering **media cross-ownership** rules that, for example, would allow broadcasters to own newspapers as well as broadcast stations in the same geographic area. The concept of media cross-ownership remains under study, and FCC rules still prohibit media cross-ownership of a daily newspaper and a full-power broadcast station (AM, FM, or TV) in the same market.

Encouraged Local Phone Competition

Due to deregulation, cable, satellite and telephone companies today are competing to deliver telecommunications services to home customers.

To encourage competition for delivery of video services, the act allowed local telephone companies to enter the video delivery business and repealed the FCC's "telco-cable cross-ownership" restrictions (**telco** is an abbreviation for "telephone company"). Local telephone companies now can deliver video services either by making an agreement with a cable or satellite operator or by creating their own delivery system.

In turn, cable companies were allowed to enter the local telephone business. Large cable companies also may deliver new types of telephone services, such as carrying messages to and from mobile phones.

The act also allowed long-distance carriers to offer local telephone service. Within two months of the act's passage, the long-distance carrier AT&T filed to be allowed to offer local telephone service in all 50 states. "If we get this right," said former FCC Chairman Reed Hundt, "you'll be buying communications services like shoes. Different styles, different vendors."

Ends Cable Rate Regulation

In an attempt to control spiraling cable charges to consumers, Congress passed the 1992 Cable Act to regulate rates. Cable companies, facing competition from telephone companies, argued that Congress should remove rate regulation to allow them to compete and increase cable income.

The act removed most rate regulation for all cable companies. All that remains is FCC regulation to monitor the "basic tier" of cable service, often called "basic cable." Overall, this resulted in rate increases for most cable consumers.

Broadcast Cross-Ownership The practice of one company owning TV and radio stations in the same broadcast market.

Media Cross-Ownership Government rules that would allow a broadcast company to own a newspaper business in the same geographic area.

Telco An abbreviation for "telephone company."

TV Industry Agrees to Ratings and the V-Chip

Under pressure from Congress, television executives agreed to implement a voluntary ratings system for television programs by January 1997. The new ratings system *applies to all programming except sports, news magazines and news shows.*

The ratings divide programs into six categories, ranging from TV-Y (appropriate for all children but specifically designed for a very young audience, including children between the ages of 2 and 6) to TV-MA (specifically designed to be viewed by adults and therefore possibly unsuitable for children younger than 17).

Producers, networks, cable channels, syndicators and other people who originate TV shows rate their own programs, unlike movies (which are rated by an independent board). TV ratings evaluate violence and sexual content, and the results are displayed on the screen at the beginning of each program and coded into each TV program. The codes are read by a v-chip, a microchip device that must be included in all new TV sets. The v-chip allows parents to program the TV set to eliminate shows they find objectionable, although follow-up studies have shown that few parents use this option.

Six months after this rating system was adopted, the TV networks added a more specific rating for violent or sexual content. Today, the broadcast networks and program services display content ratings on most programs.

Congress Attempts to Control Access to Indecent Content

Along with the major provisions of the Telecommunications Act to increase competition, Congress added several provisions to try to control content. These provisions, together called the Communications Decency Act (CDA), attempted to define and control users' access to specific content.

The CDA made it a felony to send indecent material over computer networks and relied on a very broad definition of the word *indecent*. Under the act's provisions, violators could have been fined up to $250,000.

On June 12, 1996, a three-judge panel unanimously declared that the Internet indecency provisions were unconstitutional, and the judges blocked the law's enforcement. They issued a restraining order, which meant that the Internet indecency provisions could not be enforced and that violations could not even be investigated.

In 1997, the U.S. Supreme Court struck down the indecency provision of the Communications Decency Act, making it much harder for Congress to limit Internet access in the future.

This decision is important because Congress and the president, through the FCC, historically have regulated the broadcast industries, but none of the regulations that apply to the broadcast media apply to print. The content of the print media, by law and by practice, has historically remained unregulated because of the First Amendment's protection of free expression. What is interesting is that, in striking down the CDA, the courts defined and protected free expression through an electronic delivery system—the Internet—as if it were a print medium.

Supreme Court Upholds Internet Filters for Public Libraries

In 2003, the U.S. Supreme Court upheld another law that said that libraries that accept federal funds must

Kevin Schafer/Getty Images

In 2003, the U.S. Supreme Court voted 5-4 to uphold a law that said that libraries that accept federal funding must equip their computers with content filters. The American Library Association argued that Internet filters are a form of censorship. Patrons at the Seattle Public Library access the Internet in January 2015.

equip their computers with content filters to block pornography, a blow for freedom of expression. The case was defended in court on behalf of 13-year-old Emalyn Rood, who logged onto the Internet in an Oregon library to research information on lesbianism, and Mark Brown, who researched information about his mother's breast cancer on a Philadelphia library computer—information that may have been blocked by a commonly used Internet filter.

In a close 5-4 decision in *United States v. American Library Association*, the U.S. Supreme Court said the requirement for Internet filters is "a valid exercise of Congress' spending power." This decision allows the U.S. government to require Internet filters at libraries that receive federal funding. Librarians argued that Internet filters are a form of censorship that blocks valuable information from people who need it.

Government Monitors Broadcast Indecency

In early 2004, responding to congressional pressure for more government control over the airwaves, the FCC proposed a $775,000 fine against Clear Channel Communications for a Florida radio broadcast of various episodes of *Bubba the Love Sponge Show*. The FCC fined Clear Channel the maximum amount then allowed—$27,500 for each time the episode ran (a total of $715,000) plus $40,000 for record-keeping violations at the station. Clear Channel said the programs were meant to entertain, not to offend its listeners.

FCC Chairman Michael Powell also urged Congress to increase the maximum fine for indecency to $275,000 per incident, saying the maximum fine of $27,500 per episode wasn't large enough to discourage objectionable programming.

Just a few days later, singers Janet Jackson and Justin Timberlake, performing on CBS-TV during Super Bowl halftime, provoked controversy when Timberlake reached over and ripped off part of Jackson's costume, exposing her breast to an estimated 90 million Americans and a much bigger worldwide audience.

Jackson and Timberlake apologized for the incident, but the FCC launched an investigation. FCC rules say that radio and over-the-air TV stations may not air obscene material at any time. The rules also bar stations from broadcasting indecent material—references to sex or excretions—between 6 a.m. and 10 p.m., when the FCC says children are more likely to be listening or watching. (Cable and satellite programming is not covered by the restrictions.) The FCC fined CBS $550,000 for the Janet Jackson incident.

In 2007, CBS appealed the Jackson fine before the 3rd U.S. Circuit Court of Appeals in Philadelphia, saying the network had taken precautions beforehand to avoid any

In 2002, singer Cher appeared on the Billboard Music Awards and made some impromptu comments that included a profanity. The FCC fined Fox television network, which broadcast the awards, for indecency. In July 2010, a three-judge panel in New York, hearing the Billboard Music Awards case and several others dealing with the issue of fleeting expletives, struck down the indecency rule, saying it had a "chilling effect" that interfered with freedom of expression.

incidents, including a five-second audio delay. In 2008, a federal appeals court overturned the decision, saying, "The FCC cannot impose liability on CBS for the acts of Janet Jackson and Justin Timberlake, independent contractors hired for the limited purposes of the Halftime Show."

Then in a July 2010 ruling on a group of indecency cases, a federal appeals court in New York found that the FCC's indecency policy violated the First Amendment. The cases involved *fleeting expletives*, profanity uttered without warning on live television. In the instances cited, celebrities including Cher and Bono made impromptu remarks during awards shows on live television, and the FCC fined the networks that aired the shows.

The court said that the FCC's policy against indecency had a chilling effect on free speech "because broadcasters have no way of knowing what the FCC will find offensive."

> **Fleeting Expletives** Profanity uttered without warning on live television.

These controversies highlight the difficulties that arise when a federal government agency attempts to monitor free expression without an established national legal standard for obscenity. The definition of broadcast indecency often is based on politics and public pressure at the FCC, which shifts emphasis from one presidential administration to another.

The main issues are these: Should a government entity have the power to decide what's obscene or indecent and then to enforce those restrictions? And what effect, if any, could these decisions have in a media environment where there are so many alternative, unregulated outlets available to consumers of all ages?

Don Arnold/Getty Images

To combat video piracy, the music and movie industries launched the Copyright Alert System in 2013. The Sydney, Australia, premiere of *Game of Thrones* on April 13, 2015, features a fire-breathing dragon. In March 2015, Torrentfreak.com, which tracks online piracy, reported that *Game of Thrones* was on track to become the most-pirated TV show of the year.

Intellectual Property Rights Affirmed

The right of ownership for creative ideas in the U.S. is legally governed by what are called ***intellectual property rights***. Four recent developments—the Digital Millennium Copyright Act, the U.S. Supreme Court decision in *New York Times Co. v. Tasini* and decisions in *Metro-Goldwyn-Mayer Studios Inc. v. Grokster Ltd.* and *Arista Records LLC v. Lime Group LLC*—are beginning to define the issues of electronic copyright in the digital era.

Digital Millennium Copyright Act

Passed in 1998, the Digital Millennium Copyright Act (***DMCA***), which became effective on October 28, 2000, begins to address copyright issues provoked by the Internet. The law makes several changes in U.S. copyright law to bring it into compliance with two World Intellectual Property Organization (***WIPO***) treaties about digitally transmitted copyrighted and stored material. (The WIPO is responsible for promoting the protection of intellectual property throughout the world.)

The DMCA, designed to prevent illegal copying of material that is published and distributed on the Internet, makes it illegal to circumvent technology that protects or controls access to copyrighted materials, such as music shared on the Internet. The DMCA also makes it illegal to manufacture materials that will help people gain access to copyrighted materials. The DMCA became effective on October 28, 2000.

Supporters of the DMCA—which includes most media industries that hold copyrights on creative works, such as movies, books and music—say the DMCA is an important

law that must be enforced to protect intellectual property. Opponents say the law goes too far and limits technological development.

In March 2007, media conglomerate Viacom, whose media properties included MTV, Comedy Central and Nickelodeon, sued Google and YouTube, saying the companies deliberately gathered a library of copyrighted video clips without permission. Earlier in 2007, Viacom asked YouTube to remove 100,000 clips that it said infringed on Viacom copyrights.

Google said the "safe harbor" provisions of the DMCA covered YouTube. Generally these provisions say that Web site owners are not liable for copyrighted material that others upload to their site if the Web site owners promptly remove the material when the copyright owner asks them to do so.

However, Google announced four months later that it was developing video recognition technology to detect and remove copyrighted material from its site before it was posted.

Still, illegal video sharing is very difficult to monitor and prevent. In March 2015, Torrentfreak.com, which

---

Intellectual Property Rights The legal right of ownership of ideas and content published in any medium.

DMCA Digital Millennium Copyright Act.

WIPO World Intellectual Property Organization.

tracks online piracy, reported that *Game of Thrones* was on track to become the most pirated TV program of 2015 after there were 7 million pirated downloads in the first three months of the year. "The majority of TV-show piracy," reported Torrentfreak, "occurs outside the U.S.," by people who cannot receive the programs legally until after the shows air in America. *Game of Thrones*, aired on HBO, is available only to subscribers.

In February 2013, the music and movie industries launched the Copyright Alert System, administered by the Center for Copyright Information. Music and movie companies monitor online traffic and then alert an Internet provider when a file is downloaded illegally.

The Internet provider is authorized to issue an escalating series of six warnings after which the provider may slow down or block the offender's Internet access. "We think there is a positive impact of (alert) programs like this, and that they can put money in the pocket of artists and labels," Jonathan Lamy, a spokesman for the Recording Industry Association, told *The New York Times*.

New York Times Co. v. Tasini

In 2001, a U.S. Supreme Court decision in *New York Times Co. v. Tasini* affirmed that freelance writers separately own the electronic rights to material they have written, even though a publisher had first issued their writing in printed form. In 1993, freelance writer Jonathan Tasini, president of the National Writers Union, discovered that an article he had written for *The New York Times* was available on a database for Mead Data Center Corporation, which was paying royalties for the material to the *Times*. Tasini hadn't been paid for this use, so Tasini sued the *Times* and several other publishing companies.

The suit claimed that publishers violated copyright law by using writers' work on electronic databases without their permission and that this limited the rights of freelance authors to separately publish their work digitally and be paid for it. The *Times* claimed the digital versions of written works were simply "revisions" of paper copies, which meant the rights belonged to the publisher so the writers deserved no further compensation.

On June 25, 2001, by a vote of 7-2, the U.S. Supreme Court agreed with Tasini. Writing the majority opinion, Justices Breyer and Stevens said that upholding the freelance authors' copyright would encourage the development of new technologies and the creation of new artistic work. The Court ordered the *Times* to delete thousands of articles from its database for which it had not obtained the rights.

This case is very important for anyone in the U.S. who creates intellectual property. The Court established the legal concept that the right to reproduce creative material electronically is very distinct from the right to reproduce creative material in print and that writers and other creative artists should be compensated separately for electronic and print rights to their work.

Metro-Goldwyn-Mayer Studios Inc. v. Grokster Ltd. and Arista Records LLC v. Lime Group LLC

In 2005, the U.S. Supreme Court ruled unanimously in the *Grokster* case that a software company can be held liable for copyright infringement if someone uses the company's software to illegally download songs and movies, known as illegal file sharing. The decision effectively shut down the Internet sites Grokster and StreamCast, also named in the suit. The companies provided free software that allowed users to download Internet content free.

In 2010, a New York district court ordered that the major remaining file-sharing Web site, LimeWire, shut down in response to a suit by 14 recording companies, including Arista Records, Capitol Records and Virgin Records, which alleged that LimeWire was guilty of copyright infringement. (Lime Group LLC is the parent company of the Web site LimeWire.)

The Grokster and LimeWire cases are two more examples of the strong legal tradition in the U.S. that guarantees intellectual copyright protection for creative content and the aggressiveness with which mass media companies pursue people who try to use intellectual property without permission or payment.

FCC Adopts Open Internet Rules

On February 26, 2015, following a year of public debate, the Federal Communications Commission approved groundbreaking **net neutrality** rules, called the Open Internet Order, that classify Internet services in the U.S. as a public utility. Commission Chairman Tom Wheeler said the Open Internet rules were designed to preserve the Internet as a "core of free expression and democratic principles."

The new rules cover mobile data services for smartphones and tablets as well as hardwired lines. The

> **Net Neutrality** Rules for Internet service providers that require them to keep their networks open and available to carry all legal content. Under these rules, providers cannot restrict access to their network by other providers nor can they limit the type or delivery of content they carry.

Bloomberg/Getty Images

Michael Copps, former FCC commissioner, speaks in favor of net neutrality outside the FCC's headquarters in Washington, D.C., on February 26, 2015, the day the FCC announced its Open Internet Order guaranteeing net neutrality.

commission had a choice whether to classify the Internet as an information service or as a public utility. Under an information service classification, the FCC would have had very little power to regulate Internet service providers, and the Internet would have been more vulnerable to censorship. The information service classification also would have allowed Internet service providers to create different tiers of service for commercial users versus consumers (faster service for commercial clients who use more services, for example, giving them priority over consumers).

Instead, the FCC decided 3-2 that the Internet should be regulated as a utility just like telephone service. Traffic on the Internet should not be subject to censorship and all customers should be treated equally, said the FCC. (Net neutrality also is covered in **Chapter 9.**)

Among the Open Internet Order's provisions are three new Bright Line Rules that ban "practices that are known to harm the Open Internet," according to the FCC. The Bright Line Rules are:

1. **No Blocking.** Broadband providers may not block access to legal content, applications, services or non-harmful devices.

2. **No Throttling.** Broadband providers may not impair or degrade lawful Internet traffic on the basis of content, applications, services or non-harmful devices.

3. **No Paid Prioritization.** Broadband providers may not favor some lawful Internet traffic over other lawful traffic in exchange for consideration of any kind—in other words, no "fast lanes."

The goal of the new regulations, said the FCC, is the principle that "America's broadband networks must be fast, fair and open."

Courts and Regulators Govern Advertising and PR

Advertising and public relations are governed by legal constraints and by regulation. *New York Times v. Sullivan* (see p. 287) was a crucial case for advertisers as well as for journalists. Since that decision, two other important court cases have defined the advertising and public relations businesses—the *Central Hudson* case for advertising (which is considered "commercial speech" under the law because advertisers pay for their messages) and the *Texas Gulf Sulphur* case for public relations.

Central Hudson Case

In 1980, in *Central Hudson Gas & Electric Corp. v. Public Service Commission*, the U.S. Supreme Court issued the most definitive opinion yet on commercial speech. During the energy crisis atmosphere of the 1970s, the New York Public Utilities Commission banned all advertising by public utilities that promoted the use of electricity. Central Hudson Gas & Electric wanted the ban lifted, so the company sued the commission.

The commission said the ban promoted energy conservation, but the U.S. Supreme Court disagreed, and the decision in the case forms the basis for commercial speech protection today. "If the commercial speech does not mislead, and it concerns lawful activity," explains legal scholar Ralph Holsinger, "the government's power to regulate it is limited. . . . The state cannot impose regulations that only indirectly advance its interests. Nor can it regulate commercial speech that poses no danger to a state interest." The decision prescribed standards that commercial speech must meet to be protected by the First Amendment.

The main provisions of the standards are that (1) the advertisement must be for a lawful product and (2) the advertisement must not be misleading. This has become known as the ***Hudson test***. To be protected, then, an advertisement must promote a legal product and must not lie. This would seem to have settled the issue, but controversy continues.

Should alcohol advertising be banned? What about ads for condoms or marijuana? Courts in different states have disagreed on these questions, and no Supreme Court decision about these specific issues exists, leaving many complex questions undecided. The Hudson test remains

Hudson Test   A legal test that establishes a standard for commercial speech protection.

the primary criterion for determining what is protected commercial speech.

Texas Gulf Sulphur Case

The most important civil suit involving public relations occurred in the 1960s in *Securities and Exchange Commission v. Texas Gulf Sulphur Company.* Texas Gulf Sulphur (TGS) discovered ore deposits in Canada in late 1963 but did not announce the discovery publicly. TGS quietly purchased hundreds of acres surrounding the ore deposits, and TGS officers began to accumulate more shares of the company's stock.

Meanwhile, the company issued a press release that said that the rumors about a discovery were "unreliable." When TGS announced that it had made a "major strike," which boosted the price of the company's stock, the Securities and Exchange Commission took the company to court.

The U.S. Court of Appeals, Tenth Circuit, ruled that TGS officers had violated the disclosure laws of the Securities and Exchange Commission. The court also ruled that TGS had issued "a false and misleading press release." Company officers and their friends were punished for withholding information. According to *The Practice of Public Relations*, "the case proved conclusively that a company's failure to make known material information (information likely to be considered important by reasonable investors in determining whether to buy, sell or hold securities) may be in violation of the antifraud provision of the Securities and Exchange Acts."

The *Texas Gulf Sulphur* case remains a landmark in the history of public relations law. The decision in the case means public relations people can be held legally responsible for information they do not disclose about their companies. Public relations people at publicly held corporations (businesses with stockholders) are responsible not only to their companies but also to the public.

Federal Government Regulates Advertisers

The main regulatory agency for advertising and public relations issues is the Federal Trade Commission (FTC), although other agencies such as the Securities and Exchange Commission and the Food and Drug Administration sometimes intervene to question advertising practices.

AP Images/Sandy Huffaker

In 2013, the FTC expanded its enforcement to cover online access to personal information about children. New regulations require that online operators, such as Internet gaming sites, obtain parental consent before they gather information that could be used to identify, contact or locate a young person.

In 1914, the Federal Trade Commission assumed the power to oversee deceptive interstate advertising practices under the Federal Trade Commission Act. Today, the FTC's policy covering deceptive advertising says, "The Commission will find an act or practice deceptive if there is a misrepresentation, omission or other practice that misleads the consumer acting reasonably in the circumstances, to the consumer's detriment."

The commission acts when it receives a complaint the staff feels is worth investigating. The staff can request a *letter of compliance* from the advertiser, with the advertiser promising to change the alleged deception without admitting guilt. Next, the advertiser may argue the case before an administrative law judge, who may write a consent agreement to outline what the advertiser must do to comply with the law. A cease-and-desist order may be issued against the advertiser, although this is rare. The FTC can fine an advertiser who doesn't comply with an FTC order.

The Federal Trade Commission's five members serve seven-year terms. They are appointed by the president and confirmed by the U.S. Senate, and no more than three members can be from one political party. Because the FTC's members are presidential appointees, the commission's actions often reflect the political climate under which they operate.

In 2013, under the Obama administration, the FTC announced expanded federal safeguards to extend to children's apps and Web sites. The new rules mean that online operators must obtain parental consent before they gather information (such as photos, videos and audio recordings) that could be used to identify, contact or locate a young person.

Law Must Balance Rights and Responsibilities

Legal and regulatory issues governing advertising and public relations, then, are stitched with the same conflicting values that govern all aspects of mass media. The courts, the FCC, the FTC and other government agencies that monitor the mass media industries are the major arbiters of ongoing constitutional clashes.

Important legal decisions make lasting and influential statements about the role of law in protecting the constitutional guarantee of free expression in a country with constantly shifting public values. Through the courts and regulation, government must balance the business needs of the mass media industries with the government's role as a public interest representative.

REVIEW, ANALYZE, INVESTIGATE

CHAPTER 14

U.S. Constitution Sets Free Press Precedent
- The U.S. media's role is to encourage "uninhibited, robust and wide-open" debate.
- The legal and regulatory issues that media face are attempts to balance the media's rights and responsibilities, based on the First Amendment.

Government Tries to Restrict Free Expression
- Before 1964, the First Amendment faced four notable government challenges: the Alien and Sedition Laws of 1798, the Espionage Act of 1918, the Smith Act of 1940 and the Cold War congressional investigations of suspected Communists in the late 1940s and early 1950s.
- All of these challenges were attempts to limit free expression.

Prior Restraint Rarely Used
- American courts rarely have invoked prior restraint. The two most recent cases involved the publication of the Pentagon Papers by *The New York Times* and the publication of directions to build a hydrogen bomb in *The Progressive* magazine.
- In both cases, the information eventually was printed, but the intervention of the government delayed publication.

Government Manages War Coverage
- Attempts by the Reagan administration to limit reporters' access to Grenada during the U.S. invasion in October 1983 were a subtle form of prior restraint.
- Pentagon rules that created press pools for Gulf War coverage in 1991 were reached in cooperation with journalists, but imposed stricter restrictions on reporting than in any previous U.S. war.

- In 2001, the U.S. government controlled release of information to the American public about the war in Afghanistan even more than in the Gulf War.
- During the early months of the war in Afghanistan, the military used press pools and provided its own video footage of troop landings, produced by the military's combat film teams.
- During the Iraq War in 2003, the U.S. government used a system called *embedding*, which meant that members of the press traveled with the military, but the press's movements were restricted and managed by their military units.
- During the Gulf War, the George W. Bush administration (2001–2009) banned the media from covering the return of war fatalities to the U.S., saying the administration wanted to protect the families' privacy. In 2009, the Obama administration lifted the ban and now allows press coverage of the arrival of fatally wounded soldiers, with family permission.

WikiLeaks Challenges Government Secrecy
- In 2010, WikiLeaks began releasing classified U.S. diplomatic documents about the Iraq and Afghanistan wars on its Web site.
- The U.S. government warned that the WikiLeaks postings could endanger military personnel and civilians.
- On November 28, 2010, *The New York Times* began publishing a series of articles based on a new release of U.S. State Department documents posted on WikiLeaks.
- On February 23, 2011, WikiLeaks founder Julian Assange was ordered extradited to Sweden, but eventually he found asylum at the Ecuadorian Embassy in London. The U.S. government has not filed any charges against Assange for publishing secret U.S. documents on the Internet.

- The U.S. military charged Pfc. Bradley Manning with downloading large amounts of classified information from a military database and sharing the documents with WikiLeaks.

- On August 21, 2013, Pfc. Manning was sentenced to 35 years in prison.

USA PATRIOT Act Meets Public Resistance

- Congress passed the USA PATRIOT Act in 2001, giving the U.S. government broad powers to track, detain and interrogate people deemed a threat to the country.

- Among the provisions of the PATRIOT Act was Section 215, which allowed the FBI to monitor business records, including computer log-ins and the lists of books people check out of public libraries.

- The American Library Association and the American Civil Liberties Union challenged Section 215 in court.

- In 2007, a federal district court agreed that some provisions of the PATRIOT Act went against constitutional principles of checks and balances and separation of powers.

- President Obama signed a four-year extension of the PATRIOT Act on May 30, 2011.

- The USA PATRIOT Act was renamed the USA Freedom Act when President Obama signed it on June 2, 2015.

- New provisions of the USA Freedom Act curtail the government's bulk collection of consumer data.

What Is the Standard for Obscenity?

- *Roth v. United States* defined obscenity as material that is "utterly without redeeming social importance."

- *Miller v. California* established a three-part local test for obscenity: whether "the average person, applying contemporary community standards," would find that the work, taken as a whole, appeals to prurient interest; whether the work depicts or describes, in a patently offensive way, sexual conduct specifically defined by the applicable state law; and whether the work, taken as a whole, lacks serious literary, artistic, political or scientific value (often called the LAPS test).

- Many censorship cases begin at school and local government boards.

- Most reported book challenges are reversed when appealed.

- The American Library Association compiles a list each year detailing the nation's ten Most Challenged Books.

- In the 1988 *Hazelwood* case, the U.S. Supreme Court gave public school officials considerable freedom to limit what appears in student publications.

Libel Law Outlines the Media's Public Responsibility

- In 1964, the *New York Times v. Sullivan* case set a precedent, establishing that to be successful in a libel suit, a public official must prove actual malice.

- The press can use three defenses against a libel suit: truth, privilege and fair comment.

- Most successful libel judgments eventually are reversed or reduced when they are appealed. Often the major cost of a libel suit is the defense lawyers' fees.

- *Gertz v. Robert Welch Inc.* established the concept that the expression of opinions is a necessary part of public debate.

- Because of the *Herbert v. Lando* decision, today reporters may be asked in a libel suit to identify their sources and to surrender their notes.

- The *Masson v. New Yorker Magazine* case addressed the journalist's responsibility for direct quotations.

- Businesses and public officials have used SLAPP suits to try to intimidate individuals and news organizations that write unfavorable stories or post critical comments on the Internet.

Invasion of Privacy Defined Four Ways

- Invasion-of-privacy lawsuits are much less common than libel suits.

- There is no U.S. Supreme Court decision that governs invasion of privacy, so each state has its own interpretation of the issue.

- Generally, the media can be guilty of invading someone's privacy by intruding on a person's physical or mental solitude, publishing or disclosing embarrassing personal facts, giving someone publicity that places the person in a false light or using someone's name or likeness for commercial benefit.

- In an important case for the press, *Bartnicki v. Vopper*, in 2001, the U.S. Supreme Court reaffirmed the media's right to broadcast information and to comment on that information, no matter how the information was obtained.

Debate Continues over Fair Trial, Courtroom Access and Shield Laws

- *Sheppard v. Maxwell* established the legal precedent for limiting press access to courtrooms and juries.

- Most states allow some camera access to courtroom proceedings.

- The U.S. Supreme Court does not allow cameras.

- In 1994, Court TV broadcast the entire murder trial of football star O. J. Simpson.

- In 2015, cameras were banned during the trial of James Holmes, who was charged with killing 12 people and injuring 58 in a movie theater in Aurora, Colo., but the court allowed camera coverage of closing arguments.

- Individual state shield laws protect journalists from being compelled to reveal their sources, but no federal shield law guarantees these rights to every journalist nationwide.

FCC Regulates Broadcast and Cable

- Unlike print, which is not regulated by the government, broadcast media and Internet service providers are regulated by the FCC.

- Since 1972, the concept behind broadcast regulation has been based on the belief that broadcasters are trustees operating in the public interest.

Telecommunications Act of 1996 Changes the Marketplace

- The Telecommunications Act of 1996 was the most far-reaching reform in the way the U.S. government regulates mass media since the creation of the FCC in 1934.
- Following passage of the Telecommunications Act, large companies began positioning themselves to deliver the combination of telecommunications services for consumers called The Bundle.
- The major provisions of the Telecommunications Act of 1996 affect telecommunications, broadcast, satellite and cable.

Deregulation Unleashes the Media

- The FCC under President Clinton moved to a policy of deregulation of station ownership.
- The Telecommunications Act of 1996 established a goal of universal service.
- In 2003, the FCC adopted regulations, still in place today, that allow one company to control 35 percent of the broadcast audience.
- The act allowed broadcast cross-ownership, but not media cross-ownership.
- The act encouraged local phone competition and ended cable rate regulation.

TV Industry Agrees to Ratings and the V-Chip

- Under pressure from Congress, television executives devised a voluntary system of ratings for TV programming.
- The programming codes can be read by a v-chip, which allows parents to program a TV set to eliminate objectionable programs, although few parents use this option.

Congress Attempts to Control Access to Indecent Content

- The Communications Decency Act (CDA), part of the Telecommunications Act, attempted to regulate cable and TV programming and Internet content.
- In 1997, the U.S. Supreme Court struck down the Internet indecency provisions of the CDA.
- In 2003, the U.S. Supreme Court ruled that the federal government may withhold funding from schools and libraries that refuse to install Internet filters for pornography on their computers.
- In 2004, the FCC increased fines for broadcast programs the FCC determines are indecent.
- The FCC fined CBS-TV for Janet Jackson's "wardrobe malfunction" during the 2004 Super Bowl.
- In a July 2010 ruling on a group of indecency cases concerning fleeting expletives, a federal appeals court in New York found that the FCC's indecency policy violated the First Amendment.

Intellectual Property Rights Affirmed

- The right of ownership of creative ideas in the United States is legally governed by a concept called intellectual property rights.
- The Digital Millennium Copyright Act (DMCA), the U.S. Supreme Court decision in *New York Times Co. v. Tasini*, the U.S. Supreme Court decision in *Metro-Goldwyn-Mayer Studios Inc. v. Grokster Ltd.* and *Arista Records LLC v. Lime Group LLC* have begun to define the issues of digital copyright.
- These four examples affirm the strong legal tradition in the U.S. of guaranteeing intellectual copyright for creative content.
- Internet piracy is very difficult to monitor and prevent.
- To combat video piracy, the music and movie industries launched the Copyright Alert System in 2013.

FCC Adopts Open Internet Rules

- On February 26, 2015, the FCC approved net neutrality rules called the Open Internet Order.
- The FCC decided 3-2 that the Internet should be regulated as a utility just like telephone service.
- The FCC rules mean that traffic on the Internet will not be subject to government censorship and that all customers will be treated equally.
- Among the Open Internet Order's provisions are three new Bright Line Rules for broadband, which are (1) no blocking, (2) no throttling and (3) no paid prioritization.
- The goal of the new regulations, said the FCC, is the principle that "America's broadband networks must be fast, fair and open."

Courts and Regulators Govern Advertising and PR

- The Hudson test for advertising means that to be protected by the First Amendment, an ad must promote a legal product and must not lie.
- The *Texas Gulf Sulphur* case established the concept that a publicly held company is responsible for any information it withholds from the public.
- The main government agency regulating advertising is the Federal Trade Commission.
- The agency today is becoming more aggressive about policing advertisers than it was during the previous 20 years.
- In 2013, the FTC expanded its enforcement to cover online access to personal information about children.

Law Must Balance Rights and Responsibilities

- The courts, the FCC and the FTC arbitrate the media's rights and responsibilities.
- Government must balance the media's business needs with the government's role to protect the interests of the public.

Key Terms

These terms are defined in the margins throughout this chapter and appear in alphabetical order with definitions in the Glossary, which begins on page 361.

Broadcast Cross-Ownership *297*

Bundle *296*

Censorship *285*

DMCA *300*

False Light *292*

Fleeting Expletives *299*

HUAC *279*

Hudson Test *302*

Intellectual Property Rights *300*

LAPS Test *286*

Libel *287*

Media Cross-Ownership *297*

Net Neutrality *301*

NSL *285*

Pool Reporting *282*

Prior Restraint *281*

Qualified Privilege *291*

Roth Test *286*

Shield Laws *294*

SLAPP *291*

Telco *297*

WIPO *300*

Critical Questions

1. List and explain five major events or legal decisions in the evolution of the interpretation of the First Amendment in America from its beginnings to today.

2. Why is *New York Times v. Sullivan* a precedent-setting case for the American mass media?

3. List and describe the four elements necessary to prove libel. Why are so few libel cases successful?

4. Why are the courts generally reluctant to use prior restraint to stop publication? List two cases in which the courts did invoke prior restraint. What was the outcome in each case?

5. List and explain three specific cases that demonstrate how the U.S. legal system is responding to challenges posed by consumer access to Internet media.

Working the Web

This list includes sites mentioned in the chapter and others to give you greater insight into media law and regulation.

American Booksellers for Free Expression (ABFE Group at ABA)

bookweb.org/abfe

The "bookseller's voice in the fight against censorship," ABA's Foundation for Free Expression was a stand-alone nonprofit from 1990 to 2014, when it merged with the ABA and is now the ABFE Group at ABA. ABFE participates in legal cases about First Amendment rights and provides education about the importance of free expression. Resources and information about Banned Books Week and the Free Speech Resources for Booksellers are available on the ABFE site.

American Library Association (ALA)

ala.org

Founded in 1876 as part of the Centennial Exposition in Philadelphia, the ALA's mission is to provide "leadership for the development, promotion and improvement of library and information services and the profession of librarianship to enhance learning and ensure access to information for all." The ALA is open to any interested person or organization. Among the professional tools available on the ALA site are articles, guidelines and other resources about such issues as censorship, copyright, diversity and equal access.

Federal Communications Commission (FCC)

fcc.gov

Established by the Communications Act of 1934, the FCC regulates interstate and international communications by radio, television, wire, satellite and cable. The FCC's jurisdiction covers the 50 states, the District of Columbia and all U.S. territories. The FCC provides "leadership in strengthening the defense of the nation's communications infrastructure." The site offers resources such as an FCC Encyclopedia, new rules on the Open Internet, guides on texting and driving and caller ID and spoofing, plus Connect America Phases 1 and 2.

FindLaw

findlaw.com

FindLaw provides legal information for the public on common legal topics, including intellectual property, copyright and the Internet as well as civil rights, education law, employees' rights and criminal law and blogs covering the use of social media to fight crime.

Index (Index on Censorship)

indexoncensorship.org

Inspired by poet Stephen Spender, Index on Censorship was established in 1972 to publish stories about dissidents living behind the Iron Curtain. Today, the Index is an international organization that continues to be the "voice of free expression . . . fighting for free speech around the world and challenging censorship whenever and wherever it occurs." The site contains the online edition of *Index Magazine* and information on global censorship issues and campaigns and the organization's annual Freedom of Expression Awards.

Institute for Nonprofit News (INN; formerly the Investigative News Network)

inn.org

Comprising over 100 nonprofit media organizations in North America, INN "supports mission driven journalism" and represents the "urgent need to nourish and sustain the emerging investigative journalism ecosystem to better serve the public." The site has information about INN membership plus technology training and Web hosting.

International Media Lawyers Association (IMLA)

internationalmedialawyers.org

The IMLA "is an international network of lawyers working in the areas of media law, media freedom and media policy, and committed to promoting and defending the fundamental human rights of freedom of expression and freedom of information." The site has an alphabetical listing by country of resources available throughout the world as well as links to the Open Society Justice Initiative and Synchronicity, a philanthropic environmental organization.

Media Center at New York Law School

nyls.edu/media_center/media_law_and_policy/

Founded in 1977, the Media Center is New York Law School's home for the study of telecommunications, new media and media law and policy. According to the center, it is "one of the nation's oldest training programs for media lawyers and the only one that offers a digital video lab for the production of visual media relating to justice and the law." The center offers public programs and conferences, produces a weekly cable television program on media law and policy, produces the *Media Law Reporter* and runs the center's Web site.

Media Law Resource Center (MLRC)

medialaw.org

This nonprofit association represents media content providers and members of the media law profession. Established in 1980, the MLRC closely monitors legislation at all levels of government relating to media law and the First Amendment. The more than 115 members of the association include publishers, Internet companies, cable programmers and media insurance providers. The MLRC site offers information on the association's publications such as *Media Law Daily* and the *Media Law Letter* as well as MLRC conferences held annually throughout the world.

National Freedom of Information Coalition (NFOIC)

nfoic.org

The NFOIC is a nonpartisan organization with the mission "to ensure government transparency at the state and local level through advocacy, education and resolve." Each year, NFOIC holds a two-day Freedom of Information Summit. The coalition also administers the Knight Freedom of Information Fund, which provides legal and financial assistance for open government law trials held throughout the U.S.

ProPublica

propublica.org

ProPublica is a nonprofit news organization that publishes investigative journalism in the public interest. Its mission is "to expose abuses of power and betrayals of the public trust by government, business and other institutions." ProPublica feels that investigative journalism is at risk of disappearing from for-profit media. Founded by Paul Steiger, the former managing editor of *The Wall Street Journal*, ProPublica is headquartered in New York City. ProPublica's site contains links to current and archived print stories as well as podcasts and a complete database of information and statistics from recent investigative projects.

Silha Center for the Study of Media Ethics and Law (University of Minnesota)

silha.umn.edu/

The Silha Center was established in 1984 through a grant from Otto Silha, the former president and publisher of the *Minneapolis Star* and the *Minneapolis Tribune*, and his wife, Helen Silha. The center, housed in the Department of Journalism and Mass Communication at the University of Minnesota, funds graduate student research and publishes the

Bulletin three times a year covering issues relating to media law and ethics and cosponsors *Media Ethics*, published at Emerson College.

Student Press Law Center (SPLC)

splc.org

Established in 1974 in Washington, D.C., the Student Press Law Center advocates for student free press rights, online freedom of speech and open government on U.S. high school and college campuses. SPLC provides free information and legal assistance as well as low-cost materials on the First Amendment to students and educators.

WikiLeaks

wikileaks.org

Based in Melbourne, Australia, WikiLeaks publishes and comments on leaked documents, alleging government and corporate misconduct. Unlike other wikis, source documents published on WikiLeaks cannot be edited or changed by the public. WikiLeaks claims that "transparency in government activities leads to reduced corruption, better government and stronger democracies." The site provides separate discussion and source pages for content published on the site.

Impact/Action Videos are concise news features on various topics created exclusively for *Media/Impact*. Find them in *Media/Impact*'s MindTap at cengagebrain.com.

MindTap® Log on to MindTap for *Media/Impact* to access a variety of additional material—including learning objectives, chapter readings with high-lighting and note-taking, **Impact/Action Videos**, activities, and comprehension quizzes—that will guide you through this chapter.

MASS MEDIA ETHICS
TAKING RESPONSIBILITY

"We owe you, our readers, an apology. Plagiarism is an act of disrespect to the reader. We are deeply embarrassed and sorry to have misled you."

—BEN SMITH, EDITOR-IN-CHIEF, BUZZFEED

"Most of us would rather publish a story than not," explained journalist *Anthony Brandt in an* Esquire magazine article about ethics. "We're in the business of reporting, after all; most of us believe the public should know what's going on, has a right to know, has, indeed, a responsibility to know, and that this right, this responsibility, transcends the right to privacy, excuses our own pushiness, our arrogance, and therefore ought to protect us from lawsuits even when we are wrong.

"But most reporters also know there are times when publishing can harm or ruin people's lives. Members of the press sometimes print gossip as truth, disregard the impact they have on people's lives, and are ready to believe the worst about people because the worst sells. . . . We in the media have much to answer for."

Ethics Define Responsibilities

Discussions about how journalists answer for what they do center on questions of *ethics*. The word derives from the Greek word *ethos*—the guiding spirit or traditions that govern a culture. Part of American culture is the unique protection journalists enjoy under the First Amendment, so any discussion of ethics and the American media must acknowledge the cultural and professional belief under the U.S. Constitution that First Amendment privileges carry special obligations.

But the discussion of media ethics today should be framed internationally. Worldwide access to the Internet means that the work media professionals perform—in the U.S. and abroad—travels globally, no matter where the work originates.

Professional ethics are the rules and standards that govern the conduct of people working in a specific profession. In some countries, like the U.S., professional associations have established voluntary ethics codes for people who work in the mass media industries and many corporations prescribe codes of conduct for employees who work with the media. In other countries, courts, corporations and journalists' unions enforce breaches of ethical conduct. But in many countries, media companies have no overriding ethics guidelines for media workers and rely, instead, on individuals to make ethical decisions.

It is important to understand the value of ethical standards in the mass media business because when media professionals make the wrong ethical choices, the consequences can be very damaging and very public. "It may well be that if journalism loses touch with ethical values, it will then cease to be of use to society, and cease to have any real reason for being," writes media ethics scholar John Hulteng. "But that, for the sake of all of us, must never be allowed to happen."

Mass media professionals make poor ethical judgments for many reasons. They work quickly. They sometimes act impulsively because the rush to be first with a story overrides the desire to be right. Sometimes they don't research well enough to question the reliability of what they're told. They may be rewarded with attention and monetary success by enhancing the importance of their role in the events they cover. And they can become insensitive to the consequences of their unethical actions on the people who ultimately are affected by what they do.

Ethics The rules or standards that govern someone's conduct.

Professional Ethics The rules or standards governing the conduct of the members of a profession.

The media face four types of ethical issues:

1. Truthfulness
2. Fairness
3. Privacy
4. Responsibility

Consider these actual situations and the questions that arise:

Example 1: Truthfulness. A veteran anchorperson at a major TV network falsely reported he had been shot down by rocket-propelled grenade fire while reporting in Iraq. When this falsehood was uncovered, the network began an inquiry into other stories he had reported and concluded there had been several fabrications. After an independent investigation, the network suspended him as anchor and reassigned him to a reporting job at one of its secondary news outlets. Question: Why is credibility such an important asset for a news organization?

Example 2: Fairness. A TV network host who regularly interviewed government officials on his program admitted that he had given $75,000 to a foundation run by political figures and that he did not publicly disclose the donations. The network allowed him to remain on the program but said it would consider canceling his participation in the network's 2016 presidential debate coverage. Question: Why should newspeople who cover government be required to disclose contributions to political candidates?

Example 3: Privacy. Reporters at a tabloid newspaper hacked into personal e-mail accounts and illegally obtained access to private voice mails of celebrities and public officials. Did the reporters infringe on the person's privacy, or should public figures just learn to live with this type of intrusion?

Example 4: Responsibility. At a private party, an influential Internet executive discussed plans to investigate the private life of a technology journalist who was writing unfavorable stories about his company. The conversation was reported online. The executive's boss later publicly apologized, but the incident pointed out the expectation among many venture capitalists that they will receive only flattering coverage from technology reporters because many people who write about the Internet industries work for businesses that are financed by the companies they cover. Question: Why is it important for technology companies to maintain a professional distance from reporters and for reporters to maintain editorial independence from the companies they cover?

Truth versus falsehood is the issue for the anchorperson who embellished his role in the news stories he covered in example 1. Fairness versus bias is the question for the news program host who did not publicly report his large donation in example 2.

Personal privacy versus invasion of privacy is the debate facing the Internet site that posted the video in example 3. Responsibility versus irresponsibility is the issue for technology writers who cover the world of Internet startups in example 4.

Some ethical debates are easier to resolve than others. These four incidents and several other examples outlined in this chapter demonstrate the amazing range of ethical dilemmas facing media professionals and their companies every day.

Truthfulness Affects Credibility

Truthfulness in reporting means more than being accurate and not lying. Truthfulness means not misrepresenting the people or the underlying motives of a story, as well as reporting the complete story. Another aspect of truthfulness is presenting original, complete work that is not embellished or borrowed from other sources.

Fabrications

The journalist described in example 1 is NBC anchor Brian Williams. On January 30, 2015, on *NBC Nightly News*, Williams, during a tribute to a retired military veteran who had provided security for Williams when he reported from Iraq in 2003, said he was aboard a Chinook helicopter when it was forced down.

A few days later the military paper *Stars and Stripes* reported that soldiers aboard the helicopter disagreed that Williams was aboard the helicopter and raised doubts about his story. NBC began an investigation, which turned up more questions about Williams' role in reporting during Hurricane Katrina and protests in Egypt's Tahrir Square.

NBC suspended Williams from *NBC Nightly News*, and less than six months later, the network announced that Williams had been reassigned to MSNBC. Williams publicly apologized, saying his ***fabrications*** "came from clearly a bad place, a bad urge inside of me."

In February 2015, shortly after the Williams incident, the Web site *Mother Jones* raised questions about Fox News host Bill O'Reilly's claims to have reported from an active "war zone" in Argentina in 1982, at the end of the Falklands War, as O'Reilly had repeatedly said on the air and in his 2001

Fabrication Something made up in order to deceive.

In 2015, anchor Brian Williams was suspended from *NBC Nightly News* after a network investigation showed that he had falsely claimed he was aboard a helicopter that was shot down in 2003 during the Iraq War. He was reassigned to MSNBC.

Fox News admitted that Bill O'Reilly, host of the Fox News program *The O'Reilly Factor*, did not witness bombings in Northern Ireland or murders in El Salvador, as he had claimed. But Fox maintained its "staunch support" for O'Reilly and he retained his position as host of the program.

book *The No Spin Zone: Confrontations with the Powerful and Famous in America*. Erik Engberg, a former CBS reporter who was with O'Reilly in Argentina, said in a Facebook post that O'Reilly "has displayed a willingness to twist the truth in a way that seeks to invent a battlefield that did not exist." Six other CBS journalists also challenged O'Reilly's claims.

O'Reilly responded to the charges on his show, *The O'Reilly Factor*, calling the *Mother Jones* reports "disgusting" and "a piece of garbage." "Every single thing I said is true," O'Reilly told *The New York Times*.

Within days, more inconsistencies emerged in O'Reilly's version of events in other stories he had reported. Answering questions from the *Washington Post*, Fox News admitted that O'Reilly had not witnessed any bombings in Northern Ireland or murders in El Salvador, as he had claimed, and had only seen photographs, another example of fabrication. Still, a Fox spokesperson told *The Guardian* newspaper, "Fox News maintains its staunch support of O'Reilly," and he retained his role on the network.

"Fox News has a market; the market is people who don't trust the news media," New York University journalism professor Jay Rosen told *The New York Times*. "That strategy requires personalities like Bill O'Reilly to be under attack from the rest of the news media." *The Times* reported that *The O'Reilly Factor* generated $100 million in advertising revenue in 2014.

In a third example of fabrication, *Tablet* magazine revealed in July 2012 that Jonah Lehrer, 31, author of the best-selling book *Imagine: How Creativity Works*, had fabricated quotes from musician Bob Dylan in his

book. Only a month before, Lehrer, a writer for *The New Yorker*, had publicly apologized for taking some articles he had published in *The Wall Street Journal* and other publications and republishing them on his blog at *The New Yorker*.

After the *Imagine* fabrication was discovered, Lehrer admitted he had made up the quote and resigned from *The New Yorker*. "This is a terrifically sad situation," *New Yorker* editor David Remnick said in a statement, "but, in the end, what is most important is the integrity of what we publish and what we stand for."

Lehrer's publisher, Canongate Books, asked all its retailers to return the books; *Imagine* had sold 200,000 hardcover and e-book copies before it was pulled from the shelves.

Plagiarism

Internet access to other people's work makes **plagiarism** easy, but the Internet also makes plagiarism easier to detect. At most media outlets, plagiarists who are caught are dismissed and asked to issue a public apology, so it's surprising that instances of plagiarism happen as often as they do.

Beginning on July 23, 2014, Twitter users began pointing out sentences and phrases copied by BuzzFeed writer Benny Johnson from stories that initially appeared on other

> **Plagiarism** Passing off as your own the ideas or writings of others.

In July 2012, *New Yorker* writer Jonah Lehrer resigned after it was discovered that he had fabricated quotes for his book, *Imagine: How Creativity Works.* His publisher asked retailers to return the books.

Web sites. After an investigation, BuzzFeed dismissed Johnson and posted a list of 41 examples of his plagiarized content, including unverified and unattributed entries he had used from Wikipedia.

"We owe you, our readers, an apology," wrote BuzzFeed editor Ben Smith. "This plagiarism is a breach of our fundamental responsibility to be honest with you—in this

☰ BuzzFeed

Editor's Note: An Apology To Our Readers

What we're doing about an episode of plagiarism.

Posted on July 25, 2014, at 8:32 p.m.

Ben Smith
BuzzFeed Staff

Starting this Wednesday, Twitter users began pointing out instances in which a BuzzFeed writer, Benny Johnson, had lifted phrases and sentences from other websites.

In July 2014 the news Web site BuzzFeed dismissed writer Benny Johnson after identifying 41 instances of plagiarism in the 500 stories he had written for the site.

case about who wrote the words on our site. Plagiarism, much less copying unchecked facts from Wikipedia or other sources, is an act of disrespect to the reader."

In 2010, *The New York Times* suspended reporter Zachery Kouwe after editors said Kouwe had plagiarized portions of an article he wrote for *The Times* from an earlier online article by another reporter for *The Wall Street Journal.* When editors of *The Journal* contacted *The Times* about the similarity, *Times* editors investigated some of Kouwe's other stories and found more examples of plagiarism.

"In a number of business articles in *The Times* over the past year, and in posts on the DealBook blog on nytimes.com, a *Times* reporter appears to have improperly appropriated wording and passages published by other news organizations," wrote *The Times* on its Corrections page. "A subsequent search by *The Times* found other cases of extensive overlap between passages in Mr. Kouwe's articles and other news organizations'. . . . Copying language directly from other news organizations without providing attribution—even if the facts are independently verified—is a serious violation of *Times* policy and basic journalistic standards. It should not have occurred." Kouwe resigned.

Misrepresentation

In a stunning example of ***misrepresentation***—the presentation of a false or misleading representation of something or someone—that lasted two decades, a reporter for Britain's *News of the World* disguised himself as a sheikh and enticed several famous people into compromising situations. He then reported on their wrongdoing and, if they were arrested, often testified against them in court.

Known in England as "the fake sheikh," Mazher Mahmood received several awards for his reporting and claimed responsibility for convictions in 25 criminal cases. However, in July 2014, Mahmood's behavior came under scrutiny after he testified in a case against singer Tulisa Contostavlos that she had bought him cocaine. The judge dismissed the case, saying Mahmood had been "manipulating the evidence" against the actress. Then in November 2014, the British Broadcasting Corporation presented a 30-minute documentary about his methods. Mahmood was suspended from *News of the World* and British authorities are reviewing some of the convictions. (See **Impact/Global**, "Fake Sheikh Mazher Mahmood: 25 Criminal Convictions Linked to Undercover Reporter to be Re-examined," p. 316.)

"Mazher Mahmood is part of that culture of ruthlessness," reporter Nick Davies told *The New York Times.* Davies, who works for the respected British newspaper *The Guardian*, said, "The big picture here is that

Misrepresentation The presentation of a false or misleading representation of something or someone.

IMPACT Global

Fake Sheikh Mazher Mahmood: 25 Criminal Convictions Linked to Undercover Reporter to be Re-examined

By James Rush

LONDON. Convictions in 25 criminal cases where evidence was given by undercover reporter Mazher Mahmood are being re-examined, the Crown Prosecution Service [CPS] has said.

The CPS said it had identified current and past cases where the "Fake Sheikh" was a prosecution witness following the collapse of the trial of pop singer and former *X Factor* judge Tulisa Contostavlos.

It said while past cases which resulted in a conviction were now being "considered," it had also offered no evidence in three live cases where the undercover journalist was a prosecution witness.

A CPS spokesman said: "We are now considering past cases which resulted in a conviction in criminal courts in England and Wales based on evidence provided by Mr. Mahmood, and have identified 25 cases.

"As part of this process, over the coming weeks, CPS Areas will be contacting representatives of the defendants—or defendants themselves as necessary—convicted in these cases in order to provide them with a disclosure pack—details of material which they may consider undermines the conviction in a specific case."

Mr. Mahmood, a former *News of the World* reporter, was suspended by the *Sun* on [November 30,

British authorities announced they would be reviewing convictions in several cases in which reporter Mazher Mahmood (the "Fake Sheikh") testified for the prosecution after a judge dismissed charges against singer Tulisa Contostavlos, who had been the subject of a Mahmood undercover article. The judge said there was strong evidence Mahmood had been "manipulating the evidence."

AP Images

2014] following the collapse of Ms. Contostavlos' trial in July [2014].

The former N-Dubz star went on trial after allegedly boasting that she could "sort out" cocaine for Mr. Mahmood and put the reporter in touch with her rapper friend Mike GLC—real name Michael Coombs.

But both were cleared after Judge Alistair McCreath said there were "strong grounds" to believe Mr. Mahmood lied in the witness box and "had been manipulating the evidence."

The CPS spokesman said today: "Following the halting of the trial of Ms. Contostavlos, we took steps to identify current and past cases involving Mr. Mahmood as a prosecution witness.

"We made it our immediate priority to carefully look into live prosecutions in accordance with the Code for Crown Prosecutors and any past cases which involved a defendant still in custody.

"There were no concluded cases where a defendant was still in custody, but we identified three live cases. Each case was looked at individually and no evidence was offered as we concluded that there was no longer a realistic prospect of a conviction."

the commercial pressure to deliver stories that will sell the paper and make more money is an irresistible force in those newsrooms. What it translates into is reporters' being told, 'Do whatever you need to do, and if that involves breaking the law, that's OK.'"

The classic case of several instances of journalistic misrepresentation by a prominent reporter involved Jayson Blair, a *New York Times* reporter who was forced to resign on May 1, 2003. The day he resigned, *The Times* published a front-page story, "*Times* Reporter Who Resigned Leaves Long Trail of Deception," which began: "A staff reporter for *The New York Times* committed frequent acts of journalistic fraud while covering significant news events in recent months, an investigation by *Times* journalists has found. The widespread fabrication and plagiarism represent a profound betrayal of trust and a low point in the 152-year history of the newspaper." *The Times* said that as a reporter for *The Times*, 27-year-old Blair had:

▶ Written stories purported to be filed in Maryland, Texas and other states, when often he was still in New York.

▶ Fabricated comments.

▶ Concocted scenes.

▶ Stolen material from other newspapers and wire services.

▶ Selected details from photographs to create the impression he had been somewhere or seen someone, when he hadn't.

The Times then published an exhaustive, unprecedented eight-page accounting of 73 significant falsehoods in Blair's stories *The Times* had published, detailing every traceable error, based on an internal investigation by its own reporters. In one story, for example, Blair had reported details from inside the National Naval Medical Center in Bethesda, Md., but the hospital said Blair had never been there. In another story about a stricter National Collegiate Athletic Association standard for class attendance, Blair quoted someone who said he had never talked to Blair and Blair used quotes from another newspaper as his own.

When discussing Blair's case, Alex S. Jones, a former *Times* reporter and co-author of *The Trust: The Private and Powerful Family Behind The New York Times*, told *The Times*: "To the best of my knowledge, there has never been anything like this at *The New York Times*. . . . There has never been a systematic effort to lie and

cheat as a reporter at *The New York Times* comparable to what Jayson Blair seems to have done."

Less than two months later, *The Times*' two top editors, who were responsible for hiring and supervising Blair, resigned.

When reporters misrepresent the facts or create false stories, readers and viewers question all information published by similar sources. Is the information fiction or fact? Has the subject of the story been set up? Misrepresentations also can have legal consequences for companies that publish, broadcast or post false information.

Fairness Means Evenhandedness

Fairness implies impartiality—that the writer has nothing personal to gain from a report, that there are no hidden benefits to the writer's organization or to the source from the story that is being presented or being withheld. Criticism of the press for unfairness results from:

▶ Close ties that develop between reporters and the stories they cover—called *insider friendships*.

▶ Reporters who accept personal or financial benefits from sources, sponsors or advertisers—called *conflicts of interest*.

▶ Reporters who pay their sources for stories—called *checkbook journalism*.

Insider Friendships

The person in example 2 is ABC Chief anchor George Stephanopoulos. In May 2015, Stephanopoulos acknowledged he did not publicly disclose he had donated

ABC chief anchor George Stephanopoulos acknowledged in May 2015 that he had donated $75,000 between 2012 and 2014 to the Clinton Foundation after the Web site Politico reported the gifts. On September 23, 2014, Stephanopoulos (right) interviewed former president Bill Clinton about the Clinton Global Initiative on ABC's *Good Morning America*.

Heidi Gutman/ABC via Getty Images

$75,000 to the Clinton Foundation, run by former president Bill Clinton and 2016 presidential candidate Hillary Clinton, after the Web site Politico reported the gift. Stephanopoulos had worked as communications director in the Clinton White House before going to work for ABC, and on September 23, 2014, Stephanopoulos had interviewed the former president about the Clinton Global Initiative on ABC's *Good Morning America*, an example of insider friendships.

Stephanopoulos apologized in a statement. "I thought my donations were a matter of public record. However, in hindsight I should have taken the extra step of personally disclosing my donations to my employer and to the viewers on air during the recent news stories about the foundation. I apologize." ABC retained Stephanopoulos on the program but indicated he might be barred from participating in the 2016 presidential debate coverage because of the potential candidacy of Hillary Clinton.

ABC's reaction contrasts with two other examples of undisclosed donations five years earlier that involved MSNBC. On November 5, 2010, MSNBC announced it was suspending TV political commentator Keith Olbermann without pay after MSNBC TV President Phil Griffin learned that Olbermann had violated newsroom policies by contributing to three Democratic congressional candidates.

Olbermann admitted he made three donations of $2,400 but issued a statement that said he did not use his influence in any other way. "I did not privately or publicly encourage anyone else to donate to these campaigns, nor to any others in this election or any previous ones, nor have I previously donated to any political campaign at any level," he said. MSNBC, which originally suspended him indefinitely, announced a two-day suspension. Olbermann resigned from MSNBC in January 2011.

Less than a month later, MSNBC announced another two-day suspension of the co-host of its morning program after the online site Politico reported that Joe Scarborough had donated $4,000 in recent years to three Republican candidates in Florida. The contributions, Scarborough said, "were not relevant to my work at MSNBC." He had not reported on any of the races to which he gave money, he said.

Scarborough's suspension "underscored the idiosyncrasy of a policy that seeks to protect NBC's journalistic integrity, but does not differentiate between news reporters and political commentators," wrote *The New York Times* (NBC owns MSNBC). MSNBC President Phil Griffin said, "As Joe recognizes, it is critical that we enforce our standards and policies." Scarborough said, in a statement, "There is nothing more important than maintaining the integrity" of the news.

In the Stephanopolous, Olbermann and Scarborough examples, the news organizations were dealing with the potential public perception that insider contacts might affect the overall credibility of its news coverage. The networks believed that political donations could interfere with the public's trust in news organizations, although the consequences for the people involved were different. Even the appearance of insider friendships removes the very important element of a news organization's independence from the people and events it covers, but there is no standardized response for media organizations when the conflicts are uncovered.

Conflicts of Interest

Reporters with conflicts of interest are divided between at least two loyalties, and the ethical question is this: How will the stories the reporters write and the integrity of the organizations for which they work be affected?

One type of conflict of interest involves allowing the subject of a report to alter its content before the report is broadcast, published or posted, fearing that the subject will not cooperate without control. In June 2015, PBS postponed a future season of the show *Finding Your Roots* after the network discovered that producers had omitted information about actor Ben Affleck's slave-owning ancestor from the report at Affleck's request. (See **Impact/Profile**, "Citing Ben Affleck's 'Improper Influence,' PBS Suspends *Finding Your Roots*," p. 319.)

Another type of conflict of interest happens when reporters accept free meals and passes to entertainment events (freebies) and free travel (junkets). In one survey of newspapers, nearly half said reporters accepted free tickets to athletic events, and nearly two-thirds accepted free tickets to artistic events. In an editorial about junkets, *The New York Times* said, "Accepting junkets and boondoggles does not necessarily mean that a reporter is being bought—but it inescapably creates the appearance of being bought."

Accepting junkets and freebies creates an appearance of conflict of interest—even if the reporters don't write favorably about the places they visit. In 2010, however, a newspaper took the unusual step of taking money from an advertiser to help pay for its coverage of the war in Afghanistan.

On September 27, 2010, the *New Hampshire Union Leader* (*UL*), the state's largest newspaper, announced the paper had accepted underwriting from three major New Hampshire businesses so its publisher and a staff photographer could travel to Afghanistan to report on a New Hampshire National Guard unit serving there. One of the underwriters, BAE Systems, is the state's largest manufacturing firm and works mainly in the defense industry,

IMPACT
Profile

Citing Ben Affleck's 'Improper Influence,' PBS Suspends *Finding Your Roots*

By John Koblin

PBS said on Wednesday that it was postponing a future season of "Finding Your Roots" after an investigation revealed that the actor Ben Affleck pressured producers into leaving out details about an ancestor of his who owned slaves.

PBS will not run the show's third season until staffing changes are made, including hiring a fact checker, it said.

The show, which is hosted by the Harvard professor Henry Louis Gates Jr., traces family histories of celebrities and public figures, and has run for two seasons. The concern about Mr. Affleck's relative surfaced in the WikiLeaks cache of hacked Sony emails after Mr. Gates asked a Sony executive for advice about a "megastar" who wanted to omit a detail about a slave-owning ancestor.

"We've never had anyone ever try to censor or edit what we found," Mr. Gates wrote to a Sony executive, Michael Lynton, in July 2014. Mr. Gates added that this

would violate PBS rules, and "once we open the door to censorship, we lose control of the brand."

When the episode was broadcast in October [2014], it did not mention the slave-owning ancestor. After the emails were posted to WikiLeaks, Mr. Gates said that producers had discovered more interesting ancestors from Mr. Affleck's family, including a relative from the Revolutionary War and an occult enthusiast.

Mr. Affleck said in April [2015] that he was "embarrassed" when he discovered that he was related to a slave owner. "I didn't want any television show about my family to include a guy who owned slaves," Mr. Affleck wrote on Facebook.

In the investigation, PBS said that producers violated network standards by letting Mr. Affleck have "improper influence" and "by failing to inform PBS or WNET of Mr. Affleck's efforts to affect program content."

The network said that before the third season of *Finding Your Roots* can broadcast, the show needs to make some staffing changes, including the addition of a fact checker and

PBS postponed its 2015 season of *Finding Your Roots* after the network learned the program's producers had omitted details about Ben Affleck's slave-owning ancestor under pressure from the actor.

Albert L. Ortega/Getty Images

an "independent genealogist" to review the show's contents.

PBS also said that it had not made a decision about whether to commit to a fourth season of the show.

In a statement on Wednesday, Mr. Gates said, "I sincerely regret not discussing my editing rationale with our partners at PBS and WNET and I apologize for putting PBS and its member stations in the position of having to defend the integrity of their programming."

John Koblin, "Citing Ben Affleck's 'Improper Influence,' PBS Suspends *Finding Your Roots*," June 24, 2015, nytimes.com.

according to a story about the incident published by The Newspaper Guild.

Citing declining revenue because of the recession, the newspaper's publisher wrote, "I had a hunch that I knew some companies that would feel the same way as the *Union Leader*, that the story of Charlie Company ought to be told and that, with their assistance, New Hampshire's newspaper and UnionLeader.com could and should tell it."

Many readers didn't agree. "The *UL* takes money from BAE and other companies? That is obvious conflict of interest," wrote one reader. "How can we trust the *UL* to report on these companies in an objective way when they are taking money from them? We can't. These stories will be nothing more than propaganda."

In a similar type of conflict of interest, *The Washington Post* in 2009 issued invitations to lobbyists, members of Congress and other influential people in Washington to attend a *Washington Post* "salon" at publisher Katharine Weymouth's home. Guests were invited to buy sponsorships ($25,000 for one or $250,000 for the entire series) to attend off-the-record dinners hosted by the newspaper's editor, Marcus Brauchli.

After a story on Politico (an online competitor) made the event public, *The Post* canceled it, and Weymouth apologized to *The Post*'s readers, although she said Politico had characterized the invitation incorrectly. The planned event highlights the conflicts of interest that can develop when the business side of a media organization overlaps the news side.

Checkbook Journalism

In 2012, Alliance, the film company that represented actor Brad Pitt, requested £2,000 (approximately $3,000) from journalists for a 20-minute interview with Pitt at the Cannes Film Festival, an example of ***checkbook journalism***—paying an interview source, directly or indirectly, for access. Alliance claimed it was not a direct interview payment but helped cover some of the star's costs for the trip. This is an example of checkbook journalism.

"In a way, there is nothing new about this," wrote journalist Sam Hattenstone, whose British newspaper, *The Guardian*, doesn't pay for interviews. "After all, interviews with celebrities have always been an exchange of sorts—you promote your movie, song, book, and we get pretty pictures, gossip and hopefully even insight into said star. Some newspapers always preferred the cleaner deal of paying for interviews. Then you can whisk away your subject, hold them in captivity and interview the life out of them—because you've paid for it."

In 2009, some journalists who were covering the kidnapping story of Jaycee Lee Dugard—a young girl who said she had been held in captivity for 18 years in Antioch, Calif.—offered payments to several neighbors near the place where she lived with her alleged kidnappers, Phillip and Nancy Garrido. Interview payments to witnesses are quite common in Europe, but they present serious ethical problems for reporters who cannot pay for information about the story they are covering.

According to the *Los Angeles Times*, one Garrido neighbor, Damon Robinson, was talking to reporters from CNN, the Associated Press and the *Times* when a British journalist offered Robinson $2,000 if he would stop talking with other reporters and give the British journalist an exclusive. According to the *Times*, "Robinson complied."

Two years later, when Jaycee Lee Dugard was ready to talk with the press, ABC News paid for exclusive rights to the interview.

Besides ethical questions about whether actors, newsmakers, witnesses and even criminals should profit financially from manufactured publicity, there are other hazards in any type of checkbook journalism. One danger is that a paid interviewee may sensationalize the information to bring a higher price, so the interviewee's truthfulness cannot always be trusted.

A second hazard is that paid interviews may become the exclusive property of the highest bidder, shutting out smaller news organizations and independent journalists from the information.

A third possibility is that the person who is paid by the news organization to comment could carry a hidden agenda.

Privacy Involves Respect

Private Acts That Become Public

Privacy for e-mail and voice communications is a very important ethical and legal issue (see also **Chapter 14**). In July 2011, the British newspaper The Guardian reported that journalists at the competing British tabloid *News of the World* (owned by a subsidiary of Rupert Murdoch's News Corp.) repeatedly hacked e-mails and voice mails belonging to British and U.S. celebrities and government officials. This is the case listed as example 3 on p. 313. There were at least 800 documented hacking victims, allegedly including Queen Elizabeth II and former Prime Minister Gordon Brown as well as actor Jude Law.

Murdoch printed a public apology and then shut down the 168-year-old newspaper. In January 2012, News Corp.

Vittorio Zunino Celotto/WireImage for Electrolux

The film company Alliance requested £2,000 for a 20-minute interview with actor Brad Pitt at Cannes in 2012, an example of checkbook journalism.

> **Checkbook Journalism** The practice of a news organization paying for an interview or a photograph.

Jeff J Mitchell/Getty Images

In 2012, Andy Coulson, editor of the now-defunct British tabloid *News of the World* (owned by Rupert Murdoch), was charged with paying bribes of up to $160,000 for access to public officials' e-mails and voice mails. In 2015, Coulson was convicted in the phone hacking and required to pay up to £750,000 to cover the trial's court costs.

agreed to pay substantial damages to 37 victims, including actor Jude Law.

In November 2012, prosecutors in London charged two former top executives at the newspaper, Rebekah Brooks and Andy Coulson, with paying bribes of up to $160,000 to public officials for information, in addition to several earlier charges. Brooks eventually was acquitted, but Coulson was convicted in 2015 and required to pay up to £750,000 to help cover court costs.

Reporting on Rape

Reporting on rape is another example of a complex ethical dilemma of privacy: How does the press balance the goal of truthfulness and fact-finding with the need for personal privacy? Is the pain that such a report may cause worth the public good that can result from publishing the information?

Traditionally, common newsroom practice forbids the naming of rape victims in stories. But in 1989, *Des Moines Register* editor Geneva Overholser startled the press community when she wrote an editorial arguing that newspapers contribute to the public's misunderstanding of the crime by withholding not only the woman's name but an explicit description of what happened.

In 1990, *The Register* published a five-part series about the rape of Nancy Ziegenmeyer, with

Ziegenmeyer's full cooperation. Ziegenmeyer had contacted *The Register* after Overholser's column appeared, volunteering to tell her story. The Ziegenmeyer series provoked wide-ranging debate among editors about this aspect of privacy.

Twenty-five years later, in July 2015, *New York* magazine reignited the controversy about identifying rape victims when the magazine's cover showed photos of 35 women who alleged that entertainer Bill Cosby sexually assaulted them. The magazine also posted detailed personal accounts from each woman on its Web site. Cosby has denied the charges.

The women consented to the coverage and the magazine commissioned a photographer to take the photos. The cover story reinvigorated a long-running debate about whether the media should identify victims who claim sexual assault, as it does with victims of other crimes, or whether their identities should remain private.

Is there more benefit to society by publishing a victim's name, with the victim's permission, than by withholding it? Should the press explicitly describe sexual crimes, or is that merely sensationalism, feeding the public's salacious curiosity?

The Bollea, Coulson, Ziegenmeyer and *New York* magazine examples demonstrate how complex privacy issues have become. When do journalists' efforts to get a story go too far? Is it ever in the public interest to divulge personal information about private individuals? How important is the public's right to know?

Responsibility Generates Trust

The stories that reporters choose and the ways they use the information they gather reflect on the profession's sense of public responsibility. Most reporters realize that

Richard Levine/Corbis News/Corbis

In July 2015, *New York* magazine reignited the debate about the ethics of identifying rape victims when the magazine's cover showed photos of 35 women, with their consent, who alleged that entertainer Bill Cosby sexually assaulted them. Cosby has denied the charges.

the way they characterize an event can affect how the public perceives the story. The mere presence of the media also magnifies the consequences of what is reported.

Many Internet venture capitalists, for example, have come to expect positive coverage from Internet media companies. In this interdependent culture, where positive press may generate millions from investors, technology companies bristle at any negative coverage, which can hinder investment and decrease revenue. With the financial stakes so high, venture capitalists and the people who report on them sometimes find it difficult to maintain a responsible distance.

Example 4 concerns the Internet ride-sharing company Uber. On Monday, November 17, 2014, the Web site BuzzFeed reported that Uber senior vice president Emil Michael suggested at a private dinner that the company had considered an investigation into the private life of Sarah Lacy, a technology journalist who had been critical of the company.

Uber CEO Travis Kalanick issued an apology on Twitter the next day, in a series of 13 short messages, which included the following: "Emil's comments at the recent dinner party were terrible and do not represent the company. His remarks showed a lack of leadership, a lack of humanity, and a departure from our values and ideas. His duties here at Uber do not involve communications strategy or plans and are not representative in any way of the company approach. Instead, we should lead by inspiring our riders, our drivers and the public at large." (See **Impact/Society**: "Reaction to Uber Tactics Highlights Tech Journalists' Fine Line Between Critic and Booster," p. 323.)

All news organizations must accept responsibility for editorial review and oversight of stories that reach the public. Companies that work with the media should realize that it is impossible to completely control how their businesses are portrayed and that seeking retribution against reporters reflects poorly on the company.

Responsible companies encourage ethical behavior and continually remind their employees about their public and professional responsibilities.

Five Philosophical Principles Govern Media Ethics

Ethicists prescribe only general guidelines for moral decisions because each situation presents its own special dilemmas. First, it is important to understand the basic principles that underlie these philosophical discussions. In their book *Media Ethics*, Clifford G. Christians, Kim B. Rotzoll and Mark Fackler identify five major philosophical principles underlying today's ethical decisions:

(1) Aristotle's golden mean, (2) Kant's categorical imperative, (3) Mill's principle of utility, (4) Rawls' veil of ignorance and (5) the Judeo-Christian view of persons as ends in themselves.

1. Aristotle's golden mean: According to Aristotle, virtue is "the mean between two extremes." This is a philosophy of moderation and compromise, often called the *golden mean*. The journalistic concept of fairness reflects this idea.

2. Kant's categorical imperative: "Act on that maxim which you will to become a universal law." Eighteenth-century philosopher Immanuel Kant developed this idea, an extension of Aristotle's golden mean. Kant's test—that you make decisions based on principles that you want to be universally applied—is called the *categorical imperative*. This means you choose an action by asking yourself the question, what would happen if everyone acted this way?

3. Mill's principle of utility: "Seek the greatest happiness for the greatest number." In the 19th century, John Stuart Mill taught that the best decision is one with the biggest overall benefit for the most human beings.

4. Rawls' veil of ignorance: "Justice emerges when negotiating without social differentiations." John Rawls' 20th-century theory supports an egalitarian society that asks everyone to work from a sense of liberty and basic respect for everyone, regardless of social position.

5. Judeo-Christian view of persons as ends in themselves: "Love your neighbor as yourself." Under this longstanding ethic of religious heritage, people should care for one another—friends as well as enemies—equally and without favor. Trust in people and they will trust in you.

None of these five philosophies operates independently. Ethical choices in many situations are not exquisitely simple. What is predictable about ethical dilemmas is their unpredictability. Therefore, media professionals generally adopt a philosophy of situational ethics: Because each circumstance is different, a journalist must decide the best action to take in each situation.

Should the press adopt Rawls' idea of social equality and cover each person equally, or should public officials receive more scrutiny than others because they maintain a public trust? Is it a loving act in the Judeo-Christian tradition to allow bereaved parents privacy to grieve for their child's death by drowning, or is the journalist contributing to society's greater good by warning others about the dangers of leaving a child unattended? Questions like

IMPACT

Society

Reaction to Uber Tactics Highlights Tech Journalists' Fine Line Between Critic and Booster

By Leslie Kaufman

[On November 17, 2014], BuzzFeed reported that an Uber executive had considered investigating the private life of the tech journalist Sarah Lacy because of her negative coverage of the company. Ms. Lacy responded almost instantaneously—and she was not happy.

In a podcast, Ms. Lacy, the founder and editor in chief of the Silicon Valley news Web site PandoDaily, and Paul Carr, her co-host, called Uber "awful," "evil" and "nasty." They also reserved a portion of their scathing rant for their fellow tech writers, who, they said, had gone too soft on Uber.

To further complicate matters, many of these publications make a significant portion of their revenue from live events and conferences that feature appearances by the big-name tech executives they cover. Some publications also rely on investments from venture capital firms that have stakes in the start-ups they cover.

Ms. Lacy says her challenge in balancing competing interests was no different from that of reporters who cover Washington or Hollywood. "For journalists, there has always been a slippery slope between being an insider and getting really good material and being too close to your sources," she said.

She has been harder on Uber than most of her tech peers have, Ms. Lacy said, which is perhaps why she was specifically named

After BuzzFeed reported that Uber executive vice president Emil Michael suggested that the Internet ride-sharing company considered investigating the private life of a tech journalist, the company president posted a 13-part apology on Twitter.

by the Uber executive, Emil Michael.

The account of Mr. Michael's remarks came from Ben Smith, the editor in chief of BuzzFeed. Mr. Smith spoke to Mr. Michael at a private dinner last Friday [November 14, 2014]. He later reported that Mr. Michael was contemplating spending $1 million to dig up dirt on reporters who, he said, had unfairly criticized the company, mentioning Ms. Lacy in particular.

BuzzFeed reported that Mr. Michael had "expressed outrage" at Ms. Lacy's column and said that "women are far more likely to get assaulted by taxi drivers than Uber drivers." The article added that he had said he thought Ms. Lacy "should be held 'personally responsible' for any woman who

followed her lead in deleting Uber and was then sexually assaulted."

Mr. Michael apologized personally to Ms. Lacy by email on [November 18, 2014] after she refused to speak with him off the record on the phone.

Uber declined a request to discuss why Mr. Michael had singled out Ms. Lacy, but her opinionated style of journalism has made her a lightning rod for negative attention throughout her career.

Ms. Lacy said she was not going to stop pressing, saying she believes that Uber needs to be held accountable. She thinks it is particularly significant that Mr. Michael has not been fired.

"It is clear that the board of directors is not going to act," she said. "This is terrifying to me as a woman and a journalist."

Excerpted from Leslie Kaufman, "Reaction to Uber Tactics Highlights Tech Journalists' Fine Line Between Critic and Booster," November 19, 2014, nytimes.com.

these leave the press in a continually bubbling cauldron of ethical quandaries.

Media's Ethical Decisions Carry Consequences

Ethical dilemmas might seem easier to solve with a rule-book nearby, and several professional media organizations have tried to codify ethical judgments to ensure the outcomes in difficult situations.

Codes of ethics can be very general ("Seek truth and report it."—Society of Professional Journalists); some are very specific ("Do not pay sources or subjects or reward them materially or for participation."—National Press Photographers Association); and some are very personal ("Entities should not collect and use financial account numbers, Social Security numbers, pharmaceutical prescriptions, or medical records about a specific individual without consent."—Internet Advertising Bureau).

Some ethical decisions carry legal consequences—for example, when a journalist reports embarrassing facts and invades someone's privacy. First Amendment protections shield the media from government enforcement of specific codes of conduct, except when ethical mistakes also are judged by the courts to be legal mistakes. In most cases, however, a reporter or a news organization that makes an ethical mistake will not face a lawsuit.

TIM, THE IDEA WE WOULD BUG REPORTERS' PHONES AND LISTEN TO THEIR PRIVATE CALLS IS PREPOSTEROUS. INCIDENTALLY, HOW WAS YOUR WIFE'S BUNION SURGERY? AND ARE TIMMY JR'S GRADES IMPROVING?

5-29   © Dan Thompson/Distributed by Universal Uclick via CartoonStock.com

Dan Thompson/Cartoonstock.com

The consequences of bad ethical judgments usually involve damage to the reputation of newsmakers and the individual reporter, damage to the reputation of the news organization where the reporter works and ultimately damage to the profession in general.

Professional Associations Proscribe Behavior

Professional codes of ethics set a leadership tone for a profession, an organization, a company or an individual. Several media groups have published rules suggesting how the media should operate.

Ethics codes for print, broadcast and Internet organizations are voluntary, with no specific penalties for people who violate the rules. Many media organizations, such as CBS News, the *Los Angeles Times*, and *The New York Times*, maintain their own detailed standards and employ people specifically to monitor ethical conduct. Media support organizations, such as advertising and public relations agencies, usually use guidelines from professional groups as a basis for developing a company philosophy.

Five widely observed codes of ethics are the guidelines adopted by the Society of Professional Journalists, the Radio Television Digital News Association, the Interactive Advertising Bureau, the National Press Photographers Association and the Public Relations Society of America.

Society of Professional Journalists Codifies Conduct

The Society of Professional Journalists Code of Conduct is the oldest and most comprehensive. Some of the code's major points follow.

Seek Truth and Report It. Journalists should be honest, fair and courageous in gathering, reporting and interpreting information. Journalists should:

▶ Test the accuracy of information from all sources and exercise care to avoid inadvertent error. Deliberate distortion is never permissible.

▶ Identify sources whenever feasible. The public is entitled to as much information as possible on sources' reliability.

▶ Make certain that headlines, news teases and promotional material, photos, video, audio, graphics, sound bites and quotations do not misrepresent. They should not oversimplify or highlight incidents out of context.

▶ Never distort the content of news photos or video. Image enhancement for technical clarity is always permissible. Label montages and photo illustrations.

▶ Avoid misleading reenactments or staged news events.

▶ Never plagiarize.

▶ Avoid stereotyping by race, gender, age, religion, ethnicity, geography, sexual orientation, disability, physical appearance or social status.

▶ Distinguish between advocacy and news reporting. Analysis and commentary should be labeled and not misrepresent fact or context.

▶ Distinguish news from advertising and shun hybrids that blur the lines between the two.

▶ Recognize a special obligation to ensure that the public's business is conducted in the open and that government records are open to inspection.

Minimize Harm. Ethical journalists treat sources, subjects and colleagues as human beings deserving of respect. Journalists should:

▶ Show compassion for those who may be affected adversely by news coverage. Use special sensitivity when dealing with children and inexperienced sources or subjects.

▶ Be sensitive when seeking or using interviews or photographs of those affected by tragedy or grief.

▶ Recognize that gathering and reporting information may cause harm or discomfort. Pursuit of the news is not a license for arrogance. . . .

▶ Show good taste. Avoid pandering to lurid curiosity.

▶ Balance a criminal suspect's fair trial rights with the public's right to be informed.

Act Independently. Journalists should be free of obligation to any interest other than the public's right to know. Journalists should:

▶ Avoid conflicts of interest, real or perceived.

▶ Remain free of associations and activities that may compromise integrity or damage credibility.

▶ Refuse gifts, favors, fees, free travel and special

treatment, and shun secondary employment, political involvement, public office and service in community organizations if they compromise journalistic integrity. . . .

Be Accountable. Journalists are accountable to their readers, listeners, viewers and each other. Journalists should:

▶ Clarify and explain news coverage and invite dialogue with the public over journalistic conduct.

▶ Encourage the public to voice grievances against the news media.

▶ Admit mistakes and correct them promptly.

▶ Expose unethical practices of journalists and the news media.

▶ Abide by the same high standards to which they hold others.

Radio Television Digital News Association (RTDNA) Code Covers Electronic News

The RTDNA Code of Ethics and Professional Conduct offers general principles for electronic news reporters ("Professional electronic journalists should recognize that their first obligation is to the public"), as well as specific guidelines ("Professional electronic journalists should not manipulate images or sounds in any way that is misleading"). Following are some major points from the RTDNA ethics code.

Ethics codes adopted by media organizations are voluntary, with no specific penalties suggested for people who violate the rules. The codes are meant as guidelines only. Attorney Douglas Hallward-Dreimeier speaks with reporters outside the U.S. Supreme Court on April 28, 2015, after arguing before the court that states must recognize same sex marriages performed elsewhere.

PREAMBLE: Professional electronic journalists should operate as trustees of the public, seek the truth, report it fairly and with integrity and independence, and stand accountable for their actions.

PUBLIC TRUST: Professional electronic journalists should recognize that their first obligation is to the public.

TRUTH: Professional electronic journalists should pursue truth aggressively and present the news accurately, in context, and as completely as possible.

FAIRNESS: Professional electronic journalists should present the news fairly and impartially, placing primary value on significance and relevance.

INTEGRITY: Professional electronic journalists should present the news with integrity and decency, avoiding real or perceived conflicts of interest, and respect the dignity and intelligence of the audience as well as the subjects of news.

INDEPENDENCE: Professional electronic journalists should defend the independence of all journalists from those seeking influence or control over news content.

ACCOUNTABILITY: Professional electronic journalists should recognize that they are accountable for their actions to the public, the profession, and themselves.

National Press Photographers Association Addresses Visual Journalism

The National Press Photographers Association is "a professional society that promotes the highest standards in visual journalism, acknowledges concern for every person's need both to be fully informed about public events and to be recognized as a part of the world in which we live."

The association's ethics code lists a series of goals for visual journalists, including the following:

1. Be accurate and comprehensive in the representation of subjects.

2. Resist being manipulated by stated photo opportunities.

3. Be complete and provide context when photographing or recording subjects.

4. Treat all subjects with respect and dignity.

5. While photographing subjects do not intentionally contribute to, alter, or seek to alter or influence events.

6. Editing should maintain the integrity of the photographic images' content and context.

7. Do not pay sources or subjects or reward them materially for information or participation.

8. Do not accept gifts, favors, or compensation from those who might to influence coverage.

9. Do not sabotage the efforts of other journalists.

Interactive Advertising Bureau Addresses Digital Ads

The Interactive Advertising Bureau (IAB) Code of Conduct is the most recent set of media guidelines, first established in 1996 to cover businesses that advertise on the Internet. The guidelines, last updated in 2003, are voluntary and self-regulatory and apply to all members of the IAB.

The IAB says that more than 80 percent of interactive display ads follow IAB standards. Some principles of the IAB Code of Conduct are excerpted here.

I. Education

Entities should participate in efforts to educate individuals and businesses about online behavioral advertising, including the actors in the ecosystem, how data may be collected, and how consumer choice and control may be exercised.

II. Transparency

Third parties and service providers should give clear, meaningful, and prominent notice on their own Web sites that describes their online behavioral advertising data collection and use practices.

III. Consumer Control

A third party should provide consumers with the ability to exercise choice with respect to the collection and use of data for online behavioral advertising purposes or the transfer of such data to a non-affiliate for such purpose.

IV. Data Security

A. Safeguards

Entities should maintain appropriate physical, electronic, and administrative safeguards to protect the data collected and used for online behavioral advertising purposes.

Unethical advertising uses falsehoods to deceive the public. Ethical advertising uses the truth to deceive the public.

Mark Dubowski/Cartoonstock.com

B. Data Retention

Entities should retain data that is collected and used for online behavioral advertising only as long as necessary to fulfill a legitimate business need, or as required by law.

V. Material Changes to Existing Online Behavioral Advertising Policies and Practices

Entities should obtain consent before applying any material change to their online behavioral advertising data collection and use policies and practices prior to such material change.

VI. Sensitive Data

A. Children

Entities should not collect "personal information," as defined in the Children's Online Privacy Protection Act (COPPA), from children they have actual knowledge are under the age of 13 or from sites directed to children under the age of 13 for online behavioral advertising, or engage in online behavioral advertising directed to children they have actual knowledge are under the age of 13 except as compliant with the COPPA.

B. Health and Financial Data

Entities should not collect and use financial account numbers, Social Security numbers, pharmaceutical prescriptions, or medical records about a specific individual for online behavioral advertising without consent.

Public Relations Society of America Sets Standards

The Code of Professional Standards, first adopted in 1950 by the Public Relations Society of America, has been revised several times. Here are some excerpts:

▶ A member shall deal fairly with clients or employers, past, present, or potential, with fellow practitioners and with the general public.

▶ A member shall adhere to truth and accuracy and to generally accepted standards of good taste.

▶ A member shall not intentionally communicate false or misleading information, and is obligated to use care to avoid communication of false or misleading information.

▶ A member shall be prepared to identify publicly the name of the client or employer on whose behalf any public communication is made.

▶ A member shall not guarantee the achievement of specified results beyond the member's direct control.

Media Organizations Respond to Criticism

Prescriptive codes of ethics are helpful in describing what media professionals should do, and informal guidelines can supplement professional codes. Many media professionals use good judgment, but what happens when they don't? People with serious complaints against broadcasters sometimes appeal to the Federal Communications Commission, but what about complaints that must be handled more quickly? The press has offered three solutions: news councils, readers' representatives and correction boxes.

News Councils

News councils originated in Great Britain. They are composed of people who formerly worked or currently work in the news business, as well as some laypeople. The council reviews complaints from the public, and when the members determine that a mistake has been made, the council reports its findings to the offending news organization.

In 1973, the Twentieth-Century Fund established a National News Council in the U.S., but the council disbanded in 1984.

Today, only two news councils exist in the United States—the Minnesota News Council and the Honolulu Community Media Council. The Minnesota council is older. Since 1970, the council's 24 members, half of them journalists and half of them public members such as lawyers and teachers, have reviewed complaints about the state's media. Half the complaints have been ruled in favor of the reporters. The council has no enforcement power, only the power of public scrutiny.

Readers' Representatives

The *readers' representative* (also called an ombudsperson or public reporter) is a go-between at a media company who responds to complaints from the public and regularly publishes answers to criticism.

About two dozen newspapers throughout the country, including *The Washington Post, The New York Times,* the *Los Angeles Times* and *The Sacramento Bee*, have tried the idea, but most news organizations still funnel complaints directly to the editor.

Correction Boxes

The *correction box* is a device that often is handled by a readers' representative but also has been adopted by media organizations without a readers' representative. The box is published in the newspaper and on the newspaper's Web site near the corrected story with a note about the correction.

As a permanent fixture of the newspaper, the correction box is used to counter criticism that corrections sometimes receive less attention from readers than the original stories.

The New York Times, for example, regularly publishes a small correction box to fix small errors in its stories. But when *The Times* discovered in 2010 that its reporter Zachery Kouwe had plagiarized stories from *The Wall Street Journal* (see p. 315), *The Times* published a specific explanation as a lengthy Editor's Note, which gave the incident more prominence.

Professional Codes Preserve Media Credibility

Ethics codes, news councils, readers' representatives and correction boxes help media organizations handle criticism and avert possible legal problems, but no single solution can address all the ethical issues these businesses face. In media organizations every day, people face the same ethical decisions all people face in their daily lives—whether to be honest, how to be fair, how to be sensitive and how to be responsible.

The difference is that, unlike personal ethical dilemmas that people can debate privately, reporters and editors publish, broadcast and post the results of their ethical judgments, and those judgments quickly become public.

A profession that accepts ethical behavior as a standard helps guarantee its future. The major commodity the media profession has to offer is information, and when the presentation of that information is weakened by untruth, bias, intrusiveness or irresponsibility, the media gain few advocates and acquire more enemies.

Writes John Hulteng:

> The primary objective of the press and those who work with it is to bring readers, listeners and viewers as honest, accurate and complete an account of the day's events as possible. . . . The need to be informed is so great that the Constitution provides the press with a First Amendment standing that is unique among business enterprises. But as with most grants of power, there is an accompanying responsibility, not constitutionally mandated but nonetheless well understood: that the power of the press must be used responsibly and compassionately.

REVIEW, ANALYZE, INVESTIGATE

CHAPTER 15

Ethics Define Responsibilities

- The word *ethics* derives from the Greek word *ethos*, which means the guiding spirit or traditions that govern a culture.
- When journalists make the wrong ethical choices, the consequences are very public.
- Journalists' ethical dilemmas can be discussed using four categories: truthfulness, fairness, privacy and responsibility.

Truthfulness Affects Credibility

- Truthfulness means more than telling the truth to get a story. Truthfulness also means not misrepresenting the people or the situations in the story for readers or viewers.
- In 2015, NBC anchor Brian Williams and Fox News personality Bill O'Reilly embellished stories they reported, examples of fabrication.
- In July 2012, *New Yorker* writer Jonah Lehrer resigned after it was discovered that he fabricated quotes for his book, *Imagine: How Creativity Works*.
- In 2014, BuzzFeed dismissed writer Benny Johnson after identifying 41 examples of plagiarism.
- In 2010, *The New York Times* suspended reporter Zachery Kouwe after editors said Kouwe had plagiarized portions of an article he had written for *The Times* from an article by another reporter that had appeared online in *The Wall Street Journal*. Kouwe resigned.
- For two decades British reporter Mazher Mahmood wrote stories about the wrongdoings of many famous people and then testified against them in court. In 2014, the Crown Prosecution Service announced an investigation of Mahmood's role in at least 25 criminal convictions.
- A classic example of a journalistic misrepresentation is Jayson Blair, a reporter for *The New York Times*, who admitted in May 2003 that he had fabricated comments, concocted scenes, stolen material from other newspapers and news services and selected details from photos to create an impression he had been in certain places and interviewed people when he hadn't.

Fairness Means Evenhandedness

- Fairness implies impartiality—that the journalist has nothing personal to gain from a report and that there are no hidden benefits to the reporter or to the source from the story being presented.
- Criticism of the press for unfairness results from insider friendships, conflicts of interest and checkbook journalism.
- In May 2015, ABC chief anchor George Stephanopoulos acknowledged he had donated $75,000 to the Clinton Foundation and did not publicly disclose the donation, an example of insider friendships.
- In more examples of insider friendships, MSNBC commentators Keith Olbermann and Joe Scarborough were suspended in 2010 for two days after it was discovered that they had made campaign contributions to political candidates.
- In 2015, PBS postponed broadcast of the program *Finding Your Roots* after PBS learned producers had omitted information about Ben Affleck's slave-owning ancestor, at Affleck's request.
- In another example of insider friendship, in 2010, the *New Hampshire Union Leader* accepted underwriting from three major New Hampshire businesses including BAE Systems, a defense contractor, so the newspaper's publisher and a staff photographer could travel to Afghanistan to report on a New Hampshire National Guard unit serving there.
- In 2009, *The Washington Post* lost credibility when its publisher invited sponsorships in exchange for attendance at an exclusive "salon" at her home. *The Post* eventually canceled the event and printed an apology.
- In 2012, Alliance, the film company that represented actor Brad Pitt, requested £2,000 (approximately $3,000) from journalists who wanted to interview Pitt at the Cannes Film Festival, an example of checkbook journalism.
- In another example of checkbook journalism, in 2011 ABC News paid kidnapping victim Jaycee Lee Dugard for exclusive rights to an interview.

Privacy Involves Respect

- Privacy for personal communications such as e-mails and voice mails became a big issue in 2011 when reporters at Rupert Murdoch's *News of the World* hacked celebrity e-mails and voice mails.

- In November 2012, prosecutors charged two former top executives at *News of the World*, Rebekah Brooks and Andy Coulson, with paying bribes of up to $160,000 to public officials, in addition to several earlier charges levied against them.

- Brooks was acquitted but Coulson was convicted and required to pay up to £750,000 in court costs.

- An important invasion-of-privacy issue is the publication of names of rape victims.

- Reporters must decide whether the public interest is served by revealing victims' names.

- In 1990, the *Des Moines Register* published a five-part series about rape victim Nancy Ziegenmayer, with her consent.

- In 2015, *New York* magazine reignited the controversy about identifying rape victims when the magazine's cover showed photos of 35 women, with their permission, who alleged that entertainer Bill Cosby sexually assaulted them. He denied the charges.

Responsibility Generates Trust

- Responsibility means that reporters and editors must be careful about how they use the information they gather.

- In 2014, the Web size BuzzFeed reported that Uber senior vice president Emil Michael said the company had considered investigating the private life of Sarah Lacy, a technology reporter who had written critically about the company. Uber's CEO eventually apologized.

Five Philosophical Principles Govern Media Ethics

- Five philosophical principles underlying the practical application of ethical decisions are (1) Aristotle's golden mean, (2) Immanuel Kant's categorical imperative, (3) John Stuart Mill's principle of utility, (4) John Rawls' veil of ignorance and (5) the Judeo-Christian view of persons as ends in themselves.

- Journalists adopt a philosophy of situational ethics.

Media's Ethical Decisions Carry Consequences

- Some ethical decisions carry legal consequences, such as when a journalist reports embarrassing facts and invades someone's privacy.

- In most cases, a reporter or a news organization that makes an ethical mistake will not face a lawsuit.

Professional Associations Proscribe Behavior

- Several media professions have adopted ethics codes to guide their conduct.

- Five of these ethics codes are the guidelines adopted by the Society of Professional Journalists, the Radio Television Digital News Association, the National Press Photographers Association, the Interactive Advertising Bureau and the Public Relations Society of America.

Media Organizations Respond to Criticism

- The three responses of the U.S. press to criticism have been to create news councils, to employ readers' representatives and to publish correction boxes in the printed newspaper and online.

- The National Press Council, created to hear consumer complaints about the press, disbanded in 1984.

- Today only two news councils still exist in the United States—the Minnesota News Council and the Honolulu Community Media Council.

Professional Codes Preserve Media Credibility

- The media's ethical decisions can broadly affect society.

- The major commodity the American press has to offer is credibility, and when the presentation of information is weakened by untruth, bias, intrusiveness or irresponsibility, the press gains few advocates and acquires more enemies.

Key Terms

These terms are defined in the margins throughout this chapter and appear in alphabetical order with definitions in the Glossary, which begins on page 361.

Critical Questions

1. When you read about high-profile media ethics cases like the ones in this chapter, what should you remember about the possibility that what you read, hear or see in the mass media may not be true, or at least not what you understand it to be? How does this affect the way you obtain or critically analyze print, broadcast and Internet information?

2. List and explain three ways that checkbook journalism may affect the quality of reporting.

3. Choose any of the ethical situations specified in this chapter and describe how each of the following philosophical principles would define your decision.

   a. Aristotle's golden mean
   b. Kant's categorical imperative
   c. Mill's principle of utility
   d. Rawls' veil of ignorance
   e. Judeo-Christian persons-as-ends

4. Explain the consequences of plagiarism, fabrication and misrepresentation on reporters, the companies they work for and the public.

5. What effect do you believe ethics codes, such as those described in this chapter, have on the professionals for whom they have been developed? Do they work? Explain.

Working the Web

This list includes sites mentioned in the chapter and others to give you greater insight into media ethics.

Center for Journalism Ethics

ethics.journalism.wisc.edu

Established in 2008 at the School of Journalism and Mass Communication at the University of Wisconsin, the center applies an interdisciplinary approach to studying the issues of best media practices. Resources on the site include hyperlinks to topics such as Ethics in a Nutshell, Holding Media Accountable and Digital and Global Media Ethics.

College Media Association (CMA)

collegemedia.org

Originally founded in 1954 as the National Council of College Publications Advisors, the College Media Association is headquartered in Nashville, Tenn. at Vanderbilt University. Through social media and the listserv on the CMA Web site, members can discuss, study and learn more about current issues trending at college print and digital publications throughout the U.S. The association also publishes the *College Media Review*, an academic journal on advising college media.

Columbia Journalism Review (CJR)

cjr.org

The main emphasis of the flagship publication from the Columbia University Graduate School of Journalism is "to encourage and stimulate excellence in journalism in the service of a free society." The *Review* is published six times a year. The Web site promises fresh media analysis and criticism as well as interactive features about the performance and problems of the press, including *CJRDaily.org*, which hosts daily discussions on current trends and issues affecting all forms of media throughout the world. The discussions include Who Owns What (a regularly updated listing of media ownership worldwide), Magazines and Their Web Sites, and a Guide to Online News Startups.

EthicNet, European Ethics Codes

ethicnet.uta.fi/

This databank primarily holds links to English translations of journalism codes of ethics from most European countries (maintained by the Department of Journalism and Mass Communication, University of Tampere, Finland) as well as some countries outside Europe. Links are available on the site to two other media code databases—Media Accountability Systems and MediaWise Trust.

Fairness & Accuracy in Reporting (FAIR)

fair.org

An anticensorship and media watchdog group, FAIR advocates "greater diversity in the press by scrutinizing media practices that marginalize public interest, minority and dissenting viewpoints." FAIR's main premise is that the media relies on the economics of profit rather than its originally intended purpose to be an institution that helps maintain free and open societies throughout the world. Resources on the site include links to "Extra!"—a newsletter of media criticism—and "CounterSpin"—a weekly radio program that reports "the news behind the headlines."

Freedom Forum

newseuminstitute.org/freedom-forum/

This nonpartisan foundation based in Washington, D.C., is dedicated to promoting the five freedoms contained in the First Amendment of the U.S. Constitution—freedom of speech, press, religion, and assembly and freedom to petition the government. The Freedom Forum provides the majority of funding for the Newseum, an interactive museum of news in Washington, D.C.; the First Amendment Center, which features current news and commentary; and the Diversity Institute, based at the John Seigenthaler Center at Vanderbilt University in Nashville, Tenn. Resources on the site include links to a library of books and periodicals on the First Amendment that can be downloaded and a listing of online and in-person courses available through the Freedom Center.

Journalism Ethics Cases Online

journalism.indiana.edu/resources/ethics/

Hosted by the School of Journalism at Indiana University, this set of cases was created to help teachers, researchers, professional journalists and news consumers explore ethical issues in journalism. The issues include sensitive news topics, such as covering politics, invading privacy and aiding law enforcement.

National Press Photographers Association (NPPA)

nppa.org

Tracing its origins to the days of "sheet film box cameras and newsreels," the NPPA is the professional trade association for those who work in the visual media, including news photographers, videographers and multimedia journalists. NPPA lobbies Congress and state and local governments as well as filing friend of the court briefs in legal cases affecting the practices and regulation of all aspects of visual media. The association hosts several competitions each year for photojournalists, videographers and NPPA student members. Resources include a digital news archive, a listing for professional visual journalists and access to the online version of *News Photographer Magazine*, published by the NPPA.

Poynter Online

poynter.org

This Web site of the St. Petersburg, Florida-based Poynter Institute, a learning center for journalists, future journalists and journalism teachers, features news and tips for students about reporting and writing, ethics and diversity and journalism education. The training section includes information on seminars and webinars, career coaching and Poynter publications. Users can connect with an online community based on various journalism topics.

Radio Television Digital News Association (RTDNA; formerly Radio-Television News Directors Association)

rtdna.org

RTDNA is the U.S. professional organization that serves the digital news profession. Its membership consists of news directors, associates, educators and students. The association's educational foundation, RTDNF, was created to help members uphold ethical journalism standards in the newsroom. Ethics information—including the association's Code of Ethics and Professional Conduct, details on the Journalism Ethics Project and coverage guidelines—is available in the Web site's Best Practices section.

Society of Professional Journalists (SPJ)

spj.org

Originally established in 1909 on the DePauw University campus in Greendale, Ind., under the Greek fraternal name Sigma Delta Chi, SPJ is the nation's most broad-based journalism organization. SPJ is dedicated to "encouraging the free practice of journalism and stimulating high standards of ethical behavior." Features include freedom of information; ethics (including the SPJ Code of Ethics); *Rainbow Diversity Sourcebook*, *Journalists Toolbox*, SPJ blogs and current issues of the association's online magazine, *Quill*.

Impact/Action Videos are concise news features on various topics created exclusively for *Media/Impact*. Find them in *Media/Impact*'s MindTap at cengagebrain.com.

MindTap® Log on to MindTap for *Media/Impact* to access a variety of additional material—including learning objectives, chapter readings with highlighting and note-taking, **Impact/Action Videos**, activities, and comprehension quizzes—that will guide you through this chapter.

GLOBAL MEDIA
COMMUNICATING
CHANGE

Mobile media are a central factor in the global
expansion of mass media. A giant billboard in
Riyadh, Saudi Arabia, shows King Salman on a
giant mobile phone.

What's Ahead?

- World Media Systems Vary
- Five Political Theories Describe How World Media Operate
- Western Europe and Canada Are Similar to the U.S.
- Eastern Europe Is in Transition
- Middle Eastern and North African Media Work Under Government Controls
- African Media Find a New Voice
- Media Explode in Asia and the Pacific
- Government, Corporations and Dynasties Control Latin American and Caribbean Media
- *International New York Times* Seeks a Global Audience
- Critics Cite Western Communications Bias
- Internet Expands Mass Media's Global Reach
- Mobile Media Open Communications Channels
- Reporters Risk Lives to Report World Events
- Global Media Chase International Consumers
- Ideas Transcend Borders

"International communications is often considered a mixed blessing by rulers. Usually they want technical progress. But at the same time they do not want the ideas that come with them."

—ITHIEL DE SOLA POOL, AUTHOR OF *TECHNOLOGIES OF FREEDOM*

In the United States, many students assume that mass media in most countries operate like the U.S. media, but media industries in different countries are as varied as the countries they serve. Can you identify the countries in the following media situations?

1. People in this country have access to more wireless Internet **hot spots** than anywhere else in the world. (A hot spot is a public area such as a restaurant or hotel where a wireless Internet router allows people with laptops and hand-held Internet devices, such as smart phones, to use the Internet without a wired connection.)

2. This country produces more movies every year—1,100—than any other nation in the world.

3. This company is the world's biggest advertiser and spends more than $11.5 billion a year to market its products.

4. This country's citizens must pay the government an annual TV license fee, the equivalent of $225, and can be fined if they are caught using an unlicensed TV set.

5. In this country, viewers can watch TV news presented by rap-orters, hip-hop artists who use rhyme to convey the day's events.

World Media Systems Vary

The country with the largest number of wireless locations (example 1) is South Korea. In the United States, the place with the most wireless locations (hot spots) is New York City with 1,657—nearly three times the number of hot spots that are available in Los Angeles (637).

The country that produces the most movies (example 2) is India, which celebrated its 100th year of moviemaking in 2013.

The company that spends the most money to advertise globally (example 3) is Procter & Gamble, makers of Tide detergent, among other household products. Procter & Gamble is also the biggest advertiser in the U.S.

People who live in the United Kingdom are responsible for paying a yearly TV license fee (example 4). The fee is due at the post office each year, and the collectors who enforce the fee are actually employees of the post office. The government collects more than $2 billion a year from

Hot Spot A public area such as a restaurant or hotel where people with laptops and hand-held Internet devices can connect to the Internet without a wire.

the fees, which allows the British Broadcasting Corporation to operate several radio and TV stations without advertising.

The rap-orters are news presenters on the Ugandan TV program *NewzBeat* (example 5). Every Saturday, three popular hip-hop artists use their five-minute news program as a way around government censorship. One of the artists' favorite topics is the country's widespread corruption.

These examples demonstrate the complexity of defining today's international media marketplace, which clearly is a marketplace in rapid transition as the Internet blurs global borders. It is very difficult to control the flow of digital information, although some countries try.

This chapter examines various aspects of global media, including political theories and the media, world media systems, news and information flow and global media markets.

Five Political Theories Describe How World Media Operate

No institution as sizable and influential as the mass media can escape involvement with government and politics. The media are not only channels for the transmission of political information and debate but also significant players with a direct stake in government's regulatory and economic policies, as well as government's attitude toward free speech and dissent.

Remember that *the way a country's political system is organized affects the way the mass media within that country operate.* Media systems can be divided broadly into those systems that allow dissent and those that do not.

In Britain, radio and TV users pay an annual license fee to support the British Broadcasting Corporation (BBC). On May 15, 2015, BBC Northern Ireland Presenter Noel Thompson moderates a general election candidates' debate in Belfast, United Kingdom.

To categorize the political organization of media systems, scholars often begin with the 1956 book *Four Theories of the Press*, by Fred S. Siebert, Theodore Peterson and Wilbur Schramm. These four theories, which originally were used to describe the political systems under which media operated in different countries, were (1) the Soviet theory, (2) the authoritarian theory, (3) the libertarian theory and (4) the social responsibility theory. Scholars recently added a fifth description, the more modern (5) developmental theory, to update the original categories used to help describe the world's mass media systems.

The Soviet Theory

Historically in the Soviet Union (which dissolved in 1991 into several independent nations and states), the government owned and operated the mass media. All media employees were government employees, expected to serve the government's interests.

Top media executives also served as leaders in the Communist Party. Even when the press controls loosened in the 1980s, the mass media were part of the government's policy. Government control came *before* the media published or broadcast; people who controlled the media could exercise *prior restraint*. They could review copy and look at programs before they appeared.

This description of the Soviet press system was conceived before the events of the 1990s challenged the basic assumptions of Soviet government. Many Eastern bloc countries, such as Romania, Slovakia and the Czech Republic, which once operated under Soviet influence, based their media systems on the Communist model. Today, the media systems in these countries are in transition and Russian media are once again under strong government controls.

The Authoritarian Theory

Media that operate under the authoritarian theory can be either publicly or privately owned. This concept of the press developed in Europe after Gutenberg. Until the 1850s, presses in Europe were privately owned, and the aristocracy (which governed the countries) wanted some sort of control over what was printed about them. The aristocracy had the financial and political power necessary to make the rules about what would be printed.

The first idea was to license everyone who owned a printing press so the license could be revoked if someone published something unfavorable about the government. The British crown licensed the first colonial newspapers in America. Licensing wasn't very successful in the United States, however, because many people who owned presses didn't apply for licenses.

The next authoritarian attempt to control the press was to review material after it was published. A printer who was discovered publishing material that strongly challenged the government could be heavily fined or even put to death. Today, many governments still maintain this type of rigid control over the media.

Most monarchies, for example, operate in an authoritarian tradition, which tolerates very little dissent. Media systems that serve at the government's pleasure and with the government's approval are common.

YOSHIKAZU TSUNO/Getty Images

Japanese telecommunications giant Softbank introduced Pepper, a mobile marketing robot. Pepper is promoting the sale of watermelons in a market in Tokyo. Japanese media combine libertarianism and social responsibility.

The Libertarian Theory

The concept of a libertarian press evolved from the idea that people who are given all the information on an issue will be able to discern what is true and what is false and will make good choices. This is an idea embraced by the writers of the U.S. Constitution and by other democratic governments.

This theory assumes, of course, that the media's main goal is to convey the truth and that the media will not cave in to outside pressures, such as from advertisers or corporate owners. This theory also assumes that people with opposing viewpoints will be heard—that the media will present all points of view, in what is commonly called the free marketplace of ideas.

The First Amendment to the U.S. Constitution concisely advocates the idea of freedom of the press. Theoretically, America today operates under the libertarian theory, although this ideal has been challenged often by changes in the media industries since the Constitution was adopted.

The Social Responsibility Theory

This theory accepts the concept of a libertarian press but prescribes what the media should do. Someone who believes in the social responsibility theory believes that members of the media will do their jobs well only if periodically reminded about their duties.

The theory grew out of the 1947 Hutchins Commission Report on the Free and Responsible Press. The commission listed five goals for the media, including the need for truthful

and complete reporting of all sides of an issue. The commission concluded that the American press's privileged position in the Constitution means that the press must always work to be responsible to society.

If the media fail to meet their responsibilities to society, the social responsibility theory holds that the government should encourage the media to comply. In this way, the libertarian and the social responsibility theories differ. The libertarian theory assumes members of

Hagen/Cartoonstock.com

I know we're a long way from anywhere, but I still like to know what's going on in the World...

the media will work well without government interference; the social responsibility theory advocates government oversight for media that don't act in society's best interest.

The Developmental Theory

The most recent description for media systems is the developmental theory. Under this theory, named for the developing nations where it is most often found, the media *may* be privately owned but usually are owned by the government.

The mass media in the developmental category are used to promote the country's social and economic goals and to direct a sense of national purpose. For example, a developmental media system might be used to promote birth control or to encourage children to attend school. The media are an outlet for some types of government propaganda, then, but in the name of economic and social progress, as defined by the government.

Although the theory that best describes the American media is the libertarian theory, throughout their history the American media have struggled with both authoritarian and social responsibility debates: Should the press be free to print secret government documents, for example? What responsibility do television networks have to provide worthwhile programming to their audiences? The media, the government and the public continually modify and adjust their interpretations of just how the media should operate.

It has been nearly seven decades since scholars began using the political theories of the press to define the world's media systems. With today's transitional period in global history, even the recent addition of the developmental theory still leaves many media systems beyond convenient categorization.

Media systems vary throughout the world. The print media form the basis for press systems that developed in North America, Australia, Western Europe and Eastern Europe—where two-thirds of the world's newspapers are published. Many developing countries matured after broadcast media were introduced in the 1920s, and newsprint in these countries often is scarce or government-controlled, making radio their dominant communications medium. Radio receivers are inexpensive, and many people can share one radio.

Television, which relies on expensive equipment, is widely used in prosperous nations and in developing countries' urban areas. Yet many countries still have only one television service, usually run by the government. In many developing countries, all broadcasting—television and radio—is owned and controlled by the government.

The Internet is blurring international media borders because it is very difficult to control the flow of digital information across geographical and ideological boundaries, although some countries try.

What follows is a description of today's media systems by geographic region: Western Europe and Canada; Eastern Europe; the Middle East and North Africa; Africa; Asia and the Pacific; and Latin America and the Caribbean.

Western Europe and Canada Are Similar to the U.S.

Western European and Canadian media prosper under guarantees of freedom of expression similar to the First Amendment, but each nation has modified the idea to reflect its values. For example, in Great Britain the media are prohibited from commenting on a trial until the trial is finished, and in 2003, Britain banned all tobacco advertising in newspapers, on billboards and on the Internet.

France and Greece, unlike the United States, give more libel protection to public figures than to private citizens. Scandinavian journalists enjoy the widest press freedoms of all of Western Europe, including almost unlimited access to public documents.

Of the Western nations, Canada is the most recent country to issue an official decree supporting the philosophy of press freedom. In 1982, Canada adopted the Canadian Charter of Rights and Freedoms. Before 1982, Canada did not have its own constitution and instead operated under the 1867 British North America Act,

AP Images/Kay Nietfeld

In Western European countries like Greece, newspapers tend to be partisan, and journalists often reflect political points of view. On July 5, 2015, Greek Prime Minister Alexis Tsipras meets the press during a referendum vote on Greece's financial crisis.

sharing the British free press philosophy. In 2010, however, Canada's Supreme Court ruled that Canadian reporters do not have a constitutional right to offer their sources blanket confidentiality. Like the United States, Canada does not have a national shield law.

Print Media

Johannes Gutenberg's invention of movable type rooted the print media in Western Europe. Today, Western European and Canadian media companies produce many fine newspapers. *The Globe and Mail* of Toronto, *The Times* of London, *Frankfurter Allgemeine* of Germany, *Le Monde* of France and Milan's *Corriere della Sera* enjoy healthy circulations.

Whereas Canadian journalists have adopted the U.S. values of fairness and balance as a journalistic ethic, Western European newspapers tend to be much more partisan than the U.S. or Canadian press, and newspapers (and journalists) are expected to reflect strong points of view.

Broadcast Media

As in the United States, the print media in Western Europe are losing audiences to the broadcast media, cable and the Internet. Government originally controlled most of Western Europe's broadcast stations. A board of governors, appointed by the queen, supervises the British Broadcasting Corporation (**BBC**), for example.

To finance the government-run broadcast media, countries like the United Kingdom tax the sale of radios and TVs or charge users an annual license fee, which funds the broadcasts. The BBC collects more than $2 billion annually in license fees, but government controls the budget. In 2010, the BBC governing board reduced staff positions and proposed cuts to employee pensions. The BBC's 4,100 reporters, who are members of the National Union of Journalists, announced a series of 48-hour strikes in protest, and BBC management was forced to replace scheduled live shows with pre-recorded programs during the strikes. The government continues to threaten further budget cuts.

ITV is the largest commercial network in the United Kingdom, with four separate channels. ITV is a "public service broadcaster," which means the network is required to offer public service programming and is regulated by the government, but the channels are very similar to commercial networks in the United States.

Western Europeans watch less television than people in the United States—an average of three hours a day per household in Europe, compared with seven hours a day per household in the United States. One reason for the difference in viewing time is that some Western European TV stations don't go on the air until late afternoon.

In many countries, commercials are shown back to back at the beginning or the end of a program.

Europe gets some of its programming from the United States. Of the 125,000 hours of TV broadcast in Western Europe each year, less than half are produced in Europe. Many of the programs come from America, with a few shows imported from Australia and Japan. U.S. imports are attractive because buying U.S. programs is cheaper than producing new programming within the country.

The European Union (EU) constitutes a single, unified European market. The policy adopted by the EU is Television Without Frontiers, which promotes an open marketplace for television programs among countries in the EU and between EU countries and the United States.

Some members of the EU (especially France) have proposed quotas to limit imported TV programs, charging that U.S. imports are an example of "cultural imperialism." Countries that favor quotas fear that the importation of U.S. programs imposes a concentration of U.S. values on their viewers.

The United States opposes such quotas, of course, because Western European commercial broadcasting offers a seemingly insatiable market for recycled U.S. programs. Broadcasting in Western Europe is slowly evolving to private ownership and commercial sponsorship. In 2015, the European Union challenged the distribution system of five U.S. film companies, charging them with antitrust violations (See **Impact/Money**, "Film Studios Respond to European Antitrust Allegations," p. 341.)

Eastern Europe Is in Transition

The democratization of Eastern Europe is transforming the print and broadcast media in these countries at an unprecedented pace. Everette E. Dennis, executive director of the Gannett Center for Media Studies, and Jon Vanden Heuvel described the Eastern European challenges in a report issued after a Gannett-sponsored fact-finding trip:

> Mass communication in the several countries of the region was reinventing itself. While grassroots newspapers and magazines struggled for survival, new press laws were being debated and enacted; elements of a market economy were coming into view; the media system itself and its role in the state and society were being redefined, as was the very nature of journalism and the job description of the journalist, who was no longer a propagandist for the state.

BBC British Broadcasting Corporation, the government-funded British broadcast network.

In many Eastern European countries like Russia, the government tightly controls mass media outlets. On April 25, 2015, Russian President Vladimir Putin speaks at a commemorative ceremony in Yerevan, Armenia.

AP Images/Briquet Nicolas

Eastern Europe today is in transition, defining a new balance between people's desire for free expression and the indigenous remnants of government-controlled systems. In many of these countries, mass media played a central role in upsetting the established power structure. Often one of the first targets of the revolutionary movements is a nation's broadcast operation.

For example, in Romania in 1989, opposition leaders of the National Salvation Committee and sympathetic employees barricaded themselves in a Bucharest TV station, rallying the audience to action. "Romania was governed from a hectic studio littered with empty bottles, cracked coffee mugs and half-eaten sandwiches, and run by people who had not slept in days," the Associated Press reported.

Print Media

Print media were strictly controlled under Communism, with high-ranking party officials forming the core of media management. Because paper supplies were limited, newspapers rarely exceeded 12 pages. Revolutionary leader Vladimir Lenin, who said a newspaper should be a "collective propagandist," a "collective agitator" and a "collective organizer," founded *Pravda*, the Soviet Union's oldest newspaper, in 1912. The Eastern European nations developed their press policies following the Soviet model.

In the late 1980s, Soviet President Mikhail Gorbachev eased media controls as part of his policy of *glasnost*. In 1988, the first paid commercials (for Pepsi-Cola, Sony and Visa credit cards) appeared on Soviet TV, and in 1989, the Soviet daily newspaper *Izvestia* published its first Western ads (including ads for perfume and wines from the French firm Pechiney and for Dresdner, a German bank).

In 1990, the Supreme Soviet, the legislative body, outlawed media censorship and gave every citizen the right to publish a newspaper. Within 5 months, more than 100 newspapers began publication. Then, showing how quickly government positions can change, in early 1991, Gorbachev asked the Supreme Soviet to suspend these press freedoms, but it refused. Less than a year later, Gorbachev's successor, President Boris Yeltsin, again began to relax government control of the press. In 1996, facing bankruptcy, *Pravda* ceased publication.

Today Russian officials, such as Prime Minister Vladimir Putin, maintain a tight rein on the press, and several reporters who have written critically about the government have been brutally injured or killed, although the government disavows any connection to the attacks. Putin "thinks that democracy stands in his way," former Soviet leader Mikhail S. Gorbachev told *The New York Times* in an interview published on October 26, 2010. "I am afraid that they have been saddled with this idea that this unmanageable country needs authoritarianism. They think they cannot do without it."

Broadcast Media

Television in the Eastern bloc countries developed under Communist direction because the Communist governments were in power before TV use was widespread. Radio broadcasting also was tightly controlled, although foreign broadcasts directed across Eastern European borders, such as Voice of America and Radio Free Europe, usually evaded jamming attempts by Radio Moscow. Today Eastern Europe is creating a new media environment.

As Eastern European governments change and realign themselves, the adjustments facing Eastern European media are unprecedented. According to Everette E. Dennis and Jon Vanden Heuvel:

Once the revolution came, among the first acts of new government was to take (they would say liberate) electronic media and open up the print press. Permitting free and eventually independent media was a vital beginning for democracy in several countries and a clear break with the past. The freeing up of the media system, speedily in some countries and incrementally in others, was the lifting of an ideological veil without saying just what would replace it.

Middle Eastern and North African Media Work Under Government Controls

Press history in the Middle East and North Africa begins with the newspaper *Al-Iraq*, first published in 1817, although the first *daily* newspaper didn't begin publishing until 1873. With one exception, development of the press throughout this region follows the same pattern as in most developing countries: More newspapers and magazines are published in regions with high literacy rates than in regions with low literacy rates.

The exception is Egypt, where less than half the people are literate. Yet Cairo is the Arab world's publishing center. *Al Ahram* and *Al Akhbar* are Egypt's leading government-controlled daily newspapers.

AP Images/Amr Nabil

Egypt is one of the most dangerous countries for journalists. More reporters have been imprisoned under the current administration of President Abdel Fattah el-Sisi than at any other time in Egypt's recent history. On July 12, 2014, journalists called for the release of reporter Abou Zeid, known as Shawkan. He was arrested in 2013 for photographing demonstrators who opposed the current government and remains in custody although he has never officially been charged with a crime.

Print Media

The Middle Eastern press is tightly controlled by government restrictions through ownership and licensing, and it is not uncommon for opposition newspapers to suddenly disappear and for journalists to be jailed or forced to leave the country following political upheaval.

According to global media scholar Christine Ogan, "Following the revolution in Iran, all opposition and some moderate newspapers were closed, and according to the National Union of Iranian Journalists (now an illegal organization), more than 75 percent of all journalists left the country, were jailed, or no longer work in journalism." The Palestinian press was subject to censorship by the Israeli government, and all Palestinian newspapers and magazines at one time required permission from the Israeli government to be published.

In Syria, where rebels were fighting the government of President Bashar al-Assad, opposition journalists began publishing weeklies in 2012, hoping to counteract government-controlled media. The papers are supported by donations and distributed free in Syria and by paid subscription abroad.

Broadcast Media

The foreign-language press is especially strong in the Middle East because of the large number of immigrants in the area, and foreign radio is very popular. Governments within each country control radio and television almost completely, and television stations in Sudan and Yemen, for example, broadcast for only a few hours a day beginning in mid-afternoon.

In the larger Arab states (Jordan, Lebanon, Saudi Arabia and Egypt), TV stations typically broadcast from early morning until midnight. Radio signals beamed from Europe are one of the region's alternative, affordable sources of news. According to the *Los Angeles Times*, "Because of tight censorship, newspapers and television stations in the Arab world frequently reflect the biases or outright propaganda of their governments. But radio broadcasts from outside the region travel easily across borders and long distances, and many Arabs regard those stations as the most reliable sources of unbiased news." The BBC (based in London) and Radio Monte Carlo Middle East (based in Paris) are the main Western European across-the-border program sources.

In the Middle East, as in other developing regions, government-owned media are often perceived as instruments of each country's social and political structure. When demonstrators calling for the ouster of President Hosni Mubarak filled Tahrir Square in Cairo, Egypt, in late January 2011, the government quickly shut down access to the Internet. Officials blamed social media, such as Twitter and Facebook, for mobilizing the demonstrators. This marked the first time that a government had deliberately denied Internet communications access to an entire country.

Within 24 hours of the Internet shutdown, a new voice-based social media platform, Saynow, joined with Google and Twitter to create an alternative way to communicate. Saynow distributed three phone numbers Egyptians could call to record messages that were then distributed using cell phone access, a modern telephone tree.

IMPACT

Money

Film Studios Respond to European Antitrust Allegations

By Daniel Miller

While five of the six major film studios targeted by European regulators in an antitrust case considered their responses Thursday to what could eventually become a drawn-out legal fight, Walt Disney Co. vowed to fight the action.

The case, filed by regulators of the European Union, alleges that the studios and British pay-TV provider Sky UK have blocked consumers in much of Europe from watching U.S. films, television programs and other content.

The studios—Disney, NBCUniversal, Paramount Pictures, Sony Pictures Entertainment, 20th Century Fox and Warner Bros.—are alleged to have entered into improper licensing agreements with Sky UK. Those contracts prohibit viewers outside Britain and Ireland from accessing Sky UK's programming via satellite or the Internet.

The case aims to remove barriers to the consumption of digital content across Europe. A Sky TV subscriber from London cannot watch a Warner Bros. film on his laptop while vacationing in Paris because the satellite TV service prohibits access using a practice called geo-blocking.

Burbank-based Disney touted its role as a "leader in embracing new and innovative digital technologies that bring its unique entertainment to

Bloomberg/Getty Images

Warner Brothers is one of five American film companies that have been charged with blocking consumer access to U.S. films and TV programs in Europe. The companies deny any wrongdoing.

families and fans worldwide," and said it would oppose the action brought by the European Commission, the region's executive arm.

"Our approach is one that supports local creative industries, local digital and broadcast partners and most importantly consumers in every country across the EU," a Disney spokesperson said in a statement. "The impact of the commission's analysis is destructive of consumer value and we will oppose the proposed action vigorously."

Warner Bros., Hollywood's biggest movie studio, offered a muted

response. "We are cooperating fully with the European Commission's investigation," a Warner Bros. spokesperson said. "It is premature to comment further at this time."

NBCUniversal responded in kind. "NBCUniversal confirms that it has received the notice and will respond and cooperate with the European Commission," a company spokesman said.

Fox, Sony and Paramount declined to comment.

Each studio faces fines of as much as 10 percent of annual revenue.

Daniel Miller, "Film Studios Respond to European Antitrust Allegations," July 23, 2015, latimes.com.

Today, under the current government of President Abdel Fattah el-Sisi, journalists are constantly under threat, and Egypt has been named by the worldwide organization Reporters Without Borders as the most dangerous country for working journalists.

In July 2013, i24news went on the air in Israel, the first international broadcast channel dedicated to an Israeli point of view. It is privately funded and its founders say they hope to provide a multidimensional view of the country. "What I want to do is to connect Israel to the world and connect the world to the Israeli reality," i24news' chief executive Frank Melloni told the Associated Press.

The Arabic-language channel Al Jazeera, founded in 1996 as an independent satellite TV channel based in Doha, Qatar, is the Middle East's most-watched TV network. Al Jazeera, available since 2006 in an English-language version at english.aljazeera.net, has made its reputation through comparatively independent news reporting and coverage of events in the region. Al Jazeera was widely credited with extensive video coverage of the January 2011 Cairo protests, although the network experienced continued disruptions in transmission of its signal during its live coverage of the demonstrations.

Al Jazeera blamed the interruptions on "powers that do not want our important images pushing for democracy and reform to be seen by the public," but did not specify who the "powers" were. In an unprecedented show of solidarity with Al Jazeera, ten other channels in the region interrupted their own programming to simulcast Al Jazeera coverage of the demonstrations live to their viewers. The government efforts failed to stop the demonstrations and eventually President Mubarak resigned.

The rapid spread of technological developments, such as the growing availability of the Internet and the ongoing influence of new media outlets such as the satellite network Al Jazeera, represent ongoing challenges to traditional government authority over mass media in the Middle East.

African Media Find a New Voice

Most of the new nations of Africa were born after 1960. African history is a record of colonialism, primarily by the British, French, Dutch and Portuguese, and the early print media were created to serve the colonists, not the native population.

SAUL LOEB/Getty Images

Radio is a very important mass medium in Africa because less than 5 percent of Africa's population has access to the Internet. On July 26, 2015, Olive Burrows, producer at Kenya's Capital FM radio, interviews President Obama during his landmark visit to the East African nation.

Print Media

The first English-language newspaper in sub-Saharan Africa, the *Capetown Gazette and African Advertiser*, appeared in South Africa in 1800. A year later, the first black newspaper, the *Royal Gazette and Sierra Leone Advertiser*, appeared in Sierra Leone.

French settlement in Africa is reflected in the pages of more than 60 newspapers, including *Fraternité-Matin*, French Africa's major daily. A Portuguese settler founded *Noticias*, published in Mozambique. In Kenya, three tabloid newspapers enjoy wide circulations with relative independence: the English-language *Daily Nation, The Standard* and the Swahili daily *Taifa Leo*.

According to media scholar L. John Martin, Africans have never had an information press. Theirs has always been an opinion press. Advocacy journalism comes naturally to them. To the extent that they feel a need for hard news, that need is satisfied by the minimal coverage of the mass media, especially radio.

African culture is very diverse, with an estimated 800 to 2,000 language dialects, making it impossible to create a mass circulation newspaper that can appeal to a wide readership. One publication with a wide circulation in the continent is a magazine called *Drum*, published in South Africa but also distributed throughout Africa.

From 1985 to 1990, the South African government demonstrated its distaste for dissident speech when it instituted strict limits on domestic and international news coverage in the region. Because of violent demonstrations supporting the opposition African National Congress,

President P. W. Botha declared a state of emergency in the country in 1985. In 1988, the government suspended the *New Nation* and four other alternative publications. The suspensions and regulations that prevented journalists from covering unrest show the power of government to limit reporting on dissent.

Today, most newspapers in South Africa, for example, are published either in English or in Afrikaans, a language that evolved from South Africa's 17th-century Dutch settlers. South Africa's first Afrikaans newspaper, *Di Patriot*, began in 1875. South Africa's highest circulation newspaper is *The Star*.

Avusa Limited publishes the *Sowetan*, a handsome newspaper based in Johannesburg, with color graphics, an appealing design and a healthy circulation. Many of the *Sowetan*'s original editors spent time in jail for speaking out against apartheid. Avusa also owns South Africa's biggest-selling weekly newspaper, the *Sunday Times*, and a daily print and Internet newspaper, *The Times*.

Broadcast Media

Radio is a very important medium in Africa. One reason for radio's dominance over print is that literacy rates are lower in Africa than in many other regions of the world. Radio is also very accessible and the cheapest way for people to follow the news.

Some governments charge license fees for radio sets, which are supposed to be registered, but many sets go unregistered. Most stations accept advertising, but the majority of funding for radio comes from government subsidies. Government censorship is very active, and journalists look for innovative ways to circumvent government interference. (See **Impact/Society**, "From Headlines to Hip-Hop: The Ugandan TV Show Rapping the News," p. 344.)

A relatively small percentage of the African public owns a TV set, and less than 5 percent of Africa's population has access to the Internet. "Attempts to bring affordable high-speed Internet service to the masses have made little headway on the [African] continent," according to journalist Ron Nixon. "A lack of infrastructure is the biggest problem. In many countries, communications networks were destroyed during years of civil conflict, and continuing political instability deters governments or companies from investing in new systems."

Media in the region are concentrated in urban areas, although the growing availability of cellular signals throughout Africa has the potential to expand communications rapidly, once the political unrest subsides.

Media Explode in Asia and the Pacific

The development of media in this region centers primarily in four countries: Japan, with its prosperous mix of public and private ownership; Australia, where media barons contributed their entrepreneurial fervor; India, which has seen phenomenal media growth; and the People's Republic of China, with its sustained government-controlled media monopoly.

Japan

Japan boasts more newspaper readers than any other nation in the world. Japan's four major newspapers—*Asahi Shimbun, Yomiuri Shimbun, Mainichi Shimbun* and *The Nikkei*—are based in Tokyo. These four papers, each of them more than 100 years old, account for almost half the nation's newspaper circulation.

In 2015, the Japanese media company Nikkei Inc. surprised the global publishing community when it purchased the *Financial Times*, Britain's leading business newspaper, in a $1.3 billion acquisition deal. In this unprecedented move, company president Naotoshi Okada signaled his intention to expand Nikkei's reach beyond Asia. Nikkei Inc. also owns broadcast and Internet properties.

In a surprising move, on July 24, 2015, Japanese media company Nikkei Inc. announced it had purchased the British business newspaper *Financial Times* as part of a $1.3 billion deal, an example of the expanding global ambition of this Asian media corporation.

IMPACT

Society

From Headlines to Hip-Hop: The Ugandan TV Show Rapping the News

By Amy Fallon, Agence France-Presse

Ugandan broadcasters calling themselves "rap-orters" are changing the way news is delivered, after a team of hip-hop artists teamed up to deliver a weekly TV bulletin.

NewzBeat is screened in both English and the local language Luganda on NTV every Saturday before the station's traditional news bulletins, and first aired [in 2014].

Hearing hip-hop news may sound strange, but in Uganda, where the press faces government censorship and the country's growing youth population often takes little interest in current affairs, a programme where self-styled rap-orters broadcast with "rhyme and reason" has become hugely popular.

The show is presented by Sharon Bwogi, Uganda's "queen of hip hop" known as Lady Slyke; Daniel Kisekka, dubbed the "Survivor"; and teenage rapper Zoe Kabuye, or MC Loy.

It aims to: "promote diversity and visibility for marginalised groups" and "push the boundaries of press limitations" in Uganda, according to Lady Slyke.

Bwogi, who started rapping when she was 13, added that today people from all walks of life follow the programme, including businessmen and government ministers.

"People keep asking for more and asking me questions about certain topics," said Bwogi, 28,

NewzBeat's host Sharon Bwogi a.k.a. Lady Slyke (*left*), producer Daniel Kisekka a.k.a. Survivor (*center*) and 14-year-old rapper Zoe Kabuye in Kampala.

ISAAC KASAMANI/Getty Images

who also raps at venues across Uganda professionally.

NewzBeat, which runs for five minutes an episode, usually features four local, regional and international stories.

Nothing is off limits. The programme has covered stories on Uganda's anti-pornography laws, the political situation in Ukraine and Ebola updates from west Africa.

Corruption is another favourite topic. "All around the world this problem remains/The abuse so far is keeping people in chains," rapped Kisekka in a recent bulletin on graft.

Bwogi says the programme talks about corruption because it's a major problem facing Uganda which journalists are becoming increasingly unable to cover. Uganda's Human Rights Network for Journalists and other activist groups have repeatedly warned that the space for reporters to operate

freely in the east African country is shrinking.

Kabuye, 14, has rapped about a wide range of issues—from the Egyptian single mother who spent 43 years living as a man to Uganda's ID card programme—and says many of her friends are disinterested in the news.

"They *used* to say it's boring," said the student, who has been rapping since 2009 and now juggles her presenting commitments with her homework.

Kisekka, 40, said that in the beginning many viewers dismissed the show as "just entertainment," but they have come to "appreciate the art form and start listening to the news."

"Media belongs to the power of the day," Bwogi rapped in one episode. "The Chinese have CCTV/the British have BBC/and we too are making our voices heard on NTV."

Excerpted from Amy Fallon, "From Headlines to Hip-Hop: The Ugandan TV Show Rapping the News, June 10, 2015, theguardian.com.

Broadcast media in Japan originated as a public corporation called the Japanese Broadcasting Corporation (NHK). During World War II, NHK became a propaganda arm of the government, but after the Japanese surrender, the United States helped establish the direction for Japanese broadcasting.

Japan created a licensing board similar to the Federal Communications Commission, but an operating board similar to that of Great Britain's BBC. Japan also decided to allow private broadcast ownership. As a result, Japan today has a mixed system of privately owned and publicly held broadcast media. NHK continues to prosper and, according to broadcast scholar Sydney W. Head, "NHK enjoys more autonomy than any other major public broadcasting corporation. In a rather literal sense, the general public 'owns' it by virtue of paying receiver fees.

"The government cannot veto any program or demand that any program be aired. It leaves the NHK free to set the level of license fees and to do its own fee collecting (which may be why it rates as the richest of the world's fee-supported broadcasting organizations)."

Private ownership is an important element in the Japanese media, and newspaper publishers own many broadcasting operations. NHK owns many more radio properties than private broadcasters do; NHK shares television ownership about equally with private investors. Japan has very few cable systems, which has hindered access to global communications networks in the past, but its cellular and Internet networks are growing rapidly.

Japan is ranked eighth in the world in the number of wireless hot spots available to the public (see **Illustration 16.1** on p. 350). Tokyo also is the home of Sony Corp., which owns Sony Music and Sony Pictures and is one of the world's largest manufacturers of electronic products, including television sets and PlayStation. Sony has 167,000 employees worldwide.

Australia

In Australia, acquisitions by media moguls such as Rupert Murdoch skyrocketed in the 1980s. The Murdoch empire controls 60 percent of Australia's newspaper circulation, which includes the *Daily Telegraph* in Sydney and *The Herald-Sun* in Melbourne. Murdoch, although somewhat burdened with debt because of his media investments in the 1980s, emerged in the 1990s as Australia's uncontested print media baron.

ANNA ZIEMINSKI/Getty Images

India has a rich media history, with an especially prosperous film industry, but the country has lagged behind in digital development. In 2015, Prime Minister Narendra Modi announced an ambitious Digital India campaign, a government initiative to expand the Internet's reach beyond the nation's urban areas.

Australian Broadcasting Corporation (***ABC***), modeled after the BBC, dominates broadcasting in Australia. Three nationwide commercial networks operate in the country. All three suffered financial difficulty in the 1990s, a legacy "of the heydays of the 1980s, when aspiring buyers, backed by eager bank lenders, paid heady prices for broadcast and print assets," reported *The Wall Street Journal*. But they have recovered and today are very prosperous.

India

Entrepreneurship is an important element in the print media of India, which gained independence from Britain in 1947. Forty years after independence, in 1987, Indian print media had multiplied 1,000 times—from 200 publications in 1947 to nearly 25,000.

Broadcasting in India follows its British colonial beginnings, with radio operating under the name All India Radio (AIR) and TV as Doordarshan ("distance view"). Doordarshan uses satellite service to reach remote locations, bringing network TV to four out of five people in the country. As in most developing countries, the network regularly broadcasts programs aimed at improving public life, covering subjects such as family planning, health and hygiene.

One of the most prosperous industries in India today is filmmaking. The film industry, which produces 1,100 films a year (more than twice as many as Hollywood), is centered around Film City near Mumbai, where 16 film

ABC Australian Broadcasting Corporation.

studios employ thousands of people working at dozens of sprawling sets. The industry popularly is known as Bollywood, a merger of Bombay, the former name of Mumbai, and Hollywood.

In July 2015, Indian Prime Minister Narendra Modi announced the Digital India campaign, designed to expand Internet access beyond the country's urban areas. India has seriously lagged behind other Asian countries in digital development, with only 100 million broadband subscribers in a country of 1.2 billion people.

People's Republic of China

Social responsibility is a very important element of media development in the People's Republic of China, where a media monopoly gives government the power to influence change. At the center of Chinese media are the two Communist Party information sources, the newspaper *People's Daily* and Xinhua, the Chinese news agency. These two sources set the tone for the print media throughout China, where self-censorship maintains the government's direction.

Broadcasting in China, as in India, offers important potential for social change in a vast land of rural villages. China's 3-tier system for radio includes a central national station; 100 regional, provincial and municipal networks; and grassroots stations that send local announcements and bulletins by wire to loudspeakers in outdoor markets and other public gathering places.

The Chinese government has bought some U.S. TV programs and accepted some U.S. commercials, but the government still produces most of the nation's programming. Chinese media today sometimes use information and entertainment shows from the West to show the dangers of Western influence, proving the power and the reach of a government media monopoly. In the new market economy in China, there are at least ten times as many newspapers and magazines today as there were in 1978, but all operate under government sanctions.

With the increased competition for readers, some of the print media are beginning to look like Western tabloids, running sensationalist stories. This sensationalism has angered Communist Party officials, who are trying to maintain control over what is published.

With the inevitable influx of Western media during the 2008 Beijing Olympics, the Chinese government originally pledged to open up media outlets completely but still restricted journalists' access to many Western news outlets. In 2012, when *The New York Times* reported that Chinese premier Wen Jiabao's family controlled assets worth

In Latin America, broadcast media operate under a mix of public and private control, and sports is a very important part of TV programming, just as in the U.S. On June 12, 2014, photographers gather around one of the doves released during the opening ceremonies of the 2014 FIFA World Cup in São Paulo, Brazil.

Adrian Dennis/Getty Images

at least $2.7 billion, the country blocked the *Times'* main and Chinese-language Web sites and banned English- and Chinese-language searches for "New York Times" on blogs.

The State Administration of Press, Publication, Radio, Film and Television regulates Chinese media. In 2014, a directive on its Web site warned local journalists not to cooperate with foreign news agencies and issued rules that required journalists to submit stories critical of the government for prior review.

Some Chinese business reporters also have been known to take advantage of the companies they cover, by demanding payment to keep unfavorable stories from being reported. In September 2014, the government arrested eight journalists and charged them with extortion. (See **Impact/Money**, "Journalists in China Describe Extortion," p. 347.)

China has 538 million Internet users, and the government has placed various controls on Web site access, especially for social networking sites, such as Facebook and Twitter, but technology-savvy people in the country often manage to find ways around government censorship.

Government, Corporations and Dynasties Control Latin American and Caribbean Media

In Latin America, where hectic political change is the norm, media have been as volatile as the region. Media are part of the same power structure that controls politics, business and industry. In some Latin American countries, such as Brazil, a family dynasty dominates the

IMPACT

Money

Journalists in China Describe Extortion

By Chris Buckley

HONG KONG—Journalists who worked for a business news Web site under investigation in Shanghai have described a scheme of extorting Chinese companies, which were pressed to pay in return for the production of flattering articles or the burying of damaging ones, according to reports in the state-run news media.

The accusations against the site, 21st Century Net, came after the arrests of eight people [in September 2014] in the case. On China Central Television, the president of the Web site and several arrested reporters described how they had colluded with public relations firms to identify vulnerable Chinese companies.

China's corporate landscape is pitted with scandals involving corruption, nepotism, bribery and false company results. The CCTV accounts from the 21st Century Net journalists added vivid detail to claims that some members of China's news media have become a part of the problem by turning self-censorship and skewed reporting into a source of revenue.

"These kinds of problems have kicked around for a long time," said Paul Gillis, a professor at the Guanghua School of Management of Peking University, who follows Chinese corporate and accounting problems. "As widespread as corruption can be in China, I'm sure somebody's also figured this out."

AFP/Getty Images

Chinese journalist Zhao Jing, who writes for the business magazine *Caixin* under the pen name Michael Anti, describes a media culture in China that supports corruption among reporters.

Zhou Bin, a journalist who was arrested, said many companies were willing to pay in return for favorable coverage.

The site's president and the reporters said the targets were presented with a proposition: Pay up in the form of advertising orders or become the subjects of damning reports that could unsettle investors and deter regulators from approving plans for initial public offerings of stock or restructuring.

"Using negative reports to extort businesses is a hidden rule of the industry," Xinhua, the state-run news agency, paraphrased Wang Zhuoming, one of the arrested reporters, as saying. "This was collective behavior, and companies all did it, from top to bottom."

The legal affairs office for the Web site and newspaper declined to comment on Thursday. Last week, the Web site issued a statement

that it would cooperate with the police investigation.

In the broadcast, the arrested journalists did not appear to be speaking freely as they contritely described the misdeeds. The interviews, in which the journalists wore orange T-shirts, appeared to be more of the paraded confessions that have become a staple of law enforcement in China. But the journalists' descriptions of corrupted coverage nonetheless rang true, said several people who follow business journalism in China.

"In the Chinese financial media, there's usually no firewall between the business side and the editorial side," Zhao Jing, a journalist who writes regularly for *Caixin*, a weekly business magazine based in Beijing, said in a telephone interview. Mr. Zhao, better known by his pen name, Michael Anti, said *Caixin* had safeguards to deter such practices.

Excerpted from Chris Buckley, "Journalists in China Describe Extortion," September 11, 2014, nytimes.com.

Overnight on October 14, 2013, *The New York Times* (which bought the *International Herald Tribune* in 2003) changed the *Tribune*'s name to the *International New York Times* (seen on October 15, 2013, with its new masthead).

media, and in many countries one corporation is allowed to control several different types of media outlets.

For example, Televisa, based in Mexico, owns more than 258 affiliated TV stations, 31 pay TV channels and 158 publications. Organization Editorial Mexicana owns 70 newspapers, 24 radio stations and 43 Internet sites.

Print Media

In Santiago, Chile, the newspaper *El Mercurio* was founded in 1827. Today the El Mercurio company owns 9 newspapers and 32 radio stations. *O Estado de São Paulo* in Brazil, owned by the Mesquita family, has represented editorial independence in the region for more than 100 years and often is mentioned as one of the country's best newspapers. Argentina's *La Prensa* refuses government subsidies and has survived great conflicts with people like dictator Juan Perón, who shut down the newspaper from 1951 to 1955.

Home delivery for newspapers and magazines is uncommon in Latin America; the centers of print media merchandising are street-corner kiosks, where vendors offer a variety of publications. *Manchete*, published in Brazil, is one of the most widely circulated national magazines, filled with photos and celebrity profiles.

Broadcast Media

Broadcasting operates in a mix of government and private control, with government often owning a few key stations and regulating stations that are privately owned, but the pattern varies.

Cuba's broadcast media are controlled totally by the government, for example. In Costa Rica and Ecuador, almost all the broadcast media are privately owned. In Brazil, private owners hold most of the radio stations and television networks, including TV Globo Network, which claims to be the world's fourth-largest television network (after the United States' original three TV networks—ABC, CBS and NBC).

International New York Times
Seeks a Global Audience

One of the largest global media presences is the *International New York Times*, originally called the *International Herald Tribune* (**IHT**), based in Paris and published in English. Called "the world's daily newspaper," the *International Herald Tribune* was founded in 1887 by American entrepreneur J. Gordon Bennett Jr., and today is the world's largest English-language newspaper. Known for its independence, the newspaper was co-owned by *The Washington Post* and *The New York Times* until 2003, when *The New York Times* became the paper's sole owner. In 2013, it changed the paper's name to the *International New York Times*.

IHT *International Herald Tribune*, the world's largest English-language newspaper, renamed the *International New York Times* in 2013.

The *International New York Times* is the first truly global newspaper, published at 35 sites around the world and covering international news every day. With a global outlook and available by subscription in an electronic edition, the *International New York Times* counts most of the world's opinion leaders and decision makers among its subscribers.

The paper has a circulation of 241,000 and an international readership in 180 countries throughout Europe, Asia, the Middle East, Russia, Africa and the Americas. The biggest regular audience for the print edition is American tourists traveling abroad, and the Internet edition receives 7 million visitors a month.

Critics Cite Western Communications Bias

Countries in many developing areas of the world historically have criticized what they believe is a Western bias to the flow of information throughout the world. These countries charge that this practice imposes cultural imperialism, centered in Western ideology because many of the major international news services are based in the West.

The Associated Press, Reuters (Great Britain), Agence France-Presse (France), Deutsche Presse-Agentur (Germany) and Agencia Efe (Spain) supply news to the print and broadcast media. Visnews, based in Great Britain, the U.S.-based Cable News Network and World International Network (WIN) offer international video services. Sky TV in Europe and Star TV in Asia deliver programs by satellite. The Internet, of course, ignores all national borders.

Despite Western dominance of global news organizations, many regions of the world support information services within their own countries and even within their regions. Middle East News Agency (MENA), based in Egypt, serves all the countries of the Middle East, while News Agency of Nigeria (NAN) limits services to Nigeria, for example.

Within the past 50 years, news services outside the Western orbit have been created—Russian Information Agency (RIA); Asian-Pacific News Network in Japan; Caribbean News Agency (CANA); Pan-African News Agency (PANA); Non-Aligned News Agency (NANA), linking the nonaligned nations with the national news agencies, based in Yugoslavia; and Inter Press Service (IPS), based in Rome as an "information bridge" between Europe and Latin America.

Even with the creation of these added sources of information and the Internet, Western news services dominate. Critics of the system of news and information flow suggested a New World Information and Communications

Order (**NWICO**) should be created because the existing system is **ethnocentric**, or promotes the superiority of one ethnic group (in this case, the Western world) over another.

According to Robert G. Picard in *Global Journalism: Survey of International Communication*, "Developing world media and governments have argued that Western ethnocentrism creates an unequal flow of information by providing a large stream of information about events in the developed world but only a very small flow from the developing world."

Today, online access to a variety of news outlets and the availability of mobile media throughout the world is quickly changing the balance. (See **Impact/Convergence: Illustration 16.1**, "Top 10 Countries with Public Wireless Locations (Hot Spots)," p. 350.)

Internet Expands Mass Media's Global Reach

When communication stays within borders, it is easier for governments to control information, but the Internet makes it possible for information and entertainment to travel effortlessly across borders.

Until recently, most developing countries were limited to traditional mass media delivery systems—print and broadcast. These systems were regional by nature because they were confined by geography and economics. Print media could travel only through the mail and by carrier. Radio and television were limited by the reach of their towers and depended on people having enough money to purchase receivers. Information from outside the country was limited to reports filtered through each nation's print and broadcast outlets; similarly, news and information about other countries reached the U.S. only through traditional print and broadcast organizations.

A country with government controls on the mass media can use those controls to try to combat dissent and limit awareness, but digital signals carried on the Internet break down international barriers because the delivery system knows no limits. Information on the Internet is controlled by individuals rather than by institutions, which is precisely why many governments

NWICO New World Information and Communications Order. The concept that mass media should include all areas of the world, not just the West.

Ethnocentric Promoting the superiority of one ethnic group over another.

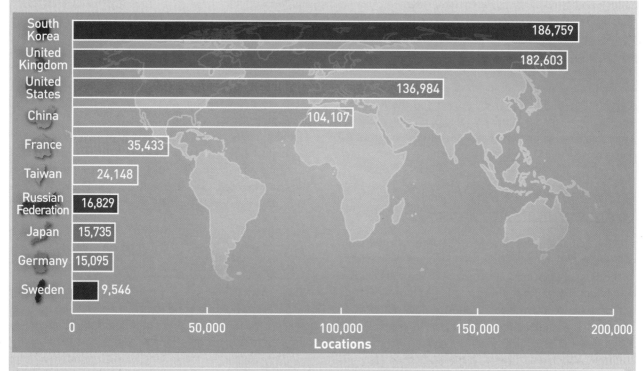

ILLUSTRATION 16.1

Top 10 Countries with Public Wireless Locations (Hot Spots)

South Korea has more public wireless locations (hot spots) than any other country, and the U.K. (ranked second) has more hot spots than the United States. South Korea has 20 times more hot spots than Sweden, which is ranked tenth.

Hotstats as of April 22, 2013, Jiwire.com.

are afraid of the influence that access to the Internet will have if allowed to operate unchecked within their countries.

Governments that are accustomed to controlling information, especially in developing countries, have tried to stop the information flow by pricing Internet access beyond what most people can afford. According to the World Bank, the average consumer pays about $22 a month for Internet access, but in Tanzania, for example, the price is $95 a month, and in South Africa the cost is $60 a month.

Also, many countries simply don't yet have reliable telecommunications technology in place—telephone, broadband, cellular or satellite connections—to handle Internet traffic. None of the countries in South America or Africa is listed among the countries with the highest number of wireless hot spots available to the public, for example.

This often means that in poorer countries, Internet access to the international flow of information is limited to the rich and powerful. As digital technology grows more affordable, however, it will be difficult even for developing countries to stop information from seeping across their borders. The most promising new and simplest technology today is mobile media.

Mobile Media Open Communications Channels

In 2002, for the first time, the number of mobile phones in the world exceeded the number of landline phones, according to the World Bank. Wireless networks offer the easiest way for developing countries to modernize their communications systems because these countries have never had extensive wired networks.

"The mobility, ease of use, flexible deployment, and relatively low and declining rollout costs of wireless technologies enable them to reach rural populations with low levels of income and literacy," reports the World Bank.

"From Kenya to Colombia to South Africa . . . cell phones are becoming the truly universal technology," according to Anand Giridharadas, reporting for *The New York Times*. "The number of mobile subscriptions in the world is expected to pass five billion this year [2010], according to the International Telecommunication Union, an intergovernmental organization. That would mean more human beings today have access to a cell phone than the United Nations says have access to a clean toilet."

According to Giridharadas, "The phone has also moved to the center of community life in many places. In Africa, churches record sermons with cell phones and then transmit them to villages to be replayed. In Iran and Moldova, phones helped to organize popular uprisings against authoritarian governments."

The World Bank points out the interrelationship between reliable communications systems and economic development. Farmers can price and sell goods to markets they could never reach otherwise; city dwellers can transfer money to rural relatives through an online banking network; and smart phones give users access to the Internet, music downloads, movies, radio, games and information services.

Although access to information from outside the country is a major benefit of wireless networks, many governments consider outsiders—and the information they offer—a threat. Digital technology is much more difficult for governments to restrict. Governments often try to restrict the messages sent past the country's borders, usually with little success. Today, information can travel from anywhere in the world to almost anywhere in the world and back again via the Internet.

The Internet is as near as a smart phone, which is becoming an indispensable tool in the developing world for individuals, businesses and governments. For developing countries especially, today's digital technology offers

Bloomberg/Getty Images

Today mobile media are the world's fastest-growing communications technology. An attendee walks through a virtual video display of the Tower Bridge in London at the Mobile World Congress in Barcelona, Spain, on March 3, 2015.

a faster path to economic growth, increased literacy and freedom of expression.

Reporters Risk Lives to Report World Events

Journalists in many developing countries are often targets for political and terrorist threats, making a reporter's life very hazardous.

According to *Global Journalism: Survey of International Communication*, "Threats to journalists come not only from governments but from terrorist groups, drug lords and quasi-government hit squads as well. Numerous news organizations have been bombed, ransacked and destroyed by opponents." (See **Impact/Society**, "Reporters Without Borders Monitors Journalists Killed and Kidnapped in 2014," p. 352.)

Journalists face danger because the mass media often represent a challenge to the political power of a country's leadership or they uncover criminal activity that is being ignored by the government. In all parts of the world, the dangers that journalists face to report unraveling news events form a central part of each nation's media history.

Global Media Chase International Consumers

International communication on the Internet is just the beginning of an easy, affordable and accessible transfer of information and entertainment back and forth between other countries and the United States. Media companies in

IMPACT / *Society*

Reporters Without Borders Monitors Journalists Killed and Kidnapped in 2014

The international organization Reporters Without Borders, based in France, issues a yearly report that documents the number of journalists killed and kidnapped each year while on assignment.

Reporters Without Borders statistics are divided into journalists, media workers (such as translators and drivers) and citizen journalists (freelancers).

Reporters Without Borders also maintains the Press Freedom Index on its Web site, an interactive country-by-country map of 180 countries that tracks reporters who have been killed or are being held hostage. Kidnappings increased 37 percent in 2014, the organization reported. It also was a particularly gruesome year that included the beheading of three journalists by the militant group ISIS, who had demanded ransom in exchange for their release but their demands were not met.

The organization says the report "highlights an evolution in the nature of violence against journalists and the way certain kinds, including carefully-staged threats and beheadings, are being used for very clear purposes.

"The murders are becoming more and more barbaric and the number of abductions is growing rapidly, with those carrying them out seeking to prevent independent news coverage and deter scrutiny by the outside world."

71	**Journalists Killed**
11	**Media Workers Killed**
20	**Citizen Journalists Killed**
119	**Journalists Kidnapped**
221	**Total Number of Journalists and Media Workers Killed and Kidnapped in 2014**

Source: Reporters Without Borders, en.rsf.org.

Reporters At Risk

Ruben Espinosa

Yuri Cortez/AFP/Getty Images

Jason Rezaian

AP Images/Vahid Salemi

Kenji Goto

Ahmed Muhammed Ali/Anadolu Agency/Getty Images

Kathy Gannon & Anja Niedringhaus

AP Images

Steven Sotloff

Handout/Getty Images

James Foley

Jonathan Wiggs/Boston Globe/Getty Images

Top row (left to right): Photojournalist Ruben Espinosa, who reported on the drug trade for the magazine *Proseco*, was found dead in Mexico City on July 31, 2015. *Washington Post* reporter Jason Rezaian, an Iranian-American, was arrested in 2014 by Iran and prosecuted for spying. Japanese journalist Kenji Goto was beheaded by the militant Syrian organization ISIS on February 1, 2015. *Bottom row (left to right)*: Veteran Associated Press Correspondent Kathy Gannon (on the left in first photo) was wounded, and Pulitzer Prize–winning AP photographer Anja Niedringhaus (on the right in first photo) was killed on April 4, 2014, in Afghanistan, shot by a local police commander. U.S. journalist Steven Sotloff was kidnapped in Syria in 2013 and beheaded by ISIS on September 2, 2014, two weeks after reporter James Foley, missing in Syria since 2012, met the same fate on August 19, 2014.

the U.S. also are looking at the large populations in other countries that are just beginning to acquire the tools of communication, creating millions of potential consumers for all types of products and services. (See **Impact/Money: Illustration 16.2**, "Top 10 Global Advertisers," below.)

Today's media markets are increasingly global. U.S. media companies are searching for new markets overseas at the same time that overseas media companies are purchasing pieces of media industries in the United States and other countries. Here are some recent examples:

▶ In Saudi Arabia, young women, who aren't allowed to drive, can schedule rides online from car services like Uber.

▶ Estonians have embraced a national identity card embedded with a microchip that they can use to do their banking, get access to medical care, vote and file their taxes.

▶ Walt Disney Co. has joined China's largest Internet company, Tencent Holdings Ltd., to develop China's animation industry. "Our philosophy is to operate as the Chinese Walt Disney Company," according to Stanley Cheung, managing director of Disney China.

▶ IBM announced plans to supply computing technology and services to upgrade the cell phone network across 16 nations in sub-Saharan Africa.

The global media marketplace includes news and information services, print, broadcast programming, movies and music, as well as products and services plus the advertising to sell them.

Fueling the move to global marketing is the decision by the European countries to eliminate all trade barriers. A further sign of the times is the shrinking proportion of worldwide advertising expenditures

IMPACT
Money

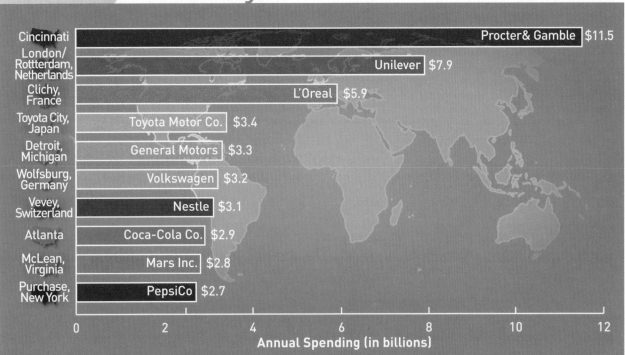

Location	Company	Annual Spending (in billions)
Cincinnati	Procter & Gamble	$11.5
London/Rottterdam, Netherlands	Unilever	$7.9
Clichy, France	L'Oreal	$5.9
Toyota City, Japan	Toyota Motor Co.	$3.4
Detroit, Michigan	General Motors	$3.3
Wolfsburg, Germany	Volkswagen	$3.2
Vevey, Switzerland	Nestle	$3.1
Atlanta	Coca-Cola Co.	$2.9
McLean, Virginia	Mars Inc.	$2.8
Purchase, New York	PepsiCo	$2.7

ILLUSTRATION 16.2

Top 10 Global Advertisers—Annual Spending

Half the world's top 10 global advertisers are U.S.-based companies. Three of the top 10 advertisers sell cars (Toyota, General Motors and Volkswagen), and 4 of the top 10 sell food and beverages (Nestlé, Coca-Cola, candy maker Mars Inc. and PepsiCo). The top 2 global marketers (Procter & Gamble and Unilever) sell household cleaning products, and 1 (L'Oréal) sells cosmetics. Listed is the annual spending by the top 10 global advertisers.

"100 Largest Global Marketers," *Advertising Age*, December 6, 2014, p. 26.

generated by the U.S., which has long been the world's advertising colossus. In recent years, advertising spending by companies *outside* the United States has begun to overtake the amount spent by companies *in* the United States.

Ideas Transcend Borders

Along with the transfer of information in the new global communications future, however, comes the transfer of ideas. Says the *Los Angeles Times*:

> *Historically, the empowered elite have always sought to suppress the wider distribution of ideas, wealth, rights and, most of all, knowledge. This is as true today as it was . . . when the German printer Gutenberg invented movable type to print the Bible. Can't tell it's an excerpt. For two centuries afterward, government tightly controlled what people could read through the widespread use of "prior restraint." . . .*
>
> *Just as censorship of the printed word could not continue with the emergence of democracy in 17th century Britain and 18th century America, so today suppression of the electronic media is thwarted by technology and rapidly growing economies around the world.*

Governments that are accustomed to controlling the information that crosses their borders face unprecedented access within their countries to global information sources. According to author Ithiel de Sola Pool, "International communications is often considered a mixed blessing by rulers. Usually they want technical progress. They want computers. They want satellites. They want efficient telephones. They want television. But at the same time they do not want the ideas that come with them."

Many governments that control their country's mass media, especially broadcast media and the Internet, will continue to try to control access as long as they can regulate newsprint and satellites, but this is becoming increasingly difficult. As more national media boundaries disappear throughout the world, news, information and entertainment will be able to move instantly from each home country as part of an interactive global dialogue. Today the mass media industries operate in a media marketplace without boundaries, using a global delivery system that is truly "transnational."

CSL, CartoonStock Ltd

May

"Okay, you can have freedom of speech, but watch your language!"

REVIEW, ANALYZE, INVESTIGATE

CHAPTER 16

World Media Systems Vary

- Media industries in different countries are as varied as the countries they serve.

Five Political Theories Describe How World Media Operate

- Media systems can be divided into systems that allow dissent and those that do not.

- The original four theories on the press (the Soviet theory, the authoritarian theory, the libertarian theory and the social responsibility theory) plus the developmental theory still leave many press systems beyond specific categorization.

- The global media theory that best describes the American media is the libertarian theory, although American media also have struggled with authoritarian and social responsibility debates.

- The Internet is blurring international media borders because it is very difficult to control the flow of digital information across geographical and ideological boundaries, although some countries try.

Western Europe and Canada Are Similar to the U.S.

- Until the 1850s, presses in Europe were privately owned.

- The print media form the basis for press development in North America, Australia, Western Europe and Eastern Europe.

- Today Western European and Canadian media prosper under guarantees of freedom of expression similar to the First Amendment of the U.S. Constitution, although each nation has modified the idea to reflect differing values.

- In 1982, Canada adopted the Canadian Charter of Rights and Freedoms, becoming the most recent Western country to issue an official decree supporting the philosophy of press freedom.

- Scandinavian journalists enjoy the widest press freedoms of all of Western Europe, including almost unlimited access to public documents.

- Of the Western nations, Canada is the most recent country to adopt an official decree supporting press freedom.

- Western European newspapers tend to be much more partisan than U.S. or Canadian newspapers.

- To finance the government-run broadcast media, countries such as the United Kingdom tax the sale of radios and TVs or charge users an annual license fee, which funds the broadcasts.

- ITV, a "public service broadcaster," is the largest commercial network in the United Kingdom, with four separate channels.

- Western Europeans watch less television than do people in the United States.

- Some TV stations in Europe don't go on the air until late afternoon.

- Some Western European programming comes from the United States.

- U.S. programs are attractive to European broadcasters because buying U.S. programs is cheaper than producing their own.

- Some members of the European community have proposed quotas on the importation of U.S. programs.

Eastern Europe Is in Transition

- Many Eastern European nations developed their press policies following the Soviet model.

- Eastern Europe is defining a new balance between the desire for free expression and the remnants of government control.

- In many Eastern European countries, the media play a central role in upsetting the established power structure.

- Television in the Eastern bloc countries developed under Communist direction because the Communist governments were in power before TV use was widespread; radio broadcasting also was tightly controlled.

- *Pravda*, the Soviet Union's oldest newspaper, was founded in 1912. In 1996, facing bankruptcy, *Pravda* ceased publication.

- Today Russian officials, such as Prime Minister Vladimir Putin, maintain a tight rein on the press.

Middle Eastern and North African Media Work Under Government Controls

- Press history in the Middle East and North Africa begins with the newspaper *Al-Iraq*, first published in 1817, although the first daily newspaper didn't begin publishing until 1873.

- In the Middle East and North Africa, more newspapers and magazines are published in regions with high literacy rates than in regions with low literacy rates; the one exception is Cairo, Egypt, which is the Arab world's publishing center.

- Radio often is the dominant medium in developing countries; television is in widespread use in prosperous nations and in urban areas of developing countries. Yet many countries still have only one TV service, usually run by the government.

- Radio Monte Carlo and the BBC offer alternative radio programming across Middle Eastern borders.

- The Middle Eastern press is tightly controlled by government restrictions, through ownership and licensing.

- Al Jazeera is the Middle East's most-watched TV network and has made its controversial reputation by promising independent news reporting and coverage.

- In the Middle East, as in other developing regions, the mass media are perceived as instruments of each country's social and political agendas.

- In Syria, where rebels were fighting the government of President Bashar al-Assad, opposition journalists began publishing weeklies in 2012, hoping to counteract government-controlled media.

- Egypt is the most dangerous country for journalists to work, according to the worldwide organization Reporters Without Borders.

African Media Find a New Voice

- The first English-language newspaper in sub-Saharan Africa appeared in Capetown, South Africa, in 1800; a year later, the first black newspaper appeared in Sierra Leone.

- African culture is very diverse, making it impossible to create a mass circulation newspaper that can appeal to a wide readership.

- In Africa, radio is a much more important medium than print because it is an inexpensive way for people to follow the news.

- Suspension of five publications in South Africa throughout the state of emergency from 1985 to 1990 demonstrates the power of government to limit reporting on dissent.

- People in Africa have limited access to the Internet, which is mostly available in urban areas.

- In Uganda, rap-orters host a news program called *NewzBeat* where they deliver a hip-hop newscast as a way around government censorship.

Media Explode in Asia and the Pacific

- The four major Japanese national dailies account for almost half the nation's newspaper circulation.

- Japan today has a mixed system of privately owned and publicly held broadcast media.

- In 2015, Nikkei Inc. bought the British business newspaper *Financial Times* in a move to expand the company's global reach beyond Asia.

- Entrepreneurs, including Rupert Murdoch, control large segments of Australia's media.

- The Australian Broadcasting Corporation (ABC) dominates broadcasting in Australia.

- Since India's independence in 1947, the number of publications has increased 1,000 times.

- Broadcasting in India follows its British colonial beginnings.

- The most successful media business in India is filmmaking, an industry nicknamed Bollywood. The industry is based in Film City, a settlement near Mumbai.

- In July 2015, Indian Prime Minister Narendra Modi announced the Digital India campaign, designed to expand Internet access beyond the country's urban areas.

- Chinese media operate under a government monopoly, supported by a belief in the media's social responsibility.

- China has 538 million Internet users.

- In 2014, the Chinese government arrested eight journalists and charged them with extorting business owners for favorable media coverage.

Government, Corporations and Dynasties Control Latin American and Caribbean Media

- Media in Latin America are part of the power structure, and family dynasties as well as large corporations control many media industries.

- Dictator Juan Perón shut down Argentina's independent newspaper *La Prensa* from 1951 to 1955.

- In Santiago, Chile, the Edwards family has owned *El Mercurio* since 1880.

International New York Times Seeks a Global Audience

- The *International Herald Tribune* was founded in 1887 by American entrepreneur J. Gordon Bennett Jr., and today is the world's largest English-language newspaper.

- The *IHT* was co-owned by the *Washington Post* and *The New York Times* until 2003, when *The New York Times* became the paper's sole owner.

- The paper was renamed the *International New York Times* in 2013.

- The *International New York Times* is the first truly global newspaper, published at 35 sites around the world and covering world news every day.

Critics Cite Western Communications Bias

- Some developing nations criticize the news media for their Western slant.

- Despite Western dominance of global news organizations, many regions of the world have their own news services.

- Critics of the system of news and information flow have called for a New World Information and Communications Order (NWICO).

Internet Expands Mass Media's Global Reach

- Governments that are used to controlling information, especially in developing countries, have tried to stop the information flow by making Internet access too expensive for the average consumer.

- South Korea has more public wireless locations (hot spots) than any other country, and the U.K. (ranked second) has more hot spots than the U.S.

- Many countries simply don't have reliable telecommunications technology in place—telephone, broadband, cellular or satellite connections—to handle Internet traffic.

- More than any other factor, the economic potential of the Internet guarantees its future as a global communications medium.

Mobile Media Open Communications Channels

- In 2002, for the first time, the number of mobile phones in the world exceeded the number of landline phones.

- Wireless networks offer the easiest way for developing countries to modernize their communications systems because these countries have never had extensive wired networks.

- Access to information through wireless networks can be a major benefit, but many countries consider outsiders a threat.

Reporters Risk Lives to Report World Events

- Journalists in many developing countries face danger because the media represent a challenge to political power.

- In 2014, 221 journalists and media workers were killed or kidnapped on the job.

- Kidnappings increased 37 percent in 2014.

- The year 2014 was particularly gruesome because three journalists held for ransom by the militant organization ISIS were beheaded when the ransom demands were not met.

Global Media Chase International Consumers

- U.S. media companies are looking for markets overseas at the same time that overseas media companies are purchasing pieces of media industries in the United States and other countries.

- Procter & Gamble spends more money on global advertising than any other company.

- Fueling the move to global marketing is the decision by the European countries to eliminate all trade barriers.

- The global media marketplace includes news and information services, print, broadcast programming, movies and music, as well as advertising.

Ideas Transcend Borders

- Along with the transfer of information in the new global communications future comes the transfer of ideas.

- Governments that are accustomed to controlling the information that crosses their borders face unprecedented access within their borders to global information sources.

- Today the media industries operate in a marketplace that is "transnational."

Key Terms

These terms are defined in the margins throughout this chapter and appear in alphabetical order with definitions in the Glossary, which begins on page 361.

ABC *345*	Ethnocentric *349*	IHT *348*
BBC *338*	Hot Spot *334*	NWICO *349*

Critical Questions

1. In what ways might a nation's media system be shaped by its government's political philosophy? Cite three specific examples.

2. Compare the evolution of mass media in the various regions of the world. Give three specific examples.

3. Discuss the role of radio in developed and less-developed countries. Cite three specific examples.

4. Explain how the *International New York Times* became one of the largest global media presences. What do you think the *International New York Times* has to do to stay competitive in the growing global media market?

5. List and explain three examples of the global consequences of international access to the Internet, including the impact of the Internet on government control of information and ways that developing countries attempt to deal with the loss of control.

Working the Web

This list includes sites mentioned in the chapter and others to give you greater insight into global media.

BBC News
bbc.com

With an enormous depth and breadth of content, the British Broadcasting Company's site includes news, sports, entertainment and weather as well as an international version, which offers news and audio in 27 languages. The site has links to streaming content from BBC TV and BBC radio channels reporting from Britain and worldwide.

Foreign Policy Magazine
foreignpolicy.com

Founded more than 40 years ago, *Foreign Policy* magazine is a bimonthly print and digital publication about global politics and economics. *Foreign Policy's* mission is to explain "how the process of globalization is reshaping nations, institutions, cultures, and, more fundamentally, our daily lives." Articles from current issues are available along with topical stories and columns from international and regional news sources.

Global Media Journal (GMJ)
globalmediajournal.com

Launched in 2002, GMJ's main intent is to address the global "diverse interests of media and journalism scholars, researchers, teachers, students, and institutions engaged in international activities, particularly communication." The GMJ site has links to a wide variety of information and specialized content, including media structures and practices, global media and culture, the role of media in democratic governance, commercialization of news, new media technologies, media regulations and regional and alternative media.

Global Online Video Association
gova.cc

Founded in 2014 by a group of media companies, the Global Online Video Association is a nonprofit trade association for the online video industry. The association lobbies and advocates throughout the U.S. regarding the industry, including advertising, licensing, production, distribution and best business practices. The site offers current issues and events from the online video industry and updates about the annual Streamy Awards, which honors the best online videos and the creators behind them.

International Association for Media and Communication Research (IAMCR)
iamcr.org

IAMCR is a professional organization for global media and communication academics from more than 100 countries throughout the world. The United Nations Educational, Scientific and Cultural Organization (UNESCO) helped facilitate the establishment of IAMCR in 1957. IAMCR promotes freedom of academic thought in all areas of communication research worldwide. Information is available on the site about published works by IAMCR and IAMCR members, grants and awards and the annual IAMCR conference.

International Center for Journalists (ICFJ)
icfj.org

Believing that "better journalism leads to better lives," the International Center for Journalists promotes quality journalism worldwide. As a direct result of constantly improving, cutting-edge communication technology, ICFJ has established a network of citizen and professional journalists as well as alliances with media companies that allow news reporting from all across the globe. ICFJ offers programs, seminars and fellowships for journalists in the U.S. and abroad, as well as online resources and instructor-led and distance courses and training in Arabic, Chinese, English, Persian, Portuguese, Russian and Spanish.

International New York Times
international.nytimes.com

Formerly the *International Herald Tribune*, the *International New York Times* is the global English-language daily of its parent U.S. publisher, *The New York Times*. Online content includes an ambitious array of print and video news stories with a global focus, the only publication of its kind in the world.

International News Media Association (INMA)
inma.org

The International News Media Association offers members best practices on all aspects of news reporting in a global media environment. Members can access professional contacts using blogs, case studies, conferences, publications, sales and marketing campaigns and networking tools.

International Women's Media Foundation (IWMF)

iwmf.org

Founded in 1990 and based in Washington, D.C., the IWMF raises awareness about, creates opportunities for and builds networks of female journalists around the world. "The news media worldwide are not truly free and representative without the equal voice of women" is its motto. Online resources include links to online training, tips and guides, statistics and studies; links to Web sites of interest to women in the media; and publications and newsletter articles.

Internews

internews.org

An international media development organization, Internews has administrative offices in California; Washington, D.C.; and London along with global hubs in Bangkok and Nairobi. The site has information on the Media Map Project, a joint research project by Internews and the World Bank Institute on the correlation and the relationship between the media and democratic or non-democratically governed countries.

Reporters Without Borders

rsf.org

An international organization that works for freedom of the press around the world, Reporters Without Borders defends and represents journalists who are threatened, imprisoned or persecuted; works to improve the safety of journalists in war zones; and opposes censorship. The Web site's main feature is the Press Freedom Barometer, a current and archived listing of professional, citizen and online journalists killed worldwide. The site also provides news in five languages about attacks on press freedom and journalists in Africa, the Americas, Asia, Europe and the former USSR, the Middle East and Northern Africa.

Worldpress.org

worldpress.org

Worldpress.org is a compilation of articles from the world's newspapers. The site contains originally written material and articles reprinted from the press outside the U.S., translated from more than 20 different languages. Site resources include daily world headlines, a directory of world newspapers, real-time news feeds, country maps and profiles (from the *CIA World Factbook*), the texts of documents in the news and links to think tanks and nongovernmental organizations.

 **Impact/Action Videos** are concise news features on various topics created exclusively for *Media/Impact*. Find them in *Media/Impact*'s MindTap at cengagebrain.com.

MindTap® Log on to MindTap for *Media/Impact* to access a variety of additional material—including learning objectives, chapter readings with highlighting and note-taking, **Impact/Action Videos**, activities, and comprehension quizzes—that will guide you through this chapter.

GLOSSARY

30-Year Rule Developed by Paul Saffo, the theory that it takes about 30 years for a new technology to be completely adopted within a culture.

3-D Printing A process that uses a large commercial printer and liquid plastic to fabricate individual, custom-designed pieces of equipment based on computer-generated designs.

AAM Alliance for Audited Media (formerly Audit Bureau of Circulations). An independent agency of media market research that verifies and publishes circulation figures for member magazines.

ABC Australian Broadcasting Corporation.

Accreditation The process by which the government certifies members of the press to cover government-related news events.

Advance An amount the publisher pays the author before the book is published.

Advertising Campaign A planned advertising effort, coordinated for a specific time period.

Advertorial Paid advertising supplements in newspapers and magazines that often look similar to the regular news pages.

Affiliates Stations that use network programming but are owned by companies other than the networks.

Agenda-Setting The belief that journalists don't tell you *what* to think but do tell you *what and whom to think about.*

All-Platform Journalists Broadcast journalists who act as their own producer, cameraperson and editor, and sometimes also transmit live video.

Alternative (Dissident) Press Media that present alternative viewpoints that challenge the mainstream press.

Analog In mass communications, a type of technology used in broadcasting, whereby video or audio information is sent as continuous signals through the air on specific airwave frequencies.

Ancillary Rights Marketing opportunities related to a movie, in addition to direct income from the movie itself.

App Mobile application.

ASCAP American Society of Composers, Authors and Publishers.

Audiobooks Abridged or complete versions of classic books and popular new titles available on CDs and as Internet downloads.

BBC British Broadcasting Corporation, the government-funded British broadcast network.

Blacklisting Studio owners' refusal to hire someone who was alleged to have taken part in subversive activities.

Blanket Licensing Agreement An arrangement whereby radio stations become authorized to use recorded music for broadcast by paying a fee.

Blind Booking The practice of renting films to exhibitors without letting them see the films first.

Block Booking The practice of requiring theaters to take a package of movies instead of showing the movies individually.

Blockbuster A book that achieves outstanding financial success.

Blog Short for Web log. A running Internet discussion group where items are posted in reverse chronological order. Blogs usually focus on a specific topic.

BMI Broadcast Music, Inc., a cooperative music licensing organization.

Branded Content, Content Marketing, Branded Entertainment A program or story that mimics regular commercial programming or standard journalism but is custom-produced by an advertiser to promote a specific product and may or may not be labeled as an advertisement.

Broadcast Cross-Ownership The practice of one company owning TV and radio stations in the same broadcast market.

Browser Software that allows people to display and interact with information on Web pages.

Bundle The combination of telecommunications services that the media industries can offer consumers.

CATV Community antenna television or cable television.

CDA Communications Decency Act.

CD-RW (Re-Writable) Drives Computer drives that read data and music encoded in digital form and can be used to record more than once.

Censorship The practice of suppressing material that is considered morally, politically or otherwise objectionable.

Checkbook Journalism   The practice of a news organization paying for an interview or a photograph.

Click-Through Rate   The rate at which people who see an ad on an Internet site click through to learn more.

Cloud Computing   The remote use by one business of another company's computer space, operating "in the cloud."

Company Magazines   Magazines produced by businesses for their employees, customers and stockholders.

Compatible   Media that can function well with one another to exchange and integrate text, pictures, sound and video.

Concentration of Ownership   The current trend of large companies buying smaller companies so that fewer companies own more types of media businesses.

Conglomerates   Companies that own media companies as well as businesses that are unrelated to the media business.

Consensus Journalism   The tendency among many journalists covering the same event to report similar conclusions about the event.

Consumer Magazines   All magazines sold by subscription or at newsstands, supermarkets and bookstores.

Convergence   The melding of the communications, computer and electronics industries. Also used to describe the economic alignment of the various media companies with each other to take advantage of technological advancements.

Cooperative News Gathering   Member news organizations that share the expense of getting the news.

Copyright Alert System (CAS)   A government-mandated warning to alert consumers who try to download copyrighted material.

CPM   Cost per thousand, the cost of an ad per 1,000 people reached. (M is the Roman numeral for 1,000.)

Crisis Communication   A timely public relations response to a critical situation that could damage a company's reputation.

Cross-Ownership   The practice of one company owning radio and TV stations in the same broadcast market.

Cybersmears   Negative information organized and presented on the Internet as continuing attacks against a corporation.

Data Compression   The process of squeezing digital content into a smaller electronic space.

Data Farms   Locations that house data centers for the servers that process data flowing over the Internet.

Data Streaming   A common type of cloud computing that allows the user to play back an audio or video file without first completely downloading it.

DBS   Direct broadcast satellite.

Demographics   Data about consumers' characteristics, such as age, gender, income level, marital status, geographic location and occupation.

Deregulation   Government action that reduces restrictions on the business operations of an industry.

Digital Audio Broadcast   A new form of audio transmission that eliminates all static and makes more program choices possible.

Digital Communication   Data in a form that can be transmitted and received electronically.

Digital Divide   The gap between people who have Internet access and those who do not.

Digital Media   All emerging communications media that combine text, graphics, sound and video using electronic technology.

Digital Replica Magazines   Magazines that are published in both printed and digital versions.

Direct Sponsorship   A program that carries an advertiser's name in the program title.

DMCA   Digital Millennium Copyright Act.

Drive-Time Audiences   People who listen to the radio in their cars during 6 to 9 a.m. and 4 to 7 p.m.

DVR   Digital video recorder.

E-books   Electronic books.

E-mail   Mail that is delivered electronically over the Internet.

Embed   During the Iraq War, a term used to describe journalists who were allowed to cover the war on the frontlines, supervised by the U.S. military.

Ethics   The rules or standards that govern someone's conduct.

Ethnocentric   Promoting the superiority of one ethnic group over another.

Fabrication   Something made up in order to deceive.

False Light   The charge that what was implied in a story about someone is incorrect.

FCC   Federal Communications Commission.

Feedback   A response sent back to the sender from the person who receives the communication.

File Sharing   The distribution of copyrighted material on the Internet. *Illegal* file sharing is distribution of copyrighted material *without* the copyright owner's permission.

Fleeting Expletives   Profanity uttered without warning on live television.

Freelancers   Writers who are not on the staff of a magazine but who are paid for each individual article published.

HD Radio   Hybrid digital technology that improves sound quality and makes it possible for radio stations to transmit real-time text messaging along with their programming.

High-Definition Television (HDTV)   The industry standard for digital television transmission as of 2009; it provides a picture with a clearer resolution than earlier TV sets.

Home Page   The first page of a Web site, which welcomes the user.

Hot Spot   A public area like a restaurant or hotel where people with laptops and hand-held Internet devices can connect to the Internet without a wire.

HTML   Hypertext markup language.

HTTP   Hypertext transfer protocol.

HUAC   House Un-American Activities Committee.

Hudson Test   A legal test that establishes a standard for commercial speech protection.

IHT   *International Herald Tribune*, the world's largest English-language newspaper, renamed the *International New York Times* in 2013.

Illuminations   Hand-colored decorative drawings used to enhance printed text.

Intellectual Property Rights   The legal right of ownership of ideas and content published in any medium.

Interactive   A message system that allows senders and receivers to communicate simultaneously.

Internet   An international web of computer networks.

Internet of Things (IoT)   A computing concept that envisions a society where all electronic devices are interconnected through the Internet and, in turn, can process and share information and interact globally.

ISP   Internet service provider, also called an Internet access provider.

LAPS Test   A yardstick for local obscenity judgments, which evaluates an artistic work's literary, artistic, political or scientific value.

Libel   A false statement that damages a person's character or reputation by exposing that person to public ridicule or contempt.

Libelous   A statement is libelous if it is false and damages a person's character or reputation by exposing that person to public ridicule or contempt.

Links   Electronic connections from one source of information to another.

LP   Long-playing record.

Magic Bullet Theory   The assertion that media messages directly and measurably affect people's behavior.

Mass Communication   Communication from one person or group of persons through a transmitting device (a medium) to large audiences or markets.

Mass Media Content Analysis   An attempt to analyze how mass media programming influences behavior.

Mass Media Effects Research   An attempt to analyze how people use the information they receive from the media.

Mass Media Industries   Eight types of media businesses: books, newspapers, magazines, recordings, radio, movies, television and the Internet.

Media   Plural of the word *medium*.

Media Cross-Ownership   Government rules that would allow broadcasters to own newspapers located in the same media market as their broadcast station(s).

Medium   The means by which a message reaches the audience. Also, the singular form of the word *media*.

Message Pluralism   The availability to an audience of a variety of information and entertainment sources.

Misrepresentation   The presentation of a false or misleading representation of something or someone.

MOOCs   Massive open online courses.

MPA   The Association of Magazine Media, originally the Magazine Publisher's Association.

MPAA   Motion Picture Association of America.

Muckrakers   Investigative magazine journalists who targeted abuses by government and big business.

Narrowcasting   Segmenting the radio audience.

Net Neutrality   Rules for Internet service providers that require them to keep their networks open and available to carry all legal content. Under these rules, providers cannot exclude other providers from access to their network nor can they limit the type or delivery of content they carry.

Network   A collection of radio or TV stations that offers programs, usually simultaneously, throughout the country, during designated program times.

News Aggregators   Technology-based companies that primarily gather and re-format viral news content borrowed from traditional news organizations and social networks, then post the content as news on their own sponsored sites.

NII   National Information Infrastructure.

Noise   Distortion (such as static) that interferes with clear communication.

NSL   National Security Letter.

NWICO   New World Information and Communications Order. The concept that mass media should include all areas of the world, not just the West.

O & Os   TV stations that are *o* wned and *o* perated by the networks.

Pass-Along Readership   People who share a magazine with the original recipient.

Payola   The practice of accepting payment to play specific recordings on the air.

Paywall   A fee-for-access system set up by a newspaper to charge readers for Internet content.

Penny Press or Penny Paper   A newspaper produced by dropping the price of each copy to a penny and supporting the production cost through advertising.

Persuasion   The act of using argument or reasoning to induce someone to do something.

Phonetic Writing   The use of symbols to represent sounds.

Photojournalism   Using photographs to accompany text to capture a news story.

Pictograph   A symbol of an object that is used to convey an idea.

Plagiarism   Passing off as your own the ideas or writings of others.

Podcast   An audio or video file made available on the Internet for anyone to download, often by subscription.

Point-of-Purchase Magazines   Magazines that consumers buy directly, not by subscription. They are sold mainly at checkout stands in supermarkets.

Pool Reporting   An arrangement that places reporters in small, government-supervised groups to cover an event.

Pop-Up   An advertisement on a Web site that appears on the screen either behind a Web page when someone leaves the site or on top of the Web site home page when someone first visits.

Prime Time   The TV time period from 7 to 11 p.m. when more people watch TV than at any other time.

Prior Restraint   Government censorship of information before the information is published or broadcast.

Professional Ethics   The rules or standards governing the conduct of the members of a profession.

Public Domain   Publications, products and processes that are not protected by copyright and thus are available free to the public.

Public Relations   Creating understanding for, or goodwill toward, a company, a person or a product.

Publicity   Uncontrolled free use of media by a public relations firm to create events and present information to capture press and public attention.

Publishing   Placing items on the Web.

Qualified Privilege   The freedom of the press to report what is discussed during legislative and court proceedings.

Rating   The percentage of the total number of households *with TV sets* tuned to a particular program.

Recording Industry Association of America (RIAA)   Industry association that lobbies for the interests of the nation's major recording companies. Member companies account for 95 percent of all U.S. recording company sales.

Roth Test   A standard court test for obscenity, named for one of the defendants in an obscenity case.

Royalty   An amount the publisher pays an author, based on an established percentage of the book's price; royalties run anywhere from 6 to 15 percent.

RPM   Revolutions per minute.

Satellite Radio   Radio transmission by satellite, with or without advertising, available by subscription.

Search Advertising   Advertising in the form of a list and/or link to a company's site domain name through a specific online search word or phrase.

Search Engine   The tool used to locate information in a computer database.

Search Marketing   Positioning Internet advertising prominently next to consumers' related online search results.

Seditious Language   Language that authorities believe could incite rebellion against the government.

Selective Perception   The concept that each person processes messages differently.

Server   The equipment that delivers programs from their source to the programs' subscribers.

Share   The percentage of the audience *with TV sets turned on* that is watching a particular program.

Shield Laws   Laws that protect journalists from revealing their sources and the information that is communicated between reporters and their sources in a journalistic relationship.

Situation Comedy   A TV program that establishes a regular cast of characters typically in a home or work situation. Also called a sitcom.

SLAPP   Strategic lawsuit against public participation.

Social Network   An Internet community where users share information, ideas, personal messages, photographs, audio and video.

Spiral of Silence   The belief that people with divergent views may be reluctant to challenge the consensus of opinion offered by the media.

Star System   Promoting popular movie personalities to lure audiences.

Studio System   An early method of hiring a stable of salaried stars and production people under exclusive contracts to a specific studio.

Subscription Television   A new term used to describe consumer services delivered by cable and satellite program delivery.

Subsidiary Rights   The rights to market a book for other uses—to make a movie or to print a character from the book on T-shirts, for example.

Sweeps   The months when TV ratings services gather their most important ratings—February, May and November.

Syndicates   News agencies that sell articles for publication to several newspapers simultaneously.

Syndicators   Services that sell programming to broadcast stations and cable.

Tabloid   A small-format newspaper that features large photographs and illustrations along with sensational stories.

Telco   An abbreviation for "telephone company."

Time-Shifting   Recording a television program on a DVR to watch at a more convenient time.

Touch Technology   Uses computing power to digitally enhance the five senses—touch, sight, hearing, taste and smell.

Trade, Technical and Professional Magazines   Magazines dedicated to a particular business or profession.

Two-Step Flow   The transmission of information and ideas from mass media to opinion leaders and then to friends.

UAV   Unstaffed aerial vehicle, commonly called a *drone.*

Vertical Integration   An attempt by one company to simultaneously control several related aspects of the media business.

Viral Marketing   Creating an online message that is entertaining enough to get consumers to pass it on over the Internet like a virus.

Wi-Fi   An abbreviation for *Wi*reless *Fi*delity, which makes it possible to transmit Internet data wirelessly to any compatible device.

Wiki   An Internet location where registered users collaborate to create, review and compile information on a shared site.

WIPO   World Intellectual Property Organization.

Yellow Journalism   News that emphasizes crime, sex and violence; also called jazz journalism and tabloid journalism.

Zero TV Consumers   People who do not use a traditional TV set to watch programs via antenna, cable or satellite, but instead access TV programs only through video streaming on the Internet.

MEDIA INFORMATION RESOURCE GUIDE

This guide offers a selection of current information sources to help research mass media topics. Many of these are print resources that also are available as e-books and online. Also included is a list of associations that provide information, including job listings, for specific media industries.

The study of mass media covers a wide range of scholarship besides journalism and mass communication. Historians, psychologists, economists, political scientists and sociologists, for example, often contribute ideas to media studies. This guide therefore includes a variety of research sources from academic and industry publications as well as from popular periodicals.

These Research Sources Give a Good Overview

The New York Times is the best daily source of information about the media industries, especially the paper's Business section, where you will find regular reports on earnings, acquisitions and leaders in the media industries. *The New York Times* archive online helps locate the articles you need. *The International Herald Tribune*, published by *The New York Times*, offers the best global English-language coverage of mass media worldwide.

The *Los Angeles Times*' daily Calendar section follows the media business very closely, especially television and movies, because many video production companies are based in Los Angeles.

The Wall Street Journal and *The Washington Post* also carry media information, and both archives are indexed online. *The Wall Street Journal* charges users for access to most of its articles.

Advertising Age publishes special issues throughout the year focusing on newspapers, magazines, broadcasting and the Internet, as well as periodic estimates of total advertising revenue in each industry throughout the year. *Advertising Age* has an online index at *adage.com* but charges a fee and requires user registration for some articles and most statistical tables.

Columbia Journalism Review and *American Journalism Review* regularly critique developments in the print, broadcast and Internet industries. *Columbia Journalism Review* is published by New York's Columbia University Graduate School of Journalism. *American Journalism* is

published by the University of Maryland Foundation with offices in the Philip Merrill College of Journalism.

Communication Abstracts, *Communication Research*, *Journal of Communication* and *Journalism Quarterly* offer scholarly articles and article summaries about media issues. Journals that cover specific media topics include *Journal of Advertising Research*, *Newspaper Research Journal* and *Public Relations Review*.

These Resources Offer Specific Media Industry Information

Editor & Publisher, updated regularly online at *editorandpublisher.com*, follows the newspaper business, including information about industry revenue.

Broadcasting & Cable Yearbook was an annual compilation of material about the broadcast industry that also included syndicators, brokers, advertising agencies and associations. The yearbook stopped publishing in 2010, but an archive of issues is available free online at *americanradiohistory.com*.

Encyclopedia of American Journalism, edited by Stephen L. Vaughn (Routledge, 2007) is the only single-volume reference work covering the history of journalism in the United States and is available in paperback and as a Kindle e-book. The *Encyclopedia* documents the historical distinctions between print media, radio, television and the Internet and their roles in the formation of a variety of social movements in the United States, including peace and protest, civil and consumer rights, environmentalism and globalization.

Ulrich's Periodicals Directory lists journals, magazines and newspapers alphabetically and by subject and is available in most libraries. Its online counterpart, *Ulrichsweb.com*, is continually updated with new information and includes an archive.

ASCAP (The American Society of Composers, Authors and Publishers) publishes a magazine called *Playback* that chronicles the recording industry.

Hollywood Screenwriting Directory is a compilation of contact information for what the publisher calls "Hollywood buyers," including street and e-mail addresses.

For annual compilations of movie listings and reviews, check *Roger Ebert's Movie Yearbook* (Andrews McMeel, 2012) and *Leonard Maltin's 2014 Movie Guide* (Signet, 2013).

The National Association of Broadcasters (NAB) produces some publications that cover the radio and television industries, including advocacy papers on subjects the NAB lobbies in Congress.

Advertising Red Books is a database of advertisers and advertising agencies, available at *redbooks.com*.

Digital Media Wire publishes daily online newsletters and updated directories covering the business of digital media (including music, videos, gaming and mobile media).

These Resources Help Uncover U.S. Media History and Culture

John P. Dessauer's *Book Publishing: What It Is, What It Does* (R. R. Bowker, 1981) succinctly explains the history of the book publishing business. Another historical perspective and overview is available in *Books: The Culture & Commerce of Publishing* by Lewis A. Coser et al. (Basic Books, 1982). *Book Business: Publishing Past, Present and Future* by Jason Epstein (Norton, 2002) assesses the past and present book business. *The Book Publishing Industry* by Albert N. Greco, 2nd edition (Erlbaum, 2004) discusses marketing, production and changing technology.

The Journalist's Bookshelf by Roland E. Wolseley and Isabel Wolseley (Berg, 1986) is a comprehensive listing of resources about American print journalism.

The classic early history of American magazines is Frank Luther Mott's *History of American Magazines* (Appleton, 1930). *Pages from the Past: History and Memory in American Magazines* by Carolyn Kitch (University of North Carolina Press, 2008) examines the role of magazines in creating collective memory and identity for Americans.

The Music Business and Recording Industry by Geoffrey Hull, Thomas Hutchinson and Richard Strasser (Routledge, 2010) is a textbook that examines the economics of today's recording industry. *Appetite for Self-Destruction: The Spectacular Crash of the Record Industry in the Digital Age* by Steve Kopper (Soft Skull Press, 2009) offers a critical look at the last 30 years of the music business. *This Business of Music* by M. William Krasilovsky, Sidney Shemel, John M. Gross and Jonathan Feinstein (Billboard Publications, 2007) explains how the recording industry works.

Listening In: Radio and American Imagination by Susan J. Douglas (University of Minnesota Press, 2004) and *Radio Reader: Essays in the Cultural History of Radio* by Michele Hilmes (Routledge, 2001) specifically discuss the cultural impact of radio in the 20th century.

A History of Films by John L. Fell (Holt, Rinehart & Winston, 1979) and *Movie-Made America: A Cultural History of American Movies*, revised edition (Vintage, 1994) by Robert Sklar provide a good introduction to the history of movies. Works examining the cultural, social and economic impacts on American society include *Movies and American Society* edited by Steven J. Ross (Wiley-Blackwell, 2002) and *American Film: A History* by Jon Lewis (Norton, 2007). *Hollywood Stories: A Book about Celebrities, Gossip, Directors, Famous People and More!* by Stephen Schochet (Hollywood Stories Publishing, 2010) is a chatty compilation of stories and useful information, available in hardback and as an e-book.

International Film Guide (International Film Guide, 2012) is an encyclopedic source for global movie information. Another good movie information resource is *The Film Encyclopedia* (Collins, 2012), currently in its 7th edition, by Ephraim Katz.

The Columbia History of American Television by Gary Edgerton (Columbia University Press, 2009) follows the technological developments and cultural relevance of TV from its early days to today. *From Daytime to Primetime: The History of American Television Programs* by James W. Roman (Greenwood, 2008) offers comprehensive coverage of TV history before 2008. The classic television history is Eric Barnouw's *Tube of Plenty* (Oxford University Press, 1975). Christopher H. Sterling and John M. Kittross provide another overview of radio and television history in *Stay Tuned: A History of American Broadcasting*, 3rd edition (Routledge, 2001).

Confessions of an Advertising Man by David Ogilvy (Southbank, 2004) is the classic insider's view of the business. Three other histories of American advertising are *The Making of Modern Advertising* by Daniel Pope (Basic Books, 1983), *Advertising the American Dream* by Roland Marchand (University of California Press, 1986) and *The Mirror Makers: A History of American Advertising and Its Creators* by Stephen Fox (University of Illinois Press, 1997). In 2011, Yale University Press published a current critique of advertising by Joseph Turow, *The Daily You: How the New Advertising Industry Is Defining Your Identity and Your Worth*.

In 1923, Edward L. Bernays wrote the first book specifically about public relations, *The Engineering of Consent* (University of Oklahoma Press, reprinted in 1955). For an understanding of today's public relations business, you can read *This Is PR: The Realities of Public Relations* by Doug Newsom, Judy Turk and Dean Kruckeberg (Cengage, 2012).

A Social History of the Media: From Gutenberg to the Internet by Peter Burke and Asa Briggs, 2nd edition (Polity, 2005) and *Convergence Culture: Where Old and New Media Collide* by Henry Jenkins (NYU Press, 2008) discuss the emergence and evolution of communications media, their social impact and the relationship between media producers and consumers. For recent analysis of the Internet's effects on society, read *The Filter Bubble: How the New Personalized Web Is Changing What We Read and How We Think* by Eli Pariser (Penguin, 2011) and *The Shallows: What the Internet Is Doing to Our Brains* by Nicholas Carr (W. W. Norton, 2011).

To learn more about newsreels and to view the actual films, visit the University of South Carolina Web site, *sc.edu/library/newsfilm*. Other major newsreel collections exist at the National Archives and Records Administration Web site at *archives.gov* and at the Library of Congress, *loc.gov/library/libarch-digital.html*. British Pathé newsreels are located at *britishpathe.com*.

The most comprehensive academic journals specifically devoted to media history are *American Journalism*, published by the American Journalism Historians Association, and *Journalism History*, published by the E. W. Scripps School of Journalism at Ohio University, with support from the History Division of the Association for Education in Journalism and Mass Communication.

For information about historical events and people in the media who often are omitted from traditional histories, you can refer to *Up from the Footnote: A History of Women Journalists* by Marion Marzolf (Hastings House, 1977); *Great Women of the Press* by Madelon Golden Schilpp and Sharon M. Murphy (Southern Illinois University Press, 1983); *Taking Their Place: A Documentary History of Women and Journalism* by Maurine Hoffman Beasley and Sheila Jean Gibbons, 2nd edition (Strata Publishing, 2002); *Journalistas: 100 Years of the Best Writing and Reporting by Women Journalists*, edited by Eleanor Mills (Seal Press, 2005); *Black Journalists: The NABJ Story* by Wayne Dawkins, updated edition (August Press, 1997); *Ladies' Pages: African American Women's Magazines and the Culture that Made Them* by Noliwe M. Rooks (Rutgers University Press, 2004); *Minorities and Media: Diversity and the End of Mass Communication* by Clint C. Wilson and Felix Gutiérrez (Sage, 1985); *Gender, Race and Class in Media* by Gail Dines and Jean M. Humez (Sage, 2002); and *Facing Difference: Race, Gender and Mass Media* by Shirley Biagi and Marilyn Kern-Foxworth (Pine Forge Press, 1997).

These Web Sites Follow Current Media Industry News

Thousands of Web sites on the Internet offer useful material about the mass media. What follows is an alphabetical list of the specific sites that also appear at the end of each chapter. If you can't reach the Web site at the address listed, search using the site's name, listed in **bold type**. To find Web sites on a specific media topic, check **Working the Web** at the end of each chapter.

Academy of Motion Picture Arts and Sciences
oscars.org

Adrants
adrants.com

Advertising Age
adage.com

Advertising Council
adcouncil.org

All About Public Relations
aboutpublicrelations.net

AllYouCanRead.com
allyoucanread.com

Amazon
amazon.com

American Advertising Federation (AAF)
aaf.org

American Association of Advertising Agencies
aaaa.org

American Booksellers Association (ABA)
bookweb.org

American Booksellers for Free Expression (ABFE Group at ABA)
bookweb.org/abfe

American Journalism Historians Association (AJHA)
ajha.wildapricot.org

American Library Association (ALA)
ala.org

American Marketing Association (AMA)
ama.org

American Society of Journalists and Authors (ASJA)
asja.org

American Society of News Editors (ASNE)
asne.org

American Top 40 (AT40) with Ryan Seacrest
at40.com

AOL (formerly America Online)
aol.com

AOL Radio (formerly AOL Music)
aolradio.slacker.com

Apple.com/iTunes
apple.com/itunes

Apple Inc.
apple.com

Association for Education in Journalism and Mass Communication (AEJMC)
aejmc.org

Association of American Publishers
publishers.org

Association of Hispanic Advertising Agencies (AHAA)
ahaa.org

Barnes & Noble
barnesandnoble.com

BBC News
bbc.com

Benton Foundation
benton.org

Biblio
biblio.com

Billboard and Billboard Business
billboard.com and *billboard.com/biz*

BookFinder
bookfinder.com

The Broadcast Archive
oldradio.com

BuzzFeed
buzzfeed.com

Canadian Broadcasting Corporation (CBC) Radio-Canada
cbc.ca/radio

The Cartoon Bank
cartoonbank.com

CBS Corporation
cbscorporation.com

CBS Radio
cbsradio.com

CBS Television
cbs.com

Center for Investigative Reporting (CIR)
revealnews.org

Center for Journalism Ethics
ethics.journalism.wisc.edu

Center for Media and Democracy (CMD)
prwatch.org

Center on Media and Child Health (CMCH)
cmch.tv

Chartered Institute of Public Relations (CIPR)
cipr.co.uk

Clio Awards
clioawards.com

CNET
cnet.com

College Media Association (CMA)
collegemedia.org

Columbia Journalism Review (CJR)
cjr.org

Comcast Corporation
comcast.com

Committee to Protect Journalists (CPJ)
cpj.org

Condé Nast Media Company
condenast.com

C-SPAN
c-span.org

CyberJournalist.net
cyberjournalist.net

The Dallas Morning News
dallasnews.com

DEG Digital Entertainment Group
degonline.org

Digital Content Next (formerly the Online Publishers Association)
onlinepub.org

Directors Guild of America
dga.org

Disney/ABC Television Group
disneyabcpress.com

Electronic Frontier Foundation (EFF)
eff.org

EthicNet, European Ethics Codes
ethicnet.uta.fi/

Facebook
facebook.com

Fairness & Accuracy in Reporting (FAIR)
fair.org

Federal Communications Commission (FCC)
fcc.gov

Federal Trade Commission (FTC)
ftc.gov

FindLaw
findlaw.com

Folio: The Magazine for Magazine Management
foliomag.com

***Foreign Policy* Magazine**
foreignpolicy.com

Forrester Research
forrester.com

Fox Movietone News
foxnews.com/on-air/movietone-news/index.html

Freedom Forum
newseuminstitute.org/freedom-forum/

Friday Morning Quarterback (FMQB)
fmqb.com

Gannett Company
gannett.com

***Global Media Journal* (GMJ)**
globalmediajournal.com

Global Online Video Association

gova.cc

HBO (Home Box Office)

hbo.com

Hearst Corporation

hearst.com

Honolulu Star-Advertiser

staradvertiser.com

Index (Index on Censorship)

indexoncensorship.org

IndieBound

indiebound.org

Inside Radio

insideradio.com

Institute for Nonprofit News (INN; formerly the Investigative News Network)

inn.org

Institute for Public Relations (IPR)

instituteforpr.com

Institute of Electrical and Electronics Engineers (IEEE)

ieee.org

Interactive Advertising Bureau (IAB)

iab.net

International Association for Media and Communication Research (IAMCR)

iamcr.org

International Center for Journalists (ICFJ)

icfj.org

International Media Lawyers Association (IMLA)

internationalmedialawyers.org

International New York Times

international.nytimes.com

International News Media Association (INMA)

inma.org

International Public Relations Association (IPRA)

ipra.org

International Women's Media Foundation (IWMF)

iwmf.org

Internet Movie Database (IMDb)

imdb.com

Internews

internews.org

Investigative Reporters and Editors (IRE)

ire.org

Joan Shorenstein Center on Media, Politics and Public Policy (Harvard University)

shorensteincenter.org

Journal of Electronic Publishing (JEP)

journalofelectronicpublishing.org

Journalism Ethics Cases Online

journalism.indiana.edu/resources/ethics/

La Opinión

laopinion.com/

Los Angeles Times

latimes.com

Lucasfilm

lucasfilm.com

Media Center at New York Law School

nyls.edu/media_center/media_law_and_policy/

Media Effects Research Lab (MERL) at Penn State University

comm.psu.edu/research/centers/medialab

Media Law Resource Center (MLRC)

medialaw.org

MediaPost Communications

mediapost.com

MediaSmarts

mediasmarts.ca

The Miami Herald

miamiherald.com

MIT Media Lab Project

media.mit.edu

Moorland-Spingarn Research Center (MSRC) at Howard University

library.howard.edu/MSRC

Motion Picture Association of America (MPAA) and Motion Picture Association (MPA)

mpaa.org

MPA—The Association of Magazine Media

magazine.org

National Association of Black Journalists (NABJ)

nabj.org

National Association of Broadcasters (NAB)

nab.org

National Association of Hispanic Journalists (NAHJ)

nahj.org

National Cable & Telecommunications Association (NCTA)

ncta.com

National Freedom of Information Coalition (NFOIC)

nfoic.org

National Journal

nationaljournal.com

National Lesbian and Gay Journalists Association (NLGJA), also known as the Association of Lesbian, Gay, Bisexual and Transgender (LGBT) Journalists

nlgja.org

National Press Club

press.org

National Press Photographers Association (NPPA)
nppa.org

National Public Radio
npr.org

Native American Journalists Association (NAJA)
naja.com

NBC
nbc.com

Netflix
netflix.com

News Corporation
newscorp.com

Newspaper Association of America (NAA)
naa.org

The New York Times
nytimes.com

The New Yorker
newyorker.com

Nielsen Media Research
nielsen.com

Nieman Foundation for Journalism at Harvard University
nieman.harvard.edu

Online News Association (ONA)
journalists.org

Online Public Relations
online-pr.com

Pandora Radio
pandora.com

Parental Guide
parentalguide.org

Pearson Education
pearson.com

Pew Internet, Science and Technology Project
pewinternet.org

Pew Research Center: Journalism and Media
journalism.org

Pew Research Center: U.S. Politics and Policy
people-press.org

Pinterest
pinterest.com

Poynter Institute
poynter.org

Poynter Online
poynter.org

PR Newswire
prnewswire.com

ProPublica
propublica.org

PRWeb
prweb.com

PRWeek
prweek.com/us

Public Broadcasting Service (PBS)
pbs.org

Public Relations Society of America (PRSA)
prsa.org

Public Relations Student Society of America (PRSSA)
prssa.prsa.org

Radio Advertising Bureau (RAB)
rab.com

Radio Lovers
radiolovers.com

Radio Television Digital News Association (RTDNA; formerly Radio-Television News Directors Association)
rtdna.org

Recording Industry Association of America (RIAA)
riaa.com

Reed Elsevier
relxgroup.com

Reddit
reddit.com

Reporters Without Borders
rsf.org

Rhapsody Inc.
rhapsody.com

Salon
salon.com

Scholastic Corporation
scholastic.com

Screenwriters Federation of America (SFA)
screenwritersfederation.org

Silha Center for the Study of Media Ethics and Law (University of Minnesota)
silha.umn.edu/

Sirius XM
siriusxm.com

Skype
skype.com

Slate
slate.com

Society of Professional Journalists (SPJ)
spj.org

Sony Corporation of America (SCA)
sony.com

SoundCloud
soundcloud.com

Sports Illustrated
si.com

Student Press Law Center (SPLC)
splc.org

Sundance Institute
sundance.org

Talking Points Memo (TPM)
talkingpointsmemo.com

Television Bureau of Advertising (TVB)
tvb.org

Time Inc.
timeinc.com

Time Warner Inc.
timewarner.com

Topix
topix.net

Tribune Media
tribunemedia.com

Tribune Publishing
tribpub.com

TuneIn
tunein.com

TV.com
tv.com

21st Century Fox
21cf.com

Twitter
twitter.com

UNITY: Journalists for Diversity
unityjournalists.org

Universal Music Group (UMG)
universalmusic.com

University of Iowa Department of Communication Studies: Political Communication and Campaigns
clas.uiowa.edu/commstudies/political-communication-campaigns

Vanderbilt Television News Archive
tvnews.vanderbilt.edu

The Verge
theverge.com

Viacom Incorporated
viacom.com

Vine
vine.co

The Walt Disney Company
thewaltdisneycompany.com

Warner Bros.
warnerbros.com

Washington Center for Politics and Journalism
wcpj.org

The Washington Post
washingtonpost.com

WikiLeaks
wikileaks.org

Worldpress.org
worldpress.org

YouTube
youtube.com

More Media Research Sources You Can Use

Many magazines and journals publish information about the mass media industries. The following is a listing of the major magazine and journal titles in each subject area. All these publications offer companion Web sites.

Advertising

Adweek
adweek.com

Journal of Advertising
tandfonline.com

Journal of Advertising Research
journalofadvertisingresearch.com

Broadcasting

Broadcasting & Cable
broadcastingcable.com

Emmy (published by the Academy of Television Arts and Sciences)
emmys.com/emmy-magazine

Journal of Broadcasting & Electronic Media
beaweb.org/jobem.htm

RTDNA Communicator
rtdna.org

TV Guide
tvguide.com

Magazine and Book Publishing

Folio: **Magazine**
foliomag.com

Publishers Weekly
publishersweekly.com

Movies

Film Comment
filmcomment.com

Hollywood Reporter
hollywoodreporter.com

Variety
variety.com/

VideoAge
videoageinternational.com

Newspapers

Editor & Publisher
editorandpublisher.com

Journalism and Communication Monographs
jmo.sagepub.com

Newspaper Research Journal
newspaperresearchjournal.org

PRESSTIME Update
naa.org/news-and-media/presstime-update.aspx

Quill
spj.org/quill.asp

Public Relations

PRWeek
prweek.com/us

Public Relations Journal
prsa.org/Intelligence/PRJournal

Recordings

Billboard
billboard.com

Down Beat
downbeat.com

Music Index
ebscohost.com/public/music-index

Rolling Stone
rollingstone.com

Digital Media and the Web

AI Magazine
aaai.org/Magazine/magazine.php

Communications Daily
warren-news.com

Information Today
infotoday.com

Macworld
macworld.com

PC Magazine
pcmag.com

PCWorld
pcworld.com

Technical Communication
techcomm.stc.org

Wired
wired.com

Global Media

Advertising

International Journal of Advertising
tandfonline.com

Broadcasting

Cable and Satellite International
csimagazine.com/csi/index.php

Ofcom (independent regulator and competition authority for the UK communications industries)
ofcom.org.uk

Movies

CineAction (Canada)
cineaction.ca

Empire Magazine
empireonline.com/magazine

Film Ink (Australia)
filmink.com.au

Film Ireland
filmireland.net

Recordings

Musical America Worldwide
musicalamerica.com

Other

OPMA Overseas Media Guide (England)
opma.co.uk

Media-Related Topics

Censorship News (published by the National Coalition Against Censorship—available to download as a PDF or by e-mail subscription)
ncac.org

Communication Research (online editions available through Sage Publications)
crx.sagepub.com/

The News Media and the Law (published by Reporters Committee for Freedom of the Press)
rcfp.org/magazine-archive

Nieman Reports (published by the Nieman Foundation for Journalism at Harvard University)
niemanreports.org/

SELECTED REFERENCES

Chapter 1   Mass Media and Everyday Life

Association of American Publishers. (2014, June 16). U.S. publishing industry annual survey reports $27 billion in net revenue, 2.6 billion units for 2013. publishers.org.

Association of Magazine Media. *MPA factbook 2014.* magazine.org.

Bagdikian, B. (1983). *The media monopoly.* Boston: Beacon Press.

Bowker. (2014, August 5). Traditional print book production dipped slightly in 2013. bowker.com.

Dormehl, L. (2014, June 7). Internet of Things: It's all coming together for a tech revolution. theguardian.com.

Federal Communications Commission. (2014, December 31). Broadcast station totals as of December 31, 2014. fcc.gov.

Friedlander, J. (2014). News and notes on 2013 RIAA music industry shipment and revenue statistics. riaa.com.

Gilder, G. (1994, February 28). Life after television, updated. *Forbes,* 17.

Gustin, S. (2010, February 23). One-third of Americans lack high-speed Internet access. dailyfinance.com.

Interactive Advertising Bureau. (2014, April 10). 2013 Internet ad revenues soar to $42.8 billion, hitting landmark high and surpassing broadcast television for the first time. iab.net.

Ives, N. (2010, June 28). Mounting web woes pummel newspapers. *Advertising Age,* 6.

James, M. (2015, January 29). NBC scores a record haul from Super Bowl ad sales. latimes.com.

Jenkins, H. (2000, March). Digital land grab. *Technology Review,* 103.

Kim, R. (2005, May 28). Sales of cell phones totally off the hook. *San Francisco Chronicle,* C1.

Lang, B. (2010, September 20). Ipsos OTX study: People spend more than half their day consuming media. thewrap.com.

Liebling, A. J. (1961). *The press.* New York: Ballantine.

Los Angeles Times. (2011, January 26). Mobile app revenue will triple to $15 billion this year, Gartner says. latimes.com.

Macmillan, D. (2014, August 28). Snapchat is said to have more than 100 million monthly active users. wsj.com.

Morgan, J. (2013, May 13). A simple explanation of "The Internet of Things." forbes.com.

Nakashima, R. (2014, February 13). Comcast strikes deal to buy Time Warner Cable. sfgate.com.

National Association of Theatre Owners. (2014). Number of U.S. movie screens. natoonline.org.

Nielsenwire. (2009, December 21). Study: More cellular-only homes as Americans expand mobile media usage. nielsenwire.com.

Plato. (1961). *Collected works.* Princeton, N.J.: Phaedrus.

Raine, G. (2005, September 27). Net ad revenues grow steadily. *San Francisco Chronicle,* D1.

Scott, A. O. (2008, November 23). The screening of America. *The New York Times Magazine,* 21.

Smith, A. (1980). *Goodbye Gutenberg.* New York: Oxford University Press.

Soto, M. (2000, May 4). Microsoft executive Nathan Myhrvold resigns. seattletimes.nwsource.com.

Thielman, S. (2015, July 21). FCC approves $48.6bn sale of DirecTV to AT&T. theguardian.com.

Timberg, C. (2013, February 25). Mobile device connections growing quickly. washingtonpost.com.

United States Census Bureau. (2014, November). Computer and Internet use in the United States 2013. census.gov.

Verrier, R. (2011, January 28). Movie ticket prices reach new milestone. latimes.com.

Chapter 2   Books: Rearranging the Page

Alter, A. (2014, September 9). Barnes & Noble revenue is off, but loss narrows. nytimes.com.

Andriani, L. (2009, August 14). Cengage Learning to rent print textbooks. publishersweekly.com.

Anton, M. (2012, April 14). Even e-reader owners still like printed books, survey finds. latimes.com.

Associated Press. (2009, August 20). Microsoft, Yahoo, Amazon to fight Google book deal. sfgate.com.

Associated Press. (2010, November 9). Publishers to get 70 percent of sales on Kindle. wsj.com.

Associated Press. (2011, August 30). Books-A-Million will assume 14 Borders leases. sfgate.com.

Auletta, K. (2010, April 26). Publish or perish. NewYorker.com.

Bosman, J. (2010, December 8). Lusty tales and hot sales: Romance e-books thrive. nytimes.com.

Bosman, J. (2012, June 4). Amazon buys Avalon Books, publisher in romance and mysteries. nytimes.com.

Bradley, T. (2009, September 21). Opposition mounting against Google books settlement. sfgate.com.

Clifford, S., & Bosman, J. (2011, February 27). Publishers look beyond bookstores. nytimes.com.

Coser, L. A., Kadushin, C., & Powell, W. F. (1982). *Books: The culture and commerce of publishing.* New York: Basic Books.

Davis, K. C. (1984). *Two-bit culture: The paperbacking of America.* Boston: Houghton Mifflin.

Dessauer, J. P. (1974). *Book publishing: What it is, what it does.* New York: R. R. Bowker.

Donadio, R. (2008, April 27). You're an author? Me too! *The New York Times Book Review*, 27.

Galassi, J. (2010, January 3). There's more to publishing than meets the screen. nytimes.com.

Hart, J. D. (1950). *The popular book*. Berkeley: University of California Press.

Helft, M. (2011, March 22). Judge rejects Google's deal to digitize books. nytimes.com.

Hyde, C. R. (2010, November 2). The (paltry) economics of being a novelist. dailyfinance.com.

Kaufman, L. (2013, February 20). Independent booksellers sue Amazon and publishers over e-books. nytimes.com.

Mackay, R. (2010, December 27). Julian Assange's 1.3 million reasons to write. nytimes.com.

Mason, P. (2015, August 10). Ebooks are changing the way we read, and the way novelists write. theguardian.com.

Miller, C. C., & Bosman, J. (2011, May 19). E-books outsell print books at Amazon. nytimes.com.

Milliot, J. (2014, July 27). Book sales dipped in 2013. publishersweekly.com.

Publishers Weekly. (2014). The world's 56 largest book publishers, 2014. publishersweekly.com.

Streitfield, D. (2005, July 17). Publisher loses ruling on e-books. latimes.com.

Streitfeld, D. (2014, March 23). Web fiction, serialized and social. nytimes.com.

Sweeney, M. (2013, March 26). *Fifty Shades of Grey* publisher Random House posts record profits. guardiannews.com.

Trachtenberg, J. A. (2010, May 21). E-books rewrite bookselling. wsj.com.

Trachtenberg, J. A. (2010, September 28). Authors feel pinch in age of e-books. wsj.com.

Turow, S. (2013, April 7). The slow death of the American author. nytimes.com.

Weber, P. J. (2014, January 3). Texas library offers glimpse of bookless future. sfgate.com.

Weinberg, S. (2010, March 16). Enhanced e-books: A boon for readers, a headache for agents. dailyfinance.com.

Weinberg, S. (2010, August 2). Amazon's new Kindles sell out in just five days. dailyfinance.com.

White, E. B. (1976). *Letters of E. B. White*. New York: Harper & Row.

Chapter 3   Newspapers: Mobilizing Delivery

Ahrens, F. (2009, March 26). *Washington Post* to offer new buyouts to employees. washingtonpost.com.

Associated Press. (2010, January 16). MediaNews holding company filing Chapter 11. sfgate.com.

Associated Press. (2010, February 12). *USA Today* mandates staff furloughs to save money. nytimes.com.

Associated Press. (2012, December 30). Tribune to leave bankruptcy after four years. sacbee.com.

Associated Press. (2013, August 3). Red Sox owner enters $70M deal for *Boston Globe*. sfgate.com.

Carr, D. (2014, August 10). Print is down, and now out. nytimes.com.

Chang, A. (2015, May 7). LA Times parent to buy San Diego paper, expanding reach in Southern California. latimes.com.

De Falco, B. (2011, January 11). Gannett to cut staff at 3 N.J. papers by nearly half. sfgate.com.

De La Merced, M. (2009, December 8). Tribune files for bankruptcy. nytimes.com.

Dertouzos, J., & Quinn, T. (1985, September). Bargaining responses to the technology revolution: The case of the newspaper industry. *Labor management cooperation brief*. Washington, D.C.: U.S. Department of Labor.

Halliday, J. (2013, January 6). 11 things you need to know about BuzzFeed. theguardian.com.

Hawaii Reporter. (2014, July 7). The Garden Island to resume publishing Saturday edition. hawaiireporter.com.

Isaac, M. (2014, August 10). 50 million new reasons BuzzFeed wants to take its content far beyond lists. nytimes.com.

Johnson, K. (2009, February 27). Part of Denver's past, the Rocky says goodbye. nytimes.com.

Kessler, K. (1984). *The dissident press*. Beverly Hills, Calif.: Sage.

Kirchhoff, S. M. (2010, September 9). *The U.S. newspaper industry in transition*. Washington, D.C.: Congressional Research Service.

Marzolf, M. (1977). *Up from the footnote*. New York: Hastings House.

Mitchell, A. (2014, March 26). State of the news media 2014. Pew Research Center. journalism.org.

Neate, R. (2015, February 26). New York Daily News up for grabs as billionaire Mort Zuckerman looks to sell. theguardian.com.

Oneal, M., & Puzzanghera, J. (2012, July 14). Bankruptcy judge to confirm Tribune reorganization plan. latimes.com.

Perez-Peña, R. (2007, May 1). Newspaper circulation in steep slide across nation. *The New York Times*, C10.

Perez-Peña, R. (2010, January 21). *The Times* to charge for frequent access to its web site. nytimes.com.

Peters, J. W. (2010, October 25). Newspaper circulation falls broadly but at slower pace. nytimes.com.

Peters, J. W. (2012, February 11). A newspaper, and a legacy, reordered. washingtonpost.com.

Pew Research Center (2014, March 26). Revenue sources: A heavy dependence on advertising. pewresearch.org.

Pfeifer, S. (2015, May 26). San Diego Union-Tribune lays off 178, mostly in printing, delivery. latimes.com

Rainey, J. (2011, February 5). Consolidation seen as inevitable for Southern California newspapers. latimes.com.

Rice, Andrew (2013, April 17). Does BuzzFeed know the secret? newyork.com.

Richman, D., & James, A. (2009, March 16). *Seattle P-I* to publish last edition Tuesday. SeattlePI.com.

Rutherford, L. (1963). *John Peter Zenger*. Gloucester, Mass.: Peter Smith.

Schilpp, M. G., & Murphy, S. M. (1983). *Great women of the press*. Carbondale: Southern Illinois University Press.

Seelye, K. Q. (2005, September 21). Times company announces 500 job cuts. *The New York Times*, C5.

Seelye, K. Q., & Sorkin, A. R. (2007, April 2). Tribune accepts real estate magnate's bid. nytimes.com.

Smith, A. (1980). *Goodbye Gutenberg*. New York: Oxford University Press.

Somaiya, R. (2014, October 1). *New York Times* plans to eliminate 100 jobs in the newsroom. nytimes.com.

Swanberg, W. A. (1971). *Citizen Hearst*. New York: Bantam Books.

Wells, I. B. (1970). *The crusade for justice: The autobiography of Ida B. Wells*. Chicago: University of Chicago Press.

Woodward, C. (2013, August 6). A family dynasty gives up *The Washington Post*. sfgate.com.

Zezima, K. (2005, August 8). Abolitionist's family celebrates a legacy of nonconformity. *The New York Times*, A10.

Chapter 4 Magazines: Chasing the Audience

Alliance for Audited Media. (2014, August 7). Top 25 U.S. consumer magazines for June 2014. auditedmedia.com.

Association of Magazine Media. *MPA factbook 2014*. magazine.org.

Bercovici, J. (2009, October 5). Condé Nast closes beloved *Gourmet* magazine and three others. DailyFinance.com.

Bercovici, J. (2010, August 2). *Newsweek* gets sold to Sidney Harman. So long, *Newsweek*. dailyfinance.com.

Biagi, S. (1987). *NewsTalk I*. Belmont, Calif.: Wadsworth.

Chozick, A. (2013, March 6). Time Warner ends talks with Meredith and will spin off Time Inc. into separate company. nytimes.com.

Haber, M. (2012, December 7). *Ebony* looks to its past as it moves forward. nytimes.com.

Haughney, C. (2013, August 6). Magazine newsstand sales plummet, but digital editions thrive. nytimes.com.

Haughney, C. (2014, August 7). Celebrity magazine sales plummet on newsstands. nytimes.com.

Ives, N. (2012, November 30). Digital subs rising, *The Economist* unbundles tablet editions from print. adage.com.

Ives, N. (2013, January 3). Digital cracks 50% of ad revenue at *Wired* magazine. adage.com.

Ives, N. (2013, February 7). Magazines' digital circ soars . . . to 2.4% of total. adage.com.

Kaufman, L. (2014, May 7). *Jet* magazine to shift to digital publishing next month. nytimes.com.

Kobak, J. B. (1985, April). 1984: A billion-dollar year for acquisitions. *Folio*, 14, 82–95.

Lee, F. R. (2005, August 10). He created a mirror for black America. *The New York Times*, B1.

Madrigal, A. C. (2015, February 3). Welcome to the real future. fusion.net.

O'Brien, K. J. (2007, March 18). Magazine publishers see future, but no profit in shift to Internet. iht.com.

Paneth, D. (1983). *Encyclopedia of American journalism*. New York: Facts on File.

Paschyn, C. M. (2015, March 24). Ida Tarbell: The woman who pioneered investigative journalism. ms.newsletter.com.

Peters, J. W. (2011, November 20). At 154, a digital milestone. nytimes.com.

Pilkington, E. (2014, April 24). *Ladies' Home Journal* ending regular publication after 130 years. theguardian.com.

Pogue, D. (2012, April 11). A buffet of magazines on a tablet. nytimes.com.

Rose, M. (2000, November 6). Problems for magazines come into view. *The Wall Street Journal*, B18.

Sarno, D. (2012, April 5). Five magazine publishers jointly release tablet app. latimes.com.

Schilpp, M. G., & Murphy, S. M. (1983). *Great women of the press*. Carbondale: Southern Illinois University Press.

Sebastian, M. (2015, January 12). *Vice* magazine brand of the year. *Advertising Age*, 23.

Seelye, K. Q. (2007, March 27). *Life* magazine, its pages dwindling, will cease publication. nytimes.com.

Smith, S. (2010, December 14). Has the age of uber-cocooning begun? Digital media October boxscores. MinOnline.com.

Somaiya, R. (2015, February 1). After turmoil, *The New Republic* re-emerges on newsstands. nytimes.com.

Swanberg, W. A. (1972). *Luce and his empire*. New York: Scribner's.

Tarbell, I. (1939). *All in the day's work*. New York: MacMillan.

Chapter 5 Recordings: Streaming Sounds

Associated Press. (2015, February 13). Estonian man pleads guilty in Megaupload piracy case. nytimes.com.

Denisoff, R. S. (1975). *Solid gold*. New Brunswick, N.J.: Transaction Books.

Dredge, S. (2015, June 8). Apple unveils streaming service Apple Music and 24-hour radio stations. theguardian.com.

Evangelista, B. (2003, April 25). Apple kicks off online music store. *San Francisco Chronicle*, B1.

Faughnder, R. (2015, June 26). Music piracy is down but still very much in play. latimes.com.

Friedlander, J. P. News and notes on 2014 RIAA music industry shipment and revenue statistics. riaa.com.

Gomes, L. (2001, February 13). Napster suffers a rout in appeals court. *The Wall Street Journal*, A3.

Gomes, L. (2001, March 5). Judge starts process of silencing Napster. *The Wall Street Journal*, B6.

Hann, M. (2015, April 21). Who destroyed the music industry? A blue-collar worker in a small North Carolina town. theguardian.com.

Holloway, L. (2003, June 26). Recording industry to sue Internet music swappers. *The New York Times*, C4.

Jesdanun, A. (2015, April 1). Who's who in music streaming: Tidal, Spotify, Pandora & More. sfgate.com.

Karnowski, S. (2009, June 18). Jury rules against Minn. woman in download case. sfgate.com.

Kopytoff, V. (2003, September 4). Music lawsuits snare 18 in Bay Area. *San Francisco Chronicle*, A1.

Kravels, D. (2013, March 18). Supreme Court OKs $222K verdict for sharing 24 songs. wired.com.

Lee, E. (2007, March 22). Music industry threatens student downloaders at UC. sfgate.com.

Leeds, J. (2007, May 28). Plunge in CD sales shakes up big labels. *The New York Times*, B1.

Leeds, J. (2007, October 5). Labels win suit against song sharer. nytimes.com.

Lowensohn, J. (2013, January 17). *Rolling Stone* lands on iPad with iTunes integration in tow. cnet.com.

Metz, R. (1975). *CBS: Reflections in a bloodshot eye*. Chicago: Playboy Press.

Mostrous, A. (2010, March 1). Music industry needs clear strategy and control over illegal downloads. Business. timesonline.co.uk.

Pfanner, E. (2013, February 26). Music industry records first revenue increase since 1999. nytimes.com.

Pham, A. (2011, May 10). Warner Music Group debt is downgraded. latimes.com.

Plambeck, J. (2010, February 26). 10 billionth download for iTunes. *The New York Times*, C5.

Plaugic, L. (2015, February 14). Megaupload copyright infringement case sees its first conviction. theverge.com.

Recording Industry Association of America. (2010, May 12). Federal court issues landmark ruling against LimeWire. riaa.com.

Recording Industry Association of America. (2014). #labelsatwork: American music's digital revolution. riaa.com.

Sabbagh, D. (2008, June 18). Music sales fall to their lowest level in over 20 years. timesonline.com.

Satter, R. G. (2011, January 21). IFPI: Growth in digital music sales is slowing. sfgate.com.

Sisario, B. (2012, September 21). U.S. and European regulators approve Universal's purchase of EMI. nytimes.com.

Sisario, B. (2013, January 28). As music streaming grows, royalties slow to a trickle. nytimes.com.

Sisario, B. (2015, March 30). Jay Z reveals plans for Tidal, a streaming music service. nytimes.com.

Sisario, B. (2015, June 4). SoundCloud reaches royalty deal with 20,000 record labels. nytimes.com.

Sisario, B. (2015, June 30). Apple Music makes debut with d.j. carrying the flag. nytimes.com.

Sloan, P. (2013, March 12). Spotify: Growing like mad, yet so far to go. cnet.com.

Smart, J. R. (1977). *A wonderful invention: A brief history of the phonograph from tinfoil to the LP*. Washington, D.C.: Library of Congress.

Sweeney, M., & Sabbagh, D. (2011, November 11). Universal and Sony reach deal to buy EMI for 2.5 billion British pounds. guardian.co.uk.

Chapter 6   Radio: Riding New Waves

Advertising Age. (2014, September 23). How Pandora thinks about advertising in the connected car. adage.com.

Advertising Age. (2014, October 22, 2014). Pandora opens listener data to let musicians target fans. adage.com.

Associated Press. (2007, April 14). $12.5 million "payola" fine. *San Francisco Chronicle*, C2.

Barnouw, E. (1978). *Tube of plenty*. New York: Oxford University Press.

Bittner, J. (1982). *Broadcast law and regulation*. Englewood Cliffs, N.J.: Prentice Hall.

De La Merced, M. J. (2012, December 18). Nielsen to buy Arbitron for $1.26 billion. nytimes.com.

Engleman, E., & Fixmer, A. (2012, November 27). Pandora, musicians clash over fees. sfgate.com.

Farhi, P. (2011, November 16). CBS Radio to start all-news station in D.C. area. washingtonpost.com.

Feder, B. J. (2002, October 11). FCC approves a digital radio technology. *The New York Times*, B1.

Fixmer, A. (2013, February 28). Pandora caps free listening as royalty costs soar. bloomberg.com.

Fornatale, P., & Mills, J. E. (1980). *Radio in the television age*. New York: Overlook Press.

James, M. (2014, June 12). Two months of L.A. radio data may be wrong, Nielsen says. latimes.com.

Leeds, J. (2007, March 6). Broadcasters agree to fine over payoffs. *The New York Times*, C1.

MacFarland, D. R. (1979). *The development of the top 40 radio format*. New York: Arno Press.

McMahan, T. (2009, July 14). Pandora sings new tune with royalty agreement, funding. blogs.wsj.com.

Mindlin, A. (2007, May 7). Counting radio listeners stirs controversy. *The New York Times*, C4.

Nielsen. (2014, February). State of the media: Audio today 2014. nielsen.com.

Radio Advertising Bureau. (2011). Digital audio usage trends: A highly engaged listenership. rab.com.

Rainey, J. (2010, October 20). Public radio is enjoying boom times. latimes.com.

Settel, L. (1960). *A pictorial history of radio*. New York: Citadel Press.

Shenon, P. (2008, March 25). Justice Dept. approves XM merger with Sirius. *The New York Times*, C1.

Sperber, A. M. (1986). *Murrow: His life and times*. New York: Freundlich.

Stimson, L. (2010, September 1). AM HD radio has stalled; now what? *Radio World*. rwonline.com.

Chapter 7   Movies: Digitizing Dreams

Associated Press. (2012, September 6). Small theaters struggle as Hollywood goes digital. sfgate.com.

Associated Press. (2014, November 28). Watch: Fans go wild over 88-second "Star Wars" teaser. sacbee.com.

Balio, T. (1976). *The American film industry*. Madison: University of Wisconsin Press.

Barnes, B. (2014, December 7). Hollywood tracks social media chatter to target hit films. nytimes.com.

Barnes, B. (2015, June 2). Antitrust scrutiny for 3 big U.S. theater chains. nytimes.com.

Burrows, P. (2010, December 5). Will Netflix kill the Internet? *Bloomberg Businessweek*. sfgate.com.

Child, B. (2013, February 5). Yoda not far, soon you will be with him—when his own *Star Wars* movie he has. theguardian.com.

Chinnock, C. (1999, August 9). Lights! Camera! Action! It's the dawn of digital cinema. *Electronic Design*, 32F.

Chmielewski, D. C. (2011, June 6). Disney film studio lay-offs expected soon. latimes.com.

Cieply, M. (2010, March 3). 3-D films fuel a rise in box office revenues. *The New York Times*, C2.

Cieply, M. (2012, October 30). Disney buying Lucasfilm for $4 billion. nytimes.com.

Denby, D. (2007, January 8). Big pictures. *The New Yorker*, 54.

Ellis, J. C. (1985). *A history of American film*, 2nd ed. Englewood Cliffs, N.J.: Prentice Hall.

Fabrikant, G., & Waxman, S. (2005, December 9). Viacom's Paramount to buy DreamWorks for $1.6 billion. nytimes.com.

Fritz, B. (2010, May 31). Summer box office sees its worst Memorial Day weekend in 17 years. latimes.com.

Fritz, B. (2011, July 9). Not much demand yet for premium video on demand. latimes.com.

Goldstein, P. (2010, January 30). Is this a box-office record with an *? latimes.com.

Hamedy, S. (2014, July 31). Kodak to keep making movie film, with Hollywood's support. latimes.com.

LaSalle, M. (2005, July 13). Blame the economy, the product, the theaters—We're just not going to movies the way we used to. sfgate.com.

Motion Picture Association of America. (1954). *Motion picture production code*.

Motion Picture Association of America. (2013). Theatrical Market Statistics 2013. mpaa.com.

Nagourney, A. (2015, February 12). Hollywood gets its groove back. nytimes.com.

Nakashima, R. (2009, March 10). Sony Pictures to cut nearly 350 jobs. sfgate.com.

Richter, F. (2015, April 19). Netflix blows past 60 million subscribers. statista.com.

Schuker, L. A. E., & Smith, E. (2010, May 22). Hollywood eyes shortcut to TV. wsj.com.

Sklar, R. (1975). *Movie-made America*. New York: Random House.

Smith, D. (2010, April 23). Streaming putting video stores out of business. sacbee.com.

Solomon, C. (2011, August 16). A little lamp lights the way for Pixar's success. latimes.com.

Squire, J. E. (ed.). (1983). *The movie business book*. New York: Simon & Schuster.

Trumbo, D. (1962). *Additional dialogue: Letters of Dalton Trumbo, 1942–1962*. New York: M. Evans.

Verrier, R. (2010, May 7). FCC paves way for studios to push movies into the home, rattling theaters. latimes.com.

Verrier, R. (2014, March 28). Global movie ticket sales climb. latimes.com.

Verrier, R. (2015, February 10). Digital jobs help drive Hollywood employment to highest level in decade. latimes.com.

Verrier, R. (2015, April 16). Department of Justice probes major theater chains over antitrust claims. latimes.com.

Waxman, S. (2007, April 26). Hollywood's shortage of female power. *The New York Times*, B1.

Chapter 8 Television: Changing Channels

Anderson, M., & Ledtke, M. (2014, October 15). HBO going away from cable, will stand on its own. Associated Press, retrieved from sacbee.com.

Associated Press. (2013, June 13). 3-D TV falls flat; ESPN to kill 3-D broadcasts. sacbee.com.

Barnouw, E. (1975). *Tube of plenty*. New York: Oxford University Press.

Biagi, S. (1987). *NewsTalk II*. Belmont, Calif.: Wadsworth.

Brown, L. (1971). *Television: The business behind the box*. New York: Harcourt Brace Jovanovich.

Carter, B. (2011, February 21). Networks have lost key viewers at 10 p.m. *The New York Times*, B1.

Chen, K., & Peers, M. (1999, August 6). FCC relaxes its rules on TV station ownership. *The Wall Street Journal*, A3.

Chozick, A., & Stelter, B. (2013, February 12). Comcast buys rest of NBC in early sale. nytimes.com.

FitzGerald, T. (2011, May 4). Pac-12 gets richest TV deal. sfgate.com.

Flint, J. (2012, August 28). ESPN shells out $5.6 billion to keep Major League Baseball. latimes.com.

Fritz, B., & Verrier, R. (2011, March 2). DirecTV prepares to launch premium video on demand; theater executives alarmed. latimes.com.

Greenfield, J. (1977). *Television: The first fifty years*. New York: Abrams.

Helft, M. (2010, September 5). Apple faces many rivals for streaming to TVs. nytimes.com.

Jensen, E. (2011, February 28). Public broadcasters start to sweat, as a budget threat looks serious. *The New York Times*, B4.

Jensen, E. (2011, May 30). PBS plans promotional breaks within programs. nytimes.com.

Minow, N. (1964). *Equal time: The private broadcaster and the public interest*. New York: Atheneum.

Nakashima, R. (2013, April 7). Broadcasters worry about "zero TV" homes. Associated Press, retrieved from sacbee.com.

Nielsen. (2013, March). Free to move between screens: The cross-platform report. nielsen.com.

Nielsen. (2014, Q4). The total audience report. nielsen.com.

Puzzanghera, J. (2014, March 6). FCC to consider tougher rules for local TV stations. latimes.com.

Sandomir, R. (2011, June 7). NBC wins TV rights to four more Olympics. nytimes.com.

Severo, R. (2003, June 13). David Brinkley, 82, newsman model, dies. *The New York Times*, A26.

Sherr, I. (2010, September 1). Apple makes Internet-TV push. wsj.com.

Steel, E. (2014, October 16). Cord-cutters rejoice: CBS joins web stream. nytimes.com.

Steel, E. (2015, April 19). Netflix is betting its future on exclusive programming. nytimes.com.

Steel, E. (2015, August 6). Viacom's weak results pile on more bad news for TV industry. nytimes.com.

Stelter, B. (2013, February 11). A CBS deal bolsters Amazon's challenge to Netflix. nytimes.com.

Stelter, B. (2013, March 4). Don't touch that remote: TV pilots turn to net, not networks. nytimes.com.

Stelter, B. (2013, April 9). Two networks hint at leaving the airwaves. nytimes.com.

Sterling, C., & Kittross, J. (1990). *Stay tuned: A concise history of American broadcasting*, 2nd ed. Belmont, Calif.: Wadsworth.

Tracy, M., & Rohan, T. (2014, December 30). What made college football more like the pros? $7.3 billion, for a start. nytimes.com.

Tsukayama, H. (2011, October 5). TV on your Xbox, coming soon. washingtonpost.com.

Villarreal, Y. (2012, October 27). TV giant Don Francisco celebrates 50 years of "Sabado Gigante." latimes.com.

Williams, A. (2014, November 7). For millennials, the end of the TV viewing party. nytimes.com.

Chapter 9 Internet Media: Widening the Web

Alkhatib, H., Faraboschi, P., Frachtenburg, E., Kasahara, H., Lange, D., Laplante, P., Merchant, A., Milojicic, D., & Schwan, K. (2014, February). *IEEE CS 2022 Report*. IEEE Computer Society. ieee.org.

Arango, T. (2010, October 28). Judge tells LimeWire, the file-trading service, to disable its software. nytimes.com.

Arthur, C. (2012, September 5). Tim Berners-Lee: The Internet has no off switch. guardiannews.com.

Barnes, R. (2011, June 28). Court strikes down law on violent video games. washingtonpost.com.

Dewey, C. (2012, December 21). Holiday smartphone shoppers set records for mobile retail. washingtonpost.com.

Duggan, M., Ellison, N. B., Lampe, C., Lenhart, A., & Madden, M. (2015, January 9). *Social Media Update 2014*. Pew Research Center. pewinternet.org.

Ebin, B. (2014, December 16). In an all-digital future, it's the new movies that will be in trouble. vulture.com.

Edwards, J. (2012, August 15). People now spend more time watching their phones than watching TV. businessinsider.com.

Fidler, R. (1997). *Mediamorphosis*. Thousand Oaks, Calif.: Pine Forge Press.

Gnatek, T. (2005, October 5). Darknets: Virtual parties with a select group of invitees. *The New York Times*, E2.

Helmore, E. (2014, April 12). Ethical gaming: Can video games be a force for good? theguardian.com.

Hooper, M. (2014, July 21). Amazon at 20: Billions, bestsellers and legal battles. theguardian.com.

Isaacson, W. (2011, October 29). The genius of Jobs. nytimes.com.

Itzkoff, D. (2012, December 24). "Game of Thrones" is named year's most pirated show. nytimes.com.

Kang, C. (2011, October 11). U.S. has more cell phones than people. washingtonpost.com.

Kim, R. (2010, June 17). Keeping core gamers while expanding audience. sfgate.com.

Kiss, J. (2014, March 11). An online Magna Carta: Berners-Lee calls for bill of rights for the web. theguardian.com.

L2 Inc. (2014, November 4). *Social Platforms*. L2ThinkTank.com.

Lewsin, T., & Markoff, J. (2013, January 15). California to give web courses a big trial. nytimes.com.

Markoff, J. (2011, October 5). Steve Jobs, Apple visionary, dies at 56. nytimes.com.

Nielsen. (2012, December 3). State of the media: The social media report. nielsen.com.

Nielsen. (2013, February). The mobile consumer: A global snapshot. nielsen.com.

Nielsen. (2014, December 18). Tops of 2014: Digital. nielsen.com.

Paresh, D. (2015, March 13). Alibaba investment puts Snapchat valuation at $15 billion. latimes.com.

Sanger, D. E. (2014, December 23). Countering cyberattacks without a playbook. nytimes.com.

Sherr, I. (2012, November 17). Activision's "Call of Duty" sets sales record. wsj.com.

Sommer, J. (2014, May 10). Defending the open Internet. nytimes.com.

Tang, D. (2014, December 30). Chinese access to Gmail cut, regulators blamed. Associated Press, retrieved from sacbee.com.

Urbina, I. (2013, March 18). Unwanted electronic gear rising in toxic piles. nytimes.com.

Wollman, D. (2010, October 20). UN report: Internet users to surpass 2B in 2010. washingtonpost.com.

Wood, N. (2015, January 4). At the International CES, the Internet of Things hits home. nytimes.com.

Woolf, M. (2015, June 29). How television won the Internet. nytimes.com.

Wright, R. (1997, May 19). The man who invented the Web. *Time*, 68.

Chapter 10 Advertising: Catching Consumers

Advertising Age. (2014, May 4). Agency Report 2015. *Advertising Age*, 45.

Advertising Age. (2014, December 29). *Marketing Fact Pack*, 2015 edition.

Associated Press. (2010, November 15). Facebook enters e-mail, messaging arena. latimes.com.

Atwan, R. (1979). Newspapers and the foundations of modern advertising. In *The commercial connection*, ed. J. W. Wright. New York: Doubleday.

Beatty, S. G. (1996, June 11). Seagram flouts ban on TV ads pitching liquor. *The Wall Street Journal*, B1.

Boorstin, D. J. (1986). The rhetoric of democracy. In *American mass media: Industries and issues*, 3rd ed., ed. R. Atwan, B. Orton, & W. Vesterman. New York: Random House.

Doyle, M. (2014, January 30). Court upholds deception claims against POM Wonderful. sacbee.com.

Dredge, S. (2015, April 9). YouTube reveals plans for monthly subscription to remove ads. theguardian.com.

Flint, J., Branch, S., & O'Connell, V. (2001, December 14). Breaking longtime taboo, NBC network plans to accept liquor ads. *The Wall Street Journal*, B1.

Fowles, J. (1985). Advertising's fifteen basic appeals. In *American mass media: Industries and issues*, 3rd ed., ed. R. Atwan, B. Orton, & W. Vesterman. New York: Random House.

Fox, S. (1984). *The mirror makers: A history of American advertising and its creators*. New York: Morrow.

Guynn, J., & Sarno, D. (2010, April 8). Apple launches ad system for mobile devices in race with Google. latimes.com.

Hof, R. (2013, January 9). Online ad spending tops $100 billion in 2012. forbes.com.

James, M. (2012, July 8). Digital advertising agencies are built for the Internet age. latimes.com.

Jones, E. R. (1979). *Those were the good old days*. New York: Simon & Schuster.

Kaufman, L. (1987). *Essentials of advertising*, 2nd ed. New York: Harcourt Brace Jovanovich.

Li, S., & Sarno, D. (2011, August 21). Advertisers start using facial recognition to tailor pitches. latimes.com.

Nielsen. (2013, March 22). January 2013: Top US entertainment sites and web brands. nielsen.com.

Nielsenwire. (2010, January 20). Survey: Most Super Bowl viewers tune in for the commercials. blog.nielsen.com.

Schudson, M. (1984). *Advertising: The uneasy persuasion*. New York: Basic Books.

Silverstein, B. (2012, December). Branding in 2013: Convergence, content, gaming, big data and other big trends. brandchannel.com.

Steel, E. (2012, December 3). Ad groups cut 2013 growth outlook. ft.com.

Steel, E. & Ember, S. (2015, May 10). Networks fret as ad dollars flow to digital media. nytimes.com.

Strategy Analytics. (2015, May 2). The United States tops ad spending per capita in 2014 at USD$567 per person. strategyanalytics.com.

Strom, S. (2012, May 21). Judge says Pom Wonderful's advertising is misleading. nytimes.com.

Turow, J. (2011). *The daily you: How the new advertising industry is defining your identity and your worth*. New Haven, Conn. & London: Yale University Press.

Vega, T. (2013, February 25). Twitter hackings put focus on security for brands. *The New York Times*, B1.

Vega, T. (2013, April 7). Sponsors now pay for online articles, not just ads. nytimes.com.

Walker, P. (2014, December 9). Everyone for tennis? Women's game signs record broadcast deal. theguardian.com.

Chapter 11 Public Relations: Promoting Ideas

Ambrosio, J. (1980, March/April). It's in the *Journal*, but this is reporting? *Columbia Journalism Review*, 18, 35.

Associated Press. (2012, March 22). Komen executives resign in aftermath of decision to eliminate money for Planned Parenthood. washingtonpost.com.

Bernays, E. L. (1955). *The engineering of consent*. Norman: University of Oklahoma Press.

Berr, J. (2010, January 28). Facing its "Tylenol Moment," Toyota needs to move fast. DailyFinance.com.

Blyskal, B., & Blyskal, M. (1985). *PR: How the public relations industry writes the news*. New York: Morrow.

Bush, M. (2010, March 1). The cult of Toyota. *Advertising Age*, 1.

Bush, M. (2010, March 1). Internal communication is key to repairing Toyota reputation. *Advertising Age*, 1.

Council of Public Relations Firms. (2012, November 12). The PR factor 2012: The expanding power of public relations. adage.com.

Fleischman, D. E. (1931, February). Public relations—A new field for women. *Independent woman*. As quoted in S. Henry, *In her own name: Public relations pioneer Doris Fleischman Bernays*. Paper presented to the Committee on the Status of Women Research Session, Association for Education in Journalism and Mass Communication, Portland, Ore., July 1988.

Foster, L. G. (1983, March). The role of public relations in the Tylenol crisis. *Public Relations Journal*, 13.

Glover, M. (1996, March 6). Juice maker in PR mode: Odwalla's ads explain status. *The Sacramento Bee*, B6.

Goldsborough, R. (2001, June). Dealing with Internet smears. *Campaigns & Elections*, 50B6.

Goodman, P. S. (2010, August 21). In case of emergency: What not to do. nytimes.com.

Graham, J. (2007, March 9). Apple buffs marketing savvy to a high shine. *USA Today*, 1B.

Krauss, C. (2010, May 7). For BP, a technological battle to contain leak and an image fight, too. *The New York Times*, A16.

Los Angeles Times Staff. (2012, December). Toyota to pay at least $1.2 billion to settle sudden-acceleration lawsuit. latimes.com.

Marken, A. (1998, Spring). The Internet and the web: The two-way public relations highway. *Public Relations Quarterly*, 31–34.

Miller, C. (2009, July 5). Spinning the web: PR in Silicon Valley. nytimes.com.

Morse, S. (1906, September). An awakening on Wall Street. *American Magazine*, 460.

Newsom, D., Turk, J., & Kruckeberg, D. (2009). *This is PR: The realities of public relations*, 11th ed. Boston: Cengage Learning.

Parekh, R., & Lee, E. (2010, May 10). How to succeed when it's time to make your social-media mea culpa. *Advertising Age*, 1.

Pilon, M., & Lehren, A. W. (2013, February 15). Livestrong not immune from turmoil surrounding its founder. nytimes.com.

Pizzi, P. (2001, July 23). Grappling with "cybersmear." *New Jersey Law Journal*, S12.

Randall, C. (1985, November). The father of public relations: Edward Bernays, 93, is still saucy. *United*, 50.

Rushe, D. (2015, July 2). BP set to pay largest environmental fine in U.S. history for Gulf oil spill. theguardian.com.

Rutten, T. (2010, February 20). Tiger and Toyota: Rebuilding the brands. latimes.com.

Seitel, F. P. (1984). *The practice of public relations*, 2nd ed. Columbus, Ohio: Merrill.

Starkman, D. (2015, August 11). SEC says hacked news releases were used to make illegal trades. latimes.com.

Stengle, J. (2015, January 4). Komen sees big drop in contributions after dispute. sfgate.com.

Tracy, T. (2010, September 1). BP tripled its ad budget after oil spill. wsj.com.

Trop, J. (2013, July 19). Toyota will pay $1.6 billion over faulty accelerator suit. nytimes.com.

Vellinga, M. L. (2012, May 7). Komen race numbers show sharp decline. sacbee.com.

Vittachi, I. (2011, June 13). Horse marches through John Wayne Airport to mark air service to Canada. latimes.com.

Wallis, D. (2012, November 8). Komen Foundation struggles to regain wide support. nytimes.com.

White, R. D. (2010, April 30). For BP, oil spill is a public relations catastrophe. latimes.com.

Yui, M. (2015, April 16). McDonald's Japan closing stores after forecasting wider loss. bloombergbusiness.com.

Chapter 12 News and Information: Staying Connected

Barthel, M. (2015, April 29). 5 key takeaways from State of the News Media 2015. Pew Research Center. pewresearch.org.

Carr, D. (2014, November 2). Journalism, independent and not. nytimes.com.

Charles, D. (2005, September 7). Federal government seeks to block photos of dead. Reuters on AOL News. aol.com.

Chmielewski, D. C. (2010, May 4). Murdoch to unveil paywall for news content soon. latimes.com.

Fathi, N., & Landler, M. (2009, May 12). Iran releases journalist convicted of spying for U.S. nytimes.com.

Gans, H. (1985, December). Are U.S. journalists dangerously liberal? *Columbia Journalism Review*, 32–33.

Gans, H. (1986). *The messages behind the news*. In *Readings in mass communication*, 6th ed., ed. M. Emery & T. Smythe. Dubuque, Iowa: Brown.

Goel, V., & Somaiya, R. (2015, March 13). Facebook begins texting instant articles from news publishers. nytimes.com.

Goodman, T. (2011, March 18). Japan disaster shows U.S. journalists unprepared. sfgate.com.

Gordon, M. (2001, October 31). Military is putting heavier limits on reporters' access. *The New York Times*, B3.

Irvine, M. (2015, March 16). Young adults want news every day, survey shows. sfgate.com.

Jurkowitz, M. (2014, March 26). The growth in digital reporting. Pew Research Center. pewresearch.org.

Lippmann, W. (1965). *Public opinion*. New York: Free Press.

Liptak, A. (2014, June 2). Supreme Court rejects appeal from *Times* reporter over refusal to identify sources. nytimes.com.

McDermott, T. (2007, March 17). Blogs can top the presses. latimes.com.

Mitchell, A. (2015, April 29). State of the news media 2015. Pew Research Center. pewresearch.org.

Olmstead, K. (2015, April 29). Digital news—audience fact sheet. Pew Research Center. pewresearch.org.

Perez-Peña, R. (2010, February 3). Some news sites to try charging readers. *The New York Times*, B2.

Raines, H. (2010, March 14). Why don't honest journalists take on Roger Ailes and Fox News? washingtonpost.com.

Rutenberg, J. (2003, April 20). Spectacular success or incomplete picture? Views of TV's war coverage are split. *The New York Times*, B15.

Schmitt, E. (2005, December 13). Military admits planting news in Iraq. *The New York Times*, A11.

Seelye, K. Q. (2005, March 14). Fewer sources go nameless in the press, survey shows. *The New York Times*, C6.

Stelter, B. (2012, May 26). You can change the channel, but local news is the same. nytimes.com.

Chapter 13 Social and Political Issues: Shaping the Arguments

Alexander, H. E. (1983). *Financing the 1980 election*. Lexington, Mass.: Heath.

Alexander, H. E., & Haggerty, B. (1987). *Financing the 1984 election*. Lexington, Mass.: Heath.

Barber, J. D. (1986). *The pulse of politics: Electing presidents in the media age*. New York: Norton.

Bauder, D., Elber, L., & Moore, F. (2015, January 21). TV networks make unequal progress toward onscreen diversity. Associated Press, retrieved from sacbee.com.

Carey, B. (2011, October 18). Parents urged again to limit TV for youngest. nytimes.com.

Carr, D. (2012, November 20). Election audience votes, and web clobbers print. nytimes.com.

Cieply, M. (2007, April 13). Report says the young readily buy violent games and movies. *The New York Times*, C3.

Collins, S. (2015, April 22). Broadcast networks touting diversity, at least in fall pilots. latimes.com.

Contreras, R. (2015, April 23). American Indian actors quit Adam Sandler movie over names. Associated Press, retrieved from sfgate.com.

Fetler, M. (1985). Television viewing and school achievement. *Mass communication review yearbook*, vol. 5. Beverly Hills, Calif.: Sage.

Flood, A. (2012, May 31). Gay superheroes under fire from US pressure group. Guardiannews.com.

Gresko, J. (2015, June 4). Report: Women produce about a third of U.S. news content. Associated Press, retrieved from sfgate.com.

Hamburger, T. (2012, December 6). Manic spending marked end of 2012 campaigns, FEC reports show. washingtonpost.com.

Healy, M. (2010, May 4). Toddler TV time linked to poorer fourth-grade classroom attention, math and exercise. latimes.com.

James, M. (2010, October 29). TV still the favored medium for political ad spending. latimes.com.

Khimm, S. (2013, January 17). POW! CRACK! What we know about video games and violence. washingtonpost.com.

Liebert, R. M., & Sprafkin, J. (1988). *The early window*, 3rd ed. New York: Pergamon Press.

Linn, S. (2013, January 22). Invitation to a dialogue: Media violence. nytimes.com.

Lippmann, W. (1965). *Public opinion*. New York: Free Press.

Martindale, C. (1995, August). *Only in glimpses: Portrayal of America's largest minority groups by* The New York Times *1934–1994.* Paper presented at the Association for Education in Journalism and Mass Communication Annual Convention, Washington, D.C.

Meyrowitz, J. (1985). *No sense of place*. New York: Oxford University Press.

Modleski, T. (1982). *Loving with a vengeance: Mass-produced fantasies for women*. New York: Methuen.

Moore, M. (2012, May 23). Marvel comics plans wedding for gay hero Northstar. sacbee.com.

Nauman, A. (1993, April 11). Comics page gets serious. *The Sacramento Bee*, B1.

Patterson, T., & McClure, R. (1976). *The unseeing eye: The myth of television power in national elections*. New York: Putnam.

Pham, A., Zeitchik, S., & Fritz, B. (2012, July 28). Hollywood trying to avoid villain role in film violence. latimes.com.

Pham, S. (2010, November 8). Political TV ad spending sets record. abcnews.go.com.

Postman, N. (1985). *Amusing ourselves to death*. New York: Viking Penguin.

Potter, D. M. (1954). *People of plenty*. Chicago: University of Chicago Press.

Rivers, W. L., & Schramm, W. (1986). The impact of mass communications. In *American mass media: Industries and issues*, 3rd ed., ed. R. Atwan, B. Orton, & W. Vesterman. New York: Random House.

Scott, A. O. (2010, April 18). Brutal truths about violence. *The New York Times*, AR1.

Simon, S., & Stein, P. (2010, September 4). From grass roots to goofball: Politicians pitch on YouTube. wsj.com.

Spear, J. (1984). *Presidents and the press*. Cambridge, Mass.: M.I.T. Press.

Stanley, A. (2008, June 8). No debate: It's great TV. *The New York Times*, MT1.

Stein, M. L. (1994, August 6). Racial stereotyping and the media. *Editor & Publisher*, 6.

Terdiman, D. (2012, October 4). Obama, Romney debate (and Big Bird) generate 10 million tweets. cnet.com.

Vega, T. (2011, September 19). Newsroom diversity groups in partnership. nytimes.com.

Wright, J. W. (1979). *The commercial connection*. New York: Dell. (Synopsis of FTC staff report on television advertising to children.)

Chapter 14 Law and Regulation: Reforming the Rules

Abrams, J. (2011, May 30). Obama, in Europe, signs Patriot Act extension. Associated Press, retrieved from sfgate.com.

Aitkenhead, D. (2012, December). Julian Assange: The fugitive. guardiannews.com.

Arbel, T. (2015, May 30). FCC head unveils proposal to narrow "digital divide." Associated Press, retrieved from sacbee.com.

Associated Press. (2006, June 8). Fines to rise for indecency in broadcasts. *The New York Times*, C7.

Associated Press. (2007, September 6). Judge strikes down part of Patriot Act. nytimes.com.

Associated Press. (2007, December 18). FCC relaxes media ownership rule. nytimes.com.

Associated Press. (2009, May 4). High court throws out ruling on Janet Jackson. washingtonpost.com.

Associated Press. (2010, October 31). Supreme Court to hear violent video game case. nytimes.com.

Associated Press. (2012, July 24). Judge bars cameras from shooting suspect's hearing. sacbee.com.

Benton Foundation. (1996). *The Telecommunications Act of 1996 and the changing communications landscape*. Washington, D.C.: Benton Foundation.

Birnbaum, M. (2010, March 17). Historians blast proposed Texas social studies curriculum. washingtonpost.com.

Bode, C. (1969). *Mencken*. Carbondale: Southern Illinois University Press.

Braestrup, P. (1985). *Battle lines: Report of the Twentieth Century Fund Task Force on the Military and the Media*. New York: Priority Press.

Chu, H. (2011, November 2). Julian Assange ordered extradited in sex case. latimes.com.

Climan, L. (2001, September). Writers battle media companies. *Dollars & Sense*, 6.

Cloud, D. S. (2011, March 2). Soldier in WikiLeaks case charged with aiding the enemy. latimes.com.

Coile, Z. (2007, February 17). House Dems back federal shield law. *San Francisco Chronicle*, A5.

Congressional Research Service. (2005, March 8). Journalists' privilege to withhold information in judicial and other proceedings: State shield statutes. Washington, D.C.: Library of Congress.

Cowan, A. L. (2005, September 10). Plaintiffs win round in Patriot Act lawsuit. nytimes.com.

Crawford, K. (2005, June 27). Hollywood wins Internet piracy battle. money.cnn.com.

Davis, J. (2001, April 9). Decision: A defining moment in libel law. *Editor & Publisher*, 9.

Dishneau, D., & Jelinek, P. (2013, August 21). Manning sentenced to 35 years in WikiLeaks case. sacbee.com.

Dombey, D. (2010, December 3). U.S. counts cost in week of leaks. ft.com.

Federal Communications Commission. (2015, February 26). FCC adopts strong, sustainable rules to protect the open Internet. fcc.gov.

Fitzgerald, M. (2001, July 2). "Tasini" reality test. *Editor & Publisher*, 11.

Flaherty, A. (2013, February 26). Music, movie industry to warn copyright infringers. sfgate.com.

Flint, J. (2014, May 20). FCC chairman expresses concern about TV networks blocking websites. latimes.com.

Gerhardt-Powals, J. (2000, November 27). The Digital Millennium Copyright Act: A compromise in progress. *New Jersey Law Journal*, 28.

Greenwald, G. (2013, June 6). NSA collecting phone records of millions of Verizon customers daily. Guardiannews.com.

Holsinger, R. (1996). *Media law*, 4th ed. New York: McGraw-Hill.

Johnson, K., & Hall, K. G. (2015, March 13). New players replacing newspapers in seeking government info. sfgate.com.

Kasperkevic, J. (2015, February 22). Cord cutters on net neutrality: "It would be the end of wild west of the Internet." theguardian.com.

Khatchadourian, R. (2010, June 7). No secrets: Julian Assange's mission for total transparency. newyorker.com.

Kitigaki, P. (2003, September 22). Librarians step up. *The Sacramento Bee*, A1.

Levin, M. (2005, January 27). Lawsuits take aim at ads for alcohol. latimes.com.

Levine, R. (2007, March 12). Old concerts on new media lead to lawsuits. iht.com.

Levy, L. (2004). *Emergence of a free press*. Lanham, Md.: Ivan R. Dee.

Lewis, P. (1996, June 13). Judges turn back law intended to regulate Internet decency. *The New York Times*, A1.

Lichtblau, E. (2005, August 26). FBI demands library records. *San Francisco Chronicle*, A5.

Lichtblau, E. (2013, January 11). Makers of violent video games marshal support to fend off regulation. nytimes.com.

Liptak, A. (2012, June 21). Supreme Court rejects FCC fines for indecency. nytimes.com.

McKinley, J. C. (2010, March 13). Conservatives on Texas panel carry the day on curriculum changes. *The New York Times*, A9.

McMasters, P. K. (2006, January 1). Prying by the press exposes spying on Americans. FirstAmendmentCenter.org.

New York Times, The (2010, November 28). A note to readers: The decision to publish diplomatic documents. nytimes.com.

Peek, T. (1999, January). Taming the Internet in three acts. *Information Today*, 28.

Penenberg, A. L. (2011, January 28). WikiLeaks' Julian Assange: "Anarchist," "agitator," "arrogant," and a journalist. washingtonpost.com.

Pike, G. H. (2001, October). Understanding and surviving *Tasini*. *Information Today*, 18.

Pilkington, E. (2013, February 28). Manning plea statement: Americans had a right to know "true cost of war." guardiannews.com.

Puzzanghera, J. (2015, March 12). Net neutrality regulations released by FCC; industry lawsuit expected. theguardian.com.

Puzzanghera, J., & James, M. (2010, July 14). FCC indecency rule struck down by appeals court. latimes.com.

Reid, C. (2001, October 15). Writers 2, publishers 0. *Publishers Weekly*, 12.

Reuters. (2014, September 15). FCC receives record 3m comments about "net neutrality" issue. theguardian.com.

Roberts, D. (2015, June 5). NSA surveillance: How librarians have been on the front line to protect privacy. theguardian.com.

Ruiz, R. R., & Lohr, S. (2015, February 26). FCC approves net neutrality rules, classifying broadband Internet service as a utility. nytimes.com.

Rushe, D. (2012, June 22). Google reports "alarming" rise in censorship by governments. guardiannews.com.

Savage, C. (2013, July 30). Manning is acquitted of aiding the enemy. nytimes.com.

Savage, C., & Weisman, J. (2015, May 7). NSA collection of bulk call data is ruled illegal. nytimes.com.

Singer, N. (2012, December 19). FTC broadens rules for online privacy of children. nytimes.com.

Sisario, B. (2013, February 25). Online piracy alert system to begin this week. nytimes.com.

Smolla, R. (1987). *Suing the press*. New York: Oxford University Press.

Steinhauer, J., & Weisman, J. (2015, June 2). U.S. surveillance in place since 9/11 is sharply limited. nytimes.com.

Stern, C. (1996, February 12). The V-chip First Amendment infringement vs. empowerment tool. *Broadcasting & Cable*, 8.

Ungar, S. (1975). *The papers and the papers: An account of the legal and political battle over the Pentagon papers*. New York: Dutton.

Woodward, C., & Lardner, R. (2011, June 13). 40 years after leak, the Pentagon Papers are out. Associated Press, retrieved from sfgate.com.

Yuhas, A. (2015, May 15). More than 10,000 websites "blackout" Congress in protest of NSA surveillance laws. theguardian.com.

Chapter 15 Mass Media Ethics: Taking Responsibility

Alter, J., & McKillop, P. (1986, August). AIDS and the right to know. *Newsweek*, 46.

Associated Press. (2007, March 12). *New York Times* says former reporter's link to source included a $2,000 payment. iht.com.

Associated Press. (2010, November 19). MSNBC suspends host Scarborough for GOP donations. sfgate.com.

Barry, D. (2003, May 1). *Times* reporter who resigned leaves long trail of deception. *The New York Times*, A1.

Battaglio, S. (2015, June 18). Brian Williams will leave *NBC Nightly News* and join MSNBC. latimes.com.

Bennhold, K. (2014, November 19). A tabloid "fake sheikh," bane of crooks and royalty, finds he's now the story. nytimes.com.

Brandt, A. (1984, October). Truth and consequences. *Esquire*, 27.

Buettner, R. (2011, February 24). Affidavits say Fox News chief told employee to lie. nytimes.com.

Carr, D. (2010, November 8). Olbermann, impartiality and MSNBC. *The New York Times*, B1.

Carter, B. (2010, November 9). Olbermann, on air again, criticizes NBC for its policy. *The New York Times*, B2.

Christians, C., Rotzoll, K., & Fackler, M. (1987). *Media ethics*, 2nd ed. New York: Longman.

Chu, H. (2011, September 6). James Murdoch knew of wider phone hacking, ex-colleagues say. latimes.com.

Cowell, A., & Burns, J. F. (2012, November 20). Two former top Murdoch aides will be charged with bribery of public officials. nytimes.com.

Deans, J., Hill, A., & O'Carroll, L. (2012, January 19). Phone hacking: News International to pay out to 37 victims. guardiannews.com.

Farhi, P. (2014, November 25). Bill Cosby story shows media's evolution on willingness to report on allegations of rape. latimes.com.

Farhi, P. (2015, May 19). Stephanopoulos was also involved with offshoot of Clinton Foundation. washingtonpost.com.

Glenza, J. (2015, July 27). #TheEmptyChair: *New York* magazine's Cosby cover ignites dialogue on rape. theguardian.com.

Hulteng, J. (1985). *The messenger's motives: Ethical problems of the news media*. Englewood Cliffs, N.J.: Prentice Hall.

Koblin, J. (2015, June 24). Citing Ben Affleck's "improper influence," PBS suspends *Finding Your Roots*. nytimes.com.

Kurtz, H. (2009, October 18). *Post*'s canceled series of "salon" dinners again called into question. washingtonpost.com.

Lee, K. (2014, November 18). Uber CEO issues 13-part Twitter apology, clarifies data privacy policy. latimes.com.

Lunzer, B. (2010, October 5). New Hampshire newspaper publishes Afghanistan series with corporate backers. newsguild.org.

Maerz, M. (2011, January 24). Keith Olbermann's departure and the unanswered questions. latimes.com.

New York Times, The (2010, February 17). *Times* business reporter accused of plagiarism is said to resign. nytimes.com.

O'Carroll, L. (2011, December 10). Phone-hacking victims to number 800. guardian.co.uk.

O'Carroll, L. (2015, March 1). Rebekah Brooks about to be rehired by Rupert Murdoch for US operation. theguardian.com.

Oluo, I. (2015, July 28). The Cosby accusers were taught to be silent. We must learn to hear rape victims. theguardian.com.

Prendergast, A. (1987, January/February). Mickey Mouse journalism. *Washington Journalism Review*, 9, 32.

Smith, B. (2014, June 25). Editor's note: An apology to our readers. BuzzFeed.com.

Somaiya, R. (2014, July 26). BuzzFeed politics writer is fired over plagiarism. nytimes.com.

Sonne, P., Whalen, J., & Orwall, B. (2011, August 17). New issues emerge for News Corp. in Britain. wsj.com.

Steel, E. (2015, February 6). Brian Williams faces "fact-checking" inquiry at NBC. nytimes.com.

Steel, E. (2015, June 19). Brian Williams says fabrications came from "bad urge inside of me." nytimes.com.

Steinberg, J. (2003, June 6). *Times*' top editors resign after furor on writer's fraud. *The New York Times*, A1.

Stelter, B. (2010, November 10). 2nd MSNBC host suspended over campaign donations. *The New York Times*, B1.

Swaine, J. (2015, February 27). Bill O'Reilly twisted truth on "war zone" account, says former CBS colleague. theguardian.com.

Yuhas, A. (2015, March 2). Fox News forced to backtrack again over Bill O'Reilly's reporting claims. theguardian.com.

Chapter 16 Global Media: Communicating Change

Advertising Age. (2014, December 8). Global marketers 2014. *Advertising Age*, 26.

Ana, C. (2014, December 23). Report: At least 60 journalists killed in 2014. Associated Press, retrieved from sacbee.com.

Arthur, C. (2013, June 4). Turkish protesters using encryption software to evade censors. guardiannews.com.

Associated Press. (2010, November 10). Rights groups blast Egypt detention of blogger. washingtonpost.com.

Associated Press. (2011, January 30). Egypt bans Arabic broadcaster Al Jazeera. AOLNews.com.

Associated Press. (2014, April 4). AP photographer killed, reporter wounded. sacbee.com.

Associated Press. (2014, June 25). Egypt's attacks on press freedom unprecedented, says watchdog. theguardian.com.

Branigan, T. (2012, October 26). *New York Times* blocked in China after report on wealth of Wen Jiabao's family. guardiannews.com.

Bulos, N. (2013, August 2). Syria opens new front in social media war: Instagram. latimes.com.

Callimachi R. (2014, August 20). Before killing James Foley, ISIS demanded ransom from U.S. nytimes.com.

Carr, D. (2012, November 25). Using war as cover to target journalists. nytimes.com.

Chang, A. (2014, September 5). Alibaba sets price range, hopes to raise record-breaking $24.3 billion. latimes.com.

Chen, A. C., & Chaudhary, A. G. (1991). Asia and the Pacific. In *Global journalism: Survey of international communication*, 2nd ed. New York: Longman.

Cowell, A. (2003, July 31). Independent for 81 years, the BBC is facing a challenge. *The New York Times*, A3.

Deghan, S. K. (2015, July 13). Iran trial of *Washington Post* correspondent Jason Rezaian resumes. theguardian.com.

DeGiorgio, E. (2000, April). The African Internet revolution. *African Business*, 30.

Dennis, E., & Vanden Heuvel, J. (1990, October). Emerging voices: East European media in transition. *Gannett Center for Media Studies*, 2.

Fackler, M., & Nordland, R. (2015, February 1). Hostage's apparent beheading by ISIS stirs outrage in Japan. nytimes.com.

Fanner, E. (2013, February 10). With a focus on its future, *Financial Times* turns 125. nytimes.com.

Foster, P. (2010, February 26). BBC signals an end to era of expansion. business.timesonline.co.uk.

Goel, V., & Kramer, A. E. (2015, January 1). Web freedom is seen as growing global issue. nytimes.com.

Hamilton, R. (2010, November 10). In Radio Dabanga raid, Sudan targets last uncensored media outlet on the ground. washingtonpost.com.

Hassan, A. (2010, June 1). Arabic Web addresses expected to draw millions of new users to Internet. latimes.com.

Hays, L., & Rutherford, A. (1991, January 1). Gorbachev bids to crack down on Soviet press. *The Wall Street Journal*, A8.

Head, S. W. (1985). *World broadcasting systems*. Belmont, Calif.: Wadsworth.

Heller, A. (2013, July 31). New TV channel tells Israel's side of the story. sfgate.com.

Hindley, A. (1999, April 23). Breaking the taboos. *Middle East Economic Digest*, 6.

Hindley, A. (2000, February 11). Internet usage: The boom in access. *Middle East Economic Digest*, 27.

Karam, Z., & Satter, R. (2014, August 21). Social media pushes back at militant propaganda. Associated Press.

Khalil, M., Dongier, P., & Zhen-Wei Qiang, C. (2009). *Information and communications for development 2009: Extending reach and increasing impact*. Washington, D.C.: World Bank Publications.

Kingsley, P. (2014, December 26). Worse than the dictators: Egypt's leaders bring pillars of freedom crashing down. theguardian.com.

Kirkpatrick, D. D., & Goodman, J. D. (2011, February 3). Reporters in Egypt under broad assault. nytimes.com.

Landay, J. S. (2014, August 19). Islamic State posts video of beheading of U.S. journalist, warns Obama to halt strikes. sacbee.com.

Lowndes, F. S. (1991). The world's media systems: An overview. In *Global journalism: Survey of international communication*, 2nd ed. New York: Longman.

Lyall, S., & Pfanner, E. (2011, April 23). BBC, under criticism, struggles to tighten its belt. nytimes.com.

Martin, L. J. (1991). Africa. In *Global journalism: Survey of international communication*, 2nd ed. New York: Longman.

McDowall, A. (2001, April 20). Uncorking the bottlenecks. *Middle East Economic Digest*, 45.

Mista, N. (2003, September 15). India's film city is gobbling tribal land. *San Francisco Chronicle*, D1.

Najar, N. (2015, July 5). India's leader maps out a more robust digital future. nytimes.com.

Ogan, C. (1991). Middle East and North Africa. In *Global journalism: Survey of international communication*, 2nd ed. New York: Longman.

Paraschos, M. (1991). Europe. In *Global journalism: Survey of international communication*, 2nd ed. New York: Longman.

Picard, R. G. (1991). Global communications controversies. In *Global journalism: Survey of international communication*, 2nd ed. New York: Longman.

Pierson, D. (2010, January 16). Despite censorship, cracks in China's great firewall. latimes.com.

Pintak, L. (2007, April 27). Reporting a revolution: The changing Arab media landscape. ArabMediaSociety.com.

Press Association. (2014, December 29). Protests outside Egyptian embassy in London against imprisonment of journalists. theguardian.com.

Richburg, K. B. (2011, April 12). Chinese editors detail censors' hidden hand. washingtonpost.com.

Sabbagh, D. (2009, March 20). BBC must cut spending by £400 million, says Mark Thompson. timesonline.co.uk.

Sabbagh, D. (2009, April 16). Digital economy bill to pave way for shake-up of rules governing media mergers. timesonline.co.uk.

Salwen, M. B., Garrison, B., & Buckman, R. (1991). Latin America and the Caribbean. In *Global journalism: Survey of international communication*, 2nd ed. New York: Longman.

Scola, N. (2014, December 9). In the "global struggle for Internet freedom," the Internet is losing, report finds. washingtonpost.com.

Scott, M. (2014, October 8). Estonians embrace life in a digital world. nytimes.com.

Siebert, F., Peterson, T., & Schramm, W. (1963). *Four theories of the press*. Urbana: University of Illinois Press.

Sobranes, R., & Palafox, G. G. (2013, April 28). Mexican journalists march against attacks on press. sacbee.com.

Somaiya, R., Soble, J., & Jolly, D. (2015, July 23). Nikkei to buy *Financial Times* from Pearson for $1.3 billion. nytimes.com.

Stevens, R. (2014, August 21). Slain American journalist remembered as driven. Associated Press.

Strobel, W. P. (2005, April 18). Arab satellite channel Al Jazeera goes global. mercurynews.com.

Tunstall, J. (2008). *The media were American*. New York: Oxford University Press.

Villiamy, E. (2015, April 11). "They want to erase journalists in Mexico." theguardian.com.

Wallace, C. (1988, January 7). Radio: Town crier of the Arab world. *Los Angeles Times*, 1.

Wan, W. (2011, March 4). Egypt's Facebook revolution faces identity crisis. washingtonpost.com.

Warren, M. (2010, August 28). Argentine president moves to control newsprint. sfgate.com.

Werdigier, J. (2010, November 5). BBC staff strikes over changes to pension plan. nytimes.com.

Werth, C. (2014, November 21). British journalists slam police surveillance in lawsuit. latimes.com.

Wilkinson, T. (2012, May 20). Six journalists killed in Mexico in under a month. latimes.com.

INDEX